Bilingual Dictionary

W I T H D R A W N
★ F R O M ★
S T O C K

English-Ukrainian
Ukrainian-English
Dictionary

Compiled by
Katerina Volobuyeva

STAR Foreign Language BOOKS

© Publishers

ISBN : 978 1 912826 02 5

This Edition : 2022

Published by

STAR Foreign Language BOOKS

a unit of

Star Books

56, Langland Crescent
Stanmore HA7 1NG, U.K.
info@starbooksuk.com
www.bilingualbooks.co.uk

Printed in India at
Star Print-O-Bind, New Delhi-110 020

About this Dictionary

Developments in science and technology today have narrowed down distances between countries, and have made the world a small place. A person living thousands of miles away can learn and understand the culture and lifestyle of another country with ease and without travelling to that country. Languages play an important role as facilitators of communication in this respect.

To promote such an understanding, **STAR Foreign Language BOOKS** has planned to bring out a series of bilingual dictionaries in which important English words have been translated into other languages, with Roman transliteration in case of languages that have different scripts. This is a humble attempt to bring people of the word closer through the medium of language, thus making communication easy and convenient.

Under this series of *one-to-one dictionaries*, we have published almost 57 languages, the list of which has been given in the opening pages. These have all been compiled and edited by teachers and scholars of the relative languages.

Publishers

Bilingual Dictionaries in this Series

English-Afrikaans / Afrikaans-English	Abraham Venter
English-Albanian / Albanian-English	Theodhora Blushi
English-Amharic / Amharic-English	Girun Asanke
English-Arabic / Arabic-English	Rania-al-Qass
English-Bengali / Bengali-English	Amit Majumdar
English-Bosnian / Bosnian-English	Boris Kazanegra
English-Bulgarian / Bulgarian-English	Vladka Kocheshkova
English-Burmese (Myanmar) / Burmese (Myanmar)-English	Kyaw Swar Aung
English-Cambodian / Cambodian-English	Engly Sok
English-Cantonese / Cantonese-English	Nisa Yang
English-Chinese (Mandarin) / Chinese (Mandarin)-Eng	Y. Shang & R. Yao
English-Croatian / Croatain-English	Vesna Kazanegra
English-Czech / Czech-English	Jindriska Poulova
English-Danish / Danish-English	Rikke Wend Hartung
English-Dari / Dari-English	Amir Khan
English-Dutch / Dutch-English	Lisanne Vogel
English-Estonian / Estonian-English	Lana Haleta
English-Farsi / Farsi-English	Maryam Zaman Khani
English-French / French-English	Aurélie Colin
English-Georgian / Georgina-English	Eka Goderdzishvili
English-Gujarati / Gujarati-English	Sujata Basaria
English-German / German-English	Bicskei Hedwig
English-Greek / Greek-English	Lina Stergiou
English-Hindi / Hindi-English	Sudhakar Chaturvedi
English-Hungarian / Hungarian-English	Lucy Mallows
English-Italian / Italian-English	Eni Lamllari
English-Japanese / Japanese-English	Miruka Arai & Hiroko Nishimura
English-Korean / Korean-English	Mihee Song
English-Latvian / Latvian-English	Julija Baranovska
English-Levantine Arabic / Levantine Arabic-English	Ayman Khalaf
English-Lithuanian / Lithuanian-English	Regina Kazakeviciute
English-Malay / Malay-English	Azimah Husna
English-Nepali / Nepali-English	Anil Mandal
English-Norwegian / Norwegian-English	Samuele Narcisi
English-Pashto / Pashto-English	Amir Khan
English-Polish / Polish-English	Magdalena Herok
English-Portuguese / Portuguese-English	Dina Teresa
English-Punjabi / Punjabi-English	Teja Singh Chatwal
English-Romanian / Romanian-English	Georgeta Laura Dutulescu
English-Russian / Russian-English	Katerina Volobuyeva
English-Serbian / Serbian-English	Vesna Kazanegra
English-Sinhalese / Sinhalese-English	Naseer Salahudeen
English-Slovak / Slovak-English	Zuzana Horvathova
English-Slovenian / Slovenian-English	Tanja Turk
English-Somali / Somali-English	Ali Mohamud Omer
English-Spanish / Spanish-English	Cristina Rodriguez
English-Swahili / Swahili-English	Abdul Rauf Hassan Kinga
English-Swedish / Swedish-English	Madelene Axelsson
English-Tagalog / Tagalog-English	Jefferson Bantayan
English-Tamil / Tamil-English	Sandhya Mahadevan
English-Thai / Thai-English	Suwan Kaewkongpan
English-Tigrigna / Tigrigna-English	Tsegazeab Hailegebriel
English-Turkish / Turkish-English	Nagme Yazgin
English-Ukrainian / Ukrainian-English	Katerina Volobuyeva
English-Urdu / Urdu-English	S. A. Rahman
English-Vietnamese / Vietnamese-English	Hoa Hoang
English-Yoruba / Yoruba-English	O. A. Temitope

STAR Foreign Language BOOKS

ENGLISH-UKRAINIAN

abolish *v.t* покласти кінець poklasty kinets
abominable *a* жахливий zhakhlyvyi
abound *v.i.* бути у великій кількості buty u velykii kilkosti
about *adv* кругом kruhom
about *prep* про pro
above *adv* нагорі nahori
above *prep.* над nad
abreast *adv* в ряд v riad
abridge *v.t* скорочувати skorochuvaty
abridgement *n* скорочення skorochennia
abroad *adv* за кордоном za kordonom
abscond *v.i* уникати unykaty
absence *n* відсутність vidsutnist
absent *a* відсутній vidsutnii
absent *v.t* не бути ne buty
absolute *a* абсолютний absoliutnyi
absolutely *adv* абсолютно absoliutno
absorb *v.t* поглинати pohlynaty
abstract *v.t* абстрагувати abstrahuvaty
abstract *a* абстрактний abstraktnyi
abstract *n* абстракція abstraktsiia
abstraction *n.* узагальнення uzahalnennia
absurd *a* абсурдний absurdnyi
absurdity *n* безглуздість bezhluzdist
abundance *n* надлишок nadlyshok
abundant *a* більш ніж достатній bilsh nizh dostatnii

abuse *n* зловживання zlovzhyvannia
abuse *v.t.* ображати obrazhaty
abusive *a* жорстокий zhorstokyi
academic *a* науковий naukovyi
academy *n* академія akademiia
accede *v.t.* приєднуватися pryiednuvatysia
accelerate *v.t* прискорювати pryskoriuvaty
acceleration *n* прискорення pryskorennia
abaction *n* скотокрадство skotokradstvo
abactor *n* скотокрад skotokrad
abandon *v.t.* покидати pokydaty
abase *v.t.* понижувати ponyzhuvaty
abasement *n* приниження prynyzhennia
abash *v.t.* соромити soromyty
abate *v.t.* ослабляти oslabliaty
abatement *n.* послаблення poslablennia
abbey *n.* абатство abatstvo
abbreviate *v.t.* скорочувати skorochuvaty
abbreviation *n* абревіатура abreviatura
abdicate *v.t,* відрікатися vidrikatysia
abdication *n* зречення zrechennia
abdomen *n* черево cherevo
abdominal *a.* черевний cherevnyi
abduct *v.t.* викрадати vykradaty
abduction *n* викрадення vykradennia
abed *adv.* у ліжку u lizhku
aberrance *n.* відхилення vidkhylennia
abet *v.t.* підбурювати pidburiuvaty
abetment *n.* сприяння spryiannia

abeyance *n.* стан непевності stan nepevnosti

abhor *v.t.* ненавидіти nenavydity

abhorrence *n.* відраза vidraza

abide *v.i* очікувати ochikuvaty

abiding *a* постійний postiinyi

ability *n* здатність zdatnist

abject *a.* підлий pidlyi

ablactate *v. t* віднімати від грудей vidnimaty vid hrudei

ablactation *n* відібрання дитини від грудей vidibrannia dytyny vid hrudei

ablaze *adv.* палаючий palaiuchyi

able *a* спроможній spromozhnii

ablepsy *n* сліпота slipota

ablush *adv* збентежений zbentezhenyi

ablution *n* обмивання obmyvannia

abnegate *v. t* відмовляти собі в чому-небудь vidmovliaty sobi v chomu-nebud

abnegation *n* відмова vidmova

abnormal *a* ненормальний nenormalnyi

aboard *adv* на борту na bortu

abode *n* житло zhytlo

abolition *n.* анулювання anuliuvannia

aboriginal *a* аборигенний aboryhennyi

aborigines *n. pl* аборигени aboryheny

abort *v.i* перервати perervaty

abortion *n* аборт abort

abortive *adv* викидень vykyden

abrogate *v. t.* анулювати anuliuvaty

abrupt *a* раптовий raptovyi

abruption *n* розрив rozryv

abscess *n* абсцес abstses

absolve *v.t* звільняти zvilniaty

absonant *adj* різкий rizkyi

abstain *v.i.* утримуватися utrymuvatysia

abutted *v* прилягати pryliahaty

abyss *n* безодня bezodnia

acarpous *adj.* що не має плодів shcho ne maie plodiv

accent *n* акцент aktsent

accent *v.t* виділяти vydiliaty

accept & приймати pryimaty

acceptable *a* прийнятний pryiniatnyi

acceptance *n* прийняття pryiniattia

access *n* доступ dostup

accession *n* вступ vstup

accessory *n* співучасник spivuchasnyk

accident *n* випадок vypadok

accidental *a* випадковий vypadkovyi

accipitral *adj* хижий khyzhyi

acclaim *v.t* бурхливо аплодувати burkhlyvo aploduvaty

acclaim *n* гучне вітання huchne vitannia

acclamation *n* вітальні вигуки vitalni vyhuky

acclimatise *v.t* акліматизуватися aklimatyzuvatysia

accommodate *v.t* пристосовувати prystosovuvaty

accommodation *n.* приміщення prymishchennia

accompaniment *n* супровід suprovid

accompany *v.t.* супроводжувати suprovodzhuvaty

accomplice *n* спільник spilnyk

accomplish *v.t.* здійснювати zdiisniuvaty

accomplished *a* доповнений dopovnenyi

accomplishment *n.* освіченість osvichenist

accord *n.* згода zhoda

accord *v.t.* узгоджувати uzhodzhuvaty

accordingly *adv.* відповідно vidpovidno

account *v.t.* вважати за vvazhaty za

account *n.* рахунок rakhunok

accountable *a* відповідальний vidpovidalnyi

accountancy *n.* бухгалтерська справа bukhhalterska sprava

accountant *n.* відповідач vidpovidach

accredit *v.t.* уповноважувати upovnovazhuvaty

accrementition *n* розростання тканини rozrostannia tkanyny

accrete *v.t.* зростатися zrostatysia

accrue *v.i.* збільшуватися zbilshuvatysia

accumulate *v.t.* акумулювати akumuliuvaty

accumulation *n* акумуляція akumuliatsiia

accuracy *n.* точність tochnist

accurate *a.* точний tochnyi

accursed *a.* проклятий prokliatyi

accusation *n* звинувачення zvynuvachennia

accuse *v.t.* обвинувачити obvynuvachyty

accused *n.* обвинувачений obvynuvachenyi

accustom *v.t.* привчати pryvchaty

accustomed *a.* звиклий zvyklyi

ace *n* туз tuz

acentric *adj* той, що не має центру toi, shcho ne maie tsentru

acephalous *adj.* позбавлений голови pozbavlenyi holovy

acephalus *n.* безголовий bezholovyi

acetify *v.* перетворюватися на оцет peretvoriuvatysia na otset

ache *n.* біль bil

ache *v.i.* хворіти khvority

achieve *v.t.* досягати dosiahaty

achievement *n.* виконання vykonannia

achromatic *adj* ахроматичний akhromatychnyi

acid *a* кислий kyslyi

acid *n* кислота kyslota

acidity *n.* кислотність kyslotnist

acknowledge *v.* усвідомлювати usvidomliuvaty

acknowledgement *n.* визнання vyznannia

acne *n* прищ pryshch

acorn *n.* жолудь zholud

acoustic *a* акустичний akustychnyi

acoustics *n.* акустика akustyka

acquaint *v.t.* познайомити poznaiomyty

acquaintance *n.* знайомство znaiomstvo

acquest *n* набуття чинності nabuttia chynnosti

acquiesce *v.i.* неохоче згоджуватися neokhoche zhodzhuvatysia

acquiescence *n.* покірність pokirnist

acquire *v.t.* набувати nabuvaty

acquirement *n.* придбання prydbannia

acquisition *n.* привласнення pryvlasnennia

acquit *v.t.* виносити виправдальний вирок vynosyty vypravdalnyi vyrok
acquittal *n.* виправдання vypravdannia
acre *n.* акр akr
acreage *n.* площа землі в акрах ploshcha zemli v akrakh
acrimony *n* жовчність zhovchnist
acrobat *n.* акробат akrobat
across *adv.* впоперек vpoperek
across *prep.* через cherez
act *n.* акт akt
act *v.i.* діяти diiaty
acting *n.* виконання vykonannia
action *n.* вчинок vchynok
activate *v.t.* активувати aktyvuvaty
active *a.* активний aktyvnyi
activity *n.* діяльність diialnist
actor *n.* актор aktor
actress *n.* актриса aktrysa
actual *a.* фактичний faktychnyi
actually *adv.* фактично faktychno
acumen *n.* кмітливість kmitlyvist
acute *a.* різкий rizkyi
adage *n.* прислів'я pryslivia
adamant *n.* адамант adamant
adamant *a.* непохитний nepokhytnyi
adapt *v.t.* адаптуватися adaptuvatysia
adaptation *n.* адаптація adaptatsiia
adays *adv* щоденно shchodenno
add *v.t.* додати dodaty
addict *v.t.* залежати zalezhaty
addict *n.* наркоман narkoman
addiction *n.* залежність zalezhnist
addition *n.* додаток dodatok
additional *a.* додатковий dodatkovyi

addle *adj* зіпсований zipsovanyi
address *n.* адреса adresa
address *v.t.* звернутися zvernutysia
addressee *n.* адресат adresat
adduce *v.t.* наводити докази navodyty dokazy
adept *n.* знавець znavets
adept *a.* обізнаний obiznanyi
adequacy *n.* адекватність adekvatnist
adequate *a.* адекватний adekvatnyi
adhere *v.i.* дотримуватися dotrymuvatysia
adherence *n.* дотримання dotrymannia
adhesion *n.* прилипання prylypannia
adhesive *n.* клей klei
adhesive *a.* клейкий kleikyi
adhibit *v.t.* прикладати prykladaty
adieu *interj.* прощавай(те)! proshchavai(te)!
adieu *n.* прощання proshchannia
adiure *v.t.* благати blahaty
adjacent *a.* прилеглий prylehlyi
adjective *n.* прикметник prykmetnyk
adjoin *v.t.* примикати prymykaty
adjourn *v.t.* відкладати vidkladaty
adjournment *n.* відкладення vidkladennia
adjudge *v.t.* виносити вирок vynosyty vyrok
adjunct *n.* доповнення dopovnennia
adjuration *n* благання blahannia
adjust *v.t.* упорядковувати uporiadkovuvaty
adjustment *n.* врегулювання vrehuliuvannia

administer *v.t.* управляти
upravliaty
administration *n.* управління
upravlinnia
administrative *a.*
адміністративний
administratyvnyi
administrator *n.* адміністратор
administrator
admirable *a.* прекрасний
prekrasnyi
admiral *n.* адмірал admiral
admiration *n.* предмет
захоплення predmet
zakhoplennia
admire *v.t.* захоплюватися
zakhopliuvatysia
admissible *a.* допустимий
dopustymyi
admission *n.* допущення
dopushchennia
admit *v.t.* допускати dopuskaty
admittance *n.* доступ dostup
admonish *v.t.* застерігати
zasterihaty
admonition *n.* застереження
zasterezhennia
adnascent *adj.* той, що зростає
toi, shcho zrostaie
ado *n.* шум shum
adobe *n.* цегла повітряного
сушіння tsehla povitrianoho
sushinnia
adolescence *n.* молодість
molodist
adolescent *a.* юний yunyi
adopt *v.t.* переймати pereimaty
adoption *n* добір dobir
adorable *a.* обожнюваний
obozhniuvanyi
adoration *n.* обожнювання
obozhniuvannia

adore *v.t.* обожнювати
obozhniuvaty
adorn *v.t.* прикрашати
prykrashaty
adscititious *adj* привнесений
pryvnesenyi
adscript *adj.* приписаний
prypysanyi
adulation *n* лестощі lestoshchi
adult *n.* доросла людина dorosla
liudyna
adult *a* дорослий doroslyi
adulterate *v.t.* перелюбствувати
pereliubstvuvaty
adulteration *n.* перелюб pereliub
adultery *n.* адюльтер adiulter
advance *n.* аванс avans
advance *v.t.* крокувати krokuvaty
advancement *n.* прогрес prohres
advantage *v.t.* давати перевагу
davaty perevahu
advantage *n.* перевага perevaha
advantageous *a.* виграшний
vyhrashnyi
advent *n.* прихід prykhid
adventure *n* авантюра avantiura
adventurous *a.* авантюрний
avantiurnyi
adverb *n.* прислівник pryslivnyk
adverbial *a.* прислівниковий
pryslivnykovyi
adversary *n.* противник protyvnyk
adverse *a* несприятливий
nespryiatlyvyi
adversity *n.* негаразди neharazdy
advert *v.* звертатися zvertatysia
advertise *v.t.* рекламувати
reklamuvaty
advertisement *n* реклама
reklama
advice *n* порада porada
advisability *n* доцільність
dotsilnist

advisable *a.* доцільний dotsilnyi
advise *v.t.* консультувати konsultuvaty
advocacy *n.* адвокатура advokatura
advocate *n* адвокат advokat
advocate *v.t.* захищати zakhyshchaty
aerial *n.* антена antena
aerial *a.* повітряний povitrianyi
aeriform *adj.* газоподібний hazopodibnyi
aerify *v.t.* аерувати aeruvaty
aerodrome *n* аеродром aerodrom
aeronautics *n.pl.* аеронавтика aeronavtyka
aeroplane *n.* аероплан aeroplan
aesthetic *a.* естетичний estetychnyi
aesthetics *n.pl.* естетика estetyka
aestival *adj* річний richnyi
afar *adv.* удалині udalyni
affable *a.* привітний pryvitnyi
affair *n.* справа sprava
affect *v.t.* впливати vplyvaty
affectation *n* афектація afektatsiia
affection *n.* поразка porazka
affectionate *a.* люблячий liubliachyi
affidavit *n* письмове свідчення pysmove svidchennia
affiliation *n.* приєднання pryiednannia
affinity *n* спорідненість sporidnenist
affirm *v.t.* стверджувати stverdzhuvaty
affirmation *n* затвердження zatverdzhennia
affirmative *a* ствердний stverdnyi
affix *v.t.* наклеювати nakleiuvaty

afflict *v.t.* засмучувати zasmuchuvaty
affliction *n.* гіркота hirkota
affluence *n.* достаток dostatok
affluent *a.* який вільно тече yakyi vilno teche
afford *v.t.* давати davaty
afforest *v.t.* засадити лісом zasadyty lisom
affray *n* бешкет beshket
affront *n* ганьба hanba
affront *v.t.* образити obrazyty
afield *adv.* у полі u poli
aflame *adv.* у вогні u vohni
afloat *adv.* на воді na vodi
afoot *adv.* в русі v rusi
afore *prep.* вище vyshche
afraid *a.* переляканий pereliakanyi
afresh *adv.* знову znovu
after *prep.* за za
after *conj.* згідно з zhidno z
after *a* майбутній maibutnii
after *adv* позаду pozadu
afterwards *adv.* згодом zhodom
again *adv.* з другого боку z druhoho boku
against *prep.* проти proty
agamist *n* переконаний холостяк perekonanyi kholostiak
agape *adv.,* роззявивши рот rozziavyvshy rot
agaze *adv* у подиві u podyvi
age *n.* вік vik
aged *a.* літній litnii
agency *n.* агентство ahentstvo
agenda *n.* повістка povistka
agent *n* агент ahent
aggravate *v.t.* ускладнювати uskladniuvaty
aggravation *n.* загострення zahostrennia
aggregate *v.t.* збирати zbyraty

13

aggression *n* агресія ahresiia
aggressive *a.* агресивний ahresyvnyi
aggressor *n.* агресор ahresor
aggrieve *v.t.* кривдити kryvdyty
aghast *a.* вражений жахом vrazhenyi zhakhom
agile *a.* рухливий rukhlyvyi
agility *n.* спритність sprytnist
agist *v.t.* брати на відгодівлю braty na vidhodivliu
agitate *v.t.* агітувати ahituvaty
agitation *n* агітація ahitatsiia
aglow *adv.* палаючий palaiuchyi
agnus *n* Агні Ahni
ago *adv.* тому tomu
agog *adj.* збуджений zbudzhenyi
agonist *n* суперник supernyk
agonize *v.t.* мучитися muchytysia
agony *n.* агонія ahoniia
agoraphobia *n.* агорафобія ahorafobiia
agrarian *a.* аграрний ahrarnyi
agree *v.i.* погоджуватися pohodzhuvatysia
agreeable *a.* згодний zhodnyi
agreement *n.* угода uhoda
agricultural *a* сільськогосподарський silskohospodarskyi
agriculture *n* сільське господарство silske hospodarstvo
agriculturist *n.* агроном ahronom
agronomy *n.* агрономія ahronomiia
ague *n* гарячковий озноб hariachkovyi oznob
ahead *adv.* попереду poperedu
aheap *adv* в купі v kupi
aid *n* допомога dopomoha
aid *v.t* допомогти dopomohty
aigrette *n* плюмаж pliumazh

ail *v.t.* турбувати turbuvaty
ailment *n.* хвороба khvoroba
aim *n.* мета meta
aim *v.i.* цілити tsilyty
air *n* повітря povitria
aircraft *n.* літальний апарат litalnyi aparat
airy *a.* повітряний povitrianyi
ajar *adv.* відкритий vidkrytyi
akin *a.* споріднений sporidnenyi
alacrious *adj* запопадливий zapopadlyvyi
alacrity *n.* жвавість zhvavist
alamort *adj.* при смерті pry smerti
alarm *v.t* сигнальний syhnalnyi
alarm *n* тривога tryvoha
alas *interj.* на жаль na zhal
albeit *conj.* хоча khocha
albion *n* Альбіон Albion
album *n.* альбом albom
albumen *n* яєчний білок yaiechnyi bilok
alchemy *n.* алхімія alkhimiia
alcohol *n* алкоголь alkohol
ale *n* ель el
alegar *n* солодовий оцет solodovyi otset
alert *a.* насторожений nastorozhenyi
alertness *n.* настороженість nastorozhenist
algebra *n.* алгебра alhebra
alias *adv.* інакше inakshe
alias *n.* прізвисько prizvysko
alibi *n.* алібі alibi
alien *a.* прибулець prybulets
alienate *v.t.* відчужувати vidchuzhuvaty
aliferous *adj.* крилатий krylatyi
alight *v.i.* злізти zlizty
align *v.t.* вибудовувати в лінію vybudovuvaty v liniiu

alignment *n.* регулювання
rehuliuvannia
alike *adv* подібно podibno
alike *a.* схожий skhozhyi
aliment *n.* зміст zmist
alimony *n.* аліменти alimenty
alin *adj* благородний blahorodnyi
aliquot *n.* певна кількість pevna
kilkist
alive *a* живий zhyvyi
alkali *n* луг luh
all *a.* весь ves
all *pron* все vse
all *n* всі vsi
all *adv* цілком tsilkom
allay *v.t.* вгамовувати
vhamovuvaty
allegation *n.* твердження
tverdzhennia
allege *v.t.* посилатися на
posylatysia na
allegiance *n.* вірність virnist
allegorical *a.* алегоричний
alehorychnyi
allegory *n.* алегорія alehoriia
allergy *n.* алергія alerhiia
alleviate *v.t.* пом'якшувати
pomiakshuvaty
alleviation *n.* полегшення
polehshennia
alley *n.* алея aleia
alliance *n.* альянс alians
alligator *n* алігатор alihator
alliterate *v.* алітерувати
aliteruvaty
alliteration *n.* алітерація
aliteratsiia
allocate *v.t.* призначати
pryznachaty
allocation *n.* асигнування
asyhnuvannia
allot *v.t.* наділяти nadiliaty
allotment *n.* наділ nadil

allow *v.t.* дозволяти dozvoliaty
allowance *n.* порція portsiia
alloy *n.* сплавляти splavliaty
allude *v.i.* зпосилатися
zposylatysia
alluminate *v.t.* висвітлювати
vysvitliuvaty
allure *v.t.* заманювати
zamaniuvaty
allurement *n* спокуса spokusa
allusion *n* натяк natiak
allusive *a.* алегоричний
alehorychnyi
ally *v.t.* вступати у союз vstupaty
u soiuz
ally *n.* союзник soiuznyk
almanac *n.* альманах almanakh
almighty *a.* всемогутній
vsemohutnii
almond *n.* мигдаль myhdal
almost *adv.* майже maizhe
alms *n.* милостиня mylostynia
aloft *adv.* в горі v hori
alone *a.* самотній samotnii
along *adv.* уздовж uzdovzh
along *prep.* через cherez
aloof *adv.* осторонь ostoron
aloud *adv.* вголос vholos
alp *n.* гірська вершина hirska
vershyna
alpha *n* альфа alfa
alphabet *n.* алфавіт alfavit
alphabetical *a.* алфавітний
alfavitnyi
alphonsion *n.* берікс beriks
alpinist *n* альпініст alpinist
already *adv.* вже vzhe
also *adv.* також takozh
altar *n.* вівтар vivtar
alter *v.t.* переробляти pererobliaty
alteration *n* зміна zmina
altercation *n.* сперечання
sperechannia

alternate *a.* переміжний peremizhnyi
alternate *v.t.* чергувати cherhuvaty
alternative *n.* альтернатива alternatyva
alternative *a.* змінний zminnyi
although *conj.* хоча khocha
altimeter *n* альтиметр altymetr
altitude *n.* висота vysota
altivalent *adj* той, що високо літає toi, shcho vysoko lыtaie
alto *n* альт alt
altogether *adv.* всі разом vsi razom
aluminium *n.* алюміній aliuminii
alumna *n* колишня вихованка kolyshnia vykhovanka
alveary *n* зовнішній слуховий прохід zovnishnii slukhovyi prokhid
alvine *adj.* кишковий kyshkovyi
always *adv* завжди zavzhdy
am *adv* актор-аматор aktor-amator
amalgam *n* амальгама amalhama
amalgamate *v.t.* зливатися zlyvatysia
amalgamation *n* злиття zlyttia
amass *v.t.* скупчувати skupchuvaty
amateur *n.* любитель liubytel
amatory *adj* аматорський amatorskyi
amauriosis *n* сліпота slipota
amaze *v.t.* дивувати dyvuvaty
amazement *n.* дивування dyvuvannia
ambassador *n.* посол posol
amberite *n.* амберіт amberit
ambient *adj.* навколо navkolo
ambiguity *n.* двозначність dvoznachnist

ambiguous *a.* двозначний dvoznachnyi
ambition *n.* честолюбство chestoliubstvo
ambitious *a.* честолюбний chestoliubnyi
ambry *n.* комора komora
ambulance *n.* машина швидкої допомоги mashyna shvydkoi dopomohy
ambulant *adj* що переходить з одного місця на інше shcho perekhodyt z odnoho mistsia na inshe
ambulate *v.t* пересуватися peresuvatysia
ambush *n.* засідка zasidka
ameliorate *v.t.* поліпшуватися polipshuvatysia
amelioration *n.* амеліорація amelioratsiia
amen *interj.* амінь! amin!
amenable *a* зговірливий zhovirlyvyi
amend *v.t.* змінити zminyty
amendment *n.* зміна zmina
amends *n.pl.* поправки popravky
amenorrhoea *n* аменорея amenoreia
amiability *n.* люб'язність liubaznist
amiable *a.* люб'язний liubiaznyi
amicable *adj.* доброзичливий dobrozychlyvyi
amid *prep.* в середені v seredeni
amiss *adv.* невірно nevirno
amity *n.* дружні стосунки druzhni stosunky
ammunition *n.* боєприпаси boieprypasy
amnesia *n* амнезія amneziia
amnesty *n.* амністія amnistiia
among *prep.* серед sered

amongst *prep.* між mizh
amoral *a.* аморальний amoralnyi
amorous *a.* влюбливий vliublyvyi
amount *v.* зводитися zvodytysia
amount *v.i* становити stanovyty
amount *n* сума suma
amour *n* любовний зв'язок liubovnyi zviazok
ampere *n* Ампер Amper
amphibious *adj* десантний desantnyi
amphitheatre *n* амфітеатр amfiteatr
ample *a.* місткий mistkyi
amplification *n* зусилля zusyllia
amplifier *n* підсилювач pidsyliuvach
amplify *v.t.* перебільшувати perebilshuvaty
amuck *adv.* шалений shalenyi
amulet *n.* амулет amulet
amuse *v.t.* забавляти zabavliaty
amusement *n* звеселяння zveseliannia
an *art* невизначений артикль nevyznachenyi artykl
anabaptism *n* анабаптизм anabaptyzm
anachronism *n* анахронізм anakhronizm
anaclisis *n* анаклаза anaklaza
anadem *n* гірлянда hirlianda
anaemia *n* анемія anemiia
anaesthesia *n* анестезія anesteziia
anaesthetic *n.* анестетик anestetyk
anal *adj.* анальний analnyi
analogous *a.* подібний podibnyi
analogy *n.* аналогія analohiia
analyse *v.t.* аналізувати analizuvaty
analysis *n.* аналіз analiz

analyst *n* аналітик analityk
analytical *a* аналітичний analitychnyi
anamnesis *n* пригадування pryhaduvannia
anamorphous *adj* анаморфний anamorfnyi
anarchism *n.* анархізм anarkhizm
anarchist *n* анархіст anarkhist
anarchy *n* анархія anarkhiia
anatomy *n.* анатомія anatomiia
ancestor *n.* предок predok
ancestral *a.* спадковий spadkovyi
ancestry *n.* походження pokhodzhennia
anchor *n.* якір yakir
anchorage *n* якірна стоянка yakirna stoianka
ancient *a.* стародавній starodavnii
ancon *n* лікоть likot
and *conj.* і i
androphagi *n.* андрофаг androfah
anecdote *n.* анекдот anekdot
anemometer *n* анемометр anemometr
anew *adv.* по-новому po-novomu
anfractuous *adj* кривий kryvyi
angel *n* янгол yanhol
anger *n.* гнів hniv
angina *n* ангіна anhina
angle *n.* кут kut
angle *n* точка зору tochka zoru
angry *a.* злий zlyi
anguish *n.* страждання strazhdannia
angular *a.* кутовий kutovyi
anigh *adv.* близько blyzko
animal *n.* тварина tvaryna
animate *a.* натхненний natkhnennyi
animate *v.t.* оживити ozhyvyty

animation *n* пожвавлення pozhvavlennia
animosity *n* ворожість vorozhist
animus *n* намір namir
aniseed *n* аніс anis
ankle *n.* гомілка homilka
anklet *n* ножний браслет nozhnyi braslet
annalist *n.* літописець litopysets
annals *n.pl.* літописі litopysi
annectant *adj.* проміжний promizhnyi
annex *v.t.* крило krylo
annexation *n* анексія aneksiia
annihilate *v.t.* знищувати znyshchuvaty
annihilation *n* знищення znyshchennia
anniversary *n.* річниця richnytsia
announce *v.t.* оголошувати oholoshuvaty
announcement *n.* оголошення oholoshennia
annoy *v.t.* досаждати dosazhdaty
annoyance *n.* досада dosada
annual *a.* щорічний shchorichnyi
annuitant *n* аннуітент annuitent
annuity *n.* щорічна рента shchorichna renta
annul *v.t.* анулювати anuliuvaty
annulet *n* поясок колони poiasok kolony
anoint *v.t.* мазати mazaty
anomalous *a* неправильний nepravylnyi
anomaly *n* аномалія anomaliia
anon *adv.* скоро skoro
anonymity *n.* анонімність anonimnist
anonymity *n.* безликість bezlykist
anonymous *a.* анонімний anonimnyi
another *a* інший inshyi

answer *n* вирішення vyrishennia
answer *v.t* відповісти vidpovisty
answerable *a.* який несе відповідальність yakyi nese vidpovidalnist
ant *n* мураха murakha
antacid *adj.* антацидний antatsydnyi
antagonism *n* антагонізм antahonizm
antagonist *n.* антагоніст antahonist
antagonize *v.t.* ворогувати vorohuvaty
antarctic *a.* антарктичний antarktychnyi
antecede *v.t.* передувати pereduvaty
antecedent *n.* минуле mynule
antecedent *a.* апріорний apriornyi
antedate *n* датувати більш раннім числом datuvaty bilsh rannim chyslom
antelope *n.* антилопа antylopa
antenatal *adj.* який відбувся до народження yakyi vidbuvsia do narodzhennia
antennae *n.* чуття chuttia
antenuptial *adj.* дошлюбний doshliubnyi
anthem *n* гімн himn
anthology *n.* антологія antolohiia
anthropoid *adj.* людиноподібний liudynopodibnyi
anti *pref.* анти anty
anti-aircraft *a.* зенітний zenitnyi
antic *n* гримаси hrymasy
anticardium *n* ямка під грудьми yamka pid hrudmy
anticipate *v.t.* передбачити peredbachyty
anticipation *n.* побоювання poboiuvannia

antidote *n.* антидот antydot
antinomy *n.* протиріччя в законі protyrichchia v zakoni
antipathy *n.* антипатія antypatiia
antiphony *n.* антифон antyfon
antipodes *n.* антиподи antypody
antiquarian *n* антиквар antykvar
antiquarian *a.* антикварний antykvarnyi
antiquary *n.* збирач старовинних речей zbyrach starovynnykh rechei
antiquated *a.* старезний stareznyi
antique *a.* давній davnii
antiquity *n.* старовина starovyna
antiseptic *n.* антисептик antyseptyk
antiseptic *a.* антисептичний antyseptychnyi
antitheist *n* атеїст ateist
antithesis *n.* антитеза antyteza
antler *n.* оленячий ріг oleniachyi rih
antonym *n.* антонім antonim
anus *n.* задній прохід zadnii prokhid
anvil *n.* ковадло kovadlo
anxiety *n* тривога tryvoha
anxious *a.* заклопотаний zaklopotanyi
any *adv.* взагалі vzahali
any *a.* який-небудь yakyi-nebud
anyhow *adv.* так чи інакше tak chy inakshe
apace *adv.* швидко shvydko
apart *adv.* на віддалі na viddali
apartment *n.* квартира kvartyra
apathy *n.* апатія apatiia
ape *n* мавпа mavpa
ape *v.t.* мавпувати mavpuvaty
aperture *n.* отвір otvir
apex *n.* верхівка verkhivka
aphorism *n* афоризм aforyzm

apiary *n.* пасіка pasika
apiculture *n.* бджільництво bdzhilnytstvo
apish *a.* мавпячий mavpiachyi
apnoea *n* задуха zadukha
apologize *v.i.* вибачатися vybachatysia
apologue *n* повчальна база povchalna baza
apology *n.* вибачення vybachennia
apostle *n.* апостол apostol
apostrophe *n.* апостроф apostrof
apotheosis *n.* прославляння proslavliannia
apparatus *n.* апарат aparat
apparel *n.* предмети одягу predmety odiahu
apparel *v.t.* споряджати sporiadzhaty
apparent *a.* видимий vydymyi
appeal *v.t.* апеляція apeliatsiia
appeal *n.* заклик zaklyk
appear *v.i.* показуватися pokazuvatysia
appearance *n* поява poiava
appease *v.t.* полегшувати polehshuvaty
appellant *n.* аппелянт appeliant
append *v.t.* приєднувати pryiednuvaty
appendage *n.* придаток prydatok
appendicitis *n.* апендицит apendytsyt
appendix *n.* апендикс apendyks
appendix *n.* додаток dodatok
appetence *n.* потяг potiah
appetent *adj.* спраглий sprahlyi
appetite *n.* апетит apetyt
appetite *n.* пристрасть prystrast
appetizer *n* аперитив aperytyv
applaud *v.t.* аплодувати aploduvaty

applause *n.* оплески oplesky
apple *n.* яблуко yabluko
appliance *n.* прилад prylad
applicable *a.* застосовний zastosovnyi
applicant *n.* заявник zaiavnyk
application *n.* застосовність zastosovnist
apply *v.t.* застосовувати zastosovuvaty
appoint *v.t.* затверджувати zatverdzhuvaty
appointment *n.* побачення pobachennia
apportion *v.t.* розподіляти rozpodiliaty
apposite *a.* відповідний vidpovidnyi
apposite *adj* доречно dorechno
appositely *adv* до речі do rechi
appraise *v.t.* розцінювати roztsiniuvaty
appreciable *a.* помітний pomitnyi
appreciate *v.t.* усвідомлювати usvidomliuvaty
appreciation *n.* оцінка otsinka
apprehend *v.t.* передчувати peredchuvaty
apprehension *n.* розуміння rozuminnia
apprehensive *a.* кмітливий kmitlyvyi
apprentice *n.* підмайстер pidmaister
apprise *v.t.* сповіщати spovishchaty
approach *n.* підхід pidkhid
approach *v.t.* підходити pidkhodyty
approbate *v.t* санкціонувати sanktsionuvaty
approbation *n.* схвалення skhvalennia

appropriate *a.* доречний dorechnyi
appropriate *v.t.* привласнювати pryvlasniuvaty
appropriation *n.* асигнування asyhnuvannia
approval *n.* розгляд rozhliad
approve *v.t.* затверджувати zatverdzhuvaty
approximate *a.* приблизно pryblyzno
appurtenance *n* приналежність prynalezhnist
apricot *n.* абрикос abrykos
apron *n.* фартух fartukh
apt *a.* здібний zdibnyi
aptitude *n.* придатність prydatnist
aquarium *n.* акваріум akvarium
aquarius *n.* Водолій Vodolii
aqueduct *n* акведук akveduk
arable *adj* орний ornyi
arbiter *n.* арбітр arbitr
arbitrary *a.* довільний dovilnyi
arbitrate *v.t.* виносити третейське рішення vynosyty treteiske rishennia
arbitration *n.* третейський суд treteiskyi sud
arbitrator *n.* третейський суддя treteiskyi suddia
arc *n.* арка arka
arcade *n* аркада arkada
arch *n.* звід zvid
arch *v.t.* згинати zhynaty
arch *a* опуклий opuklyi
archaic *a.* архаїчний arkhaichnyi
archangel *n* архангел arkhanhel
archbishop *n.* архієпископ arkhiiepyskop
archer *n* лучник luchnyk
architect *n.* архітектор arkhitektor
architecture *n.* архітектура arkhitektura

archives *n.pl.* архіви arkhivy
Arctic *n* Арктика Arktyka
ardent *a.* палкий palkyi
ardour *n.* запал zapal
arduous *a.* важкий vazhkyi
area *n* площа ploshcha
areca *n* арека areka
arefaction *n* осушення osushennia
arena *n* місце подій mistse podii
argil *n* глина hlyna
argue *v.t.* сперечатися sperechatysia
argument *n.* довід dovid
argute *adj* гострий hostryi
arid *adj.* сухий sukhyi
aries *n* Овен Oven
aright *adv.* вірно virno
aright *adv* правильно pravylno
arise *v.i.* виникати vynykaty
aristocracy *n.* аристократія arystokratiia
aristocrat *n.* аристократ arystokrat
aristophanic *adj* той, що відноситься до Аристофана toi, shcho vidnosytsia do Arystofana
arithmetic *n.* арифметика aryfmetyka
arithmetical *a.* числовий chyslovyi
ark *n* ящик yashchyk
arm *v.t.* озброювати ozbroiuvaty
arm *n.* рука ruka
armada *n.* армада armada
armament *n.* озброєння ozbroiennia
armature *n.* арматура armatura
armistice *n.* припинення військових дій prypynennia viiskovykh dii
armlet *a* нарукавник narukavnyk

armour *n.* броня bronia
armoury *n.* склад зброї sklad zbroi
army *n.* армія armiia
around *adv* крізь kriz
around *prep.* по ро
arouse *v.t.* будити budyty
arraign *v.* притягати до суду prytiahaty do sudu
arrange *v.t.* влаштовувати vlashtovuvaty
arrangement *n.* впорядкування vporiadkuvannia
arrant *n.* запеклий zapeklyi
array *n.* бойовий порядок boiovyi poriadok
array *v.t.* вишиковувати в бойовий порядок vyshykovuvaty v boiovyi poriadok
arrears *n.pl.* борги borhy
arrest *n.* арешт aresht
arrest *v.t.* заарештовувати zaareshtovuvaty
arrival *n.* прибуття prybuttia
arrive *v.i.* прибути prybuty
arrogance *n.* гордовитість hordovytist
arrogant *a.* зарозумілий zarozumilyi
arrow *n* стріла strila
arrowroot *n.* арроурут arrourut
arsenal *n.* арсенал arsenal
arsenic *n* арсен arsen
arson *n* підпал pidpal
art *n.* мистецтво mystetstvo
artery *n.* магістраль mahistral
artful *a.* вправний vpravnyi
arthritis *n* артрит artryt
artichoke *n.* артишок artyshok
article *n* стаття stattia
articulate *a.* артикулювати artykuliuvaty

artifice *n.* винахід vynakhid
artificial *a.* штучний shtuchnyi
artillery *n.* артилерія artyleriia
artisan *n.* ремісник remisnyk
artist *n.* художник khudozhnyk
artistic *a.* художній khudozhnii
artless *a.* простий prostyi
as *conj.* так як tak yak
as *adv.* як yak
as *pron.* який yakyi
asafoetida *n.* асафетида asafetyda
asbestos *n.* азбест azbest
ascend *v.t.* сходити skhodyty
ascent *n.* сходження skhodzhennia
ascertain *v.t.* з'ясовувати ziasovuvaty
ascetic *n.* аскет asket
ascetic *a.* аскетичний asketychnyi
ascribe *v.t.* приписувати prypysuvaty
ash *n.* попіл popil
ashamed *a.* совісно sovisno
ashore *adv.* до берега do bereha
aside *n.* зауваження, зроблене «про себе» zauvazhennia, zroblene «pro sebe»
aside *adv.* окремо okremo
asinine *adj.* ослячий osliachyi
ask *v.t.* просити prosyty
asleep *adv.* сплячий spliachyi
aspect *n.* аспект aspekt
asperse *v.* ганьбити hanbyty
aspirant *n.* честолюбець chestoliubets
aspiration *n.* прагнення prahnennia
aspire *v.t.* прагнути prahnuty
ass *n.* дупа dupa
assail *v.* штурмувати shturmuvaty
assassin *n.* вбивця vbyvtsia
assassinate *v.t.* вбити vbyty

assassination *n* вбивство vbyvstvo
assault *v.t.* атакувати atakuvaty
assault *n.* напад napad
assemble *v.t.* збиратися zbyratysia
assembly *n.* асамблея asambleia
assent *n.* дозвіл dozvil
assent *v.i.* згоджуватися zhodzhuvatysia
assert *v.t.* відстоювати vidstoiuvaty
assess *v.t.* визначати vyznachaty
assessment *n.* обкладання obkladannia
asset *n.* актив aktyv
assibilate *v.* вимовляти з шипінням vymovliaty z shypinniam
assign *v.t.* уповноважувати upovnovazhuvaty
assignee *n.* уповноважений upovnovazhenyi
assimilate *v.* засвоювати zasvoiuvaty
assimilation *n* засвоєння zasvoiennia
assist *v.t.* допомагати dopomahaty
assistance *n.* сприяння spryiannia
assistant *n.* асистент asystent
associate *a.* асоціативний asotsiatyvnyi
associate *v.t.* асоціювати asotsiiuvaty
associate *n.* спільник spilnyk
association *n.* асоціація asotsiatsiia
assoil *v.t.* виправдовувати по суду vypravdovuvaty po sudu
assort *v.t.* сортувати sortuvaty

assuage *v.t.* заспокоїти zaspokoity

assume *v.t.* удавати udavaty

assumption *n.* самовпевненість samovpevnenist

assurance *n.* страхування strakhuvannia

assure *v.t.* завіряти zaviriaty

astatic *adj.* нестабільний nestabilnyi

asterisk *n.* зірочка zirochka

asterism *n.* астеризм asteryzm

asteroid *adj.* зіркоподібний zirkopodibnyi

asthma *n.* астма astma

astir *adv.* що перебуває в русі shcho perebuvaie v rusi

astonish *v.t.* вражати vrazhaty

astonishment *n.* здивування zdyvuvannia

astound *v.i.* дивуватися dyvuvatysia

astray *adv.*, той, що заблукав toi, shcho zablukav

astrologer *n.* астролог astroloh

astrology *n.* астрологія astrolohiia

astronaut *n.* астронавт astronavt

astronomer *n.* астроном astronom

astronomy *n.* астрономія astronomiia

asunder *adv.* нарізно narizno

asylum *n* психіатрична лікарня psykhiatrychna likarnia

at *prep.* при pry

atheism *n* атеїзм ateizm

atheist *n* безбожник bezbozhnyk

athirst *adj.* прагнучий prahnuchyi

athlete *n.* атлет atlet

athletic *a.* атлетичний atletychnyi

athletics *n.* атлетика atletyka

athwart *prep.* наперерік napererik

atlas *n.* атлас atlas

atmosphere *n.* атмосфера atmosfera

atoll *n.* атол atol

atom *n.* атом atom

atomic *a.* атомний atomnyi

atone *v.i.* спокутувати spokutuvaty

atonement *n.* спокута spokuta

atrocious *a.* звірячий zviriachyi

atrocity *n* звірство zvirstvo

attach *v.t.* вкладати vkladaty

attache *n.* аташе atashe

attachment *n.* вкладення vkladennia

attack *v.t.* нападати napadaty

attack *n.* наступ nastup

attain *v.t.* домагатися domahatysia

attainment *n.* досягнення dosiahnennia

attaint *v.t.* оголошувати поза законом oholoshuvaty poza zakonom

attempt *v.t.* намагатися namahatysia

attempt *n.* спроба sproba

attend *v.t.* відвідувати vidviduvaty

attendance *n.* відвідуваність vidviduvanist

attendant *n.* відвідувач vidviduvach

attention *n.* увага uvaha

attentive *a.* уважний uvazhnyi

attest *v.t.* свідчити svіdchyty

attire *n.* наряд nariad

attire *v.t.* наряджати nariadzhaty

attitude *n.* ставлення stavlennia

attorney *n.* прокурор prokuror

attract *v.t.* залучати zaluchaty

attraction *n.* принада prynada

attractive *a.* привабливий pryvablyvyi

attribute *n.* визначення vyznachennia
attribute *v.t.* приписувати prypysuvaty
auction *v.t.* продавати з аукціону prodavaty z auktsionu
auction *n* торг torh
audible *a* чутний chutnyi
audience *n.* публіка publika
audit *n.* аналіз analiz
audit *v.t.* перевіряти звітність pereviriaty zvitnist
auditive *adj.* слуховий slukhovyi
auditor *n.* аудитор audytor
auditorium *n.* зал для глядачів zal dlia hliadachiv
auger *n.* шнек shnek
aught *n.* щось shchos
augment *v.t.* збільшувати zbilshuvaty
augmentation *n.* збільшення zbilshennia
august *a.* величний velychnyi
August *n.* серпень serpen
aunt *n.* тітка titka
auriform *adj.* що має форму вуха shcho maie formu vukha
aurilave *n.* апарат для промивання вуха aparat dlia promyvannia vukha
aurora *n* ранкова зоря rankova zoria
auspicate *v.t.* починати pochynaty
auspice *n.* заступництво zastupnytstvo
auspicious *a.* сприятливий spryiatlyvyi
austere *a.* суворий suvoryi
authentic *a.* достовірний dostovirnyi
author *n.* автор avtor
authoritative *a.* авторитетний avtorytetnyi

authority *n.* влада vlada
authorize *v.t.* уповноважувати upovnovazhuvaty
autobiography *n.* автобіографія avtobiohrafiia
autocracy *n* самодержавство samoderzhavstvo
autocrat *n* самодержець samoderzhets
autocratic *a* самодержавний samoderzhavnyi
autograph *n.* автограф avtohraf
automatic *a.* несвідомий nesvidomyi
automobile *n.* автомобіль avtomobil
autonomous *a* автономний avtonomnyi
autumn *n.* осінь osin
auxiliary *a.* допоміжний dopomizhnyi
auxiliary *n.* допоміжний механізм dopomizhnyi mekhanizm
avail *v.t.* бути корисним buty korysnym
available *a* наявний naiavnyi
avale *v.t.* опускати opuskaty
avarice *n.* скупість skupist
avenge *v.t.* мстити mstyty
avenue *n.* проспект prospekt
average *a.* звичайний zvychainyi
average *n.* середня величина serednia velychyna
average *v.t.* усереднювати useredniuvaty
averse *a.* неприхильний neprykhylnyi
aversion *n.* відраза vidraza
avert *v.t.* відвести vidvesty
aviary *n.* пташник ptashnyk
aviation *n.* авіація aviatsiia
aviator *n.* пілот pilot
avid *adj.* жадібний zhadibnyi

avidity *n.* пожадливість
  pozhadlyvist
avidly *adv* жадібно zhadibno
avoid *v.t.* уникати unykaty
avoidance *n.* уникнути unyknuty
avow *v.t.* визнавати vyznavaty
avulsion *n.* відрив vidryv
await *v.t.* чекати chekaty
awake *a* бадьорий badoryi
awake *v.t.* пробуджуватися
  probudzhuvatysia
award *n.* нагорода nahoroda
award *v.t.* нагороджувати
  nahorodzhuvaty
aware *a.* свідомий svidomyi
away *adv.* геть het
awe *n.* благоговіння
  blahohovinnia
awful *a.* що викликає страх
  shcho vyklykaie strakh
awhile *adv.* ненадовго nenadovho
awkward *a.* незграбний
  nezhrabnyi
axe *n.* сокира sokyra
axis *n.* вісь vis
axle *n.* вісь vis

babble *n.* лепет lepet
babble *v.i.* лепетати lepetaty
babe *n.* маля malia
babel *n* галас halas
baboon *n.* бабуїн babuin
baby *n.* дитина dytyna
bachelor *n.* холостяк kholostiak
back *adv.* назад nazad
back *n.* спина spyna
backbite *v.t.* обмовляти
  obmovliaty
backbone *n.* хребет khrebet
background *n.* фон fon

backhand *n.* тильна сторона
  руки tylna storona ruky
backslide *v.i.* відмовлятися від
  переконань vidmovliatysia vid
  perekonan
backward *adv.* на гірше na hirshe
backward *a.* темний temnyi
bacon *n.* сало salo
bacteria *n.* бактерія bakteriia
bad *a.* зіпсований zipsovanyi
badge *n.* значок znachok
badger *n.* борсук borsuk
badly *adv.* погано pohano
badminton *n.* бадмінтон
  badminton
baffle *v. t.* спантеличувати
  spantelychuvaty
bag *n.* сумка sumka
bag *v. i.* класти у мішок klasty u
  mishok
baggage *n.* майно maino
bagpipe *n.* волинка volynka
bail *v. t.* брати на поруки braty na
  poruky
bail *n.* застава zastava
bailable *a.* який має право на
  звільнення з ув'язнення під
  заставу yakyi maie pravo na
  zvilnennia z uviaznennia pid
  zastavu
bailiff *n.* судовий пристав sudovyi
  prystav
bait *n* наживка nazhyvka
bait *v.t.* перепочинок
  perepochynok
bake *v.t.* пекти pekty
baker *n.* пекар pekar
bakery *n* пекарня pekarnia
balance *n.* баланс balans
balance *v.t.* балансувати
  balansuvaty
balcony *n.* балкон balkon
bald *a.* лисий lysyi

bale *v.t.* в'язати у вузли viazaty u vuzly
bale *n.* зв'язка zviazka
baleen *n.* китовий вус kytovyi vus
baleful *a.* ліховісний likhovisnyi
ball *n.* м'яч miach
ballad *n.* балада balada
ballet *sn.* балет balet
balloon *n.* повітряна куля povitriana kulia
ballot *n* бюлетень biuleten
ballot *v.i.* голосувати holosuvaty
balm *n.* бальзам balzam
balsam *n.* розрада rozrada
bam *n.* розіграш rozihrash
bamboo *n.* бамбук bambuk
ban *n* анафема anafema
ban *n.* заборона zaborona
banal *a.* банальний banalnyi
banana *n.* банан banan
band *n.* стрічка strichka
bandage *~n.* бинт bynt
bandage *v.t* бинтувати byntuvaty
bandit *n.* розбійник rozbiinyk
bang *v.t.* стукнути stuknuty
bang *n.* удар udar
bangle *n.* браслет braslet
banish *v.t.* виганяти vyhaniaty
banishment *n.* висилка vysylka
banjo *n.* банджо bandzho
bank *n.* банк bank
bank *v.t.* згрібати в купу zhribaty v kupu
banker *n.* банкір bankir
bankrupt *n.* банкрут bankrut
bankruptcy *n.* неспроможність nespromozhnist
banner *n.* прапор prapor
banquet *n.* банкет banket
banquet *v.t.* бенкетувати benketuvaty
bantam *n.* забіяка-коротун zabiiaka-korotun

banter *v.t.* добродушно жартувати dobrodushno zhartuvaty
banter *n.* жартівлива бесіда zhartivlyva besida
bantling *n.* кодло kodlo
banyan *n.* баніан banian
baptism *n.* хрещення khreshchennia
baptize *+v.t.* хрестити khrestyty
bar *n.* бочка bochka
bar *v.t* виключати, не рахуючи vykliuchaty, ne rakhuiuchy
barb *n.* колючка koliuchka
barbarian *n.* варвар varvar
barbarian *a.* варварський varvarskyi
barbarism *n.* варварство varvarstvo
barbarity *n* нелюдяність neliudianist
barbarous *a.* дикий dykyi
barbed *a.* колючий koliuchyi
barber *n.* перукар perukar
bard *n.* бард bard
bare *a.* голий holyi
bare *v.t.* оголювати oholiuvaty
barely *adv.* ледь led
bargain *n.* угода uhoda
bargain *v.t.* укладати угоду ukladaty uhodu
barge *n.* баржа barzha
bark *n.* кора kora
bark *v.t.* нарощувати кору naroshchuvaty koru
barley *n.* ячмінь yachmin
barn *n.* сарай sarai
barnacles *n* докучлива людина dokuchlyva liudyna
barometer *n* барометр barometr
barouche *n.* ландо lando
barrack *n.* барак barak
barrage *n.* гребля hreblia

barrator *ns.* хабарник khabarnyk
barrel *n.* бочка bochka
barren *n* пустир pustyr
barricade *n.* барикада barykada
barrier *n.* бар'єр barier
barrister *n.* адвокат найвищого рангу advokat naivyshchoho ranhu
barter1 *v.t.* міняти miniaty
barter2 *n.* товарообмін tovaroobmin
barton *n.* садиба sadyba
basal *adj.* що лежить в основі shcho lezhyt v osnovi
base *a.* базовий bazovyi
base *v.t.* заснувати zasnuvaty
base *n.* основа osnova
baseless *a.* безпідставний bezpidstavnyi
basement *n.* підстава pidstava
bashful *a.* сором'язливий soromiazlyvyi
basial *adv.* базіоальвеолярний bazioalveoliarnyi
basic *a.* головний holovnyi
basil *n.* базилік bazylik
basin *n.* резервуар rezervuar
basis *n.* базис bazys
bask *v.i.* грітися hritysia
basket *n.* кошик koshyk
baslard *n.* кинджал kyndzhal
bass *n.* бас bas
bastard *n.* ублюдок ubliudok
bastard *a* позашлюбний pozashliubnyi
bat *v. i* бити палицею byty palytseiu
bat *n* дубина dubyna
bat *n* кажан kazhan
batch *n* пачка pachka
bath *n* ванна vanna
bathe *v. t* купати kupaty
baton *n* жезл zhezl

batsman *n.* гравець биткою hravets bytkoiu
battalion *n* дивізіон dyvizion
battery *n* батарея batareia
battle *n* бій bii
battle *v. i.* боротися borotysia
bawd *n.* звідник zvidnyk
bawl *n.* крик kryk
bawn *n.* загін для худоби zahin dlia khudoby
bay *n* бухта bukhta
bayard *n.* відчайдушна голова vidchaidushna holova
bayonet *n* багнет bahnet
be *pref.* обез- obez-
be *v.t.* бути buty
beach *n* пляж pliazh
beacon *n* маяк maiak
bead *n* бусинка busynka
beadle *n.* церковний сторож tserkovnyi storozh
beak *n* дзьоб dzob
beaker *n* кубок kubok
beam *n* промінь promin
beam *v. i* сяяти siaiaty
bean *n.* квасоля kvasolia
bear *n* ведмідь vedmid
bear *v.t* переносити perenosyty
beard *n* борода boroda
bearing *n* народження narodzhennia
beast *n* чудовисько chudovysko
beastly *a* тваринний tvarynnyi
beat *v. t.* бити byty
beat *n* удар udar
beautiful *a* красивий krasyvyi
beautify *v. t* прикрашати prykrashaty
beauty *n* краса krasa
beaver *n* бобер bober
because *conj.* тому що tomu shcho
beck *n.* кивок kyvok

beckon *v.t.* вабити vabyty
beckon *v. t* зробити знак zrobyty
  znak
become *v. i* ставати stavaty
becoming *a* який пасує yakyi
  pasuie
bed *n* ліжко lizhko
bedding *n.* постільні
  приналежності postilni
  prynalezhnosti
bedevil *v. t* мучити muchyty
bedight *v.t.* одягати odiahaty
bed-time *n.* час лягати спати
  chas liahaty spaty
bee *n.* бджола bdzhola
beech *n.* бук buk
beef *n* яловичина yalovychyna
beehive *n.* вулик vulyk
beer *n* пиво pyvo
beet *n* буряк buriak
beetle *n* жук zhuk
befall *v. t* траплятися trapliatysia
before *prep* до do
before *adv.* перш persh
before *conj* швидше, ніж
  shvydshe, nizh
beforehand *adv.* завчасно
  zavchasno
befriend *v. t.* ставитися дружньо
  stavytysia druzhno
beg *v. t.* благати blahaty
beget *v. t* народжувати
  narodzhuvaty
beggar *n* жебрак zhebrak
begin *v.t.* розпочинати
  rozpochynaty
beginning *n.* початок pochatok
begird *v.t.* оперізувати
  operizuvaty
beguile *v. t* сорочити sorochyty
behalf *n* підтримка pidtrymka
behave *v. i.* надходити
  nadkhodyty

behaviour *n* поведінка povedinka
behead *v. t.* обезголовити
  obezholovyty
behind *prep* позаду pozadu
behind *adv* ззаду zzadu
behold *v. t* бачити bachyty
being *n* буття buttia
belabour *v. t* лупцювати
  luptsiuvaty
belated *adj.* запізнілий zapiznilyi
belch *v. t* вивергати vyverhaty
belch *n* відрижка vidryzhka
belief *n* віра vira
believe *v. t* вірити viryty
bell *n* дзвін dzvin
belle *n* красуня krasunia
bellicose *a* войовничий
  voiovnychyi
belligerency *n* стан війни stan
  viiny
belligerent *a* той, що
  знаходиться в стані війни toi,
  shcho znakhodytsia v stani viiny
belligerent *n* учасник бійки
  uchasnyk biiky
bellow *v. i* ревіти revity
bellows *n.* міхи mikhy
belly *n* живіт zhyvit
belong *v. i* належати nalezhaty
belongings *n.* деталі detali
beloved *n* коханий kokhanyi
beloved *a* улюблений uliublenyi
below *adv* нижче nyzhche
below *prep* нижче nyzhche
belt *n* ремінь remin
belvedere *n* альтанка altanka
bemask *v. t* замовчувати
  zamovchuvaty
bemire *v. t* забризкувати брудом
  zabryzkuvaty brudom
bemuse *v. t* приголомшити
  pryholomshyty
bench *n* лава lava

bend *n* згин zhyn
bend *v. t* напружувати
  napruzhuvaty
beneath *adv* внизу vnyzu
beneath *prep* під pid
benefaction *n.* благодіяння
  blahodiiannia
benefice *n* бенефіцій benefitsii
beneficial *a* благотворний
  blahotvornyi
benefit *n* привілей pryvilei
benefit *v. t.* мати користь maty
  koryst
benevolence *n* доброзичливість
  dobrozychlyvist
benevolent *a* доброзичливий
  dobrozychlyvyi
benight *v. t* ввергати у морок
  vverhaty u morok
benign *adj* милостивий
  mylostyvyi
benignly *adv* милостиво
  mylostyvo
benison *n* благословення
  blahoslovennia
bent *n* схильність skhylnist
bequeath *v. t.* заповідати
  zapovidaty
bereave *v. t.* віднімати vidnimaty
bereavement *n* втрата vtrata
berth *n* койка koika
beside *prep.* поруч з poruch z
besides *prep* крім krim
besides *adv* крім того krim toho
besiege *v. t* облягати obliahaty
beslaver *v. t* слинити slynyty
bestow *v. t* дарувати daruvaty
bestrew *v. t* всипати vsypaty
bet *v.i* сперечатися sperechatysia
bet *n* ставка stavka
betel *n* бетель betel
betray *v.t.* зраджувати
  zradzhuvaty

betrayal *n* зрада zrada
betroth *v. t* обручити obruchyty
betrothal *n.* заручини zaruchyny
better *a* кращий krashchyi
better *adv.* набагато nabahato
better *v. t* поліпшувати
  polipshuvaty
betterment *n* видатки на
  збільшення вартості власності
  vydatky na zbilshennia vartosti
  vlasnosti
between *prep* між mizh
beverage *n* напій napii
bewail *v. t* оплакувати oplakuvaty
beware *v.i.* берегтися berehtysia
bewilder *v. t* заплутувати
  zaplutuvaty
bewitch *v.t* зачарувати
  zacharuvaty
beyond *prep.* за za
beyond *adv.* понад ponad
bi *pref* бі bi
biangular *adj.* двуугольний
  dvuuholnyi
bias *v. t* настроювати nastroiuvaty
bias *n* нахил nakhyl
biaxial *adj* двохосьовий
  dvokhosovyi
bibber *n* п'яниця pianytsia
bible *n* біблія bibliia
bibliographer *n* бібліограф
  bibliohraf
bibliography *+n* бібліографія
  bibliohrafiia
bicentenary *adj* двохсотріччя
  dvokhsotrichchia
biceps *n* біцепс bitseps
bicker *v. t* сперечатися
  sperechatysia
bicycle *n.* велосипед velosyped
bid *v.t* пропонувати ціну
  proponuvaty tsinu

bid *n* конкурсна пропозиція konkursna propozytsiia
bidder *n* учасник торгів uchasnyk torhiv
bide *v. t* проживати prozhyvaty
biennial *adj* дворічний dvorichnyi
bier *n* одр odr
big *a* великий velykyi
bigamy *n* двоєженство dvoiezhenstvo
bight *n* закрут zakrut
bigot *n* фанатик fanatyk
bigotry *n* фанатизм fanatyzm
bile *n* жовч zhovch
bilingual *a* двомовний dvomovnyi
biliteral *adj* двобуквений dvobukvenyi
bilk *v. t.* вислизати vyslyzaty
bill *n* список spysok
billion *n* мільярд miliard
billow *v.i* здійматися zdiimatysia
billow *n* лавина lavyna
bimenasl *adj* оманливий omanlyvyi
bimonthly *adj.* двічі на місяць dvichi na misiats
binary *adj* двійковий dviikovyi
bind *v.t* пов'язувати poviazuvaty
binding *a* сполучний spoluchnyi
binocular *n.* бінокулярний binokuliarnyi
biographer *n* біограф biohraf
biography *n* біографія biohrafiia
biologist *n* біолог bioloh
biology *n* біологія biolohiia
bioscope *n* біоскоп bioskop
biped *n* двоноге dvonohe
birch *n.* береза bereza
bird *n* птах ptakh
birdlime *n* пташиний клей ptashynyi klei
birth *n.* зародження zarodzhennia
biscuit *n* печиво pechyvo

bisect *v. t* ділити навпіл dilyty navpil
bisexual *adj.* двостатевий dvostatevyi
bishop *n* єпископ yepyskop
bison *n* бізон bizon
bisque *n* фора в тенісі fora v tenisi
bit *n* шматок shmatok
bitch *n* самка samka
bite *v. t.* жалити zhalyty
bite *n* укус ukus
bitter *a* гіркий hirkyi
bi-weekly *adj* раз на два тижні raz na dva tyzhni
bizarre *adj* химерний khymernyi
blab *v. t. & i* базікати bazikaty
black *a* чорний chornyi
blacken *v. t.* чорнити chornyty
blackmail *n* шантаж shantazh
blackmail *v.t* шантажувати shantazhuvaty
blacksmith *n* коваль koval
bladder *n* сечовий міхур sechovyi mikhur
blade *n.* лезо lezo
blain *n* нарив naryv
blame *v. t* вважати винним vvazhaty vynnym
blame *n* осуд osud
blanch *v. t. & i* відбілювати vidbiliuvaty
bland *adj.* ввічливий vvichlyvyi
blank *a* порожній porozhnii
blank *n* пробіл probil
blanket *n* ковдра kovdra
blare *v. t* сурмити surmyty
blast *n* вибух vybukh
blast *v.i* шкодити shkodyty
blaze *n* полум'я polumia
blaze *v.i* палати palaty
bleach *v. t* відбілювати vidbiliuvaty

blear *v. t* затуманювати zatumaniuvaty
bleat *n* бекання bekannia
bleat *v. i* бекати bekaty
bleb *n* пухир pukhyr
bleed *v. i* кровоточити krovotochyty
blemish *n* недолік nedolik
blend *v. t* змішувати zmishuvaty
blend *n* суміш sumish
bless *v. t* благословляти blahoslovliaty
blether *v. i* тріщати trishchaty
blight *n* занепад zanepad
blind *a* сліпий slipyi
blindage *n* бліндаж blindazh
blindfold *v. t* зав'язувати очі zaviazuvaty ochi
blindness *n* сліпота slipota
blink *v. t. & i* блимати blymaty
bliss *n* блаженство blazhenstvo
blister *n* пузир puzyr
blizzard *n* заметіль zametil
bloc *n* блок blok
block *n* колода koloda
block *v.t* примусити prymusyty
blockade *n* затор zator
blockhead *n* дурень duren
blood *n* кров krov
bloodshed *n* кровопролиття krovoprolyttia
bloody *a* кривавий kryvavyi
bloom *n* розквіт rozkvit
bloom *v.i.* розквітати rozkvitaty
blossom *v.i* цвісти tsvisty
blossom *n* цвітіння tsvitinnia
blot *v. t* бруднити brudnyty
blot *n.* ляпка liapka
blouse *n* блуза bluza
blow *v.i.* надути naduty
blow *n* удар udar
blue *a* блакитний blakytnyi
blue *n* синій колір synii kolir

bluff *n* блеф blef
bluff *v. t* блефувати blefuvaty
blunder *n* промах promakh
blunder *v.i* промахуватися promakhuvatysia
blunt *a* тупий tupyi
blur *n* неразні обриси nerazni obrysy
blurt *v. t* бовкнути bovknuty
blush *n* рум'янець rumianets
blush *v.i* червоніти chervonity
boar *n* кабан kaban
board *v. t.* сісти на корабель sisty na korabel
board *n* управління upravlinnia
boast *v.i* хвастати khvastaty
boast *n* хвастощі khvastoshchi
boat *v.i* кататися на човні katatysia na chovni
boat *n* човен choven
bodice *n* корсаж korsazh
bodily *adv.* особисто osobysto
bodily *a* цілком tsilkom
body *n* тіло tilo
bodyguard *n.* охоронець okhoronets
bog *n* трясовина triasovyna
bog *v.i* вигинати спину vyhynaty spynu
bogle *n* страховище strakhovyshche
bogus *a* підроблений pidroblenyi
boil *n* кипіння kypinnia
boil *v.i.* кипіти kypity
boiler *n* бак bak
bold *a.* зухвалий zukhvalyi
boldness *n* сміливість smilyvist
bolt *v. t* замикати на засув zamykaty na zasuv
bolt *n* засув zasuv
bomb *n* бомба bomba
bomb *v. t* бомбити bombyty

bombard *v. t* бомбардувати bombarduvaty
bombardment *n* бомбардування bombarduvannia
bomber *n* бомбардувальник bombarduvalnyk
bonafide *a* сумлінний sumlinnyi
bonafide *adv* сумлінно sumlinno
bond *n* кайдани kaidany
bondage *n* кабала kabala
bone *n*. кістка kistka
bonfire *n* багаття bahattia
bonnet *n* капот kapot
bonten *n* хутро khutro
bonus *n* премія premiia
book *v. t.* записуватися zapysuvatysia
book *n* книга knyha
bookish *n*. книжковий knyzhkovyi
book-keeper *n* бухгалтер bukhhalter
booklet *n* буклет buklet
book-mark *n*. закладка zakladka
book-seller *n* книгопродавець knyhoprodavets
book-worm *n* книжковий хробак knyzhkovyi khrobak
boon *n* добродіяння dobrodiiannia
boor *n* мужик muzhyk
boost *v. t* прискорювати pryskoriuvaty
boost *n* рекламування reklamuvannia
boot *n* чобіт chobit
booth *n* палатка palatka
booty *n* видобуток vydobutok
booze *v. i* випивка vypyvka
border *n* кордон kordon
border *v.t* межувати mezhuvaty
bore *n* калібр kalibr
bore *v. t* набридати nabrydaty
born *v*. перенести perenesty

born rich *adj.* багатий за народженням bahatyi za narodzhenniam
borne *adj.* обмежений obmezhenyi
borrow *v. t* запозичувати zapozychuvaty
bosom *n* груди hrudy
boss *n* бос bos
botany *n* ботаніка botanika
botch *v. t* робити недбало robyty nedbalo
both *pron* і один і другий i odyn i druhyi
both *adj.* обидва obydva
both *conj* так само, як tak samo, yak
bother *v. t* набридати nabrydaty
botheration *n* неспокій nespokii
bottle *n* пляшка pliashka
bottler *n* розливочна машина rozlyvochna mashyna
bottom *n* дно dno
bough *n* сук suk
boulder *n* валун valun
bouncer *n* хвалько khvalko
bound *n*. кидок kydok
boundary *n* межа mezha
bountiful *a* щедрий shchedryi
bounty *n* щедрість shchedrist
bouquet *n* букет buket
bout *n* мах makh
bow *v. t* гнутися hnutysia
bow *n* лук для стрільби luk dlia strilby
bow *n* уклін uklin
bowel *n*. кишечник kyshechnyk
bower *n* дача dacha
bowl *v.i* подавати м'яч podavaty miach
bowl *n* чаша chasha
box *n* коробка korobka
boxing *n* бокс boks

boy *n* хлопчик khlopchyk
boycott *n* бойкот boikot
boycott *v. t.* бойкотувати boikotuvaty
boyhood *n* отроцтво otrotstvo
brace *n* скоба skoba
bracelet *n* браслет braslet
brag *n* хвалько khvalko
brag *v. i* хвастати khvastaty
braille *n* шрифт Брайля shryft Brailia
brain *n* мозок mozok
brake *n* гальмо halmo
brake *v. t* гальмувати halmuvaty
branch *n* філія filiia
brand *n* головешка holoveshka
brandy *n* бренді brendi
brangle *v. t* шумно сваритися shumno svarytysia
brass *n.* латунь latun
brave *a* хоробрий khorobryi
bravery *n* хоробрість khorobrist
brawl *v. i. & n* сваритися svarytysia
bray *n* ревіння revinnia
bray *v. i* пронизливо кричати pronyzlyvo krychaty
breach *n* порушення porushennia
bread *n* хліб khlib
breaden *v. t. & i* панірувати paniruvaty
breadth *n* ширина shyryna
break *v. t* ламати lamaty
break *n* прорив proryv
breakage *n* поломка polomka
breakdown *n* аварія avariia
breakfast *n* сніданок snidanok
breakneck *n* запаморочлива швидкість zapamorochlyva shvydkist
breast *n* джерело харчування dzherelo kharchuvannia
breath *n* дихання dykhannia

breathe *v. i.* дихати dykhaty
breeches *n.* бриджі brydzhi
breed *n* порода poroda
breed *v.t* розводити rozvodyty
breeze *n* бриз bryz
breviary *n.* скорочення skorochennia
brevity *n* стислість styslist
brew *v. t.* варити пиво varyty pyvo
brewery *n* пивоварня pyvovarnia
bribe *v. t.* давати хабар davaty khabar
bribe *n* хабар khabar
brick *n* цегла tsehla
bride *n* наречена narechena
bridegroom *n.* жених zhenykh
bridge *n* міст mist
bridle *n* узда uzda
brief *a.* короткий korotkyi
brigade *n.* бригада bryhada
brigadier *n* бригадир bryhadyr
bright *a* яскравий yaskravyi
brighten *v. t* кращати krashchaty
brilliance *n* яскравість yaskravist
brilliant *a* блискучий blyskuchyi
brim *n* край krai
brine *n* розсіл rozsil
bring *v. t* нести nesty
brinjal *n* баклажан baklazhan
brink *n.* берег bereh
brisk *adj* жвавий zhvavyi
bristle *n* щетина shchetyna
british *adj* британський brytanskyi
brittle *a.* тендітний tenditnyi
broad *a* широкий shyrokyi
broadcast *n* радіопередача radioperedacha
broadcast *v. t* транслювати transliuvaty
brocade *n* парча parcha
broccoli *n.* броколі brokkoli
brochure *n* брошура broshura

brochure *n* брошура broshura
broker *n* брокер broker
bronze *n. & adj* бронза bronza
brood *n* виводок vyvodok
brook *n.* струмок strumok
broom *n* мітла mitla
broth *n* юшка yushka
brothel *n* бордель bordel
brother *n* брат brat
brotherhood *n* братство bratstvo
brow *n* брова brova
brown *a* коричневий korychnevyi
brown *n* коричневий колір korychnevyi kolir
browse *n* огляд ohliad
bruise *n* синяк syniak
bruit *n* чутки chutky
brush *n* пензлик penzlyk
brustle *v. i* тріщати trishchaty
brutal *a* брутальний brutalnyi
brute *n* тварина tvaryna
bubble *n* міхур mikhur
bucket *n* відро vidro
buckle *n* пряжка priazhka
bud *n* брунька brunka
budge *v. i. & n* ворушитися vorushytysia
budget *n* бюджет biudzhet
buff *n* буйволяча шкіра buivoliacha shkira
buffalo *n.* буйвол buivol
buffoon *n* блазень blazen
bug *n.* блошиця bloshytsia
bugle *n* ріжок rizhok
build *n* будова тіла budova tila
build *v. t* будувати buduvaty
building *n* будівництво budivnytstvo
bulb *n.* лампа lampa
bulk *n* обсяг obsiah
bulky *a* громіздкий hromizdkyi
bull *n* бик byk

bull's eye *n* точний постріл tochnyi postril
bulldog *n* бульдог buldoh
bullet *n* куля kulia
bulletin *n* зведення zvedennia
bullock *n* віл vil
bully *v. t.* задирати zadyraty
bully *n* хуліган khulihan
bulwark *n* бастіон bastion
bumper *n.* бампер bamper
bumpy *adj* вибоїстий vyboistyi
bunch *n* компанія kompaniia
bundle *n* вузол vuzol
bungalow *n* бунгало bunhalo
bungle *v. t* невміло працювати nevmilo pratsiuvaty
bungle *n* погана робота pohana robota
bunk *n* спальне місце spalne mistse
bunker *n* ямка yamka
buoy *n* буй bui
buoyancy *n* плавучість plavuchist
burden *n* ноша nosha
burden *v. t* обтяжувати obtiazhuvaty
burdensome *a* обтяжливий obtiazhlyvyi
Bureacracy *n.* бюрократія biurokratiia
bureau *n.* бюро biuro
bureaucrat *n* бюрократ biurokrat
burglar *n* зломщик zlomshchyk
burglary *n* крадіжка зі зломом kradizhka zi zlomom
burial *n* захоронення zakhoronennia
burk *v. t* дуже тверда брила duzhe tverda bryla
burn *v. t* горіти hority
burn *n* опік opik
burrow *n* нора nora
burst *v. i.* зламувати zlamuvaty

burst *n* спалах spalakh
bury *v. t.* ховати khovaty
bus *n* автобус avtobus
bush *n* кущ kushch
business *n* бізнес biznes
businessman *n* бізнесмен biznesmen
bustle *v. t* підганяти pidhaniaty
busy *a* зайнятий zainiatyi
but *prep* але ale
but *conj.* але ale
butcher *v. t* забивати zabyvaty
butcher *n* м'ясник miasnyk
butter *v. t* мазати mazaty
butter *n* масло maslo
butterfly *n* метелик metelyk
buttermilk *n* пахта pakhta
buttock *n* зад zad
button *n* ґудзик gudzyk
button *v. t.* застібати zastibaty
buy *v. t.* купувати kupuvaty
buyer *n.* покупець pokupets
buzz *v. i* дзижчати dzyzhchaty
buzz *n.* дзижчання dzyzhchannia
by *prep* біля bilia
by *adv* біля bilia
bye-bye *interj.* бувай buvai
by-election *n* додаткові вибори dodatkovi vybory
bylaw, bye-law *n* постанова postanova
bypass *n* обхід obkhid
by-product *n* субпродукти subprodukty
byre *n* корівник korivnyk
byword *n* приказка prykazka

C

cab *n.* таксі taksi
cabaret *n.* кабаре kabare
cabbage *n.* капуста kapusta
cabin *n.* хатина khatyna

cabinet *n.* група міністрів hrupa ministriv
cable *v. t.* закріплювати канатом zakripliuvaty kanatom
cable *n.* кабель kabel
cache *n* тайник tainyk
cachet *n* відбиток vidbytok
cackle *v. i* кудкудакати kudkudakaty
cactus *n.* кактус kaktus
cad *n* хам kham
cadet *n.* курсант kursant
cadge *v. i* жебракувати zhebrakuvaty
cadmium *n* кадмій kadmii
cafe *n.* кафе kafe
cage *n.* клітина klityna
cain *n* братовбивця bratovbyvtsia
cake *n.* пиріг pyrih
calamity *n.* біда bida
calcium *n* кальцій kaltsii
calculate *v. t.* розраховувати rozrakhovuvaty
calculation *n.* обчислення obchyslennia
calculator *n* калькулятор kalkuliator
calendar *n.* календар kalendar
calf *n.* теля telia
call *v. t.* кликати klykaty
call *n.* дзвінок dzvinok
caller *n* візитер vizyter
calligraphy *n* каліграфія kalihrafiia
calling *n.* покликання poklykannia
callous *a.* черствий cherstvyi
callow *adj* незрілий nezrilyi
calm *v. t.* заспокоювати zaspokoiuvaty
calm *n.* спокій spokii
calm *n.* заспокоєння zaspokoiennia

calmative *adj* заспокійливий
zaspokiilyvyi
calorie *n.* калорія kaloriia
calumniate *v. t.* обумовлювати
obumovliuvaty
camel *n.* верблюд verbliud
camera *n.* камера kamera
camlet *n* камлот kamlot
camp *v. i.* розбивати табір
rozbyvaty tabir
camp *n.* табір tabir
campaign *n.* кампанія kampaniia
camphor *n.* камфора kamfora
can *v.* бути в змозі buty v zmozi
can *v. t.* могти mohty
can *n.* бідон bidon
canal *n.* канал kanal
canard *n* качка kachka
cancel *v. t.* закреслювання
zakresliuvannia
cancellation *n* скасування
skasuvannia
cancer *n.* рак rak
candid *a.* щирий shchyryi
candidate *n.* кандидат kandydat
candle *n.* свічка svichka
candour *n.* відвертість vidvertist
candy *v. t.* зацукровувати
zatsukrovuvaty
candy *n.* цукерка tsukerka
cane *v. t.* плести з очерету plesty
z ocheretu
cane *n.* ціпок tsipok
canister *n.* каністра kanistra
cannon *n.* гармата harmata
cannonade *v. t.* обстрілювати
артилерійським вогнем
obstriliuvaty artyleriiskym
vohnem
canon *n* критерій kryterii
canopy *n.* полог poloh
canteen *n.* їдальня yidalnia
canter *n* ханжа khanzha

canton *n* кантон kanton
cantonment *n.* розквартирування
rozkvartyruvannia
canvas *n.* парусина parusyna
canvass *v. t.* агітувати ahituvaty
cap *v. t.* закривати кришкою
zakryvaty kryshkoiu
cap *n.* кепка kepka
capability *n.* здібність zdibnist
capable *a.* здатний zdatnyi
capacious *a.* ємний yemnyi
capacity *n.* місткість mistkist
cape *n.* накидка nakydka
capital *n.* столиця stolytsia
capital *a.* столичний stolychnyi
capitalist *n.* капіталіст kapitalist
capitulate *v. t* капітулювати
kapituliuvaty
caprice *n.* каприз kapryz
capricious *a.* вередливий
veredlyvyi
Capricorn *n* Козеріг Kozerih
capsicum *n* перець червоний
perets chervonyi
capsize *v. i.* перекидатися
perekydatysia
capsular *adj* капсульний
kapsulnyi
captain *n.* капітан kapitan
captaincy *n.* звання капітана
zvannia kapitana
caption *n.* титр tytr
captivate *v. t.* полонити polonyty
captive *a.* полонений polonenyi
captive *n.* бранець branets
captivity *n.* полонення
polonennia
capture *n.* здобич zdobych
capture *v. t.* захоплювати силою
zakhopliuvaty syloiu
car *n.* вагон трамвая vahon
tramvaia
carat *n.* карат karat

caravan *n.* караван karavan
carbide *n.* карбід karbid
carbon *n.* вуглець vuhlets
card *n.* гральна карта hralna karta
cardamom *n.* кардамон kardamon
cardboard *n.* картон karton
cardiacal *adjs* серцевий sertsevyi
cardinal *n.* кардинал kardynal
cardinal *a.* головний holovnyi
care *v. i.* піклуватися pikluvatysia
care *n.* догляд dohliad
career *n.* кар'єра kariera
careful *a* ретельний retelnyi
careless *a.* недбалий nedbalyi
caress *v. t.* пестити pestyty
cargo *n.* вантаж vantazh
caricature *n.* карикатура karykatura
carious *adj* каріозний karioznyi
carl *n* селюк seliuk
carnage *n* кривава бійня kryvava biinia
carnival *n* карнавал karnaval
carol *n* весела пісня vesela pisnia
carpal *adj* кистьовий kystovyi
carpenter *n.* тесляр tesliar
carpentry *n.* теслярські роботи tesliarski roboty
carpet *n.* килим kylym
carriage *n.* коляска koliaska
carrier *n.* носильник nosylnyk
carrot *n.* морква morkva
carry *v. t.* триматися trymatysia
cart *n.* візок vizok
cartage *n.* перевезення perevezennia
carton *n* картонка kartonka
cartoon *n.* мультфільм multfilm
cartridge *n.* патрон patron
carve *v. t.* вирізати vyryzaty
cascade *n.* водоспад vodospad

case *n.* положення polozhennia
cash *v. t.* перетворювати в готівку peretvoriuvaty v hotivku
cash *n.* готівка hotivka
cashier *n.* касир kasyr
casing *n.* кожух kozhukh
cask *n* барило barylo
casket *n* шкатулка shkatulka
cassette *n.* касета kaseta
cast *v. t.* метати metaty
cast *n.* тип typ
caste *n* каста kasta
castigate *v. t.* карати karaty
casting *n* кидання kydannia
cast-iron *n* чавун chavun
castle *n.* замок zamok
castor oil *n.* касторове масло kastorove maslo
castral *adj* табірний tabirnyi
casual *a.* тимчасовий tymchasovyi
casualty *n.* втрати vtraty
cat *n.* кішка kishka
catalogue *n.* каталог kataloh
cataract *n.* каскад kaskad
catch *n.* піймання piimannia
catch *v. t.* ловити lovyty
categorical *a.* категорічний katehorichnyi
category *n.* категорія katehoriia
cater *v. i* поставляти провізію postavliaty proviziiu
caterpillar *n* гусениця husenytsia
cathedral *n.* собор sobor
catholic *a.* католицький katolytskyi
cattle *n.* худоба khudoba
cauliflower *n.* кольорова капуста kolorova kapusta
causal *adj.* причинний prychynnyi
causality *n* причинність prychynnist

cause *v.t* заподіювати zapodiiuvaty
cause *n.* підстава pidstava
causeway *n* бруківка brukivka
caustic *a.* їдливий uidlyvyi
caution *v. t.* робити попередження robyty poperedzhennia
caution *n.* застереження zasterezhennia
cautious *a.* передбачливий peredbachlyvyi
cavalry *n.* кавалерія kavaleriia
cave *n.* печера pechera
cavern *n.* дупло duplo
cavil *v. t* чіплятися chipliatysia
cavity *n.* порожнина porozhnyna
caw *v. i.* каркати karkaty
caw *n.* каркання karkannia
cease *v. i.* переставати perestavaty
ceaseless *~a.* невпинний nevpynnyi
cedar *n.* кедр kedr
ceiling *n.* стеля stelia
celebrate *v. t. & i.* святкувати sviatkuvaty
celebration *n.* святкування sviatkuvannia
celebrity *n* славетна людина slavetna liudyna
celestial *adj* небесний nebesnyi
celibacy *n.* безшлюбність bezshliubnist
celibacy *n.* целібат tselibat
cell *n.* осередок oseredok
cellar *n* погріб pohrib
cellular *adj* клітинний klitynnyi
cement *v. t.* цементувати tsementuvaty
cement *n.* цемент tsement
cemetery *n.* цвинтар tsvyntar
cense *v. t* кадити kadyty

censer *n* кадило kadylo
censor *v. t.* цензурувати tsenzuruvaty
censor *n.* цензор tsenzor
censorious *adj* прискіпливий pryskiplyvyi
censorship *n.* цензура tsenzura
censure *n.* цензура tsenzura
censure *v. t.* осуджувати osudzhuvaty
census *n.* перепис perepys
cent *n* цент tsent
centenarian *n* довгожитель dovhozhytel
centenary *n.* сторіччя storichchia
centennial *adj.* столітній stolitnii
center *n* центр tsentr
centigrade *a.* стоградусний stohradusnyi
centipede *n.* сороконіжка sorokonizhka
central *a.* центральний tsentralnyi
centre *n* центр tsentr
centrifugal *adj.* відцентровий vidtsentrovyi
centuple *n. & adj* стократний stokratnyi
century *n.* століття stolittia
ceramics *n* кераміка keramika
cerated *adj.* воскований voskovanyi
cereal *a* злаковий zlakovyi
cereal *n.* каша kasha
cerebral *adj* церебральний tserebralnyi
ceremonial *a.* церемоніальний tseremonialnyi
ceremonious *a.* церемонний tseremonnyi
ceremony *n.* церемонія tseremoniia
certain *a* якийсь yakyis
certainly *adv.* звичайно zvychaino

certainty *n.* безсумнівний факт
bezsumnivnyi fakt
certificate *n.* сертифікат sertyfikat
certify *v. t.* засвідчувати
zasvidchuvaty
cerumen *n* вушна сірка vushna
sirka
cesspool *n.* вигрібна яма
vyhribna yama
chaice *n* чаша chasha
chain *n* ланцюг lantsiuh
chair *n.* стілець stilets
chairman *n* головуючий
holovuiuchyi
chaise *n* фаетон faeton
challenge *v. t.* викликати
vyklykaty
challenge *n.* виклик vyklyk
chamber *n.* кімната kimnata
chamberlain *n* камергер
kamerher
champion *v. t.* захищати
zakhyshchaty
champion *n.* чемпіон chempion
chance *n.* шанс shans
chancellor *n.* канцлер kantsler
chancery *n* канцелярія
kantseliariia
change *n.* заміна zamina
change *v. t.* переробляти
pererobliaty
channel *n* річище richyshche
chant *n* хорал khoral
chaos *n.* хаос khaos
chaotic *adv.* хаотичний
khaotychnyi
chapel *n.* каплиця kaplytsia
chapter *n.* глава hlava
character *n.* характер kharakter
charge *n.* заряд zariad
charge *v. t.* заряджати
zariadzhaty

chariot *n* легка коляска lehka
koliaska
charitable *a.* благодійний
blahodiinyi
charity *n.* милосердя myloserdia
charm1 *n.* чарівність charivnist
charm2 *v. t.* заклинати zaklynaty
chart *n.* графік hrafik
charter *n* грамота hramota
chase1 *v. t.* погоня pohonia
chase2 *n.* полювання poliuvannia
chaste *a.* цнотливий tsnotlyvyi
chastity *n.* цнотливість tsnotlyvist
chat1 *n.* бесіда besida
chat2 *v. i.* розмовляти rozmovliaty
chatter *v. t.* цокотіти tsokotity
chauffeur *n.* шофер shofer
cheap *a* дешевий deshevyi
cheapen *v. t.* дешевшати
deshevshaty
cheat *n.* шахрайство shakhraistvo
cheat *v. t.* шахраювати
shakhraiuvaty
check *n* відмітка vidmitka
check *v. t.* зазначити zaznachyty
checkmate *n* шах і мат shakh i
mat
cheek *n* щока shchoka
cheep *v. i* пропищати
propyshchaty
cheer *v. t.* вітати vitaty
cheer *n.* схвальний вигук
skhvalnyi vyhuk
cheerful *a.* безжурний bezzhurnyi
cheerless *a* сумовитий sumovytyi
cheese *n.* сир syr
chemical *n.* хімікат khimikat
chemical *a.* хімічний khimichnyi
chemise *n* жіноча сорочка
zhinocha sorochka
chemist *n.* хімік khimik
chemistry *n.* хімія khimiia
cheque *n.* чек chek

cherish *v. t.* плекати plekaty
cheroot *n* сигара syhara
chess *n.* віконна рама vikonna rama
chest *n* ящик yashchyk
chestnut *n.* каштан kashtan
chevalier *n* кавалер kavaler
chew *v. t* жувати zhuvaty
chicken *n.* курча kurcha
chide *v. t.* сварити svaryty
chief *a.* головний holovnyi
chieftain *n.* вождь vozhd
child *n* маля malia
childhood *n.* дитинство dytynstvo
childish *a.* дитячий dytiachyi
chiliad *n.* тисяча tysiacha
chill *n.* холод kholod
chilli *n.* перець гострий perets hostryi
chilly *a* мерзлякуватий merzliakuvatyi
chimney *n.* труба truba
chimpanzee *n.* шимпанзе shympanze
chin *n.* підборіддя pidboriddia
china *n.* фарфор farfor
chirp *n* цвірінькання tsvirinkannia
chirp *v.i.* цвірінькати tsvirinkaty
chisel *v. t.* працювати стамескою pratsiuvaty stameskoiu
chisel *n* стамеска stameska
chit *n.* крихта krykhta
chivalrous *a.* лицарський lytsarskyi
chivalry *n.* лицарство lytsarstvo
chlorine *n* хлор khlor
chloroform *n* хлороформ khloroform
chocolate *n* шоколад shokolad
choice *n.* асортимент asortyment
choir *n* хор khor
choke *v. t.* душитися dushytysia
cholera *n.* холера kholera

choose *v. t.* вибирати vybyraty
chop *v. t* кришити kryshyty
chord *n.* струна struna
choroid *n* судинна оболонка sudynna obolonka
chorus *n.* хор khor
Christ *n.* Христос Khrystos
Christendom *n.* християнський світ khrystyianskyi svit
Christian *n* християнин khrystyianyn
Christian *a.* християнський khrystyianskyi
Christianity *n.* християнство khrystyianstvo
Christmas *n* Різдво Rizdvo
chrome *n* жовта фарба zhovta farba
chronic *a.* хронічний khronichnyi
chronicle *n.* хроніка khronika
chronograph *n* хронограф khronohraf
chronology *n.* хронологія khronolohiia
chuckle *v. i* посміюватися posmiiuvatysia
chum *n* приятель pryiatel
church *n.* церква tserkva
churchyard *n.* кладовище kladovyshche
churl *n* селюк seliuk
churn *n.* олійниця oliinytsia
churn *v. t. & i.* збивати zbyvaty
cigar *n.* сигара syhara
cigarette *n.* сигарета syhareta
cinema *n.* кінотеатр kinoteatr
cinnabar *n* кіновар kinovar
cinnamon *n* кориця korytsia
cipher, cipher *n.* шифр shyfr
circle *n.* коло kolo
circuit *n.* кругообіг kruhoobih
circular *a* круговой kruhovoi
circular *n.* циркуляр tsyrkuliar

circulate v. i. циркулювати tsyrkuliuvaty
circulation n круговорот kruhovorot
circumference n. коло kolo
circumfluence n. обтікання obtikannia
circumspect adj. обережний oberezhnyi
circumstance n обставина obstavyna
circus n. цирк tsyrk
cist n гробниця hrobnytsia
citadel n. цитадель tsytadel
cite v. t згадувати zhaduvaty
citizen n громадянин hromadianyn
citizenship n громадянство hromadianstvo
citric adj. лимонний lymonnyi
city n місто misto
civic a цивільний tsyvilnyi
civics n основи громадянськості osnovy hromadianskosti
civil a цивільний tsyvilnyi
civilian n цивільна особа tsyvilna osoba
civilization n. цивілізація tsyvilizatsiia
civilize v. t цивілізувати tsyvilizuvaty
clack n. & v. i тріщати trishchaty
claim v. t вимагати vymahaty
claim n позов pozov
claimant n позивач pozyvach
clamber v. i дертися dertysia
clamour v. i. бурхливо виражати протест burkhlyvo vyrazhaty protest
clamour n шум shum
clamp n хомут khomut
clandestine adj. таємний taiemnyi

clap n бавовна bavovna
clap v. i. ляпати liapaty
clarification n прояснення proiasnennia
clarify v. t прояснити proiasnyty
clarion n. звук ріжка zvuk rizhka
clarity n чистота chystota
clash v. t. зіштовхуватися zishtovkhuvatysia
clash n. зіткнення zitknennia
clasp n застібка zastibka
class n клас klas
classic n класик klasyk
classic a класичний klasychnyi
classical a гуманітарний humanitarnyi
classification n класифікація klasyfikatsiia
classify v. t класифікувати klasyfikuvaty
clause n стаття stattia
claw n пазур pazur
clay n глинозем hlynozem
clean v. t чистити chystyty
clean чистий chystyi
cleanliness n чистота chystota
cleanse v. t чистити chystyty
clear a чистий chystyi
clear v. t очищати ochyshchaty
clearance n очищення ochyshchennia
clearly adv ясно yasno
cleft n тріщина trishchyna
clergy n духовенство dukhovenstvo
clerical a клерикальний klerykalnyi
clerk n клерк klerk
clever a. розумний rozumnyi
clew n. клубок klubok
click n. клацання klatsannia
client n.. клієнт kliient
cliff n. стрімчак strimchak

climate *n.* клімат klimat
climax *n.* клімакс klimaks
climb *v.i* видиратися vydyratysia
climb1 *n.* підйом pidiom
cling *v. i.* прилипати prylypaty
clinic *n.* клініка klinika
clink *n.* віршик virshyk
cloak *n.* плащ plashch
clock *n.* годинник hodynnyk
clod *n.* ком kom
cloister *n.* монастир monastyr
close *v. t* закрити zakryty
close *a.* закритий zakrytyi
close *n.* завершення
    zavershennia
closet *n.* кабінет kabinet
closure *n.* закриття zakryttia
clot *n.* грудка hrudka
clot *v. t* запікатися zapikatysia
cloth *n* тканина tkanyna
clothe *v. t* вкривати vkryvaty
clothes *n.* убрання ubrannia
clothing *n* обмундирування
    obmundyruvannia
cloud *n.* хмара khmara
cloudy *a* хмарний khmarnyi
clove *n* гвоздика hvozdyka
clown *n* клоун kloun
club *n* клуб klub
clue *n* ключ kliuch
clumsy *a* нетактовний
    netaktovnyi
cluster *v. i.* зростати гронами
    zrostaty hronamy
cluster *n* китиця kytytsia
clutch *n* зчеплення zcheplennia
clutter *v. t* спричиняти безлад
    sprychyniaty bezlad
coach *n* тренер trener
coachman *n* кучер kucher
coal *n* вугілля vuhillia
coalition *n* коаліція koalitsiia
coarse *a* грубий hrubyi

coast *n* узбережжя uzberezhzhia
coat *n* пальто palto
coating *n* шар shar
coax *v. t* умовляти umovliaty
cobalt *n* кобальт kobalt
cobbler *n* швець shvets
cobra *n* кобра kobra
cobweb *n* павутина pavutyna
cocaine *n* кокаїн kokain
cock *n* півень piven
cocker *v. t* балувати baluvaty
cockle *v. i* морщитися
    morshchytysia
cock-pit *n.* кокпіт kokpit
cockroach *n* тарган tarhan
coconut *n* кокос kokos
code *n* код kod
co-education *n.* спільне
    навчання spilne navchannia
coefficient *n.* коефіцієнт
    koefitsiient
co-exist *v. i* співіснувати
    spivisnuvaty
co-existence *n* співіснування
    spivisnuvannia
coffee *n* кава kava
coffin *n* труна truna
cog *n* зубець zubets
cogent *adj.* переконливий
    perekonlyvyi
cognate *adj* споріднений
    sporidnenyi
cognizance *n* знання znannia
cohabit *v. t* співмешкати
    spivmeshkaty
coherent *a* зчеплений zcheplenyi
cohesive *adj* здатний до
    зчеплення zdatnyi do
    zcheplennia
coif *n* стрижка stryzhka
coin *n* монета moneta
coinage *n* карбування монети
    karbuvannia monety

coincide v. i збігатися zbihatysia
coir n кокосові волокна kokosovi volokna
coke v. t кокс koks
cold n холод kholod
cold a холодний kholodnyi
collaborate v. i співпрацювати spivpratsiuvaty
collaboration n співробітництво spivrobitnytstvo
collapse v. i обвал obval
collar n комір komir
colleague n колега koleha
collect v. t колекціонувати kolektsionuvaty
collection n колекція kolektsiia
collective a колективний kolektyvnyi
collector n складальник skladalnyk
college n коледж koledzh
collide v. i. зіштовхувати zishtovkhuvaty
collision n сутичка sutychka
collusion n таємна угода taiemna uhoda
colon n двокрапка dvokrapka
colon n Колон Kolon
colonel n. полковник polkovnyk
colonial a колоніальний kolonialnyi
colony n колонія koloniia
colour v. t розфарбовувати rozfarbovuvaty
colour n колір kolir
colter n різак rizak
column n колона kolona
coma n. голова комети holova komety
comb n гребінь hrebin
combat v. t. боротися borotysia
combat1 n сутичка sutychka
combatant a. стройовий stroiovyi

combatant1 n той, хто бореться toi, khto boretsia
combination n комбінація kombinatsiia
combine v. t комбінувати kombinuvaty
come v. i. приходити prykhodyty
comedian n. комедіант komediant
comedy n. комедія komediia
comet n комета kometa
comfit n. драже drazhe
comfort v. t втішати vtishaty
comfort1 n. комфорт komfort
comfortable a зручний zruchnyi
comic n комік komik
comic a комічний komichnyi
comical a смішний smishnyi
comma n кома koma
command n команда komanda
command v. t командувати komanduvaty
commandant n комендант komendant
commander n командир komandyr
commemorate v. t. відзначати vidznachaty
commemoration n. святкування sviatkuvannia
commence v. t починатися pochynatysia
commencement n набуття nabuttia
commend v. t рекомендувати rekomenduvaty
commendable a. похвальний pokhvalnyi
commendation n похвала pokhvala
comment n коментар komentar
comment v. i коментувати komentuvaty

commentary *n* коментар komentar
commentator *n* коментатор komentator
commerce *n* торгівля torhivlia
commercial *a* торговий torhovyi
commiserate *v. t* співчувати spivchuvaty
commission *n.* доручення doruchennia
commissioner *n.* уповноважений upovnovazhenyi
commissure *n.* спайка spaika
commit *v. t.* доручати doruchaty
committee *n* комітет komitet
commodity *n.* товар tovar
common *a.* загальний zahalnyi
commoner *n.* людина незнатного походження liudyna neznatnoho pokhodzhennia
commonplace *a.* загальне місце zahalne mistse
commonwealth *n.* держава derzhava
commotion *n* хвилювання khvyliuvannia
commove *v. t* турбувати turbuvaty
communal *a* комунальний komunalnyi
commune *v. t* спілкуватися spilkuvatysia
communicate *v. t* спілкуватися spilkuvatysia
communication *n.* комунікація komunikatsiia
communiqué *n.* комюніке komiunike
communism *n* комунізм komunizm
community *n.* суспільство suspilstvo
commute *v. t* перемикати peremykaty

compact *n.* договір dohovir
compact *a.* щільний shchilnyi
companion *n.* супутник suputnyk
company *n.* компанія kompaniia
comparative *a* порівняльний porivnialnyi
compare *v. t* порівнювати porivniuvaty
comparison *n* порівняння porivniannia
compartment *n.* купе kupe
compass *n* компас kompas
compassion *n* співчуття spivchuttia
compel *v. t* змушувати zmushuvaty
compensate *v.t* компенсувати kompensuvaty
compensation *n* компенсація kompensatsiia
compete *v. i* конкурувати konkuruvaty
competence *n* компетентність kompetentnist
competent *a.* компетентний kompetentnyi
competition *n.* змагання zmahannia
competitive *a* конкурентоспроможний konkurentospromozhnyi
compile *v. t* компілювати kompiliuvaty
complacent *adj.* послужливий posluzhlyvyi
complain *v. i* скаржитися skarzhytysia
complaint *n* скарга skarha
complaisance *n.* ввічливість vvichlyvist
complaisant *adj.* послужливий posluzhlyvyi

complement *n* повний комплект
povnyi komplekt
complementary *a* неконкуруючий
nekonkuruiuchyi
complete *v. t* завершувати
zavershuvaty
complete *a* повний povnyi
completion *n.* вивершення
vyvershennia
complex *n* комплекс kompleks
complex *a* комплексний
kompleksnyi
complexion *n* колір обличчя kolir
oblychchia
compliance *n.* щзгода shchzhoda
compliant *adj.* сумісний sumisnyi
complicate *v. t* ускладнювати
uskladniuvaty
complication *n.* складність
skladnist
compliment *n.* комплімент
kompliment
compliment *v. t* хвалити khvalyty
comply *v. i* підкорятися
pidkoriatysia
component *adj.* складовий
skladovyi
compose *v. t* складати skladaty
composition *n* складання
skladannia
compositor композитор
kompozytor
compost *n* удобрювати
компостом udobriuvaty
kompostom
composure *n.* холоднокровність
kholodnokrovnist
compound *a* складений
skladenyi
compound *n* сполука spoluka
compound *v. i* з'єднувати
ziednuvaty

compound *n* сполучення
spoluchennia
compounder *n.* мировий
посередник myrovyi
poserednyk
comprehend *v. t* включати
vkliuchaty
comprehension *n* розуміння
rozuminnia
comprehensive *a* всебічний
vsebichnyi
compress *v. t.* стискати styskaty
compromise *v. t* компрометувати
komprometuvaty
compromise *n* компроміс
kompromis
compulsion *n* примус prymus
compulsory *a* обов'язковий
oboviazkovyi
compunction *n.* каяття kaiattia
computation *n.* розрахунок
rozrakhunok
compute *v.t.* рахувати rakhuvaty
comrade *n.* товариш tovarysh
conation *n.* здатність до
вольового руху zdatnist do
volovoho rukhu
concave *adj.* увігнутий uvihnutyi
conceal *v. t.* ховати khovaty
concede *v.t.* погоджуватися
pohodzhuvatysia
conceit *n* марнославство
marnoslavstvo
conceive *v. t* задумувати
zadumuvaty
concentrate *v. t* концентруватися
kontsentruvatysia
concentration *n.* концентрація
kontsentratsiia
concept *n* концепція kontseptsiia
conception *n* задум zadum
concern *n* справа sprava

concern v. t стосуватися stosuvatysia
concert n. концерт kontsert
concert2 v. t змовлятися zmovliatysia
concession n поступка postupka
conch n. абсида absyda
conciliate v.t. примиряти prymyriaty
concise a стислий styslyi
conclude v. t укладати ukladaty
conclusion n. висновок vysnovok
conclusive a заключний zakliuchnyi
concoct v. t куховарити kukhovaryty
concoction n. куховарство kukhovarstvo
concord n. узгодження uzhodzhennia
concrescence n. зрощення zroshchennia
concrete n бетон beton
concrete a бетонний betonnyi
concrete v. t твердіти tverdity
concubinage n. позашлюбне співжиття pozashliubne spivzhyttia
concubine n співмешанка spivmeshanka
conculcate v.t. топати topaty
condemn v. t засудити zasudyty
condemnation n вирок vyrok
condense v. t згущувати zhushchuvaty
condite v.t. солити solyty
condition n умова umova
conditional a обумовлений obumovlenyi
condole v. i. співчувати spivchuvaty
condolence n співчуття spivchuttia

condonation n. потурання poturannia
conduct v. t вести vesty
conduct n керувати keruvaty
conductor n кондуктор konduktor
cone n. шишка shyshka
confectioner n кондитер kondyter
confectionery n кондитерські вироби kondyterski vyroby
confer v. i радитися radytysia
conference n конференція konferentsiia
confess v. t. сповідувати spoviduvaty
confession n сповідь spovid
confidant n довірена особа dovirena osoba
confide v. i довіряти doviriaty
confidence n довіра dovira
confident a. впевнений vpevnenyi
confidential a. конфіденційний konfidentsiinyi
confine v. t обмежувати obmezhuvaty
confinement n. позбавлення волі pozbavlennia voli
confirm v. t санкціонувати sanktsionuvaty
confirmation n підтвердження pidtverdzhennia
confiscate v. t конфіскувати konfiskuvaty
confiscation n конфіскація konfiskatsiia
conflict v. i бути в конфлікті buty v konflikti
conflict n. конфлікт konflikt
confluence n скупчення народу skupchennia narodu
confluent adj. який зливається yakyi zlyvaietsia

conformity *n.* погодженість
pohodzhenist
conformity *n.* підпорядкування
pidporiadkuvannia
confraternity *n.* товариство
tovarystvo
confrontation *n.* конфронтація
konfrontatsiia
confuse *v. t* змішувати
zmishuvaty
confusion *n* замішування
zamishuvannia
confute *v.t.* спростовувати
sprostovuvaty
conge *n.* наказ nakaz
congenial *a* сприятливий
spryiatlyvyi
conglutinat *v.t.* склеювати
skleiuvaty
congratulate *v. t* поздоровляти
pozdorovliaty
congratulation *n* поздоровлення
pozdorovlennia
congress *n* конгрес konhres
conjecture *n* здогад zdohad
conjecture *v. t* гадати hadaty
conjugal *a* шлюбний shliubnyi
conjugate *v.t. & i.* відмінюватися
vidminiuvatysia
conjunct *adj.* з'єднаний ziednanyi
conjunctiva *n.* кон'юнктива
koniunktyva
conjuncture *n.* кон'юктура
koniuktura
conjure *v.i.* заклинати zaklynaty
conjure *v.t.* чаклувати chakluvaty
connect *v. t.* з'єднуватися
ziednuvatysia
connection *n* зв'язок zv'iazok
connivance *n.* попуск popusk
conquer *v. t* завойовувати
zavoiovuvaty

conquest *n* завоювання
zavoiuvannia
conscience *n* совість sovist
conscious *a* який усвідомлює
yakyi usvidomliuie
consecrate *v.t.* присвячувати
prysviachuvaty
consecutive *adj.* послідовний
poslidovnyi
consecutively *adv* послідовно
poslidovno
consensus *n.* згода zhoda
consent *v. i* дозволяти dozvoliaty
consent *n.* угода uhoda
consent3 *v.t.* бути задоволеним
buty zadovolenym
consequence *n* наслідок naslidok
consequent *a* логічний lohichnyi
conservative *n* консерватор
konservator
conservative *a* консервативний
konservatyvnyi
conserve *v. t* консервувати
konservuvaty
consider *v. t* обмірковувати
obmirkovuvaty
considerable *a* достатній
dostatnii
considerate *a.* уважний uvazhnyi
consideration *n* розгляд rozhliad
considering *prep.* враховуючи
vrakhovuiuchy
consign *v. t.* доручати doruchaty
consign *v.t.* ввіряти vviriaty
consignment *n.* партія partiia
consist *v. i* полягати poliahaty
consistence,-cy *n.* логічність
lohichnist
consistent *a* щільний shchilnyi
consolation *n* утіха utikha
console *v. t* заспокоювати
zaspokoiuvaty

consolidate v. t. консолідувати
konsoliduvaty
consolidation n консолідація
konsolidatsiia
consonance n. співзвуччя
spivzvuchchia
consonant n. приголосний
pryholosnyi
consort n. чоловік cholovik
conspectus n. конспект konspekt
conspicuous a. показний
pokaznyi
conspiracy n. змова zmova
conspirator n. змовник zmovnyk
conspire v. i. вчиняти змову
vchyniaty zmovu
constable n констебль konstebl
constant a сталий stalyi
constellation n. сукупність
sukupnist
constipation n. закреп zakrep
constituency n електорат
elektorat
constituent n. виборець vyborets
constituent adj. який обирає
yakyi obyraie
constitute v. t складати skladaty
constitution n конституція
konstytutsiia
constrict v.t. стискати styskaty
construct v. t. конструювати
konstruiuvaty
construction n спорудження
sporudzhennia
consult v. t довідуватися
doviduvatysia
consultation n консультація
konsultatsiia
consume v. t споживати
spozhyvaty
consumption n витрата vytrata
consumption n споживання
spozhyvannia

contact n. контакт kontakt
contact v. t контактувати
kontaktuvaty
contagious a заразливий
zarazlyvyi
contain v.t. містити mistyty
contaminate v.t. забруднювати
zabrudniuvaty
contemplate v. t споглядати
spohliadaty
contemplation n споглядання
spohliadannia
contemporary a сучасний
suchasnyi
contempt n презирство
prezyrstvo
contemptuous a презирливий
prezyrlyvyi
contend v. i твердити tverdyty
content a. який голосує «за»
yakyi holosuie «za»
content n. задоволення
zadovolennia
content v. t задовольняти
zadovolniaty
content n суть sut
contention n твердження
tverdzhennia
contentment n задоволеність
zadovolenist
contest v. t оскаржувати
oskarzhuvaty
contest n. суперечка superechka
context n контекст kontekst
continent n континент kontynent
continental a континентальний
kontynentalnyi
contingency n. випадковість
vypadkovist
continual adj. безперервний
bezperervnyi
continuation n. продовження
prodovzhennia

continue *v. i.* продовжувати prodovzhuvaty
continuity *n* безперервність bezperervnist
continuous *a* безперервний bezperervnyi
contour *n* контур kontur
contra *pref.* проти- proty-
contraception *n.* контрацепція kontratseptsiia
contract *n* контракт kontrakt
contract *v. t* скорочувати skorochuvaty
contractor *n* підрядник pidriadnyk
contradict *v. t* суперечити superechyty
contradiction *n* протиріччя protyrichchia
contrapose *v.t.* протиставляти protystavliaty
contrary *a* супротивний suprotyvnyi
contrast *n* контраст kontrast
contrast *v. t* суперечити superechyty
contribute *v. t* сприяти spryiaty
contribution *n* внесок vnesok
control *n* контроль kontrol
control *v. t* контролювати kontroliuvaty
controller *n.* контролер kontroler
controversy *n* спір spir
contuse *v.t.* контузія kontuziia
conundrum *n.* загадка zahadka
convene *v. t* скликати sklykaty
convener *n* керівник конференції kerivnyk konferentsii
convenience *n.* зручність zruchnist
convenient *a* придатний prydatnyi

convent *n* католіцька жіноча школа katolitska zhinocha shkola
convention *n.* угода uhoda
conversant *adj.* добре знайомий dobre znaiomyi
conversant *a* досвічений dosvichenyi
conversation *n* бесіда besida
converse *v.t.* спілкуватися spilkuvatysia
conversion *n* зміна zmina
convert *v. t* перетворювати peretvoriuvaty
convert *n* новонавернений novonavernenyi
convey *v. t.* переправляти perepravliaty
conveyance *n* перевізни засоби perevizny zasoby
convict *n* арештант areshtant
convict *v. t.* визнанти винним vyznanty vynnym
conviction *n* переконаність perekonanist
convince *v. t* переконати perekonaty
convivial *adj.* бенкетний benketnyi
convocation *n.* скликання sklykannia
convoke *v.t.* скликати sklykaty
convolve *v.t.* згортати zhortaty
coo *n* воркування vorkuvannia
coo *v. i* ніжно воркувати nizhno vorkuvaty
cook *v. t* готувати hotuvaty
cook *n* кухар kukhar
cooker *n* кухонна плита kukhonna plyta
cool *v. i.* охолоджувати okholodzhuvaty
cool *a* прохолодний prokholodnyi

cooler *n* холодильник kholodylnyk
coolie *n* чорнороб chornorob
co-operate *v. i* співпрацювати spivpratsiuvaty
co-operation *n* співробітництво spivrobitnytstvo
co-operative *a* кооперативний kooperatyvnyi
co-ordinate *v.t* координувати koordynuvaty
co-ordinate *a* координований koordynovanyi
co-ordination *n* координація koordynatsiia
coot *n.* лисуха lysukha
co-partner *n* член товариства chlen tovarystva
cope *v. i* справитися spravytysia
coper *n.* баришник baryshnyk
copper *n* мідь mid
coppice *n.* підлісок pidlisok
coprology *n.* копрологія koprolohiia
copulate *v.i.* спаровуватися sparovuvatysia
copy *n* копія kopiia
copy *v. t* копіювати kopiiuvaty
coral *n* корал koral
corbel *n.* кронштейн kronshtein
cord *n* шнур shnur
cordate *adj.* серцеподібний sertsepodibnyi
cordial *a* серцевий sertsevyi
core *n.* ядро yadro
coriander *n.* коріандр koriandr
Corinth *n.* Коринф Korynf
cork *n.* затикати zatykaty
cormorant *n.* ненажера nenazhera
corn *n* зерно zerno
cornea *n* рогівка rohivka
corner *n* район raion

cornet *n.* корнет kornet
cornicle *n.* вусик vusyk
coronation *n* коронація koronatsiia
coronet *n.* віночок vinochok
corporal *a* тілесний tilesnyi
corporate *adj.* корпоративний korporatyvnyi
corporation *n* корпорація korporatsiia
corps *n* корпус korpus
corpse *n* труп trup
correct *v. t* виправляти vypravliaty
correct *a* правильний pravylnyi
correction *n* виправлення vypravlennia
correlate *v.t.* зіставляти zistavliaty
correlation *n.* взаємозв'язок vzaiemozviazok
correspond *v. i* відповідати vidpovidaty
correspondence *n.* відповідність vidpovidnist
correspondent *n.* кореспондент korespondent
corridor *n.* коридор korydor
corroborate *v.t.* підтверджувати pidtverdzhuvaty
corrosive *adj.* корозійний koroziinyi
corrupt *v. t.* спотворювати spotvoriuvaty
corrupt *a.* зіпсований zipsovanyi
corruption *n.* псування psuvannia
cosier *n.* затишне місце zatyshne mistse
cosmetic *n.* косметика kosmetyka
cosmetic *a.* косметичний kosmetychnyi
cosmic *adj.* космічний kosmichnyi
cost *n.* вартість vartist
cost *v.t.* коштувати koshtuvaty

costal *adj.* реберний rebernyi
costly *a.* дорогий dorohyi
costume *n.* одяг odiah
cosy *a.* приємний pryiemnyi
cot *n.* дитяче ліжко dytiache lizhko
cote *n.* хлів khliv
cottage *n* котедж kotedzh
cotton *n.* бавовна bavovna
couch *n.* диван dyvan
cough *n.* кашель kashel
cough *v. i.* кашляти kashliaty
council *n.* рада rada
councillor *n.* радник radnyk
counsel *v. t.* дати пораду daty poradu
counsel *n.* обговорення obhovorennia
counsellor *n.* радник radnyk
count *n.* позовна pozovna
count *v. t.* підраховувати pidrakhovuvaty
countenance *n.* обличчя oblychchia
counter *n.* прилавок prylavok
counter *v. t* протистояти protystoiaty
counteract *v.t.* протидіяти protydiiaty
countercharge *n.* зустрічне звинувачення zustrichne zvynuvachennia
counterfeit *a.* підробляти pidrobliaty
counterfeiter *n.* підроблювач pidrobliuvach
countermand *v.t.* відкликати vidklykaty
counterpart *n.* двійник dviinyk
countersign *v. t.* скріплювати підписом skripliuvaty pidpysom
countess *n.* графиня hrafynia

countless *a.* незчисленний nezchyslennyi
country *n.* країна kraina
county *n.* жителі графства zhyteli hrafstva
coup *n.* подвиг podvyh
couple *n* пара para
couple *v. t* спарюватися spariuvatysia
couplet *n.* куплет kuplet
coupon *n.* відривний талон vidryvnyi talon
courage *n.* хоробрість khorobrist
courageous *a.* сміливий smilyvyi
courier *n.* кур'єр kurier
course *n.* курс kurs
court *v. t.* спокушати spokushaty
court *n.* суд sud
courteous *a.* чемний chemnyi
courtesan *n.* куртизанка kurtyzanka
courtesy *n.* чемність chemnist
courtier *n.* придворний prydvornyi
courtship *n.* залицяння zalytsiannia
courtyard *n.* двір dvir
cousin *n.* двоюрідний брат dvoiuridnyi brat
covenant *n.* домовленість domovlenist
cover *v. t.* закривати zakryvaty
cover *n.* покришка pokryshka
coverlet *n.* покривало pokryvalo
covet *v.t.* жадати zhadaty
cow *v. t.* залякувати zaliakuvaty
cow *n.* корова korova
coward *n.* боягуз boiahuz
cowardice *n.* боягузтво boiahuztvo
cower *v.i.* зіщулюватися zishchuliuvatysia
cozy *adj.* затишний zatyshnyi

crab *n* краб krab
crack *v. i* розтріскування roztriskuvannia
crack *n* тріск trisk
cracker *n* сухар sukhar
crackle *v.t.* потріскувати potriskuvaty
cradle *n* колиска kolyska
craft *n* ремесло remeslo
craftsman *n* вправний майстер vpravnyi maister
crafty *a* хитрий khytryi
cram *v. t* втискувати vtyskuvaty
crambo *n.* ріфмоплетство rifmopletstvo
crane *n* підйомний кран pidiomnyi kran
crankle *v.t.* звиватися zvyvatysia
crash *v. i* розбити з грюкотом rozbyty z hriukotom
crash *n* тріск trьsk
crass *adj.* повний povnyi
crate *n.* кліть klit
crave *v.t.* палко бажати palko bazhaty
craw *n.* зоб zob
crawl *n* повзання povzannia
crawl *v. t* плентатися plentatysia
craze *n* манія maniia
crazy *a* божевільний bozhevilnyi
creak *v. i* скрипіти skrypity
creak *n* скрип skryp
cream *n* вершки vershky
crease *n* складка skladka
create *v. t* створювати stvoriuvaty
creation *n* створення stvorennia
creative *adj.* творчий tvorchyi
creator *n* творець tvorets
creature *n* створіння stvorinnia
credible *a* ймовірний ymovirnyi
credit *n* кредит kredyt
creditable *a* похвальний pokhvalnyi

creditor *n* кредитор kredytor
credulity *adj.* довірливість dovirlyvist
creed *n.* кредо kredo
creed *n* віросповідання virospovidannia
creek *n.* струмок strumok
creep *v. i* плазувати plazuvaty
creeper *n* повзуча рослина povzucha roslyna
cremate *v. t* кремувати kremuvaty
cremation *n* кремація krematsiia
crest *n* гребінець hrebinets
crevet *n.* плавильна чаша plavylna chasha
crew *n.* екіпаж ekipazh
crib *n.* ясла yasla
cricket *n* цвіркун tsvirkun
crime *n* злочин zlochyn
criminal *n* злочинець zlochynets
criminal *a* кримінальний kryminalnyi
crimp *n* агент, що вербує на військову службу обманом ahent, shcho verbuie na vьiskovu sluzhbu obmanom
crimple *v.t.* робити складки robyty skladky
crimson *n* малиновий колір malynovyi kolir
cringe *v. i.* раболіпствувати rabolipstvuvaty
cripple *n* каліка kalika
crisis *n* криза kryza
crisp *a* розсипчастий rozsypchastyi
criterion *n* мірило mirylo
critic *n* критик krytyk
critical *a* критичний krytychnyi
criticism *n* критика krytyka
criticize *v. t* критикувати krytykuvaty
croak *n.* кумкання kumkannia

crockery *n.* посуд posud
crocodile *n* крокодил krokodyl
croesus *n.* Крез Krez
crook *a* несправедливий nespravedlyvyi
crop *n* урожай urozhai
cross *v.* *t* перетинати peretynaty
cross *a* поперечний poperechnyi
cross *n* хрест khrest
crossing *n.* перетин peretyn
crotchet *n.* гачок hachok
crouch *v.* *i.* раболіпствувати rabolipstvuvaty
crow *n* ворона vorona
crow *v.* *i* кукурікати kukurikaty
crowd *n* натовп natovp
crown *v.* *t* вінчати vinchaty
crown *n* корона korona
crucial *adj.* вирішальний vyrishalnyi
crude *a* необроблений neobroblenyi
cruel *a* жорстокий zhorstokyi
cruelty *n* жорстокість zhorstokist
cruise *v.* *i.* круїз kruiz
cruiser *n* крейсер kreiser
crumb *n* крихітка krykhitka
crumble *v.* *t* кришити kryshyty
crump *adj.* зхрусткий zkhrustkyi
crusade *n* похід pokhid
crush *v.* *t* роздавити rozdavyty
crust *n.* скоринка skorynka
crutch *n* опора opora
cry *n* благання blahannia
cry *v.* *i* кричати krychaty
cryptography *n.* криптографія kryptohrafiia
crystal *n* кришталь kryshtal
cub *n* дитинча dytyncha
cube *n* куб kub
cubical *a* кубічний kubichnyi
cubiform *adj.* кубовидний kubovydnyi

cuckold *n.* рогоносець rohonosets
cuckoo *n* зозуля zozulia
cucumber *n* огірок ohirok
cudgel *n* дрючок driuchok
cue *n* репліка replika
cuff *v.* *t* бити рукою byty rukoiu
cuff *n* манжета manzheta
cuisine *n.* кулінарне мистецтво kulinarne mystetstvo
cullet *n.* склобій sklobii
culminate *v.i.* досягати найвищої точки dosiahaty naivyshchoi tochky
culpable *a* винний vynnyi
culprit *n* винуватець vynuvatets
cult *n* культ kult
cultivate *v.* *t* обробляти obrobliaty
cultrate *adj.* загострений zahostrenyi
cultural *a* культурний kulturnyi
culture *n* культура kultura
culvert *n.* дренажна труба drenazhna truba
cunning *a* хитрий khytryi
cunning *n* хитрість khytrist
cup *n.* чашка chashka
cupboard *n* буфет bufet
Cupid *n* Купідон Kupidon
cupidity *n* скнарість sknarist
curable *a* виліковний vylikovnyi
curative *a* цілющий tsiliushchyi
curb *v.* *t* приборкувати pryborkuvaty
curb *n* узбіччя uzbichchia
curcuma *n.* куркума kurkuma
curd *n* сир syr
cure *v.* *t.* виліковувати vylikovuvaty
cure *n* ліки liky
curfew *n* комендантська година komendantska hodyna
curiosity *n* цікавість tsikavist

curious *a* цікавий tsikavyi
curl *n.* локон lokon
currant *n.* смородина smorodyna
currency *n* валюта valiuta
current *n* електричний струм elektrychnyi strum
current *a* поточний potochnyi
curriculum *n* навчальний план navchalnyi plan
curse *v. t* проклинати proklynaty
curse *n* прокляття prokliattia
cursory *a* поверховий poverkhovyi
curt *a* уривчастий uryvchastyi
curtail *v. t* скорочувати skorochuvaty
curtain *n* заслона zaslona
curve *v. t* вигинати vyhynaty
curve *n* дуга duha
cushion *n* диванна подушка dyvanna podushka
cushion *v. t* підкладати подушку pidkladaty podushku
custard *n* заварний крем zavarnyi krem
custodian *n* зберігач zberihach
custody *v* опіка opika
custom *n.* звичай zvychai
customary *a* звичайний zvychainyi
customer *n* замовник zamovnyk
cut *n* поріз poriz
cut *v. t* різати rizaty
cutis *n.* шкіра shkira
cuvette *n.* кювета kiuveta
cycle *n* цикл tsykl
cyclic *a* циклічний tsyklichnyi
cyclist *n* велосипедист velosypedyst
cyclone *n.* циклон tsyklon
cyclostyle *n* розмножувальний апарат rozmnozhuvalnyi aparat

cyclostyle *v. t* розмножувати rozmnozhuvaty
cylinder *n* циліндр tsylindr
cynic *n* цинік tsynik
cypher cypress *n* кипарис kyparys

dabble *v. i.* займатися чимсь поверхово zaimatysia chyms poverkhovo
dacoit *n.* бандит bandyt
dacoity *n.* розбій rozbii
dad, daddy *n* тато, татусь tato, tatus
daffodil *n.* нарцис жовтий nartsys zhovtyi
daft *adj.* божевільний bozhevilnyi
dagger *n.* кинджал kyndzhal
daily *n.* щоденна газета shchodenna hazeta
daily *a* щоденний shchodennyi
daily *adv.* щоденно shchodenno
dainty *a.* витончений vytonchenyi
dainty *n.* ласощі lasoshchi
dairy *n* маслоробня maslorobnia
dais *n.* поміст pomist
daisy *n* маргаритка marharytka
dale *n* ділянка землі dilianka zemli
dam *n* дамба damba
damage *v. t.* пошкоджувати poshkodzhuvaty
damage *n.* пошкодження poshkodzhennia
dame *n.* дама dama
damn *v. t.* лаятися laiatysia
damnation *n.* проклін proklin
damp *a* вологий volohyi
damp *v. t.* сиріти syrity
damp *n* вогкість vohkist
damsel *n.* грілка hrilka

dance *n* танець tanets
dance *v. t.* танцювати tantsiuvaty
dandelion *n.* кульбаба kulbaba
dandle *v.t.* гойдати hoidaty
dandruff *n* лупа lupa
dandy *n* денді dendi
danger *n.* небезпека nebezpeka
dangerous *a* небезпечний nebezpechnyi
dangle *v. t* гойдатися hoidatysia
dank *adj.* неприємно вологий nepryiemno volohyi
dap *v.i.* ударяти про землю udariaty pro zemliu
dare *v. i.* сміти smity
daring *n.* сміливість smilyvist
daring *a* хоробрий khorobryi
dark *n* таємниця taiemnytsia
dark *a* темний temnyi
darkle *v.i.* темніти temnity
darling *n* улюбленець uliublenets
darling *a* улюблений uliublenyi
dart *n.* стріла strila
dash *v. i.* жбурнути zhburnuty
dash *n* рішучість rishuchist
date *n* дата data
date *v. t* ставити число stavyty chyslo
daub *n.* мазок mazok
daub *v. t.* обмазувати obmazuvaty
daughter *n* дочка dochka
daunt *v. t* приборкати pryborkaty
dauntless *a* безстрашний bezstrashnyi
dawdle *v.i.* байдикувати baidykuvaty
dawn *n* світанок svitanok
dawn *v. i.* світати svitaty
day *n* день den
daze *v. t* здивувати zdyvuvaty
daze *n* подив podyv
dazzle *v. t.* засліплювати блиском zaslipliuvaty blyskom

dazzle *n* сліпучий блиск slipuchyi blysk
deacon *n.* диякон dyiakon
dead *a* мертвий mertvyi
deadlock *n* тупик tupyk
deadly *a* смертельний smertelnyi
deaf *a* глухий hlukhyi
deal *n* справа sprava
deal *v. i* роздати rozdaty
dealer *n* дилер dyler
dealing *n.* роздача rozdacha
dean *n.* декан dekan
dear *a* милий mylyi
dearth *n* голод holod
death *n* смерть smert
debar *v. t.* не дозволяти ne dozvoliaty
debase *v. t.* знижувати якість znyzhuvaty yakist
debate *v. t.* дебатувати debatuvaty
debate *n.* дебати debaty
debauch *n* дебош debosh
debauch *v. t.* спокушати spokushaty
debauchee *n* розпусник rozpusnyk
debauchery *n* оргія orhiia
debility *n* слабкість slabkist
debit *n* дебет debet
debit *v. t* дебетувати debetuvaty
debris *n* уламки ulamky
debt *n* борг borh
debtor *n* боржник borzhnyk
decade *n* група з десяти hrupa z desiaty
decadent *a* занепадницький zanepadnytskyi
decamp *v. i* тікати tikaty
decay *v. i* руйнуватися ruinuvatysia
decay *n* розпад rozpad
decease *v. i* померти pomerty

decease *n* смерть smert
deceit *n* хитрість khytrist
deceive *v. t* навмисно вводити в оману navmysno vvodyty v omanu
december *n* грудень hruden
decency *n* пристойність prystoinist
decennary *n.* десятиліття desiatylittia
decent *a* славний slavnyi
deception *n* облуда obluda
decide *v. t* вирішувати vyrishuvaty
decillion *n.* децілліон detsillion
decimal *a* десятковий desiatkovyi
decimate *v.t.* стратити stratyty
decision *n* рішення rishennia
decisive *a* певний pevnyi
deck *n* палуба paluba
deck *v. t* настилати палубу nastylaty palubu
declaration *n* заява zaiava
declare *v. t.* визнавати vyznavaty
decline *n* занепад zanepad
decline *n* захід zakhid
decline *v. t.* відхиляти vidkhyliaty
declivous *adj.* похилий pokhylyi
decompose *v. t.* розкладати rozkladaty
decomposition *n.* розкладання rozkladannia
decontrol *v.t.* зняти контроль zniaty kontrol
decorate *v. t* нагороджувати орденами nahorodzhuvaty ordenamy
decoration *n* декорація dekoratsiia
decorum *n* благопристойність blahoprystoinist
decrease *n* зниження znyzhennia
decrease *v. t* знижувати znyzhuvaty

decree *n* рішення rishennia
decree *v. i* видавати декрет vydavaty dekret
decrement *n.* зменшення zmenshennia
dedicate *v. t.* відкривати vidkryvaty
dedication *n* відданість viddanist
deduct *v.t.* утримувати utrymuvaty
deed *n* документ про передачу права власності dokument pro peredachu prava vlasnosti
deem *v.i.* вважати vvazhaty
deep *a.* глибокий hlybokyi
deer *n* олень olen
defamation *n* наклеп naklep
defame *v. t.* брехати brekhaty
default *n.* замовчування zamovchuvannia
defeat *n* припинення prypynennia
defeat *v. t.* перемогти peremohty
defect *n* дефект defekt
defence *n* аргументація захисту arhumentatsiia zakhystu
defend *v. t* обороняти oboroniaty
defendant *n* підсудний pidsudnyi
defensive *adv.* оборона oborona
deference *n* повага povaha
defiance *n* зухвала поведінка zukhvala povedinka
deficient *adj.* недостатній nedostatnii
deficit *n* дефіцит defitsyt
defile *n.* дефіле defile
define *v. t* характеризувати kharakteryzuvaty
definite *a* певний pevnyi
definition *n* дефініція definitsiia
deflation *n.* дефляція defliatsiia
deflect *v.t. & i.* заломлювати zalomliuvaty
deft *adj.* моторний motornyi

degrade v. t деградувати dehraduvaty
degree n ступінь stupin
dehort v.i. переконувати perekonuvaty
deist n. деїст deist
deity n. божество bozhestvo
deject v. t пригнічувати pryhnichuvaty
dejection n зневіра znevira
delay v.t. & i. затримувати zatrymuvaty
delegate v. t делегувати delehuvaty
delegation n делегація delehatsiia
delete v. t видалити vydalyty
delibate v.t. зменшувати zmenshuvaty
deliberate a обдуманий obdumanyi
deliberate v. i обговорювати obhovoriuvaty
deliberation n нарада narada
delicate a слабкий slabkyi
delicious a дуже смачний duzhe smachnyi
deligate1 n пов'язка poviazka
delight n захват zakhvat
delight v. t. захоплювати zakhopliuvaty
deliver v. t доставляти dostavliaty
delivery n доставка dostavka
delta n дельта delta
delude n.t. зваблювати zvabliuvaty
delusion n. зваба zvaba
demand n вимога vymoha
demand v. t висувати вимогу vysuvaty vymohu
demarcation n. демаркація demarkatsiia

dement v.t зводити з розуму zvodyty z rozumu
demerit n вада vada
democracy n демократія demokratiia
democratic a демократичний demokratychnyi
demolish v. t. зносити znosyty
demon n. демон demon
demonetize v.t. вилучати з обігу vyluchaty z obihu
demonstrate v. t демонструвати demonstruvaty
demonstration n. демонстрація demonstratsiia
demoralize v. t. деморалізувати demoralizuvaty
demur n вагання vahannia
demur v. t вагатися vahatysia
demurrage n. плата за простій plata za prostii
den n притон pryton
dengue n. тропічна лихоманка tropichna lykhomanka
denial n заперечення zaperechennia
denote v. i позначати poznachaty
denounce v. t доносити donosyty
dense a густий hustyi
density n щільність shchilnist
dentist n дантист dantyst
denude v.t. позбавляти pozbavliaty
denunciation n. донос donos
deny v. t. заперечувати zaperechuvaty
depart v. i. відбувати vidbuvaty
department n відділення viddilennia
departure n виліт vylit
depauperate v.t. виснажувати vysnazhuvaty
depend v. i. залежати zalezhaty

dependant *n* нахлібник nakhlibnyk
dependence *n* підпорядкованість pidporiadkovanist
dependent *a* залежний zalezhnyi
depict *v. t.* зображати zobrazhaty
deplorable *a* прикрий prykryi
deploy *v.t.* розгортати rozhortaty
deponent *n.* свідок, який дає показання під присягою svidok, yakyi daie pokazannia pid prysiahoiu
deport *v.t.* депортувати deportuvaty
depose *v. t* позбавити влади pozbavyty vlady
deposit *n.* депозит depozyt
deposit *v. t* класти в банк klasty v bank
depot *n* депо depo
depreciate *v.t.i.* знецінювати znetsiniuvaty
depredate *v.t.* спустошувати spustoshuvaty
depress *v. t* пригноблювати pryhnobliuvaty
depression *n* депресія depresiia
deprive *v. t* позбавити pozbavyty
depth *n* глибина hlybyna
deputation *n* депутація deputatsiia
depute *v. t* доручати doruchaty
deputy *n.*депутат deputat
derail *v. t.* пускати під укіс puskaty pid ukis
derive *v. t.* виводити vyvodyty
descend *v. i.* зійти ziity
descendant *n* нащадок nashchadok
descent *n.* спуск spusk
describe *v. t* описувати opysuvaty
description *n* опис opys
descriptive *a* описовий opysovyi

desert *v. t.* залишати zalyshaty
desert *n* пустеля pustelia
deserve *v. t.* бути гідним buty hidnym
design *n.* намір namir
design *v. t.* проектувати proektuvaty
desirable *a* бажаний bazhanyi
desire *v.t* бажати bazhaty
desire *n* предмет бажання predmet bazhannia
desirous *a* бажаючий bazhaiuchyi
desk *n* парта parta
despair *n* відчай vidchai
despair *v. i* зневірятися zneviriatysia
desperate *a* відчайдушний vidchaidushnyi
despicable *a* мерзенний merzennyi
despise *v. t* зневажати znevazhaty
despot *n* деспот despot
destination *n* призначення pryznachennia
destiny *n* доля dolia
destroy *v. t* знищити znyshchyty
destruction *n* руйнування ruinuvannia
detach *v. t* відряджати vidriadzhaty
detachment *n* відряджання vidriadzhannia
detail *n* деталь detal
detail *v. t* деталізувати detalizuvaty
detain *v. t* тримати під вартою trymaty pid vartoiu
detect *v. t* виявляти vyiavliaty
detective *a* детектив detektyv
detective *n.* детективний detektyvnyi

determination *n.* рішимість rishymist
determine *v. t* вимірювати vymiriuvaty
dethrone *v. t* скидати з трону skydaty z tronu
develop *v. t.* розвивати rozvyvaty
development *n.* розвиток rozvytok
deviate *v. i* відхилятися vidkhyliatysia
deviation *n* девіація deviatsiia
device *n* метод metod
devil *n* диявол dyiavol
devise *v. t* вигадати vyhadaty
devoid *a* позбавлений pozbavlenyi
devote *v. t* віддаватися viddavatysia
devotee *n* прихильник prykhylnyk
devotion *n* відданість viddanist
devour *v. t* знищувати znyshchuvaty
dew *n.* роса rosa
diabetes *n* цукровий діабет tsukrovyi diabet
diagnose *v. t* діагностувати diahnostuvaty
diagnosis *n* діагноз diahnoz
diagram *n* графік hrafik
dial *n.* циферблат tsyferblat
dialect *n* діалект dialekt
dialogue *n* діалог dialoh
diameter *n* диметр dymetr
diamond *n* діамант diamant
diarrhoea *n* пронос pronos
diary *n* щоденник shchodennyk
dice *n.* гральні кості hralni kosti
dice *v. i.* грати в кості hraty v kosti
dictate *v. t* диктувати dyktuvaty
dictation *n* диктування dyktuvannia
dictator *n* диктатор dyktator

diction *n* дикція dyktsiia
dictionary *n* словник slovnyk
dictum *n* вислів vysliv
didactic *a* дидактичний dydaktychnyi
die *n* гральна кість hralna kist
die *v. i* померти pomerty
diet *n* дієта diieta
differ *v. i* відрізнятися vidrizniatysia
difference *n* різниця riznytsia
different *a* відмінний vidminnyi
difficult *a* складний skladnyi
difficulty *n* труднощі trudnoshchi
dig *v.t.* копати kopaty
dig *n* тичок tychok
digest *v. t.* переварювати perevariuvaty
digest *n.* збірник zbirnyk
digestion *n* травлення travlennia
digit *n* цифра tsyfra
dignify *v.t* облагороджувати oblahorodzhuvaty
dignity *n* гідність hidnist
dilemma *n* дилема dylema
diligence *n* старанність starannist
diligent *a* старанний starannyi
dilute *a* розбавлений rozbavlenyi
dilute *v. t* розбавляти rozbavliaty
dim *a* матовий matovyi
dim *v. t* потьмяніти potmianity
dimension *n* вимір vymir
diminish *v. t* опадати opadaty
din *n* гомін homin
dine *v. t.* вечеряти vecheriaty
dinner *n* вечеря vecheria
dip *n.* занурення zanurennia
dip *v. t* занурюватися zanuriuvatysia
diploma *n* диплом dyplom
diplomacy *n* дипломатія dyplomatiia
diplomat *n* дипломат dyplomat

diplomatic *a* дипломатичний
dyplomatychnyi
dire *a* жахливий zhakhlyvyi
direct *a* безпосередній
bezposerednii
direct *v. t* направляти napravliaty
direction *n* напрям napriam
director *n.* директор dyrektor
directory *n* довідник dovidnyk
dirt *n* бруд brud
dirty *a* нечесний nechesnyi
disability *n* нездатність
nezdatnist
disable *v. t* робити непридатним
robyty neprydatnym
disabled *a* непрацездатний
nepratsezdatnyi
disadvantage *n* збиток zbytok
disagree *v. i* не сходитися в
поглядах ne skhodytysia v
pohliadakh
disagreeable *a.* неприємний
nepryiemnyi
disagreement *n.* розбіжність
rozbizhnist
disappear *v. i* зникнути znyknuty
disappearance *n* зникнення
znyknennia
disappoint *v. t.* розчаровувати
rozcharovuvaty
disapproval *n* несхвалення
neskhvalennia
disapprove *v. t* не схвалювати ne
skhvaliuvaty
disarm *v. t* обеззброювати
obezzbroiuvaty
disarmament *n.* роззброєння
rozzbroiennia
disaster *n* катастрофа katastrofa
disastrous *a* катастрофічний
katastrofichnyi
disc *n.* диск dysk
discard *v. t* звільняти zvilniaty

discharge *n.* розвантаження
rozvantazhuvannia
discharge *v. t* розряджати
rozriadzhaty
disciple *n* апостол apostol
discipline *n* дисципліна
dystsyplina
disclose *v. t* розкрити rozkryty
discomfort *n* незручність
nezruchnist
disconnect *v. t* роз'єднувати
roziednuvaty
discontent *n* незадоволеність
nezadovolenist
discontinue *v. t* припиняти
prypyniaty
discord *n* розлад rozlad
discount *n* знижка znyzhka
discourage *v. t.* відраджувати
vidradzhuvaty
discourse *n* мова mova
discourteous *a* непоштивий
neposhtyvyi
discover *v. t* знаходити
znakhodyty
discovery *n.* відкриття vidkryttia
discretion *n* розсуд rozsud
discriminate *v. t.* дискримінувати
dyskryminuvaty
discrimination *n* дискримінація
dyskryminatsiia
discuss *v. t.* обговорювати
obhovoriuvaty
disdain *v. t.* нехтувати nekhtuvaty
disdain *n* зневажання
znevazhannia
disease *n* захворювання
zakhvoriuvannia
disguise *n* маскування
maskuvannia
disguise *v. t* маскувати
maskuvaty
dish *n* блюдо bliudo

dishearten v. t приводити у
відчай pryvodyty u vidchai
dishonest a нечесний nechesnyi
dishonesty n. несумлінність
nesumlinnist
dishonour v. t безчестити
bezchestyty
dishonour n безчестя bezchestia
dislike v. t не любити ne liubyty
dislike n неприязнь nepryiazn
disloyal a нелояльний neloialnyi
dismiss v. t. відпускати
vidpuskaty
dismissal n зняття zniattia
disobey v. t не підкорятися ne
pidkoriatysia
disorder n безлад bezlad
disparity n нерівність nerivnist
dispensary n диспансер
dyspanser
disperse v. t розбігатися
rozbihatysia
displace v. t витісняти vytisniaty
display n прояв proiav
display v. t проявляти proiavliaty
displease v. t не подобатися ne
podobatysia
displeasure n невдоволеність
nevdovolenist
disposal n розпорядження
rozporiadzhennia
dispose v. t розташовувати
roztashovuvaty
disprove v. t спростовувати
sprostovuvaty
dispute v. i сперечатися
sperechatysia
dispute n спір spir
disqualification n
дискваліфікація
dyskvalifikatsiia
disqualify v. t. дискваліфікувати
dyskvalifikuvaty

disquiet n хвилювання
khvyliuvannia
disregard n зневага znevaha
disregard v. t знехтувати
znekhtuvaty
disrepute n погана слава pohana
slava
disrespect n неповага nepovaha
disrupt v. t зривати zryvaty
dissatisfaction n невдоволення
nevdovolennia
dissatisfy v. t. викликати
невдоволення vyklykaty
nevdovolennia
dissect v. t розсікати rozsikaty
dissection n розсічення
rozsichennia
dissimilar a несхожий neskhozhyi
dissolve v.t розчиняти
rozchyniaty
dissuade v. t відмовляти
vidmovliaty
distance n відстань vidstan
distant a далекий dalekyi
distil v. t гнати hnaty
distillery n спиртогорілчаний
завод spyrtohorilchanyi zavod
distinct a чіткий chitkyi
distinction n відмінність
vidminnist
distinguish v. i розрізняти
rozrizniaty
distort v. t спотворювати
spotvoriuvaty
distress n нужда nuzhda
distress v. t крушити krushyty
distribute v. t роздавати
rozdavaty
distribution n розподіл rozpodil
district n округ okruh
distrust n сумнів sumniv
distrust v. t. сумніватися
sumnivatysia

disturb *v. t* турбувати turbuvaty
ditch *n* канава kanava
ditto *n.* точна копія tochna kopiia
dive *v. i* пірнати pirnaty
dive *n* кубло kublo
diverse *a* різноманітний riznomanitnyi
divert *v. t* відволікати vidvolikaty
divide *v. t* розділяти rozdiliaty
divine *a* божественний bozhestvenyi
divinity *n* богослов'я bohoslovia
division *n* дівізія diviziia
divorce *v. t* розлучати rozluchaty
divorce *n* розлучення rozluchennia
divulge *v. t* оприлюднити opryliudnyty
do *v. t* робити robyty
docile *a* тямущий tiamushchyi
dock *n.* док dok
doctor *n* лікар likar
doctorate *n* докторська ступінь doktorska stupin
doctrine *n* доктрина doktryna
document *n* документ dokument
dodge *n* виверт vyvert
dodge *v. t* лукавити lukavyty
doe *n* лань lan
dog *n* собака sobaka
dog *v. t* цькувати собаками tskuvaty sobakamy
dogma *n* догма dohma
dogmatic *a* догматичний dohmatychnyi
doll *n* лялька lialka
dollar *n* долар dolar
domain *n* область oblast
dome *n* купол kupol
domestic *a* домашній domashnii
domestic *n* домашня робота domashnia robota

domicile *n* постійне місце проживання postiine mistse prozhyvannia
dominant *a* домінуючий dominuiuchyi
dominate *v. t* домінувати dominuvaty
domination *n* панування panuvannia
dominion *n* домініон dominion
donate *v. t* жертвувати zhertvuvaty
donation *n.* дар dar
donkey *n* осел osel
donor *n* донор donor
doom *n* загибель zahybel
doom *v. t.* прирікати pryrikaty
door *n* двері dveri
dose *n* доза doza
dot *v. t* ставити крапки над stavyty krapky nad
dot *n* точка tochka
double *n* двійник dviinyk
double *a* подвійний podviinyi
double *v. t.* роздвоюватися rozdvoiuvatysia
doubt *n* сумнів sumniv
doubt *v. i* сумніватися sumnivatysia
dough *n* тісто tisto
dove *n* голуб holub
down *v. t* збити zbyty
down *adv* вниз vnyz
down *prep* по ро
downfall *n* розвал rozval
downpour *n* злива zlyva
downright *a* повний povnyi
downright *adv* явно yavno
downward *adv* донизу donyzu
downward *a* який спускається yakyi spuskaietsia
downwards *adv* під уклон pid uklon

dowry *n* придане prydane
doze *v. i* дрімати drimaty
doze *n.* дрімота drimota
dozen *n* дюжина diuzhyna
draft *n* креслення kreslennia
draft *v. t* робити ескіз robyty eskiz
draftsman *n* укладач ukladach
drag *n* волочіння volochinnia
drag *v. t* тягти tiahty
dragon *n* дракон drakon
drain *n* відтік vidtik
drain *v. t* осушувати osushuvaty
drainage *n* дренаж drenazh
dram *n* драхма drakhma
drama *n* драма drama
dramatic *a* драматичний dramatychnyi
dramatist *n* драматург dramaturh
draper *n* драпірувальник drapiruvalnyk
drastic *a* сильнодійний sylnodiinyi
draught *n* складати законопроект skladaty zakonoproekt
draw *n* розіграш rozihrash
draw *v.t* малювати maliuvaty
drawback *n* перешкода pereshkoda
drawer *n* буфетник bufetnyk
drawing *n* креслення kreslennia
drawing-room *n* вітальня vitalnia
dread *n* жуть zhut
dread *v.t* боятися boiatysia
dread *a* страхатися strakhatysia
dream *v. i.* мріяти mriiaty
dream *n* сон son
drench *v. t* доза ліків doza likiv
dress *n* плаття plattia
dress *v. t* причісувати prychisuvaty
dressing *n* прикраса prykrasa
drill *v. t.* свердлити sverdlyty

drill *n* свердло sverdlo
drink *v. t* випивати vypyvaty
drink *n* питво pytvo
drip *n* капання kapannia
drip *v. i* капати kapaty
drive *n* виїзд vyizd
drive *v. t* водити автомобіль vodyty avtomobil
driver *n* водій vodii
drizzle *n* мжичка mzhychka
drizzle *v. i* мрячити mriachyty
drop *v. i* крапати krapaty
drop *n* крапля kraplia
drown *v.i* тонути tonuty
drug *n* медикамент medykament
druggist *n* фармацевт farmatsevt
drum *n* барабан baraban
drum *v.i.* бити в барабан byty v baraban
drunkard *n* алкоголік alkoholik
dry *n* посуха posukha
dry *v. i.* сохнути sokhnuty
dry *a* сухий sukhyi
dual *a* двоїстий dvoistyi
duck *n.* качка kachka
duck *v.i.* присідати prysidaty
due *n* належне nalezhne
due *adv* належний nalezhnyi
due *a* належний nalezhnyi
duel *n* дуель duel
duel *v. i* битися на дуелі bytysia na dueli
duke *n* герцог hertsoh
dull *a* тупий tupyi
dull *v. t.* притуплятися prytupliatysia
duly *adv* належним чином nalezhnym chynom
dumb *a* німий nimyi
dunce *n* йолоп yolop
dung *n* кал kal
duplicate *n* дублікат dublikat

duplicate *v. t* дублювати dubliuvaty
duplicate *a* запасний zapasnyi
duplicity *n* лукавість lukavist
durable *a* довговічний dovhovichnyi
duration *n* тривалість tryvalist
during *prep* під час pid chas
dusk *n* сутінковий sutinkovyi
dust *n* пил pyl
dust *v.t.* порошити poroshyty
duster *n* ганчірка hanchirka
dutiful *a* покірний pokirnyi
duty *n* податок podatok
dwarf *n* зупиняти розвиток zupyniaty rozvytok
dwell *v. i* мешкати meshkaty
dwelling *n* оселя oselia
dwindle *v. t* скорочуватися skorochuvatysia
dye *n* барвник barvnyk
dye *v. t* фарбувати farbuvaty
dynamic *a* динамічний dynamichnyi
dynamics *n.* динаміка dynamika
dynamite *n* динаміт dynamit
dynamo *n* генератор henerator
dynasty *n* династія dynastiia
dysentery *n* дизентерія dyzenteriia

E

each *pron.* один одного odyn odnoho
each *a* кожен kozhen
eager *a* старанний starannyi
eagle *n* орел orel
ear *n* вухо vukho
early *a* ранній rannii
early *adv* рано rano
earn *v. t* заробляти zarobliaty

earnest *a* переконаний perekonanyi
earth *n* земля zemlia
earthen *a* земний zemnyi
earthly *a* земляний zemlianyi
earthquake *n* землетрус zemletrus
ease *n* легкість lehkist
ease *v. t* полегшувати polehshuvaty
east *adv* на схід na skhid
east *n* схід skhid
east *a* східний skhidnyi
easter *n* великдень velykden
eastern *a* східний skhidnyi
easy *a* легкий lehkyi
eat *v. t* є ye
eatable *n.* їстівне yistivne
eatable *a* їстівний yistivnyi
ebb *n* відлив vidlyv
ebb *v. i* відлити vidlyty
ebony *n* чорне дерево chorne derevo
echo *n* луна luna
echo *v. t* лунати lunaty
eclipse *n* затемнення zatemnennia
economic *a* економічний ekonomichnyi
economical *a* ощадливий oshchadlyvyi
economics *n.* економіка ekonomika
economy *n* економія ekonomiia
edge *n* грань hran
edible *a* придатний для їжи prydatnyi dlia yizhy
edifice *n* будівля budivlia
edit *v. t* редагувати redahuvaty
edition *n* видання vydannia
editor *n* видавець vydavets
editorial *a* редакторскій redaktorckii

editorial *n* передовиця peredovytsia
educate *v. t* давати освіту davaty osvitu
education *n* освіта osvita
efface *v. t* стерти sterty
effect *v. t* впливати vplyvaty
effect *n* ефект efekt
effective *a* ефективний efektyvnyi
effeminate *a* подібний до жінки podibnyi do zhinky
efficacy *n* дієвість diievist
efficiency *n* ефективність efektyvnist
efficient *a* ефективний efektyvnyi
effigy *n* зображення zobrazhennia
effort *n* спроба sproba
egg *n* яйце yaitse
ego *n* егоїзм ehoizm
egotism *n* зарозумілість zarozumilist
eight *n* вісім visim
eighteen *n* вісімнадцять visimnadtsiat
eighty *n* вісімдесят visimdesiat
either *a.,* або ... або abo ... abo
either *adv.* будь-який bud-iakyi
eject *v. t.* вигнати vyhnaty
elaborate *a* вдосконалений vdoskonalenyi
elaborate *v. t* детально розробляти detalno rozrobliaty
elapse *v. t* проходити prokhodyty
elastic *a* еластичний elastychnyi
elbow *n* підлокітник pidlokitnyk
elder *n* староста starosta
elder *a* старший starshyi
elderly *a* похилого віку pokhyloho viku
elect *v. t* обрати obraty
election *n* вибори vybory

electorate *n* контингент виборців kontynhent vybortsiv
electric *a* електричний elektrychnyi
electricity *n* електрика elektryka
electrify *v. t* електрифікувати elektryfikuvaty
elegance *n* елегантність elehantnist
elegant *adj* елегантний elehantnyi
elegy *n* елегія elehiia
element *n* елемент element
elementary *a* елементарний elementarnyi
elephant *n* слон slon
elevate *v. t* підвищувати по службі pidvyshchuvaty po sluzhbi
elevation *n* піднесення pidnesennia
eleven *n* одинадцять odynadtsiat
elf *n* ельф elf
eligible *a* підхожий pidkhozhyi
eliminate *v. t* усувати usuvaty
elimination *n* усунення usunennia
elope *v. i* втекти vtekty
eloquence *n* красномовство krasnomovstvo
eloquent *a* красномовний krasnomovnyi
else *adv* а то a to
else *a* інший inshyi
elucidate *v. t* з'ясувати ziasuvaty
elude *v. t* уникати unykaty
elusion *n* викрут vykrut
elusive *a* невловимий nevlovymyi
emancipation *n.* емансипація emansypatsiia
embalm *v. t* забальзамувати zabalzamuvaty
embankment *n* насип nasyp
embark *v. t* вантажити на корабель vantazhyty na korabel

embarrass *v. t* ускладнювати
uskladniuvaty
embassy *n* посольство posolstvo
embitter *v. t* озлобляти ozlobliaty
emblem *n* емблема emblema
embodiment *n* втілення vtilennia
embody *v. t.* втілювати vtiliuvaty
embolden *v. t.* заохочувати
zaokhochuvaty
embrace *n* обійми obiimy
embrace *v. t.* обійняти obiiniaty
embroidery *n* вишивання
vyshyvannia
embryo *n* ембріон embrion
emerald *n* смарагд smarahd
emerge *v. i* з'явитися ziavytysia
emergency *n* крайність krainist
eminance *n* високе положення
vysoke polozhennia
eminent *a* іменитий imenytyi
emissary *n* шпигун shpyhun
emit *v. t* видавати vydavaty
emolument *n* зароботок
zarobotok
emotion *n* емоція emotsiia
emotional *a* емоційний emotsiinyi
emperor *n* імператор imperator
emphasis *n* акцентування
aktsentuvannia
emphasize *v. t* акцентувати
aktsentuvaty
emphatic *a* виразний vyraznyi
empire *n* імперія imperiia
employ *v. t* наймати naimaty
employee *n* працівник pratsivnyk
employer *n* роботодавець
robotodavets
employment *n* зайнятість
zainiatist
empower *v. t* уповноважити
upovnovazhyty
empress *n* імператриця
imperatrytsia

empty *v* спорожнити sporozhnyty
empty *a* марний marnyi
emulate *v. t* змагатися
zmahatysia
enable *v. t* давати можливість
davaty mozhlyvist
enact *v. t* пропонувати
proponuvaty
enamel *n* емаль emal
enamour *v. t* закохувати
zakokhuvaty
encase *v. t* укладати ukladaty
enchant *v. t* чарувати charuvaty
encircle *v. t.* обводити obvodyty
enclose *v. t* оточувати otochuvaty
enclosure *n.* огорожа ohorozha
encompass *v. t* стосуватися
stosuvatysia
encounter *v. t* зустріти zustrity
encounter *n.* сутичка sutychka
encourage *v. t* підбадьорювати
pidbadoriuvaty
encroach *v. i* зазіхати zazikhaty
encumber *v. t.* забудовувати
zabudovuvaty
encyclopaedia *n.* енциклопедія
entsyklopediia
end *v. t* кінчатися kinchatysia
end *n.* смерть smert
endanger *v. t.* піддавати
небезпеці piddavaty nebezpetsi
endear *v.t* пеститися pestytysia
endearment *n.* ласка laska
endeavour *v.i* спроба sproba
endeavour *n* старання starannia
endorse *v. t.* надписувати
nadpysuvaty
endow *v. t* забезпечувати
постійним доходом
zabezpechuvaty postiinym
dokhodom
endurable *a* стерпний sterpnyi

endurance *n.* терплячість terpliachist
endure *v.t.* витерпіти vyterpity
enemy *n* ворог voroh
energetic *a* енергійний enerhiinyi
energy *n.* енергія enerhiia
enfeeble *v. t.* послаблювати poslabliuvaty
enforce *v. t.* нав'язувати naviazuvaty
enfranchise *v.t.* відпускати на волю vidpuskaty na voliu
engage *v. t* привертати pryvertaty
engagement *n.* зобов'язання zoboviazannia
engine *n* двигун dvyhun
engineer *n* інженер inzhener
English *n* англійська мова anhliiska mova
engrave *v. t* гравірувати hraviruvaty
engross *v.t* скупити skupyty
engulf *v.t* засмоктувати zasmoktuvaty
enigma *n* таємниця taiemnytsia
enjoy *v. t* отримувати задоволення otrymuvaty zadovolennia
enjoyment *n* задоволення zadovolennia
enlarge *v. t* розширювати rozshyriuvaty
enlighten *v. t.* просвіщати prosvishchaty
enlist *v. t* завербуватися zaverbuvatysia
enliven *v. t.* оживляти ozhyvliaty
enmity *n* ворожнеча vorozhnecha
ennoble *v. t.* надавати дворянський титул nadavaty dvorianskyi tytul
enormous *a* величезний velycheznyi

enough *adv.* досить dosyt
enough *adv* достатньо dostatno
enrage *v. t* бісити bisyty
enrapture *v. t* викликати захоплення vyklykaty zakhoplennia
enrich *v. t* збагачувати zbahachuvaty
enrol *v. t* вносити до списку vnosyty do spysku
enshrine *v. t* зберігати zberihaty
enslave *v.t.* поневолювати ponevoliuvaty
ensue *v.i* слідувати sliduvaty
ensure *v. t* гарантувати harantuvaty
entangle *v. t* замішувати zamishuvaty
enter *v. t* входити vkhodyty
enterprise *n* ініціативність initsiatyvnist
entertain *v. t* розважати rozvazhaty
entertainment *n.* видовище vydovyshche
enthrone *v. t* зводити на престол zvodyty na prestol
enthusiasm *n* ентузіазм entuziazm
enthusiastic *a* захоплений zakhoplenyi
entice *v. t.* спокушати spokushaty
entire *a* цілий tsilyi
entirely *adv* повністю povnistiu
entitle *v. t.* надавати право nadavaty pravo
entity *n* суб'єкт sub'iekt
entomology *n.* ентомологія entomolohiia
entrails *n.* нутрощі nutroshchi
entrance *n* вхід vkhid
entrap *v. t.* заманити zamanyty
entreat *v. t.* молити molyty

entreaty *n.* прохання prokhannia
entrust *v. t* надавати nadavaty
entry *n* вступ vstup
enumerate *v. t.* переписувати
perepysuvaty
envelop *v. t* огортати ohortaty
envelope *n* конверт konvert
enviable *a* завидний zavydnyi
envious *a* заздрісний zazdrisnyi
environment *n.* навколишнє
середовище navkolyshnie
seredovyshche
envy *v. t* заздрити zazdryty
envy *n* об`єкт заздрощів ob`iekt
zazdroshchiv
epic *n* епічна поема epichna
poema
epidemic *n* епідемія epidemiia
epigram *n* епіграма epihrama
epilepsy *n* епілепсія epilepsiia
epilogue *n* епілог epiloh
episode *n* епізод epizod
epitaph *n* епітафія epitafiia
epoch *n* доба doba
equal *n* рівня rivnia
equal *v. t* дорівнювати
dorivniuvaty
equal *a* однаковий odnakovyi
equality *n* рівність rivnist
equalize *v. t.* зрівнювати
zrivniuvaty
equate *v. t* зрівнювати zrivniuvaty
equation *n* рівняння rivniannia
equator *n* екватор ekvator
equilateral *a* рівносторонній
rivnostoronnii
equip *v. t* екіпірувати ekipiruvaty
equipment *n* обладнання
obladnannia
equitable *a* справедливий
spravedlyvyi
equivalent *a* еквівалентний
ekvivalentnyi

equivocal *a* неясний neiasnyi
era *n* епоха epokha
eradicate *v. t* викорінювати
vykoriniuvaty
erase *v. t* прати praty
erect *a* піднятий pidniatyi
erect *v. t* спорудити sporudyty
erection *n* спорудження
sporudzhennia
erode *v. t* знецінюватися
znetsiniuvatysia
erosion *n* ерозія eroziia
erotic *a* еротичний erotychnyi
err *v. i* помилятися pomyliatysia
errand *n* завдання zavdannia
erroneous *a* неправильний
nepravylnyi
error *n* помилка pomylka
erupt *v. i* вивергатися
vyverhatysia
eruption *n* виверження
vyverzhennia
escape *n* минути mynuty
escape *v.i* тікати tikaty
escort *n* конвой konvoi
escort *v. t* супроводжувати
suprovodzhuvaty
especial *a* особливий osoblyvyi
essay *v. t.* випробовувати
vyprobovuvaty
essay *n.* есе ese
essayist *n* есеїст eseist
essence *n* есенція esentsiia
essential *a* істотний istotnyi
establish *v. t.* закладати
zakladaty
establishment *n* пристрій prystrii
estate *n* майно maino
esteem *n* шана shana
esteem *v. t* поважати povazhaty
estimate *n.* кошторис koshtorys
estimate *v. t* складати кошторис
skladaty koshtorys

estimation *n* розрахунок rozrakhunok
etcetera *a* і так далі і tak dali
eternal *a* вічний vichnyi
eternity *n* вічність vichnist
ether *n* ефір efir
ethical *a* етичний etychnyi
ethics *n.* етика etyka
etiquette *n* етикет etyket
etymology *n.* етимологія etymolohiia
eunuch *n* євнух yevnukh
evacuate *v. t* евакуювати evakuiuvaty
evacuation *n* евакуація evakuatsiia
evade *v. t* уникати unykaty
evaluate *v. t* атестувати atestuvaty
evaporate *v. i* випаровувати vyparovuvaty
evasion *n* ухиляння ukhyliannia
even *v. t* вирівнювати vyrivniuvaty
even *a* рівномірний rivnomirnyi
even *adv* хоча khocha
evening *n* вечір vechir
event *n* випадок vypadok
eventually *adv.* врешті-решт vreshti-resht
ever *adv* коли-небудь koly-nebud
evergreen *n* вічнозелена рослина vichnozelena roslyna
evergreen *a* вічнозелений vichnozelenyi
everlasting *a.* безсмертний bezsmertnyi
every *a* будь-який bud-iakyi
evict *v. t* виселяти vyseliaty
eviction *n* виселення vyselennia
evidence *n* доказ dokaz
evident *a.* очевидний ochevydnyi
evil *a* лихий lykhyi
evil *n* лихо lykho

evoke *v. t* витребувати справу з нижчого суду до вищого vytrebuvaty spravu z nyzhchoho sudu do vyshchoho
evolution *n* розвиток rozvytok
evolve *v.t* виділяти vydiliaty
ewe *n* вівця vivtsia
exact *a* точний tochnyi
exaggerate *v. t.* перебільшувати perebilshuvaty
exaggeration *n.* перебільшення perebilshennia
exalt *v. t* звеличувати zvelychuvaty
examination *n.* дослідження doslidzhennia
examine *v. t* розглядати rozhliadaty
examinee *n* екзаменований ekzamenovanyi
examiner *n* екзаменатор ekzamenator
example *n* приклад pryklad
excavate *v. t.* рити ryty
excavation *n.* розкопка rozkopka
exceed *v.t* перевищувати perevyshchuvaty
excel *v.i* перевищувати perevyshchuvaty
excellence *n.* висока якість vysoka yakist
excellency *n* ясновельможність yasnovelmozhnist
excellent *a.* відмінний vidminnyi
except *v. t* виключати vykliuchaty
except *prep* за винятком za vyniatkom
exception *n* виняток vyniatok
excess *a* зайвий zaivyi
excess *n* надлишок nadlyshok
exchange *n* обмін obmin
exchange *v. t* обмінювати obminiuvaty

excise *n* акциз aktsyz
excite *v. t* хвилювати khvyliuvaty
exclaim *v.i* вигукувати vyhukuvaty
exclamation *n* вигук vyhuk
exclude *v. t* вимикати vymykaty
exclusive *a* винятковий vyniatkovyi
excommunicate *v. t.* відлучити від церкви vidluchyty vid tserkvy
excursion *n.* екскурсія ekskursiia
excuse *n* звільнення від обов'язку zvilnennia vid oboviazku
excuse *v.t* прощати proshchaty
execute *v. t* стратити stratyty
execution *n* страта strata
executioner *n.* кат kat
exempt *v. t.* вилучати vyluchaty
exempt *a* звільнений від zvilnenyi vid
exercise *n.* вправа vprava
exercise *v. t* виправляти vypravliaty
exhaust *v. t.* вичерпувати vycherpuvaty
exhibit *n.* експонат eksponat
exhibit *v. t* виявляти vyiavliaty
exhibition *n.* виставка vystavka
exile *n.* засланець zaslanets
exile *v. t* заслати zaslaty
exist *v.i* бути buty
existence *n* існування isnuvannia
exit *n.* смерть smert
expand *v.t.* розвивати rozvyvaty
expansion *n.* експансія ekspansiia
ex-parte *a* односторонній odnostoronnii
ex-parte *a* який йде лише від однієї сторони yakyi yde lyshe vid odniiei storony
expect *v. t* чекати chekaty

expectation *n.* очікування ochikuvannia
expedient *a* раціональний ratsionalnyi
expedite *v. t.* швидко виконувати shvydko vykonuvaty
expedition *n* експедиція ekspedytsiia
expel *v. t.* виштовхувати vyshtovkhuvaty
expend *v. t* витрачати vytrachaty
expenditure *n* споживання spozhyvannia
expense *n.* ціна tsina
expensive *a* який дорого коштує yakyi doroho koshtuie
experience *v. t.* довідатися з досвіду dovidatysia z dosvidu
experience *n* досвід dosvid
experiment *n* експеримент eksperiment
expert *a* знаючий znaiuchyi
expert *n* експерт ekspert
expire *v.i.* кінчатися kinchatysia
expiry *n* витікання vytikannia
explain *v. t.* пояснювати poiasniuvaty
explanation *n* пояснення poiasnennia
explicit *a.* явний yavnyi
explode *v. t.* вибухнути vybukhnuty
exploit *v. t* експлуатувати ekspluatuvaty
exploit *n* подвиг podvyh
exploration *n* розвідка rozivdka
explore *v.t* досліджувати doslidzhuvaty
explosion *n.* вибух vybukh
explosive *n.* вибухова речовина vybukhova rechovyna
explosive *a* вибуховий vybukhovyi

exponent *n* інтерпретатор
interpretator
export *n* вивезення vyvezennia
export *v. t.* вивозити vyvozyty
expose *v. t* викладати vykladaty
express *v. t.* висловлювати
vyslovliuvaty
express *a* кур'єрський kurierskyi
express *n* нарочний narochnyi
expression *n.* вираз vyraz
expressive *a.* який служить до
вираження yakyi sluzhyt do
vyrazhennia
expulsion *n.* вигнання vyhnannia
extend *v. t* спростягати
sprostiahaty
extent *n.* ступінь stupin
external *a* зовнішній zovnishnii
extinct *a* згаслий zhaslyi
extinguish *v.t* гасити hasyty
extol *v. t.* розхвалювати
rozkhvaliuvaty
extra *adv* додатково dodatkovo
extra *a* спеціальний spetsialnyi
extract *v. t* витягати vytiahaty
extract *n* настій nastii
extraordinary *a.*
екстраординарний
ekstraordynarnyi
extravagance *n* марнотратність
marnotratnist
extravagant *a* марнотратний
marnotratnyi
extreme *a* екстремальний
ekstremalnyi
extreme *n* надмірність nadmirnist
extremist *n* екстреміст ekstremist
exult *v. i* тріумфувати triumfuvaty
eye *n* око oko
eyeball *n* очне яблуко ochne
yabluko
eyelash *n* вія viia
eyelet *n* петелька petelka

eyewash *n* окозамилювання
okozamyliuvannia

fable *n.* байка baika
fabric *n* матерія materiia
fabricate *v.t* вигадувати
vyhaduvaty
fabrication *n* виготовлення
vyhotovlennia
fabulous *a* нечуваний nechuvanyi
facade *n* фасад fasad
face *n* лице lytse
face *v.t* стояти обличчям до
stoiaty oblychchiam do
facet *n* аспект aspekt
facial *a* лицьовий lytsovyi
facile *a* гнучкий hnuchkyi
facilitate *v.t* полегшувати
polehshuvaty
facility *n* нескладність
neskladnist
facsimile *n* факсиміле faksymile
fact *n* факт fakt
faction *n* фракція fraktsiia
factious *a* фракційний fraktsiinyi
factor *n* фактор faktor
factory *n* фабрика fabryka
faculty *n* факультет fakultet
fad *n* коник konyk
fade *v.i* в'янути vianuty
faggot *n* в'язанка viazanka
fail *v.i* зазнавати невдачі
zaznavaty nevdachi
failure *n* неуспіх neuspikh
faint *a* слабкий slabkyi
faint *v.i* слабнути slabnuty
fair *a* справедливий spravedlyvyi
fair *n.* ярмарок yarmarok
fairly *adv.* чесно chesno
fairy *n* фея feia
faith *n* довіра dovira

faithful *a* вірний virnyi
falcon *n* сокіл sokil
fall *v.i.* падати padaty
fall *n* падіння padinnia
fallacy *n* омана omana
fallow *n* земля під паром zemlia
  pid parom
false *a* штучний shtuchnyi
falter *v.i* зам'яти zamiaty
fame *n* слава slava
familiar *a* знайомий znaiomyi
family *n* сім'я simia
famine *n* голодовка holodovka
famous *a* славетний slavetnyi
fan *n* в, віяло viialo
fanatic *n* фанатик fanatyk
fanatic *a* фанатичний fanatychnyi
fancy *n* уява uiava
fancy *v.t* фантазійний fantaziinyi
fantastic *a* фантастичний
  fantastychnyi
far *n* далека відстань daleka
  vidstan
far *adv.* далеко daleko
far *a* дальній dalnii
farce *n* фарс fars
fare *n* вартість проїзду vartist
  proizdu
farewell *interj.* прощавай!
  proshchavai!
farewell *n* прощальний прийом
  гостей proshchalnyi pryiom
  hostei
farm *n* ферма ferma
farmer *n* фермер fermer
fascinate *v.t* зачаровувати
  поглядом zacharovuvaty
  pohliadom
fascination *n.* чарівність
  charivnist
fashion *n* мода moda
fashionable *a* модний modnyi
fast *n* голодування holoduvannia

fast *v.i* голодувати holoduvaty
fast *a* пісний pisnyi
fast *a* швидкий shvydkyi
fasten *v.t* зав'язувати zaviazuvaty
fat *n* жир zhyr
fat *a* масний masnyi
fatal *a* фатальний fatalnyi
fate *n* фатум fatum
father *n* батько batko
fathom *n* морська сажень morska
  sazhen
fathom *v.t* вимірювати глибину
  vymiriuvaty hlybynu
fatigue *n* втома vtoma
fatigue *v.t* стомлювати
  stomliuvaty
fault *n* хиба khyba
faulty *a* недосконалий
  nedoskonalyi
fauna *n* фауна fauna
favour *v.t* сприяти spryiaty
favour1 *n* прихильність
  prykhylnist
favourable *a* сприятливий
  spryiatlyvyi
favourite *a* улюблений uliublenyi
favourite *n* фаворит favoryt
fear *v.i* побоюватися
  poboiuvatysia
fear *n* страх strakh
fearful *a.* страшний strashnyi
feasible *a* здійсненний
  zdiisnennyi
feast *n* бенкет benket
feast *v.i* вшановувати
  vshanovuvaty
feat *n* фах fakh
feather *n* перо pero
feature *n* ознака oznaka
February *n* лютий liutyi
federal *a* федеральний federalnyi
federation *n* федерація
  federatsiia

fee *n* гонорар honorar
feeble *a* слабкий slabkyi
feed *n* годування hoduvannia
feed *v.t* годувати hoduvaty
feel *v.t* відчувати vidchuvaty
feeling *n* почуття pochuttia
feign *v.t* прикидатися
 prykydatysia
felicitate *v.t* бажати щастя
 bazhaty shchastia
felicity *n* вдалість vdalist
fell *v.t* валити valyty
fellow *n* хлопець khlopets
female *a* жіночий zhinochyi
female *n* самиця samytsia
feminine *a* властивий жінкам
 vlastyvyi zhinkam
fence *v.t* огороджувати
 ohorodzhuvaty
fence *n* паркан parkan
fend *v.t* відображати vidobrazhaty
ferment *v.t* бродити brodyty
ferment *n* фермент ferment
fermentation *n* бродіння
 brodinnia
ferocious *a* лютий liutyi
ferry *v.t* переганяти літаки
 perehaniaty litaky
ferry *n* переправа pereprava
fertile *a* рясний riasnyi
fertility *n* родючість rodiuchist
fertilize *v.t* удобрювати
 udobriuvaty
fertilizer *n* добриво dobryvo
fervent *a* гарячий hariachyi
fervour *n* палкість palkist
festival *n* свято sviato
festive *a* святковий sviatkovyi
festivity *n* веселість veselist
festoon *n* фестон feston
fetch *v.t* принести prynesty
fetter *n* кайдани kaidany
fetter *v.t* сковувати skovuvaty

feud *n.* тривала ворожнеча
 tryvala vorozhnecha
feudal *a* феодальний feodalnyi
fever *n* лихоманка lykhomanka
few *a* нечисленний nechyslennyi
fiasco *n* фіаско fiasko
fibre *n* волокно volokno
fickle *a* мінливий minlyvyi
fiction *n* вигадка vyhadka
fictitious *a* вигаданий vyhadanyi
fiddle *v.i* хімічити khimichyty
fiddle *n* скрипка skrypka
fidelity *n* лояльність loialnist
fie *interj* фу fu
field *n* поле pole
fiend *n* лиходій lykhodii
fierce *a* шалений shalenyi
fiery *a* вогненний vohnennyi
fifteen *n* п'ятнадцять piatnadtsiat
fifty *n.* п'ятьдесят piatdesiat
fig *n* інжир inzhyr
fight *v.t* битися bytysia
fight *n* боротьба borotba
figment *n* фікція fiktsiia
figurative *a* фігуральний
 fihuralnyi
figure *v.t* зобразити zobrazyty
figure *n* фігура fihura
file *v.i.* пересуватися колоною
 peresuvatysia kolonoiu
file *n* досьє dosie
file *v.t* підшити pidshyty
file *v.t* пиляти pyliaty
file *n* справа sprava
file *n* файл fail
fill *v.t* заповнювати zapovniuvaty
film *n* плівка plivka
film *v.t* покривати тонкою
 плівкою pokryvaty tonkoiu
 plivkoiu
filter *n* фільтр filtr
filter *v.t* фільтрувати filtruvaty
filth *n* мерзота merzota

filthy *a* мерзотний merzotnyi
fin *n* плавник plavnyk
final *a* остаточний ostatochnyi
finance *n* фінансова справа
finansova sprava
finance *v.t* фінансувати
finansuvaty
financial *a* фінансовий finansovyi
financier *n* фінансист finansyst
find *v.t* знаходити znakhodyty
fine *a* тонкий tonkyi
fine *n* штраф shtraf
fine *v.t* штрафувати shtrafuvaty
finger *v.t* встановити vstanovyty
finger *n* палець palets
finish *n* закінчення zakinchennia
finish *v.t* закінчувати
zakinchuvaty
finite *a* особовий osobovyi
fir *n* ялина yalyna
fire *n* вогонь vohon
fire *v.t* запалювати zapaliuvaty
firm *a* міцний mitsnyi
firm *n.* фірма firma
first *a* перший pershyi
first *n* перший примірник pershyi
prymirnyk
first *adv* по-перше po-pershe
fiscal *a* фіскальний fiskalnyi
fish *v.i* вудити vudyty
fish *n* риба ryba
fisherman *n* рибалка rybalka
fissure *n* тріщина trishchyna
fist *n* кулак kulak
fistula *n* фістула fistula
fit *v.t* годитися hodytysia
fit *n* підгонка pidhonka
fit *n* припадок prypadok
fitful *a* переривчастий
pereryvchastyi
fitter *n* придатний prydatnyi
five *n* п'ять piat
fix *n* угода uhoda

fix *v.t* фіксувати fiksuvaty
flabby *a* відвислий vidvyslyi
flag *n* стяг stiah
flagrant *a* жахливий zhakhlyvyi
flame *n* полум'я polumia
flame *v.i* полум'яніти polumianity
flannel *n* фланель flanel
flare *n* блискотіння blyskotinnia
flare *v.i* яскраво спалахнути
yaskravo spalakhnuty
flash *v.t* виблискувати
vyblyskuvaty
flash *n* спалах spalakh
flask *n* фляга fliaha
flat *a* млявий mliavyi
flat *n* площина ploshchyna
flatter *v.t* лестити lestyty
flattery *n* самообман samoobman
flavour *n* смак smak
flaw *n* тріщина trishchyna
flea *n.* блоха blokha
flee *v.i* бігти bihty
fleece *n* руно runo
fleece *v.t* стригти овець stryhty
ovets
fleet *n* флот flot
flesh *n* плоть plot
flexible *a* гнучкий hnuchkyi
flicker *n* мерехтіння merekhtinnia
flicker *v.t* мерехтіти merekhtity
flight *n* переліт perelit
flimsy *a* неміцний nemitsnyi
fling *v.t* рішуче братися rishuche
bratysia
flippancy *n* легковажність
lehkovazhnist
flirt *n* флірт flirt
flirt *v.i* фліртувати flirtuvaty
float *v.i* плавати plavaty
flock *n* пушинка pushynka
flock *v.i* скупчуватися
skupchuvatysia
flog *v.t* стьобати stobaty

flood *v.t* затопляти zatopliaty
flood *n* повінь povin
floor *v.t* настилати підлогу
nastylaty pidlohu
floor *n* підлога pidloha
flora *n* флора flora
florist *n* квітникар kvitnykar
flour *n* борошно boroshno
flourish *v.i* розростатися
rozrostatysia
flow *n* потік potik
flow *v.i* текти tekty
flower *n* квітка kvitka
flowery *a* барвистий barvystyi
fluent *a* вільний vilnyi
fluid *n* флюїд fliuid
fluid *a* текучий tekuchyi
flush *v.i* бити струминою byty
strumynoiu
flush *n* приступ prystup
flute *v.i* грати на флейті hraty na
fleiti
flute *n* флейта fleita
flutter *n* пурхання purkhannia
flutter *v.t* махати крилами
makhaty krylamy
fly *v.i* летіти letity
fly *n* муха mukha
foam *n* піна pina
foam *v.t* вспінювати vspiniuvaty
focal *a* фокальний fokalnyi
focus *n* фокус fokus
focus *v.t* фокусуватися
fokusuvatysia
fodder *n* фураж furazh
foe *n* недруг nedruh
fog *n* туман tuman
foil *v.t* фольга folha
fold *n* складка skladka
fold *v.t* схрещувати
skhreshchuvaty
foliage *n* листя lystia
follow *v.t* послідувати posliduvaty

follower *n* послідовник
poslidovnyk
folly *n* дурість durist
foment *v.t* підбурювати
pidburiuvaty
fond *a* марний marnyi
fondle *v.t* голубити holubyty
food *n* їжа yizha
fool *n* блазень blazen
foolish *a* нерозсудливий
nerozsudlyvyi
foolscap *n* блазенський ковпак
blazenskyi kovpak
foot *n* нога noha
for *prep* для dlia
for *conj.* протягом protiahom
forbid *v.t* не дозволяти ne
dozvoliaty
force *v.t* примушувати
prymushuvaty
force *n* сила syla
forceful *a* дієвий diievyi
forcible *a* насильницький
nasylnytskyi
forearm *v.t* заздалегідь
озброюватися zazdalehid
ozbroiuvatysia
forearm *n* передпліччя
peredplichchia
forecast *v.t* завбачення
zavbachennia
forecast *n* прогноз prohnoz
forefather *n* прабатько prabatko
forefinger *n* вказівний палець
vkazivnyi palets
forehead *n* лоб lob
foreign *a* іноземний inozemnyi
foreigner *n* іноземець inozemets
foreknowledge *n.* передбачення
peredbachennia
foreleg *n* передня лапа perednia
lapa
forelock *n* чуб chub

foreman *n* майстер maister
foremost *a* передовий peredovyi
forenoon *n* час до полудня chas do poludnia
forerunner *n* попередник poperednyk
foresee *v.t* передбачити peredbachyty
foresight *n* мушка mushka
forest *n* ліс lis
forestall *v.t* передбачати peredbachaty
forester *n* лісник lisnyk
forestry *n* лісництво lisnytstvo
foretell *v.t* завбачати zavbachaty
forethought *n* передбачливість peredbachlyvist
forever *adv* назавжди nazavzhdy
forewarn *v.t* попереджати заздалегідь poperedzhaty zazdalehid
foreword *n* передмова peredmova
forfeit *v.t* позбутися pozbutysia
forfeit *n* штраф shtraf
forfeiture *n* позбавлення pozbavlennia
forge *v.t* кувати kuvaty
forge *n* кузня kuznia
forgery *n* фальсифікація falsyfikatsiia
forget *v.t* забувати zabuvaty
forgetful *a* забудькуватий zabudkuvatyi
forgive *v.t* вибачати vybachaty
forgo *v.t* утримуватися від utrymuvatysia vid
forlorn *a* нещасний neshchasnyi
form *v.t.* утворювати utvoriuvaty
form *n* форма forma
formal *a* формальний formalnyi
format *n* формат format

formation *n* формування formuvannia
former *a* колишній kolyshnii
former *n.* укладач ukladach
formerly *adv* раніше ranishe
formidable *a* грізний hriznyi
formula *n* формула formula
formulate *v.t* формулювати formuliuvaty
forsake *v.t.* відмовлятися vidmovliatysia
forswear *v.t.* зарікатися zarikatysia
fort *n.* піднесеність pidnesenist
forte *n.* сильна сторона sylna storona
forth *adv.* вперед vpered
forthcoming *a.* наступний nastupnyi
forthwith *adv.* зараз zaraz
fortify *v.t.* зводити укріплення zvodyty ukriplennia
fortitude *n.* сила духу syla dukhu
fort-night *n.* два тижні dva tyzhni
fortress *n.* фортеця fortetsia
fortunate *a.* щасливий shchaslyvyi
fortune *n.* стан stan
forty *n.* сорок sorok
forum *n.* збори zbory
forward *v.t* передавати peredavaty
forward *a.* передовий peredovyi
forward *adv* уперед upered
fossil *n.* скам'янілість skamianilist
foster *v.t.* виховувати vykhovuvaty
foul *a.* брудний brudnyi
found *v.t.* засновувати zasnovuvaty
foundation *n.* установа ustanova
founder *n.* засновник zasnovnyk
foundry *n.* плавильня plavylnia

fountain *n.* фонтан fontan
four *n.* чотири chotyry
fourteen *n.* чотирнадцять
chotyrnadtsiat
fowl *n.* птиця ptytsia
fowler *n.* птахолов ptakholov
fox *n.* лисиця lysytsia
fraction *n.* частка chastka
fracture *v.t* розколюватися
rozkoliuvatysia
fracture *n.* пролом prolom
fragile *a.* тендітний tenditnyi
fragment *n.* фрагмент frahment
fragrance *n.* аромат aromat
fragrant *a.* ароматний aromatnyi
frail *a.* крихкий krykhkyi
frame *v.t.* обрамовувати
obramovuvaty
frame *n* рама rama
franchise *n.* привілей pryvilei
frank *a.* щирий shchyryi
frantic *a.* шалений shalenyi
fraternal *a.* братерський
braterskyi
fraternity *n.* громада hromada
fratricide *n.* братовбивство
bratovbyvstvo
fraud *n.* шахрайство shakhraistvo
fraudulent *a.* шахрайський
shakhraiskyi
fraught *a.* обтяжений obtiazhenyi
fray *n* сварка svarka
free *a.* відкритий vidkrytyi
free *v.t* визволяти vypzvoliaty
freedom *n.* свобода svoboda
freeze *v.i.* заморожувати
zamorozhuvaty
freight *n.* фрахт frakht
French *a.* французький
frantsuzkyi
French *n* французька мова
frantsuzka mova
frenzy *n.* божевілля bozhevillia

frequency *n.* частота chastota
frequent *a.* частий chastyi
fresh *a.* свіжий svizhyi
fret *v.t.* підточувати pidtochuvaty
fret *n.* хвилювання khvyliuvannia
friction *n.* тертя tertia
Friday *n.* п'ятниця piatnytsia
fridge *n.* холодильник
kholodylnyk
friend *n.* приятель pryiatel
fright *n.* жах zhakh
frighten *v.t.* налякати naliakaty
frigid *a.* холодний kholodnyi
frill *n.* оборка oborka
fringe *n.* бахрома bakhroma
fringe *v.t* облямовувати
obliamovuvaty
frivolous *a.* легковажний
lehkovazhnyi
frock *n.* плаття plattia
frog *n.* жаба zhaba
frolic *n.* пустощі pustoshchi
frolic *v.i.* пустувати pustuvaty
from *prep.* від vid
front *a* передній perednii
front *v.t* виходити на vykhodyty
na
front *n.* чоло cholo
frontier *n.* рубіж rubizh
frost *n.* мороз moroz
frown *n.* похмурий погляд
pokhmuryi pohliad
frown *v.i* хмуритися khmurytysia
frugal *a.* скромний skromnyi
fruit *n.* фрукт frukt
fruitful *a.* плідний plidnyi
frustrate *v.t.* розладнувати
rozladnuvaty
frustration *n.* розлад rozlad
fry *n* смажене smazhene
fry *v.t.* смажити smazhyty
fuel *n.* паливо palyvo
fugitive *a.* побіжний pobizhnyi

fugitive *n.* утікач utikach
fulfill *v.t.* виконувати vykonuvaty
fulfilment *n.* здійснення zdiisnennia
full *a.* нескорочений neskorochenyi
full *adv.* пухкий pukhkyi
fullness *n.* повнота povnota
fully *adv.* цілком tsilkom
fumble *v.i.* нишпорити nyshporyty
fun *n.* розвага rozvaha
function *v.i* функціонувати funktsionuvaty
function *n.* функція funktsiia
functionary *n.* функціонер funktsioner
fund *n.* фонд fond
fundamental *a.* фундаментальний fundamentalnyi
funeral *n.* похорон pokhoron
fungus *n.* грибок hrybok
funny *n.* забавний zabavnyi
fur *n.* хутро khutro
furious *a.* скажений skazhenyi
furl *v.t.* кріпити kripyty
furlong *n.* восьма частина милі vosma chastyna myli
furnace *n.* горн horn
furnish *v.t.* обставляти obstavliaty
furniture *n.* обстановка obstanovka
furrow *n.* борозна borozna
further *adv.* подалі podali
further *a* подальший podalshyi
further *v.t* сприяти spryiaty
fury *n.* лють liut
fuse *v.t.* плавити plavyty
fuse *n* плавка plavka
fusion *n.* плавлення plavlennia
fuss *v.i* метушитися metushytysia
fuss *n.* метушня metushnia
futile *a.* марний marnyi

futility *n.* марність marnist
future *a.* майбутній maibutnii
future *n* майбутнє maibutnie

gabble *v.i.* бурмотати burmotaty
gadfly *n.* сліпень slipen
gag *v.t.* затикати рот zatykaty rot
gag *n.* кляп kliap
gaiety *n.* нарядність nariadnist
gain *n* виграш vyhrash
gain *v.t.* здобувати zdobuvaty
gainsay *v.t.* суперечити superechyty
gait *n.* хода khoda
galaxy *n.* галактика halaktyka
gale *n.* шторм shtorm
gallant *a.* галантний halantnyi
gallant *n* кавалер kavaler
gallantry *n.* галантність halantnist
gallery *n.* галерея halereia
gallon *n.* галон halon
gallop *n.* галоп halop
gallop *v.t.* скакати skakaty
gallows *n.* . шибениця shybenytsia
galore *adv.* удосталь udostal
galvanize *v.t.* гальванізувати halvanizuvaty
gamble *n* азартна гра azartna hra
gamble *v.i.* грати в азартні ігри hraty v azartni ihry
gambler *n.* гравець hravets
game *n.* гра hra
game *v.i* грати hraty
gander *n.* йолоп yolop
gang *n.* банда banda
gangster *n.* гангстер hanhster
gap *n* пролом prolom
gape *v.i.* позіхати pozikhaty
garage *n.* гараж harazh
garb *n.* одіяння odiiannia

garb *v.t* одягатися odiahatysia
garbage *n.* сміття smittia
garden *n.* сад sad
gardener *n.* садівник sadivnyk
gargle *v.i.* полоскати poloskaty
garland *n.* вінок vinok
garland *v.t.* прикрашати гірляндою prykrashaty hirliandoiu
garlic *n.* часник chasnyk
garment *n.* предмет одягу predmet odiahu
garter *n.* підв'язка pidviazka
gas *n.* газ haz
gasket *n.* набивка nabyvka
gasp *v.i* важко дихати vazhko dykhaty
gasp *n.* утруднене дихання utrudnene dykhannia
gassy *a.* балакучий balakuchyi
gastric *a.* шлунковий shlunkovyi
gate *n.* ворота vorota
gather *v.t.* рвати rvaty
gaudy *a.* яскравий yaskravyi
gauge *n.* розмір rozmir
gauntlet *n.* рукавиця rukavytsia
gay *a.* безтурботний bezturbotnyi
gaze *v.t.* дивитися dyvytysia
gaze *n* погляд pohliad
gazette *n.* газета hazeta
gear *n.* швидкість shvydkist
geld *v.t.* обкладати податком obkladaty podatkom
gem *n* коштовність koshtovnist
gender *n.* рід rid
general *a.* широкий shyrokyi
generally *adv.* як правило yak pravylo
generate *v.t.* породжувати porodzhuvaty
generation *n.* покоління pokolinnia

generator *n.* джерело енергії dzherelo enerhii
generosity *n.* щедрість shchedrist
generous *a.* щедрий shchedryi
genius *n.* геній henii
gentle *a.* м'який miakyi
gentleman *n.* джентльмен dzhentlmen
gentry *n.* дрібнопомісне дворянство dribnopomisne dvorianstvo
genuine *a.* справжній spravzhnii
geographer *n.* географ heohraf
geographical *a.* географічний heohrafichnyi
geography *n.* географія heohrafiia
geological *a.* геологічний heolohichnyi
geologist *n.* геолог heolóh
geology *n.* геологія heolohiia
geometrical *a.* геометричний heometrychnyi
geometry *n.* геометрія heometriia
germ *n.* мікроб mikrob
germicide *n.* бактерицид bakterytsyd
germinate *v.i.* прорости prorosty
germination *n.* пророщування proroshchuvannia
gerund *n.* герундій herundii
gesture *n.* жест zhest
get *v.t.* приносити prynosyty
ghastly *a.* мертво-блідий mertvo-blidyi
ghost *n.* тінь tin
giant *n.* гігант hihant
gibbon *n.* гібон hibon
gibe *n* колючість koliuchist
gibe *v.i.* насміхатися nasmikhatysia
giddy *a.* запаморочливий zapamorochlyvyi

gift *n.* дар dar
gifted *a.* обдарований obdarovanyi
gigantic *a.* гігантський hihantskyi
giggle *v.i.* хихикати khykhykaty
gild *v.t.* прикрашати prykrashaty
gilt *a.* позолота pozolota
ginger *n.* імбир imbyr
giraffe *n.* жираф zhyraf
gird *v.t.* підперізувати pidperizuvaty
girder *n.* перекладина perekladyna
girdle *v.t* кільцювати kiltsiuvaty
girdle *n.* кушак kushak
girl *n.* дівчина divchyna
girlish *a.* дівочий divochyi
gist *n.* суть sut
give *v.t.* піддатливість piddatlyvist
glacier *n.* льодовик lodovyk
glad *a.* приємний pryiemnyi
gladden *v.t.* радувати raduvaty
glamour *n.* чарівність charivnist
glance *v.i.* окинути поглядом okynuty pohliadom
glance *n.* швидкий погляд shvydkyi pohliad
gland *n.* залоза zaloza
glare *n.* блискуча мішура blyskucha mishura
glare *v.i* пильно дивитися pylno dyvytysia
glass *n.* скло sklo
glaucoma *n.* глаукома hlaukoma
glaze *n* глазур hlazur
glaze *v.t.* склити sklyty
glazier *n.* скляр skliar
glee *n.* радість radist
glide *v.t.* плавно рухатися plavno rukhatysia
glider *n.* глісер hliser
glimpse *n.* просвіт prosvit
glitter *n* блиск blysk

glitter *v.i.* виблискувати vyblyskuvaty
global *a.* глобальний hlobalnyi
globe *n.* глобус hlobus
gloom *n.* заволікатися zavolikatysia
gloomy *a.* темний temnyi
glorification *n.* вихваляння vykhvaliannia
glorify *v.t.* славити slavyty
glorious *a.* славний slavnyi
glory *n.* слава slava
gloss *n.* лиск lysk
glossary *n.* глосарій hlosarii
glossy *a.* лискучий lyskuchyi
glove *n.* рукавичка rukavychka
glow *v.i.* розжарюватися rozzhariuvatysia
glow *n* спека speka
glucose *n.* глюкоза hliukoza
glue *n.* клей klei
glut *v.t.* завалювати товарами zavaliuvaty tovaramy
glut *n* затоварення zatovarennia
glutton *n.* росомаха rosomakha
gluttony *n.* обжерливість obzherlyvist
glycerine *n.* гліцерин hlitseryn
go *v.i.* йти yty
goad *v.t* спонукати sponukaty
goad *n.* стимул stymul
goal *n.* завдання zavdannia
goat *n.* коза koza
gobble *n.* жерти zherty
goblet *n.* келих kelykh
god *n.* бог boh
goddess *n.* богиня bohynia
godhead *n.* божественність bozhestvennist
godly *a.* праведний pravednyi
godown *n.* склад товарів sklad tovariv
godsend *n.* удача udacha

goggles *n.* здивований погляд zdyvovanyi pohliad
gold *n.* золото zoloto
golden *a.* золотий zolotyi
goldsmith *n.* ювелір yuvelir
golf *n.* гольф holf
gong *n.* гонг honh
good *a.* добрий dobryi
good *n* товар tovar
good-bye *interj.* до побачення do pobachennia
goodness *n.* доброта dobrota
goodwill *n.* благовоління blahovolinnia
goose *n.* гусак husak
gooseberry *n.* аґрус agrus
gorgeous *a.* яскравий yaskravyi
gorilla *n.* горила horyla
gospel *n.* проповідь propovid
gospel *n.* Євангеліє Yevanheliie
gossip *n.* плітка plitka
gourd *n.* горлянка horlianka
gout *n.* подагра podahra
govern *v.t.* управляти upravliaty
governance *n.* керівництво kerivnytstvo
governess *n.* гувернантка huvernantka
government *n.* управління upravlinnia
governor *n.* губернатор hubernator
gown *n.* сукня suknia
grab *v.t.* хапати khapaty
grace *n.* грація hratsiia
grace *v.t.* удостоювати udostoiuvaty
gracious *a.* милостивий mylostyvyi
gradation *n.* градація hradatsiia
grade *v.t* сортувати sortuvaty
grade *n.* ступінь stupin
gradual *a.* поступовий postupovyi

graduate *v.i.* випускати vypuskaty
graduate *n* випускний vypusknyi
graft *v.t* пересаджувати peresadzhuvaty
graft *n.* щеплення shcheplennia
grain *n.* крупи krupy
grammar *n.* граматика hramatyka
grammarian *n.* граматисти hramatysty
gramme *n.* грам hram
gramophone *n.* грамофон hramofon
granary *n.* житниця zhytnytsia
grand *a.* грандіозний hrandioznyi
grandeur *n.* велич velych
grant *n* видача vydacha
grant *v.t.* надавати nadavaty
grape *n.* виноград vynohrad
graph *n.* крива kryva
graphic *a.* графічний hrafichnyi
grapple *n.* сутичка sutychka
grapple *v.i.* чепляти chepliaty
grasp *v.t.* розібратися rozibratysia
grasp *n* стискання styskannia
grass *n* трава trava
grate *n.* ґрати graty
grate *v.t* терти terty
grateful *a.* благодатний blahodatnyi
gratification *n.* винагорода vynahoroda
gratis *adv.* безкоштовний bezkoshtovnyi
gratitude *n.* подяка podiaka
gratuity *n.* грошовий подарунок hroshovyi podarunok
grave *a.* вагомий vahomyi
grave *n.* могила mohyla
gravitate *v.i.* тяжіти tiazhity
gravitation *n.* гравітація hravitatsiia
gravity *n.* серйозність serioznist
graze *v.i.* пасти pasty

graze *n* садно sadno
grease *n* мастило mastylo
grease *v.t* змастити zmastyty
greasy *a.* жирний zhyrnyi
great *a* значний znachnyi
greed *n.* жадібність zhadibnist
greedy *a.* пожадливий pozhadlyvyi
Greek *n.* грецька мова hretska mova
Greek *a* грецький hretskyi
green *a.* зелений zelenyi
green *n* зелений колір zelenyi kolir
greenery *n.* оранжерея oranzhereia
greet *v.t.* вітатися vitatysia
grenade *n.* граната hranata
grey *a.* сірий siryi
greyhound *n.* хортиця khortytsia
grief *n.* горе hore
grievance *n.* скарга skarha
grieve *v.t.* горювати horiuvaty
grievous *a.* сумний sumnyi
grind *v.i.* размелювати razmeliuvaty
grinder *n.* шліфувальник shlifuvalnyk
grip *n* затиснення zatysnennia
grip *v.t.* схоплювати skhopliuvaty
groan *n* стогін stohin
groan *v.i.* стогнати stohnaty
grocer *n.* бакалійник bakaliinyk
grocery *n.* бакалійна лавка bakaliina lavka
groom *n.* грум hrum
groom *v.t* чистити коня chystyty konia
groove *n.* вибоїна vyboina
groove *v.t* жалоби zhaloby
grope *v.t.* намацувати namatsuvaty
gross *n.* брутто brutto

gross *a* огрядний ohriadnyi
grotesque *a.* гротеск hrotesk
ground *n.* майданчик maidanchyk
group *n.* група hrupa
group *v.t.* групувати hrupuvaty
grow *v.t.* робитися robytysia
grower *n.* садівник sadivnyk
growl *n* бурчання burchannia
growl *v.i.* бурчати burchaty
growth *n.* зростання zrostannia
grudge *n* заздрість zazdrist
grudge *v.t.* шкодувати shkoduvaty
grumble *v.i.* гуркотіти hurkotity
grunt *n.* рохкання rokhkannia
grunt *v.i.* рохкати rokhkaty
guarantee *n.* поручитель poruchytel
guarantee *v.t* ручатися ruchatysia
guard *n.* охорона okhorona
guard *v.i.* охороняти okhoroniaty
guardian *n.* страж strazh
guava *n.* гуава huava
guerilla *n.* партизан partyzan
guess *n.* здогадка zdohadka
guess *v.i* здогадуватися zdohaduvatysia
guest *n.* гість hist
guidance *n.* керівництво kerivnytstvo
guide *v.t.* провести provesty
guide *n.* розвідник rozvidnyk
guild *n.* гільдія hildiia
guile *n.* підступність pidstupnist
guilt *n.* провина provyna
guilty *a.* винуватий vynuvatyi
guise *n.* личина lychyna
guitar *n.* гітара hitara
gulf *n.* затока zatoka
gull *v.t* дурити duryty
gull *n* чайка chaika
gull *n.* чайка chaika
gulp *n.* ковток kovtok
gum *n.* десна desna

gun *n.* зброя zbroia
gust *n.* шквал shkval
gutter *n.* жолоб zholob
guttural *a.* горловий horlovyi
gymnasium *n.* гімнастичний зал himnastychnyi zal
gymnast *n.* гімнаст himnast
gymnastic *a.* гімнастичний himnastychnyi
gymnastics *n.* гімнастика himnastyka

habeas corpus *n.* судовий наказ про передачу арештованого до суду для належного судового розгляду sudovyi nakaz pro peredachu areshtovanoho do sudu dlia nalezhnoho sudovoho rozhliadu
habit *n.* будова тіла budova tila
habitable *a.* придатний для житла prydatnyi dlia zhytla
habitat *n.* батьківщина batkivshchyna
habitation *n.* проживання prozhyvannia
habituate *v. t.* привчати pryvchaty
hack *v.t.* мотика motyka
hag *n.* чаклунка chaklunka
haggard *a.* виснажений vysnazhenyi
haggle *v.i.* торгуватися torhuvatysia
hail *v.t* поздоровляти pozdorovliaty
hail *v.i* сипатися sypatysia
hail *n.* слава slava
hair *n* волосся volossia
hale *a.* здоровий zdorovyi
half *n.* половина polovyna
half *a* половинний polovynnyi

hall *n.* зал zal
hallmark *n.* проба proba
hallow *v.t.* шанувати shanuvaty
halt *v. t.* зробити привал zrobyty pryval
halt *n* привал pryval
halve *v.t.* поділити навпіл podilyty navpil
hamlet *n.* селище selyshche
hammer *n.* молоток molotok
hammer *v.t* прибивати prybyvaty
hand *v.t* передати peredaty
hand *n* рука ruka
handbill *n.* рекламний листок reklamnyi lystok
handbook *n.* довідник туриста dovidnyk turysta
handcuff *v.t* надіти наручники nadity naruchnyky
handcuff *n.* наручник naruchnyk
handful *n.* жменя zhmenia
handicap *n* фізична вада fizychna vada
handicap *v.t.* ускладнювати uskladniuvaty
handicraft *n.* ручна робота ruchna robota
handiwork *n.* ручна робота ruchna robota
handkerchief *n.* носовичок nosovychok
handle *v.t* поратися poratysia
handle *n.* рукоятка rukoiatka
handsome *a.* гарний harnyi
handy *a.* портативний portatyvnyi
hang *v.t.* вішати vishaty
hanker *v.i.* прагнути prahnuty
haphazard *a.* необдуманий neobdumanyi
happen *v.t.* статися statysia
happening *n.* подія podiia
happiness *n.* щастя shchastia
happy *a.* щасливий shchaslyvyi

harass *v.t.* турбувати turbuvaty
harassment *n.* залякування zaliakuvannia
harbour *n.* гавань havan
harbour *v.t* стати на якір staty na yakir
hard *a.* жорсткий zhorstkyi
harden *v.t.* робити твердим robyty tverdym
hardihood *n.* зухвальство zukhvalstvo
hardly *adv.* насилу nasylu
hardship *n.* нестатки nestatky
hardy *adj.* відважний vidvazhnyi
hare *n.* заєць zaiets
harm *n.* шкода shkoda
harm *v.t* шкодити shkodyty
harmonious *a.* гармонійний harmoniinyi
harmonium *n.* фісгармонія fisharmoniia
harmony *n.* гармонія harmoniia
harness *v.t* запрягати zapriahaty
harness *n.* упряж upriazh
harp *n.* арфа arfa
harsh *a.* твердий tverdyi
harverster *n.* збирач врожаю zbyrach vrozhaiu
harvest *n.* урожай urozhai
haste *n.* поспіх pospikh
hasten *v.i.* поспішати pospishaty
hasty *a.* запальний zapalnyi
hat *n.* капелюх kapeliukh
hatchet *n.* сокирка sokyrka
hate *v.t.* ненавидіти nenavydity
hate *n.* ненависть nenavyst
haughty *a.* гордовитий hordovytyi
haunt *n* улюблене місце uliublene mistse
haunt *v.t.* часто бувати chasto buvaty
have *v.t.* мати maty
haven *n.* притулок prytulok

havoc *n.* спустошення spustoshennia
hawk *n* яструб yastrub
hawker *n* сокільник sokilnyk
hawthorn *n.* глід hlid
hay *n.* сіно sino
hazard *n.* загроза zahroza
hazard *v.t* ставити на карту stavyty na kartu
haze *n.* легкий туман lehkyi tuman
hazy *a.* туманний tumannyi
he *pron.* він vin
head *n.* голова holova
head *v.t* вести vesty
headache *n.* головний біль holovnyi bil
heading *n.* заголовок zaholovok
headlong *adv.* невтримний nevtrymnyi
headstrong *a.* свавільний svavilnyi
heal *v.i.* сприяти заєнню spryiaty zaienniu
health *n.* здоров'я zdorovia
healthy *a.* корисний korysnyi
heap *n.* купа kupa
heap *v.t* нагромаджувати nahromadzhuvaty
hear *v.t.* чути chuty
hearsay *n.* слух slukh
heart *n.* серце sertse
hearth *n.* вогнище vohnyshche
heartily *adv.* серцево sertsevo
heat *v.t* зігрівати zihrivaty
heat *n.* спека speka
heave *v.i.* піднімати pidnimaty
heaven *n.* небеса nebesa
heavenly *a.* священний sviashchennyi
hedge *n.* дивопліт dyvoplit
hedge *v.t* підрізати живопліт podrizaty zhyvoplit

heed *v.t.* звернути увагу zvernuty uvahu
heed *n* увага uvaha
heel *n.* п'ята piata
hefty *a.* неабиякий neabyiakyi
height *n.* зріст zrist
heighten *v.t.* підвищувати pidvyshchuvaty
heinous *a.* огидний ohydnyi
heir *n.* спадкоємець spadkoiemets
hell *a.* пекло peklo
helm *n.* кермо kermo
helmet *n.* шолом sholom
help *v.t.* допомагати dopomahaty
help *n* помічник pomichnyk
helpful *a.* корисний korysnyi
helpless *a.* безпомічний bezpomichnyi
helpmate *n.* товариш tovarysh
hemisphere *n.* півкуля pivkulia
hemp *n.* пенька penka
hen *n.* курка kurka
hence *adv.* звідси zvidsy
henceforth *adv.* з цього часу z tsoho chasu
henceforward *adv.* відтепер vidteper
henchman *n.* зброєносець zbroienosets
henpecked *n.* підкаблучник pidkabluchnyk
her *a* її yii
her *pron.* їй yii
herald *n.* вісник visnyk
herald *v.t* сповіщати spovishchaty
herb *n.* трава trava
herculean *a.* дуже сильний duzhe sylnyi
herd *n.* стадо stado
herdsman *n.* пастух pastukh
here *adv.* тут tut

hereabouts *adv.* десь поруч des poruch
hereafter *adv.* тут і далі tut i dali
hereditary *a.* спадковий spadkovyi
heredity *n.* спадковість spadkovist
heritable *a.* наслідуваний nasliduvanyi
heritage *n.* спадщина spadshchyna
hermit *n.* самітник samitnyk
hermitage *n.* пустинь pustyn
hernia *n.* грижа hryzha
hero *n.* герой heroi
heroic *a.* героїчний heroichnyi
heroine *n.* героїня heroinia
heroism *n.* героїзм heroizm
herring *n.* оселедець oseledets
hesitant *a.* коливний kolyvnyi
hesitate *v.i.* коливатися kolyvatysia
hesitation *n.* коливання kolyvannia
hew *v.t.* прорубувати prorubuvaty
heyday *n.* розквіт rozkvit
hibernation *n.* зимівля zymivlia
hiccup *n.* гикавка hykavka
hide *n.* укриття ukryttia
hide *v.t* ховати khovaty
hideous *a.* потворний potvornyi
hierarchy *n.* ієрархія iierarkhiia
high *a.* високий vysokyi
highly *adv.* дуже duzhe
Highness *n.* високість vysokist
highway *n.* шосе shose
hilarious *a.* галасливий halaslyvyi
hilarity *n.* гучні веселощі huchni veseloshchi
hill *n.* пагорб pahorb
hillock *n.* горбок horbok
him *pron.* йому yomu
hinder *v.t.* заважати zavazhaty

hindrance *n.* завада zavada
hint *v.i* натякати natiakaty
hint *n.* натяк natiak
hip *n* стегно stehno
hire *v.t* знімати znimaty
hire *n.* наймання naimannia
hireling *n.* найманець naimanets
his *pron.* його yoho
hiss *n* шипіння shypinnia
hiss *v.i* шипіти shypity
historian *n.* історик istoryk
historic *a*. історичний istorychnyi
historical *a.* пов'язаний з
    історією poviazanyi z ictoriieiu
history *n.* історія istoriia
hit *n* удар udar
hit *v.t.* ударяти udariaty
hitch *n.* ривок ryvok
hither *adv.* сюди siudy
hitherto *adv.* досі dosi
hive *n.* саджати у вулик sadzhaty
    u vulyk
hoarse *a.* хрипкий khrypkyi
hoax *v.t* дурити duryty
hoax *n.* містифікація mistyfikatsiia
hobby *n.* хобі khobi
hobby-horse *n.* коник konyk
hockey *n.* хокей khokei
hoist *v.t.* підняти pidniaty
hold *n.* володіння volodinnia
hold *v.t* тримати trymaty
hole *n* діра dira
hole *v.t* дірявити diriavyty
holiday *n.* день відпочинку den
    vidpochynku
hollow *v.t* видовбувати
    vydovbuvaty
hollow *a.* глухий hlukhyi
hollow *n.* пустота pustota
holocaust *n.* масове винищення
    masove vynyshchennia
holy *a.* святий sviatyi

homage *n.* шанування
    shanuvannia
home *n.* будинок budynok
homeopathy *n.* гомеопатія
    homeopatiia
homicide *n.* позбавлення життя
    pozbavlennia zhyttia
homoeopath *n.* гомеопат
    homeopat
homogeneous *a.* однорідний
    odnoridnyi
honest *a.* чесний chesnyi
honesty *n.* чесність chesnist
honey *n.* мед med
honeycomb *n.* медові соти
    medovi soty
honeymoon *n.* медовий місяць
    medovyi misiats
honorarium *n.* винагорода
    vynahoroda
honorary *a.* почесний pochesnyi
honour *n.* честь chest
honour *v. t* поважати povazhaty
honourable *a.* шановний
    shanovnyi
hood *n.* капюшон kapiushon
hoodwink *v.t.* ввести в оману
    vvesty v omanu
hoof *n.* бити копитом byty
    kopytom
hook *n.* гак hak
hooligan *n.* хуліган khulihan
hoot *n.* гикання hykannia
hoot *v.i* улюлюкати uliuliukaty
hop *v. i* стрибати strybaty
hop *n* стрибок strybok
hope *n* надія nadiia
hope *v.t.* сподіватися spodivatysia
hopeful *a.* який сподівається
    yakyi spodivaietsia
hopeless *a.* безнадійний
    beznadiinyi
horde *n.* орда orda

horizon *n.* горизонт horyzont
horn *n.* ріг rih
hornet *n.* шершень shershen
horrible *a.* бридкий brydkyi
horrify *v.t.* шокувати shokuvaty
horror *n.* огида ohyda
horse *n.* коняка koniaka
horticulture *n.* садівництво sadivnytstvo
hose *n.* шланг shlanh
hosiery *n.* панчішні вироби panchishni vyroby
hospitable *a.* гостинний hostynnyi
hospital *n.* лікарня likarnia
hospitality *n.* гостинність hostynnist
host *n.* господар hospodar
hostage *n.* заручник zaruchnyk
hostel *n.* гуртожиток hurtozhytok
hostile *a.* ворожий vorozhyi
hostility *n.* вороже ставлення vorozhe stavlennia
hot *a.* пекучий pekuchyi
hotchpotch *n.* рагу з м'яса з овочами rahu z miasa z ovochamy
hotel *n.* готель hotel
hound *n.* мисливський собака myslyvskyi sobaka
hour *n.* година hodyna
house *v.t* надавати житло nadavaty zhytlo
house *n* хата khata
how *adv.* як yak
however *adv.* тим не менш tym ne mensh
however *conj* при цьому pry tsomu
howl *v.t.* вити vyty
howl *n* завивання zavyvannia
hub *n.* втулка vtulka
hubbub *n.* шум shum

huge *a.* величезний velycheznyi
hum *n* гудіння hudinnia
hum *v.* і гудіти hudity
human *a.* людський liudskyi
humane *a.* гуманний humannyi
humanitarian *a* гуманітарій humanitarii
humanity *n.* людство liudstvo
humanize *v.t.* олюднювати oliudniuvaty
humble *a.* скромний skromnyi
humdrum *a.* загальне місце zahalne mistse
humid *a.* сирий syryi
humidity *n.* вологість volohist
humiliate *v.t.* принижувати prynyzhuvaty
humiliation *n.* приниженість prynyzhenist
humility *n.* покірність pokirnist
humorist *n.* гуморист humoryst
humorous *a.* гумористичний humorystychnyi
humour *n.* гумор humor
hunch *n.* горб horb
hundred *n.* сотня sotnia
hunger *n* тривале недоїдання tryvale nedoidannia
hungry *a.* голодний holodnyi
hunt *n* полювання poliuvannia
hunt *v.t.* полювати poliuvaty
hunter *n.* мисливець myslyvets
huntsman *n.* єгер yeher
hurdle1 *n.* гатка hatka
hurdle2 *v.t* обгороджувати тином obhorodzhuvaty tynom
hurl *v.t.* жбурляти zhburliaty
hurrah *interj.* ура ura
hurricane *n.* ураган urahan
hurry *n* квапливість kvaplyvist
hurry *v.t.* квапити kvapyty
hurt *v.t.* заподіювати біль zapodiiuvaty bil

hurt *n* образа obraza
husband *n* чоловік cholovik
husbandry *n.* землеробство zemlerobstvo
hush *v.i* змушувати замовчати zmushuvaty zamovchaty
hush *n* тиша tysha
husk *n.* лушпайка lushpaika
husky *a.* сухий sukhyi
hut *n.* хатина khatyna
hyaena, hyena *n.* гієна hiiena
hybrid *n* гібрид hibryd
hybrid *a.* гібридний hibrydnyi
hydrogen *n.* водень voden
hygiene *n.* гігієна hihiiena
hygienic *a.* гігієнічний hihiienichnyi
hymn *n.* церковний гімн tserkovnyi himn
hyperbole *n.* гіпербола hiperbola
hypnotism *n.* гіпнотизм hipnotyzm
hypnotize *v.t.* гіпнотизувати hipnotyzuvaty
hypocrisy *n.* лицемірство lytsemirstvo
hypocrite *n.* лицемір lytsemir
hypocritical *a.* лицемірний lytsemirnyi
hypothesis *n.* гіпотеза hipoteza
hypothetical *a.* можливий mozhlyvyi
hysteria *n.* істерія isteriia
hysterical *a.* істеричний isterychnyi

I *pron.* я ya
ice *n.* лід lid
iceberg *n.* айсберг aisberh
icicle *n.* бурулька burulka
icy *a.* крижаний kryzhanyi

idea *n.* ідея ideia
ideal *n* ідеал ideal
ideal *a.* ідеальний idealnyi
idealism *n.* ідеалізм idealizm
idealist *n.* ідеаліст idealist
idealistic *a.* ідеалістичний idealistychnyi
idealize *v.t.* ідеалізувати idealizuvaty
identical *a.* ідентичний identychnyi
identify *v.t.* ідентифікувати identyfikuvaty
identity *n.* ідентичність identychnist
ideocy *n.* ідіотизм idiotyzm
idiom *n.* ідіома idioma
idiomatic *a.* ідіоматичний idiomatychnyi
idiot *n.* ідіот idiot
idiotic *a.* ідіотський idiotskyi
idle *a.* незайнятий nezainiatyi
idleness *n.* ледарство ledarstvo
idler *n.* нероба neroba
idol *n.* ідол idol
idolater *n.* ідолопоклонник idolopoklonnyk
if *conj.* якщо yakshcho
ignoble *a.* низький nyzkyi
ignorance *n.* неуцтво neutstvo
ignorant *a.* неосвічений neosvichenyi
ignore *v.t.* ігнорувати ihnoruvaty
ill *a.* хворий khvoryi
ill *adv.* навряд чи navriad chy
ill *n* шкода shkoda
illegal *a.* незаконний nezakonnyi
illegibility *n.* неможливість прочитати nemozhlyvist prochytaty
illegible *a.* який важко читається yakyi vazhko chytaietsia

illegitimate *a.* неправильний nepravylnyi
illicit *a.* недозволений nedozvolenyi
illiteracy *n.* неграмотність nehramotnist
illiterate *a.* неписьменний nepysmennyi
illness *n.* хвороба khvoroba
illogical *a.* нелогічний nelohichnyi
illuminate *v.t.* опромінювати oprominiuvaty
illumination *n.* ілюмінація iliuminatsiia
illusion *n.* ілюзія iliuziia
illustrate *v.t.* ілюструвати iliustruvaty
illustration *n.* ілюстрація iliustratsiia
image *n.* образ obraz
imagery *n.* різьба rizba
imaginary *a.* уявний uiavnyi
imagination *n.* уява uiava
imaginative *a.* творчий tvorchyi
imagine *v.t.* уявляти uiavliaty
imitate *v.t.* копіювати kopiiuvaty
imitation *n.* наслідування nasliduvannia
imitator *n.* наслідувач nasliduvach
immaterial *a.* нематеріальний nematerialnyi
immature *a.* нестиглий nestyhlyi
immaturity *n.* незрілість nezrilist
immeasurable *a.* незмірний nezmirnyi
immediate *a.* спішний spishnyi
immemorial *a.* древній drevnii
immense *a.* неосяжний neosiazhnyi
immensity *n.* безмір bezmir
immerse *v.t.* занурювати zanuriuvaty
immersion *n.* занурення zanurennia
immigrant *n.* іммігрант immihrant
immigrate *v.i.* іммігрувати immihruvaty
immigration *n.* імміграція immihratsiia
imminent *a.* насувається nasuvaietsia
immodest *a.* нескромне neskromne
immodesty *n.* нескромність neskromnist
immoral *a.* розпутний rozputnyi
immorality *n.* аморальність amoralnist
immortal *a.* безсмертний bezsmertnyi
immortality *n.* безсмертя bezsmertia
immortalize *v.t.* увічнити uvichnyty
immovable *a.* байдужий baiduzhyi
immune *a.* імунний imunnyi
immunity *n.* несприйнятливість nespryiniatlyvist
immunize *v.t.* імунізувати imunizuvaty
impact *n.* імпульс impuls
impart *v.t.* давати davaty
impartial *a.* неупереджений neuperedzhenyi
impartiality *n.* неупередженість neuperedzhenist
impassable *a.* непрохідний neprokhidnyi
impasse *n.* безвихідне становище bezvykhidne stanovyshche
impatience *n.* нетерпимість neterpymist

impatient *a.* дратівливий
drativlyvyi
impeach *v.t.* брати під сумнів
braty pid sumniv
impeachment *n.* вияв сумніву
vyiav sumnivu
impede *v.t.* затримувати
zatrymuvaty
impediment *n.* ускладнення
uskladnennia
impenetrable *a.* недоступний
nedostupnyi
imperative *a.* наказовий
nakazovyi
imperfect *a.* незавершений
nezavershenyi
imperfection *n.* недосконалість
nedoskonalist
imperial *a.* імперський imperskyi
imperialism *n.* імперіалізм
imperializm
imperil *v.t.* наражати на
небезпеку narazhaty na
nebezpeku
imperishable *a.* нерушимий
nerushymyi
impersonal *a.* безособовий
bezosobovyi
impersonate *v.t.* уособлювати
uosobliuvaty
impersonation *n.* уособлення
uosoblennia
impertinence *n.* зухвалість
zukhvalist
impertinent *a.* нахабний
nakhabnyi
impetuosity *n.* імпульсивність
impulsyvnist
impetuous *a.* стрімкий strimkyi
implement *n.* знаряддя
znariaddia

implement *v.t.* щзабезпечувати
інструментами
shchzabezpechuvaty
instrumentamy
implicate *v.t.* вплутувати
vplutuvaty
implication *n.* залучення
zaluchennia
implicit *a.* котрого kotroho
implore *v.t.* просити prosyty
imply *v.t.* містити в собі mistyty
v sobi
impolite *a.* неввічливий
nevvichlyvyi
import *n.* імпорт import
import *v.t.* імпортувати
importuvaty
importance *n.* важливість
vazhlyvist
important *a.* важливий vazhlyvyi
impose *v.t.* накласти naklasty
imposing *a.* імпозантний
impozantnyi
imposition *n.* накладення
nakladennia
impossibility *n.* неможливість
nemozhlyvist
impossible *a.* неможливий
nemozhlyvyi
impostor *n.* обманщик
obmanshchyk
imposture *n.* обман obman
impotence *n.* безсилля bezsyllia
impotent *a.* слабкий slabkyi
impoverish *v.t.* довести до
бідності dovesty do bidnosti
impracticability *n.*
нездійсненність nezdiisnennist
impracticable *a.* нездійсненний
nezdiisnennyi
impress *v.t.* віддруковувати
viddrukovuvaty

impression *n.* враження
vrazhennia
impressive *a.* вражаючий
vrazhaiuchyi
imprint *v.t.* удруковане
udrukovane
imprint *n.* штамп shtamp
imprison *v.t.* ув'язнювати
uviazniuvaty
improper *a.* невідповідний
nevidpovidnyi
impropriety *n.* недоречність
nedorechnist
improve *v.t.* вдосконалювати
vdoskonaliuvaty
improvement *n.* поліпшення
polipshennia
imprudence *n.* нерозсудливість
nerozsudlyvist
imprudent *a.* необережний
neoberezhnyi
impulse *n.* збудження
zbudzhennia
impulsive *a.* імпульсивний
impulsyvnyi
impunity *n.* безкарність
bezkarnist
impure *a.* нечистий nechystyi
impurity *n.* нечистота nechystota
impute *v.t.* ставити stavyty
in *prep.* у u
inability *n.* нездібність nezdibnist
inaccurate *a.* помилковий
pomylkovyi
inaction *n.* бездіяльність
bezdiialnist
inactive *a.* бездіяльний
bezdiialnyi
inadmissible *a.* неприпустимий
neprypustymyi
inanimate *a.* неживий nezhyvyi
inapplicable *a.* непридатний
neprydatnyi

inattentive *a.* неуважний
neuvazhnyi
inaudible *a.* нечутний nechutnyi
inaugural *a.* урочиста промова
urochysta promova
inauguration *n.* урочисте
відкриття urochyste vidkryttia
inauspicious *a.* зловісний
zlovisnyi
inborn *a.* уроджений urodzhenyi
incalculable *a.* незліченні
nezlichenni
incapable *a.* невмілий nevmilyi
incapacity *n.* нездатність
nezdatnist
incarnate *a.* втілений vtilenyi
incarnate *v.t.* втілювати vtiliuvaty
incarnation *n.* уособлення
uosoblennia
incense *v.t.* дратувати dratuvaty
incense *n.* ладан ladan
incentive *n.* спонукання
sponukannia
inception *n.* народження
narodzhennia
inch *n.* дюйм diuim
incident *n.* інцидент intsydent
incidental *a.* побічний pobichnyi
incite *v.t.* порушувати
porushuvaty
inclination *n.* нахилення
nakhylennia
incline *v.i.* схиляти skhyliaty
include *v.t.* включати vkliuchaty
inclusion *n.* включення
vkliuchennia
inclusive *a.* містить mistyt
incoherent *a.* незв'язних
nezviaznykh
income *n.* дохід dokhid
incomparable *a.* непорівнянний
neporivniannyi

incompetent *a.* некомпетентний
nekompetentnyi
incomplete *a.* неповний
nepovnyi
inconsiderate *a.* необдуманий
neobdumanyi
inconvenient *a.* незручний
nezruchnyi
incorporate *a.* об'єднаний
obiednanyi
incorporate *v.t.* реєструвати
reiestruvaty
incorporation *n.* корпорація
korporatsiia
incorrect *a.* невірний nevirnyi
incorrigible *a.* невиправний
nevypravnyi
incorruptible *a.* псується
psuietsia
increase *n* збільшуватися
zbilshuvatysia
increase *v.t.* зростати zrostaty
incredible *a.* неймовірний
neimovirnyi
increment *n.* приріст pryrist
incriminate *v.t.* інкримінувати
inkryminuvaty
incubate *v.i.* висиджувати
vysydzhuvaty
inculcate *v.t.* впроваджувати
vprovadzhuvaty
incumbent *n.* особа, що займає
посаду osoba, shcho zaimaie
posadu
incumbent *a* покладений
pokladenyi
incur *v.t.* брати на себе braty na
sebe
incurable *a.* невиліковний
nevylikovnyi
indebted *a.* знаходиться в боргу
znakhodytsia v borhu

indecency *n.* безсоромна дія
bezsoromna diia
indecent *a.* непорядний
neporiadnyi
indecision *n.* нерішучість
nerishuchist
indeed *adv.* невже nevzhe
indefensible *a.* незахищений
nezakhyshchenyi
indefinite *a.* невизначений
nevyznachenyi
indemnity *n.* гарантія від збитків
harantiia vid zbytkiv
indentification *n.* ідентифікація
identyfikatsiia
independence *n.* незалежність
nezalezhnist
independent *a.* самостійний
samostiinyi
indescribable *a.* неясний
neiasnyi
index *n.* покажчик pokazhchyk
Indian *a.* індійський indiiskyi
indicate *v.t.* вказувати vkazuvaty
indication *n.* вказівка vkazivka
indicative *a.* який вказує yakyi
vkazuie
indicator *n.* індикатор indykator
indict *v.t.* висувати
обвинувачення vysuvaty
obvynuvachennia
indictment *n.* обвинувальний акт
obvynuvalnyi akt
indifference *n.* байдужість
baiduzhist
indifferent *a.* байдужий baiduzhyi
indigenous *a.* місцевий mistsevyi
indigestible *a.* нестравний
nestravnyi
indigestion *n.* порушення
травлення porushennia
travlennia
indignant *a.* обурений oburenyi

indignation *n.* обурення oburennia

indigo *n.* індиго indyho

indirect *a.* непрямий nepriamyi

indiscipline *n.* недисциплінованість nedystsyplinovanist

indiscreet *a.* нескромний neskromnyi

indiscretion *n.* нечемність nechemnist

indiscriminate *a.* нерозбірливий nerozbirlyvyi

indispensable *a.* необхідний neobkhidnyi

indisposed *a.* неприхильність neprykhylnist

indisputable *a.* безперечний bezperechnyi

indistinct *a.* неясний neiasnyi

individual *a.* особистий osobystyi

individualism *n.* індивідуалізм indyvidualizm

individuality *n.* індивідуальність indyvidualnist

indivisible *a.* неподільний nepodilnyi

indolent *a.* пустопорожнє pustoporozhnie

indomitable *a.* неприборканий nepryborkanyi

indoor *a.* внутрішній vnutrishnii

indoors *adv.* всередині vseredyni

induce *v.t.* спонукати sponukaty

inducement *n.* спонукання sponukannia

induct *v.t.* вводити в посаду vvodyty v posadu

induction *n.* офіційно вводити на посаду ofitsiino vvodyty na posadu

indulge *v.t.* давати собі волю davaty sobi voliu

indulgence *n.* поблажливість poblazhlyvist

indulgent *a.* поблажливий poblazhlyvyi

industrial *a.* виробничий vyrobnychyi

industrious *a.* працьовитий pratsovytyi

industry *n.* виробництво vyrobnytstvo

ineffective *a.* безрезультатний bezrezultatnyi

inert *a.* інертний inertnyi

inertia *n.* сила інерції syla inertsii

inevitable *a.* неминучий nemynuchyi

inexact *a.* неточний netochnyi

inexorable *a.* невблаганний nevblahannyi

inexpensive *a.* недорогий nedorohyi

inexperience *n.* недосвідченість nedosvidchenist

inexplicable *a.* незрозумілий nezrozumilyi

infallible *a.* безпомилковий bezpomylkovyi

infamous *a.* має погану репутацію maie pohanu reputatsiiu

infamy *n.* ганьба hanba

infancy *n.* раннє дитинство rannie dytynstvo

infant *n.* немовля nemovlia

infanticide *n.* дітовбивство ditovbyvstvo

infantile *a.* інфантільний infantilnyi

infantry *n.* піхота pikhota

infatuate *v.t.* закрутити голову zakrutyty holovu

infatuation *n.* сліпе захоплення slipe zakhoplennia

infect *v.t.* заражати zarazhaty
infection *n.* зараження zarazhennia
infectious *a.* інфекційний infektsiinyi
infer *v.t.* укладати ukladaty
inference *n.* виведення vyvedennia
inferior *a.* підлеглий pidlehlyi
inferiority *n.* неповноцінність nepovnotsinnist
infernal *a.* пекельний pekelnyi
infinite *a.* безмежний bezmezhnyi
infinity *n.* нескінченність neskinchennist
infirm *a.* немічний nemichnyi
infirmity *n.* неміч nemich
inflame *v.i.* запалюватися zapaliuvatysia
inflammable *a.* горюча речовина horiucha rechovyna
inflammation *n.* займання zaimannia
inflammatory *a.* збудливий zbudlyvyi
inflation *n.* надування naduvannia
inflexible *a.* негнучкий nehnuchkyi
inflict *v.t.* наносити nanosyty
influence *n.* вплив vplyv
influence *v.t.* впливова особа vplyvova osoba
influential *a.* впливовий vplyvovyi
influenza *n.* грип hryp
influx *n.* приплив pryplyv
inform *v.t.* повідомляти povidomliaty
informal *a.* неофіційний neofitsiinyi
information *n.* інформація informatsiia

informative *a.* інформаційний informatsiinyi
informer *n.* інформатор informator
infringe *v.t.* посягати posiahaty
infringement *n.* обмеження obmezhennia
infuriate *v.t.* приводити в лють pryvodyty v liut
infuse *v.t.* вливати vlyvaty
infusion *n.* вливання vlyvannia
ingrained *a.* проникаючий pronykaiuchyi
ingratitude *n.* невдячність nevdiachnist
ingredient *n.* інгредієнт inhrediient
inhabit *v.t.* населяти naseliaty
inhabitable *a.* жилий zhylyi
inhabitant *n.* житель zhytel
inhale *v.i.* вдихати vdykhaty
inherent *a.* властивий vlastyvyi
inherit *v.t.* успадковувати uspadkovuvaty
inheritance *n.* успадкування uspadkuvannia
inhibit *v.t.* забороняти zaboroniaty
inhibition *n.* стримування strymuvannia
inhospitable *a.* негостинний nehostynnyi
inhuman *a.* нелюдський neliudskyi
inimical *a.* неприязний nepryiaznyi
inimitable *a.* неповторний nepovtornyi
initial *n.* ініціал initsial
initial *a.* початковий pochatkovyi
initial *v.t* ставити ініціали stavyty initsialy

initiate *v.t.* ознайомити oznaiomyty
initiative *n.* ініціатива initsiatyva
inject *v.t.* вводити vvodyty
injection *n.* упорскування uporskuvannia
injudicious *a.* несвоєчасний nesvoiechasnyi
injunction *n.* припис prypys
injure *v.t.* забити zabyty
injurious *a.* шкідливий shkidlyvyi
injury *n.* рана rana
injustice *n.* неправосуддя nepravosuddia
ink *n.* чорнило chornylo
inkling *n.* слабка підозра slabka pidozra
inland *adv.* углиб країни uhlyb krainy
inland *a.* розташований усередені країни roztashovanyi useredeni krainy
in-laws *n.* свояки svoiaky
inmate *n.* мешканець meshkanets
inmost *a.* лежить глибоко усередині lezhyt hlyboko useredyni
inn *n.* трактир traktyr
innate *a.* вроджений vrodzhenyi
inner *a.* інтелектуальний intelektualnyi
innermost *a.* найглибший naihlybshyi
innings *n.* подача podacha
innocence *n.* невинність nevynnist
innocent *a.* безвинний bezvynnyi
innovate *v.t.* запроваджувати нововведення zaprovadzhuvaty novovvedennia

innovation *n.* нововведення novovvedennia
innovator *n.* новатор novator
innumerable *a.* незлічний nezlichnyi
inoculate *v.t.* робити щеплення robyty shcheplennia
inoculation *n.* щеплення shcheplennia
inoperative *a.* недіючий nediiuchyi
inopportune *a.* недоречний nedorechnyi
input *n.* введення vvedennia
inquest *n.* слідство slidstvo
inquire *v.t.* розпитувати rozpytuvaty
inquiry *n.* запит zapyt
inquisition *n.* вивчення vyvchennia
inquisitive *a.* допитливий dopytlyvyi
insane *a.* душевнохворий dushevnokhvoryi
insanity *n.* божевілля bozhevillia
insatiable *a.* ненаситно nenasytno
inscribe *v.t.* вписувати vpysuvaty
inscription *n.* напис napys
insect *n.* комаха komakha
insecticide *n.* інсектицид insektytsyd
insecure *a.* небезпечний nebezpechnyi
insecurity *n.* небезпечність nebezpechnist
insensibility *n.* нечутливість nechutlyvist
insensible *a.* нечутливий nechutlyvyi
inseparable *a.* нероздільний nerozdilnyi
insert *v.t.* вставляти vstavliaty

insertion *n.* вкладання
vkladannia
inside *a* прихований prykhovanyi
inside *adv.* у середині u seredyni
inside *prep.* усередині useredyni
inside *n.* внутрішня сторона
vnutrishnia storona
insight *n.* інтуїція intuitsiia
insignificance *n.* незначність
neznachnist
insignificant *a.* дрібний dribnyi
insincere *a.* нещирий neshchyryi
insincerity *n.* нещирість
neshchyrist
insinuate *v.t.* непомітно вселяти
nepomitno vseliaty
insinuation *n.* інсинуація
insynuatsiia
insipid *a.* несмачний nesmachnyi
insipidity *n.* відсутність смаку
vidsutnist smaku
insist *v.t.* наполягати napoliahaty
insistence *n.* нестійкість nestiikist
insistent *a.* наполегливий
napolehlyvyi
insolence *n.* нахабство
nakhabstvo
insolent *a.* пихатий pykhatyi
insoluble *n.* нерозчинний
nerozchynnyi
insolvency *n.* банкрутство
bankrutstvo
insolvent *a.* неплатоспроможний
neplatospromozhnyi
inspect *v.t.* уважно оглядати
uvazhno ohliadaty
inspection *n.* інспекція inspektsiia
inspector *n.* інспектор inspektor
inspiration *n.* натхнення
natkhnennia
inspire *v.t.* навіювати naviiuvaty
instability *n.* несталість nestalist

install *v.t.* офіційно празначувати
на посаду ofitsiino
praznachuvaty na posadu
installation *n.* інтсоляція
intsoliatsiia
instalment *n.* випуск vypusk
instance *n.* інстанція instantsiia
instant *a.* миттєвий myttievyi
instant *n.* мить myt
instantaneous *a.* негайний
nehainyi
instantly *adv.* відразу vidrazu
instigate *v.t.* спонукати sponukaty
instigation *n.* підбурювання
pidburiuvannia
instil *v.t.* вливати по краплині
vlyvaty po kraplyni
instinct *n.* інстинкт instynkt
instinctive *a.* інстинктивний
instynktyvnyi
institute *n.* інститут instytut
institution *n.* установа ustanova
instruct *v.t.* вчити vchyty
instruction *n.* інструктаж
instruktazh
instructor *n.* інструктор instruktor
instrument *n.* інструмент
instrument
instrumental *a.*
інструментальний
instrumentalnyi
instrumentalist *n.*
інструменталіст instrumentalist
insubordinate *a.* непокірливий
nepokirlyvyi
insubordination *n.* непокора
nepokora
insufficient *a.* незадовільний
nezadovilnyi
insular *a.* острівний ostrivnyi
insularity *n.* відособленість
vidosoblenist
insulate *v.t.* роз'єднати roziednaty

insulation *n.* відокремлення vidokremlennia
insulator *n.* ізолятор izoliator
insult *v.t.* завдавати образи zavdavaty obrazy
insult *n.* знущання znushchannia
insupportable *a.* нестерпний nesterpnyi
insurance *n.* страховка strakhovka
insure *v.t.* страхувати strakhuvaty
insurgent *n.* повстанець povstanets
insurgent *a.* повсталий povstalyi
insurmountable *a.* непереборний neperebornyi
insurrection *n.* заколот zakolot
intact *a.* незайманий nezaimanyi
intangible *a.* невідчутний nevidchutnyi
integral *a.* всеосяжний vseosiazhnyi
integrity *n.* прямота priamota
intellect *n.* інтелект intelekt
intellectual *a.* розумовий rozumovyi
intellectual *n.* інтелігент intelihent
intelligence *n.* розвідка rozvidka
intelligent *a.* кмітливий kmitlyvyi
intelligentsia *n.* інтелігенція intelihentsiia
intelligible *a.* зрозумілий zrozumilyi
intend *v.t.* мати намір maty namir
intense *a.* вразливий vrazlyvyi
intensify *v.t.* посилюватися posyliuvatysia
intensity *n.* інтенсивність intensyvnist
intensive *a.* інтенсивний intensyvnyi
intent *n.* призначення pryznachennia

intent *a.* схильний skhylnyi
intention *n.* прагнення prahnennia
intentional *a.* навмисний navmysnyi
intercept *v.t.* перехопити perekhopyty
interception *n.* перехоплювання perekhopliuvannia
interchange *v.* обмінюватися obminiuvatysia
interchange *n.* операції operatsii
intercourse *n.* спілкування spilkuvannia
interdependence *n.* взаємозалежність vzaiemozalezhnist
interdependent *a.* взаємозалежний vzaiemozalezhnyi
interest *n.* інтерес interes
interested *a.* упереджений uperedzhenyi
interesting *a.* цікавий tsikavyi
interfere *v.i.* перешкоджати pereshkodzhaty
interference *n.* втручання vtruchannia
interim *n.* інтервал interval
interior *a.* віддалений від моря viddalenyi vid moria
interior *n.* внутрішність vnutrishnist
interjection *n.* втручання vtruchannia
interlock *v.t.* блокування blokuvannia
interlude *n.* антракт antrakt
intermediary *n.* посередник poserednyk
intermediate *a.* проміжний promizhnyi

interminable *a.* нескінченний neskinchennyi

intermingle *v.t.* спілкуватися spilkuvatysia

intern *v.t.* стажист stazhyst

internal *a.* національний natsionalnyi

international *a.* міжнародний mizhnarodnyi

interplay *n.* взаємодія vzaiemodiia

interpret *v.t.* тлумачити tlumachyty

interpreter *n.* перекладач perekladach

interrogate *v.t.* допитувати dopytuvaty

interrogation *n.* питання pytannia

interrogative *n* дізнання diznannia

interrogative *a.* питальний pytalnyi

interrupt *v.t.* переривати pereryvaty

interruption *n.* перерва pererva

intersect *v.t.* перетинатися peretynatysia

intersection *n.* перехрестя perekhrestia

interval *n.* проміжок promizhok

intervene *v.i.* втручатися vtruchatysia

intervention *n.* інтервенція interventsiia

interview *v.t.* проводити співбесіду provodyty spivbesidu

interview *n.* співбесіда spivbesida

intestinal *a.* кишковий kyshkovyi

intestine *n.* кишка kyshka

intimacy *n.* тісний зв'язок tisnyi zviazok

intimate *v.t.* говорити натяками hovoryty natiakamy

intimate *a.* інтимний intymnyi

intimation *n.* повідомлення povidomlennia

intimidate *v.t.* лякати liakaty

intimidation *n.* залякування zaliakuvannia

into *prep.* у u

intolerable *a.* непереносний neperenosnyi

intolerance *n.* нетолерантність netolerantnist

intolerant *a.* нетерпимий neterpymyi

intoxicant *n.* токсична речовина toksychna rechovyna

intoxicate *v.t.* одурманювати odurmaniuvaty

intoxication *n.* сп'яніння spianinnia

intransitive *a. (verb)* неперехідний neperekhidnyi

intrepid *a.* відважний vidvazhnyi

intrepidity *n.* сміливість smilyvist

intricate *a.* заплутаний zaplutanyi

intrigue *n* інтрига intryha

intrigue *v.t.* інтригувати intryhuvaty

intrinsic *a.* інстінктивний instinktyvnyi

introduce *v.t.* знайомити znaiomyty

introduction *n.* знайомство znaiomstvo

introductory *a.* вступний vstupnyi

introspect *v.i.* дивитися всередину dyvytysia vseredynu

introspection *n.* інтроспекція introspektsiia

intrude *v.t.* вторгатися vtorhatysia

intrusion *n.* вторгнення vtorhnennia

intuition *n.* інтуїція intuitsiia

intuitive *a.* інтуїтивний intuityvnyi

invade *v.t.* вражати vrazhaty
invalid *a.* необґрунтований neobhruntovanyi
invalid *n* інвалід invalid
invalid *a.* недійсний nediisnyi
invalidate *v.t.* позбавляти законної сили pozbavliaty zakonnoi syly
invaluable *a.* неоціненний neotsinennyi
invasion *n.* навала navala
invective *n.* лайка laika
invent *v.t.* винаходити vynakhodyty
invention *n.* створення stvorennia
inventive *a.* винахідливий vynakhidlyvyi
inventor *n.* винахідник vynakhidnyk
invert *v.t.* перевертати perevertaty
invest *v.t.* інвестувати investuvaty
investigate *v.t.* розслідувати rozsliduvaty
investigation *n.* розслідування rozsliduvannia
investment *n.* інвестиції investytsii
invigilate *v.t.* наглядати nahliadaty
invigilation *n.* спостереження за тими, хто проходить іспит sposterezhennia za tymy, khto prokhodyt ispyt
invigilator *n.* той, кто слідкує за тим, щоб студенти не списували під час іспитів toi, kto slidkuie za tym, shchob studenty ne spysuvaly pid chas ispytiv
invincible *a.* непереможний neperemozhnyi

inviolable *a.* який користується недоторнканістю yakyi korystuietsia nedotornkanistiu
invisible *a.* невидимий nevydymyi
invitation *n.* запрошення zaproshennia
invite *v.t.* запрошувати zaproshuvaty
invocation *n.* заклинання zaklynannia
invoice *n.* рахунок-фактура rakhunok-faktura
invoke *v.t.* закликати zaklykaty
involve *v.t.* ускладнювати uskladniuvaty
inward *a.* внутрішній vnutrishnii
inwards *adv.* усередину useredynu
irate *a.* гнівний hnivnyi
ire *n.* роздратування rozdratuvannia
Irish *n.* ірландська мова irlandska mova
Irish *a.* ірландський irlandskyi
irksome *a.* дратівний drativnyi
iron *v.t.* залізний zaliznyi
iron *n.* праска praska
ironical *a.* іронічний ironichnyi
irony *n.* іронія ironiia
irradiate *v.i.* роз'яснити roziasnyty
irrational *a.* нераціональний neratsionalnyi
irreconcilable *a.* непримиренний neprymyrennyi
irrecoverable *a.* непоправний nepopravnyi
irrefutable *a.* незаперечний nezaperechnyi
irregular *a.* нерегулярний nerehuliarnyi
irregularity *n.* неправильність nepravylnist

irrelevant *a.* недоречний nedorechnyi
irrespective *a.* незалежний nezalezhnyi
irresponsible *a.* невідповідальний nevidpovidalnyi
irrigate *v.t.* зрошувати zroshuvaty
irrigation *n.* зрошення zroshennia
irritable *a.* дратівливий drativlyvyi
irritant *a.* касувальний kasuvalnyi
irritant *n.* подразник podraznyk
irritate *v.t.* дратувати dratuvaty
irritation *n.* роздратування rozdratuvannia
irruption *n.* набіг nabih
island *n.* острів ostriv
isle *n.* острівець ostrivets
isobar *n.* изобар yzobar
isolate *v.t.* ізолювати izoliuvaty
isolation *n.* ізоляція izoliatsiia
issue *n.* виходити vykhodyty
issue *v.i.* закінчуватися zakinchuvatysia
it *pron.* воно vono
Italian *a.* італійський italiiskyi
Italian *n.* італійська мову italiiska movu
italic *a.* курсивний kursyvnyi
italics *n.* курсив kursyv
itch *n.* свербіж sverbizh
itch *v.i.* свербіти sverbity
item *n.* параграф parahraf
ivory *n.* бивень byven
ivy *n* плющ pliushch

jab *v.t.* пхати pkhaty
jabber *v.t.* плескати язиком pleskaty yazykom
jack *v.t.* залишити zalyshyty
jack *n.* простолюдин prostoliudyn

jackal *n.* шакал shakal
jacket *n.* куртка kurtka
jade *n.* шкапа shkapa
jail *n.* в'язниця viaznytsia
jailer *n.* тюремник tiuremnyk
jam *n.* джем dzhem
jam *v.t.* затискати zatyskaty
jar *n.* неприємний звук nepryiemnyi zvuk
jargon *n.* жаргон zharhon
jasmine, jessamine *n.* жасмин zhasmyn
jaundice *v.t.* викликати ревнощі vyklykaty revnoshchi
jaundice *n.* жовтяниця zhovtianytsia
javelin *n.* метальний спис metalnyi spys
jaw *n.* щелепа shchelepa
jay *n.* базіка bazika
jealous *a.* ревнивий revnyvyi
jealousy *n.* ревнощі revnoshchi
jean *n.* джинсова тканина dzhynsova tkanyna
jeer *v.i.* глумитися hlumytysia
jelly *n.* желе zhele
jeopardize *v.t.* ризикувати ryzykuvaty
jeopardy *n.* небезпека nebezpeka
jerk *n.* різкий рух rizkyi rukh
jerkin *n.* жакет zhaket
jerky *a.* труський truskyi
jersey *n.* фуфайка fufaika
jest *n.* дотеп dotep
jest *v.i.* кепкувати kepkuvaty
jet *n.* реактивний двигун reaktyvnyi dvyhun
Jew *n.* єврей yevrei
jewel *v.t.* вставляти камені vstavliaty kameni
jewel *n.* дорогоцінний камінь dorohotsinnyi kamin
jeweller *n.* ювелір yuvelir

jewellery *n.* коштовності koshtovnosti
jingle *v.i.* дзвеніти dzvenity
jingle *n.* передзвін peredzvin
job *n.* робота robota
jobber *n.* маклер makler
jobbery *n.* спекуляція spekuliatsiia
jocular *a.* жартівливий zhartivlyvyi
jog *v.t.* штовхати shtovkhaty
join *v.t.* приєднуватися pryiednuvatysia
joiner *n.* столяр stoliar
joint *n.* шов shov
jointly *adv.* спільно spilno
joke *n.* жарт zhart
joke *v.i.* жартувати zhartuvaty
joker *n.* насмішник nasmishnyk
jollity *n.* гулянка hulianka
jolly *a.* жвавий zhvavyi
jolt *n.* трясіння triasinnia
jolt *v.t.* трясти triasty
jostle *n.* давка davka
jostle *v.t.* натрапити natrapyty
jot *n.* йота yota
jot *v.t.* стисло записати styslo zapysaty
journal *n.* журнал zhurnal
journalism *n.* журналістика zhurnalistyka
journalist *n.* журналіст zhurnalist
journey *v.i.* подорожувати podorozhuvaty
journey *n.* поїздка poizdka
jovial *a.* товариський tovaryskyi
joviality *n.* товариськість tovaryskist
joy *n.* успіх uspikh
joyful, joyous *a.* щасливий shchaslyvyi
jubilant *a.* задоволений zadovolenyi

jubilation *n.* торжество torzhestvo
jubilee *n.* свято sviato
judge *n.* суддя suddia
judge *v.i.* судити sudyty
judgement *n.* розум rozum
judicature *n.* судочинство sudochynstvo
judicial *a.* судовий sudovyi
judiciary *n.* судоустрій sudoustrii
judicious *a.* розсудливий rozsudlyvyi
jug *n.* глечик hlechyk
juggle *v.t.* обманювати obmaniuvaty
juggler *n.* фокусник fokusnyk
juice *n* сік sik
juicy *a.* соковитий sokovytyi
jumble *n.* тряска triaska
jumble *v.t.* трястися triastysia
jump *v.i* стрибати strybaty
jump *n.* стрибок strybok
junction *n.* злиття zlyttia
juncture *n.* стан справ stan sprav
jungle *n.* джунглі dzhunhli
junior *a.* молодий molodyi
junior *n.* молодший за званням molodshyi za zvanniam
junk *n.* утиль utyl
jupiter *n.* Юпітер Yupiter
jurisdiction *n.* юрисдикція yurysdyktsiia
jurisprudence *n.* юриспруденція yurysprudentsiia
jurist *n.* юрист yuryst
juror *n.* член журі chlen zhuri
jury *n.* журі zhuri
juryman *n.* присяжний prysiazhnyi
just *a.* справедливий spravedlyvyi
just *adv.* тільки tilky
justice *n.* справедливість spravedlyvist

justifiable *a.* законний zakonnyi
justification *n.* обставини, що виправдовують obstavyny, shcho vypravdovuiut
justify *v.t.* виправдовувати vypravdovuvaty
justly *adv.* недарма nedarma
jute *n.* джут dzhut
juvenile *a.* юнацький yunatskyi

keen *a.* тонко сприймаючий tonko spryimaiuchyi
keenness *n.* гострота hostrota
keep *v.t.* тримати trymaty
keeper *n.* сторож storozh
keepsake *n.* подарунок на пам'ять podarunok na pamiat
kennel *n.* будка budka
kerchief *n.* хустка khustka
kernel *n.* зернятко zerniatko
kerosene *n.* гас has
ketchup *n.* кетчуп ketchup
kettle *n.* чайник chainyk
key *v.t* замикати zamykaty
key *n.* ключ kliuch
kick *v.t.* вдарити ногою vdaryty nohoiu
kick *n.* удар ногою udar nohoiu
kid *n.* дитя dytia
kidnap *v.t.* викрасти vykrasty
kidney *n.* характер kharakter
kill *v.t.* вбивати vbyvaty
kill *n.* здобич zdobych
kiln *n.* промислова піч для сушіння promyslova pich dlia sushinnia
kin *n.* рідня ridnia
kind *n.* різновид riznovyd
kind *a* сорт sort
kindergarten ; *n.* дитячий сад dytiachyi sad

kindle *v.t.* загорітися zahoritysia
kindly *adv.* доброзичливо dobrozychlyvo
king *n.* король korol
kingdom *n.* королівство korolivstvo
kinship *n.* спорідненість sporidnenist
kiss *n.* поцілунок potsilunok
kiss *v.t.* цілувати tsiluvaty
kit *n.* екіпірування ekipiruvannia
kitchen *n.* кухня kukhnia
kite *n.* паперовий змій paperovyi zmii
kith *n.* друзі druzi
kitten *n.* кошеня koshenia
knave *n.* шахрай shakhrai
knavery *n.* шахрайство shakhraistvo
knee *n.* коліно kolino
kneel *v.i.* стояти на колінах stoiaty na kolinakh
knife *n.* ніж nizh
knight *n.* лицар lytsar
knight *v.t.* посвячувати в лицарі posviachuvaty v lytsari
knit *v.t.* в'язати viazaty
knock *v.t.* стукати stukaty
knot *n.* бант bant
knot *v.t.* зав'язати вузлом zaviazaty vuzlom
know *v.t.* знати znaty
knowledge *n.* пізнання piznannia

label *v.t.* позначати poznachaty
label *n.* ярлик yarlyk
labial *a.* губний hubnyi
laboratory *n.* лабораторія laboratoriia
laborious *a.* стомлюючий stomliuiuchyi

labour *v.i.* працювати pratsiuvaty
labour *n.* праця pratsia
laboured *a.* вимучений vymuchenyi
labourer *n.* чорнороб chornorob
labyrinth *n.* лабіринт labirynt
lac, lakh *n* сто тисяч sto tysiach
lace *v.t.* шнурувати shnuruvaty
lace *n.* мереживо merezhyvo
lacerate *v.t.* рвати rvaty
lachrymose *a.* плаксивий plaksyvyi
lack *v.t.* відчувати брак vidchuvaty brak
lack *n.* нестача nestacha
lackey *n.* лакей lakei
lacklustre *a.* тьмяний tmianyi
laconic *a.* лаконічний lakonichnyi
lactate *v.i.* виділяти молоко vydiliaty moloko
lactometer *n.* лактометр laktometr
lactose *n.* лактоза laktoza
lacuna *n.* прогалина prohalyna
lacy *a.* мереживний merezhyvnyi
lad *n.* хлопець khlopets
ladder *n.* сходи skhody
lade *v.t.* вантажити vantazhyty
ladle *n.* ківш kivsh
ladle *v.t.* черпати cherpaty
lady *n.* леді ledi
lag *v.i.* запізнюватися zapizniuvatysia
laggard *n.* телепень telepen
lagoon *n.* лагуна lahuna
lair *n.* барліг barlih
lake *n.* озеро ozero
lama *n.* лама lama
lamb *n.* ягня yahnia
lambaste *v.t.* шмагати shmahaty
lambkin *n.* ягнятко yahniatko
lame *v.t.* калічити kalichyty
lame *a.* кульгавий kulhavyi

lament *n* скарги skarhy
lament *v.i.* стогнати stohnaty
lamentable *a.* сумний sumnyi
lamentation *n.* нарікання narikannia
laminate *v.t.* розщеплювати на тонкі шари rozshchepliuvaty na tonki shary
lamp *n.* світило svitylo
lampoon *n.* зла сатира zla satyra
lampoon *v.t.* писати памфлети pysaty pamflety
lance *v.t.* пронизувати списом pronyzuvaty spysom
lance *n.* спис spys
lancer *n.* улан ulan
lancet *a.* ланцет lantset
land *v.i.* висаджувати vysadzhuvaty
land *n.* суша susha
landing *n.* висадка vysadka
landscape *n.* ландшафт landshaft
lane *n.* стежка stezhka
language *n.* стиль styl
languish *v.i.* слабшати slabshaty
lank *a.* худий khudyi
lantern *n.* ліхтар likhtar
lap *n.* пола pola
lapse *v.i.* впадати vpadaty
lapse *n* плин plyn
lard *n.* свиняче сало svyniache salo
large *a.* крупний krupnyi
largesse *n.* щедрий дар shchedryi dar
lark *n.* проказа prokaza
lascivious *a.* хтивий khtyvyi
lash *n* канчук kanchuk
lash *v.t.* хльостати khlostaty
lass *n.* дівчинка divchynka
last *adv.* після всіх pislia vsikh
last *n* кінець kinets

last *v.i.* продовжуватися prodovzhuvatysia
last1 *a.* крайній krainii
lasting *a.* тривалість tryvalist
lastly *adv.* на закінчення na zakinchennia
latch *n.* клямка kliamka
late *a.* пізній piznii
late *adv.* пізно pizno
lately *adv.* останнім часом ostannim chasom
latent *a.* латентний latentnyi
lath *n.* рейка reika
lathe *n.* верстат verstat
lathe *n.* токарний верстат tokarnyi verstat
lather *n.* мильна піна mylna pina
latitude *n.* широта shyrota
latrine *n.* відхоже місце vidkhozhe mistse
latter *a.* недавній nedavnii
lattice *n.* решітка reshitka
laud *v.t.* прославляти proslavliaty
laud *n* хвала khvala
laudable *a.* доброякісний dobroiakisnyi
laugh *n.* сміх smikh
laugh *v.i* сміятися smiiatysia
laughable *a.* смішний smishnyi
laughter *n.* регіт rehit
launch *n.* спуск spusk
launch *v.t.* спускати spuskaty
launder *v.t.* прати і прасувати praty i prasuvaty
laundress *n.* прачка prachka
laundry *n.* пральня pralnia
laureate *a.* видатний vydatnyi
laureate *n* лауреат laureat
laurel *n.* лавр lavr
lava *n.* лава lava
lavatory *n.* туалет tualet
lavender *n.* лаванда lavanda
lavish *a.* щедрий shchedryi

lavish *v.t.* щедро раздавати shchedro razdavaty
law *n.* закон zakon
lawful *a.* законний zakonnyi
lawless *a.* беззаконний bezzakonnyi
lawn *n.* галявина haliavyna
lawyer *n.* юрист yuryst
lax *a.* слабкий slabkyi
laxative *n.* проносний засіб pronosnyi zasib
laxative *a* проносний pronosnyi
laxity *n.* слабкість slabkist
lay *n* коротенька пісенька korotenka pisenka
lay *v.t.* класти klasty
lay *a.* непрофесійний neprofesiinyi
layer *n.* шар shar
layman *n.* мирянин myrianyn
laze *v.i.* ледарювати ledariuvaty
laziness *n.* лінь lin
lazy *n.* лінивий linyvyi
lea *n.* пасовищі pasovyshchi
leach *v.t.* ропа ropa
lead *n.* грузило hruzylo
lead *n.* провідна позиція providna pozytsiia
lead *v.t.* управляти upravliaty
leaden *a.* свинцевий svyntsevyi
leader *n.* керівник kerivnyk
leadership *n.* керівна посада kerivna posada
leaf *n.* листок lystok
leaflet *n.* листочок lystochok
leafy *a.* покритий листям pokrytyi lystiam
league *n.* ліга liha
leak *n.* витік vytik
leak *v.i.* текти tekty
leakage *n.* просочування prosochuvannia
lean *v.i.* притуляти prytuliaty

lean *n.* худий khudyi
leap *v.i.* стрибати strybaty
leap *n* стрибок strybok
learn *v.i.* вчитися vchytysia
learned *a.* вчений vchenyi
learner *n.* учень uchen
learning *n.* навчання navchannia
lease *v.t.* здавати в оренду zdavaty v orendu
lease *n.* оренда orenda
least *a.* малий malyi
least *adv.* менш за все mensh za vse
leather *n.* шкіра shkira
leave *n.* дозвіл dozvil
leave *v.t.* припиняти prypyniaty
lecture *n.* лекція lektsiia
lecture *v* читати лекцію chytaty lektsiiu
lecturer *n.* лектор lektor
ledger *n.* надгробна плита nadhrobna plyta
lee *n.* укриття ukryttia
leech *n.* п'явка piavka
leek *n.* цибуля-порей tsybulia-porei
left *a.* лівий livyi
left *adv.* ліво livo
leftist *n* лівак livak
leg *n.* нога noha
legacy *n.* спадщина spadshchyna
legal *a.* дозволений dozvolenyi
legality *n.* легальність lehalnist
legalize *v.t.* узаконити uzakonyty
legend *n.* легенда lehenda
legendary *a.* легендарний lehendarnyi
leghorn *n.* італійська соломка italiiska solomka
legible *a.* розбірливий rozbirlyvyi
legibly *adv.* розбірливо rozbirlyvo
legion *n.* легіон lehion
legionary *n.* легіонер lehioner

legislate *v.i.* видавати закони vydavaty zakony
legislation *n.* законодавство zakonodavstvo
legislative *a.* законодавчий zakonodavchyi
legislator *n.* законодавець zakonodavets
legislature *n.* законодавча влада zakonodavcha vlada
legitimacy *n.* законність zakonnist
legitimate *a.* закононароджений zakononarodzhenyi
leisure *n.* вільний час vilnyi chas
leisure *n.* дозвілля dozvillia
leisurely *a.* неквапливий nekvaplyvyi
leisurely *adv.* неквапливо nekvaplyvo
lemon *n.* лимон lymon
lemonade *n.* лимонад lymonad
lend *v.t.* позичати pozychaty
length *n.* довжина dovzhyna
lengthen *v.t.* подовжувати podovzhuvaty
lengthy *a.* тривалий tryvalyi
lenience, leniency *n.* м'якість miakist
lenient *a.* терпимий terpymyi
lens *n.* лінза linza
lentil *n.* сочевиця sochevytsia
Leo *n.* Лев Lev
leonine *a* левиний levynyi
leopard *n.* леопард leopard
leper *n.* парія pariia
leprosy *n.* проказа prokaza
leprous *a.* прокажений prokazhenyi
less *prep.* без bez
less *adv.* за вирахуванням za vyrakhuvanniam
less *a.* маленький malenkyi

less *adv.* менше menshe
lessee *n.* наймач naimach
lessen *v.t* зменшуватися
zmenshuvatysia
lesser *a.* менший menshyi
lesson *n.* урок urok
lest *conj.* щоб... не shchob... ne
let *v.t.* здавати внайм zdavaty
vnaim
lethal *a.* летальний letalnyi
lethargic *a.* летаргічний
letarhichnyi
lethargy *n.* млявість mliavist
letter *n* лист lyst
level *n.* рівень riven
level *a* плоский ploskyi
level *v.t.* робити рівним robyty
rivnym
lever *n.* важіль vazhil
lever *v.t.* піднімати за допомогою
важіля pidnimaty za
dopomohoiu vazhilia
leverage *n.* дія важеля diia
vazhelia
levity *n.* недоречна веселість
nedorechna veselist
levy *v.t.* обкладати obkladaty
levy *n.* збирання zbyrannia
lewd *a.* безсоромний
bezsoromnyi
lexicography *n.* лексикографія
leksykohrafiia
lexicon *n.* лексикон leksykon
liability *n.* відповідальність
vidpovidalnist
liable *a.* зобов'язаний
zoboviazanyi
liaison *n.* взаємодія vzaiemodiia
liar *n.* брехун brekhun
libel *n.* пасквіль paskvil
libel *v.t.* писати пасквілі pysaty
paskvili
liberal *a.* ліберальний liberalnyi

liberalism *n.* лібералізм
liberalizm
liberality *n.* щедрість shchedrist
liberate *v.t.* виізволяти viyzvoliaty
liberation *n.* визволення
vyzvolennia
liberator *n.* визволитель
vyzvolytel
libertine *n.* вільнодумець
vilnodumets
liberty *n.* свобода svoboda
librarian *n.* бібліотекар bibliotekar
library *n.* бібліотека biblioteka
licence *n.* ліцензія litsenziia
license *v.t.* ліцензувати
litsenzuvaty
licensee *n.* ліцензіат litsenziat
licentious *a.* розпущений
rozpushchenyi
lick *v.t.* лизати lyzaty
lick *n* облизування oblyzuvannia
lid *n.* кришка kryshka
lie *n* брехня brekhnia
lie *v.i* брехати brekhaty
lie *v.i.* лежати lezhaty
lien *n.* заставне право zastavne
pravo
lieu *n.* місце mistse
lieutenant *n.* лейтенант leitenant
life *n* життя zhyttia
lifeless *a.* нудний nudnyi
lifelong *a.* довічний dovichnyi
lift *n.* ліфт lift
lift *v.t.* скасовувати skasovuvaty
light *v.t.* засвічувати zasvichuvaty
light *a* світлий svitlyi
light *n.* світло svitlo
lighten *v.i.* полегшувати
polehshuvaty
lightening *n.* освітлення
osvitlennia
lighter *n.* легше lehshe
lightly *adv.* злегка zlehka

lignite *n.* буре вугілля bure vuhillia
like *adv.* начебто nachebto
like *v.t.* любити liubyty
like *a.* схожий skhozhyi
like *n.* щось подібне shchos podibne
likelihood *n.* ймовірність ymovirnist
likely *a.* багатонадійний bahatonadiinyi
liken *v.t.* уподібнювати upodibniuvaty
likeness *n.* подібність podibnist
likewise *adv.* також takozh
liking *n.* смак smak
lilac *n.* бузок buzok
lily *n.* лілія liliia
limb *n.* кінцівка kintsivka
limber *v.t.* робити гнучким robyty hnuchkym
limber *n* сучкоруб suchkorub
lime *n.* лайм laim
lime *v.t* білити вапном bilyty vapnom
lime *n.* вапно vapno
limelight *n.* центр уваги tsentr uvahy
limit *v.t.* встановлювати межі vstanovliuvaty mezhi
limit *n.* границя hranytsia
limitation *n.* строк давності strok davnosti
limited *a.* з обмеженою відповідальністю z obmezhenoiu vidpovidalnistiu
limitless *a.* безмежний bezmezhnyi
line *v.t.* лініювати liniiuvaty
line *n.* лінія liniia
line *v.t.* проводити лінію provodyty liniiu
lineage *n.* родовід rodovid

linen *n.* полотно polotno
linger *v.i.* затримуватися zatrymuvatysia
lingo *n.* іноземна мова inozemna mova
lingua franca *n.* лінгва франка linhva franka
lingual *a.* мовний movnyi
linguist *n.* лінгвіст linhvist
linguistic *a.* лінгвістичний linhvistychnyi
linguistics *n.* мовознавство movoznavstvo
lining *n* підкладка pidkladka
link *n.* посилання posylannia
link *v.t* посилатися posylatysia
linseed *n.* лляне насіння lliane nasinnia
lintel *n.* перемички peremychky
lion *n* лев lev
lioness *n.* левиця levytsia
lip *n.* губа huba
liquefy *v.t.* перетворювати на рідину peretvoriuvaty na ridynu
liquid *n* рідка їжа ridka yizha
liquid *a.* рідкий ridkyi
liquidate *v.t.* ліквідувати likviduvaty
liquidation *n.* ліквідація likvidatsiia
liquor *n.* алкогольний напій alkoholnyi napii
lisp *v.t.* шепелявити shepeliavyty
lisp *n* шепелявість shepeliavist
list *v.t.* вносити до списку vnosyty do spysku
list *n.* список spysok
listen *v.i.* слухати slukhaty
listener *n.* слухач slukhach
listless *a.* апатичний apatychnyi
lists *n.* арена arena
literacy *n.* грамотність hramotnist
literal *a.* буквальний bukvalnyi

literary *a.* літературний literaturnyi

literate *a.* освічений osvichenyi

literature *n.* література literatura

litigant *n.* сторона у справі storona u spravi

litigate *v.t.* судитися sudytysia

litigation *n.* судовий процес sudovyi protses

litre *n.* літр litr

litter *v.t.* виносити на ношах vynosyty na noshakh

litter *n.* ноші noshi

litterateur *n.* літератор literator

little *n.* невелика кількість nevelyka kilkist

little *adv.* мало malo

little *a.* слабкий slabkyi

littoral *a.* прибережний pryberezhnyi

liturgical *a.* літургійний liturhiinyi

live *a.* діяльний diialnyi

live *v.i.* жити zhyty

livelihood *n.* зарплатня zarplatnia

lively *a.* швидкий shvydkyi

liver *n.* печінка pechinka

livery *n.* ліврея livreia

living *a.* невгаслий nevhaslyi

living *n* спосіб життя sposib zhyttia

lizard *n.* ящірка yashchirka

load *n.* навантаження navantazhennia

load *v.t.* навантажувати navantazhuvaty

loadstar *n.* Полярна зірка Poliarna zirka

loadstone *n.* магнетит mahnetyt

loaf *n.* буханець bukhanets

loaf *v.i.* ледарювати ledariuvaty

loafer *n.* ледар ledar

loan *v.t.* давати в борг davaty v borh

loan *n.* позика pozyka

loath *a.* неохочий neokhochyi

loathe *v.t.* ненавидіти nenavydyty

loathsome *a.* що викликає відразу shcho vyklykaie vidrazu

lobby *n.* фойє foiie

lobe *n.* мочка вуха mochka vukha

lobster *n.* омар omar

local *a.* місцевий mistsevyi

locale *n.* місце дії mistse dii

locality *n.* місцевість mistsevist

localize *v.t.* локалізувати lokalizuvaty

locate *v.t.* розмістити rozmistyty

location *n.* місце розташування mistse roztashuvannia

lock *v.t* замикати на замок zamykaty na zamok

lock *n.* замок zamok

lock *n* засув zasuv

locker *n.* шафа shafa

locket *n.* медальйон medalion

locomotive *n.* локомотив lokomotyv

locus *n.* місцеположення mistsepolozhennia

locust *n.* сарана sarana

locution *n.* ідіома idioma

lodge *n.* будиночок budynochok

lodge *v.t.* тимчасово жити tymchasovo zhyty

lodging *n.* тимчасове житло tymchasove zhytlo

loft *n.* горище horyshche

lofty *a.* ставний stavnyi

log *n.* колода koloda

logarithim *n.* логарифм loharyfm

loggerhead *n.* болван bolvan

logic *n.* логіка lohika

logical *a.* логічний lohichnyi

logician *n.* логік lohik

loin *n.* поперек poperek

loiter *v.i.* тинятися без діла
tyniatysia bez dila
loll *v.i.* ніжитися nizhytysia
lollipop *n.* льодяник на паличці
lodianyk na palychtsi
lone *a.* відокремлений
vidokremlenyi
loneliness *n.* самотність
samotnist
lonely *a.* який навіває тугу yakyi
navivaie tuhu
lonesome *a.* занедбаний
zanedbanyi
long *adv* довго dovho
long *v.i* сумувати sumuvaty
long *a.* довгий dovhyi
longevity *n.* довговічність
dovhovichnist
longing *n.* сильне бажання sylne
bazhannia
longitude *n.* довгота dovhota
look *v.i* глянути hlianuty
look *n.* зовнішність zovnishnist
loom *v.i.* маячити maiachyty
loom *n* ткацький верстат tkatskyi
verstat
loop *n.* петля petlia
loop-hole *n.* бійниця biinytsia
loose *a.* вільний vilnyi
loose *v.t.* розв'язувати
rozviazuvaty
loosen *v.t.* розв`язувати
rozv`iazuvaty
loot *v.i.* забирати награбоване
добро zabyraty nahrabovane
dobro
loot *n.* трофей trofei
lop *v.t.* обкраяти obkraiaty
lop *n.* суки suky
lord *n.* пан pan
lordly *a.* панський panskyi
lordship *n.* світлість svitlist

lore *n.* практичні знання
praktychni znannia
lorry *n.* вантажівка vantazhivka
lose *v.t.* втрачати vtrachaty
loss *n.* втрата vtrata
lot *n.* багато bahato
lot *n.* жереб zhereb
lotion *n.* лосьйон losion
lottery *n.* лотерея lotereia
lotus *n.* лотос lotos
loud *a.* гучний huchnyi
lounge *v.i.* розсістися rozsistysia
lounge *n.* хол khol
louse *n.* воша vosha
lovable *a.* привабливий
pryvablyvyi
love *v.t.* любити liubyty
love *n* любов liubov
lovely *a.* прекрасний prekrasnyi
lover *n.* коханець kokhanets
loving *a.* люблячий liubliachyi
low *n.* низина nyzyna
low *v.i.* волати volaty
low *n.* мукання mukannia
low *a.* ниций nytsyi
lower *v.t.* нижче nyzhche
lowliness *n.* смиренність
smyrennist
lowly *a.* невибагливий
nevybahlyvyi
loyal *a.* лояльний loialnyi
loyalist *n.* вірнопідданий
virnopiddanyi
loyalty *n.* лояльність loialnist
lubricant *n.* примиритель
prymyrytel
lubricate *v.t.* мастити mastyty
lubrication *n.* змащування
zmashchuvannia
lucent *a.* яскравий yaskravyi
lucerne *n.* люцерна liutserna
lucid *a.* ясний yasnyi
lucidity *n.* ясність yasnist

luck *n.* удача udacha
luckily *adv.* на щастя na shchastia
luckless *a.* невдачливий nevdachlyvyi
lucky *a.* щасливий shchaslyvyi
lucrative *a.* прибутковий prybutkovyi
lucre *n.* корисливість koryslyvist
luggage *n.* багаж bahazh
lukewarm *a.* теплий teplyi
lull *n.* затишшя zatyshshia
lull *v.t.* колихати kolykhaty
lullaby *n.* колискова kolyskova
luminary *n.* знаменитість znamenytist
luminous *a.* світиться svitytsia
lump *v.t.* важко ступати vazhko stupaty
lump *n.* шматок shmatok
lunacy *n.* сомнабулізм somnabulizm
lunar *a.* місячний misiachnyi
lunatic *n.* безумець bezumets
lunatic *a.* схиблений skhyblenyi
lunch *n.* обід obid
lunch *v.i.* обідати obidaty
lung *n* легке lehke
lunge *n.* випад vypad
lunge *v.i* робити випад robyty vypad
lurch *n.* крен kren
lurch *v.i.* кренитися krenytysia
lure *n.* приманка prymanka
lure *v.t.* приманювати prymaniuvaty
lurk *v.i.* таїтися taitysia
luscious *a.* солодкий solodkyi
lush *a.* соковитий sokovytyi
lust *n.* жага zhaha
lustful *a.* хтивий khtyvyi
lustre *n.* слава slava

lustrous *a.* глянсуватий hliansuvatyi
lusty *a.* здоровий zdorovyi
lute *n.* лютня liutnia
luxuriance *n.* буйний ріст buinyi rist
luxuriant *a.* пишний pyshnyi
luxurious *a.* який любит розкіш yakyi liubyt rozkish
luxury *n.* насолода nasoloda
lynch *v.t.* лінчувати linchuvaty
lyre *n.* ліра lira
lyric *n.* ліричний вірш lirychnyi virsh
lyric *a.* ліричний lirychnyi
lyrical *a.* захоплений zakhoplenyi´
lyricist *n.* лірик liryk

maddle *v.i.* звихнутися zvykhnutysia
magical *a.* магічний mahichnyi
magician *n.* маг mah
magisterial *a.* суддівський suddivskyi
magistracy *n.* магістратура mahistratura
magistrate *n.* суддя suddia
magnanimity *n.* великодушність velykodushnist
magnanimous *a.* великодушний velykodushnyi
magnate *n.* магнат mahnat
magnet *n.* магніт mahnit
magnetic *a.* магнітний mahnitnyi
magnetism *n.* магнетизм mahnetyzm
magnificent *a.* пишний pyshnyi
magnify *v.t.* збільшувати zbilshuvaty
magnitude *n.* величина velychyna

magpie *n.* сорока soroka
mahogany *n.* червоне дерево
chervone derevo
mahout *n.* погонич слонів
pohonych sloniv
maid *n.* покоївка pokoivka
maiden *n.* діва diva
maiden *a* незаміжня nezamizhnia
mail *v.t.* відправляти поштою
vidpravliaty poshtoiu
mail *n* кореспонденція
korespondentsiia
mail *n.* пошта poshta
main *n* відкрите море vidkryte
more
main *a* основний osnovnyi
mainly *adv.* головним чином
holovnym chynom
mainstay *n.* головна підтримка
holovna pidtrymka
maintain *v.t.* підтримувати
pidtrymuvaty
maintenance *n.* технічне
обслуговування tekhnichne
obsluhovuvannia
maize *n.* кукурудза kukurudza
majestic *a.* величний velychnyi
majesty *n.* величність velychnist
major *n* майор maior
major *a.* повнолітній povnolitnii
majority *n.* повноліття povnolittia
make *n* модель model
make *v.t.* робити robyty
maker *n.* виробник vyrobnyk
maladjustment *n.*
невідповідність nevidpovidnist
maladministration *n.*
неправильні адміністративні
дії nepravylni administratyvni dii
maladroit *a.* невдалий nevdalyi
malady *n.* хвороба khvoroba
malafide *a.* несумлінний
nesumlinnyi

malafide *adv* нечесно nechesno
malaise *n.* нездужання
nezduzhannia
malaria *n.* малярія maliariia
malcontent *a.* незадоволений
nezadovolenyi
malcontent *n* опозиціонер
opozytsioner
male *n* чоловік cholovik
male *a.* чоловічий cholovichyi
malediction *n.* лайка laika
malefactor *n.* зловмисник
zlovmysnyk
maleficent *a.* згубний zhubnyi
malice *n.* злий умисел zlyi umysel
malicious *a.* зловмисний
zlovmysnyi
malign *v.t.* злословити zloslovyty
malign *a* злоякісний zloiakisnyi
malignancy *n.* злоякісність
zloiakisnist
malignant *a.* злісний zlisnyi
malleable *a.* ковкий kovkyi
malmsey *n.* мальвазія malvaziia
malnutrition *n.* недоїдання
nedoidannia
malpractice *n.* зловживання
довірою zlovzhyvannia doviroiu
malt *n.* солод solod
mal-treatment *n.* ппогане
поводження ppohane
povodzhennia
mamma *n.* грудна залоза hrudna
zaloza
mammal *n.* ссавець ssavets
mammary *a.* грудний hrudnyi
mammon *n.* багатство bahatstvo
mammoth *n.* мамонт mamont
mammoth *a* схожий на мамонта
skhozhyi na mamonta
man *v.t.* ставити людей (до
гармати) stavyty liudei (do
harmaty)

man *n.* людина liudyna
manage *v.t.* управляти upravliaty
manageable *a.* керований kerovanyi
management *n.* управління upravlinnia
manager *n.* менеджер menedzher
managerial *a.* управлінський upravlinskyi
mandate *n.* мандат mandat
mandatory *a.* примусовий prymusovyi
mane *n.* грива hryva
manes *n.* патли patly
manful *a.* рішучий rishuchyi
manganese *n.* марганець marhanets
manger *n.* ясла yasla
mangle *v.t.* шматувати shmatuvaty
mango *n* манго manho
manhandle *v.t.* тягти tiahty
manhole *n.* люк liuk
manhood *n.* змужнілість zmuzhnilist
mania *n* маніакальний синдром maniakalnyi syndrom
maniac *n.* маніяк maniiak
manicure *n.* манікюр manikiur
manifest *v.t.* робити очевидним robyty ochevydnym
manifest *a.* явний yavnyi
manifestation *n.* виявлення vyiavlennia
manifesto *n.* маніфест manifest
manifold *a.* колектор kolektor
manipulate *v.t.* маніпулювати manipuliuvaty
manipulation *n.* маніпуляція manipuliatsiia
mankind *n.* людський рід liudskyi rid

manlike *a.* чоловічий cholovichyi
manliness *n* мужність muzhnist
manly *a.* мужній muzhnii
manna *n.* манна manna
mannequin *n.* манекен maneken
manner *n.* манера manera
mannerism *n.* манірність manirnist
mannerly *a.* з гарними манерами z harnymy maneramy
manoeuvre *n.* маневр manevr
manoeuvre *v.i.* маневрувати manevruvaty
manor *n.* маєток maietok
manorial *a.* маноріальний manorialnyi
mansion *n.* особняк osobniak
mantel *n.* камінна дошка kaminna doshka
mantle *n* мантія mantiia
mantle *v.t* огорнути ohornuty
manual *n* посібник posibnyk
manual *a.* ручний ruchnyi
manufacture *n* обробка obrobka
manufacture *v.t.* штампувати shtampuvaty
manufacturer *n* виробник vyrobnyk
manumission *n.* відпускна грамота vidpuskna hramota
manumit *v.t.* звільняти zvilniaty
manure *n.* органічне добриво orhanichne dobryvo
manure *v.t.* удобрювати udobriuvaty
manuscript *n.* рукопис rukopys
many *a.* багато хто bahato khto
map *v.t.* наносити на карту nanosyty na kartu
map *n* карта karta
mar *v.t.* спотворювати spotvoriuvaty
marathon *n.* марафон marafon

maraud *v.i.* мародерствувати
maroderstvuvaty
marauder *n.* мародер maroder
marble *n.* мармур marmur
march *n.* березень berezen
march *n* марш marsh
march *v.i* марширувати
marshyruvaty
mare *n.* кобила kobyla
margarine *n.* маргарин marharyn
margin *n.* маржа marzha
marginal *a.* граничний hranychnyi
marigold *n.* чорнобривці
chornobryvtsi
marine *a.* морський morskyi
mariner *n.* моряк moriak
marionette *n.* маріонетка
marionetka
marital *a.* сімейний simeinyi
maritime *a.* приморський
prymorskyi
mark *v.t* позначати poznachaty
mark *n.* позначка poznachka
marker *n.* маркер marker
market *n* ринок rynok
market *v.t* ринок rynok
marketable *a.* товарний tovarnyi
marksman *n.* вправний стрілець
vpravnyi strilets
marl *n.* мергель merhel
marmalade *n.* мармелад
marmelad
maroon *v.t* залишатися в
безвихідному становищі
zalyshatysia v bezvykhidnomu
stanovyshchi
maroon *a* темно-бордовий
temno-bordovyi
maroon *n.* темно-бордовий колір
temno-bordovyi kolir
marriage *n.* шлюб shliub
marriageable *a.* шлюбний
shliubnyi

marry *v.t.* одружуватися
odruzhuvatysia
Mars *n* Марс Mars
marsh *n.* болото boloto
marshal *n* маршал marshal
marshal *v.t* вибудовувати
vybudovuvaty
marshy *a.* болотистий bolotystyi
marsupial *n.* сумчастий
sumchastyi
mart *n.* аукціонний зал
auktsionnyi zal
marten *n.* куниця kunytsia
martial *a.* військовий viiskovyi
martinet *n.* прихильник суворої
дисципліни prykhylnyk suvoroi
dystsypliny
martyr *n.* мученик muchenyk
martyrdom *n.* мучеництво
muchenytstvo
marvel *v.i* дивуватися dyvuvatysia
marvel *n.* чудо chudo
marvellous *a.* незбагнений
nezbahnenyi
mascot *n.* талісман talisman
masculine *a.* чоловічий
cholovichyi
mash *v.t* роздавлювати
rozdavliuvaty
mash *n.* пюре piure
mask *n.* маска maska
mask *v.t.* маскувати maskuvaty
mason *n.* муляр muliar
masonry *n.* кам'яна укладка
kamiana ukladka
masquerade *n.* маскарад
maskarad
mass *v.i* збиратися натовпом
zbyratysia natovpom
mass *n.* маса masa
massacre *n.* масове вбивство
masove vbyvstvo

massacre *v.t.* влаштувати різанину vlashtuvaty rizanynu
massage *n.* масаж masazh
massage *v.t.* масажувати masazhuvaty
masseur *n.* масажист masazhyst
massive *a.* масивний masyvnyi
massy *a.* солідний solidnyi
mast *n.* щогла shchohla
master *v.t.* володіти volodity
master *n.* хазяїн khaziain
masterly *a.* віртуозний virtuoznyi
masterpiece *n.* шедевр shedevr
mastery *n.* майстерність maisternist
masticate *v.t.* пережовувати perezhovuvaty
masturbate *v.i.* мастурбувати masturbuvaty
mat *n.* циновка tsynovka
matador *n.* матадор matador
match *n* підбір pidbir
match *v.i.* співпадати spivpadaty
match *n.* матч match
matchless *a.* неоднаковий neodnakovyi
mate *v.t.* зробити мат zrobyty mat
mate *n* мат mat
mate *n.* напарник naparnyk
mate *v.t.* поєднувати poiednuvaty
material *n* матеріал material
material *a.* речовий rechovyi
materialism *n.* матеріалізм materializm
materialize *v.t.* матеріалізувати materializuvaty
maternal *a.* властивий матері vlastyvyi materi
maternity *n.* материнство materynstvo
mathematical *a.* математичний matematychnyi

mathematician *n.* математик matematyk
mathematics *n* математика matematyka
matinee *n.* денний спектакль dennyi spektakl
matriarch *n.* матриарх matryarkh
matricidal *a.* матеревбивчий materevbyvchyi
matricide *n.* матеревбивство materevbyvstvo
matriculate *v.t.* зарахувати до вищого навчального закладу zarakhuvaty do vyshchoho navchalnoho zakladu
matriculation *n.* атестат зрілості atestat zrilosti
matrimonial *a.* матрімоніальний matrimonialnyi
matrimony *n.* подружжя podruzhzhia
matrix *n* матриця matrytsia
matron *n.* заміжня жінка zamizhnia zhinka
matter *v.i.* означати oznachaty
matter *n.* предмет predmet
mattock *n.* киркомотика kyrkomotyka
mattress *n.* матрац matrats
mature *a.* зрілий zrilyi
mature *v.i* зріти zrity
maturity *n.* зрілість zrilist
maudlin *a* сентиментальнй sentymentalni
maul *n.* кувалда kuvalda
maul *v.t* терзати terzaty
maulstick *n.* муштабель mushtabel
maunder *v.t.* незв'язно говорити nezviazno hovoryty
mausoleum *n.* мавзолей mavzolei
mawkish *a.* нудотний nudotnyi

maxilla *n.* верхня щелепа verkhnia shchelepa
maxim *n.* сентенція sententsiia
maximize *v.t.* максимізувати maksymizuvaty
maximum *n* максимум maksymum
maximum *a.* максимальний maksymalnyi
may *v* мати можливість maty mozhlyvist
May *n.* травень traven
mayor *n.* мер mer
maze *n.* плутанина plutanyna
me *pron.* мені meni
mead *n.* луг luh
meadow *n.* лучка luchka
meagre *a.* убогий ubohyi
meal *n.* прийняття їжи pryiniattia yizhy
mealy *a.* борошнистий boroshnystyi
mean *n.* засіб zasib
mean *v.t* мати на увазі maty na uvazi
mean *v.t.* призначатися pryznachatysia
mean *a.* скупий skupyi
meander *v.i.* блукати навмання blukaty navmannia
meaning *n.* сенс sens
meaningful *a.* багатозначний bahatoznachnyi
meaningless *a.* безглуздий bezhluzdyi
meanness *n.* підлість pidlist
means *n* кошти koshty
meanwhile *adv.* тим часом tym chasom
measles *n* кір kir
measurable *a.* вимірний vymirnyi
measure *v.t* вимірювати vymiriuvaty

measure *n.* міра mira
measureless *a.* безмірний bezmirnyi
measurement *n.* нормування normuvannia
meat *n.* м'ясо miaso
mechanic *a* автоматичний avtomatychnyi
mechanic *n.* механік mekhanik
mechanical *a.* механічний mekhanichnyi
mechanics *n.* механіка mekhanika
mechanism *n.* механізм mekhanizm
medal *n.* медаль medal
medallist *n.* медаліст medalist
median *a.* медіана mediana
mediate *v.i.* бути посередником buty poserednykom
mediation *n.* посередництво poserednytstvo
mediation *n.* посередництво poserednytstvo
mediator *n.* посередник poserednyk
medical *a.* медичний medychnyi
medicament *n.* ліки liky
medicinal *a.* лікарський likarskyi
medicine *n.* медицина medytsyna
medico *n.* доктор doktor
medieval *a.* середньовічний serednovichnyi
medieval *a.* середньовічний serednovichnyi
mediocre *a.* середній serednii
mediocrity *n.* посередність poserednist
meditate *v.t.* міркувати mirkuvaty
meditative *a.* медитативний medytatyvnyi
medium *n* шлях shliakh
medium *a* помірний pomirnyi

meek *a.* лагідний lahidnyi
meet *n.* збір zbir
meet *v.t.* зустрічатися
zustrichatysia
meeting *n.* дуель duel
megalith *n.* мегаліт mehalit
megalithic *a.* мегалітичний
mehalitychnyi
megaphone *n.* мегафон mehafon
melancholia *n.* меланхолія
melankholiia
melancholic *a.* меланхолійний
melankholiinyi
melancholy *n.* зневіра znevira
melancholy *adj* тужливий
tuzhlyvyi
melee *n.* рукопашна rukopashna
meliorate *v.t.* меліорували
melioruvaly
mellow *a.* спілий spilyi
melodious *a.* мелодійний
melodiinyi
melodrama *n.* мелодрама
melodrama
melodramatic *a.*
мелодраматичний
melodramatychnyi
melody *n.* мелодія melodiia
melon *n.* диня dynia
melt *v.i.* танути tanuty
member *n.* член chlen
membership *n.* членство
chlenstvo
membrane *n.* мембрана
membrana
memento *n.* сувенір suvenir
memoir *n.* мемуари memuary
memorable *a.* пам'ятний
pamiatnyi
memorandum *n* меморандум
memorandum
memorial *n.* меморіал memorial

memorial *a* меморіальний
memorialnyi
memory *n.* пам'ять pamiat
menace *v.t* загрожувати
zahrozhuvaty
menace *n* небезпека nebezpeka
mend *v.t.* лагодити lahodyty
mendacious *a.* брехливий
brekhlyvyi
menial *a.* лакейський lakeiskyi
menial *n* слуга sluha
meningitis *n.* менінгіт meninhit
menopause *n.* менопауза
menopauza
menses *n.* менструації
menstruatsii
menstrual *a.* менструальний
menstrualnyi
menstruation *n.* менструація
menstruatsiia
mental *a.* розумовий rozumovyi
mentality *n.* менталітет mentalitet
mention *n.* згадка zhadka
mention *v.t.* згадувати zhaduvaty
mentor *n.* наставник nastavnyk
menu *n.* меню meniu
mercantile *a.* меркантильний
merkantylnyi
mercenary *a.* корисливий
koryslyvyi
mercerise *v.t.* мерсиризувати
mersyryzuvaty
merchandise *n.* товар tovar
merchant *n.* купець kupets
merciful *a.* милосердний
myloserdnyi
merciless *adj.* немилосердний
nemyloserdnyi
mercurial *a.* ртутний rtutnyi
mercury *n.* ртуть rtut
mercy *n.* милосердя myloserdia
mere *a.* цілковитий tsilkovytyi
merge *v.t.* зливатися zlyvatysia

merger *n.* поглинення pohlynennia

meridian *a.* меридіан merydian

merit *n.* заслуга zasluha

merit *v.t* заслуговувати zasluhovuvaty

meritorious *a.* виграшний vyhrashnyi

mermaid *n.* русалка rusalka

merman *n.* водяний vodianyi

merriment *n.* веселощі veseloshchi

merry *a* веселий veselyi

mesh *n.* сіті siti

mesh *v.t* піймати в сіті piimaty v siti

mesmerism *n.* гіпноз hipnoz

mesmerize *v.t.* гіпнотизувати hipnotyzuvaty

mess *n.* безладдя bezladdia

mess *v.i* зробити безлад zrobyty bezlad

message *n.* лист lyst

messenger *n.* посильний posylnyi

messiah *n.* месія mesiia

Messrs *n.* Господа Hospoda

metabolism *n.* обмін речовин obmin rechovyn

metal *n.* метал metal

metallic *a.* металевий metalevyi

metallurgy *n.* металургія metalurhiia

metamorphosis *n.* метаморфоза metamorfoza

metaphor *n.* метафора metafora

metaphysical *a.* метафізичний metafizychnyi

metaphysics *n.* метафізика metafizyka

mete *v.t* відміряти vidmiriaty

meteor *n.* метеор meteor

meteoric *a.* метеорний meteornyi

meteorologist *n.* метеоролог meteoroloh

meteorology *n.* метеорологія meteorolohiia

meter *n.* метр metr

method *n.* метод metod

methodical *a.* методичний metodychnyi

metre *n.* метр metr

metric *a.* метричний metrychnyi

metrical *a.* вимірювальний vymiriuvalnyi

metropolis *n.* метрополія metropoliia

metropolitan *n.* митрополит mytropolyt

metropolitan *a.* столичний stolychnyi

mettle *n.* характер kharakter

mettlesome *a.* завзятий zavziatyi

mew *n.* нявкання niavkannia

mew *v.i.* нявкати niavkaty

mezzanine *n.* мезонін mezonin

mica *n.* слюда sliuda

microfilm *n.* мікрофільм mikrofilm

micrology *n.* мікроскопія mikroskopiia

micrometer *n.* мікрометр mikrometr

microphone *n.* мікрофон mikrofon

microscope *n.* мікроскоп mikroskop

microscopic *a.* мікроскопічний mikroskopichnyi

microwave *n.* мікрохвильова піч mikrokhvylova pich

mid *a.* середній serednii

midday *n.* полудень poluden

middle *n* гуща hushcha

middle *a.* середній serednii

middleman *n.* комісіонер komisioner

middling *a.* другосортний druhosortnyi
midget *n.* карлик karlyk
midland *n.* центральний tsentralnyi
midnight *n.* північ pivnoch
mid-off *n.* польовий гравець на лівій стороні від боулера в крикеті polovyi hravets na livii storoni vid boulera v kryketi
mid-on *n.* польовий гравець на правій стороні від боулера в крикеті polovyi hravets na pravii storoni vid boulera v kryketi
midriff *n.* діафрагма diafrahma
midst серед sered
midsummer *n.* середина літа seredyna lita
midwife *n.* акушерка akusherka
might *n.* могутність mohutnist
mighty *adj.* могутній mohutnii
migraine *n.* мігрень mihren
migrant *n.* мігрант mihrant
migrate *v.i.* мігрувати mihruvaty
migration *n.* міграція mihratsiia
milch *a.* молочний molochnyi
mild *a.* несуворий nesuvoryi
mildew *n.* цвіль tsvil
mile *n.* миля mylia
mileage *n.* пробіг probih
milestone *n.* віха vikha
milieu *n.* оточення otochennia
militant *n* боєць boiets
militant *a.* бойовий boiovyi
military *n* війська viiska
military *a.* призовний pryzovnyi
militate *v.i.* свідчити проти svidchyty proty
militia *n.* міліція militsiia
milk *v.t.* доїти doity
milk *n.* молоко moloko
milky *a.* молочний molochnyi
mill *v.t.* молоти moloty

mill *n.* млин mlyn
millennium *n.* тисячоліття tysiacholittia
miller *n.* мельник melnyk
millet *n.* просо proso
milliner *n.* капелюшник kapeliushnyk
milliner *n.* модистка modystka
millinery *n.* модні товари modni tovary
million *n.* мільйон milion
millionaire *n.* мільйонер milioner
millipede *n.* багатоніжка bahatonizhka
mime *n.* мім mim
mime *v.i* наслідувати nasliduvaty
mimesis *n.* мімікрія mimikriia
mimic *n* імітатор imitator
mimic *v.t* імітувати imituvaty
mimic *a.* мімічний mimichnyi
mimicry *n* міміка mimika
minaret *n.* мінарет minaret
mince *v.t.* рубати м'ясо rubaty miaso
mind *v.t.* пам'ятати pamiataty
mind *n.* розум rozum
mindful *a.* уважний uvazhnyi
mindless *a.* дурний durnyi
mine *pron.* мій mii
mine *n* шахта shakhta
miner *n.* шахтар shakhtar
mineral *a* мінеральний mineralnyi
mineral *n.* мінерал mineral
mineralogist *n.* мінералог mineraloh
mineralogy *n.* мінералогія mineralohiia
mingle *v.t.* змішуватися zmishuvatysia
miniature *a.* мініатюрний miniatiurnyi
miniature *n.* мініатюра miniatiura

minim *n.* дрібна частка dribna chastka
minimal *a.* мінімальний minimalnyi
minimize *v.t.* мінімізувати minimizuvaty
minimum *a* мінімальний minimalnyi
minimum *n.* мінімум minimum
minion *n.* фаворит favoryt
minister *v.i.* сприяти spryiaty
minister *n.* міністр ministr
ministrant *a.* священик sviashchenyk
ministry *n.* міністерство ministerstvo
mink *n.* норка norka
minor *n* неповнолітній підліток nepovnolitnii pidlitok
minor *a.* неповнолітній nepovnolitnii
minority *n.* меншість menshist
minster *n.* кафедральний собор kafedralnyi sobor
mint *v.t.* карбувати karbuvaty
mint *n.* м'ята miata
mint *n* м'ятний miatnyi
minus *n* мінус minus
minus *a* негативний nehatyvnyi
minus *prep.* за мінусом za minusom
minuscule *a.* мізерний mizernyi
minute *a.* дріб'язковий dribiazkovyi
minute *n.* хвилина khvylyna
minutely *adv.* докладно dokladno
minx *n.* кокетка koketka
miracle *n.* чудо chudo
miraculous *a.* чудотворний chudotvornyi
mirage *n.* міраж mirazh
mire *v.t.* зав'язнути в багнюці zaviaznuty v bahniutsi

mire *n.* грязь hriaz
mirror *v.t.* відображати vidobrazhaty
mirror *n* дзеркало dzerkalo
mirth *n.* веселість veselist
mirthful *a.* радісний radisnyi
misadventure *n.* нещасний випадок neshchasnyi vypadok
misalliance *n.* мезальянс mezalians
misanthrope *n.* мізантроп mizantrop
misapplication *n.* зловживання zlovzhyvannia
misapprehend *v.t.* зрозуміти неправильно zrozumity nepravylno
misapprehension *n* непорозуміння neporozuminnia
misappropriate *v.t.* незаконно привласнювати nezzakonno pryvlasniuvaty
misappropriation *n.* незаконне привласнення nezakonne pryvlasnennia
misbehave *v.i.* погано поводитися pohano povodytysia
misbehaviour *n.* неналежна поведінка nenalezhna povedinka
misbelief *n.* помилкова думка pomylkova dumka
miscalculate *v.t.* прорахуватися prorakhuvatysia
miscalculation *n.* прорахунок prorakhunok
miscall *v.t.* невірно називати nevirno nazyvaty
miscarriage *n.* помилка pomylka
miscarry *v.i.* викинути vykynuty
miscellaneous *a.* різноманітний riznomanitnyi

miscellany *n.* мішанина
mishanyna
mischance *n.* невдача nevdacha
mischief *n* витівка vytivka
mischievous *a.* пустотливий
pustotlyvyi
misconceive *v.t.* мати
неправильне уявлення maty
nepravylne uiavlennia
misconception *n.* неправильне
уявлення nepravylne uiavlennia
misconduct *n.* проступок
prostupok
misconstrue *v.t.* неправильно
тлумачити nepravylno
tlumachyty
miscreant *n.* єретик yeretyk
misdeed *n.* злочин zlochyn
misdemeanour *n.* судово
караний проступок sudovo
karanyi prostupok
misdirect *v.t.* неправильно
адресувати nepravylno
adresuvaty
misdirection *n.* неправильне
nepravylne
miser *n.* скнара sknara
miserable *a.* бідолашний
bidolashnyi
miserly *a.* скупий skupyi
misery *n.* убозтво uboztvo
misfire *v.i.* давати осічку davaty
osichku
misfit *n.* той, хто не підходить toi,
khto ne pidkhodyt
misfortune *n.* невдача nevdacha
misgive *v.t.* вселяти побоювання
vseliaty poboiuvannia
misgiving *n.* побоювання
poboiuvannia
misguide *v.t.* вводити в оману
vvodyty v omanu

mishap *n.* нещасний випадок
neshchasnyi vypadok
misjudge *v.t.* недооцінювати
nedootsiniuvaty
mislead *v.t.* збивати з шляху
zbyvaty z shliakhu
mismanagement *n.* неправильне
керівництво nepravylne
kerivnytstvo
mismatch *v.t.* не відповідати ne
vidpovidaty
misnomer *n.* неправильна назва
nepravylna nazva
misplace *v.t.* класти не на місце
klasty ne na mistse
misprint *v.t.* зробити помилку
zrobyty pomylku
misprint *n.* друкарська помилка
drukarska pomylka
misrepresent *v.t.* спотворювати
spotvoriuvaty
misrule *n.* погане управління
pohane upravlinnia
miss *v.t.* не потрапити ne
potrapyty
miss *n.* осічка osichka
missile *n.* ракета raketa
mission *n.* місія misiia
missionary *n.* місіонер misioner
missis, missus *n..* місіс misis
missive *n.* послання poslannia
mist *n.* туман tuman
mistake *v.t.* помилятися
pomyliatysia
mistake *n.* непорозуміння
neporozuminnia
mister *n.* містер mister
mistletoe *n.* омела omela
mistreat *d* брутально поводитися
brutalno povodytysia
mistress *n.* пані pani
mistrust *v.t.* не довіряти ne
doviriaty

mistrust *n.* недовіра nedovira
misty *a.* туманний tumannyi
misunderstand *v.t.* неправильно
зрозуміти nepravylno zrozumity
misunderstanding *n.*
непорозуміння neporozuminnia
misuse *v.t.* зловживати
zlovzhyvaty
misuse *n.* погане ставлення
pohane stavlennia
mite *n.* гріш hrish
mite *n* кліщ klishch
mithridate *n.* протиотрута
protyotruta
mitigate *v.t.* послабляти
poslabliaty
mitigation *n.* пом'якшення
pomiakshennia
mitre *n.* митра mytra
mitten *n.* рукавиця rukavytsia
mix *v.i* вводитися vvodytysia
mixture *n.* суміш sumish
moan *n.* стогін stohin
moan *v.i.* стогнати stohnaty
moat *v.t.* обносити ровом
obnosyty rovom
moat *n.* кріпосний рів kriposnyi riv
mob *v.t.* товпитися tovpytysia
mob *n.* юрба yurba
mobile *a.* мобільний mobilnyi
mobility *n.* мобільність mobilnist
mobilize *v.t.* мобілізувати
mobilizuvaty
mock *v.i.* знущатися
znushchatysia
mock *adj* удаваний udavanyi
mockery *n.* знущання
znushchannia
modality *n.* модальність
modalnist
mode *n.* режим rezhym
model *v.t.* ліпити lipyty
model *n.* макет maket

moderate *a.* помірний pomirnyi
moderate *v.t.* стримувати
strymuvaty
moderation *n.* сповільнення
spovilnennia
modern *a.* сучасний suchasnyi
modernity *n.* сучасність
suchasnist
modernize *v.t.* модернізувати
modernizuvaty
modest *a.* скромний skromnyi
modesty *n* скромність skromnist
modicum *n.* трішки trishky
modification *n.* модифікація
modyfikatsiia
modify *v.t.* змінювати zminiuvaty
modulate *v.t.* модулювати
moduliuvaty
moil *v.i.* важка робота vazhka
robota
moist *a.* дощовий doshchovyi
moisten *v.t.* зволожувати
zvolozhuvaty
moisture *n.* волога voloha
molar *a* молярний moliarnyi
molar *n.* корінний зуб korinnyi
zub
molasses *n* патока patoka
mole *n.* моль mol
molecular *a.* молекулярний
molekuliarnyi
molecule *n.* молекула molekula
molest *v.t.* приставати prystavaty
molestation *n.* настирливість
nastyrlyvist
molten *a.* розплавлений
rozplavlenyi
moment *n.* момент moment
momentary *a.* короткочасний
korotkochasnyi
momentous *a.* найважливіший
naivazhlyvishyi

momentum *n.* рушійна сила rushiina syla
monarch *n.* монарх monarkh
monarchy *n.* монархія monarkhiia
monastery *n.* монастир monastyr
monasticism *n* чернецтво chernetstvo
Monday *n.* понеділок ponedilok
monetary *a.* монетний monetnyi
money *n.* гроші hroshi
monger *n.* торговець torhovets
mongoose *n.* мангуста manhusta
mongrel *a* нечістокровний nechistokrovnyi
monitor *n.* староста starosta
monitory *a.* застережливий zasterezhlyvyi
monk *n.* чернець chernets
monkey *n.* кривляка kryvliaka
monochromatic *a.* монохроматичний monokhromatychnyi
monocle *n.* монокль monokl
monocular *a.* монокуляр monokuliar
monody *n.* похоронна пісня pokhoronna pisnia
monogamy *n.* моногамія monohamiia
monogram *n.* монограма monohrama
monograph *n.* монографія monohrafiia
monogynous *a.* моногінний monohinnyi
monolatry *n.* поклоніння одному Богу pokloninnia odnomu Bohu
monolith *n.* моноліт monolit
monologue *n.* монолог monoloh
monopolist *n.* монополіст monopolist
monopolize *v.t.* монополізувати monopolizuvaty

monopoly *n.* монополія monopoliia
monostrous *a.* жахливо монотонний zhakhlyvo monotonnyi
monosyllabic *a.* односкладовий odnoskladovyi
monosyllable *n.* односкладове слово odnoskladove slovo
monotheism *n.* монотеїзм monoteizm
monotheist *n.* монотеїст monoteist
monotonous *a.* одноманітний odnomanitnyi
monotony *n* монотонність monotonnist
monsoon *n.* мусон muson
monster *n.* монстр monstr
monstrous *a.* величезний velycheznyi
month *n.* місяць misiats
monthly *n* щомісячник shchomisiachnyk
monthly *adv* щомісячно shchomisiachno
monthly *a.* щомісячний shchomisiachnyi
monument *n.* пам'ятник pamiatnyk
monumental *a.* монументальний monumentalnyi
moo *v.i* мукати mukaty
mood *n.* настрій nastrii
moody *a.* похмурий pokhmuryi
moon *n.* місяць misiats
moor *n.* мохове болото mokhove boloto
moor *v.t* швартуватися shvartuvatysia
moorings *n.* причал prychal

moot *n.* навчальний судовий процес navchalnyi sudovyi protses

mop *v.t.* чистити шваброю chystyty shvabroiu

mop *n.* швабра shvabra

mope *v.i.* хандрити khandryty

moral *n.* мораль moral

moral *a.* моральний moralnyi

morale *n.* бойовий дух boiovyi dukh

moralist *n.* мораліст moralist

morality *n.* моральність moralnist

moralize *v.t.* моралізувати moralizuvaty

morbid *a.* хворобливий khvoroblyvyi

morbidity *n* захворюваність zakhvoriuvanist

more *adv* більше bilshe

more *a.* численніший chyslennishyi

moreover *adv.* більше того bilshe toho

morganatic *a.* морганатичний morhanatychnyi

morgue *n.* морг morh

moribund *a.* вмираючий vmyraiuchyi

morning *n.* ранок ranok

moron *n.* слабоумний slaboumnyi

morose *a.* понурий ponuryi

morphia *n.* морфій morfii

morrow *n.* наступний день nastupnyi den

morsel *n.* шматочок shmatochok

mortal *n* смертний smertnyi

mortal *a.* смертний smertnyi

mortality *n.* смертність smertnist

mortar *v.t.* товкти в ступі tovkty v stupi

mortgage *v.t.* заставляти zastavliaty

mortgage *n.* заставна zastavna

mortgagee *n.* кредитор по заставній kredytor po zastavnii

mortgagor *n.* боржник за заставною borzhnyk za zastavnoiu

mortify *v.t.* вгамовувати vhamovuvaty

mortuary *n.* могильник mohylnyk

mosaic *n.* мозаїка mozaika

mosque *n.* мечеть mechet

mosquito *n.* комар komar

moss *n.* мох mokh

most *n* більшість bilshist

most *adv.* найбільш naibilsh

most *a.* самий samyi

mote *n.* цяточка tsiatochka

motel *n.* мотель motel

moth *n.* нічний метелик nichnyi metelyk

mother *v.t.* плекати plekaty ˙

mother *n* матінка matinka

motherhood *n.* материнство materynstvo

motherlike *adj.* як мати yak maty

motherly *a.* материнський materynskyi

motif *n.* мотив motyv

motion *v.i.* показувати жестом pokazuvaty zhestom

motion *n.* рух rukh

motionless *a.* нерухомий nerukhomyi

motivate *v* мотивувати motyvuvaty

motivation *n.* мотивація motyvatsiia

motive *n.* мотив motyv

motley *a.* строкатий strokatyi

motor *v.i.* везти на автомобілі vezty na avtomobili

motor *n.* електромотор elektromotor

motorist *n.* автомобіліст avtomobilist
mottle *n.* цятка tsiatka
motto *n.* девіз deviz
mould *n* виливок vylyvok
mould *v.t.* відливати у форму vidlyvaty u formu
mould *n* форма forma
mould *n.* зліпок zlipok
mouldy *a.* запліснілий zaplisnilyi
moult *v.i.* линька lynka
mound *n.* курган kurhan
mount *v.t.* встановлювати vstanovliuvaty
mount *n* установка ustanovka
mount *n.* гора hora
mountain *n.* маса masa
mountaineer *n.* альпініст alpinist
mountainous *a.* гористий horystyi
mourn *v.i.* сумувати sumuvaty
mourner *n.* плакальники plakalnyky
mournful *n.* скорботний skorbotnyi
mourning *n.* траур traur
mouse *n.* миша mysha
moustache *n.* вус vus
mouth *v.t.* вирікати vyrikaty
mouth *n.* рот rot
mouthful *n.* шматок shmatok
movable *a.* рухомий rukhomyi
movables *n.* рухоме майно rukhome maino
move *n.* зміна положення zmina polozhennia
move *v.t.* рухатися rukhatysia
movement *n.* пересування peresuvannia
mover *n.* рушійна сила rushiina syla
movies *n.* кіно kino
mow *v.t.* скиртувати skyrtuvaty
much *adv* майже maizhe

much *adv.* багато bahato
mucilage *n.* рослинний слиз roslynnyi slyz
muck *n.* погань pohan
mucous *a.* слизовий slyzovyi
mucus *n.* слиз slyz
mud *n.* твань tvan
muddle *v.t.* плутати plutaty
muddle *n.* безладдя bezladdia
muffle *v.t.* глушити hlushyty
muffler *n.* кашне kashne
mug *n.* гуртка hurtka
muggy *a.* важкий vazhkyi
mulatto *n.* мулат mulat
mulberry *n.* шовковиця shovkovytsia
mule *n.* мул mul
mulish *a.* впертий vpertyi
mull *v.t.* переплутати pereplutaty
mull *n.* тонкий муслін tonkyi muslin
mullah *n.* мулла mulla
mullion *n.* середник serednyk
multifarious *a.* багатогранний bahatohrannyi
multiform *a.* різноманітний riznomanitnyi
multilateral *a.* багатосторонній bahatostoronnii
multiparous *a.* та, що народжувала ta, shcho narodzhuvala
multiped *n.* тварина, що має багато ніг tvaryna, shcho maie bahato nih
multiple *n* стисле число stysle chyslo
multiple *a.* множинний mnozhynnyi
multiplex *a.* складний skladnyi
multiplicand *n.* множене mnozhene

124

multiplication *n.* множення mnozhennia
multiplicity *n.* множинність mnozhynnist
multiply *v.t.* помножити pomnozhyty
multitude *n.* безліч bezlich
mum *n* мама mama
mum *a.* мовчазний movchaznyi
mumble *v.i.* шамкати shamkaty
mummer *n.* фігляр fihliar
mummy *n* мамаша mamasha
mummy *n.* мумія mumiia
mumps *n.* свинка svynka
munch *v.t.* плямкати pliamkaty
mundane *a.* мирський myrskyi
municipal *a.* муніципальний munitsypalnyi
municipality *n.* муніципалітет munitsypalitet
munificent *a.* надзвичайно щедрий nadzvychaino shchedryi
muniment *n.* документ про права dokument pro prava
munitions *n.* спорядження sporiadzhennia
mural *n.* фреска freska
mural *a.* стінний stinnyi
murder *n.* навмисне вбивство navmysne vbyvstvo
murder *v.t.* вбивати vbyvaty
murderer *n.* убивця ubyvtsia
murderous *a.* вбивчий vbyvchyi
murmur *v.t.* нарікати narikaty
murmur *n.* бурмотання burmotannia
muscle *n.* м'яз miaz
muscovite *n.* москвич moskvych
muscular *a.* м'язистий miazystyi
muse *n* муза muza
muse *v.i.* споглядати spohliadaty
museum *n.* музей muzei

mush *n.* м'якуш m'iakush
mushroom *n.* гриб hryb
music *n.* музика muzyka
musical *a.* музичний muzychnyi
musician *n.* музикант muzykant
musk *n.* мускус muskus
musket *n.* мушкет mushket
musketeer *n.* мушкетер mushketer
muslin *n.* муслін muslin
must *n* зобов'язання zobovzannia
must *n.* необхідність neobkhidnist
must *v.* повинен povynen
mustache *n.* вуса vusa
mustang *n.* мустанг mustanh
mustard *n.* гірчиця hirchytsia
muster *n* переклик pereklyk
muster *v.t.* робити переклик robyty pereklyk
musty *a.* затхлий zatkhlyi
mutation *n.* мутація mutatsiia
mutative *a.* мутаційний mutatsiinyi
mute *a.* мовчазний movchaznyi
mute *n.* статист statyst
mutilate *v.t.* нівечити nivechyty
mutilation *n.* каліцтво kalitstvo
mutinous *a.* заколотний zakolotnyi
mutiny *v. i* бунтувати buntuvaty
mutiny *n.* заколот zakolot
mutter *v.i.* мимрити mymryty
mutton *n.* баранина baranyna
mutual *a.* взаємний vzaiemnyi
muzzle *v.t* надягати намордник nadiahaty namordnyk
muzzle *n.* морда morda
my *a.* мій mii
myalgia *n.* біль у м'язах bil u miazakh
myopia *n.* короткозорість korotkozorist

myopic *a.* короткозорий korotkozoryi
myosis *n.* міозіс miozis
myriad *a* незліченний nezlichennyi
myriad *n.* міріади miriady
myrrh *n.* мирра myrra
myrtle *n.* мирт myrt
myself *pron.* сам sam
mysterious *a.* таємничий taiemnychyi
mystery *n.* таємниця taiemnytsia
mystic *n* містик mistyk
mystic *a.* містичний mistychnyi
mysticism *n.* містицизм mistytsyzm
mystify *v.t.* містифікувати mistyfikuvaty
myth *n.* міф mif
mythical *a.* міфічний mifichnyi
mythological *a.* міфологічний mifolohichnyi
mythology *n.* міфологія mifolohiia

N

nab *v.t.* заарештувати zaareshtuvaty
nabob *n.* набоб nabob
nadir *n.* найнижчий рівень nainyzhchyi riven
nag *v.t.* чіплятися chipliatysia
nag *n.* шкапа shkapa
nail *v.t.* придушувати prydushuvaty
nail *n.* ніготь nihot
naive *a.* наївний naivnyi
naivete *n.* наївність naivnist
naivety *n.* простацтво prostatstvo
naked *a.* оголений oholenyi
name *n.* ім'я imia
name *v.t.* назвати nazvaty
namely *adv.* а саме a same

namesake *n.* тезка tezka
nap *n.* легкий сон lehkyi son
nap *n* начіс nachis
nap *v.i.* подрімати podrimaty
nape *n.* потилиця potylytsia
napkin *n.* серветка servetka
narcissism *n.* самозакоханість samozakokhanist
narcissus *n* нарцис nartsys
narcosis *n.* наркоз narkoz
narcotic *n.* наркотичний narkotychnyi
narrate *v.t.* оповідати opovidaty
narration *n.* розповідь rozpovid
narrative *a.* розповідний rozpovidnyi
narrative *n.* оповідання opovidannia
narrator *n.* розповідач rozpovidach
narrow *v.t.* звужувати zvuzhuvaty
narrow *a.* вузький vuzkyi
nasal *n* носова кістка nosova kistka
nasal *a.* носовий nosovyi
nascent *a.* який народжується yakyi narodzhuietsia
nasty *a.* противний protyvnyi
natal *a.* натальний natalnyi
natant *a.* плавучий plavuchyi
nation *n.* нація natsiia
national *a.* національний natsionalnyi
nationalism *n.* націоналізм natsionalizm
nationalist *n.* націоналістичний natsionalistychnyi
nationality *n.* національність natsionalnist
nationalization *n.* націоналізація natsionalizatsiia
nationalize *v.t.* націоналізувати natsionalizuvaty

native *n* місцевий житель mistsevyi zhytel
native *a.* рідний ridnyi
nativity *n.* гороскоп horoskop
natural *a.* природний pryrodnyi
naturalist *n.* натураліст naturalist
naturalize *v.t.* натуралізувати naturalizuvaty
naturally *adv.* природно pryrodno
nature *n.* природа pryroda
naughty *a.* неслухняний neslukhnianyi
nausea *n.* нудота nudota
nautic(al) *a.* морехідний morekhidnyi
naval *a.* військово-морський viiskovo-morskyi
nave *n.* неф nef
navigable *a.* судноплавний sudnoplavnyi
navigate *v.i.* літати litaty
navigation *n.* навігація navihatsiia
navigator *n.* навігатор navihator
navy *n.* військово-морський флот viiskovo-morskyi flot
nay *adv.* мало того malo toho
neap *a.* дишло dyshlo
near *v.i.* наближатися nablyzhatysia
near *adv.* поблизу poblyzu
near *prep.* мало не malo ne
near *a.* ближній blyzhnii
nearly *adv.* ледве не ledve ne
neat *a.* акуратний akuratnyi
nebula *n.* туманність tumannist
necessary *a* потрібний potribnyi
necessary *n.* необхідно neobkhidno
necessitate *v.t.* робити необхідним robyty neobkhidnym
necessity *n.* бідність bidnist
neck *n.* шия shyia

necklace *n.* намисто namysto
necklet *n.* боа boa
necromancer *n.* некромант nekromant
necropolis *n.* некрополь nekropol
nectar *n.* нектар nektar
need *v.t.* потребувати potrebuvaty
need *n.* необхідність neobkhidnist
needful *a.* необхідне neobkhidne
needle *n.* голка holka
needless *a.* непотрібний nepotribnyi
needs *adv.* потреби potreby
needy *a.* скрутний skrutnyi
nefandous *a.* невимовний nevymovnyi
nefarious *a.* підлий pidlyi
negation *n.* заперечення zaperechennia
negative *v.t.* відкидати vidkydaty
negative *n.* негатив nehatyv
negative *a.* заперечний zaperechnyi
neglect *n* зневага znevaha
neglect *v.t.* зневажати znevazhaty
negligence *n.* халатність khalatnist
negligent *a.* халатний khalatnyi
negligible *a.* який не береться до уваги yakyi ne beretsia do uvahy
negotiable *a.* оборотний oborotnyi
negotiate *v.t.* вести переговори vesty perehovory
negotiation *n.* переговори perehovory
negotiator *n.* учасник переговорів uchasnyk perehovoriv
negress *n.* негритянка nehrytianka
negro *n.* негр nehr

neigh *n.* іржання irzhannia
neigh *v.i.* іржати irzhaty
neighbour *n.* сусід susid
neighbourhood *n.* сусідство susidstvo
neighbourly *a.* добросусідський dobrosusidskyi
neither *a.* жоден zhoden
nemesis *n.* відплата vidplata
neolithic *a.* неолітичний neolitychnyi
neon *n.* неоновий neonovyi
nephew *n.* племінник pleminnyk
nepotism *n.* кумівство kumivstvo
Neptune *n.* Нептун Neptun
Nerve *n.* Нерв Nerv
nerveless *a.* боягузливий boiahuzlyvyi
nervous *a.* нервовий nervovyi
nescience *n.* незнання neznannia
nest *v.t.* гніздитися hnizdytysia
nest *n.* гніздо hnizdo
nestle *v.i.* притиснутися prytysnutysia
nestling *n.* пташеня ptashenia
net *v.t.* ловити сіткою lovyty sitkoiu
net *v.t.* покривати мережею pokryvaty merezheiu
net *a* чистий chystyi
net *n.* сіть sit
nether *a.* нижній nyzhnii
nettle *n.* кропива kropyva
nettle *v.t.* ужалити кропивою uzhalyty kropyvoiu
network *n.* мережа merezha
neurologist *n.* невролог nevroloh
neurology *n.* неврологія nevrolohiia
neurosis *n.* невроз nevroz
neuter *a.* неперехідний neperekhidnyi
neuter *n* середній рід serednii rid

neutral *a.* нейтральний neitralnyi
neutralize *v.t.* нейтралізувати neitralizuvaty
neutron *n.* нейтрон neitron
never *adv.* ніколи nikoly
nevertheless *conj.* хоча khocha
new *a.* недавній nedavnii
news *n.* новини novyny
next *adv.* потім potim
next *a.* наступний nastupnyi
nib *n.* кінчик пера kinchyk pera
nibble *n* клювання kliuvannia
nibble *v.t.* гризти hryzty
nice *a.* витончений vytonchenyi
nicety *n.* пунктуальність punktualnist
niche *n.* ніша nisha
nick *n.* зарубка zarubka
nickel *n.* нікель nikel
nickname *v.t.* прозвати prozvaty
nickname *n.* зменшене ім`я zmenshene im`ia
nicotine *n.* нікотин nikotyn
niece *n.* племінниця pleminnytsia
niggard *n.* скнара sknara
niggardly *a.* скупий skupyi
nigger *n.* чорношкірий chornoshkiryi
nigh *adv.* поруч poruch
nigh *prep.* майже maizhe
night *n.* ніч nich
nightie *n.* ночнушка nochnushka
nightingale *n.* соловей solovei
nightly *adv.* вночі vnochi
nightmare *n.* кошмар koshmar
nihilism *n.* нігілізм nihilizm
nil *n.* нуль nul
nimble *a.* спритний sprytnyi
nimbus *n.* німб nimb
nine *n.* дев'ять deviat
nineteen *n.* дев'ятнадцять deviatnadtsiat

nineteenth *a.* дев'ятнадцятого deviatnadtsiatoho
ninetieth *a.* дев'яностий devianostyi
ninety *n.* дев'яносто devianosto
ninth *a.* дев'ятий deviatyi
nip *v.t* щипати shchypaty
nipple *n.* сосок sosok
nitrogen *n.* азот azot
no *n* відмова vidmova
no *a.* ні ni
no *adv.* ніякий niiakyi
nobility *n.* дворянство dvorianstvo
noble *n.* ханжа khanzha
noble *a.* шляхетний shliakhetnyi
nobleman *n.* дворянин dvorianyn
nobody *pron.* ніхто nikhto
nocturnal *a.* нічний nichnyi
nod *v.i.* кивати головою kyvaty holovoiu
node *n.* вузловий пункт vuzlovyi punkt
noise *n.* шум shum
noisy *a.* шумний shumnyi
nomad *n.* кочівник kochivnyk
nomadic *a.* кочовий kochovyi
nomenclature *n.* номенклатура nomenklatura
nominal *a.* номінальний nominalnyi
nominate *v.t.* іменувати imenuvaty
nomination *n.* висування vysuvannia
nominee *n* претендент pretendent
non-alignment *n.* нейтралізм neitralizm
nonchalance *n.* безтурботність bezturbotnist
nonchalant *a.* недбалий nedbalyi
none *adv.* ні один ni odyn

none *pron.* жоден zhoden
nonentity *n.* нікчема nikchema
nonetheless *adv.* проте prote
nonpareil *n.* ідеал ideal
nonpareil *a.* незрівнянний nezrivniannyi
nonplus *v.t.* приводити в замішання pryvodyty v zamishannia
nonsense *n.* нісенітниця nisenitnytsia
nonsensical *a.* нісенітний nisenitnyi
nook *n.* затишний куточок zatyshnyi kutochok
noon *n.* полудень poluden
noose *v.t.* заарканити zaarkanyty
noose *n.* зашморг zashmorh
nor *conj* не ne
norm *n.* норма norma
norm *n.* стандарт standart
normal *a.* нормальний normalnyi
normalcy *n.* нормальність normalnist
normalize *v.t.* нормалізувати normalizuvaty
north *adv.* на північ na pivnich
north *a* який виходить на північ yakyi vykhodyt na pivnich
north *n.* північ pivnich
northerly *adv.* на північ na pivnich
northerly *a.* північний pivnichnyi
northern *a.* який дме з півночі yakyi dme z pivnochi
nose *v.t* чуття chuttia
nose *n.* ніс nis
nosegay *n.* букетик квітів buketyk kvitiv
nosey *a.* цікавий tsikavyi
nostalgia *n.* ностальгія nostalhiia
nostril *n.* ніздря nizdria
nostrum *n.* патентований засіб patentovanyi zasob

nosy *a.* пронирливий pronyrlyvyi
not *adv.* не ne
notability *n.* відома людина vidoma liudyna
notable *a.* примітний prymitnyi
notary *n.* нотаріус notarius
notation *n.* позначення poznachennia
notch *n.* паз paz
note *v.t.* зауважити zauvazhyty
note *n.* примітка prymitka
noteworthy *a.* визначний vyznachnyi
nothing *adv.* нічого nichoho
nothing *n.* порожнє місце porozhnie mistse
notice *v.t.* звертати увагу zvertaty uvahu
notice *v.t.* посилати повідомлення posylaty povidomlennia
notification *n.* попередження poperedzhennia
notify *v.t.* давати відомості davaty vidomosti
notion *n.* поняття poniattia
notional *a.* смисловий smyslovyi
notoriety *n.* особа, яка зажила дурної слави osoba, yaka zazhyla durnoi slavy
notorious *a.* горезвісний horezvisnyi
notwithstanding *prep.* всупереч vsuperech
notwithstanding *conj.* незважаючи на nezvazhaiuchy na
notwithstanding *adv.* однак odnak
nought *n.* нікчема nikchema
noun *n.* іменник imennyk
nourish *v.t.* живити zhyvyty

nourishment *n.* харчування kharchuvannia
novel *a.* новий novyi
novel *n* роман roman
novelette *n.* повість povist
novelist *n.* романіст romanist
novelty *n.* новинка novynka
november *n.* листопад lystopad
novice *n.* початківець pochatkivets
now *conj.* коли koly
now *adv.* зараз zaraz
nowhere *adv.* ніде nide
noxious *a.* шкідливий shkidlyvyi
nozzle *n.* сопло soplo
nuance *n.* нюанс niuans
nubile *a.* шлюбний shliubnyi
nuclear *a.* ядерний yadernyi
nucleus *n.* ядро yadro
nude *n* оголене тіло oholene tilo
nude *a.* голий holyi
nudge *v.t.* підштовхнути pidshtovkhnuty
nudity *n.* нагота nahota
nugget *n.* самородок samorodok
nuisance *n.* неприємність nepryiemnist
null *a.* нульовий nulovyi
nullification *n.* анулювання anuliuvannia
nullify *v.t.* скасувати skasuvaty
numb *a.* онімілий onimilyi
number *v.t.* випуск vypusk
number *n.* номер nomer
numberless *a.* що не має номера shcho ne maie nomera
numeral *a.* цифра tsyfra
numerator *n.* чисельник chyselnyk
numerical *a.* чисельний chyselnyi
numerous *a.* численний chyslennyi
nun *n.* монахиня monakhynia

nunnery *n.* жіночий монастир zhinochyi monastyr
nuptial *a.* шлюбний shliubnyi
nuptials *n.* весілля vesillia
nurse *v.t* вигодовувати дитину vyhodovuvaty dytynu
nurse *n.* медсестра medsestra
nursery *n.* розплідник rozplidnyk
nurture *v.t.* вирощувати vyroshchuvaty
nurture *n.* виховання vykhovannia
nut *n* горіх horikh
nutrition *n.* харчування kharchuvannia
nutritious *a.* живильний zhyvylnyi
nutritive *a.* поживний pozhyvnyi
nuzzle *v.* притиснутися prytysnutysia
nylon *n.* нейлон neilon
nymph *n.* німфа nimfa

O

oak *n.* дуб dub
oar *n.* весляр vesliar
oarsman *n.* майстер веслування maister vesluvannia
oasis *n.* оазис oazys
oat *n.* овес oves
oath *n.* присяга prysiaha
obduracy *n.* черствість cherstvist
obdurate *a.* заскнілий zasknilyi
obedience *n.* слухняність slukhnianist
obedient *a.* слухняний slukhnianyi
obeisance *n.* реверанс reverans
obesity *n.* ожиріння ozhyrinnia
obey *v.t.* коритися korytysia
obituary *a.* некролог nekroloh
object *v.t.* заперечувати zaperechuvaty

object *n.* об`єкт ob`iekt
objection *n.* несхвалення neskhvalennia
objectionable *a.* спірний spirnyi
objective *a.* об`єктивний obiektyvnyi
objective *n.* ціль tsil
oblation *n.* жертвопринесення zhertvoprynesennia
obligation *n.* облігація oblihatsiia
obligatory *a.* борговий borhovyi
oblige *v.t.* зобов'язувати zoboviazuvaty
oblique *a.* косий kosyi
obliterate *v.t.* викреслювати vykresliuvaty
obliteration *n.* облітерація obliteratsiia
oblivion *n.* забуття zabuttia
oblivious *a.* який не пам'ятає yakyi ne pamiataie
oblong *a.* довгастий dovhastyi
oblong *n.* довгастий предмет dovhastyi predmet
obnoxious *a.* неприємний nepryiemnyi
obscene *a.* хуліганський khulihanskyi
obscenity *n.* лайка laika
obscure *v.t.* затемнювати zatemniuvaty
obscure *a.* непомітний nepomitnyi
obscurity *n.* невідомість nevidomist
observance *n.* дотримання dotrymannia
observant *a.* спостережливий sposterezhlyvyi
observation *n.* спостереження sposterezhennia
observatory *n.* обсерваторія observatoriia

131

observe *v.t.* спостерігати sposterihaty
obsess *v.t.* гнітити hnityty
obsession *n.* нав'язлива ідея naviazlyva ideia
obsolete *a.* атрофований atrofovanyi
obstacle *n.* перепона perepona
obstinacy *n.* упертість upertist
obstinate *a.* впертий vpertyi
obstruct *v.t.* чинити обструкцію chynyty obstruktsiiu
obstruction *n.* непрохідність neprokhidnist
obstructive *a.* перешкоджаючий pereshkodzhaiuchyi
obtain *v.t.* досягати dosiahaty
obtainable *a.* доступний dostupnyi
obtuse *a.* тупий tupyi
obvious *a.* неприхований neprykhovanyi
occasion *v.t* давати привід davaty pryvid
occasion *n.* можливість mozhlyvist
occasional *a.* нерегулярний nerehuliarnyi
occasionally *adv.* час від часу chas vid chasu
occident *n.* країни Заходу krainy Zakhodu
occidental *a.* західний zakhidnyi
occult *a.* окультний okultnyi
occupancy *n.* заняття zaniattia
occupant *n.* пожилець pozhylets
occupation *n.* вид дияльності vyd dyialnosti
occupier *n.* окупант okupant
occupy *v.t.* захоплювати zakhopliuvaty
occur *v.i.* відбуватися vidbuvatysia

occurrence *n.* пригода pryhoda
ocean *n.* океан okean
oceanic *a.* океанічний okeanichnyi
octagon *n.* восьмикутник vosmykutnyk
octangular *a.* восьмикутний vosmykutnyi
octave *n.* октава oktava
October *n.* жовтень zhovten
octogenarian *n.* вісімдесятирічний старий visimdesiatyrichnyi staryi
octogenarian *a.* вісімдесятирічний visimdesiatyrichnyi
octroi *n.* міська митниця miska mytnytsia
ocular *a.* очний ochnyi
oculist *n.* окуліст okulist
odd *a.* непарний neparnyi
oddity *n.* дивина dyvyna
odds *n.* шанси shansy
ode *n.* ода oda
odious *a.* одіозний odioznyi
odium *n.* ганьба hanba
odorous *a.* запашний zapashnyi
odour *n.* запах zapakh
offence *n.* кривда kryvda
offend *v.t.* ображати obrazhaty
offender *n.* кривдник kryvdnyk
offensive *n* наступ nastup
offensive *a.* агресивний ahresyvnyi
offer *n* наведення navedennia
offer *v.t.* траплятися trapliatysia
offering *n.* підношення pidnoshennia
office *n.* офіс ofis
officer *n.* офіцер ofitser
official *n* чиновник chynovnyk
official *a.* офіційний ofitsiinyi
officially *adv.* офіційно ofitsiino

officiate *v.i.* виконувати обов'язки vykonuvaty oboviazky

officious *a.* офіціозний ofitsioznyi

offing *n.* узмор'я uzmoria

offset *n* зміщення zmishchennia

offset *v.t.* зводити баланс zvodyty balans

offshoot *n.* відгалуження vidhaluzhennia

offspring *n.* потомство potomstvo

oft *adv.* часто chasto

often *adv.* найчастіше naichastishe

ogle *v.t.* дивитися закоханими очима dyvytysia zakokhanymy ochyma

ogle *n* око oko

oil *v.t* змащувати zmashchuvaty

oil *n.* олія oliia

oily *a.* маслянистий maslianystyi

ointment *n.* мазь maz

old *a.* старий staryi

oligarchy *n.* олігархія oliharkhiia

olive *n.* оливковий olyvkovyi

olympiad *n.* олімпіада olimpiada

omega *n.* омега omeha

omelette *n.* омлет omlet

omen *n.* ознака oznaka

ominous *a.* загрозливий zahrozlyvyi

omission *n.* недогляд nedohliad

omit *v.t.* опустити opustyty

omnipotence *n.* всемогутність vsemohutnist

omnipotent *a.* всесильний vsesylnyi

omnipresence *n.* всюдисущість vsiudysushchist

omnipresent *a.* всюдисущий vsiudysushchyi

omniscience *n.* всевідання vsevidannia

omniscient *a.* всезнаючий vseznaiuchyi

on *adv.* на na

on *prep.* на na

once *adv.* раз raz

one *pron.* один odyn

one *a.* єдиний yedynyi

oneness *n.* тотожність totozhnist

onerous *a.* скрутний skrutnyi

onion *n.* цибуля tsybulia

on-looker *n.* глядач hliadach

only *conj.* лише lyshe

only *adv.* тільки tilky

only *a.* єдиний yedynyi

onomatopoeia *n.* звуконаслідування zvukonasliduvannia

onrush *n.* натиск natysk

onset *n.* натиск natysk

onslaught *n.* стрімка атака strimka ataka

onus *n.* тягар tiahar

onward *a.* поступальний postupalnyi

onwards *adv.* далі dali

ooze *v.i.* виділятися vydiliatysia

ooze *n.* липка грязь lypka hriaz

opacity *n.* непрозорість neprozorist

opal *n.* опал opal

opaque *a.* непрозорий neprozoryi

open *v.t.* відкрити vidkryty

open *a.* розкритий rozkrytyi

opening *n.* щілина shchilyna

openly *adv.* відкрито vidkryto

opera *n.* опера opera

operate *v.t.* діяти diiaty

operation *n.* операція operatsiia

operative *a.* оперативний operatyvnyi

operator *n.* оператор operator

opine *v.t.* висловлювати думку vyslovliuvaty dumku

opinion *n.* думка dumka
opium *n.* опіум opium
opponent *n.* опонент oponent
opportune *a.* сприятливий spryiatlyvyi
opportunism *n.* опортунізм oportunizm
opportunity *n.* перспектива perspektyva
oppose *v.t.* виступати проти vystupaty proty
opposite *a.* протилежний protylezhnyi
opposition *n.* опозиція opozytsiia
oppress *v.t.* гнітити hnityty
oppression *n.* пригнічення pryhnichennia
oppressive *a.* гнітючий hnitiuchyi
oppressor *n.* гнобитель hnobytel
opt *v.i.* робити вибір robyty vybir
optic *a.* оптичний optychnyi
optician *n.* оптик optyk
optimism *n.* оптимізм optymizm
optimist *n.* оптиміст optymist
optimistic *a.* оптимістичний optymistychnyi
optimum *a* оптимальний optymalnyi
optimum *n.* оптимум optymum
option *n.* опція optsiia
optional *a.* необов'язковий neoboviazkovyi
opulence *n.* достаток dostatok
opulent *a.* багатий bahatyi
oracle *n.* оракул orakul
oracular *a.* догматичний dohmatychnyi
oral *a.* усний usnyi
orally *adv.* усно usno
orange *a* помаранчевий pomaranchevyi
orange *n.* апельсин apelsyn
oration *n.* благання blahannia

orator *n.* оратор orator
oratorical *a.* ораторський oratorskyi
oratory *n.* ораторське мистецтво oratorske mystetstvo
orb *n.* шар shar
orbit *n.* орбіта orbita
orchard *n.* фруктовий сад fruktovyi sad
orchestra *n.* оркестр orkestr
orchestral *a.* оркестровий orkestrovyi
ordeal *n.* випробування vyprobuvannia
order *v.t* наказувати nakazuvaty
order *n.* порядок poriadok
orderly *n.* прибиральник вулиць prybyralnyk vulyts
orderly *a.* упорядкований uporiadkovanyi
ordinance *n.* указ ukaz
ordinarily *adv.* зазвичай zazvychai
ordinary *a.* посередній poserednii
ordnance *n.* артилерія artyleriia
ore *n.* руда ruda
organ *n.* орган orhan
organic *a.* органічний orhanichnyi
organism *n.* організм orhanizm
organization *n.* організація orhanizatsiia
organize *v.t.* організувати orhanizuvaty
orient *v.t.* орієнтувати oriientuvaty
orient *n.* схід skhid
oriental *n* житель Сходу zhytel Skhodu
oriental *a.* східний skhidnyi
orientate *v.t.* орієнтуватися oriientuvatysia
origin *n.* джерело dzherelo
original *n* оригінал oryhinal

original *a.* початковий pochatkovyi
originality *n.* оригінальність oryhinalnist
originate *v.t.* започатковувати zapochatkovuvaty
originator *n.* творець tvorets
ornament *n.* орнамент ornament
ornament *v.t.* оздоблювати ozdobliuvaty
ornamental *a.* декоративний dekoratyvnyi
ornamentation *n.* оздоблення ozdoblennia
orphan *v.t* робити сиротою robyty syrotoiu
orphan *n.* сирота syrota
orphanage *n.* дитячий будинок dytiachyi budynok
orthodox *a.* ортодоксальний ortodoksalnyi
orthodoxy *n.* ортодоксальність ortodoksalnist
oscillate *v.i.* гойдатися hoidatysia
oscillation *n.* вібрація vibratsiia
ossify *v.t.* костеніти kostenity
ostracize *v.t.* піддавати остракізму piddavaty ostrakizmu
ostrich *n.* страус straus
other *a.* додатковий dodatkovyi
other *pron.* інакший inakshyi
otherwise *conj.* або ж abo zh
otherwise *adv.* в іншому випадку v inshomu vypadku
otter *n.* видра vydra
ottoman *n.* тахта takhta
ounce *n.* унція untsiia
our *pron.* наш nash
oust *v.t.* скидати skydaty
out *adv.* зовні zovni
out-balance *v.t.* перевершувати perevershuvaty

outbid *v.t.* перебити ціну perebyty tsinu
outbreak *n.* спалах spalakh
outburst *n.* спалах spalakh
outcast *a* знедолений znedolenyi
outcast *n.* вигнанець vyhnanets
outcome *n.* наслідок naslidok
outcry *n.* вигук vyhuk
outdated *a.* застарілий zastarilyi
outdo *v.t.* перевершити perevershyty
outdoor *a.* поза межами poza mezhamy
outer *a.* зовнішній zovnishnii
outfit *n.* обмундирування obmundyruvannia
outfit *v.t* обмундирувати obmundyruvaty
outgrow *v.t.* виростати з vyrostaty z
outhouse *n.* флігель flihel
outing *n.* прогулянка за мужі міста prohulianka za muzhi mista
outlandish *a.* дивовижний dyvovyzhnyi
outlaw *v.t* оголошувати поза законом oholoshuvaty poza zakonom
outlaw *n.* ізгой izhoi
outline *v.t.* окреслити okreslyty
outline *n.* обрис obrys
outlive *v.t.* пережити perezhyty
outlook *n.* плани на майбутнє plany na maibutnie
outmoded *a.* старомодний staromodnyi
outnumber *v.t.* перевершувати чисельно perevershuvaty chyselno
outpatient *n.* амбулаторний хворий ambulatornyi khvoryi
outpost *n.* аванпост avanpost

output *n.* зникнення znyknennia
outrage *n.* наруга naruha
outrage *v.t.* порушувати закон porushuvaty zakon
outright *a* цілеспрямований tsilespriamovanyi
outright *adv.* наповал napoval
outrun *v.t.* випереджати vyperedzhaty
outset *n.* гирло шахти hyrlo shakhty
outshine *v.t.* затьмарювати zatmariuvaty
outside *adv* за межами za mezhamy
outside *n* лицьова сторона lytsova storona
outside *prep* назовні nazovni
outside *a.* крайній krainii
outsider *n.* стороння людина storonnia liudyna
outsize *a.* нестандартний nestandartnyi
outskirts *n.* околиця okolytsia
outspoken *a.* відвертий vidvertyi
outstanding *a.* знаменитий znamenytyi
outward *adv* назовні nazovni
outward *a.* поверхневий poverkhnevyi
outwardly *adv.* зовні zovni
outwards *adv* за межі za mezhi
outweigh *v.t.* переважувати perevazhuvaty
outwit *v.t.* перехитрити perekhytryty
oval *n* футбольний м'яч futbolnyi miach
oval *a.* овальний ovalnyi
ovary *n.* яєчник yaiechnyk
ovation *n.* овація ovatsiia
oven *n.* піч pich
over *n* пух pukh

over *adv* через cherez
over *prep.* через cherez
overact *v.t.* перегравати perehravaty
overall *a* граничний hranychnyi
overall *n.* спецодяг spetsodiah
overawe *v.t.* вселяти шанобливий страх vseliaty shanoblyvyi strakh
overboard *adv.* за борт za bort
overburden *v.t.* переобтяжувати pereobtiazhuvaty
overcast *a.* хмарність khmarnist
overcharge *n* перезаряд perezariad
overcharge *v.t.* перезаряджати perezariadzhaty
overcoat *n.* шинель shynel
overcome *v.t.* подолати podolaty
overdo *v.t.* перестаратися perestaratysia
overdose *v.t.* прийняти дуже велику дозу pryiniaty duzhe velyku dozu
overdose *n.* передозування peredozuvannia
overdraft *n.* овердрафт overdraft
overdraw *v.t.* перевитрачати perevytrachaty
overdue *a.* прострочений prostrochenyi
overhaul *n.* капітальний ремонт kapitalnyi remont
overhaul *v.t.* ремонтувати remontuvaty
overhear *v.t.* підслуховувати pidslukhovuvaty
overjoyed *a* дуже задоволений duzhe zadovolenyi
overlap *n* перекриття perekryttia
overlap *v.t.* перекривати perekryvaty
overleaf *adv.* на звороті na zvoroti

overload *n* перевантаження perevantazhennia
overload *v.t.* перевантажувати perevantazhuvaty
overlook *v.t.* упускати з уваги upuskaty z uvahy
overnight *a* що триває всю ніч shcho tryvaie vsiu nich
overnight *adv.* всю ніч vsiu nich
overpower *v.t.* пересилювати peresyliuvaty
overrate *v.t.* переоцінювати pereotsiniuvaty
overrule *v.t.* пересилювати peresyliuvaty
overrun *v.t* переливатися через край perelyvatysia cherez krai
oversee *v.t.* здійснявати нагляд zdiisniavaty nahliad
overseer *n.* наглядач nahliadach
overshadow *v.t.* затінювати zatiniuvaty
oversight *n.* нагляд nahliad
overt *a.* явний yavnyi
overtake *v.t.* наздогнати nazdohnaty
overthrow *n* повалення povalennia
overthrow *v.t.* перекидати perekydaty
overtime *n* понаднормовий час ponadnormovyi chas
overtime *adv.* понаднормовий ponadnormovyi
overture *n.* увертюра uvertiura
overwhelm *v.t.* сповнювати spovniuvaty
overwork *n.* перевтома perevtoma
overwork *v.i.* перевтомлюватися perevtomliuvatysia
owe *v.t* заборгувати zaborhuvaty
owl *n.* сова sova

own *v.t.* допускати dopuskaty
own *a.* власний vlasnyi
owner *n.* власник vlasnyk
ownership *n.* власність vlasnist
ox *n.* бик byk
oxygen *n.* кисень kysen
oyster *n.* устриця ustrytsia

pace *v.i.* ходити khodyty
pace *n* темп temp
pacific *a.* миролюбний myroliubnyi
pacify *v.t.* умиротворяти umyrotvoriaty
pack *n.* стос stos
pack *v.t.* упаковувати upakovuvaty
package *n.* упакування upakuvannia
packet *n.* пакет paket
packing *n.* упаковка upakovka
pact *n.* пакт pakt
pad *v.t.* набивати nabyvaty
pad *n.* подушка podushka
padding *n.* оббивка obbyvka
paddle *n* весло veslo
paddle *v.i.* гребти веслом hrebty veslom
paddy *n.* муляр muliar
page *v.t.* нумерувати сторінки numeruvaty storinky
page *n.* сторінка storinka
pageant *n.* видовище vydovyshche
pageantry *n.* пишність pyshnist
pagoda *n.* пагода pahoda
pail *n.* цеберка tseberka
pain *v.t.* хворіти khvority
pain *n.* страждання strazhdannia
painful *a.* хворобливий khvoroblyvyi

painstaking *a.* кропіткий kropitkyi
paint *v.t.* фарбувати farbuvaty
paint *n.* фарба farba
painter *n.* художник khudozhnyk
painting *n.* живопис zhyvopys
pair *n.* пара para
pair *v.t.* розташовуватися roztashovuvatysia
pal *n.* приятель pryiatel
palace *n.* палац palats
palanquin *n.* паланкін palankin
palatable *a.* смачний smachnyi
palatal *a.* піднебінний pidnebinnyi
palate *n.* піднебіння pidnebinnia
palatial *a.* палацовий palatsovyi
pale *a* блідий blidyi
pale *v.i.* блідіти blidnuty
pale *n.* кіл kil
palette *n.* палітра palitra
palm *n.* долонь dolon
palm *n.* пальма palma
palm *v.t.* підкидати pidkydaty
palmist *n.* хіромант khiromant
palmistry *n.* хіромантія khiromantiia
palpable *a.* відчутний vidchutnyi
palpitate *v.i.* тріпотіти tripotity
palpitation *n.* серцебиття sertsebyttia
palsy *n.* стан повної безпорадності stan povnoi bezporadnosti
paltry *a.* жалюгідний zhaliuhidnyi
pamper *v.t.* балувати baluvaty
pamphlet *n.* памфлет pamflet
pamphleteer *n.* памфлетист pamfletyst
panacea *n.* панацея panatseia
pandemonium *n.* стовпотворіння stovpotvorinnia
pane *n.* віконне скло vikonne sklo
panegyric *n.* панегірик panehiryk

panel *v.t.* обшивати панелями obshyvaty paneliamy
panel *n.* панель panel
pang *n.* гострий біль hostryi bil
panic *n.* паніка panika
panorama *n.* панорама panorama
pant *n.* пихтіння pykhtinnia
pant *v.i.* тіпатися tipatysia
pantaloon *n.* рейтузи reituzy
pantheism *n.* пантеїзм panteizm
pantheist *n.* пантеїст panteist
panther *n.* пантера pantera
pantomime *n.* пантоміма pantomima
pantry *n.* буфетна bufetna
papacy *n.* папство papstvo
papal *a.* папський papskyi
paper *n.* папір papir
par *n.* номінал nominal
parable *n.* притча prytcha
parachute *n.* парашут parashut
parachutist *n.* парашутист parashutyst
parade *v.t.* хизуватися khyzuvatysia
parade *n.* парад parad
paradise *n.* рай rai
paradox *n.* парадокс paradoks
paradoxical *a.* парадоксальний paradoksalnyi
paraffin *n.* парафін parafin
paragon *n.* парагон parahon
paragraph *n.* пункт punkt
parallel *v.t.* порівнювати porivniuvaty
parallel *a.* паралельний paralelnyi
parallelism *n.* паралелізм paralelizm
parallelogram *n.* паралелограм paralelohram
paralyse *v.t.* паралізувати paralizuvaty

paralysis *n.* параліч paralich
paralytic *a.* паралітичний
  paralitychnyi
paramount *n.* першорядний
  pershoriadnyi
paramour *n.* коханка kokhanka
paraphernalia *n.* супровідне
  майно suprovidne maino
paraphrase *v.t.* переказувати
  perekazuvaty
paraphrase *n.* парафраз parafraz
parasite *n.* паразит parazyt
parcel *v.t.* загортати в пакет
  zahortaty v paket
parcel *n.* посилка posylka
parch *v.t.* підсушувати
  pidsushuvaty
pardon *n.* помилування
  pomyluvannia
pardon *v.t.* помилувати
  pomyluvaty
pardonable *a.* простимий
  prostymyi
parent *n.* названий батько
  nazvanyi batko
parentage *n.* батьківство
  batkivstvo
parental *a.* батьківський
  batkivskyi
parenthesis *n.* кругла дужка
  kruhla duzhka
parish *n.* прихід prykhid
parity *n.* паритет parytet
park *n.* парк park
park *v.t.* паркувати parkuvaty
parlance *n.* манера говорити
  manera hovoryty
parley *v.i* вести переговори vesty
  perehovory
parley *n.* переговори perehovory
parliament *n.* парламент
  parlament

parliamentarian *n.*
  парламентарій parlamentarii
parliamentary *a.* парламентський
  parlamentskyi
parlour *n.* кабінет kabinet
parody *v.t.* пародіювати
  parodiiuvaty
parody *n.* пародія parodiia
parole *v.t.* умовне звільнення
  ув'язненого з в'язниці umovne
  zvilnennia uviaznenoho z
  viaznytsi
parole *n.* слово честі slovo chesti
parricide *n.* батьковбивство
  batkovbyvstvo
parrot *n.* папуга papuha
parry *n.* парирування
  paryruvannia
parry *v.t.* парирувати paryruvaty
parson *n.* священик sviashchenyk
part *v.t.* відокремлювати
  vidokremliuvaty
part *n.* частина chastyna
partake *v.i.* брати участь braty
  uchast
partial *a.* частковий chastkovyi
partiality *n.* упередженість
  uperedzhenist
participant *n.* учасник uchasnyk
participate *v.i.* розподіляти
  rozpodiliaty
participation *n.* участь uchast
particle *a.* префікс prefiks
particular *n.* приватність
  pryvatnist
particular *a.* винятковий
  vyniatkovyi
partisan *a.* партизанів partyzaniv
partisan *n.* партизанський
  partyzanskyi
partition *v.t.* розділяти rozdiliaty
partition *n.* частина chastyna
partner *n.* партнер partner

partnership *n.* партнерство
partnerstvo
party *n.* прийом гостей pryiom
hostei
pass *n* пропуск propusk
pass *v.i.* проходити prokhodyty
passage *n.* проходження
prokhodzhennia
passenger *n.* пасажир pasazhyr
passion *n.* вибух почуттів vybukh
pochuttiv
passionate *a.* пристрасний
prystrasnyi
passive *a.* пасивний pasyvnyi
passport *n.* паспорт pasport
past *n.* життя людини zhyttia
liudyny
past *prep.* повз povz
past *a.* минулий mynulyi
paste *v.t.* клеїти kleity
paste *n.* паста pasta
pastel *n.* пастельний pastelnyi
pastime *n.* приємне проведення
часу pryiemne provedennia
chasu
pastoral *a.* пасторальний
pastoralnyi
pasture *v.t.* паша pasha
pasture *n.* пасовищі pasovyshchi
pat *n* поплескування
popleskuvannia
pat *adv* своєчасно svoiechasno
pat *v.t.* шльопати shlopaty
patch *n* клапоть klapot
patch *v.t.* латати lataty
patent *n* патент patent
patent *v.t.* патентувати
patentuvaty
patent *a.* патентований
patentovanyi
paternal *a.* по батькові po batkovi
path *n.* шлях shliakh

pathetic *a.* патетичний
patetychnyi
pathos *n.* пафос pafos
patience *n.* терпіння terpinnia
patient *n* пацієнт patsiient
patient *a.* терплячий terpliachyi
patricide *n.* вбивство батька
vbyvstvo batka
patrimony *n.* спадкоємне майно
spadkoiemne maino
patriot *n.* патріот patriot
patriotic *a.* патріотичний
patriotychnyi
patriotism *n.* патріотизм
patriotyzm
patrol *n* патруль patrul
patrol *v.i.* патрулювати
patruliuvaty
patron *n.* покровитель pokrovytel
patronage *n.* патронаж patronazh
patronize *v.t.* протегувати
protehuvaty
pattern *n.* шаблон shablon
paucity *n.* брак brak
pauper *n.* злидар zlydar
pause *v.i.* робити паузу robyty
pauzu
pause *n.* пауза pauza
pave *v.t.* мостити mostyty
pavement *n.* тротуар trotuar
pavilion *n.* павільйон pavilion
paw *v.t.* торкати лапою torkaty
lapoiu
paw *n.* лапа lapa
pay *n* оплата oplata
pay *v.t.* платити platyty
payable *a.* до сплати do splaty
payee *n.* одержувач платежу
oderzhuvach platezhu
payment *n.* сплата splata
pea *n.* горох horokh
peace *n.* мир myr
peaceable *a.* спокійний spokiinyi

peaceful *a.* мирний myrnyi
peach *n.* персик persyk
peacock *n.* павич pavych
peahen *n.* пава pava
peak *n.* пік pik
pear *n.* груша hrusha
pearl *n.* перлина perlyna
peasant *n.* селянин selianyn
peasantry *n.* селянство selianstvo
pebble *n.* галька halka
peck *v.i.* клювати kliuvaty
peck *n.* клювок kliuvok
peculiar *a.* своєрідний svoieridnyi
peculiarity *n.* особливість osoblyvist
pecuniary *a.* грошовий hroshovyi
pedagogue *n.* педагог pedahoh
pedagogy *n.* педагогіка pedahohika
pedal *v.t.* натискати педаль natyskaty pedal
pedal *n.* педаль pedal
pedant *n.* педант pedant
pedantic *n.* педантичний pedantychnyi
pedantry *n.* педантичність pedantychnist
pedestal *n.* п'єдестал piedestal
pedestrian *n.* пішохід pishokhid
pedigree *n.* родовід rodovid
peel *n.* шкірка shkirka
peel *v.t.* обдирати obdyraty
peep *n* швидкий погляд shvydkyi pohliad
peep *v.i.* підглядати pidhliadaty
peer *n.* рівний rivnyi
peerless *a.* неперевершуваний nperevershuvanyi
peg *v.t.* прикріплювати кілочком prykripliuvaty kilochkom
peg *n.* кілочок kilochok
pelf *n.* гроші hroshi

pell-mell *adv.* упереміш uperemish
pen *v.t.* творити tvoryty
pen *n.* ручка ruchka
penal *a.* карний karnyi
penalize *v.t.* робити карним robyty karnym
penalty *n.* штраф shtraf
pencil *v.t.* малювати олівцем maliuvaty olivtsem
pencil *n.* олівець olivets
pending *prep.* до do
pending *a* який розглядається yakyi rozhliadaietsia
pendulum *n.* маятник maiatnyk
penetrate *v.t.* проникати pronykaty
penetration *n.* прорив proryv
penis *n.* статевий член statevyi chlen
penniless *a.* без гроша bez hrosha
penny *n.* пенні penni
pension *v.t.* призначати пенсію pryznachaty pensiiu
pension *n.* пенсія pensiia
pensioner *n.* пенсіонер pensioner
pensive *a.* замислений zamyslenyi
pentagon *n.* п'ятикутник piatykutnyk
peon *n.* піхотинець pikhotynets
people *v.t.* заселяти zaseliaty
people *n.* люди liudy
pepper *n.* перець perets
pepper *v.t.* перчити perchyty
per *prep.* згідно zhidno
per cent *adv.* на сотню na sotniu
perambulator *n.* дитяча коляска dytiacha koliaska
perceive *v.t.* сприймати spryimaty
percentage *n.* відсоток vidsotok
perceptible *adj* помітно pomitno

perception *n.* сприйняття
spryiniattia
perceptive *a.* сприйнятливий
spryiniatlyvyi
perch *v.i.* влаштуватися
vlashtuvatysia
perch *n.* окунь okun
perennial *n.* багаторічна рослина
bahatorichna roslyna
perennial *a.* нев'янучий
nevianuchyi
perfect *a.* досконалий doskonalyi
perfect *v.t.* удосконалювати
udoskonaliuvaty
perfection *n.* удосконалення
udoskonalennia
perfidy *n.* віроломство
virolomstvo
perforate *v.t.* перфорувати
perforuvaty
perforce *adv.* волею-неволею
voleiu-nevoleiu
perform *v.t.* виконувати
vykonuvaty
performance *n.* продуктивність
produktyvnist
performer *n.* виконавець
vykonavets
perfume *n.* духи dukhy
perfume *v.t.* напахувати
парфумами napakhuvaty
parfumamy
perhaps *adv.* можливо mozhlyvo
peril *v.t.* піддавати небезпеці
piddavaty nebezpetsi
peril *n.* ризик ryzyk
perilous *a.* згубний zhubnyi
period *n.* період period
periodical *a.* періодичний
periodychnyi
periodical *n.* періодичне видання
periodychne vydannia
periphery *n.* периферія peryferiia

perish *v.i.* гинути hynuty
perishable *a.* швидкопсувний
shvydkopsuvnyi
perjure *v.i.* лжесвідчити
lzhesvidchyty
perjury *n.* лжесвідчення
lzhesvidchennia
permanence *n.* сталість stalist
permanent *a.* залишковий
zalyshkovyi
permissible *a.* дозволений
dozvolenyi
permission *n.* дозвіл dozvil
permit *v.t.* дозволити dozvolyty
permit *n.* перепустка perepustka
permutation *n.* переміщення
peremishchennia
pernicious *a.* шкідливий
shkidlyvyi
perpendicular *n.* перпендикуляр
perpendykuliar
perpendicular *a.*
перпендикулярний
perpendykuliarnyi
perpetual *a.* нескінченний
neskinchennyi
perpetuate *v.t.* увічнювати
uvichniuvaty
perplex *v.t.* спантеличувати
spantelychuvaty
perplexity *n.* ускладнення
uskladnennia
persecute *v.t.* впіддавати
гонінням vpiddavaty honinniam
persecution *n.* цькування
tskuvannia
perseverance *n.* наполегливість
napolehlyvist
persevere *v.i.* упиратися
upyratysia
persist *v.i.* зберігатися
zberihatysia

persistence *n.* завзятість zavziatist
persistent *a.* стійкий stiikyi
person *n.* людина liudyna
personage *n.* персонаж personazh
personal *a.* персональний personalnyi
personality *n.* особистість osobystist
personification *n.* персоніфікація personifikatsiia
personify *v.t.* уособлювати uosobliuvaty
personnel *n.* персонал personal
perspective *n.* вид vyd
perspiration *n.* піт pit
perspire *v.i.* потіти potity
persuade *v.t.* відмовити vidmovyty
persuasion *n.* переконання perekonannia
pertain *v.i.* ставитися stavytysia
pertinent *a.* доречний dorechnyi
perturb *v.t.* хвилювати khvyliuvaty
perusal *n.* прочитання prochytannia
peruse *v.t.* переглянути perehlianuty
pervade *v.t.* просочувати prosochuvaty
perverse *a.* збочений zbochenyi
perversion *n.* збочення zbochennia
perversity *n.* збоченість zbochenist
pervert *v.t.* збоченець zbochenets
pessimism *n.* песимізм pesymizm
pessimist *n.* песиміст pesymist
pessimistic *a.* песимістичний pesymistychnyi
pest *n.* шкідник shkidnyk

pesticide *n.* пестицид pestytsyd
pestilence *n.* пошесть poshest
pet *v.t.* обійматися obiimatysia
pet *n.* домашня тварина domashnia tvaryna
petal *n.* пелюстка peliustka
petition *v.t.* подавати прохання podavaty prokhannia
petition *n.* клопотання klopotannia
petitioner *n.* прохач prokhach
petrol *n.* бензин benzyn
petroleum *n.* нафта nafta
petticoat *n.* нижня спідниця nyzhnia spidnytsia
petty *a.* дрібний dribnyi
petulance *n.* дратівливість drativlyvist
petulant *a.* заухвалий zaukhvalyi
phantom *n.* фантом fantom
pharmacy *n.* аптека apteka
phase *n.* фаза faza
phenomenal *a.* феноменальний fenomenalnyi
phenomenon *n.* явище yavyshche
phial *n.* фіал fial
philanthropic *a.* філантропічний filantropichnyi
philanthropist *n.* філантроп filantrop
philanthropy *n.* благодійність blahodiinist
philological *a.* філологічний filolohichnyi
philologist *n.* філолог filoloh
philology *n.* філологія filolohiia
philosopher *n.* філософ filosof
philosophical *a.* філософський filosofskyi
philosophy *n.* філософія filosofiia
phone *n.* телефон telefon

phonetic *a.* фонетичний fonetychnyi
phonetics *n.* фонетика fonetyka
phosphate *n.* фосфат fosfat
phosphorus *n.* фосфор fosfor
photo *n* фото foto
photograph *n* фотографія fotohrafiia
photograph *v.t.* фотографувати fotohrafuvaty
photographer *n.* фотограф fotohraf
photographic *a.* фотографічний fotohrafichnyi
photography *n.* фотографування fotohrafuvannia
phrase *v.t.* висловити vyslovyty
phrase *n.* фраза fraza
phraseology *n.* фразеологія frazeolohiia
physic *v.t.* дати ліки daty liky
physic *n.* лікування likuvannia
physical *a.* фізичний fizychnyi
physician *n.* терапевт terapevt
physicist *n.* фізик fizyk
physics *n.* фізика fizyka
physiognomy *n.* фізіономія fizionomiia
physique *n.* статура statura
pianist *n.* піаніст pianist
piano *n.* піаніно pianino
pick *n.* кирка kyrka
pick *v.t.* відбирати vidbyraty
picket *v.t.* пікетувати piketuvaty
picket *n.* пікет piket
pickle *v.t* маринувати marynuvaty
pickle *n.* соління solinnia
picnic *v.i.* брати участь у пікніку braty uchast u pikniku
picnic *n.* пікнік piknik
pictorical *a.* ілюстрований iliustrovanyi
picture *v.t.* малювати maliuvaty

picture *n.* картина kartyna
picturesque *a.* мальовничий malovnychyi
piece *v.t.* з'єднувати ziednuvaty
piece *n.* шматок shmatok
pierce *v.t.* проколювати prokoliuvaty
piety *n.* благочестя blahochestia
pig *n.* свиня svynia
pigeon *n.* голуб holub
pigmy *n.* пігмей pihmei
pile *v.t.* навалювати navaliuvaty
pile *n.* паля palia
piles *n.* геморой hemoroi
pilfer *v.t.* красти krasty
pilgrim *n.* паломник palomnyk
pilgrimage *n.* паломництво palomnytstvo
pill *n.* пілюля piliulia
pillar *n.* стовп stovp
pillow *v.t.* служити подушкою sluzhyty podushkoiu
pillow *n* підкладка pidkladka
pilot *v.t.* пілотувати pilotuvaty
pilot *n.* досвідчений поводир dosvidchenyi povodyr
pimple *n.* вугор vuhor
pin *v.t.* приколювати prykoliuvaty
pin *n.* шпилька shpylka
pinch *n.* щіпка shchipka
pinch *v.t.* щипати shchypaty
pine *v.i.* нудитися nudytysia
pine *n.* сосна sosna
pineapple *n.* ананас ananas
pink *a* рожевий rozhevyi
pink *n.* рожевий rozhevyi
pinkish *a.* блідо-рожевий blido-rozhevyi
pinnacle *n.* вершина vershyna
pioneer *v.t.* прокладати шлях prokladaty shliakh
pioneer *n.* піонер pioner

pious *a.* благочестивий blahochestyvyi
pipe *v.i* пищати pyshchaty
pipe *n.* труба truba
piquant *a.* пікантний pikantnyi
piracy *n.* піратство piratstvo
pirate *v.t* розбійничати rozbiinychaty
pirate *n.* пірат pirat
pistol *n.* пістолет pistolet
piston *n.* поршень porshen
pit *v.t.* складати в яму skladaty v yamu
pit *n.* яма yama
pitch *v.t.* качати kachaty
pitch *n.* крок krok
pitcher *n.* брущатка brushchatka
piteous *a.* жалібний zhalibnyi
pitfall *n.* вибоїна vyboina
pitiable *a.* жалюгідний zhaliuhidnyi
pitiful *a.* сумний sumnyi
pitiless *a.* безжалісний bezzhalisnyi
pitman *n.* шатун shatun
pittance *n.* жалюгідні гроші zhaliuhidni hroshi
pity *v.t.* жаліти zhality
pity *n.* жалість zhalist
pivot *v.t.* перетворюватися peretvoriuvatysia
pivot *n.* стрижень stryzhen
place *v.t.* поміщати pomishchaty
place *n.* місце mistse
placid *a.* спокійний spokiinyi
plague *v.t.* насилати нещастя nasylaty neshchastia
plague *n.* чума chuma
plain *a.* невигадливий nevyhadlyvyi
plain *n.* рівнина rivnyna
plaintiff *n.* позивач pozyvach
plan *v.t.* планувати planuvaty

plan *n.* план plan
plane *v.t.* планерувати planeruvaty
plane *a.* плоский ploskyi
plane *n* проекція proektsiia
plane *n.* літак litak
planet *n.* планета planeta
planetary *a.* планетарний planetarnyi
plank *v.t.* настилати дошки nastylaty doshky
plank *n.* дошка doshka
plant *n.* рослина roslyna
plant *v.t.* саджати sadzhaty
plantain *n.* подорожник podorozhnyk
plantation *n.* плантація plantatsiia
plaster *v.t.* штукатурити shtukaturyty
plaster *n.* штукатурка shtukaturka
plate *n.* плита plyta
plate *v.t.* покривати металом pokryvaty metalom
plateau *n.* плато plato
platform *n.* платформа platforma
platonic *a.* платонічний platonichnyi
platoon *n.* взвод vzvod
play *v.i.* бавитися bavytysia
play *n.* спектакль spektakl
play card *n.* гральна карта hralna karta
player *n.* учасник гри uchasnyk hry
plea *n.* благання blahannia
plead *v.i.* виступати в суді vystupaty v sudi
pleader *n.* захисник zakhysnyk
pleasant *a.* приємний pryiemnyi
pleasantry *n.* жартівливість zhartivlyvist
please *v.i.* подобатися podobatysia

pleasure *n.* задоволення zadovolennia
plebiscite *n.* плебісцит plebistsyt
pledge *v.t.* запевняти zapevniaty
pledge *n.* тост tost
plenty *n.* надмір nadmir
plight *n.* заручини zaruchyny
plod *v.i.* тягтися tiahtysia
plot *v.t.* плести інтриги plesty intryhy
plot *n.* ділянка dilianka
plough *v.t.* орати oraty
plough *n.* плуг pluh
ploughman *n.* орач orach
pluck *n* смикання smykannia
pluck *v.t.* скубти skubty
plug *v.t.* затикати zatykaty
plug *n.* заглушка zahlushka
plum *n.* слива slyva
plumber *n.* водопровідник vodoprovidnyk
plunder *n* грабіж hrabizh
plunder *v.t.* пограбувати pohrabuvaty
plunge *n* пірнання pirnannia
plunge *v.t.* поринати porynaty
plural *a.* строкатий strokatyi
plurality *n.* сумісництво sumisnytstvo
plus *n* плюс plius
plus *a.* позитивний pozytyvnyi
ply *n* шар shar
ply *v.t.* засипати zasypaty
pneumonia *n.* пневмонія pnevmoniia
pocket *v.t.* привласнити pryvlasnyty
pocket *n.* кишеня kyshenia
pod *n.* стручок struchok
poem *n.* вірш virsh
poesy *n.* поезія poeziia
poet *n.* поет poet
poetaster *n.* віршомаз virshomaz

poetess *n.* поетеса poetesa
poetic *a.* поетичний poetychnyi
poetics *n.* поетика poetyka
poetry *n.* поетичність poetychnist
poignancy *n.* пікантність pikantnist
poignant *a.* пікантний pikantnyi
point *v.t.* указувати ukazuvaty
point *n.* точка tochka
poise *n* врівноваженість vrivnovazhenist
poise *v.t.* врівноважувати vrivnovazhuvaty
poison *v.t.* отруїти otruity
poison *n.* отрута otruta
poisonous *a.* отруйний otruinyi
poke *n.* тичок tychok
poke *v.t.* штовхати shtovkhaty
polar *n.* полярний poliarnyi
pole *n.* полюс polius
police *n.* поліція politsiia
policeman *n.* поліцейський politseiskyi
policy *n.* політика polityka
polish *n* поліровка polirovka
polish *v.t.* полірувати poliruvaty
polite *a.* витончений vytonchenyi
politeness *n.* чемність chemnist
politic *a.* політичний politychnyi
political *a.* пов'язаний з політикою poviazanyi z politykoiu
politician *n.* політик polityk
politics *n.* політика polityka
polity *n.* державний устрій derzhavnyi ustrii
poll *v.t.* підраховувати голоси pidrakhovuvaty holosy
poll *n.* голосування holosuvannia
pollen *n.* пилок pylok
pollute *v.t.* поганити pohanyty
pollution *n.* забруднення zabrudnennia

polo *n.* поло polo
polygamous *a.* полігамний polihamnyi
polygamy *n.* полігамія polihamiia
polyglot1 *n.* поліглот polihlot
polyglot2 *a.* багатомовний bahatomovnyi
polytechnic *n.* політехнікум politekhnikum
polytechnic *a.* політехнічний politekhnichnyi
polytheism *n.* багатобожжя bahatobozhzhia
polytheist *n.* політеїст politeist
polytheistic *a.* політеїстичний politeistychnyi
pomp *n.* пишнота pyshnota
pomposity *n.* помпезність pompeznist
pompous *a.* помпезний pompeznyi
pond *n.* ставок stavok
ponder *v.t.* зважувати zvazhuvaty
pony *n.* поні poni
poor *a.* бідний bidnyi
pop *v.i.* плескати pleskaty
pop *n* популярний populiarnyi
pope *n.* ляскання liaskannia
poplar *n.* тополя topolia
poplin *n.* поплін poplin
populace *n.* простий народ prostyi narod
popular *a.* популярний populiarnyi
popularity *n.* популярність populiarnist
popularize *v.t.* популяризувати populiaryzuvaty
populate *v.t.* населяти naseliaty
population *n.* населення naselennia
populous *a.* густонаселений hustonaselenyi

porcelain *n.* фарфор farfor
porch *n.* ганок hanok
pore *n.* пори pory
pork *n.* свинина svynyna
porridge *n.* вівсянка vivsianka
port *n.* порт port
portable *a.* переносний perenosnyi
portage *n.* провезення provezennia
portal *n.* портал portal
portend *v.t.* передвіщати peredvishchaty
porter *n.* провідник providnyk
portfolio *n.* портфель portfel
portico *n.* портик portyk
portion *v.t.* ділити dilyty
portion *n* частина chastyna
portrait *n.* опис opys
portraiture *n.* портретний живопис portretnyi zhyvopys
portray *v.t.* малювати портрет maliuvaty portret
portrayal *n* портрет portret
pose *n.* поза poza
pose *v.i.* позувати pozuvaty
position *n.* позиція pozytsiia
position *v.t.* визначати місцезнаходження vyznachaty mistseznakhodzhennia
positive *a.* позитивний pozytyvnyi
possess *v.t.* оволодівати ovolodivaty
possession *n.* залежна теріторія zalezhna teritoriia
possibility *n.* перспективи perspektyvy
possible *a.* імовірний imovirnyi
post *v.t.* відправляти vidpravliaty
post *v.t.* розклеювати rozkleiuvaty
post *n.* пост post
post *n* стовп stovp
post *adj.* спішно spishno

postage *n.* поштові витрати
poshtovi vytraty
postal *a.* поштовий poshtovyi
post-date *v.t.* датувати пізнішим
числом datuvaty piznishym
chyslom
poster *n.* плакат plakat
posterity *n.* нащадки nashchadky
posthumous *a.* народжений
після смерті батька
narodzhenyi pislia smerti batka
postman *n.* листоноша
lystonosha
postmaster *n.* поштмейстер
poshtmeister
post-mortem *n.* аналіз гри після
її закінчення analiz hry pislia yii
zakinchennia
post-mortem *a.* посмертний
posmertnyi
post-office *n.* поштове
відділення poshtove viddilennia
postpone *v.t.* відтерміновувати
vidterminovuvaty
postponement *n.* відстрочка
vidstrochka
postscript *n.* постскриптум
postskryptum
posture *n.* постава postava
pot *n.* горщик horshchyk
pot *v.t.* заготовлювати про запас
zahotovliuvaty pro zapas
potash *n.* поташ potash
potassium *n.* калій kalii
potato *n.* картопля kartoplia
potency *n.* потенція potentsiia
potent *a.* потужний potuzhnyi
potential *n.* потенціал potentsial
potential *a.* потенційний
potentsiinyi
potentiality *n.* потенційність
potentsiinist
potter *n.* гончар honchar

pottery *n.* гончарні вироби
honcharni vyroby
pouch *n.* сумка sumka
poultry *n.* домашня птиця
domashnia ptytsia
pounce *n* наскок naskok
pounce *v.i.* накидатися
nakydatysia
pound *n.* фунт funt
pound *v.t.* подрібнювати
podribniuvaty
pour *v.i.* лити lyty
poverty *n.* бідність bidnist
powder *v.t.* пудрити pudryty
powder *n.* порошок poroshok
power *n.* міць mits
powerful *a.* потужний potuzhnyi
practicability *n.* здійсненність
zdiisnennist
practicable *a.* прохідний
prokhidnyi
practical *a.* практичний
praktychnyi
practice *n.* практика praktyka
practise *v.t.* вправлятися
vpravliatysia
practitioner *n.* практикуючий
лікар praktykuiuchyi likar
pragmatic *a.* прагматичний
prahmatychnyi
pragmatism *n.* прагматизм
prahmatyzm
praise *n.* хвала khvala
praise *v.t.* хвалити khvalyty
praiseworthy *a.* гідний похвали
hidnyi pokhvaly
prank *n.* жарт zhart
prattle *n.* белькотання
belkotannia
prattle *v.i.* белькотати belkotaty
pray *v.i.* молитися molytysia
prayer *n.* молитва molytva

preach *v.i.* проповідувати
propoviduvaty
preacher *n.* проповідник
propovidnyk
preamble *n.* преамбула
preambula
precaution *n.* заходи безпеки
zakhody bezpeky
precautionary *a.*
попереджувальний
poperedzhuvalnyi
precede *v.* біти попереду bity
poperedu
precedence *n.* пріоритет priorytet
precedent *n.* прецедент
pretsedent
precept *n.* заповідь zapovid
preceptor *n.* учитель uchytel
precious *a.* дорогоцінний
dorohotsinnyi
precis *n.* конспект konspekt
precise *a.* точний tochnyi
precision *n.* точність tochnist
precursor *n.* ровісник rovisnyk
predecessor *n.* попередник
poperednyk
predestination *n.* приречення
pryrechennia
predetermine *v.t.* зумовлювати
zumovliuvaty
predicament *n.* скрутне
становище skrutne
stanovyshche
predicate *n.* предикат predykat
predict *v.t.* прогнозувати
prohnozuvaty
prediction *n.* прогноз prohnoz
predominance *n.* переважання
perevazhannia
predominant *a.* що переважає
shcho perevazhaie
predominate *v.i.* переважати
perevazhaty

pre-eminence *n.* вищість
vyshchist
pre-eminent *a.* видатний vydatnyi
preface *n.* пролог proloh
preface *v.t.* робити вступ robyty
vstup
prefect *n.* префект prefekt
prefer *v.t.* віддавати перевагу
viddavaty perevahu
preference *n.* преференція
preferentsiia
preferential *a.* пільговий pilhovyi
prefix *n.* префікс prefiks
prefix *v.t.* приставляти спереду
prystavliaty speredu
pregnancy *n.* вагітність vahitnist
pregnant *a.* вагітна vahitna
prehistoric *a.* доісторичний
doistorychnyi
prejudice *n.* упередження
uperedzhennia
prelate *n.* прелат prelat
preliminary *n* підготовчий захід
pidhotovchyi zakhid
preliminary *a.* попередній
poperednii
prelude *n.* прелюдія preliudiia
prelude *v.t.* служити вступом
sluzhyty vstupom
premarital *a.* передшлюбний
peredshliubnyi
premature *a.* передчасний
peredchasnyi
premeditate *v.t.* обмірковувати
obmirkovuvaty
premeditation *n.* навмисність
navmysnist
premier *a.* перший pershyi
premier *n* прем'єр-міністр
premier-ministr
premiere *n.* прем'єра premiera
premium *n.* плата plata

premonition *n.* передчуття
peredchuttia
preoccupation *n.* заклопотаність
zaklopotanist
preoccupy *v.t.* привертати увагу
pryvertaty uvahu
preparation *n.* підготовка
pidhotovka
preparatory *a.* підготовчий
pidhotovchyi
prepare *v.t.* підготовляти
pidhotovliaty
preponderance *n.*
перевалювання
perevaliuvannia
preponderate *v.i.* перевалювати
perevaliuvaty
preposition *n.* привід pryvid
prerequisite *n* умова umova
prerequisite *a.* який вимагається
заздалегідь yakyi vymahaietsia
zazdalehid
prerogative *n.* прерогатива
prerohatyva
prescience *n.* передбачення
peredbachennia
prescribe *v.t.* наказувати
nakazuvaty
prescription *n.* лікарський
рецепт likarskyi retsept
presence *n.* наявність naiavnist
present *v.t.* підносити pidnosyty
present *n.* подарунок podarunok
present *a.* справжній spravzhnii
presentation *n.* презентація
prezentatsiia
presently *adv.* за хвилину za
khvylynu
preservation *n.* збереження
zberezhennia
preservative *a.* запобіжний
zapobizhnyi

preservative *n.* консервант
konservant
preserve *v.t.* берегти berehty
preserve *n.* консерви konservy
preside *v.i.* головувати holovuvaty
president *n.* президент prezydent
presidential *a.* президентський
prezydentskyi
press *v.t.* здавити zdavyty
press *n* преса presa
pressure *n.* тиск tysk
pressurize *v.t.* герметизувати
hermetyzuvaty
prestige *n.* престиж prestyzh
prestigious *a.* престижний
prestyzhnyi
presume *v.t.* гадати hadaty
presumption *n.* презумпція
prezumptsiia
presuppose *v.t.* містити в собі
mistyty v sobi
presupposition *n.* передумова
peredumova
pretence *n.* удавання udavannia
pretend *v.t.* вдавати vdavaty
pretension *n.* претензійність
pretenziinist
pretentious *a.* претензійний
pretenziinyi
pretext *n* відмовка vidmovka
prettiness *n.* миловидність
mylovydnist
pretty *a* гарненький harnenkyi
pretty *adv.* досить dosyt
prevail *v.i.* існувати isnuvaty
prevalence *n.* панування
panuvannia
prevalent *a.* поширений
poshyrenyi
prevent *v.t.* запобігати zapobihaty
prevention *n.* відвернення
vidvernennia

preventive *a.* превентивний preventyvnyi

previous *a.* передчасний peredchasnyi

prey *n.* награбоване nahrabovane

prey *v.i.* терзати terzaty

price *v.t.* оцінювати otsiniuvaty

price *n.* ціна tsina

prick *v.t.* наколоти nakoloty

prick *n.* колоти koloty

pride *n.* гордість hordist

pride *v.t.* пишатися pyshatysia

priest *n.* священик sviashchenyk

priestess *n.* жриця zhrytsia

priesthood *n.* священство sviashchenstvo

prima facie *adv.* на перший погляд na pershyi pohliad

primarily *adv.* в першу чергу v pershu cherhu

primary *a.* первинний pervynnyi

prime *a.* квітучий kvituchyi

prime *n.* початок pochatok

primer *n.* грунтовка hruntovka

primeval *a.* первісний pervisnyi

primitive *a.* примітивний prymityvnyi

prince *n.* принц prynts

princely *a.* князівський kniazivskyi

princess *n.* принцеса pryntsesa

principal *n.* директор dyrektor

principal *a* провідний providnyi

principle *n.* принцип pryntsyp

print *n* друк druk

print *v.t.* друкувати drukuvaty

printer *n.* принтер prynter

prior *n* настоятель nastoiatel

prior *a.* вагоміший vahomishyi

prioress *n.* настоятелька nastoiatelka

priority *n.* старшинство starshynstvo

prison *n.* тюрма tiurma

prisoner *n.* ув'язнений uviaznenyi

privacy *n.* усамітнення usamitnennia

private *a.* приватний pryvatnyi

privation *n.* відсутність vidsutnist

privilege *n.* привілей pryvilei

prize *v.t.* високо цінувати vysoko tsinuvaty

prize *n.* приз pryz

probability *n.* можливість mozhlyvist

probable *a.* правдоподібний pravdopodibnyi

probably *adv.* ймовірно ymovirno

probation *n.* випробний термін vyprobnyi termin

probationer *n.* стажист stazhyst

probe *n* зонд zond

probe *v.t.* прощупувати proshchupuvaty

problem *n.* задача zadacha

problematic *a.* проблематичний problematychnyi

procedure *n.* процедура protsedura

proceed *v.i.* продовжити prodovzhyty

proceeding *n.* судовчинство sudovchynstvo

proceeds *n.* виручка vyruchka

process *n.* процес protses

procession *n.* процесія protsesiia

proclaim *v.t.* проголошувати proholoshuvaty

proclamation *n.* проголошення proholoshennia

proclivity *n.* схильність skhylnist

procrastinate *v.i.* простроочувати prostrochuvaty

procrastination *n.* зволікання zvolikannia

proctor *n.* проктор proktor

procure *v.t.* роздобути rozdobuty
procurement *n.* постачання postachannia
prodigal *a.* надмірний nadmirnyi
prodigality *n.* велика кількість velyka kilkist
produce *v.t.* виробляти vyrobliaty
produce *n.* продукція produktsiia
product *n.* продукт produkt
production *n.* продукція produktsiia
productive *a.* продуктивний produktyvnyi
productivity *n.* продуктивність produktyvnist
profane *v.t.* осквернити oskverniaty
profane *a.* світський svitskyi
profess *v.t.* сповідувати spoviduvaty
profession *n.* професія profesiia
professional *a.* професійний profesiinyi
professor *n.* професор profesor
proficiency *n.* уміння uminnia
proficient *a.* обізнаний obiznanyi
profile *v.t.* профанувати profanuvaty
profile *n.* профіль profil
profit *n.* вигода vyhoda
profit *v.t.* нажити nazhyty
profitable *a.* корисний korysnyi
profiteer *v.i.* спекулювати spekuliuvaty
profiteer *n.* спекулянт spekuliant
profligacy *n.* розпуста rozpusta
profligate *a.* розпусний rozpusnyi
profound *a.* море more
profundity *n.* безодня bezodnia
profuse *a.* рясний riasnyi
profusion *n.* велика кількість velyka kilkist
progeny *n.* наслідок naslidok

programme *v.t.* запрограмувати zaprohramuvaty
programme *n.* програма prohrama
progress *n.* прогрес prohres
progress *v.i.* прогресувати prohresuvaty
progressive *a.* прогресивний prohresyvnyi
prohibit *v.t.* заважати zavazhaty
prohibition *n.* заборона zaborona
prohibitive *a.* заборонний zaboronnyi
prohibitory *a.* забороняючий zaboroniaiuchyi
project *v.t.* програма prohrama
project *n.* проект proekt
projectile *a* метальний metalnyi
projectile *n.* снаряд snariad
projection *n.* проекція proektsiia
projector *n.* проектор proektor
proliferate *v.i.* швидко поширюватися shvydko poshyriuvatysia
proliferation *n.* швидке збільшення shvydke zbilshennia
prolific *a.* плідний plidnyi
prologue *n.* пролог proloh
prolong *v.t.* продовжити prodovzhyty
prolongation *n.* відстрочка vidstrochka
prominence *n.* опуклість opuklist
prominent *a.* видний vydnyi
promise *v.t* обіцяти obitsiaty
promise *n* обіцянка obitsianka
promising *a.* багатообіцяючий bahatoobitsiaiuchyi
promissory *a.* який містить зобов'язання yakyi mistyt zoboviazannia
promote *v.t.* сприяти spryiaty

promotion *n.* просування prosuvannia
prompt *v.t.* спонукати sponukaty
prompt *a.* швидкий shvydkyi
prompter *n.* суфлер sufler
prone *a.* схильний skhylnyi
pronoun *n.* займенник zaimennyk
pronounce *v.t.* вимовляти vymovliaty
pronunciation *n.* вимова vymova
proof *n.* доказ dokaz
proof *a* непроникний nepronyknyi
prop *n.* підпірка pidpirka
prop *v.t.* підпирати pidpyraty
propaganda *n.* пропаганда propahanda
propagandist *n.* пропагандист propahandyst
propagate *v.t.* плодити plodyty
propagation *n.* розведення rozvedennia
propel *v.t.* стимулювати stymuliuvaty
proper *a.* належний nalezhnyi
property *n.* майно maino
prophecy *n.* пророцтво prorotstvo
prophesy *v.t.* пророкувати prorokuvaty
prophet *n.* пророк prorok
prophetic *a.* пророчий prorochyi
proportion *v.t.* розміряти rozmiriaty
proportion *n.* пропорція proportsiia
proportional *a.* пропорційний proportsiinyi
proportionate *a.* співрозмірний spivrozmirnyi
proposal *n.* освідчення osvidchennia
propose *v.t.* висувати vysuvaty
proposition *n.* справа sprava
propound *v.t.* висувати vysuvaty

proprietary *a.* власницький vlasnytskyi
proprietor *n.* господар hospodar
propriety *n.* доречність dorechnist
prorogue *v.t.* відстрочувати vidstrochuvaty
prosaic *a.* прозаїчний prozaichnyi
prose *n.* проза proza
prosecute *v.t.* переслідувати в судовому порядку peresliduvaty v sudovomu poriadku
prosecution *n.* кримінальне переслідування kryminalne peresliduvannia
prosecutor *n.* обвинувач obvynuvach
prosody *n.* просодія prosodiia
prospect *n.* панорама panorama
prospective *a.* перспективний perspektyvnyi
prospectus *n.* публікація publikatsiia
prosper *v.i.* процвітати protsvitaty
prosperity *n.* процвітання protsvitannia
prosperous *a.* процвітаючий protsvitaiuchyi
prostitute *v.t.* займатися проституцією zaimatysia
prostitute *n.* проститутка prostytutka
prostitution *n.* проституція prostytutsiia
prostrate *v.t.* падати ниць padaty nyts
prostrate *a.* розпростертий rozprostertyi
prostration *n.* прострація prostratsiia

protagonist *n.* поборник pobornyk
protect *v.t.* захищати zakhyshchaty
protection *n.* протегування protehuvannia
protective *a.* захисний zakhysnyi
protector *n.* захисник zakhysnyk
protein *n.* білок bilok
protest *n.* протест protest
protest *v.i.* протестувати protestuvaty
protestation *n.* опротестування oprotestuvannia
prototype *n.* прототип prototyp
proud *a.* гордий hordyi
prove *v.t.* доводити dovodyty
proverb *n.* прислів'я pryslivia
proverbial *a.* провербіальний proverbialnyi
provide *v.i.* подавати podavaty
providence *n.* провидіння provydinnia
provident *a.* завбачливий zavbachlyvyi
providential *a.* провіденціальне providentsialne
province *n.* провінція provintsiia
provincial *a.* провінційний provintsiinyi
provincialism *n.* провінціалізм provintsializm
provision *n.* надання nadannia
provisional *a.* тимчасовий tymchasovyi
proviso *n.* умова umova
provocation *n.* провокація provokatsiia
provocative *a.* провокаційний provokatsiinyi
provoke *v.t.* провокувати provokuvaty
prowess *n.* доблесть doblest

proximate *a.* найближчий naiblyzhchyi
proximity *n.* близькість blyzkist
proxy *n.* довіреність dovirenist
prude *n.* ханжа khanzha
prudence *n.* розсудливість rozsudlyvist
prudent *a.* ощадливий oshchadlyvyi
prudential *a.* розважливий rozvazhlyvyi
prune *v.t.* підрізати pidrizaty
pry *v.i.* зламувати zlamuvaty
psalm *n.* псалом psalom
pseudonym *n.* псевдонім psevdonim
psyche *n.* дух dukh
psychiatrist *n.* психіатр psykhiatr
psychiatry *n.* психіатрія psykhiatriia
psychic *a.* психічний psykhichnyi
psychological *a.* психологічний psykholohichnyi
psychologist *n.* психолог psykholoh
psychology *n.* психологія psykholohiia
psychopath *n.* психопат psykhopat
psychosis *n.* психоз psykhoz
psychotherapy *n.* психотерапія psykhoterapiia
puberty *n.* статева зрілість stateva zrilist
public *a.* громадський hromadskyi
public *n.* громадськість hromadskist
publication *n.* опублікування opublikuvannia
publicity *n.* гласність hlasnist
publicize *v.t.* оголошувати oholoshuvaty

publish *v.t.* публікувати
publikuvaty
publisher *n.* видавець vydavets
pudding *n.* пудинг pudynh
puddle *v.t.* каламутити
kalamutyty
puddle *n.* калюжа kaliuzha
puerile *a.* незрілий nezrilyi
puff *v.i.* вдувати vduvaty
puff *n.* слойка sloika
pull *v.t.* дути поривами duty
poryvamy
pull *n.* смикання smykannia
pulley *n.* шків shkiv
pullover *n.* пуловер pulover
pulp *n.* м'якоть плоду miakot
plodu
pulp *v.t.* перетворити на м'яку
масу peretvoryty na miaku
masu
pulpit *a.* кафедра kafedra
pulpy *a.* м'ясистий miasystyi
pulsate *v.i.* пульсувати pulsuvaty
pulsation *n.* пульсація pulsatsiia
pulse *n.* пульс puls
pulse *v.i.* битися bytysia
pump *n.* насос nasos
pump *v.t.* працювати насосом
pratsiuvaty nasosom
pumpkin *n.* гарбуз harbuz
pun *n.* каламбур kalambur
pun *v.i.* каламбурити kalamburyty
punch *v.t.* пробити probyty
punch *n.* пунш punsh
punctual *a.* пунктуальний
punktualnyi
punctuality *n.* точність tochnist
punctuate *v.t.* перемежовувати
peremezhovuvaty
punctuation *n.* пунктуація
punktuatsiia
puncture *n.* прокол prokol

puncture *v.t.* пробивати отвір
probyvaty otvir
pungency *n.* їдкість yidkist
pungent *a.* гострокінцевий
hostrokintsevyi
punish *v.t.* карати karaty
punishment *n.* покарання
pokarannia
punitive *a.* каральний karalnyi
puny *a.* незначний neznachnyi
pupil *n.* зіниця zinytsia
puppet *n.* лялька lialka
puppy *n.* цуценя tsutsenia
purblind *n.* підсліпуватий
pidslipuvatyi
purchase *v.t.* купівля kupivlia
purchase *n.* покупка pokupka
pure *a* чистий chystyi
purgation *n.* очищення
кишечника ochyshchennia
kyshechnyka
purgative *n.* проносне pronosne
purgative *a* очисний ochysnyi
purgatory *n.* чистилище
chystylyshche
purge *v.t.* прочищати
prochyshchaty
purification *n.* ректифікація
rektyfikatsiia
purify *v.t.* очищатися
ochyshchatysia
purist *n.* пурист puryst
puritan *n.* пуританин purytanyn
puritanical *a.* пуританський
purytanskyi
purity *n.* чистота chystota
purple *adj.* фіолетовий fioletovyi
purport *n.* сенс sens
purpose *v.t.* замишляти
zamyshliaty
purpose *n.* намір namir
purposely *adv.* навмисно
navmysno

purr *n.* муркотання murkotannia
purr *v.i.* муркотіти murkotity
purse *v.t.* піджати pidzhaty
purse *n.* ридикюль rydykiul
pursuance *n.* переслідування peresliduvannia
pursue *v.t.* проводити provodyty
pursuit *n.* гонитва honytva
purview *n.* компетенція kompetentsiia
pus *n.* гній hnii
push *n.* поштовх poshtovkh
push *v.t.* штовхати shtovkhaty
put *v.t.* покласти poklasty
puzzle *n.* головоломка holovolomka
puzzle *v.t.* приводити в складне становище pryvodyty v skladne stanovyshche
pygmy *n.* карликовий karlykovyi
pyorrhoea *n.* піорея pioreia
pyramid *n.* піраміда piramida
pyre *n.* похоронне багаття pokhoronne bahattia
python *n.* пітон piton

quack *n* шарлатан sharlatan
quack *v.i.* крякати kriakaty
quackery *n.* шарлатанство sharlatanstvo
quadrangle *n.* чотирикутник chotyrykutnyk
quadrangular *a.* чотирикутний chotyrykutnyi
quadrilateral *a.* чотирикутний chotyrykutnyi
quadruped *n.* чотиринога тварина chotyrynoha tvaryna
quadruple *v.t.* множити на чотири mnozhyty na chotyry

quadruple *a.* четверний chetvernyi
quail *n.* перепел perepel
quaint *a.* химерний khymernyi
quake *n* тремтіння tremtinnia
quake *v.i.* тремтіти tremtity
qualification *n.* кваліфікація kvalifikatsiia
qualify *v.i.* кваліфікувати kvalifikuvaty
qualitative *a.* якісний yakisnyi
quality *n.* якість yakist
quandary *n.* скрутне становище skrutne stanovyshche
quantitative *a.* кількісний kilkisnyi
quantity *n.* кількість kilkist
quantum *n.* квантовий kvantovyi
quarrel *v.i.* сваритися svarytysia
quarrel *n.* сварка svarka
quarrelsome *a.* нісенітний nisenitnyi
quarry *v.i.* розробляти кар'єр rozrobliaty karier
quarry *n.* кар'єр karier
quarter *v.t.* розділити на чотири rozdilyty na chotyry
quarter *n.* чверть chvert
quarterly *a.* щоквартальний shchokvartalnyi
queen *n.* королева koroleva
queer *a.* дивний dyvnyi
quell *v.t.* заспокоювати zaspokoiuvaty
quench *v.t.* гартувати hartuvaty
query *v.t* піддавати сумніву piddavaty sumnivu
query *n.* сумнів sumniv
quest *v.t* здійснювати пошук zdiisniuvaty poshuk
quest *n.* пошук poshuk
question *v.t.* питати pytaty
question *n.* питання pytannia

questionable *a.* сумнівний sumnivnyi

questionnaire *n.* анкета anketa

queue *n.* черга cherha

quibble *v.i.* викрутас vykrutas

quibble *n.*ігра слів ihra sliv

quick *n* жива огорожа zhyva ohorozha

quick *a.* швидкий shvydkyi

quicksand *n.* пливун plyvun

quicksilver *n.* ртуть rtut

quiet *n.* мовчання movchannia

quiet *v.t.* стихнути stykhnuty

quiet *a.* тихий tykhyi

quilt *n.* стьобана ковдра stobana kovdra

quinine *n.* хінін khinin

quintessence *n.* квінтесенція kvintesentsiia

quit *v.t.* звільняти zvilniaty

quite *adv.* цілком tsilkom

quiver *v.i.* тріпотіти tripotity

quiver *n.* трепет trepet

quixotic *a.* донкіхотський donkikhotskyi

quiz *v.t.* провести опитування provesty opytuvannia

quiz *n.* вікторина viktoryna

quorum *n.* кворум kvorum

quota *n.* квота kvota

quotation *n.* цитата tsytata

quote *v.t.* цитувати tsytuvaty

quotient *n.* показник pokaznyk

R

rabato *n.* великий відкладний комір velykyi vidkladnyi komir

rabbit *n.* кролик krolyk

rabies *n.* сказ skaz

race *v.i* брати участь у скачках braty uchast u skachkakh

race *n.* гонки honky

racial *a.* расовий rasovyi

racialism *n.* расизм rasyzm

rack *n.* стелаж stelazh

rack *v.t.* класти на полицю klasty na polytsiu

racket *n.* рекет reket

radiance *n.* сяйво siaivo

radiant *a.* променистий promenystyi

radiate *v.t.* випромінювати vyprominiuvaty

radiation *n.* радіація radiatsiia

radical *a.* радикальний radykalnyi

radio *v.t.* передавати по радіо peredavaty po radio

radio *n.* радіо radio

radish *n.* редис redys

radium *n.* радій radii

radius *n.* радіус radius

rag *v.t.* дражнити drazhnyty

rag *n.* клапоть klapot

rage *v.i.* бушувати bushuvaty

rage *n.* скаженість skazhenist

raid *v.t.* здійснювати набіг zdiisniuvaty nabih

raid *n.* рейд reid

rail *v.t.* їхати залізницею yikhaty zaliznytseiu

rail *n.* перила peryla

railing *n.* поруччя poruchchia

raillery *n.* жарти zharty

railway *n.* залізниця zaliznytsia

rain *n* дощ doshch

rain *v.i.* литися lytysia

rainy *a.* дощовий doshchovyi

raise *v.t.* підвищення pidvyshchennia

raisin *n.* ізюм izium

rally *n* об'єднання obiiednannia

rally *v.t.* оволодіти собою ovolodyty soboiu

ram *v.t.* таранити taranyty

ram *n.* баран baran

ramble *n* прогулянка prohulianka
ramble *v.t.* блукати без мети
  blukaty bez mety
rampage *n.* шаленство
  shalenstvo
rampage *v.i.* шаленіти shalenity
rampant *a.* нестямний nestiamnyi
rampart *n.* вал val
rancour *n.* злопам'ятність
  zlopamiatnist
random *a.* безладний bezladnyi
range *n.* діапазон diapazon
range *v.t.* ставити по порядку
  stavyty po poriadku
ranger *n.* лісничий lisnychyi
rank *a* родючий rodiuchyi
rank *v.t.* шикувати в шеренгу
  shykuvaty v sherenhu
rank *n.* ранг ranh
ransack *v.t.* розграбувати
  rozhrabuvaty
ransom *v.t.* викуповувати
  vykupovuvaty
ransom *n.* викуп vykup
rape *v.t.* гвалтувати hvaltuvaty
rape *n.* згвалтування
  zhvaltuvannia
rapid *a.* швидкий shvydkyi
rapidity *n.* швидкість shvydkist
rapier *n.* рапіра rapira
rapport *n.* взаєморозуміння
  vzaiemorozuminnia
rapt *a.* зосереджений
  zoseredzhenyi
rapture *n.* вияв захоплення vyiav
  zakhoplennia
rare *a.* рідкісний ridkisnyi
rascal *n.* шахрай shakhrai
rash *a.* необачний neobachnyi
rat *n.* щур shchur
rate *n.* ставка stavka
rate *v.t.* обчислювати
  obchysliuvaty

rather *adv.* швидше shvydshe
ratify *v.t.* ратифікувати
  ratyfikuvaty
ratio *n.* співвідношення
  spivvidnoshennia
ration *n.* раціон ratsion
rational *a.* розсудливий
  rozsudlyvyi
rationale *n.* логічне пояснення
  lohichne poiasnennia
rationality *n.* раціональність
  ratsionalnist
rationalize *v.t.* раціоналізувати
  ratsionalizuvaty
rattle *n* брязкальце briazkaltse
rattle *v.i.* тріщати trishchaty
ravage *v.t.* спустошувати
  spustoshuvaty
ravage *n.* спустошення
  spustoshennia
rave *v.i.* марити maryty
raven *n.* ворон voron
ravine *n.* ущелина ushchelyna
raw *a.* неварений nevarenyi
ray *n.* проблиск problysk
raze *v.t.* зрівняти із землею
  zrivniaty iz zemleiu
razor *n.* бритва brytva
reach *v.t.* надходити nadkhodyty
react *v.i.* реагувати reahuvaty
reaction *n.* реакція reaktsiia
reactionary *a.* реакційний
  reaktsiinyi
read *v.t.* читати chytaty
reader *n.* читач chytach
readily *adv.* з готовністю z
  hotovnistiu
readiness *n.* спритність sprytnist
ready *a.* готовий hotovyi
real *a.* реальний realnyi
realism *n.* реалізм realizm
realist *n.* реаліст realist

realistic *a.* реалістичний realistychnyi
reality *n.* реальність realnist
realization *n.* реалізація realizatsiia
realize *v.t.* здійснити zdiisnyty
really *adv.* насправді naspravdi
realm *n.* королівство korolivstvo
ream *n.* накип nakyp
reap *v.t.* пожинати pozhynaty
reaper *n.* жнець zhnets
rear *v.t.* споруджувати sporudzhuvaty
rear *n.* огузок ohuzok
reason *v.i.* мислити myslyty
reason *n.* причина prychyna
reasonable *a.* обґрунтований obgruntovanyi
reassure *v.t.* переконувати perekonuvaty
rebel *v.i.* піднімати заколот pidnimaty zakolot
rebel *n.* бунтівник buntivnyk
rebellion *n.* бунт bunt
rebellious *a.* востанський vostanskyi
rebirth *n.* метемпсихоз metempsykhoz
rebound *n.* відскок vidskok
rebound *v.i.* рікошетувати rikoshetuvaty
rebuff *v.t.* давати відсіч davaty vidsich
rebuff *n.* відсіч vidsich
rebuke *n.* догана dohana
rebuke *v.t.* дорікати dorikaty
recall *n.* відкликання vidklykannia
recall *v.t.* відкликати vidklykaty
recede *v.i.* відступати vidstupaty
receipt *n.* отримання otrymannia
receive *v.t.* отримувати otrymuvaty

receiver *n.* одержувач oderzhuvach
recent *a.* останній ostannii
recently *adv.* недавно nedavno
reception *n.* прийом pryiom
receptive *a.* сприйнятливий spryiniatlyvyi
recess *n.* відокремлене місце vidokremlene mistse
recession *n.* рецесія retsesiia
recipe *n.* рецепт retsept
recipient *n.* реципієнт retsypiient
reciprocal *a.* аналогічний analohichnyi
reciprocate *v.t.* відповідати взаємністю vidpovidaty vzaiemnistiu
recital *n.* сольний концерт solnyi kontsert
recitation *n.* декламація deklamatsiia
recite *v.t.* декламувати deklamuvaty
reckless *a.* безрозсудний bezrozsudnyi
reckon *v.t.* підраховувати pidrakhovuvaty
reclaim *v.t.* робити кращим robyty krashchym
reclamation *n* виправлення vypravlennia
recluse *n.* самітник samitnyk
recognition *n.* дізнавання diznavannia
recognize *v.t.* дізнаватися diznavatysia
recoil *n.* віддача viddacha
recoil *v.i.* відскочити vidskochyty
recollect *v.t.* знову зібрати znovu zibraty
recollection *n.* спогад spohad
recommend *v.t.* радити radyty

recommendation *n.*
рекомендація rekomendatsiia
recompense *n.* відшкодування
vidshkoduvannia
recompense *v.t.*
винагороджувати
vynahorodzhuvaty
reconcile *v.t.* примиряти
prymyriaty
reconciliation *n.* примирення
prymyrennia
record *n.* запис zapys
record *v.t.* записувати zapysuvaty
recorder *n.* реєстратор reiestrator
recount *v.t.* розповідати
rozpovidaty
recoup *v.t.* відшкодувати
vidshkoduvaty
recourse *n.* звернення
zvernennia
recover *v.t.* видужувати
vyduzhuvaty
recovery *n.* відшкодування
vidshkoduvannia
recreation *n.* відпочинок
vidpochynok
recruit *v.t.* вербувати verbuvaty
recruit *n.* призовник pryzovnyk
rectangle *n.* прямокутник
priamokutnyk
rectangular *a.* прямокутний
priamokutnyi
rectification *n.* випрямлення
vypriamlennia
rectify *v.i.* ректіфікувати
rektifikuvaty
rectum *n.* пряма кишка priama
kyshka
recur *v.i.* рецидивувати
retsydyvuvaty
recurrence *n.* рецидив retsydyv
recurrent *a.* повторюваний
povtoriuvanyi

red *n.* червоний колір chervonyi
kolir
red *a.* червоний chervonyi
redden *v.t.* червоніти chervonity
reddish *a.* червонуватий
chervonuvatyi
redeem *v.t.* виплачувати
vyplachuvaty
redemption *n.* погашення
pohashennia
redouble *v.t.* подвоїти podvoity
redress *n* відшкодування
vidshkoduvannia
redress *v.t.* відновлювати
vidnovliuvaty
reduce *v.t.* зменшити zmenshyty
reduction *n.* перетворення
peretvorennia
redundance *n.* надмірність
nadmirnist
redundant *a.* надлишковий
nadlyshkovyi
reel *v.i.* мотати motaty
reel *n.* котушка kotushka
refer *v.t.* послатися poslatysia
referee *n.* судовий розпорядник
sudovyi rozporiadnyk
reference *n.* довідка dovidka
referendum *n.* референдум
referendum
refine *v.t.* удосконалювати
udoskonaliuvaty
refinement *n.* вишуканість
vyshukanist
refinery *n.* очисний завод
ochysnyi zavod
reflect *v.t.* відображати
vidobrazhaty
reflection *n.* відображення
vidobrazhennia
reflective *a.* рефлективний
reflektyvnyi
reflector *n.* відбивач vidbyvach

reflex *a* рефлекторний reflektornyi
reflex *n.* рефлекс refleks
reflexive *a* зворотний zvorotnyi
reform *n.* реформа reforma
reform *v.t.* реформувати reformuvaty
reformation *n.* реформування reformuvannia
reformatory *n.* виправний заклад vypravnyi zaklad
reformatory *a* виправний vypravnyi
reformer *n.* реформатор reformator
refrain *n* приспів pryspiv
refrain *v.i.* утримуватися utrymuvatysia
refresh *v.t.* оновити onovyty
refreshment *n.* закуски та напої zakusky ta napoi
refrigerate *v.t.* охолодити okholodyty
refrigeration *n.* охолодження okholodzhennia
refrigerator *n.* холодильник kholodylnyk
refuge *n.* сховище skhovyshche
refugee *n.* біженець bizhenets
refulgence *n.* сяйво siaivo
refulgent *a.* сяючий siaiuchyi
refund *v.t.* відшкодовувати vidshkodovuvaty
refund *n.* повертати гроші povertaty hroshi
refusal *n.* опціон optsion
refuse *v.t.* відмовляти vidmovliaty
refuse *n.* покидьки pokydky
refutation *n.* спростування sprostuvannia
refute *v.t.* спростувати sprostuvaty
regal *a.* королівський korolivskyi

regard *n.* увага uvaha
regard *v.t.* розцінювати roztsiniuvaty
regenerate *v.t.* регенерувати reheneruvaty
regeneration *n.* регенерація reheneratsiia
regicide *n.* царевбивство tsarevbyvstvo
regime *n.* державний стрій derzhavnyi strii
regiment *n.* полк polk
regiment *v.t.* формувати полк formuvaty polk
region *n.* регіон rehion
regional *a.* регіональний rehionalnyi
register *n.* реєстр reiestr
register *v.t.* реєструвати reiestruvaty
registrar *n.* утримувач реєстру utrymuvach reiestru
registration *n.* реєстрація reiestratsiia
registry *n.* реєстратура reiestratura
regret *n* жаль zhal
regret *v.i.* жалкувати zhalkuvaty
regular *a.* регулярний rehuliarnyi
regularity *n.* регулярність rehuliarnist
regulate *v.t.* урегульовувати urehulovuvaty
regulation *n.* норма norma
regulator *n.* регулятор rehuliator
rehabilitate *v.t.* реабілітувати reabilituvaty
rehabilitation *n.* реабілітація reabilitatsiia
rehearsal *n.* репетиція repetytsiia
rehearse *v.t.* репетирувати repetyruvaty
reign *n* князювання kniaziuvannia

reign *v.i.* царювати tsariuvaty
reimburse *v.t.* сплачувати splachuvaty
rein *v.t.* правити pravyty
rein *n.* поводи povody
reinforce *v.t.* посилювати posyliuvaty
reinforcement *n.* армування armuvannia
reinstate *v.t.* відновлювати vidnovliuvaty
reinstatement *n.* відновлення vidnovlennia
reiterate *v.t.* повторити povtoryty
reiteration *n.* повторення povtorennia
reject *v.t.* відкидати vidkydaty
rejection *n.* неприйняття nepryiniattia
rejoice *v.i.* радіти radity
rejoin *v.t.* приєднатися pryiednatysia
rejoinder *n.* відповідь vidpovid
rejuvenate *v.t.* омолоджуватися omolodzhuvatysia
rejuvenation *n.* омолодження omolodzhennia
relapse *n.* повторення povtorennia
relapse *v.i.* знову робити znovu robyty
relate *v.t.* ставитися stavytysia
relation *n.* родичка rodychka
relative *n.* родич rodych
relative *a.* відносний vidnosnyi
relax *v.t.* розслаблятися rozslabliatysia
relaxation *n.* релаксація relaksatsiia
relay *v.t.* зміняти zminiaty
relay *n.* реле rele
release *n.* звільнення zvilnennia

release *v.t.* дозволяти демонстрування dozvoliaty demonstruvannia
relent *v.i.* пом'якшуватися pomiakshuvatysia
relentless *a.* невідступний nevidstupnyi
relevance *n.* релевантність relevantnist
relevant *a.* релевантний relevantnyi
reliable *a.* надійний nadiinyi
reliance *n.* надія nadiia
relic *n.* реліквія relikviia
relief *n.* полегшення polehshennia
relieve *v.t.* позбавляти pozbavliaty
religion *n.* релігія relihiia
religious *a.* релігійний relihiinyi
relinquish *v.t.* відмовлятися vidmovliatysia
relish *n* насолода nasoloda
relish *v.t.* насолоджуватися nasolodzhuvatysia
reluctance *n.* небажання nebazhannia
reluctant *a.* неприхильний neprykhylnyi
rely *v.i.* покладатися pokladatysia
remain *v.i.* залишатися zalyshatysia
remainder *n.* залишок zalyshok
remains *n.* залишки zalyshky
remand *n* відрахування vidrakhuvannia
remand *v.t.* відрахувати vidrakhuvaty
remark *v.t.* помічати pomichaty
remark *n.* зауваження zauvazhennia
remarkable *a.* чудовий chudovyi
remedial *a.* лікувальний likuvalnyi

remedy *n.* відшкодування
vidshkoduvannia
remedy *v.t* усувати usuvaty
remember *v.t.* дарувати daruvaty
remembrance *n.* сувенір suvenir
remind *v.t.* нагадувати
nahaduvaty
reminder *n.* нагадування
nahaduvannia
reminiscence *n.* спогад spohad
reminiscent *a.* нагадуючий
nahaduiuchyi
remission *n.* ремісія remisiia
remit *v.t.* пробачити probachyty
remittance *n.* грошовий переказ
hroshovyi perekaz
remorse *n.* докори совісті dokory
sovisti
remote *a.* віддалений viddalenyi
removable *a.* змінний zminnyi
removal *n.* видалення vydalennia
remove *v.t.* прибирати prybyraty
remunerate *v.t.* оплачувати
oplachuvaty
remuneration *n.* оплата праці
oplata pratsi
remunerative *a.* вигідний vyhidnyi
renaissance *n.* ренесанс
renesans
render *v.t.* віддати viddaty
rendezvous *n.* рандеву randevu
renew *v.t.* відновити vidnovyty
renewal *n.* оновлення onovlennia
renounce *v.t.* зрікатися zrikatysia
renovate *v.t.* реставрувати
restavruvaty
renovation *n.* ремонт remont
renown *n.* слава slava
renowned *a.* знаменитий
znamenytyi
rent *v.t.* брати в оренду braty v
orendu
rent *n.* просвіт prosvit

renunciation *n.* самозречення
samozrechennia
repair *n.* загоєння zahoiennia
repair *v.t.* відправлятися
vidpravliatysia
reparable *a.* виправити vypravyty
repartee *n.* дотепна відповідь
dotepna vidpovid
repatriate *n* репатріант repatriant
repatriate *v.t.* репатріювати
repatriiuvaty
repatriation *n.* репатріація
repatriatsiia
repay *v.t.* платити вдруге platyty
vdruhe
repayment *n.* сплата splata
repeal *n* скасування skasuvannia
repeal *v.t.* скасовувати
skasovuvaty
repeat *v.t.* повторювати
povtoriuvaty
repel *v.t.* відштовхувати
vidshtovkhuvaty
repellent *n* репелент repelent
repellent *a.* який відштовхує
yakyi vidshtovkhuie
repent *v.i.* розкаюватися
rozkaiuvatysia
repentance *n.* покаяння
pokaiannia
repentant *a.* каянник kaiannyk
repercussion *n.* наслідки
naslidky
repetition *n.* копія kopiia
replace *v.t.* замінювати
zaminiuvaty
replacement *n.* заміщення
zamishchennia
replenish *v.t.* поповнювати
popovniuvaty
replete *a.* переповнений
perepovnenyi

replica *n.* репродукція
reproduktsiia
reply *v.i.* вживати відповідних
заходів vzhyvaty vidpovidnykh
zakhodiv
reply *n* відзив vidzyv
report *n.* звіт zvit
report *v.t.* описувати opysuvaty
reporter *n.* репортер reporter
repose *v.i.* давати відпочинок
davaty vidpochynok
repose *n.* спокій spokii
repository *n.* сховище
skhovyshche
represent *v.t.* зображати
zobrazhaty
representation *n.* зображення
zobrazhennia
representative *a.*
представницький
predstavnytskyi
representative *n.* представник
predstavnyk
repress *v.t.* класти край klasty
krai
repression *n.* репресія represiia
reprimand *v.t.* робити догану
robyty dohanu
reprimand *n.* догана dohana
reprint *n.* перевидання
perevydannia
reprint *v.t.* передруковувати
peredrukovuvaty
reproach *n.* докір dokir
reproach *v.t.* докоряти dokoriaty
reproduce *v.t.* відтворювати
vidtvoriuvaty
reproduction *n* відтворення
vidtvorennia
reproductive *a.* відтворювальний
vidtvoriuvalnyi
reproof *n.* докір dokir
reptile *n.* рептилія reptyliia

republic *n.* республіка respublika
republican *n* республіканець
respublikanets
republican *a.* республіканський
respublikanskyi
repudiate *v.t.* зрікатися zrikatysia
repudiation *n.* зречення
zrechennia
repugnance *n.* антипатія
antypatiia
repugnant *a.* нестерпний
nesterpnyi
repulse *n.* відмова vidmova
repulse *v.t.* відбивати vidbyvaty
repulsion *n.* відштовхування
vidshtovkhuvannia
repulsive *a.* відразливий
vidrazlyvyi
reputation *n.* репутація
reputatsiia
repute *n.* загальна думка zahalna
dumka
repute *v.t.* гадати hadaty
request *n* попит popyt
request *v.t.* попросити poprosyty
requiem *n.* реквієм rekviiem
require *v.t.* наказувати
nakazuvaty
requirement *n.* необхідна умова
neobkhidna umova
requisite *a.* належний nalezhnyi
requisite *n* потрібне potribne
requisition *n.* офіційне
розпорядження ofitsiine
rozporiadzhennia
requisition *v.t.* реквізувати
rekvizuvaty
requite *v.t.* відплачувати
vidplachuvaty
rescue *n* порятунок poriatunok
rescue *v.t.* звільняти zvilniaty
research *v.i.* збирати матеріал
zbyraty material

research *n* ретельні пошуки retelni poshuky
resemblance *n.* схожість skhozhist
resemble *v.t.* бути схожим buty skhozhym
resent *v.t.* обурюватися oburiuvatysia
resentment *n.* почуття образи pochuttia obrazy
reservation *n.* резервування rezervuvannia
reserve *v.t.* оберігати oberihaty
reservoir *n.* водойма vodoima
reside *v.i.* проживати prozhyvaty
residence *n.* місце проживання mistse prozhyvannia
resident *n* резидент rezydent
resident *a.* який постійно мешкає yakyi postiino meshkaie
residual *a.* залишковий zalyshkovyi
residue *n.* частина chastyna
resign *v.t.* йти у відставку yty u vidstavku
resignation *n.* відставка vidstavka
resist *v.t.* чинити опір chynyty opir
resistance *n.* опір opir
resistant *a.* стійкий stiikyi
resolute *a.* непохитний nepokhytnyi
resolution *n.* рішучість rishuchist
resolve *v.t.* рішати rishaty
resonance *n.* резонанс rezonans
resonant *a.* резонансний rezonansnyi
resort *v.i.* вдаватися vdavatysia
resort *n* курорт kurort
resound *v.i.* звучати zvuchaty
resource *n.* ресурс resurs
resourceful *a.* спритний sprytnyi
respect *n.* повага povaha

respect *v.t.* шанувати shanuvaty
respectful *a.* шанобливий shanoblyvyi
respective *a.* турботливий turbotlyvyi
respiration *n.* вдих vdykh
respire *v.i.* вдихати vdykhaty
resplendent *a.* сяючий siaiuchyi
respond *v.i.* робити що-небудь у відповідь robyty shcho-nebud u vidpovid
respondent *n.* відповідач vidpovidach
response *n.* реагування reahuvannia
responsibility *n.* підопічний pidopichnyi
responsible *a.* важливий vazhlyvyi
rest *v.i.* відпочивати vidpochyvaty
rest *n* сон son
restaurant *n.* ресторан restoran
restive *a.* норовливий norovlyvyi
restoration *n.* ресторація restoratsiia
restore *v.t.* повертати povertaty
restrain *v.t.* стримувати strymuvaty
restrict *v.t.* тримати в певних межах trymaty v pevnykh mezhakh
restriction *n.* обмеження obmezhennia
restrictive *a.* обмежувальний obmezhuvalnyi
result *v.i.* витікати vytikaty
result *n.* результат rezultat
resume *v.t.* брати назад braty nazad
resume *n.* резюме reziume
resumption *n.* повернення poverennnia

resurgence *n.* відродження
vidrodzhennia
resurgent *a.* який відроджується
yakyi vidrodzhuietsia
retail *adv.* в роздріб v rozdrib
retail *v.t.* продавати в роздріб
prodavaty v rozdrib
retail *n.* роздрібна торгівля
rozdribna torhivlia
retail *a* роздрібний rozdribnyi
retailer *n.* роздрібний торговець
rozdribnyi torhovets
retain *v.t.* оберігати oberihaty
retaliate *v.i.* помститися
pomstytysia
retaliation *n.* відплата vidplata
retard *v.t.* сповільнювати
spovilniuvaty
retardation *n.* уповільнення
upovilnennia
retention *n.* утримання
utrymannia
retentive *a.* який зберігає yakyi
zberihaie
reticence *n.* скритність skrytnist
reticent *a.* стриманий strymanyi
retina *n.* сітківка sitkivka
retinue *n.* свита svyta
retire *v.i.* йти на пенсію yty na
pensiiu
retirement *n.* вихід на пенсію
vykhid na pensiiu
retort *n.* заперечення
zaperechennia
retort *v.t.* різко заперечувати
rizko zaperechuvaty
retouch *v.t.* ретушувати
retushuvaty
retrace *v.t.* відновлювати у
пам`яті vidnovliuvaty u pam`iati
retread *v.t.* відновити протектор
vidnovyty protektor

retread *n.* новий протектор novyi
protektor
retreat *v.i.* відійти vidiity
retrench *v.t.* урізувати urizuvaty
retrenchment *n.* скорочення
skorochennia
retrieve *v.t.* витягувати
vytiahuvaty
retrospect *n.* погляд назад
pohliad nazad
retrospection *n.* ретроспекція
retrospektsiia
retrospective *a.* ретроспективний
retrospektyvnyi
return *n.* повернення
povernennia
return *v.i.* повернути povernuty
revel *n.* гуляння huliannia
revel *v.i.* пиячити pyiachyty
revelation *n.* одкровення
odkrovennia
reveller *n.* гуляка huliaka
revelry *n.* пиятика pyiatyka
revenge *v.t.* жадоба помсти
zhadoba pomsty
revenge *n.* помста pomsta
revengeful *a.* мстивий mstyvyi
revenue *n.* доходи dokhody
revere *v.t.* почитати pochytaty
reverence *n.* шанування
shanuvannia
reverend *a.* преподобний
prepodobnyi
reverent *a.* благоговійний
blahohoviinyi
reverential *a.* шанобливий
shanoblyvyi
reverie *n.* мрійливість mriilyvist
reversal *n.* анулювання
anuliuvannia
reverse *a.* зворотний zvorotnyi
reverse *v.t.* обертати obertaty

reverse *n* оборотна сторона oborotna storona
reversible *a.* реверсивний reversyvnyi
revert *v.i.* повертатися povertatysia
review *n* розгляд rozhliad
review *v.t.* оглядати ohliadaty
revise *v.t.* переглядати perehliadaty
revision *n.* перегляд perehliad
revival *n.* повернення до життя povernennia do zhyttia
revive *v.i.* відроджувати vidrodzhuvaty
revocable *a.* який підлягає скасуванню yakyi pidliahaie skasuvanniu
revocation *n.* ревокація revokatsiia
revoke *v.t.* брати назад braty nazad
revolt *v.i.* повставати povstavaty
revolt *n.* опір opir
revolution *n.* революція revoliutsiia
revolutionary *a.* революційний revoliutsiinyi
revolutionary *n* революціонер revoliutsioner
revolve *v.i.* обертатися obertatysia
revolver *n.* револьвер revolver
reward *n.* винагорода vynahoroda
reward *v.t.* винагороджувати vynahorodzhuvaty
rhetoric *n.* риторика rytoryka
rhetorical *a.* риторичний rytorychnyi
rheumatic *a.* ревматичний revmatychnyi
rheumatism *n.* ревматизм revmatyzm

rhinoceros *n.* носоріг nosorih
rhyme *n.* рима ryma
rhyme *v.i.* римувати rymuvaty
rhymester *n.* віршомаз virshomaz
rhythm *b.* ритм rytm
rhythmic *a.* ритмічний rytmichnyi
rib *n.* ребро rebro
ribbon *n.* стрічка strichka
rice *n.* рис rys
rich *a.* родючий rodiuchyi
riches *n.* скарби skarby
richness *n.* поживність pozhyvnist
rick *n.* стіг stih
rickets *n.* рахіт rakhit
rickety *a.* хиткий khytkyi
rickshaw *n.* рикша ryksha
rid *v.t.* рятувати riatuvaty
riddle *v.i.* говорити загадками hovoryty zahadkamy
riddle *n.* решето resheto
ride *n* поїздка poizdka
ride *v.t.* їздити yizdyty
rider *n.* вершник vershnyk
ridge *n.* хребет khrebet
ridicule *n.* насмішка nasmishka
ridicule *v.t.* піднімати на сміх pidnimaty na smikh
ridiculous *a.* смішний smishnyi
rifle *n* гвинтівка hvyntivka
rifle *v.t.* стріляти з гвинтівки striliaty z hvyntivky
rift *n.* тріщина trishchyna
right *v.t.* випрямитися vypriamytysia
right *a.* правий pravyi
right *adv* належним чином nalezhnym chynom
right *n* право pravo
righteous *a.* справедливий spravedlyvyi
rigid *a.* жорсткий zhorstkyi
rigorous *a.* суворий suvoryi

rigour *n.* строгість strohist
rim *n.* обід obid
ring *n.* кільце kiltse
ring *v.t.* оточити кільцем otochyty kiltsem
ringlet *n.* колечко kolechko
ringworm *n.* стригучий лишай stryhuchyi lyshai
rinse *v.t.* прополоскати propoloskaty
riot *v.t.* бешкетувати beshketuvaty
riot *n.* бунт bunt
rip *v.t.* розрізати rozrizaty
ripe *a* стиглий styhlyi
ripen *v.i.* дозрівати dozrivaty
ripple *n.* брижі bryzhi
ripple *v.t.* покривати брижами pokryvaty bryzhamy
rise *v.* вставати vstavaty
rise *n.* підйом pidiom
risk *n.* ризик ryzyk
risk *v.t.* наважуватися navazhuvatysia
risky *a.* ризикований ryzykovanyi
rite *n.* обряд obriad
ritual *n.* ритуал rytual
ritual *a.* ритуальний rytualnyi
rival *n.* суперник supernyk
rival *v.t.* суперничати supernychaty
rivalry *n.* суперництво supernytstvo
river *n.* річка richka
rivet *n.* заклепка zaklepka
rivet *v.t.* клепати klepaty
rivulet *n.* річечка richechka
road *n.* дорога doroha
roam *v.i.* тинятися tyniatysia
roar *n.* рев rev
roar *v.i.* ричати rychaty
roast *n* печеня pechenia
roast *a* смажений smazhenyi
roast *v.t.* смажити smazhyty

rob *v.t.* грабувати hrabuvaty
robber *n.* грабіжник hrabizhnyk
robbery *n.* пограбування pohrabuvannia
robe *v.t.* облачати oblachaty
robe *n.* халат khalat
robot *n.* робот robot
robust *a.* здоровий zdorovyi
rock *v.t.* коливати kolyvaty
rock *n.* скеля skelia
rocket *n.* реактивний снаряд reaktyvnyi snariad
rod *n.* лоза loza
rodent *n.* гризун hryzun
roe *n.* косуля kosulia
rogue *n.* шельма shelma
roguery *n.* шахрайство shakhraistvo
roguish *a.* шахрайський shakhraiskyi
role *n.* роль rol
roll *v.i.* котити kotyty
roll *n.* рулон rulon
roll-call *n.* перекличка pereklychka
roller *n.* валик valyk
romance *n.* романтика romantyka
romantic *a.* романтичний romantychnyi
romp *v.i.* возитися vozytysia
romp *n.* шибеник shybenyk
rood *n.* розп'яття rozpiattia
roof *n.* дах dakh
roof *v.t.* крити kryty
rook *n.* грак hrak
rook *v.t.* обдирати obdyraty
room *n.* приміщення prymishchennia
roomy *a.* місткий mistkyi
roost *v.i.* всістися на сідало vsistysia na sidalo
roost *n.* сідало sidalo
root *n.* корінь korin

root *v.i.* пускати коріння puskaty korinnia
rope *v.t.* зв'язати мотузкою zviazaty motuzkoiu
rope *n.* мотузка motuzka
rosary *n.* розарій rozarii
rose *n.* троянда troianda
roseate *a.* надмірно оптимістичний nadmirno optymistychnyi
rostrum *n.* трибуна trybuna
rosy *a.* рум'яний rumianyi
rot *n.* гниль hnyl
rot *v.i.* гнити hnyty
rotary *a.* обертальний obertalnyi
rotate *v.i.* чергуватися cherhuvatysia
rotation *n.* обертання obertannia
rote *n.* зубріння zubrinnia
rouble *n.* рубль rubl
rough *a.* необроблений neobroblenyi
round *a.* круглий kruhlyi
round *adv.* навколо navkolo
round *v.t.* огинати ohynaty
round *n.* щабель shchabel
rouse *v.i.* сердити serdyty
rout *v.t.* розбити вщент rozbyty vshchent
rout *n* розгром rozhrom
route *n.* маршрут marshrut
routine *a* поточний potochnyi
routine *n.* рутина rutyna
rove *v.i.* блукати blukaty
rover *n.* мандрівник mandrivnyk
row *n* веслування vesluvannia
row *v.t.* гребти hrebty
row *n.* ряд riad
row *n.* провулок provulok
rowdy *a.* буйний buinyi
royal *a.* царський tsarskyi
royalist *n.* рояліст roialist
royalty *n.* роялті roialti

rub *n* розтирання roztyrannia
rub *v.t.* терти terty
rubber *n.* гума huma
rubbish *n.* сміття smittia
rubble *n.* кругляк kruhliak
ruby *n.* рубін rubin
rude *a.* брутальний brutalnyi
rudiment *n.* рудимент rudyment
rudimentary *a.* рудиментарний rudymentarnyi
rue *v.t.* рута ruta
rueful *a.* сумний sumnyi
ruffian *n.* хуліган khulihan
ruffle *v.t.* рябити riabyty
rug *n.* килимок kylymok
rugged *a.* шорсткуватий shorstkuvatyi
ruin *n.* розорення rozorennia
ruin *v.t.* загибель zahybel
rule *v.t.* панувати panuvaty
rule *n.* правило pravylo
ruler *n.* правитель pravytel
ruling *n.* правлячий pravliachyi
rum *n.* ром rom
rum *a* чудний chudnyi
rumble *v.i.* грюкати hriukaty
rumble *n.* гуркіт hurkit
ruminant *a.* жуйний zhuinyi
ruminant *n.* жуйну тварина zhuinu tvaryna
ruminate *v.i.* жувати жуйку zhuvaty zhuiku
rumination *n.* роздум rozdum
rummage *n* пошуки poshuky
rummage *v.i.* ритися rytysia
rummy *n.* алкоголік alkoholik
rumour *v.t.* поширювати чутки poshyriuvaty chutky
rumour *n.* слух slukh
run *v.i.* бігати bihaty
run *n.* втеча vtecha
rung *n.* перекладини perekladyny
runner *n.* бігун bihun

rupee *n.* рупія rupiia
rupture *v.t.* проривати proryvaty
rupture *n.* пробій probii
rural *a.* сільський silskyi
ruse *n.* хитрість khytrist
rush *v.t.* діяти занадто поспішно diiaty zanadto pospishno
rush *n.* очерет ocheret
rush *n* схвалення skhvalennia
rust *n.* іржа irzha
rust *v.i* іржавіти irzhavity
rustic *n* селянин selianyn
rustic *a.* сільський silskyi
rusticate *v.t.* жити в селі zhyty v seli
rustication *n.* оселення в селі oselennia v seli
rusticity *n.* простота prostota
rusty *a.* іржавий irzhavyi
rut *n.* колія koliia
ruthless *a.* нещадний neshchadnyi
rye *n.* жито zhyto

S

sabbath *n.* шабаш shabash
sabotage *n.* саботаж sabotazh
sabotage *v.t.* саботувати sabotuvaty
sabre *v.t.* рубати шаблею rubaty shableiu
sabre *n.* шабля shablia
saccharin *n.* сахарин sakharyn
saccharine *a.* сахаріновий sakharinovyi
sack *v.t.* знімати з посади znimaty z posady
sack *n.* мішок mishok
sacrament *n.* таїнство tainstvo
sacred *a.* священний sviashchennyi

sacrifice *n.* пожертвування pozhertvuvannia
sacrifice *v.t.* приносити в жертву prynosyty v zhertvu
sacrificial *a.* жертовний zhertovnyi
sacrilege *n.* святотатство sviatotatstvo
sacrilegious *a.* блюзнірський bliuznirskyi
sacrosanct *a.* недоторканний nedotorkannyi
sad *a.* сумний sumnyi
sadden *v.t.* сумовати sumovaty
saddle *v.t.* сідлати sidlaty
saddle *n.* сідло sidlo
sadism *n.* садизм sadyzm
sadist *n.* садист sadyst
safe *a.* безпечний bezpechnyi
safe *n.* сейф seif
safeguard *n.* обережність oberezhnist
safety *n.* безпека bezpeka
saffron *n.* шафран shafran
saffron *a* шафранний shafrannyi
sagacious *a.* прозорливий prozorlyvyi
sagacity *n.* проникливість pronyklyvist
sage *n.* мудрець mudrets
sage *a.* мудрий mudryi
sail *v.i.* йти під вітрилами yty pid vitrylamy
sail *n.* вітрило vitrylo
sailor *n.* матрос matros
saint *n.* святий sviatyi
saintly *a.* святий sviatyi
sake *n.* саке sake
salable *a.* ходовий khodovyi
salad *n.* салат salat
salary *n.* оклад oklad
sale *n.* продаж prodazh

salesman *n.* продавець prodavets
salient *a.* випуклий vypuklyi
saline *a.* сольовий solovyi
salinity *n.* солоність solonist
saliva *n.* слина slyna
sally *n.* вилазка vylazka
sally *v.i.* робити вилазку robyty vylazku
saloon *n.* шинок shynok
salt *n.* сіль sil
salt *v.t* солити solyty
salty *a.* солоний solonyi
salutary *a.* цілющий tsiliushchyi
salutation *n.* привітання pryvitannia
salute *v.t.* привітати pryvitaty
salute *n* салют saliut
salvage *n.* вторинна сировина vtorynna syrovyna
salvage *v.t.* рятувати судно riatuvaty sudno
salvation *n.* порятунок poriatunok
same *a.* однаковий odnakovyi
sample *n.* взірець vzirets
sample *v.t.* відбирати пробу vidbyraty probu
sanatorium *n.* санаторій sanatorii
sanctification *n.* освячення osviachennia
sanctify *v.t.* освячувати osviachuvaty
sanction *v.t.* санкціонувати sanktsionuvaty
sanction *n.* санкція sanktsiia
sanctity *n.* святість sviatist
sanctuary *n.* святилище sviatylyshche
sand *n.* пісок pisok
sandal *n.* сандал sandal
sandalwood *n.* сандалове дерево sandalove derevo
sandwich *n.* бутерброд buterbrod

sandwich *v.t.* поміщати посередині pomishchaty poseredyni
sandy *a.* піщаний pishchanyi
sane *a.* нормальний normalnyi
sanguine *a.* сангвінічний sanhvinichnyi
sanitary *a.* санітарний sanitarnyi
sanity *n.* осудність osudnist
sap *n.* живиця zhyvytsia
sap *v.t.* длубатися dlubatysia
sapling *n.* паросток parostok
sapphire *n.* сапфір sapfir
sarcasm *n.* сарказм sarkazm
sarcastic *a.* саркастичний sarkastychnyi
sardonic *a.* сардонічний sardonichnyi
satan *n.* сатана satana
satchel *n.* ранець ranets
satellite *n.* супутник suputnyk
satiable *a.* який задовольняється yakyi zadovolniaietsia
satiate *v.t.* насичувати nasychuvaty
satiety *n.* ситість sytist
satire *n.* сатира satyra
satirical *a.* сатиричний satyrychnyi
satirist *n.* сатирик satyryk
satirize *v.t.* висміювати vysmiiuvaty
satisfaction *n.* сплата боргу splata borhu
satisfactory *a.* задовільний zadovilnyi
satisfy *v.t.* погашати pohashaty
saturate *v.t.* пронизувати pronyzuvaty
saturation *n.* насичення nasychennia
Saturday *n.* субота subota
sauce *n.* соус sous

saucer *n.* блюдце bliudtse
saunter *v.t.* проходжуватися prokhodzhuvatysia
savage *a.* варварський varvarskyi
savage *n* дикун dykun
savagery *n.* дикість dykist
save *prep* за винятком za vyniatkom
save *v.t.* уберігати uberihaty
saviour *n.* рятівник riativnyk
savour *n.* смак smak
savour *v.t.* смакувати smakuvaty
saw *n.* вислів vysliv
saw *v.t.* пиляти pyliaty
say *v.t.* сказати skazaty
say *n.* слово slovo
scabbard *n.* піхви pikhvy
scabies *n.* короста korosta
scaffold *n.* будівельні ліси budivelni lisy
scale *v.t.* зважувати zvazhuvaty
scale *n.* масштаб masshtab
scalp *n* скальп skalp
scamper *v.i* носитися nosytysia
scamper *n* пробіжка probizhka
scan *v.t.* сканувати skanuvaty
scandal *n* скандал skandal
scandalize *v.t.* шокувати shokuvaty
scant *a.* убогий ubohyi
scanty *a.* худий khudyi
scapegoat *n.* козел відпущення kozel vidpushchennia
scar *v.t.* залишати шрам zalyshaty shram
scar *n* шрам shram
scarce *a.* дефіцитний defitsytnyi
scarcely *adv.* навряд чи navriad chy
scarcity *n.* брак brak
scare *v.t.* налякати naliakaty
scare *n.* страх strakh
scarf *n.* шарф sharf

scatter *v.t.* розкидати rozkydaty
scavenger *n.* сміттяр smittiar
scene *n.* сцена stsena
scenery *n.* декорації dekoratsii
scenic *a.* сценічний stsenichnyi
scent *n.* запах zapakh
scent *v.t.* учувати uchuvaty
sceptic *n.* скептик skeptyk
sceptical *a.* скептичний skeptychnyi
scepticism *n.* скептицизм skeptytsyzm
sceptre *n.* скіпетр skipetr
schedule *n.* каталог kataloh
schedule *v.t.* скласти розклад sklasty rozklad
scheme *v.i.* замислити zamyslyty
scheme *n.* схема skhema
schism *n.* секта sekta
scholar *n.* вчений vchenyi
scholarly *a.* властивий вченим vlastyvyi vchenym
scholarship *n.* вченість vchenist
scholastic *a.* схоластичний skholastychnyi
school *n.* школа shkola
science *n.* наука nauka
scientific *a.* технічний tekhnichnyi
scientist *n.* науковець naukovets
scintillate *v.i.* іскритися iskrytysia
scintillation *n.* сцинтилляция stsyntylliatsyia
scissors *n.* ножиці nozhytsi
scoff *v.i.* знущатися znushchatysia
scoff *n.* посміховисько posmikhovysko
scold *v.t.* лаяти laiaty
scooter *n.* скутер skuter
scope *n.* намір namir
scorch *v.t.* палити palyty
score *v.t.* одержувати oderzhuvaty

score *n.* борг borh

scorer *n.* лічильний очків lichylnyi ochkiv

scorn *v.t.* зневажати znevazhaty

scorn *n.* об`єкт зневаги ob`iekt znevahy

scorpion *n.* скорпіон skorpion

Scot *n.* шотландець shotlandets

scotch *n.* скотч skotch

scotch *a.* шотландський shotlandskyi

scot-free *a.* безкарний bezkarnyi

scoundrel *n.* падлюка padliuka

scourge *n.* бич bych

scourge *v.t.* бичувати bychuvaty

scout *v.i* провести розвідку provesty rozvidku

scout *n* розвідник rozvidnyk

scowl *n.* похмурий вигляд pokhmuryi vyhliad

scowl *v.i.* хмуритися khmurytysia

scramble *n* видирання vydyrannia

scramble *v.i.* підніматися pidnimatysia

scrap *n.* клаптик klaptyk

scratch *v.t.* подряпати podriapaty

scratch *n.* подряпина podriapyna

scrawl *n* каракулі karakuli

scrawl *v.t.* нерозбірливо писати nerozbirlyvo pysaty

scream *n* зойк zoik

scream *v.i.* волати volaty

screen *v.t.* прикрити prykryty

screen *n.* екран ekran

screw *v.t.* пригвинчувати pryhvynchuvaty

screw *n.* гвинт hvynt

scribble *n.* карлючки karliuchky

scribble *v.t.* неакуратно писати neakuratno pysaty

script *n.* сценарій stsenarii

scripture *n.* Священне писання Sviashchenne pysannia

scroll *n.* сувій suvii

scrutinize *v.t.* вивчати vyvchaty

scrutiny *n.* розгляд rozhliad

scuffle *v.i.* битися bytysia

scuffle *n.* бійка biika

sculptor *n.* скульптор skulptor

sculptural *a.* скульптурний skulpturnyi

sculpture *n.* скульптура skulptura

scythe *v.t.* косити kosyty

scythe *n.* коса kosa

sea *n.* море more

seal *v.t.* ставити печатку stavyty pechatku

seal *n.* тюлень tiulen

seal *n.* печатка pechatka

seam *v.t.* з'єднати швами ziednaty shvamy

seam *n.* шов shov

seamy *a.* покритий швами pokrytyi shvamy

search *v.t.* шукати shukaty

search *n.* розшук rozshuk

season *v.t.* загартовувати zahartovuvaty

season *n.* сезон sezon

seasonable *a.* своєчасний svoiechasnyi

seasonal *a.* сезонний sezonnyi

seat *v.t.* сидіти sydity

seat *n.* сидіння sydinnia

secede *v.i.* відокремлюватися vidokremliuvatysia

secession *n.* розкол rozkol

secessionist *n.* сепаратист separatyst

seclude *v.t.* усамітнюватися usamitniuvatysia

secluded *a.* ізолювати izoliuvaty

seclusion *n.* усамітнення usamitnennia

second *a.* другий druhyi
second *v.t.* підтримувати
pidtrymuvaty
second *n* секунда sekunda
secondary *a.* вторинний vtorynnyi
seconder *n.* той, хто підтримує
кандидатуру toi, khto
pidtrymuie kandydaturu
secrecy *n.* секретність sekretnist
secret *n.* секрет sekret
secret *a.* секретний sekretnyi
secretariat (e) *n.* секретаріат
sekretariat
secretary *n.* секретар sekretar
secrete *v.t.* ховати khovaty
secretion *n.* секреція sekretsiia
secretive *a.* потайний potainyi
sect *n.* секта sekta
sectarian *a.* сектантський
sektantskyi
section *n.* розділ rozdil
sector *n.* сектор sektor
secure *v.t.* застрахувати
zastrakhuvaty
secure *a.* спокійний spokiinyi
security *n.* безпечність
bezpechnist
sedan *n.* носилки nosylky
sedate *v.t.* присипляти prysypliaty
sedate *a.* статечний statechnyi
sedative *n* заспокійливе
zaspokiilyve
sedative *a.* болезаспокійливий
bolezaspokiilyvyi
sedentary *a.* сидячий sydiachyi
sediment *n.* відстій vidstii
sedition *n.* підбурювання до
заколоту pidburiuvannia do
zakolotu
seditious *a.* підбурювальний
pidburiuvalnyi
seduce *n.* спокушати spokushaty
seduction *n.* зваба zvaba

seductive *a* спокусливий
spokuslyvyi
see *v.t.* знаходити znakhodyty
seed *n.* насіння nasinnia
seed *v.t.* сіяти siiaty
seek *v.t.* шукати shukaty
seem *v.i.* здаватися zdavatysia
seemly *a.* пристойний prystoinyi
seep *v.i.* просочуватися
prosochuvatysia
seer *n.* провидець provydets
seethe *v.i.* вирувати vyruvaty
segment *v.t.* ділити на сегменти
dilyty na sehmenty
segment *n.* сегмент sehment
segregate *v.t.* ізолюватися
izoliuvatysia
segregation *n.* ізоляція izoliatsiia
seismic *a.* сейсмічний
seismichnyi
seize *v.t.* заволодіти zavolodity
seizure *n.* захоплення
zakhoplennia
seldom *adv.* рідко ridko
select *a* добірний dobirnyi
select *v.t.* проводити відбір
provodyty vidbir
selection *n.* вибір vybir
selective *a.* селективний
selektyvnyi
self *n.* самість samist
selfish *a.* егоїстичний
ehoistychnyi
selfless *a.* самовідданий
samoviddanyi
sell *v.t.* продавати prodavaty
seller *n.* торговець torhovets
semblance *n.* зовнішність
zovnishnist
semen *n.* сперма sperma
semester *n.* семестр semestr
seminal *a.* насіннєвий nasinnievyi
seminar *n.* семінар seminar

174

senate *n.* сенат senat
senator *n.* сенатор senator
senatorial *a* який стосується виборів у сенат yakyi stosuietsia vyboriv u senat
senatorial *a.* сенаторський senatorskyi
send *v.t.* послати poslaty
senile *a.* старечий starechyi
senility *n.* старість starist
senior *n.* начальник nachalnyk
senior *a.* старший starshyi
seniority *n.* трудовий стаж trudovyi stazh
sensation *n.* відчуття vidchuttia
sensational *a.* сенсаційний sensatsiinyi
sense *v.t.* усвідомлювати usvidomliuvaty
sense *n.* сенс sens
senseless *a.* безглуздий bezhluzdyi
sensibility *n.* чутливість chutlyvist
sensible *a.* відчутний vidchutnyi
sensitive *a.* чутливий chutlyvyi
sensual *a.* чуттєвий chuttievyi
sensualist *n.* сластолюбець slastoliubets
sensuality *n.* чуттєвість chuttievist
sensuous *a.* плотський plotskyi
sentence *v.t.* засуджувати zasudzhuvaty
sentence *n.* вирок vyrok
sentience *n.* здатність відчувати zdatnist vidchuvaty
sentient *a.* який відчуває yakyi vidchuvaie
sentiment *n.* настрій nastrii
sentimental *a.* сентиментальний sentymentalnyi
sentinel *n.* часовий chasovyi
sentry *n.* караул karaul

separable *a.* віддільний viddilnyi
separate *v.t.* відокремлювати vidokremliuvaty
separate *a.* окремий okremyi
separation *n.* поділ podil
sepsis *n.* сепсис sepsys
September *n.* вересень veresen
septic *a.* септичний septychnyi
sepulchre *n.* склеп sklep
sepulture *n.* поховання pokhovannia
sequel *n.* наслідок naslidok
sequence *n.* послідовність poslidovnist
sequester *v.t.* накладати арешт nakladaty aresht
serene *a.* безтурботний bezturbotnyi
serenity *n.* спокій spokii
serf *n.* кріпак kripak
serge *n.* саржа sarzha
sergeant *n.* сержант serzhant
serial *n.* серіал serial
serial *a.* серійний seriinyi
series *n.* серія seriia
serious *a* серйозний serioznyi
sermonize *v.i.* повчати povchaty
serpent *n.* змія zmiia
serpentine *n.* змійовик zmiiovyk
servant *n.* слуга sluha
serve *n.* подача м`яча podacha m`iacha
serve *v.t.* служити sluzhyty
service *v.t* обслуговувати obsluhovuvaty
service *n.* обслуговування obsluhovuvannia
serviceable *a.* справний spravnyi
servile *a.* рабський rabskyi
servility *n.* піднесливість pidneslyvist
session *n.* сесія sesiia
set *a* встановлений vstanovlenyi

set *n* набір nabir
set *v.t* ставити stavyty
settle *v.i.* врегулювати
vrehuliuvaty
settlement *n.* колонізація
kolonizatsiia
settler *n.* поселенець poselenets
seven *a* семирічний semyrichnyi
seven *n.* сім sim
seventeen *n.* сімнадцять
simnadtsiat
seventeenth *a.* сімнадцятий
simnadtsiatyi
seventh *a.* сьомий somyi
seventieth *a.* сімдесятий
simdesiatyi
seventy *n.*, *a* сімдесят simdesiat
sever *v.t.* розривати rozryvaty
several *a* кілька kilka
severance *n.* відділення
viddilennia
severe *a.* твердий tverdyi
severity *n.* строгість strohist
sew *v.t.* шити shyty
sewage *n.* стічні води stichni vody
sewer *n* швець shvets
sewerage *n.* каналізація
kanalizatsiia
sex *n.* стать stat
sexual *a.* сексуальний seksualnyi
sexuality *n.* сексуальність
seksualnist
sexy *a.* сексапільний seksapilnyi
shabby *a.* потертий potertyi
shackle *v.t.* скувати skuvaty
shackle *n.* пута puta
shade *v.t.* штрихувати
shtrykhuvaty
shade *n.* тінь tin
shadow *v.t* спостерігати
sposterihaty
shadow *n.* тінь tin
shadowy *a.* темний temnyi

shaft *n.* ратище ratyshche
shake *n* тремтіння tremtinnia
shake *v.i.* трясти triasty
shaky *a.* хиткий khytkyi
shallow *a.* мілкий milkyi
sham *n* удавання udavannia
sham *a* фіктивний fiktyvnyi
sham *v.i.* симулювати symuliuvaty
shame *v.t.* соромити soromyty
shame *n.* сором sorom
shameful *a.* ганебний hanebnyi
shameless *a.* безсоромний
bezsoromnyi
shampoo *v.t.* мити шампунем
myty shampunem
shampoo *n.* шампунь shampun
shanty *n.* халупка khalupka
shape *v.t* надати форму nadaty
formu
shape *n.* форма forma
shapely *a.* стрункий strunkyi
share *n* акція aktsiia
share *v.t.* ділитися dilytysia
share *n.* пай pai
shark *n.* акула akula
sharp *adv.* сильно sylno
sharp *a.* виразний vyraznyi
sharpen *v.t.* точити tochyty
sharpener *n.* стругачка
struhachka
sharper *n.* шахрай shakhrai
shatter *v.t.* розстроюватися
rozstroiuvatysia
shave *n* гоління holinnia
shave *v.t.* голитися holytysia
shawl *n.* шаль shal
she *pron.* вона vona
sheaf *n.* сніп snip
shear *v.t.* зрушення zrushennia
shears *n. pl.* ножиці nozhytsi
shed *n* навіс navis
shed *v.t.* поширювати
poshyriuvaty

sheep *n.* паства pastva
sheepish *a.* дурнуватий durnuvatyi
sheer *a.* чистий chystyi
sheet *v.t.* покрити pokryty
sheet *n.* чохол chokhol
shelf *n.* шельф shelf
shell *v.t.* очищати від шкарлупи ochyshchaty vid shkarlupy
shell *n.* оболонка obolonka
shelter *v.t.* дати притулок daty prytulok
shelter *n.* укриття ukryttia
shelve *v.t.* відкласти vidklasty
shepherd *n.* чабан chaban
shield *v.t.* затуляти zatuliaty
shield *n.* щит shchyt
shift *n* зміна zmina
shift *v.t.* переміщати peremishchaty
shifty *a.* виверткий vyvertkyi
shilling *n.* шилінг shylinh
shilly-shally *v.i.* бути нерішучим buty nerishuchym
shilly-shally *n.* нерішучий nerishuchyi
shin *n.* рулька rulka
shine *n* сяяня siaiania
shine *v.i.* блищати blyshchaty
shiny *a.* лискучий lyskuchyi
ship *v.t.* занурити zanuryty
ship *n.* судно sudno
shipment *n.* відвантаження vidvantazhennia
shire *n.* графство hrafstvo
shirk *v.t.* ухилятися ukhyliatysia
shirker *n.* прогульник prohulnyk
shirt *n.* сорочка sorochka
shiver *v.i.* тремтіти tremtity
shoal *v.t.* міліти mility
shoal *n.* зграя zhraia
shock *v.t.* шокувати shokuvaty
shock *n.* шок shok

shoe *v.t.* взувати vzuvaty
shoe *n.* туфля tuflia
shoot *n* стрілянина strilianyna
shoot *v.t.* стріляти striliaty
shop *v.i.* робити покупки robyty pokupky
shop *n.* магазин mahazyn
shore *n.* берег bereh
short *adv.* коротко korotko
short *a.* низький nyzkyi
shortage *n.* недостача nedostacha
shortcoming *n.* дефект defekt
shorten *v.t.* скорочувати skorochuvaty
shortly *adv.* незабаром nezabarom
shorts *n. pl.* шорти shorty
shot *n.* постріл postril
shoulder *v.t.* проштовхуватися proshtovkhuvatysia
shoulder *n.* плече pleche
shout *v.i.* голосно говорити holosno hovoryty
shout *n.* вигук vyhuk
shove *n.* штовхання shtovkhannia
shove *v.t.* шпурляти shpurliaty
shovel *v.t.* вигрібати vyhribaty
shovel *n.* лопата lopata
show *n.* шоу shou
show *v.t.* показувати pokazuvaty
shower *v.t.* литися зливою lytysia zlyvoiu
shower *n.* душ dush
shrew *n.* землерийка zemleryika
shrewd *a.* проникливий pronyklyvyi
shriek *v.i.* верещати vereshchaty
shriek *n.* вереск veresk
shrill *a.* пронизливий pronyzlyvyi
shrine *n.* усипальниця usypalnytsia

shrink *v.i* скорочуватися skorochuvatysia
shrinkage *n.* усадка usadka
shroud *v.t.* загорнути в саван zahornuty v savan
shroud *n.* саван savan
shrub *n.* чагарник chaharnyk
shrug *n* знизування znyzuvannia
shrug *v.t.* знизувати плечима znyzuvaty plechyma
shudder *n* тремтіння tremtinnia
shudder *v.i.* здригатися zdryhatysia
shuffle *n.* човгання chovhannia
shuffle *v.i.* човгати chovhaty
shun *v.t.* уникати unykaty
shunt *v.t.* пересувати peresuvaty
shut *a.* шунтувальний shuntuvalnyi
shutter *n.* затвор zatvor
shuttle *v.t.* рухатися назад і вперед rukhatysia nazad i vpered
shuttle *n.* човник chovnyk
shuttlecock *n.* волан volan
shy *v.i.* полохатися polokhatysia
shy *n.* різкий випад rizkyi vypad
sick *a.* хворий khvoryi
sickle *n.* серп serp
sickly *a.* хворобливий khvoroblyvyi
sickness *n.* хвороба khvoroba
side *v.i.* вставати на чиюсь сторону vstavaty na chyius storonu
side *n.* сторона storona
siege *n.* облога obloha
siesta *n.* сієста siiesta
sieve *v.t.* відсівати vidsivaty
sieve *n.* сито syto
sift *v.t.* просівати prosivaty
sigh *v.i.* зітхати zitkhaty
sigh *n.* зітхання zitkhannia

sight *v.t.* побачити pobachyty
sight *n.* зір zir
sightly *a.* видний vydnyi
sign *v.t.* підписати pidpysaty
sign *n.* знак znak
signal *v.t.* сигналізувати syhnalizuvaty
signal *a.* сигнальний syhnalnyi
signal *n.* сигнал syhnal
signatory *n.* сторона, яка підписалася storona, yaka pidpysalasia
signature *n.* підпис pidpys
significance *n.* значення znachennia
significant *a.* багатозначний bahatoznachnyi
signification *n.* показ pokaz
signify *v.t.* виявляти vyiavliaty
silence *v.t.* заглушити zahlushyty
silence *n.* тиша tysha
silencer *n.* глушник hlushnyk
silent *a.* неактивний neaktyvnyi
silhouette *n.* силует syluet
silk *n.* шовк shovk
silken *a.* шовковий shovkovyi
silky *a.* шовковистий shovkovystyi
silly *a.* недоумкуватий nedoumkuvatyi
silt *v.t.* замулюватися zamuliuvatysia
silt *n.* шлам shlam
silver *v.t.* сріблити sriblyty
silver *n.* срібло sriblo
silver *a* срібний sribnyi
similar *a.* схожий skhozhyi
similarity *n.* тотожність totozhnist
simile *n.* порівняння porivniannia
similitude *n.* схожість skhozhist
simmer *v.i.* кипіти на повільному вогні kypyty na povilnomu vohni

simple *a.* елементарний elementarnyi
simpleton *n.* простак prostak
simplicity *n.* простодушність prostodushnist
simplification *n.* спрощення sproshchennia
simplify *v.t.* спростити sprostyty
simultaneous *a.* одночасний odnochasnyi
sin *v.i.* грішити hrishyty
sin *n.* гріх hrikh
since *conj.* з тих пір z tykh pir
since *adv.* тому tomu
since *prep.* після pislia
sincere *a.* щиросердний shchyroserdnyi
sincerity *n.* щирість shchyrist
sinful *a.* грішний hrishnyi
sing *v.i.* співати spivaty
singe *n* опік opik
singe *v.t.* обпалювати obpaliuvaty
singer *n.* співак spivak
single *v.t.* відібрати vidibraty
single *n.* холостяк kholostiak
single *a.* самотній samotnii
singular *a.* одиничний odynychnyi
singularity *n.* незвичайність nezvychainist
singularly *adv.* особливо osoblyvo
sinister *a.* поганий pohanyi
sink *n* раковина rakovyna
sink *v.i.* топити topyty
sinner *n.* грішник hrishnyk
sinuous *a.* звивистий zvyvystyi
sip *n.* маленький ковток malenkyi kovtok
sip *v.t.* куштувати kushtuvaty
sir *n.* сер ser
siren *n.* сирена syrena
sister *n.* сестра sestra

sisterhood *n.* сестринство sestrynstvo
sisterly *a.* сестринський sestrynskyi
sit *v.i.* сидіти sydity
site *n.* сайт sait
situation *n.* ситуація sytuatsiia
six *n., a* шість shist
sixteen *n., a.* шістнадцять shistnadtsiat
sixteenth *a.* шістнадцятий shistnadtsiatyi
sixth *a.* шостий shostyi
sixtieth *a.* шістдесятий shistdesiatyi
sixty *n., a.* шістьдесят shistdesiat
sizable *a.* значний znachnyi
size *n.* розмір rozmir
size *v.t.* розставляти за величиною rozstavliaty za velychynoiu
sizzle *n.* шипіння shypinnia
sizzle *v.i.* шипіти shypity
skate *v.t.* кататися на ковзанах katatysia na kovzanakh
skate *n.* санчата sanchata
skein *n.* моток пряжі motok priazhi
skeleton *n.* скелет skelet
sketch *v.t.* накидати nakydaty
sketch *n.* ескіз eskiz
sketchy *a.* уривчастий uryvchastyi
skid *n* занос zanos
skid *v.i.* буксувати buksuvaty
skilful *a.* майстерний maisternyi
skill *n.* навик navyk
skin *v.t* покривати шкірою pokryvaty shkiroiu
skin *n.* шкіра shkira
skip *n* стрибок strybok
skip *v.i.* пропускати propuskaty
skipper *n.* шкіпер shkiper

skirmish *v.t.* зав'язати
перестрілку zaviazaty
perestrilku
skirmish *n.* перестрілка
perestrilka
skirt *v.t.* обходити obkhodyty
skirt *n.* спідниця spidnytsia
skit *n.* пародія parodiia
skull *n.* череп cherep
sky *v.t.* вішати під стелю vishaty
pid steliu
sky *n.* небо nebo
slab *n.* шматок shmatok
slack *a.* слабкий slabkyi
slacken *v.t.* слабшати slabshaty
slacks *n.* слабина slabyna
slake *v.t.* втамувати vtamuvaty
slam *n* удар udar
slam *v.t.* кидати зі стуком kydaty
zi stukom
slander *n.* лихослів'я lykhoslivia
slander *v.t.* паплюжити
papliuzhyty
slanderous *a.* наклепницький
naklepnytskyi
slang *n.* сленг slenh
slant *n* схил skhyl
slant *v.t.* нахиляти nakhyliaty
slap *v.t.* шльопати shlopaty
slap *n.* ляпас liapas
slash *n* вирубка vyrubka
slash *v.t.* рубати rubaty
slate *n.* шифер shyfer
slattern *n.* грязнуля hriaznulia
slatternly *a.* неохайний
neokhainyi
slaughter *v.t.* зарізати zarizaty
slaughter *n.* різанина rizanyna
slave *v.i.* працювати, як раб
pratsiuvaty, yak rab
slave *n.* раб rab
slavery *n.* рабовласництво
rabovlasnytstvo

slavish *a.* рабський rabskyi
slay *v.t.* убити ubyty
sleek *a.* гладкий hladkyi
sleep *n.* сон son
sleep *v.i.* спати spaty
sleeper *n.* соня sonia
sleepy *a.* сонний sonnyi
sleeve *n* рукав rukav
sleight *n.* спритність sprytnist
slender *n.* стрункий strunkyi
slice *v.t.* нарізати скибками
narizaty skybkamy
slice *n.* скибочка skybochka
slick *a* мспритний msprytnyi
slide *n* ковзати kovzaty
slide *v.i.* каток katok
slight *a.* крихкий krykhkyi
slight *v.t.* нехтувати nekhtuvaty
slight *a.* тендітний tenditnyi
slim *v.i.* худнути khudnuty
slim *a.* тонкий tonkyi
slime *n.* слиз slyz
slimy *a.* слизовий slyzovyi
sling *n.* строп strop
slip *n.* сковзнути skovznuty
slip *v.i.* ковзання kovzannia
slipper *n. pl* тапочки tapochky
slippery *a.* слизький slyzkyi
slipshod *a.* недбалий nedbalyi
slit *v.t.* нарізати у довжину
narizaty u dovzhynu
slit *n.* щілина shchilyna
slogan *n.* гасло haslo
slope *v.i.* хилитися khylytysia
slope *n.* схил skhyl
sloth *n.* лінощі linoshchi
slothful *n.* недбайливий
nedbailyvyi
slough *v.t.* скинути шкіру skynuty
shkiru
slough *n.* багно bahno
slough *n.* ковбаня kovbania
slovenly *a.* неохайний neokhainyi

slow *v.i.* зволікати zvolikaty
slow *a* повільний povilnyi
slowly *adv.* повільно povilno
slowness *n.* повільність povilnist
sluggard *n.* ледар ledar
sluggish *a.* ледачий ledachyi
sluice *n.* шлюз shliuz
slum *n.* нетрі netri
slumber *n.* сон son
slumber *v.i.* не діяти ne diiaty
slump *v.i.* різко падати rizko padaty
slump *n.* спад spad
slur *n.* чорниш chornysh
slush *n.* сльота slota
slushy *a.* сльотавий slotavyi
slut *n.* шльондра shlondra
sly *a.* хитрий khytryi
smack *n.* дзвінкий поцілунок dzvinkyi potsilunok
smack *v.t.* мати присмак maty prysmak
smack *v.i.* пахнути pakhnuty
smack *n* чмоканье chmokane
smack *n.* присмак prysmak
small *n* мала величина mala velychyna
small *a.* невеликий nevelykyi
smallness *n.* малість malist
smallpox *n.* віспа vispa
smart *v.i* відчувати сильний біль vidchuvaty sylnyi bil
smart *n* пекучий біль pekuchyi bil
smart *a.* різкий rizkyi
smash *n* нищівний удар nyshchivnyi udar
smash *v.t.* громити hromyty
smear *n.* пляма pliama
smear *v.t.* натирати natyraty
smell *v.t.* нюхати niukhaty
smell *n.* нюх niukh
smelt *v.t.* виплавляти vyplavliaty

smile *v.i.* посміхатися posmikhatysia
smile *n.* усмішка usmishka
smith *n.* коваль koval
smock *n.* халат khalat
smog *n.* смог smoh
smoke *v.i.* диміти dymity
smoke *n.* дим dym
smoky *a.* димчастий dymchastyi
smooth *v.t.* пригладжувати pryhladzhuvaty
smooth *a.* плавний plavnyi
smother *v.t.* задихнутися zadykhnutysia
smoulder *v.i.* тліти tlity
smug *a.* самовдоволений samovdovolenyi
smuggle *v.t.* провозити контрабандою provozyty kontrabandoiu
smuggler *n.* контрабандист kontrabandyst
snack *n.* закуска zakuska
snag *n.* уламок зуба ulamok zuba
snail *n.* равлик ravlyk
snake *v.i.* повзти povzty
snake *n.* зрадник zradnyk
snap *n* засувка zasuvka
snap *a* поспішний pospishnyi
snap *v.t.* клацати klatsaty
snare *v.t.* піймати в пастку piimaty v pastku
snare *n.* пастка pastka
snarl *v.i.* гарчати harchaty
snarl *n.* гарчання harchannia
snatch *n.* злодійство zlodiistvo
snatch *v.t.* урвати urvaty
sneak *n* злодюжка zlodiuzhka
sneak *v.i.* крастися krastysia
sneer *n* презирлива усмішка prezyrlyva usmishka
sneer *v.i* глузливо посміхнутися hluzlyvo posmikhnutysia

sneeze *n* чхання chkhannia
sneeze *v.i.* чхати chkhaty
sniff *n* сопіння sopinnia
sniff *v.i.* сопіти sopity
snob *n.* сноб snob
snobbery *n.* снобізм snobizm
snobbish *v* снобістський snobistskyi
snore *n* хропіння khropinnia
snore *v.i.* хропіти khropity
snort *n.* пирхання pyrkhannia
snort *v.i.* фиркати fyrkaty
snout *n.* рило rylo
snow *v.i.* заносити снігом zanosyty snihom
snow *n.* сніг snih
snowy *a.* сніжний snizhnyi
snub *n.* образа obraza
snub *v.t.* принизити prynyzyty
snuff *n.* нагар на свічці nahar na svichtsi
snug *n.* затишне містечко zatyshne mistechko
so *adv.* так tak
so *conj.* таким чином takym chynom
soak *n.* замочування zamochuvannia
soak *v.t.* вбирати vbyraty
soap *v.t.* намилити namylyty
soap *n.* мило mylo
soapy *a.* мильний mylnyi
soar *v.i.* парити paryty
sob *n* ридання rydannia
sob *v.i.* ридати rydaty
sober *a.* тверезий tverezyi
sobriety *n.* тверезість tverezist
sociability *n.* товариськість tovaryskist
sociable *a.* товариський tovaryskyi
social *n.* соціальний sotsialnyi
socialism *n* соціалізм sotsializm

socialist *n,a* соціаліст, соціалістичний sotsialist, sotsialistychnyi
society *n.* суспільство suspilstvo
sociology *n.* соціологія sotsiolohiia
sock *n.* шкарпетка shkarpetka
socket *n.* розетка rozetka
sod *n.* дерен deren
sodomite *n.* педераст pederast
sodomy *n.* содомія sodomiia
sofa *n.* софа sofa
soft *n.* ніжний nizhnyi
soften *v.t.* ослабляти опір противника oslabliaty opir protyvnyka
soil *v.t.* бруднитися brudnytysia
soil *n.* грунт hrunt
sojourn *n* тимчасове перебування tymchasove perebuvannia
sojourn *v.i.* тимчасово проживати tymchasovo prozhyvaty
solace *n.* заспокоєння zaspokoiennia
solace *v.t.* утішати utishaty
solar *a.* сонячний soniachnyi
solder *v.t.* зварювання zvariuvannia
solder *n.* припій prypii
soldier *v.i.* солдат soldat
soldier *n.* споювати spoiuvaty
sole *a* винятковий vyniatkovyi
sole *v.t* ставити підметку stavyty pidmetku
sole *n.* підошва pidoshva
solemn *a.* урочистий urochystyi
solemnity *n.* урочистість urochystist
solemnize *v.t.* святкувати sviatkuvaty

solicit *v.t.* клопотатися klopotatysia
solicitation *n.* чіпляння chipliannia
solicitor *n.* повірений povirenyi
solicitous *a.* повний бажання povnyi bazhannia
solicitude *n.* дбайливість dbailyvist
solid *n* твердий tverdyi
solid *a.* згуртований zhurtovanyi
solidarity *n.* тіло tilo
soliloquy *n.* внутрішній монолог vnutrishnii monoloh
solitary *a.* занедбаний zanedbanyi
solitude *n.* самота samota
solo *adv.* незалежно nezalezhno
solo *a.* сольний solnyi
solo *n* соло solo
soloist *n.* соліст solist
solubility *n.* розчинність rozchynnist
soluble *a.* розчинний rozchynnyi
solution *n.* розчин rozchyn
solve *v.t.* вирішити vyrishyty
solvency *n.* платоспроможність platospromozhnist
solvent *n* розчинник rozchynnyk
solvent *a.* що розчиняє shcho rozchyniaie
sombre *a.* темний temnyi
some *pron.* дехто dekhto
some *a.* якийсь yakyis
somebody *n.* будь-хто bud-khto
somebody *pron.* хтось khtos
somehow *adv.* якось yakos
someone *pron.* хтось khtos
somersault *v.i.* стрибати перевертом strybaty perevertom
somersault *n.* перекидання perekydannia

something *adv.* дещо deshcho
something *pron.* щось shchos
sometime *adv.* колись kolys
sometimes *adv.* іноді inodi
somewhat *adv.* трохи trokhy
somewhere *adv.* десь des
somnambulism *n.* сомнамбулізм somnambulizm
somnambulist *n.* лунатик lunatyk
somnolence *n.* сонливість sonlyvist
somnolent *a.* сонливий sonlyvyi
son *n.* син syn
song *n.* пісня pisnia
songster *n.* співак spivak
sonic *a.* звуковий zvukovyi
sonnet *n.* сонет sonet
sonority *n.* звучність zvuchnist
soon *adv.* скоро skoro
soot *v.t.* покрити сажею pokryty sazheiu
soot *n.* сажа sazha
soothe *v.t.* втішати vtishaty
sophism *n.* софізм sofizm
sophist *n.* софіст sofist
sophisticate *v.t.* перекручувати perekruchuvaty
sophisticated *a.* позбавлений простоти pozbavlenyi prostoty
sophistication *n.* витонченість vytonchenist
sorcerer *n.* чаклун chaklun
sorcery *n.* чаклунство chaklunstvo
sordid *a.* злиденний zlydennyi
sore *n* болячка boliachka
sore *a.* запалений zapalenyi
sorrow *v.i.* засмучуватися zasmuchuvatysia
sorrow *n.* печаль pechal
sorry *a.* засмучений zasmuchenyi
sort *n.* сорт sort
sort *v.t* сортувати sortuvaty

soul *n.* душа dusha
sound *v.i.* вимірювати глибину vymiriuvaty hlybynu
sound *n* звук zvuk
sound *a.* міцний mitsnyi
soup *n.* суп sup
sour *v.t.* прокисати prokysaty
sour *a.* прокислий prokyslyi
source *n.* джерело dzherelo
south *n.* країни Півдня krainy Pivdnia
south *a.* південний pivdennyi
south *n.* південь pivden
southerly *a.* з півдня z pivdnia
southern *a.* зюйдовий ziuidovyi
souvenir *n.* сувенір suvenir
sovereign *a* суверенний suverennyi
sovereign *n.* суверен suveren
sovereignty *n.* суверенітет suverenitet
sow *n.* свиня svynia
sow *v.t.* сіяти siiaty
space *v.t.* розставити з проміжками rozstavyty z promizhkamy
space *n.* простір prostir
spacious *a.* просторий prostoryi
spade *v.t.* копати лопатою kopaty lopatoiu
spade *n.* заступ zastup
span *v.t.* простягатися prostiahatysia
span *n.* амплітуда amplituda
Spaniard *n.* іспанець ispanets
spaniel *n.* спанієль spaniiel
Spanish *n.* іспанська мова ispanska mova
Spanish *a.* іспанський ispanskyi
spanner *n.* вилочний ключ vylochnyi kliuch
spare *n.* запасні частини zapasni chastyny

spare *a* убогий ubohyi
spare *v.t.* економити ekonomyty
spark *n.* іскра iskra
spark *v.i.* іскритися iskrytysia
spark *n.* іскра iskra
sparkle *n.* іскріння iskrinnia
sparkle *v.i.* іскритися iskrytysia
sparrow *n.* горобець horobets
sparse *a.* рідкісний ridkisnyi
spasm *n.* спазм spazm
spasmodic *a.* спазматичний spazmatychnyi
spate *n.* раптова злива raptova zlyva
spatial *a.* просторовий prostorovyi
spawn *v.i.* метати ікру metaty ikru
spawn *n.* виплодок vyplodok
speak *v.i.* висловлюватися vyslovliuvatysia
speaker *n.* спікер spiker
spear *v.t.* бити остенем byty ostenem
spear *n.* спис spys
spearhead *v.t.* очолювати ocholiuvaty
spearhead *n.* вістря vistria
special *a.* спеціальний spetsialnyi
specialist *n.* спеціаліст spetsialist
speciality *n.* спеціальність spetsialnist
specialization *n.* спеціалізація spetsializatsiia
specialize *v.i.* спеціалізуватися spetsializuvatysia
species *n.* вид vyd
specific *a.* конкретний konkretnyi
specification *n.* специфікація spetsyfikatsiia
specify *v.t.* встановлювати vstanovliuvaty
specimen *n.* зразок zrazok
speck *n.* плямочка pliamochka

spectacle *n.* сцена stsena
spectacular *a.* захоплюючий zakhopliuiuchyi
spectator *n.* очевидець ochevydets
spectre *n.* примара prymara
speculate *v.i.* спекулювати spekuliuvaty
speculation *n.* міркування mirkuvannia
speech *n.* промова promova
speed *v.i.* квапити kvapyty
speed *n.* швидкість shvydkist
speedily *adv.* швидко shvydko
speedy *a.* швидкий shvydkyi
spell *v.t.* зачаровувати zacharovuvaty
spell *n* шарм sharm
spell *n.* чари chary
spend *v.t.* розтрачувати roztrachuvaty
spendthrift *n.* мот mot
sperm *n.* кашалот kashalot
sphere *n.* сфера sfera
spherical *a.* сферичний sferychnyi
spice *v.t.* приправляти prypravliaty
spice *n.* спеції spetsii
spicy *a.* пряний prianyi
spider *n.* павук pavuk
spike *v.t.* перестромлювати perestromliuvaty
spike *n.* шпилька shpylka
spill *n* затичка zatychka
spill *v.i.* проливати prolyvaty
spin *n.* кружляння kruzhliannia
spin *v.i.* ловити на блешню lovyty na bleshniu
spinach *n.* шпинат shpynat
spinal *a.* спинний spynnyi
spindle *n.* шпиндель shpyndel
spine *n.* хребет khrebet

spinner *n.* пряха priakha
spinster *n.* стара діва stara diva
spiral *a.* спіральний spiralnyi
spiral *n.* спіраль spiral
spirit *n.* дух dukh
spirited *a.* сміливий smilyvyi
spiritual *a.* духовний dukhovnyi
spiritualism *n.* спіритизм spirytyzm
spiritualist *n.* спіритуаліст spirytualist
spirituality *n.* духовність dukhovnist
spit *n* слина slyna
spit *v.i.* плювати pliuvaty
spite *n.* злість zlist
spittle *n* плювок pliuvok
spittoon *n.* плювальниця pliuvalnytsia
splash *n* сплеск splesk
splash *v.i.* плескатися pleskatysia
spleen *n.* селезінка selezinka
splendid *a.* блискучий blyskuchyi
splendour *n.* шляхетність shliakhetnist
splinter *v.t.* розщеплювати rozshchepliuvaty
splinter *n.* осколок oskolok
split *n* розщеплювання rozshchepliuvannia
split *v.i.* розколювати rozkoliuvaty
spoil *n* порожня порода porozhnia poroda
spoil *v.t.* балувати baluvaty
spoke *n.* поперечина poperechyna
spokesman *n.* промовець promovets
sponge *v.t.* чистити губкою chystyty hubkoiu
sponge *n.* губка hubka
sponsor *v.t.* спонсорувати sponsoruvaty

sponsor *n.* спонсор sponsor
spontaneity *n.* спонтанність
spontannist
spontaneous *a.* спонтанний
spontannyi
spoon *n.* ложка lozhka
spoon *v.t.* черпати ложкою
cherpaty lozhkoiu
spoonful *n.* повна ложка povna
lozhka
sporadic *a.* спорадичний
sporadychnyi
sport *v.i.* гратися hratysia
sport *n.* спорт sport
sportive *a.* спортивний sportyvnyi
sportsman *n.* спортсмен
sportsmen
spot *v.t.* плямувати pliamuvaty
spot *n.* прищик pryshchyk
spotless *a.* незаплямований
nezapliamovanyi
spousal *n.* подружній podruzhnii
spouse *n.* чоловік cholovik
spout *v.i.* бити струменем byty
strumenem
spout *n.* носик nosyk
sprain *n.* розтягнення суглоба
roztiahnennia suhloba
sprain *v.t.* розтягнути зв'язки
roztiahnuty zviazky
spray *n* гілка hilka
spray *v.t.* розпорошувати
rozporoshuvaty
spray *n.* струмінь strumin
spread *n.* поширення
poshyrennia
spread *v.i.* поширюватися
poshyriuvatysia
spree *n.* запій zapii
sprig *n.* гілочка hilochka
sprightly *a.* бадьорий badoryi
spring *n* весна vesna
spring *v.i.* скакати skakaty

sprinkle *v. t.* бризкати bryzkaty
sprint *n* спринт sprynt
sprint *v.i.* спрінтовать sprintovat
sprout *n* пагін pahin
sprout *v.i.* проростати prorostaty
spur *v.t.* пришпорити pryshporyty
spur *n.* шпора shpora
spurious *a.* паразитний
parazytnyi
spurn *v.t.* штофхати shtofkhaty
spurt *n* ривок ryvok
spurt *v.t.* викидати vykydaty
sputnik *n.* супутник suputnyk
sputum *n.* мокрота mokrota
spy *v.i.* шпигувати shpyhuvaty
spy *n.* шпигун shpyhun
squad *n.* загін zahin
squadron *n.* ескадрон eskadron
squalid *a.* убогий ubohyi
squalor *n.* убозтво uboztvo
squander *v.t.* розбазарювати
rozbazariuvaty
square *v.t.* надавати квадратну
форму nadavaty kvadratnu
formu
square *a* квадратний kvadratnyi
square *n.* консерватор
konservator
squash *n* тиснява tysniava
squash *v.t.* роздавлювати
rozdavliuvaty
squat *v.i.* сидіти навпочіпах
sydity navpochipakh
squeak *n* скрип skryp
squeak *v.i.* скрипіти skrypity
squeeze *v.t.* стиснути stysnuty
squint *n* косоокість kosookist
squint *v.i.* дивитися скоса
dyvytysia skosa
squire *n.* зброєносець
zbroienosets
squirrel *n.* білка bilka
stab *n.* удар udar

stab v.t. втикати vtykaty
stability n. стабільність stabilnist
stabilization n. стабілізація
stabilizatsiia
stabilize v.t. стабілізуватися
stabilizuvatysia
stable v.t. ставити в стайню
stavyty v stainiu
stable n стайня stainia
stable a. стабільний stabilnyi
stadium n. стадіон stadion
staff v.t. укомплектувати штат
ukomplektuvaty shtat
staff n. кий kyi
stag n. біржовий брокер birzhovyi
broker
stage v.t. інсценувати
instsenuvaty
stage n. етап etap
stagger n. похитування
pokhytuvannia
stagger v.i. хитатися khytatysia
stagnant a. застійний zastiinyi
stagnate v.i. застоюватися
zastoiuvatysia
stagnation n. застій zastii
staid a. статечний statechnyi
stain v.t. забруднити zabrudnyty
stain n. барвник barvnyk
stainless a. нержавіючий
nerzhaviiuchyi
stair n. сходинка skhodynka
stake v.t. ставити stavyty
stake n частина chastyna
stale v.t. спростовувати
sprostovuvaty
stale a. черствий cherstvyi
stalemate n. безвихідне
положення bezvykhidne
polozhennia
stalk v.i. потай просуватися potai
prosuvatysia
stalk n черешок chereshok

stalk n. стебло steblo
stall v.t. займати стійло zaimaty
stiilo
stall n. стійло stiilo
stallion n. жеребець zherebets
stalwart a. рослий roslyi
stalwart n стійкий прихильник
stiikyi prykhylnyk
stamina n. витривалість
vytryvalist
stammer n заїкання zaikannia
stammer v.i. заїкатися zaikatysia
stamp v.i. ставити печатку stavyty
pechatku
stamp n. штамп shtamp
stampede v.i панічно тікати
panichno tikaty
stampede n. панічна втеча
panichna vtecha
stand n. стояк stoiak
stand v.i. стояти stoiaty
standard a стандартний
standartnyi
standard n. стандарт standart
standardization n.
стандартизація standartyzatsiia
standardize v.t. стандартизувати
standartyzuvaty
standing n. стоячий stoiachyi
standpoint n. точка зору tochka
zoru
standstill n. зупинка zupynka
stanza n. строфа strofa
staple a основний osnovnyi
staple n. скоба skoba
star v.t. нагородити орденом
nahorodyty ordenom
star n. зірка zirka
starch v.t. крохмалити
krokhmalyty
starch n. крохмаль krokhmal
stare n. пильний погляд pylnyi
pohliad

stare *v.i.* витріщатися vytrishchatysia

stark *adv.* цілком tsilkom

stark *n.* задубілий zadubilyi

starry *a.* зоряний zorianyi

start *n.* перевага perevaha

start *v.t.* вирушати в дорогу vyrushaty v dorohu

startle *v.t.* налякати naliakaty

starvation *n.* голодна смерть holodna smert

starve *v.i.* зголодніти zholodnity

state *v.t* стверджувати stverdzhuvaty

state *n.* стан stan

stateliness *n.* величавість velychavist

stately *a.* сповнений гідності spovnenyi hidnosti

statement *n.* констатація konstatatsiia

statesman *n.* державний діяч derzhavnyi diiach

static *n.* статичний statychnyi

statics *n.* статика statyka

station *v.t.* направляти на місце роботи napravliaty na mistse roboty

station *n.* станція stantsiia

stationary *a.* стаціонарний statsionarnyi

stationer *n.* торговець канцелярським приладдям torhovets kantseliarskym pryladdiam

stationery *n.* канцелярські товари kantseliarski tovary

statistical *a.* статистичний statystychnyi

statistician *n.* статистик statystyk

statistics *n.* статистика statystyka

statue *n.* статуя statuia

stature *n.* фігура fihura

status *n.* статус status

statute *n.* статут statut

statutory *a.* законний zakonnyi

staunch *a.* стійкий stiikyi

stay *n* перебування perebuvannia

stay *v.i.* стримувати strymuvaty

steadfast *a.* стійкий stiikyi

steadiness *n.* стійкість stiikist

steady *v.t.* укріплювати ukripliuvaty

steady *a.* стійкий stiikyi

steal *v.i.* крадена річ kradena rich

stealthily *adv.* крадькома kradkoma

steam *v.i.* випускати пар vypuskaty par

steam *n* пар par

steamer *n.* пароплав paroplav

steed *n.* кінь kin

steel *n.* сталь stal

steep *v.t.* вимочувати vymochuvaty

steep *a.* крутий krutyi

steeple *n.* шпиль shpyl

steer *v.t.* управляти upravliaty

stellar *a.* зоряний zorianyi

stem *v.i.* відбутися vidbutysia

stem *n.* стебло steblo

stench *n.* сморід smorid

stencil *v.i.* фарбувати за трафаретом farbuvaty za trafaretom

stencil *n.* трафарет trafaret

stenographer *n.* стенографістка stenohrafistka

stenography *n.* стенографія stenohrafiia

step *v.i.* ступнути stupnuty

step *n.* хода khoda

steppe *n.* степ step

stereotype *v.t.* робити побитим robyty pobytym

stereotype *n.* стереотип
stereotyp
stereotyped *a.* стереотипний
stereotypnyi
sterile *a.* стерильний sterylnyi
sterility *n.* стерильність sterylnist
sterilization *n.* стерилізація
sterylizatsiia
sterilize *v.t.* стерилізувати
sterylizuvaty
sterling *n.* стерлінг sterlinh
sterling *a.* надійний nadiinyi
stern *n.* хвіст khvist
stern *a.* суворий suvoryi
stethoscope *n.* стетоскоп
stetoskop
stew *v.t.* тушкувати tushkuvaty
stew *n.* тушковане м'ясо
tushkovane miaso
steward *n.* стюард stiuard
stick *v.t.* наклеїти nakleity
stick *n.* палиця palytsia
sticker *n.* наклейка nakleika
stickler *n.* прихильник prykhylnyk
sticky *n.* липкий lypkyi
stiff *n.* негнучкий nehnuchkyi
stiffen *v.t.* надавати жорсткості
nadavaty zhorstkosti
stifle *v.t.* душити dushyty
stigma *n.* стигмат styhmat
still *adv.* до цих пір do tsykh pir
still *v.t.* переганяти perehaniaty
still *n.* фотокадр fotokadr
still *a.* непорушний neporushnyi
stillness *n.* нерухомість
nerukhomist
stilt *n.* паля palia
stimulant *n.* стимулятор
stymuliator
stimulate *v.t.* стимулювати
stymuliuvaty
stimulus *n.* стимул stymul
sting *n.* укус ukus

sting *v.t.* відчувати гострий біль
vidchuvaty hostryi bil
stingy *a.* скупий skupyi
stink *n.* сморід smorid
stink *v.i.* смердіти smerdity
stipend *n.* стипендія stypendiia
stipulate *v.t.* ставити умовою
stavyty umovoiu
stipulation *n.* умова umova
stir *v.i.* переполох perepolokh
stirrup *n.* стремено stremeno
stitch *v.t.* стьобати stobaty
stitch *n.* стібок stibok
stock *a.* біржовий birzhovyi
stock *v.t.* зберігати на складі
zberihaty na skladi
stock *n.* акції aktsii
stocking *n.* рівень запасів riven
zapasiv
stoic *n.* стоїчний stoichnyi
stoke *v.t.* підтримувати вогонь
pidtrymuvaty vohon
stoker *n.* кочегар kochehar
stomach *v.t.* стерпіти sterpity
stomach *n.* шлунок shlunok
stone *v.t.* мостити каменем
mostyty kamenem
stone *n.* камінь kamin
stony *a.* кам'янистий kamianystyi
stool *n.* стілець stilets
stoop *n.* сутулість sutulist
stoop *v.i.* сутулитися sutulytysia
stop *n.* стоп stop
stop *v.t.* зупинити zupynyty
stoppage *n* затримка zatrymka
storage *n.* склад sklad
store *v.t.* вміщувати vmishchuvaty
store *n.* резерв rezerv
storey *n.* поверх poverkh
stork *n.* лелека leleka
storm *v.i.* штурмувати
shturmuvaty
storm *n.* гроза hroza

stormy *a.* грозовий hrozovyi
story *n.* оповідання opovidannia
stout *a.* товстий tovstyi
stove *n.* піч pich
stow *v.t.* укладати ukladaty
straggle *v.i.* відставати vidstavaty
straggler *n.* відсталий vidstalyi
straight *adv.* прямо priamo
straight *a.* невигнутий nevyhnutyi
straighten *v.t.* випрямляти vypriamliaty
straightforward *a.* простий prostyi
straightway *adv.* негайно nehaino
strain *n* напруга napruha
strain *v.t.* натягувати natiahuvaty
strait *n.* протока protoka
straiten *v.t.* обмежувати obmezhuvaty
strand *n* пасмо pasmo
strand *v.i.* сісти на мілину sisty na milynu
strange *a.* дивний dyvnyi
stranger *n.* незнайомець neznaiomets
strangle *v.t.* задушити zadushyty
strangulation *n.* удушення udushennia
strap *v.t.* стягнути ременем stiahnuty remenem
strap *n.* ремінець reminets
strategem *n.* хитрість khytrist
strategic *a.* стратегічний stratehichnyi
strategist *n.* стратег strateh
strategy *n.* стратегія stratehiia
stratum *n.* шар shar
straw *n.* солома soloma
strawberry *n.* полуниця polunytsia
stray *n* бездомна собака bezdomna sobaka
stray *a* заблудлий zabludlyi

stray *v.i.* блудити bludyty
stream *v.i.* текти tekty
stream *n.* валка valka
streamer *n.* вимпел vympel
streamlet *n.* струмочок strumochok
street *n.* вулиця vulytsia
strength *n.* міцність mitsnist
strengthen *v.t.* зміцнювати zmitsniuvaty
strenuous *a.* напружений napruzhenyi
stress *v.t* ставити наголос stavyty naholos
stress *n.* стрес stres
stretch *n* розтягування roztiahuvannia
stretch *v.t.* розтягувати roztiahuvaty
stretcher *n.* носилки nosylky
strew *v.t.* посипати posypaty
strict *a.* суворий suvoryi
stricture *n.* стриктура stryktura
stride *n* великий крок velykyi krok
stride *v.i.* бігти маховим кроком bihty makhovym krokom
strident *a.* скрипучий skrypuchyi
strife *n.* розбрат rozbrat
strike *n* страйк straik
strike *v.t.* страйкувати straikuvaty
striker *n.* страйкарі straikari
string *v.t.* мотузка motuzka
string *n.* тасьма tasma
stringency *n.* строгість strohist
stringent *a.* суворий suvoryi
strip *v.t.* здирати zdyraty
strip *n.* полоса polosa
stripe *v.t.* наносити смуги nanosyty smuhy
stripe *n.* шеврон shevron
strive *v.i.* докладати зусилля dokladaty zusyllia

stroke *v.t.* погладжувати pohladzhuvaty

stroke *n* хід khid

stroke *n.* замах zamakh

stroll *n* мандри mandry

stroll *v.i.* мандрувати mandruvaty

strong *a.* сильний sylnyi

stronghold *n.* фортеця fortetsia

structural *a.* структурний strukturnyi

structure *n.* структура struktura

struggle *n* зусилля zusyllia

struggle *v.i.* відбиватися vidbyvatysia

strumpet *n.* повія poviia

strut *n* стояк stoiak

strut *v.i.* закріплювати zakripliuvaty

stub *n.* недопалок nedopalok

stubble *n.* стерня sternia

stubborn *a.* упертий upertyi

stud *v.t.* оббити obbyty

stud *n.* шпилька shpylka

student *n.* студент student

studio *n.* студія studiia

studious *a.* старанний starannyi

study *n.* вивчення vyvchennia

study *v.i.* вивчати vyvchaty

stuff *2 v.t.* нафаршировати nafarshyruvaty

stuff *n.* речовина rechovyna

stuffy *a.* задушливий zadushlyvyi

stumble *n.* запинки zapynky

stumble *v.i.* спотикатися spotykatysia

stump *v.t* обрубувати obrubuvaty

stump *n.* обрубок obrubok

stun *v.t.* оглушати ohlushaty

stunt *n* зупинка зростання zupynka zrostannia

stunt *v.t.* демонструвати сміливість demonstruvaty smilyvist

stupefy *v.t.* приголомшувати pryholomshuvaty

stupendous *a.* колосальний kolosalnyi

stupid *a.* дурний durnyi

stupidity *n.* безглуздість bezhluzdist

sturdy *a.* стійкий stiikyi

sty *n.* свинарник svynarnyk

stye *n.* ячмінь на оці yachmin na otsi

style *n.* стиль styl

subdue *v.t.* скоряти skoriaty

subject *a* залежний zalezhnyi

subject *v.t.* піддавати piddavaty

subject *n.* тема tema

subjection *n.* віддання viddannia

subjective *a.* суб'єктивний subiektyvnyi

subjudice *a.* який перебуває на розгляді yakyi perebuvaie na rozhliadi

subjugate *v.t.* колонізувати kolonizuvaty

subjugation *n.* підкорення pidkorennia

sublet *v.t.* передавати в суборенду peredavaty v suborendu

sublimate *v.t.* сублімувати sublimuvaty

sublime *n* найвища точка naivyshcha tochka

sublime *a.* піднесений pidnesenyi

sublimity *n.* піднесеність pidnesenist

submarine *a* підводний pidvodnyi

submarine *n.* підводний човен pidvodnyi choven

submerge *v.i.* затоплюватися zatopliuvatysia

submission *n.* покора pokora

submissive *a.* покірний pokirnyi

submit *v.t.* представляти predstavliaty
subordinate *n* підлеглий pidlehlyi
subordinate *a.* підрядний pidriadnyi
subordinate *v.t.* підпорядковувати pidporiadkovuvaty
subordination *n.* субординація subordynatsiia
subscribe *v.t.* підписуватися pidpysuvatysia
subscription *n.* підписка pidpyska
subsequent *a.* який випливає yakyi vyplyvaie
subservience *n.* раболіпство rabolipstvo
subservient *a.* раболіпний rabolipnyi
subside *v.i.* спадати spadaty
subsidiary *a.* дочірня компанія dochirnia kompaniia
subsidize *v.t.* субсидіювати subsydiiuvaty
subsidy *n.* субсидія subsydiia
subsist *v.i.* існувати isnuvaty
subsistence *n.* існування isnuvannia
substance *n.* субстанція substantsiia
substantial *a.* тривкий tryvkyi
substantially *adv.* в значній мірі v znachnii miri
substantiate *v.t.* обґрунтовувати obgruntovuvaty
substantiation *n.* аргумент arhument
substitute *v.t.* замінити zaminyty
substitute *n.* замінник zaminnyk
substitution *n.* заміна zamina
subterranean *a.* підземний pidzemnyi

subtle *a.* тонкий tonkyi
subtlety *n.* тонкість tonkist
subtract *v.t.* відняти vidniaty
subtraction *n.* віднімання vidnimannia
suburb *n.* передмістя peredmistia
suburban *a.* заміський zamiskyi
subversion *n.* підривна діяльність pidryvna diialnist
subversive *a.* підривний pidryvnyi
subvert *v.t.* перевертати perevertaty
succeed *v.i.* домагатися успіху domahatysia uspikhu
success *n.* успіх uspikh
successful *a* успішний uspishnyi
succession *n.* наступність nastupnist
successive *a.* наступний nastupnyi
successor *n.* наступник nastupnyk
succour *v.t.* приходити на допомогу prykhodyty na dopomohu
succour *n.* допомога dopomoha
succumb *v.i.* піддаватися piddavatysia
such *pron.* той toi
such *a.* такий takyi
suck *n.* всмоктування vsmoktuvannia
suck *v.t.* смоктати smoktaty
suckle *v.t.* годувати грудьми hoduvaty hrudmy
sudden *n.* несподіванка nespodivanka
suddenly *adv.* раптово raptovo
sue *v.t.* порушувати справу porushuvaty spravu
suffer *v.t.* страждати strazhdaty
suffice *v.i.* вистачити vystachyty

sufficiency *n.* достатність dostatnist
sufficient *a.* належний nalezhnyi
suffix *v.t.* додавати dodavaty
suffix *n.* суфікс sufiks
suffocate *v.t* душити dushyty
suffocation *n.* удушення udushennia
suffrage *n.* виборче право vyborche pravo
sugar *v.t.* обцукровувати obtsukrovuvaty
sugar *n.* цукор tsukor
suggest *v.t.* підказувати pidkazuvaty
suggestion *n.* вказівка vkazivka
suggestive *a.* навідний navidnyi
suicidal *a.* самогубний samohubnyi
suicide *n.* самогубство samohubstvo
suit *v.t.* задовольняти вимогам zadovolniaty vymoham
suit *n.* костюм kostium
suitability *n.* доцільність dotsilnist
suitable *a.* придатний prydatnyi
suite *n.* почет pochet
suitor *n.* шанувальник shanuvalnyk
sullen *a.* неяскравий neiaskravyi
sulphur *n.* сірка sirka
sulphuric *a.* сірчаний sirchanyi
sultry *a.* спекотний spekotnyi
sum *v.t.* складати skladaty
sum *n.* сума suma
summarily *adv.* сумарно sumarno
summarize *v.t.* підсумовувати pidsumovuvaty
summary *a* сумарний sumarnyi
summary *n.* конспект konspekt
summer *n.* літо lito
summit *n.* саміт samit
summon *v.t.* покликати poklykaty

summons *n.* судова повістка sudova povistka
sumptuous *a.* розкішний rozkishnyi
sun *v.t.* гріти на сонці hrity na sontsi
sun *n.* сонце sontse
Sunday *n.* неділя nedilia
sunder *v.t.* розколювати rozkoliuvaty
sundry *a.* різний riznyi
sunny *a.* сонячний soniachnyi
sup *v.i.* відсьорбувати vidsorbuvaty
superabundance *n.* надмірна кількість nadmirna kilkist
superabundant *a.* зайвий zaivyi
superb *a.* вищої якості vyshchoi yakosti
superficial *a.* наносний nanosnyi
superficiality *n.* поверховість poverkhovist
superfine *a.* найтонший naitonshyi
superfluity *n.* розкіш rozkish
superfluous *a.* зайвий zaivyi
superhuman *a.* надлюдський nadliudskyi
superintend *v.t.* управляти upravliaty
superintendence *n.* завідування zaviduvannia
superintendent *n.* керівник kerivnyk
superior *a.* вищий vyshchyi
superiority *n.* старшинство starshynstvo
superlative *n.* кульмінація kulminatsiia
superlative *a.* найвищий naivyshchyi
superman *n.* супермен supermen

supernatural *a.* надприродний nadpryrodnyi
supersede *v.t.* міняти miniaty
supersonic *a.* надзвуковий nadzvukovyi
superstition *n.* марновірство marnovirstvo
superstitious *a.* забобонний zabobonnyi
supertax *n.* податок на надприбуток podatok na nadprybutok
supervise *v.t.* контролювати kontroliuvaty
supervision *n.* переливання perelyvannia
supervisor *n.* контролер kontroler
supper *n.* причастя prychastia
supple *a.* піддатливий piddatlyvyi
supplement *v.t.* доповнювати dopovniuvaty
supplement *n.* допоміжний засоб dopomizhnyi zasob
supplementary *a.* який доповнює yakyi dopovniuie
supplier *n.* постачальник postachalnyk
supply *n* запас zapas
supply *v.t.* постачати postachaty
support *n.* оплот oplot
support *v.t.* допомагати dopomahaty
suppose *v.t.* мати певні обов'язки maty pevni obov'iazky
supposition *n.* припущення prypushchennia
suppress *v.t.* забороняти zaboroniaty
suppression *n.* придушення prydushennia
supremacy *n.* верховенство verkhovenstvo

supreme *a.* верховний verkhovnyi
surcharge *v.t.* штрафувати shtrafuvaty
surcharge *n.* доплата doplata
sure *a.* впевнений vpevnenyi
surely *adv.* твердо tverdo
surety *n.* поручительство poruchytelstvo
surf *n.* прибій prybii
surface *n.* поверхня poverkhnia
surface *v.i* приганяти pryhaniaty
surfeit *n.* непомірність nepomirnist
surge *v.i.* хлинути khlynuty
surge *n.* хвилі khvyli
surgeon *n.* хірург khirurh
surgery *n.* хірургія khirurhiia
surmise *v.t.* припускати prypuskaty
surmise *n.* підозра pidozra
surmount *v.t.* долати dolaty
surname *n.* прізвище prizvyshche
surpass *v.t.* випереджати vyperedzhaty
surplus *n.* перевищення perevyshchennia
surprise *v.t.* наскочити naskochyty
surprise *n.* сюрприз siurpryz
surrender *n* капітуляція kapituliatsiia
surrender *v.t.* поступатися postupatysia
surround *v.t.* обступати obstupaty
surroundings *n.* околиці okolytsi
surtax *n.* додатковий податок dodatkovyi podatok
surveillance *n.* спостереження sposterezhennia
survey *n.* інспектування inspektuvannia
survey *v.t.* обдивлятися obdyvliatysia

survival *n.* виживання vyzhyvannia
survive *v.i.* виживати vyzhyvaty
suspect *n* підозрюваний pidozriuvanyi
suspect *a.* підозрілий pidozrilyi
suspect *v.t.* підозрювати pidozriuvaty
suspend *v.t.* призупиняти pryzupyniaty
suspense *n.* занепокоєння zanepokoiennia
suspension *n.* призупинення pryzupynennia
suspicion *n.* підозра pidozra
suspicious *a.* який має підозру yakyi maie pidozru
sustain *v.t.* живити сили zhyvyty syly
sustenance *n.* засоби до існування zasoby do isnuvannia
swagger *n* розв'язність rozviaznist
swagger *v.i.* хвастати khvastaty
swallow *n.* ковток kovtok
swallow *n.* ластівка lastivka
swallow *v.t.* ковтати kovtaty
swamp *v.t.* затоплювати zatopliuvaty
swamp *n.* болото boloto
swan *n.* лебідь lebid
swarm *v.i.* роїтися roitysia
swarm *n.* зграя zhraia
swarthy *a.* смаглявий smahliavyi
sway *n* влада vlada
sway *v.i.* гойдати hoidaty
swear *v.t.* лаятися laiatysia
sweat *v.i.* потіти potity
sweat *n.* піт pit
sweater *n.* светр svetr
sweep *n.* підмітання pidmitannia
sweep *v.i.* підмітати pidmitaty

sweeper *n.* чистильник chystylnyk
sweet *n* цукерка tsukerka
sweet *a.* солодкий solodkyi
sweeten *v.t.* підсолоджувати pidsolodzhuvaty
sweetmeat *n.* цукати tsukaty
sweetness *n.* солодкість solodkist
swell *n* здуття zduttia
swell *v.i.* набухати nabukhaty
swift *a.* швидкий shvydkyi
swim *n* запаморочення zapamorochennia
swim *v.i.* плавати в чомусь plavaty v chomus
swimmer *n.* плавець plavets
swindle *n.* ошукування oshukuvannia
swindle *v.t.* ошукувати oshukuvaty
swindler *n.* ошуканець oshukanets
swine *n.* нахаба nakhaba
swing *n* гойдалки hoidalky
swing *v.i.* вішати vishaty
swiss *a* швейцарський shveitsarskyi
swiss *n.* швейцарець shveitsarets
switch *v.t.* бити лозиною byty lozynoiu
switch *n.* перемикач peremykach
swoon *v.i* непритомніти neprytomnity
swoon *n.* непритомність neprytomnist
swoop *n* пікірування pikiruvannia
swoop *v.i.* спрямуватися вниз spriamuvatysia vnyz
sword *n.* меч mech
sycamore *n.* платан platan
sycophancy *n.* низькопоклонство nyzkopoklonstvo

sycophant *n.* підлабузник pidlabuznyk
syllabic *a.* складовий skladovyi
syllable *n.* склад sklad
syllabus *n.* конспект konspekt
sylph *n.* сильф sylf
sylvan *a.* лісовий lisovyi
symbol *n.* символ symvol
symbolic *a.* символічний symvolichnyi
symbolism *n.* символізм symvolizm
symbolize *v.t.* символізувати symvolizuvaty
symmetrical *a.* симетричний symetrychnyi
symmetry *n.* симетрія symetriia
sympathetic *a.* симпатичний sympatychnyi
sympathize *v.i.* співчувати spivchuvaty
sympathy *n.* співчуття spivchuttia
symphony *n.* симфонія symfoniia
symposium *n.* симпозіум sympozium
symptom *n.* симптом symptom
symptomatic *a.* симптоматичний symptomatychnyi
synonym *n.* синонім synonim
synonymous *a.* синонімічний synonimichnyi
synopsis *n.* синопсис synopsys
syntax *n.* синтаксис syntaksys
synthesis *n.* синтез syntez
synthetic *n* синтетичний продукт syntetychnyi produkt
synthetic *a.* синтетичний syntetychnyi
syringe *v.t.* спринцювати spryntsiuvaty
syringe *n.* шприц shpryts
syrup *n.* сироп syrop
system *n.* система systema

systematic *a.* систематичний systematychnyi
systematize *v.t.* систематизувати systematyzuvaty

table *v.t.* класти на стіл klasty na stil
table *n.* стіл stil
tablet *n.* таблетка tabletka
taboo *a* заборонений zaboronenyi
taboo *v.t.* забороняти zaboroniaty
taboo *n.* табу tabu
tabular *a.* табличний tablychnyi
tabulate *v.t.* зводити в таблицю zvodyty v tablytsiu
tabulation *n.* складання таблиць skladannia tablyts
tabulator *n.* табулятор tabuliator
tacit *a.* який мається на увазі yakyi maietsia na uvazi
taciturn *a.* неговіркий nehovirkyi
tackle *v.t.* закріпити снастями zakripyty snastiamy
tackle *n.* снасті snasti
tact *n.* тактовність taktovnist
tactful *a.* тактовний taktovnyi
tactician *n.* тактик taktyk
tactics *n.* тактика taktyka
tactile *a.* дотиковий dotykovyi
tag *v.t.* скріпити skripyty
tag *n.* ярлик yarlyk
tail *n.* хвіст khvist
tailor *v.t.* шити shyty
tailor *n.* кравець kravets
taint *v.t.* заразити zarazyty
taint *n.* зараза zaraza
take *v.t* брати braty
tale *n.* історія istoriia
talent *n.* талант talant
talisman *n.* талісман talisman

talk *n* розмова rozmova
talk *v.i.* говорити hovoryty
talkative *a.* говіркий hovirkyi
tall *a.* хвалькуватий khvalkuvatyi
tallow *n.* сало salo
tally *v.t.* підрахувати pidrakhuvaty
tally *n.* етикетка etyketka
tamarind *n.* тамаринд tamarynd
tame *v.t.* приручати pryruchaty
tame *a.* ручний ruchnyi
tamper *v.i.* вступати в таємні відносини vstupaty v taiemni vidnosyny
tan *n., a.* загар zahar
tan *v.i.* загоряти zahoriaty
tangent *n.* дотична dotychna
tangible *a.* осяжний osiazhnyi
tangle *v.t.* заплутувати zaplutuvaty
tangle *n.* конфлікт konflikt
tank *n.* цистерна tsysterna
tanker *n.* танкер tanker
tanner *n.* дубильник dubylnyk
tannery *n.* шкіряний завод shkirianyi zavod
tantalize *v.t.* віддавати на муки viddavaty na muky
tantamount *a.* рівносильний rivnosylnyi
tap *n.* кран kran
tap *v.t.* ставити кран stavyty kran
tape *v.t* зв'язати шнуром zviazaty shnurom
tape *n.* стрічка strichka
taper *n* конус konus
taper *v.i.* звужуватися до кінця zvuzhuvatysia do kintsia
tapestry *n.* гобелен hobelen
tar *v.t.* мазати дьогтем mazaty dohtem
tar *n.* дьоготь dohot
target *n.* об'єкт obiekt
tariff *n.* тариф taryf

tarnish *v.t.* тьмяність tmianist
task *v.t.* задати роботу zadaty robotu
task *n.* завдання zavdannia
taste *v.t.* випробувати vyprobuvaty
taste *n.* смак smak
tasteful *a.* зі смаком zi smakom
tasty *a.* смачний smachnyi
tatter *v.t* рвати на шматки rvaty na shmatky
tatter *n.* лахмітник lakhmitnyk
tattoo *v.i.* татуювати tatuiuvaty
tattoo *n.* татуювання tatuiuvannia
taunt *n* образливе глузування obrazlyve hluzuvannia
taunt *v.t.* дражнити drazhnyty
tavern *n.* таверна taverna
tax *v.t.* надмірно напружувати nadmirno napruzhuvaty
tax *n.* тягар tiahar
taxable *a.* оподатковуваний opodatkovuvanyi
taxation *n.* оподаткування opodatkuvannia
taxi *v.i.* їздити на таксі yizdyty na taksi
taxi *n.* таксі taksi
tea *n* чай chai
teach *v.t.* навчати navchaty
teacher *n.* вчитель vchytel
teak *n.* тик tyk
team *n.* бригада bryhada
tear *n.* сльоза sloza
tear *v.t.* роздирати rozdyraty
tear *n.* сльоза sloza
tearful *a.* плачущий plachushchyi
tease *v.t.* ворсувати vorsuvaty
teat *n.* сосок sosok
technical *n.* технічний tekhnichnyi
technicality *n.* формальність formalnist
technician *n.* технік tekhnik

technique *n.* техніка tekhnika
technological *a.* технологічний tekhnolohichnyi
technologist *n.* технолог tekhnoloh
technology *n.* технологія tekhnolohiia
tedious *a.* виснажливий vysnazhlyvyi
tedium *n.* нудьга nudha
teem *v.i.* рясніти riasnity
teenager *n.* підліток pidlitok
teens *n.* підлітковий вік pidlitkovyi vik
teethe *v.i.* намічатися namichatysia
teetotal *a.* непитущий nepytushchyi
teetotaller *n.* непитуща людина nepytushcha liudyna
telecast *v.t.* передавати по телебаченню peredavaty po telebachenniu
telecast *n.* телепередача teleperedacha
telecommunications *n.* далекий зв'язок dalekyi zviazok
telegram *n.* телеграма telehrama
telegraph *v.t.* телеграфувати telehrafuvaty
telegraph *n.* телеграфний telehrafnyi
telegraphic *a.* телеграфний telehrafnyi
telegraphist *n.* телеграфіст telehrafist
telegraphy *n.* телеграфія telehrafiia
telepathic *a.* телепатичний telepatychnyi
telepathist *n.* телепат telepat
telepathy *n.* телепатія telepatiia
telephone *v.t.* дзвонити dzvonyty

telephone *n.* телефон telefon
telescope *n.* телескоп teleskop
telescopic *a.* телескопічний teleskopichnyi
televise *v.t.* повідомляти по телебаченню povidomliaty po telebachenniu
television *n.* телебачення telebachennia
tell *v.t.* розказати rozkazaty
teller *n.* оповідач opovidach
temper *v.t.* регулювати rehuliuvaty
temper *n.* вдача vdacha
temperament *n.* темперамент temperament
temperamental *a.* темпераментний temperamentnyi
temperance *n.* помірність pomirnist
temperate *a.* стриманий strymanyi
temperature *n.* температура temperatura
tempest *n.* буря buria
tempestuous *a.* бурхливий burkhlyvyi
temple *n* скроня skronia
temple *n.* храм khram
temporal *a.* швидкоплинний shvydkoplynnyi
temporary *a.* тимчасовий tymchasovyi
tempt *v.t.* спокушати spokushaty
temptation *n.* спокуса spokusa
tempter *n.* спокусник spokusnyk
ten *n.* десять desiat
tenable *a.* обороноздатний oboronozdatnyi
tenacious *a.* чіпкий chipkyi
tenacity *n.* чіпкість chipkist

tenancy *n.* термін оренди termin orendy

tenant *n.* орендар orendar

tend *v.i.* мати схильність maty skhylnist

tendency *n.* тенденція tendentsiia

tender *a* ніжний nizhnyi

tender *v.t.* пропонувати виконання угоди proponuvaty vykonannia uhody

tender *n* тендер tender

tender *n* пропозиція propozytsiia

tenet *n.* принцип pryntsyp

tennis *n.* теніс tenis

tense *a.* збуджений zbudzhenyi

tense *n.* збудження zbudzhennia

tension *n.* напруженість napruzhenist

tent *n.* намет namet

tentative *a.* орієнтовний oriientovnyi

tenure *n.* володіння volodinnia

term *v.t.* виражати vyrazhaty

term *n.* термін termin

terminable *a.* строковий strokovyi

terminal *n* термінал terminal

terminal *a.* семестровий semestrovyi

terminate *v.t.* припиняти prypyniaty

termination *n.* припинення prypynennia

terminological *a.* термінологічний terminolohichnyi

terminology *n.* термінологія terminolohiia

terminus *n.* вокзал vokzal

terrace *n.* тераса terasa

terrible *a.* страшенний strashennyi

terrier *n.* тер'єр terier

terrific *a.* приголомшливий pryholomshlyvyi

terrify *v.t.* жахати zhakhaty

territorial *a.* територіальний terytorialnyi

territory *n.* територія terytoriia

terror *n.* терор teror

terrorism *n.* тероризм teroryzm

terrorist *n.* терорист teroryst

terrorize *v.t.* тероризувати teroryzuvaty

terse *a.* небагатослівний nebahatoslivnyi

test *n* тест test

test *v.t.* тестувати testuvaty

testament *n.* заповіт zapovit

testicle *n.* яєчко yaiechko

testify *v.i.* давати показання davaty pokazannia

testimonial *n.* свідоцтво svidotstvo

testimony *n.* показання pokazannia

tete-a-tete *n.* віч-на-віч vich-na-vich

tether *v.t.* прив'язати pryviazaty

tether *n.* прив'язь pryviaz

text *n.* текст tekst

textile *n* тканина tkanyna

textile *a.* текстильний tekstylnyi

textual *n.* текстовий tekstovyi

texture *n.* текстура tekstura

thank *v.t.* подякувати podiakuvaty

thankful *a.* вдячний vdiachnyi

thankless *a.* невдячний nevdiachnyi

thanks *n.* подяка podiaka

that *dem. pron.* ті, хто ti, khto

that *rel. pron.* той toi

that *conj.* що shcho

that *adv.* щоб shchob

that *a.* який yakyi

thatch *v.t.* крити соломою kryty solomoiu
thatch *n.* солома soloma
thaw *n* відлига vidlyha
thaw *v.i* танути tanuty
theatre *n.* театр teatr
theatrical *a.* театральний teatralnyi
theft *n.* крадіжка kradizhka
their *a.* їх yikh
theirs *pron.* їхній yikhnii
theism *n.* теїзм teizm
theist *n.* теїст teist
them *pron.* їм yim
thematic *a.* тематичний tematychnyi
theme *n.* тема tema
then *a* тодішній todishnii
then *adv.* тоді todi
thence *adv.* звідти zvidty
theocracy *n.* теократія teokratiia
theologian *n.* богослов bohoslov
theological *a.* богословський bohoslovskyi
theology *n.* богослов'я bohoslovia
theorem *n.* теорема teorema
theoretical *a.* теоретичний teoretychnyi
theorist *n.* теоретик teoretyk
theorize *v.i.* теоретизувати teoretyzuvaty
theory *n.* теорія teoriia
therapy *n.* терапія terapiia
there *adv.* там tam
thereabouts *adv.* неподалік nepodalik
thereafter *adv.* відтоді vidtodi
thereby *adv.* тим самим tym samym
therefore *adv.* тому tomu
thermal *a.* тепловий teplovyi

thermometer *n.* термометр termometr
thermos (flask) *n.* термос (колба) termos (kolba)
thesis *n.* дисертація dysertatsiia
thick *adv.* густо husto
thick *a.* товстий tovstyi
thick *n.* центр tsentr
thicken *v.i.* згустити zhustyty
thicket *n.* гущавина hushchavyna
thief *n.* злодій zlodii
thigh *n.* стегно stehno
thimble *n.* наперсток naperstok
thin *v.t.* робити тонким robyty tonkym
thin *a.* тонкий tonkyi
thing *n.* річ rich
think *v.t.* думати dumaty
thinker *n.* мислитель myslytel
third *n.* третина tretyna
third *a.* третій tretii
thirdly *adv.* по-третє po-tretie
thirst *v.i.* хотіти пити khotity pyty
thirst *n.* спрага spraha
thirsty *a.* спраглий sprahlyi
thirteen *n.* тринадцять trynadtsiat
thirteen *n.* число тринадцять chyslo trynadtsiat
thirteenth *a.* тринадцятий trynadtsiatyi
thirtieth *n* тринадцята частина trynadtsiata chastyna
thirtieth *a.* тридцятий trydtsiatyi
thirty *n.* число тридцять chyslo trydtsiat
thirty *n.* тридцять trydtsiat
thistle *n.* чортополох chortopolokh
thither *adv.* туди tudy
thorn *n.* шип shyp
thorny *a.* тернистий ternystyi
thorough *a* ретельний retelnyi
thoroughfare *n.* проїзд proizd

though *adv.* втім vtim
though *conj.* хоча khocha
thought *n* мислення myslennia
thoughtful *a.* вдумливий
vdumlyvyi
thousand *a* тисячний tysiachnyi
thousand *n.* тисяча tysiacha
thrall *n.* раб чогось rab chohos
thralldom *n.* рабство rabstvo
thrash *v.t.* молотити molotyty
thread *v.t* нанизувати nanyzuvaty
thread *n.* нитка nytka
threadbare *a.* пошарпаний
posharpanyi
threat *n.* загроза zahroza
threaten *v.t.* погрожувати
pohrozhuvaty
three *a* третій tretii
three *n.* три try
thresh *v.t.* стібати stibaty
thresher *n.* молотарка molotarka
threshold *n.* поріг porih
thrice *adv.* тричі trychi
thrift *n.* ощадливість
oshchadlyvist
thrifty *a.* економний ekonomnyi
thrill *v.t.* тріпотіти tripotity
thrill *n.* трепет trepet
thrive *v.i.* цвісти tsvisty
throat *n.* горло horlo
throaty *a.* гортанний hortannyi
throb *n.* биття byttia
throb *v.i.* тріпотіти tripotity
throe *n.* нестерпний біль
nesterpnyi bil
throne *v.t.* займати високе
становище zaimaty vysoke
stanovyshche
throne *n.* трон tron
throng *n.* товкотнеча tovkotnecha
throng *v.t.* товпитися tovpytysia
throttle *v.t.* стискати styskaty
throttle *n.* стопор stopor

through *adv.* зовсім zovsim
through *a* прямий priamyi
through *prep.* через cherez
throughout *prep.* усюди usiudy
throughout *adv.* по всьому po
vsomu
throw *n.* шарф sharf
throw *v.t.* кидати kydaty
thrust *n* удар udar
thrust *v.t.* тикати tykaty
thud *v.i.* ударятися із глухим
стуком udariatysia iz hlukhym
stukom
thud *n.* глухий стук hlukhyi stuk
thug *n.* головоріз holovoriz
thumb *v.t.* захватати zakhvataty
thumb *n.* великий палець velykyi
palets
thump *v.t.* стукати stukaty
thump *n.* важкий удар vazhkyi
udar
thunder *v.i.* гриміти hrymity
thunder *n.* грім hrim
thunderous *a.* громовий
hromovyi
Thursday *n.* четвер chetver
thus *adv.* таким чином takym
chynom
thwart *v.t.* перешкоджати
pereshkodzhaty
tiara *n.* тіара tiara
tick *v.i.* цокати tsokaty
tick *n.* такт takt
ticket *n.* квиток kvytok
tickle *v.t.* лоскотати loskotaty
ticklish *a.* делікатне delikatne
tidal *a.* пов'язаний з приливом
poviazanyi z prylyvom
tide *n.* хвиля khvylia
tidiness *n.* охайність okhainist
tidings *n. pl.* новини novyny
tidy *v.t.* приводити в порядок
pryvodyty v poriadok

tidy *a.* охайний okhainyi
tie *v.t.* затягувати zatiahuvaty
tie *n* краватка kravatka
tier *n.* ярус yarus
tiger *n.* тигр tyhr
tight *a.* тугий tuhyi ⸱
tighten *v.t.* затягнути zatiahnuty
tigress *n.* тигриця tyhrytsia
tile *v.t.* крити кахлем kryty
kakhlem
tile *n.* кахель kakhel
till *v.t.* орати oraty
till *n. conj.* поки poky
till *prep.* до do
tilt *v.i.* займатися хліборобством
zaimatysia khliborobstvom
tilt *n.* опохиле положення
opokhyle polozhennia
timber *n.* лісоматеріали
lisomaterialy
time *v.t.* розрахувати за часом
rozrakhuvaty za chasom
time *n.* час chas
timely *a.* доречно dorechno
timid *a.* полохливий polokhlyvyi
timidity *n.* боязкість boiazkist
timorous *a.* боязкий boiazkyi
tin *v.t.* покривати оловом
pokryvaty olovom
tin *n.* олово olovo
tincture *v.t.* підфарбовувати
pidfarbovuvaty
tincture *n.* настоянка nastoianka
tinge *v.t.* надавати відтінок
nadavaty vidtinok
tinge *n.* відтінок vidtinok
tinker *n.* мідник midnyk
tinsel *n.* мішура mishura
tint *v.t.* відтіняти vidtiniaty
tint *n.* барва barva
tiny *a.* крихітний krykhitnyi
tip *n.* верхівка verkhivka
tip *v.t.* вивалювати vyvaliuvaty

tip *v.t.* давати на чай davaty na
chai
tip *n.* підказка pidkazka
tip *v.t.* ходити навшпиньки
khodyty navshpynky
tip *n.* наконечник nakonechnyk
tipsy *a.* підпилий pidpylyi
tirade *n.* тирада tyrada
tire *v.t.* надівати покришку
nadivaty pokryshku
tiresome *a.* той, що втомлює toi,
shcho vtomliuie
tissue *n.* тканина tkanyna
titanic *a.* титанічний tytanichnyi
tithe *n.* десятина desiatyna
title *n.* назва nazva
titular *a.* заголовний zaholovnyi
toad *n.* гадина hadyna
toast *v.t.* підрум'янювати
pidrumianiuvaty
toast *n.* тост tost
tobacco *n.* тютюн tiutiun
today *n.* сьогордняшній день
sohordniashnii den
today *adv.* сьогодні sohodni
toe *v.t.* торкатися носком
torkatysia noskom
toe *n.* носок nosok
toffee *n.* іриска iryska
toga *n.* тога toha
together *adv.* разом razom
toil *v.i.* тягтися tiahtysia
toil *n.* важка праця vazhka pratsia
toilet *n.* туалет tualet
toils *n. pl.* тенета teneta
token *n.* прикмета prykmeta
tolerable *a.* терпимий terpymyi
tolerance *n.* терпимість terpymist
tolerant *a.* толерантний
tolerantnyi
tolerate *v.t.* терпіти terpity
toleration *n.* терпимість terpymist

toll *v.t.* відбивати годинний vidbyvaty hodynnyi
toll *n* мито myto
toll *n.* дзвін dzvin
tomato *n.* помідор pomidor
tomb *n.* могила mohyla
tomboy *n.* шибеник shybenyk
tomcat *n.* кіт kit
tome *n.* том tom
tomorrow *adv.* завтра zavtra
tomorrow *n.* завтрашній день zavtrashnii den
ton *n.* світські люди svitski liudy
tone *v.t.* задавати тон zadavaty ton
tone *n.* тон ton
tongs *n. pl.* щипці shchyptsi
tongue *n.* язик yazyk
tonic *n.* основний тон osnovnyi ton
tonic *a.* тонізуючий tonizuiuchyi
tonight *adv.* сьогодні ввечері sohodni vvecheri
to-night *n.* сьогоднішній вечір sohodnishnii vechir
tonne *n.* тонна tonna
tonsil *n.* мигдалина myhdalyna
tonsure *n.* тонзура tonzura
too *adv.* занадто zanadto
tool *n.* верстат verstat
tooth *n.* зуб zub
toothache *n.* зубний біль zubnyi bil
toothsome *a.* смачний smachnyi
top *n.* верхній шар verkhnii shar
top *v.t.* перевищувати perevyshchuvaty
top *n.* верхня частина verkhnia chastyna
topaz *n.* топаз topaz
topic *n.* тема tema
topical *a.* актуальний aktualnyi

topographer *n.* топограф topohraf
topographical *a.* топографічний topohrafichnyi
topography *n.* топографія topohrafiia
topple *v.i.* повалити povalyty
topsy turvy *adv* вверх дном vverkh dnom
topsy turvy *a.* перевернутий perevernutyi
torch *n.* факел fakel
torment *n.* мука muka
torment *v.t.* заподіювати біль zapodiiuvaty bil
tornado *n.* торнадо tornado
torpedo *v.t.* торпедувати torpeduvaty
torpedo *n.* торпеда torpeda
torrent *n.* злива zlyva
torrential *a.* проливний prolyvnyi
torrid *a.* спекотний spekotnyi
tortoise *n.* черепаха cherepakha
tortuous *a.* ухильний ukhylnyi
torture *v.t.* катувати katuvaty
torture *n.* катування katuvannia
toss *n* метання metannia
toss *v.t.* метати metaty
total *v.t.* дорівнювати dorivniuvaty
total *n.* підсумок pidsumok
total *a.* тотальний totalnyi
totality *n.* сукупність sukupnist
touch *n* дотик dotyk
touch *v.t.* торкатися torkatysia
touchy *a.* образливий obrazlyvyi
tough *a.* щільний shchilnyi
toughen *v.t.* ставати міцним stavaty mitsnym
tour *v.i.* здійснювати поїздку zdiisniuvaty poizdku
tour *n.* тур tur
tourism *n.* туризм turyzm
tourist *n.* турист turyst

tournament *n.* турнір turnir
towards *prep.* до do
towel *v.t.* витирати рушником vytyraty rushnykom
towel *n.* рушник rushnyk
tower *v.i.* підноситися pidnosytysia
tower *n.* башта bashta
town *n.* містечко mistechko
township *a.* селище selyshche
toy *v.i.* крутити в руках krutyty v rukakh
toy *n.* іграшка ihrashka
trace *v.t.* слід slid
trace *n.* траєкторія traiektoriia
traceable *a.* якого можно відстежити yakoho mozhno vidstezhyty
track *v.t.* вистежувати vystezhuvaty
track *n.* слід slid
tract *n* тракт trakt
tract *n.* трактат traktat
traction *n.* тяга tiaha
tractor *n.* трактор traktor
trade *v.i* торгувати torhuvaty
trade *n.* торгівля torhivlia
trader *n.* торговець torhovets
tradesman *n.* крамар kramar
tradition *n.* традиція tradytsiia
traditional *a.* традиційний tradytsiinyi
traffic *v.i.* мати справу maty spravu
traffic *n.* транспорт transport
tragedian *n.* трагік trahik
tragedy *n.* трагедія trahediia
tragic *a.* трагічний trahichnyi
trail *v.t.* волочити volochyty
trail *n.* стежка stezhka
trailer *n.* трейлер treiler
train *v.t.* тренувати trenuvaty
train *n.* поїзд poizd

trainee *n.* стажист stazhyst
training *n.* навчання navchannia
trait *n.* особливість osoblyvist
traitor *n.* зрадник zradnyk
tram *n.* трамвай tramvai
trample *v.t.* топтати toptaty
trance *n.* транс trans
tranquil *a.* спокійний spokiinyi
tranquility *n.* спокій spokii
tranquillize *v.t.* заспокоюватися zaspokoiuvatysia
transact *v.t.* вести vesty
transaction *n.* угода uhoda
transcend *v.t.* долати dolaty
transcendent *a.* що перевершує shcho perevershuie
transcribe *v.t.* транскрибувати transkrybuvaty
transcription *n.* транскрипція transkryptsiia
transfer *v.t.* пересідати peresidaty
transfer *n.* перенесення perenesennia
transferable *a.* перекладний perekladnyi
transfiguration *n.* видозміна vydozmina
transfigure *v.t.* трансформувати transformuvaty
transform *v.t.* трансформувати transformuvaty
transformation *n.* трансформація transformatsiia
transgress *v.t.* переступати perestupaty
transgression *n.* провина provyna
transit *n.* транзит tranzyt
transition *n.* перехідний період perekhidnyi period
transitive *n.* перехідний perekhidnyi

transitory *a.* минущий mynushchyi
translate *v.t.* переводити perevodyty
translation *n.* переклад pereklad
transmigration *n.* переселення pereselennia
transmission *n.* передача peredacha
transmit *v.t.* відправляти vidpravliaty
transmitter *n.* передавач peredavach
transparent *a.* прозорий prozoryi
transplant *v.t.* переселяти pereseliaty
transport *n.* транспорт transport
transport *v.t.* перевозити perevozyty
transportation *n.* транспортування transportuvannia
trap *v.t.* ставити капкани stavyty kapkany
trap *n.* капкан kapkan
trash *n.* сміття smittia
travel *n* подорож podorozh
travel *v.i.* мандрувати mandruvaty
traveller *n.* комівояжер komivoiazher
tray *n.* піднос pidnos
treacherous *a.* зрадницький zradnytskyi
treachery *n.* віроломство virolomstvo
tread *n* хода khoda
tread *v.t.* протоптувати protoptuvaty
treason *n.* зрадництво zradnytstvo
treasure *v.t.* високо цінувати vysoko tsinuvaty
treasure *n.* скарб skarb

treasurer *n.* скарбник skarbnyk
treasury *n.* казначейство kaznacheistvo
treat *n* пригощання pryhoshchannia
treat *v.t.* лікувати likuvaty
treatise *n.* трактат traktat
treatment *n.* поводження povodzhennia
treaty *n.* угода uhoda
tree *n.* дерево derevo
trek *n.* перехід perekhid
trek *v.i.* переселятися pereseliatysia
tremble *v.i.* тремтіти tremtity
tremendous *a.* гігантський hihantskyi
tremor *n.* тремтіння tremtinnia
trench *v.t.* скопувати skopuvaty
trench *n.* рів riv
trend *n.* тенденція tendentsiia
trespass *n.* посягання posiahannia
trespass *v.i.* провинитися provynytysia
trial *n.* судовий розгляд sudovyi rozhliad
triangle *n.* трикутник trykutnyk
triangular *a.* трикутний trykutnyi
tribal *a.* племінний pleminnyi
tribe *n.* плем'я plemia
tribulation *n.* нещастя neshchastia
tribunal *n.* трибунал trybunal
tributary *a.* другорядний druhoriadnyi
tributary *n.* приплив pryplyv
trick *v.t.* одурювати oduriuvaty
trick *n* трюк triuk
trickery *n.* хитрість khytrist
trickle *v.i.* сочитися sochytysia
trickster *n.* спритник sprytnyk
tricky *a.* хитрий khytryi

tricolour *n* триколор trykolor
tricolour *a.* триколірний trykolirnyi
tricycle *n.* триколісний велосипед trykolisnyi velosyped
trifle *v.i* ставитися несерйозно stavytysia neseriozno
trifle *n.* дрібниця dribnytsia
trigger *n.* детонатор detonator
trim *n* оздоблення ozdoblennia
trim *v.t.* привести в порядок pryvesty v poriadok
trim *a.* наведений у порядок navedenyi u poriadok
trinity *n.* трійця triitsia
trio *n.* тріо trio
trip *n.* мандрівка mandrivka
trip *v.t.* іти легко і швидко ity lehko i shvydko
tripartite *a.* тристоронній trystoronnii
triple *a.* протироєний protyroienyi
triple *v.t.,* потроювати potroiuvaty
triplicate *v.t.* виготовляти в трьох примірниках vyhotovliaty v trokh prymirnykakh
triplicate *n* тріплікат triplikat
triplicate *a.* потрійний potriinyi
triplication *n.* потроєння potroiennia
tripod *n.* штатив shtatyv
triumph *v.i.* тріумфувати triumfuvaty
triumph *n.* тріумф triumf
triumphal *a.* тріумфальний triumfalnyi
triumphant *a.* тріумфуючий triumfuiuchyi
trivial *a.* тривіальний tryvialnyi
troop *v.i* проходити строєм prokhodyty stroiem
troop *n.* зграя zhraia

trooper *n.* кавалерист kavaleryst
trophy *n.* трофей trofei
tropic *n.* тропік tropik
tropical *a.* тропічний tropichnyi
trot *n* рись rys
trot *v.i.* йти риссю yty ryssiu
trouble *v.t.* тривожитися tryvozhytysia
trouble *n.* проблема problema
troublesome *a.* клопіткий klopitkyi
troupe *n.* трупа trupa
trousers *n. pl* брюки briuky
trowel *n.* совок sovok
truce *n.* перемир'я peremyria
truck *n.* вантажний автомобіль vantazhnyi avtomobil
true *a.* істинний istynnyi
trump *v.t.* бити козирем byty kozyrem
trump *n.* козир kozyr
trumpet *v.i.* звіщати zvishchaty
trumpet *n.* труба truba
trunk *n.* стовбур stovbur
trust *v.t* вірити viryty
trust *n.* відповідальне положення vidpovidalne polozhennia
trustee *n.* опікун opikun
trustful *a.* довірливий dovirlyvyi
trustworthy *a.* той, що заслуговує довіри toi, shcho zasluhovuie doviry
trusty *n.* надійна людина nadiina liudyna
truth *n.* правда pravda
truthful *a.* правдивий pravdyvyi
try *n* спроба sproba
try *v.i.* спробувати sprobuvaty
trying *a.* втомливий vtomlyvyi
tryst *n.* побачення pobachennia
tub *n.* діжка dizhka
tube *n.* трубка trubka

tuberculosis *n.* туберкульоз tuberkuloz
tubular *a.* трубчастий trubchastyi
tug *v.t.* буксир buksyr
tuition *n.* тренування trenuvannia
tumble *n.* сум'яття sumiattia
tumble *v.i.* ворочатися vorochatysia
tumbler *n.* тумблер tumbler
tumour *n.* пухлина pukhlyna
tumult *n.* шум shum
tumultuous *a.* галасливий halaslyvyi
tune *v.t.* налаштовувати nalashtovuvaty
tune *n.* мотив motyv
tunnel *v.i.* прокладати тунель prokladaty tunel
tunnel *n.* тунель tunel
turban *n.* тюрбан tiurban
turbine *n.* турбіна turbina
turbulence *n.* турбулентність turbulentnist
turbulent *a.* турбулентний turbulentnyi
turf *n.* торф torf
turkey *n.* індичка indychka
turmeric *n.* куркума kurkuma
turmoil *n.* метушня metushnia
turn *n* черга cherha
turn *v.i.* спрямовувати spriamovuvaty
turner *n.* токар tokar
turnip *n.* ріпа ripa
turpentine *n.* скипидар skypydar
turtle *n.* черепаха cherepakha
tusk *n.* ікло iklo
tussle *v.i.* боротися borotysia
tussle *n.* боротьба borotba
tutor *n.* репетитор repetytor
tutorial *n.* навчальний navchalnyi
tutorial *a.* підручник pidruchnyk

twelfth *n.* дванадцята частина dvanadtsiata chastyna
twelfth *a.* дванадцятий dvanadtsiatyi
twelve *n* число дванадцять chyslo dvanadtsiat
twelve *n.* дванадцять dvanadtsiat
twentieth *n* двадцята частина dvadtsiata chastyna
twentieth *a.* двадцятий dvadtsiatyi
twenty *n* число двадцять chyslo dvadtsiat
twenty *a.* двадцятий dvadtsiatyi
twice *adv.* двічі dvichi
twig *n.* лоза loza
twilight *n* сутінки sutinky
twin *a* який є близнюком yakyi ye blyzniukom
twin *n.* близнюк blyzniuk
twinkle *n.* мигання myhannia
twinkle *v.i.* виблискувати vyblyskuvaty
twist *n.* закрутити zakrutyty
twist *v.t.* вигин vyhyn
twitter *v.i.* щебетати shchebetaty
twitter *n.* щебет shchebet
two *a.* двійка dviika
two *n.* два dva
twofold *a.* вдвічі vdvichi
type *v.t.* друкувати на машинці drukuvaty na mashyntsi
type *n.* тип typ
typhoid *n.* черевний тиф cherevnyi tyf
typhoon *n.* тайфун taifun
typhus *n.* висипний тиф vysypnyi tyf
typical *a.* типовий typovyi
typify *v.t.* уособлювати uosobliuvaty
typist *n.* друкарка drukarka
tyranny *n.* тиранія tyraniia

tyrant *n.* тиран tyran
tyre *n.* шина shyna

udder *n.* вим'я vymia
uglify *v.t.* спотворювати
spotvoriuvaty
ugliness *n.* потворність potvornist
ugly *a.* потворний potvornyi
ulcer *n.* виразка vyrazka
ulcerous *a.* виразковий
vyrazkovyi
ulterior *a.* наступний nastupnyi
ultimate *a.* кінцевий kintsevyi
ultimately *adv.* в кінцевому
рахунку v kintsevomu rakhunku
ultimatum *n.* ультиматум
ultymatum
umbrella *n.* парасолька
parasolka
umpire *v.t.,* бути суддею buty
suddeiu
umpire *n.* третейський суддя
treteiskyi suddia
unable *a.* нездатний nezdatnyi
unanimity *n.* одностайність
odnostainist
unanimous *a.* одностайний
odnostainyi
unaware *a.* той, що не знає toi,
shcho ne znaie
unawares *adv.* зненацька
znenatska
unburden *v.t.* розвантажити
rozvantazhyty
uncanny *a.* моторошний
motoroshnyi
uncertain *a.* сумнівний sumnivnyi
uncle *n.* дядя diadia
uncouth *a.* необтесаний
neobtesanyi
under *adv* внизу vnyzu

under *a* нижчий nyzhchyi
under *prep.* під pid
undercurrent *n.* підводна течія
pidvodna techiia
underdog *n* невдаха nevdakha
undergo *v.t.* зазнавати zaznavaty
undergraduate *n.* студент
student
underhand *a.* закулісний
zakulisnyi
underline *v.t.* підкреслювати
pidkresliuvaty
undermine *v.t.* підривати
pidryvaty
underneath *adv.* знизу znyzu
underneath *prep.* під pid
understand *v.t.* знати znaty
undertake *v.t.* вживати vzhyvaty
undertone *n.* підтекст pidtekst
underwear *n.* натільна білизна
natilna bilyzna
underworld *n.* підземний світ
pidzemnyi svit
undo *v.t.* відмінити vidminyty
undue *a.* надмірний nadmirnyi
undulate *v.i.* рухатися
хвилеподібно rukhatysia
khvylepodibno
undulation *n.* хвилястість
khvyliastist
unearth *v.t.* розкопувати
rozkopuvaty
uneasy *a.* неспокійний
nespokiinyi
unfair *a* упереджений
uperedzhenyi
unfold *v.t.* розкриватися
rozkryvatysia
unfortunate *a.* нещасний
neshchasnyi
ungainly *a.* вайлуватий vailuvatyi
unhappy *a.* нещасливий
neshchaslyvyi

unification *n.* об'єднання obiednannia
union *n.* союз soiuz
unionist *n.* член профспілки chlen profspilky
unique *a.* унікальний unikalnyi
unison *n.* унісон unison
unit *n.* одиниця odynytsia
unite *v.t.* об'єднувати obiednuvaty
unity *n.* єдність yednist
universal *a.* універсальний universalnyi
universality *n.* універсальність universalnist
universe *n.* всесвіт vsesvit
university *n.* університет universytet
unjust *a.* необґрунтований neobgruntovanyi
unless *conj.* якщо не yakshcho ne
unlike *prep* на відміну від na vidminu vid
unlike *a* несхожий на neskhozhyi na
unlikely *a.* неймовірний neimovirnyi
unmanned *a.* безпілотний bezpilotnyi
unmannerly *a* грубий hrubyi
unprincipled *а.* безпринципний bezpryntsypnyi
unreliable *a.* ненадійний nenadiinyi
unrest *n* заворушення zavorushennia
unruly *a.* непокірний nepokirnyi
unsettle *v.t.* вибивати з колії vybyvaty z kolii
unsheathe *v.t.* виймати з піхов vyimaty z pikhov
until *prep.* до do
until *conj* до тих пір do tykh pir

untoward *a.* непокірний nepokirnyi
unwell *a.* нездоровий nezdorovyi
unwittingly *adv.* мимоволі mymovoli
up *prep.* до do
up *adv.* підвищується pidvyshchuietsia
upbraid *v.t* докоряти dokoriaty
upheaval *n.* переворот perevorot
uphold *v.t* задовольняти zadovolniaty
upkeep *n* утримання utrymannia
uplift *v.t.* піднімати pidnimaty
uplift *n* скид skyd
upon *prep* після pislia
upper *a.* верхній verkhnii
upright *a.* вертикально vertykalno
uprising *n.* повстання povstannia
uproar *n.* шум shum
uproarious *a.* бурхливий burkhlyvyi
uproot *v.t.* виривати з коренем vyryvaty z korenem
upset *v.t.* виводити з рівноваги vyvodyty z rivnovahy
upshot *n.* розв'язка rozviazka
upstart *n.* вискочка vyskochka
up-to-date *a.* новітній novitnii
upward *adv.* наверх naverkh
upwards *adv.* вгору vhoru
urban *a.* міський miskyi
urbane *a.* люб'язний liubiaznyi
urbanity *n.* чемність chemnist
urchin *n.* вуличний хлопчик vulychnyi khlopchyk
urge *v.t* примушувати prymushuvaty
urge *n* спонукання sponukannia
urgency *n.* терміновість terminovist
urgent *a.* терміновий terminovyi
urinal *n.* пісуар pisuar

urinary *a.* сечовий sechovyi
urinate *v.i.* мочитися mochytysia
urination *n.* сечовипускання
sechovypuskannia
urine *n.* сеча secha
urn *n* урна urna
usage *n.* користування
korystuvannia
use *n.* використання
vykorystannia
use *v.t.* використовувати
vykorystovuvaty
useful *a.* цінний tsinnyi
usher *v.t.* проводити provodyty
usher *n.* швейцар shveitsar
usual *a.* якій відповідає звичаю
yakii vidpovidaie zvychaiu
usually *adv.* звичайно zvychaino
usurer *n.* лихвар lykhvar
usurp *v.t.* узурпувати uzurpuvaty
usurpation *n.* узурпація
uzurpatsiia
usury *n.* лихварство lykhvarstvo
utensil *n.* начиння nachynnia
uterus *n.* матка matka
utilitarian *a.* утилітарний
utylitarnyi
utility *n.* корисність korysnist
utilization *n.* утилізація
utylizatsiia
utilize *v.t.* утилізувати utylizuvaty
utmost *n* все можливе vse
mozhlyve
utmost *a.* найвіддаленіший
naividdalenishyi
utopia *n* . утопія utopiia
utopian *a.* утопічний utopichnyi
utter *v.t.* виражати словами
vyrazhaty slovamy
utter *a* повний povnyi
utterance *n.* висловлювання
vyslovliuvannia
utterly *adv.* вкрай vkrai

vacancy *n.* вакансія vakansiia
vacant *a.* вакантний vakantnyi
vacate *v.t.* скасовувати
skasovuvaty
vacation *n.* відпустка vidpustka
vaccinate *v.t.* вакцинувати
vaktsynuvaty
vaccination *n.* вакцинація
vaktsynatsiia
vaccinator *n.* провісник provisnyk
vaccine *n.* вакцина vaktsyna
vacillate *v.i.* хитатися khytatysia
vacuum *n.* вакуум vakuum
vagabond *a* бродячий brodiachyi
vagabond *n.* бродяга brodiaha
vagary *n.* примха prymkha
vagina *n.* піхва pikhva
vague *a.* розпливчастий
rozplyvchastyi
vagueness *n.* невизначеність
nevyznachenist
vain *a.* марний marnyi
vainglorious *a.* марнославний
marnoslavnyi
vainglory *n.* хвастощі
khvastoshchi
vainly *adv.* марно marno
vale *n.* юдоль yudol
valiant *a.* доблесний doblesnyi
valid *a.* дійсний diisnyi
validate *v.t.* перевіряти pereviriaty
validity *n.* дійсність diisnist
valley *n.* долина dolyna
valour *n.* доблесть doblest
valuable *a.* цінний tsinnyi
valuation *n.* валютування
valiutuvannia
value *v.t.* цінувати tsinuvaty
value *n.* цінність tsinnist
valve *n.* клапан klapan

van *n.* фургон furhon
vanish *v.i.* зникати znykaty
vanity *n.* метушливість
metushlyvist
vanquish *v.t.* перемагати
peremahaty
vaporize *v.t.* випаровуватися
vyparovuvatysia
vaporous *a.* пароподібний
paropodibnyi
vapour *n.* туман tuman
variable *a.* змінюваний
zminiuvanyi
variance *n.* дисперсія dyspersiia
variation *n.* коливання kolyvannia
varied *a.* змінний zminnyi
variety *n.* різноманітність
riznomanitnist
various *a.* усілякий usiliakyi
varnish *v.t.* лакувати lakuvaty
varnish *n.* лак lak
vary *v.t.* змінюватися
zminiuvatysia
vasectomy *n.* вазектомія
vazektomiia
vaseline *n.* вазелін vazelin
vast *a.* численний chyslennyi
vault *v.i.* зводити склепіння
zvodyty sklepinnia
vault *n.* льох lokh
vault *n.* сховище skhovyshche
vegetable *a.* овочевий ovochevyi
vegetable *n.* овоч ovoch
vegetarian *n.* вегетаріанець
vehetarianets
vegetarian *a* вегетаріанський
vehetarianskyi
vegetation *n.* рослинність
roslynnist
vehemence *n.* гарячність
hariachnist
vehement *a.* шалений shalenyi

vehicle *n.* засоб пересування
zasob peresuvannia
vehicular *a.* автомобільний
avtomobilnyi
veil *v.t.* приховувати prykhovuvaty
veil *n.* завіса zavisa
vein *n.* вена vena
velocity *n.* швидкість shvydkist
velvet *n.* оксамит oksamyt
velvety *a.* бархатистий
barkhatystyi
venal *a.* продажний prodazhnyi
venality *n.* продажність
prodazhnist
vendor *n.* роазнощик
roaznoshchyk
venerable *a.* поважний povazhnyi
venerate *v.t.* шанувати shanuvaty
veneration *n.* шанування
shanuvannia
vengeance *n.* помста pomsta
venial *a.* пробачний probachnyi
venom *n.* злоба zloba
venomous *a.* злісний zlisnyi
vent *n.* вентиляційний
ventyliatsiinyi
ventilate *v.t.* вентилювати
ventyliuvaty
ventilation *n.* вентиляція
ventyliatsiia
ventilator *n.* вентилятор
ventyliator
venture *v.t.* ризикнути ryzyknuty
venture *n.* підприємство
pidpryiemstvo
venturesome *a.* азартний
azartnyi
venturous *a.* безстрашний
bezstrashnyi
venue *n.* місце зустрічі mistse
zustrichi
veracity *n.* правдивість pravdyvist
veranda *n.* веранда veranda

verb *n.* дієслово diieslovo
verbal *a.* словесний slovesnyi
verbally *adv.* усно usno
verbatim *adv.* дослівно doslivno
verbatim *a.* дослівний doslivnyi
verbose *a.* багатослівний bahatoslivnyi
verbosity *n.* багатослівність bahatoslivnist
verdant *a.* нестиглий nestyhlyi
verdict *n.* вердикт verdykt
verge *n.* межа mezha
verification *n.* перевірка perevirka
verify *v.t.* перевірити pereviryty
verisimilitude *n.* правдоподібність pravdopodibnist
veritable *a.* справжній spravzhnii
vermillion *a.* яскраво-червоний yaskravo-chervonyi
vermillion *n.* яскраво-червоний колір yaskravo-chervonyi kolir
vernacular *a.* народний narodnyi
vernacular *n.* рідна мова ridna mova
vernal *a.* весняний vesnianyi
versatile *a.* різносторонній riznostoronnii
versatility *n.* гнучкість hnuchkist
verse *n.* віршований рядок virshovanyi riadok
versed *a.* досвічений dosvichenyi
versification *n.* віршування virshuvannia
versify *v.t.* складати вірши skladaty virshy
version *n.* версія versiia
versus *prep.* порівнюючи з porivniuiuchy z
vertical *a.* вертикальний vertykalnyi
verve *n.* сила syla

very *a.* справжній spravzhnii
vessel *n.* судно sudno
vest *v.t.* доручити doruchyty
vest *n.* жилетка zhyletka
vestige *n.* слід slid
vestment *n.* вбрання vbrannia
veteran *a.* заслужений zasluzhenyi
veteran *n.* ветеран veteran
veterinary *a.* ветеринарний veterynarnyi
veto *v.t.* накладати вето nakladaty veto
veto *n.* вето veto
vex *v.t.* докучати dokuchaty
vexation *n* досада dosada
via *prep.* через cherez
viable *a.* життєздатний zhyttiezdatnyi
vial *n.* флакон flakon
vibrate *v.i.* вібрувати vibruvaty
vibration *n.* вібрація vibratsiia
vicar *n.* вікарій vikarii
vicarious *a.* чужий chuzhyi
vice *n.* заступник zastupnyk
viceroy *n.* віце-король vitse-korol
vice-versa *adv.* навпаки navpaky
vicinity *n.* сусідство susidstvo
vicious *a.* порочний porochnyi
vicissitude *n.* мінливість minlyvist
victim *n.* жертва zhertva
victimize *v.t.* переслідувати peresliduvaty
victor *n.* переможець peremozhets
victorious *a.* переможний peremozhnyi
victory *n.* перемога peremoha
victuals *n.* провіант proviant
vie *v.i.* суперничати supernychaty
view *v.t.* оглянути ohlianuty
view *n.* краєвид kraievyd
vigil *n.* бдіння bdinnia

vigilance *n.* пильність pylnist
vigilant *a.* пильний pylnyi
vigorous *a.* сильний sylnyi
vile *a.* бридкий brydkyi
vilify *v.t.* поносити ponosyty
villa *n.* вілла villa
village *n.* село selo
villager *n.* сільський житель silskyi zhytel
villain *n.* пустун pustun
vindicate *v.t.* довести dovesty
vindication *n.* витребування vytrebuvannia
vine *n.* виноградна лоза vynohradna loza
vinegar *n.* оцет otset
vintage *n.* марочний marochnyi
violate *v.t.* паплюжити papliuzhyty
violation *n.* правопорушення pravoporushennia
violence *n.* насильство nasylstvo
violent *a.* насильницький nasylnytskyi
violet *n.* фіолетовий колір fioletovyi kolir
violin *n.* скрипка skrypka
violinist *n.* скрипаль skrypal
virgin *n* цілина tsilyna
virgin *n.* незаймана nezaimana
virginity *n.* незайманість nezaimanist
virile *a.* чоловічий cholovichyi
virility *n.* приналежність до чоловічої статі prynalezhnist do cholovichoi stati
virtual *a* віртуальний virtualnyi
virtue *n.* доброчесність dobrochesnist
virtuous *a.* доброчесний dobrochesnyi
virulence *n.* отруйність otruinist
virulent *a.* ворожий vorozhyi
virus *n.* вірус virus

visage *n.* вираз обличчя vyraz oblychchia
visibility *n.* видимість vydymist
visible *a.* зримий zrymyi
vision *n.* проникнення pronyknennia
visionary *n.* фантазер fantazer
visionary *a.* примарний prymarnyi
visit *n.* відвідування vidviduvannia
visit *v.t.* приходити в гості prykhodyty v hosti
visitor *n.* відвідувач vidviduvach
vista *n.* алея aleia
visual *a.* візуальний vizualnyi
visualize *v.t.* візуалізувати vizualizuvaty
vital *a.* життєво важливий zhyttievo vazhlyvyi
vitality *n.* життєвість zhyttievist
vitalize *v.t.* робити життєвим robyty zhyttievym
vitamin *n.* вітамін vitamin
vitiate *v.t.* псувати psuvaty
vivacious *a.* життєрадісний zhyttieradisnyi
vivacity *n.* жвавість zhvavist
viva-voce *a* усний usnyi
viva-voce *n* усний іспит usnyi ispyt
viva-voce *adv.* усно usno
vivid *a.* яскравий yaskravyi
vixen *n.* мегера mehera
vocabulary *n.* словник slovnyk
vocal *a.* вокальний vokalnyi
vocalist *n.* вокаліст vokalist
vocation *n.* професія profesiia
vogue *n.* популярність populiarnist
voice *v.t.* вимовляти vymovliaty
voice *n.* голос holos
void *v.t.* виділити vydilyty

void *n.* почуття спушеності
pochuttia spushenosti
void *a.* недійсний nediisnyi
volcanic *a.* вулканічний
vulkanichnyi
volcano *n.* вулкан vulkan
volition *n.* воля volia
volley *v.t* стріляти залпами
striliaty zalpamy
volley *n.* залп zalp
volt *n.* вольт volt
voltage *n.* електрична напруга
elektrychna napruha
volume *n.* об`єм ob`iem
voluminous *a.* об'ємистий
obiemystyi
voluntarily *adv.* добровільно
dobrovilno
voluntary *a.* добровільний
dobrovilnyi
volunteer *v.t.* йти добровільно
yty dobrovilno
volunteer *n.* волонтер volonter
voluptuary *n.* сластолюбець
slastoliubets
voluptuous *a.* хтивий khtyvyi
vomit *n* блювота bliuvota
vomit *v.t.* нудити nudyty
voracious *a.* ненаситний
nenasytnyi
votary *n.* чернець chernets
vote *v.i.* балотувати balotuvaty
vote *n.* балотування balotuvannia
voter *n.* учасник uchasnyk
vouch *v.i.* ручатися за ruchatysia
za
voucher *n.* ваучер vaucher
vouchsafe *v.t.* удостоювати
udostoiuvaty
vow *v.t.* давати обітницю davaty
obitnytsiu
vow *n.* обітниця obitnytsia
vowel *n.* гласний hlasnyi

voyage *v.i.* робити подорож
robyty podorozh
voyage *n.* політ polit
voyager *n.* мореплавець
moreplavets
vulgar *a.* вульгарний vulharnyi
vulgarity *n.* вульгарність
vulharnist
vulnerable *a.* уразливий urazlyvyi
vulture *n.* стерв'ятник sterviatnyk

waddle *v.i.* шкандибати
shkandybaty
wade *v.i.* пробиратися
probyratysia
waft *n* віяння viiannia
waft *v.t.* навіяти naviiaty
wag *n* жартівник zhartivnyk
wag *v.i.* махати makhaty
wage *n.* розплата rozplata
wage *v.t.* вести війну vesty viinu
wager *v.i.* укладати парі ukladaty
pari
wager *n.* парі pari
wagon *n.* вагон vahon
wail *n* виття vyttia
wail *v.i.* волати volaty
wain *n.* віз viz
waist *n.* талія taliia
waistband *n.* пояс poias
waistcoat *n.* жилет zhylet
wait *n.* чекання chekannia
wait *v.i.* чекати chekaty
waiter *n.* офіціант ofitsiant
waitress *n.* офіціантка ofitsiantka
waive *v.t.* допускати відхилення
dopuskaty vidkhylennia
wake *n* кільватер kilvater
wake *n* рубець rubets
wake *v.t.* пожвавити pozhvavyty
wakeful *a.* несплячий nespliachyi

walk *n* відстань vidstan
walk *v.i.* ходити khodyty
wall *v.t.* обносити стіною obnosyty stinoiu
wall *n.* стіна stina
wallet *n.* гаманець hamanets
wallop *v.t.* побити pobyty
wallow *v.i.* валятися valiatysia
walnut *n.* волоський горіх voloskyi horikh
walrus *n.* морж morzh
wan *a.* тьмяний tmianyi
wand *n.* паличка palychka
wander *v.i.* мандрувати mandruvaty
wane *n* збиток zbytok
wane *v.i.* убувати ubuvaty
want *n* потреба potreba
want *v.t.* хотіти khotity
wanton *a.* безвідповідальний bezvidpovidalnyi
war *v.i.* вести війну vesty viinu
war *n.* війна viina
warble *n* трель trel
warble *v.i.* заливатися zalyvatysia
warbler *n.* співочий птах spivochyi ptakh
ward *v.t.* відвертати vidvertaty
ward *n.* підопічна особа pidopichna osoba
warden *n.* доглядач dohliadach
warder *n.* тюремник tiuremnyk
wardrobe *n.* плаття на шафа plattiana shafa
wardship *n.* піклування pikluvannia
ware *n. pl.* вироби vyroby
warehouse *v.t* склад sklad
warfare *n.* військові дії viiskovi dii
warlike *a.* стосовний до війни stosovnyi do viiny
warm *v.t.* гріти hrity
warm1 *a.* теплий teplyi

warmth *n.* тепло teplo
warn *v.t.* попереджати poperedzhaty
warning *n.* застереження zasterezhennia
warrant *v.t.* ручатися за ruchatysia za
warrant *n.* ордер order
warrantee *n.* особа, якій дається гарантія osoba, yakii daietsia harantiia
warrantor *n.* особа, що дає гарантію osoba, shcho daie harantiiu
warranty *n.* гарантія harantiia
warren *n.* кролячий садок kroliachyi sadok
warrior *n.* воїн voin
wart *n.* бородавка borodavka
wary *a.* насторожений nastorozhenyi
wash *n* прання prannia
wash *v.t.* мити myty
washable *a.* що стирається shcho styraietsia
washer *n.* мийник myinyk
wasp *n.* оса osa
waspish *a.* уїдливий uidlyvyi
wassail *n.* здравиця zdravytsia
wastage *n.* усушка usushka
waste *n.* відходи vidkhody
waste *v.t.* марнувати marnuvaty
waste *a.* стічний stichnyi
wasteful *a.* марнотратний marnotratnyi
watch *n.* корабельний хронометр korabelnyi khronometr
watch *v.t.* спостерігати sposterihaty
watchful *a.* обережний oberezhnyi
watchword *n.* пароль parol
water *v.t.* поїти poity

water *n.* вода voda
waterfall *n.* каскад kaskad
water-melon *n.* кавун kavun
waterproof *n* водонепроникна
тканина vodonepronykna
tkanyna
waterproof *v.t.* робити
водонепроникним robyty
vodonepronyknym
waterproof *a.* водонепроникний
vodonepronyknyi
watertight *a.* непромокальний
nepromokalnyi
watery *a.* водянистий vodianystyi
watt *n.* ват vat
wave *v.t.* завивати zavyvaty
wave *n.* хвиля khvylia
waver *v.i.* коливатися kolyvatysia
wax *v.t.* вощити voshchyty
wax *n.* віск visk
way *n.* шлях shliakh
wayfarer *n.* подорожній
podorozhnii
waylay *v.t.* підстерігати
pidsterihaty
wayward *a.* мінливий minlyvyi
weak *a.* слабкий slabkyi
weaken *v.t.* послаблювати
poslabliuvaty
weakling *n.* слабка істота slabka
istota
weakness *n.* слабкість slabkist
weal *n.* благо blaho
wealth *n.* добробут dobrobut
wealthy *a.* заможний zamozhnyi
wean *v.t.* відлучати vidluchaty
weapon *n.* знаряддя znariaddia
wear *v.t.* зносити znosyty
weary *a.* стомлений stomlenyi
weary *v.t.* стомлювати stomliuvaty
weary *v.i.* стомлюватися
stomliuvatysia
weary *a.* втомлений vtomlenyi

weather *v.t.* вивітрювати
vyvitriuvaty
weather *n* погода pohoda
weave *v.t.* ткати tkaty
weaver *n.* ткач tkach
web *n.* тасьма tasma
webby *a.* павутинний pavutynnyi
wed *v.t.* одружити odruzhyty
wedding *n.* одруження
odruzhennia
wedge *v.t.* закріплювати клином
zakripliuvaty klynom
wedge *n.* клин klyn
wedlock *n.* шлюб shliub
Wednesday *n.* середа sereda
weed *v.t.* полоти poloty
weed *n.* бур'ян burian
week *n.* тиждень tyzhden
weekly *adv.* раз на тиждень raz
na tyzhden
weekly *adv.* щотижня
shchotyzhnia
weekly *a.* тижневий tyzhnevyi
weep *v.i.* плакати plakaty
weevil *n.* довгоносик dovhonosyk
weigh *v.t.* важити vazhyty
weight *n.* вага vaha
weightage *n.* вагомість vahomist
weighty *a.* обтяжливий
obtiazhlyvyi
weir *n.* водозлив vodozlyv
weird *a.* фантастичний
fantastychnyi
welcome *v.t* привітно приймати
pryvitno pryimaty
welcome *n* гостинність hostynnist
welcome *a.* довгоочікуваний
dovhoochikuvanyi
weld *n* зварювання zvariuvannia
weld *v.t.* зварити zvaryty
welfare *n.* добробут dobrobut
well *adv.* добре dobre
well *n.* криниця krynytsia

well *v.i.* хлинути khlynuty
well *a.* хороший khoroshyi
wellington *n.* Веллінгтон Vellinhton
well-known *a.* відомий vidomyi
well-read *a.* начитаний nachytanyi
well-timed *a.* доречний dorechnyi
well-to-do *a.* забезпечений zabezpechenyi
welt *n.* бордюр bordiur
welter *n.* сумбур sumbur
wen *n.* жировик zhyrovyk
wench *n.* дівка divka
west *a.* західний zakhidnyi
west *adv.* на захід na zakhid
west *n.* вест vest
westerly *adv.* на захід na zakhid
westerly *a.* західний zakhidnyi
western *a.* вестовий vestovyi
wet *v.t.* промочити promochyty
wet *a.* мокрий mokryi
wetness *n.* вологість volohist
whack *v.t.* сильний удар sylnyi udar
whale *n.* кит kyt
wharfage *n.* портові митні збори portovi mytni zbory
what *interj.* що shcho
what *pron.* що за shcho za
what *a.* який yakyi
whatever *pron.* що б не shcho b ne
wheat *n.* пшениця pshenytsia
wheedle *v.t.* підлещуватися pidleshchuvatysia
wheel *v.t.* підкотити pidkotyty
wheel *a.* колесо koleso
whelm *v.t.* заливати zalyvaty
whelp *n.* цуценя tsutsenia
when *conj.* хоча khocha
when *adv.* коли koly
whence *adv.* звідки zvidky

whenever *adv.* *conj* коли б не koly b ne
where *conj.* де de
where *adv.* куди kudy
whereabout *adv.* місцезнаходження mistseznakhodzhennia
whereas *conj.* в той час як v toi chas yak
whereat *conj.* на що na shcho
wherein *adv.* в чому v chomu
whereupon *conj.* після чого pislia choho
wherever *adv.* де б не було de b ne bulo
whet *v.t.* точити tochyty
whether *conj.* чи chy
which *pron.* що shcho
which *a.* який yakyi
whichever *pron.* який б не yakyi b ne
whiff *n.* подув poduv
while *conj.* поки poky
while *v.t.* проводити provodyty
while *n.* час chas
whim *n.* примха prymkha
whimper *v.i.* хникати khnykaty
whimsical *a.* химерний khymernyi
whine *n* пхикання pkhykannia
whine *v.i.* скиглити skyhlyty
whip *n.* батіг batih
whip *v.t.* січ sich
whipcord *n.* габардин habardyn
whir *n.* шум shum
whirl *n* вихор vykhor
whirl *v.i.* кружляти kruzhliaty
whirligig *n.* юла yula
whirlpool *n.* вир vyr
whirlwind *n.* смерч smerch
whisk *n* віник vinyk
whisk *v.t.* снувати snuvaty
whisker *n.* борода boroda

whisky *n.* віскі viski
whisper *n* шепіт shepit
whisper *v.t.* шепотіти shepotity
whistle *n* свисток svystok
whistle *v.i.* свистіти svystity
white *n* білизна bilyzna
white *a.* білий bilyi
whiten *v.t.* чистити до білого
  chystyty do biloho
whitewash *v.t.* білити bilyty
whitewash *n.* побілка pobilka
whither *adv.* для чого dlia choho
whitish *a.* білуватий biluvatyi
whittle *v.t.* стругати struhaty
whiz *v.i.* проноситися зі свистом
  pronosytysia zi svystom
who *pron.* хто khto
whoever *pron.* хто б не khto b ne
whole *n* ціле tsile
whole *a.* цілий tsilyi
whole-hearted *a.* щирий shchyryi
wholesale *a* оптовий optovyi
wholesale *adv.* оптом optom
wholesale *n.* оптова торгівля
  optova torhivlia
wholesaler *n.* оптовик optovyk
wholesome *a.* сприятливий
  spryiatlyvyi
wholly *adv.* повністю povnistiu
whom *pron.* кому komu
whore *n.* шльондра shlondra
whose *pron.* чий chyi
why *adv.* чому chomu
wick *n.* гніт hnit
wicked *a.* неприємний
  nepryiemnyi
wicker *n.* плетіння pletinnia
wicket *n.* хвіртка khvirtka
wide *adv.* широко shyroko
wide *a.* широкий shyrokyi
widen *v.t.* розширюватися
  rozshyriuvatysia

widespread *a.* дуже поширений
  duzhe poshyrenyi
widow *v.t.* знедолити znedolyty
widow *n.* вдова vdova
widower *n.* вдівець vdivets
width *n.* ширина shyryna
wield *v.t.* вміти поводитися vmity
  povodytysia
wife *n.* дружина druzhyna
wig *n.* перука peruka
wight *n.* особа osoba
wigwam *n.* вігвам vihvam
wild *a.* некультивований
  nekultyvovanyi
wilderness *n.* цілина tsilyna
wile *n.* хитрість khytrist
will *v.t.* веліти velity
will *n.* сила волі syla voli
willing *a.* схильний skhylnyi
willingness *n.* готовність
  hotovnist
willow *n.* верба verba
wily *a.* хитрий khytryi
wimble *n.* коловорот kolovorot
wimple *n.* бурав burav
win *n* виграш vyhrash
win *v.t.* виграти vyhraty
wince *v.i.* морщитися
  morshchytysia
winch *n.* лебідка lebidka
wind *v.t.* обмотати obmotaty
wind *v.t.* вертіти vertity
wind *n.* вітер viter
windbag *n.* пустодзвін pustodzvin
winder *n.* мотальна машина
  motalna mashyna
windlass *v.t.* брашпиль brashpyl
windmill *n.* вітряк vitriak
window *n.* вікно vikno
windy *a.* вітряний vitrianyi
wine *n.* вино vyno
wing *n.* крило krylo
wink *n* моргання morhannia

wink *v.i.* підморгувати
pidmorhuvaty
winner *n.* сторона, що виграла
storona, shcho vyhrala
winnow *v.t.* віяти viiaty
winsome *a.* чарівний charivnyi
winter *v.i* проводити зиму
provodyty zymu
winter *n.* зима zyma
wintry *a.* зимовий zymovyi
wipe *n.* глузування hluzuvannia
wipe *v.t.* витирати vytyraty
wire *v.t.* телеграфувати
telehrafuvaty
wire *n.* провід provid
wireless *n* радіоприймач
radiopryimach
wireless *a.* бездротовий
bezdrotovyi
wiring *n.* проводка provodka
wisdom *n.* мудрість mudrist
wisdom-tooth *n.* мудрості зуб
mudrosti zub
wise *a.* мудрий mudryi
wish *v.t.* хотіти khotity
wish *n.* бажання bazhannia
wishful *a.* жаданий zhadanyi
wisp *n.* пучок puchok
wistful *a.* що тужить shcho tuzhyt
wit *n.* дотепність dotepnist
witch *n.* відьма vidma
witchcraft *n.* чаклунство
chaklunstvo
witchery *n.* чаклунство
chaklunstvo
with *prep.* з z
withal *adv.* вдобавок vdobavok
withdraw *v.t.* знімати znimaty
withdrawal *n.* відведення
vidvedennia
withe *n.* вербовий прут verbovyi
prut
wither *v.i.* сохнути sokhnuty

withhold *v.t.* утримувати
utrymuvaty
within *adv.* в межах v mezhakh
within *adv.* всередені vseredeni
within *prep.* в v
without *adv.* без того, щоб bez
toho, shchob
without *n* простір за межами
чогось prostir za mezhamy
chohos
without *prep.* поза poza
withstand *v.t.* витримувати
vytrymuvaty
witless *a.* нерозумний
nerozumnyi
witness *v.i.* свідчити svidchyty
witness *n.* свідок svidok
witticism *n.* жарт zhart
witty *a.* дотепний dotepnyi
wizard *n.* чарівник charivnyk
wobble *v.i* хитатися khytatysia
woe *n.* скорбота skorbota
woebegone *a.* похмурий
pokhmuryi
woeful *n.* сумний sumnyi
wolf *n.* вовк vovk
woman *n.* жінка zhinka
womanhood *n.* жіночність
zhinochnist
womanise *v.t.* жити розпусно
zhyty rozpusno
womanish *n.* власний жінкам
vlasnyi zhinkam
womb *n.* чрево chrevo
wonder *v.i.* цікавитися
tsikavytysia
wonder *n* чудо chudo
wonderful *a.* дивний dyvnyi
wondrous *a.* чудовий chudovyi
wont *n* звичка zvychka
wont *a.* що має звичай shcho
maie zvychai

wonted *a.* звиклий до нових умов zvyklyi do novykh umov
woo *v.t.* доглядати dohliadaty
wood *n.* гай hai
wooden *a.* дерев'яний derevianyi
woodland *n.* лісиста місцевість lisysta mistsevist
woods *n.* ліси lisy
woof *n.* гавкання havkannia
wool *n.* вовна vovna
woollen *n* вовняна матерія vovniana materiia
woollen *a.* вовняний vovnianyi
word *v.t* висловлювати словами vyslovliuvaty slovamy
word *n.* слово slovo
wordy *a.* словесний slovesnyi
work *v.t.* прокладати шлях prokladaty shliakh
work *n.* робота robota
workable *a.* придатний для роботи prydatnyi dlia roboty
workaday *a.* буденний budennyi
worker *n.* робітник robitnyk
workman *n.* робочий robochyi
workmanship *n.* мистецтво mystetstvo
workshop *n.* майстерня maisternia
world *n.* світ svit
worldling *n.* людина, поглинена земними інтересами liudyna, pohlynena zemnymy interesamy
worldly *a.* суєтний suietnyi
worm *n.* черв'як cherviak
wormwood *n.* полин polyn
worn *a.* зношений znoshenyi
worry *v.i.* турбуватися turbuvatysia
worry *n.* мука muka
worsen *v.t.* погіршувати pohirshuvaty

worship *v.t.* поклонятися pokloniatysia
worship *n.* поклоніння pokloninnia
worshipper *n.* шанувальник shanuvalnyk
worst *n.* найгірше naihirshe
worst *a* найгірший naihirshyi
worst *v.t.* перемогти peremohty
worsted *n.* камвольний kamvolnyi
worth *a* вартий vartyi
worth *n.* що має цінність shcho maie tsinnist
worthless *a.* даремний daremnyi
worthy *a.* гідний hidnyi
would-be *a.* передбачуваний peredbachuvanyi
wound *v.t.* поранити poranyty
wound *n.* поранення poranennia
wrack *n.* повністю руйнувати povnistiu ruinuvaty
wraith *n.* мара mara
wrangle *n.* суперечка superechka
wrangle *v.i.* сперечатися sperechatysia
wrap *n* обгортка obhortka
wrap *v.t.* обернути obernuty
wrapper *n.* пакувальник pakuvalnyk
wrath *n.* лють liut
wreath *n.* вінок vinok
wreathe *v.t.* обвивати obvyvaty
wreck *v.t.* руйнувати ruinuvaty
wreck *n.* крах krakh
wreckage *n.* уламки ulamky
wrecker *n.* шкідник shkidnyk
wren *n.* кропив'яник kropyvianyk
wrench *v.t.* вивихнути vyvykhnuty
wrench *n.* гайковий ключ haikovyi kliuch
wrest *v.t.* вирвати vyrvaty

wrestle *v.i.* вести наполегливу боротьбу vesty napolehlyvu borotbu
wrestler *n.* борець borets
wretch *n.* негідник nehidnyk
wretched *a.* кепський kepskyi
wrick *n* розтяг roztiah
wriggle *n* вигинання vyhynannia
wriggle *v.i.* просуватися вперед prosuvatysia vpered
wring *v.t* вичавлювати vychavliuvaty
wrinkle *v.t.* морщити morshchyty
wrinkle *n.* зморшка zmorshka
wrist *n.* зап'ясток zapiastok
writ *n.* судовий наказ sudovyi nakaz
write *v.t.* писати pysaty
writer *n.* письменник pysmennyk
writhe *v.i.* корчити korchyty
wrong *v.t.* бути несправедливим buty nespravedlyvym
wrong *adv.* неправильно nepravylno
wrong *a.* несправний nespravnyi
wrongful *a.* неправомірний nepravomirnyi
wry *a.* кривий kryvyi

xerox *v.t.* ксерокопіювати kserokopiiuvaty
xerox *n.* ксерокс kseroks
Xmas *n.* Різдво Rizdvo
x-ray *v.t.* просвічувати рентгенівськими променями prosvichuvaty renthenivskymy promeniamy
x-ray *n.* рентген renthen
x-ray *a.* рентгенівський renthenivskyi

xylophagous *a.* той, що живиться деревиною toi, shcho zhyvytsia derevynoiu
xylophilous *a.* зростаючий на деревині zrostaiuchyi na derevyni
xylophone *n.* ксилофон ksylofon

yacht *v.i* плавати на яхті plavaty na yakhti
yacht *n.* яхта yakhta
yak *n.* як yak
yap *n* пелька pelka
yap *v.i.* гавкати havkaty
yard *n.* подвір'я podviria
yarn *n.* пряжа priazha
yawn *n.* позіхання pozikhannia
yawn *v.i.* позіхати pozikhaty
year *n.* рік rik
yearly *a.* що триває рік shcho tryvaie rik
yearly *adv.* щорічно shchorichno
yearn *v.i.* тужити tuzhyty
yearning *n.* глибока туга hlyboka tuha
yeast *n.* дріжджі drizhdzhi
yell *v.i.* лементувати lementuvaty
yell *n* пронизливий крик pronyzlyvyi kryk
yellow *n* жовтизна zhovtyzna
yellow *a.* жовтий zhovtyi
yellow *v.t.* пожовтіти pozhovtity
yellowish *a.* жовтуватий zhovtuvatyi
Yen *n.* Ієна liena
yeoman *n.* йомен yomen
yes *adv.* так tak
yesterday *n.* вчора vchora
yesterday *adv.* учора uchora
yet *adv.* вже vzhe
yet *conj.* тільки tilky

yield *n* вихід vykhid
yield *v.t.* здати zdaty
yoke *v.t.* запрягти zapriahty
yoke *n.* ярмо yarmo
yolk *n.* жовток zhovtok
yonder *adv.* он там on tam
yonder *a.* он той on toi
young *n* молодь molod
young *a.* юний yunyi
youngster *n.* хлопчик khlopchyk
youth *n.* юнак yunak
youthful *a.* юний yunyi

Z

zany *a.* смішний smishnyi
zeal *n.* завзяття zavziattia
zealot *n.* фанатик fanatyk
zealous *a.* ревний revnyi
zebra *n.* зебра zebra
zenith *n.* зеніт zenit
zephyr *n.* зефір zefir
zero *n.* ніщо nishcho
zest *n.* родзинка rodzynka
zigzag *n.* зигзаг zyhzah
zigzag *a.* зигзагоподібний zyhzahopodibnyi
zigzag *v.i.* робити зигзаги robyty zyhzahy
zinc *n.* цинк tsynk
zip *v.t.* промайнути promainuty
zip *n.* свист кулі svyst kuli
zodiac *n* зодіак zodiak
zonal *a.* зональний zonalnyi
zone *n.* зона zona
zoo *n.* зоопарк zoopark
zoological *a.* зоологічний zoolohichnyi
zoologist *n.* зоолог zooloh
zoology *n.* зоологія zoolohiia
zoom *n.* збільшення зображення zbilshennia zobrazhennia

zoom *v.i.* рухатися з гудінням rukhatysia z hudinniam

UKRAINIAN-ENGLISH

A

a same а саме *adv.* namely
a to а то *adv* else
abatstvo абатство *n.* abbey
abo ... abo або ... або *a.*, either
abo zh або ж *conj.* otherwise
abort аборт *n* abortion
aboryhennyi аборигенний *a* aboriginal
aboryheny аборигени *n. pl* aborigines
abreviatura абревіатура *n* abbreviation
abrykos абрикос *n.* apricot
absoliutno абсолютно *adv* absolutely
absoliutnyi абсолютний *a* absolute
abstrahuvaty абстрагувати *v.t* abstract
abstraktnyi абстрактний *a* abstract
abstraktsiia абстракція *n* abstract
abstses абсцес *n* abscess
absurdnyi абсурдний *a* absurd
absyda абсида *n.* conch
adamant адамант *n.* adamant
adaptatsiia адаптація *n.* adaptation
adaptuvatysia адаптуватися *v.t.* adapt
adekvatnist адекватність *n.* adequacy
adekvatnyi адекватний *a.* adequate
adiulter адюльтер *n.* adultery
administrator адміністратор *n.* administrator
administratyvnyi адміністративний *a.* administrative

admiral адмірал *n.* admiral
adresa адреса *n.* address
adresat адресат *n.* addressee
advokat адвокат *n* advocate
advokat naivyshchoho ranhu адвокат найвищого рангу *n.* barrister
advokatura адвокатура *n.* advocacy
aerodrom аеродром *n* aerodrome
aeronavtyka аеронавтика *n.pl.* aeronautics
aeroplan аероплан *n.* aeroplane
aeruvaty аерувати *v.t.* aerify
afektatsiia афектація *n* affectation
aforyzm афоризм *n* aphorism
agrus аґрус *n.* gooseberry
ahent агент *n* agent
ahent, shcho verbuie na vyiskovu sluzhbu obmanom агент, що вербує на військову службу обманом *n* crimp
ahentstvo агентство *n.* agency
ahitatsiia агітація *n* agitation
ahituvaty агітувати *v.t.* agitate
ahituvaty агітувати *v. t.* canvass
Ahni Агні *n* agnus
ahoniia агонія *n.* agony
ahorafobiia агорафобія *n.* agoraphobia
ahrarnyi аграрний *a.* agrarian
ahresiia агресія *n* aggression
ahresor агресор *n.* aggressor
ahresyvnyi агресивний *a.* aggressive
ahresyvnyi агресивний *a.* offensive
ahronom агроном *n.* agriculturist
ahronomiia агрономія *n.* agronomy
aisberh айсберг *n.* iceberg
akademiia академія *n* academy

akhromatychnyi ахроматичний *adj* achromatic
aklimatyzuvatysia акліматизуватися *v.t* acclimatise
akr акр *n.* acre
akrobat акробат *n.* acrobat
akt акт *n.* act
aktor актор *n.* actor
aktor-amator актор-аматор *adv* am
aktrysa актриса *n.* actress
aktsent акцент *n* accent
aktsentuvannia акцентування *n* emphasis
aktsentuvaty акцентувати *v. t* emphasize
aktsii акції *n.* stock
aktsiia акція *n* share
aktsyz акциз *n* excise
aktualnyi актуальний *a.* topical
aktyv актив *n.* asset
aktyvnyi активний *a.* active
aktyvuvaty активувати *v.t.* activate
akula акула *n.* shark
akumuliatsiia акумуляція *n.* accumulation
akumuliuvaty акумулювати *v.t.* accumulate
akuratnyi акуратний *a.* neat
akusherka акушерка *n.* midwife
akustychnyi акустичний *a* acoustic
akustyka акустика *n.* acoustics
akvarium акваріум *n.* aquarium
akveduk акведук *n* aqueduct
Albion Альбіон *n* albion
albom альбом *n.* album
ale але *prep* but
ale але *conj.* but
alehoriia алегорія *n.* allegory

alehorychnyi алегоричний *a.* allegorical
alehorychnyi алегоричний *a.* allusive
aleia алея *n.* alley
aleia алея *n.* vista
alerhiia алергія *n.* allergy
alfa альфа *n* alpha
alfavit алфавіт *n.* alphabet
alfavitnyi алфавітний *a.* alphabetical
alhebra алгебра *n.* algebra
alians альянс *n.* alliance
alibi алібі *n.* alibi
alihator алігатор *n* alligator
alimenty аліменти *n.* alimony
aliteratsiia алітерація *n.* alliteration
aliteruvaty алітерувати *v.* alliterate
aliuminii алюміній *n.* aluminium
alkhimiia алхімія *n.* alchemy
alkohol алкоголь *n* alcohol
alkoholik алкоголік *n* drunkard
alkoholik алкоголік *n.* rummy
alkoholnyi napii алкогольний напій *n.* liquor
almanakh альманах *n.* almanac
alpinist альпініст *n* alpinist
alpinist альпініст *n.* mountaineer
alt альт *n* alto
altanka альтанка *n* belvedere
alternatyva альтернатива *n.* alternative
altymetr альтиметр *n* altimeter
amalhama амальгама *n* amalgam
amatorskyi аматорський *adj* amatory
amberit амберіт *n.* amberite
ambulatornyi khvoryi амбулаторний хворий *n.* outpatient

amelioratsiia амеліорація *n.* amelioration

amenoreia аменорея *n* amenorrhoea

amfiteatr амфітеатр *n* amphitheatre

amin! амінь! *interj.* amen

amneziia амнезія *n* amnesia

amnistiia амністія *n.* amnesty

amoralnist аморальність *n.* immorality

amoralnyi аморальний *a.* amoral

Amper Ампер *n* ampere

amplituda амплітуда *n.* span

amulet амулет *n.* amulet

anabaptyzm анабаптизм *n* anabaptism

anafema анафема *n* ban

anakhronizm анахронізм *n* anachronism

anaklaza анаклаза *n* anaclisis

analitychnyi аналітичний *a* analytical

analityk аналітик *n* analyst

analiz аналіз *n.* analysis

analiz аналіз *n.* audit

analiz hry pislia yii zakinchennia аналіз гри після її закінчення *n.* post-mortem

analizuvaty аналізувати *v.t.* analyse

analnyi анальний *adj.* anal

analohichnyi аналогічний *a.* reciprocal

analohiia аналогія *n.* analogy

anamorfnyi анаморфний *adj* anamorphous

ananas ананас *n.* pineapple

anarkhiia анархія *n* anarchy

anarkhist анархіст *n* anarchist

anarkhizm анархізм *n.* anarchism

anatomiia анатомія *n.* anatomy

androfah андрофаг *n.* androphagi

anekdot анекдот *n.* anecdote

aneksiia анексія *n* annexation

anemiia анемія *n* anaemia

anemometr анемометр *n* anemometer

anestetyk анестетик *n.* anaesthetic

anesteziia анестезія *n* anaesthesia

anhina ангіна *n* angina

anhliiska mova англійська мова *n* English

anis аніс *n* aniseed

anketa анкета *n.* questionnaire

annuitent аннуітент *n* annuitant

anomaliia аномалія *n* anomaly

anonimnist анонімність *n.* anonymity

anonimnyi анонімний *a.* anonymous

antahonist антагоніст *n.* antagonist

antahonizm антагонізм *n* antagonism

antarktychnyi антарктичний *a.* antarctic

antatsydnyi антацидний *adj.* antacid

antena антена *n.* aerial

antolohiia антологія *n.* anthology

antonim антонім *n.* antonym

antrakt антракт *n.* interlude

anty анти *pref.* anti

antydot антидот *n.* antidote

antyfon антифон *n.* antiphony

antykvar антиквар *n* antiquarian

antykvarnyi антикварний *a.* antiquarian

antylopa антилопа *n.* antelope

antypatiia антипатія *n.* antipathy

antypatiia антипатія *n.* repugnance

antypody антиподи *n.* antipodes

antyseptychnyi антисептичний
a. antiseptic
antyseptyk антисептик *n.*
antiseptic
antyteza антитеза *n.* antithesis
anuliuvannia анулювання *n.*
abolition
anuliuvannia анулювання *n.*
nullification
anuliuvannia анулювання *n.*
reversal
anuliuvaty анулювати *v. t.*
abrogate
anuliuvaty анулювати *v.t.* annul
aparat апарат *n.* apparatus
aparat dlia promyvannia vukha
апарат для промивання вуха
n. aurilave
apatiia апатія *n.* apathy
apatychnyi апатичний *a.* listless
apeliatsiia апеляція *v.t.* appeal
apelsyn апельсин *n.* orange
apendyks апендикс *n.* appendix
apendytsyt апендицит *n.*
appendicitis
aperytyv аперитив *n* appetizer
apetyt апетит *n.* appetite
aploduvaty аплодувати *v.t.*
applaud
apostol апостол *n.* apostle
apostol апостол *n* disciple
apostrof апостроф *n.* apostrophe
appeliant аппелянт *n.* appellant
apriornyi апріорний *a.*
antecedent
apteka аптека *n.* pharmacy
arbitr арбітр *n.* arbiter
areka арека *n* areca
arena арена *n.* lists
aresht арешт *n.* arrest
areshtant арештант *n* convict
arfa арфа *n.* harp

arhument аргумент *n.*
substantiation
arhumentatsiia zakhystu
аргументація захисту *n*
defence
arka арка *n.* arc
arkada аркада *n* arcade
arkhaichnyi архаїчний *a.* archaic
arkhanhel архангел *n* archangel
arkhiiepyskop архієпископ *n.*
archbishop
arkhitektor архітектор *n.* architect
arkhitektura архітектура *n.*
architecture
arkhivy архіви *n.pl.* archives
Arktyka Арктика *n* Arctic
armada армада *n.* armada
armatura арматура *n.* armature
armiia армія *n.* army
armuvannia армування *n.*
reinforcement
aromat аромат *n.* fragrance
aromatnyi ароматний *a.* fragrant
arrourut арроурут *n.* arrowroot
arsen арсен *n* arsenic
arsenal арсенал *n.* arsenal
artryt артрит *n* arthritis
artykuliuvaty артикулювати *a.*
articulate
artyleriia артилерія *n.* artillery
artyleriia артилерія *n.* ordnance
artyshok артишок *n.* artichoke
aryfmetyka арифметика *n.*
arithmetic
arystokrat аристократ *n.*
aristocrat
arystokratiia аристократія *n.*
aristocracy
asafetyda асафетида *n.*
asafoetida
asambleia асамблея *n.* assembly
asket аскет *n.* ascetic

asketychnyi аскетичний *a.*
ascetic
asortyment асортимент *n.* choice
asotsiatsiia асоціація *n.*
association
asotsiatyvnyi асоціативний *a.*
associate
asotsiiuvaty асоціювати *v.t.*
associate
aspekt аспект *n.* aspect
aspekt аспект *n* facet
asteryzm астеризм *n.* asterism
astma астма *n.* asthma
astroloh астролог *n.* astrologer
astrolohiia астрологія *n.*
astrology
astronavt астронавт *n.* astronaut
astronom астроном *n.*
astronomer
astronomiia астрономія *n.*
astronomy
asyhnuvannia асигнування *n.*
allocation
asyhnuvannia асигнування *n.*
appropriation
asystent асистент *n.* assistant
atakuvaty атакувати *v.t.* assault
atashe аташе *n.* attache
ateist атеїст *n* antitheist
ateizm атеїзм *n* atheism
atestat zrilosti атестат зрілості *n.*
matriculation
atestuvaty атестувати *v. t*
evaluate
atlas атлас *n.* atlas
atlet атлет *n.* athlete
atletychnyi атлетичний *a.* athletic
atletyka атлетика *n.* athletics
atmosfera атмосфера *n.*
atmosphere
atol атол *n.* atoll
atom атом *n.* atom
atomnyi атомний *a.* atomic

atrofovanyi атрофований *a.*
obsolete
audytor аудитор *n.* auditor
auktsionnyi zal аукціонний зал
n. mart
avanpost аванпост *n.* outpost
avans аванс *n.* advance
avantiura авантюра *n* adventure
avantiurnyi авантюрний *a.*
adventurous
avariia аварія *n* breakdown
aviatsiia авіація *n.* aviation
avtobiohrafiia автобіографія *n.*
autobiography
avtobus автобус *n* bus
avtohraf автограф *n.* autograph
avtomatychnyi автоматичний *a*
mechanic
avtomobil автомобіль *n.*
automobile
avtomobilist автомобіліст *n.*
motorist
avtomobilnyi автомобільний *a.*
vehicular
avtonomnyi автономний *a*
autonomous
avtor автор *n.* author
avtorytetnyi авторитетний *a.*
authoritative
azartna hra азартна гра *n* gamble
azartnyi азартний *a.* venturesome
azbest азбест *n.* asbestos
azot азот *n.* nitrogen

babuin бабуїн *n.* baboon
bachyty бачити *v. t* behold
badminton бадмінтон *n.*
badminton
badoryi бадьорий *a* awake
badoryi бадьорий *a.* sprightly
bahato багато *n.* lot

bahato багато *adv.* much
bahato khto багато хто *a.* many
bahatobozhzhia багатобожжя *n.* polytheism
bahatohrannyi багатогранний *a.* multifarious
bahatomovnyi багатомовний *a.* polyglot2
bahatonadiinyi багатонадійний *a.* likely
bahatonizhka багатоніжка *n.* millipede
bahatoobitsiaiuchyi багатообіцяючий *a.* promising
bahatorichna roslyna багаторічна рослина *n.* perennial
bahatoslivnist багатослівність *n.* verbosity
bahatoslivnyi багатослівний *a.* verbose
bahatostoronnii багатосторонній *a.* multilateral
bahatoznachnyi багатозначний *a.* meaningful
bahatoznachnyi багатозначний *a.* significant
bahatstvo багатство *n.* mammon
bahattia багаття *n* bonfire
bahatyi багатий *a.* opulent
bahatyi za narodzhenniam багатий за народженням *adj.* born rich
bahazh багаж *n.* luggage
bahnet багнет *n* bayonet
bahno багно *n.* slough
baiduzhist байдужість *n.* indifference
baiduzhyi байдужий *a.* immovable
baiduzhyi байдужий *a.* indifferent
baidykuvaty байдикувати *v.i.* dawdle

baika байка *n.* fable
bak бак *n* boiler
bakaliina lavka бакалійна лавка *n.* grocery
bakaliinyk бакалійник *n.* grocer
bakhroma бахрома *n.* fringe
baklazhan баклажан *n* brinjal
bakteriia бактерія *n.* bacteria
bakterytsyd бактерицид *n.* germicide
balada балада *n.* ballad
balakuchyi балакучий *a.* gassy
balans баланс *n.* balance
balansuvaty балансувати *v.t.* balance
balet балет *sn.* ballet
balkon балкон *n.* balcony
balotuvannia балотування *n.* vote
balotuvaty балотувати *v.i.* vote
baluvaty балувати *v. t* cocker
baluvaty балувати *v.t.* pamper
baluvaty балувати *v.t.* spoil
balzam бальзам *n.* balm
bambuk бамбук *n.* bamboo
bamper бампер *n.* bumper
banalnyi банальний *a.* banal
banan банан *n.* banana
banda банда *n.* gang
bandyt бандит *n.* dacoit
bandzho банджо *n.* banjo
banian баніан *n.* banyan
bank банк *n.* bank
banket банкет *n.* banquet
bankir банкір *n.* banker
bankrut банкрут *n.* bankrupt
bankrutstvo банкрутство *n.* insolvency
bant бант *n.* knot
baraban барабан *n* drum
barak барак *n.* barrack
baran баран *n.* ram
baranyna баранина *n.* mutton

bard бард *n.* bard
barier бар'єр *n.* barrier
barkhatystyi бархатистий *a.*
 velvety
barlih барліг *n.* lair
barometr барометр *n* barometer
barva барва *n.* tint
barvnyk барвник *n* dye
barvnyk барвник *n.* stain
barvystyi барвистий *a* flowery
barykada барикада *n.* barricade
barylo барило *n* cask
baryshnyk баришник *n.* coper
barzha баржа *n.* barge
bas бас *n.* bass
bashta башта *n.* tower
bastion бастіон *n* bulwark
batareia батарея *n* battery
batih батіг *n.* whip
batkivshchyna батьківщина *n.*
 habitat
batkivskyi батьківський *a.*
 parental
batkivstvo батьківство *n.*
 parentage
batko батько *n* father
batkovbyvstvo батьковбивство
 n. parricide
bavovna бавовна *n* clap
bavovna бавовна *n.* cotton
bavytysia бавитися *v.i.* play
bazhaiuchyi бажаючий *a*
 desirous
bazhannia бажання *n.* wish
bazhanyi бажаний *a* desirable
bazhaty бажати *v.t* desire
bazhaty shchastia бажати щастя
 v.t felicitate
bazika базіка *n.* jay
bazikaty базікати *v. t. & i* blab
bazioalveoliarnyi
 базіоальвеолярний *adv.* basial
bazovyi базовий *a.* base

bazylik базилік *n.* basil
bazys базис *n.* basis
bdinnia бдіння *n.* vigil
bdzhilnytstvo бджільництво *n.*
 apiculture
bdzhola бджола *n.* bee
bekannia бекання *n* bleat
bekaty бекати *v. i* bleat
belkotannia белькотання *n.*
 prattle
belkotaty белькотати *v.i.* prattle
benefitsii бенефіцій *n* benefice
benket бенкет *n* feast
benketnyi бенкетний *adj.*
 convivial
benketuvaty бенкетувати *v.t.*
 banquet
benzyn бензин *n.* petrol
bereh берег *n.* brink
bereh берег *n.* shore
berehty берегти *v.t.* preserve
berehtysia берегтися *v.i.* beware
bereza береза *n.* birch
berezen березень *n.* march
beriks берікс *n.* alphonsion
beshket бешкет *n* affray
beshketuvaty бешкетувати *v.t.*
 riot
besida бесіда *n.* chat1
besida бесіда *n* conversation
betel бетель *n* betel
beton бетон *n* concrete
betonnyi бетонний *a* concrete
bez без *prep.* less
bez hrosha без гроша *a.*
 penniless
bez toho, shchob без того, щоб
 adv. without
bezbozhnyk безбожник *n* atheist
bezchestia безчестя *n* dishonour
bezchestyty безчестити *v. t*
 dishonour

bezdiialnist бездіяльність *n.*
inaction
bezdiialnyi бездіяльний *a.*
inactive
bezdomna sobaka бездомна
собака *n* stray
bezdrotovyi бездротовий *a.*
wireless
bezhluzdist безглуздість *n*
absurdity
bezhluzdist безглуздість *n.*
stupidity
bezhluzdyi безглуздий *a.*
meaningless
bezhluzdyi безглуздий *a.*
senseless
bezholovyi безголовий *n.*
acephalus
bezkarnist безкарність *n.*
impunity
bezkarnyi безкарний *a.* scot-free
bezkoshtovnyi безкоштовний
adv. gratis
bezlad безлад *n* disorder
bezladdia безладдя *n.* mess
bezladdia безладдя *n.* muddle
bezladnyi безладний *a.* random
bezlich безліч *n.* multitude
bezlykist безликість *n.* anonymity
bezmezhnyi безмежний *a.* infinite
bezmezhnyi безмежний *a.*
limitless
bezmir безмір *n.* immensity
bezmirnyi безмірний *a.*
measureless
beznadiinyi безнадійний *a.*
hopeless
bezodnia безодня *n* abyss
bezodnia безодня *n.* profundity
bezosobovyi безособовий *a.*
impersonal
bezpechnist безпечність *n.*
security

bezpechnyi безпечний *a.* safe
bezpeka безпека *n.* safety
bezperechnyi безперечний *a.*
indisputable
bezperervnist безперервність *n*
continuity
bezperervnyi безперервний *adj.*
continual
bezperervnyi безперервний *a*
continuous
bezpidstavnyi безпідставний *a.*
baseless
bezpilotnyi безпілотний *a.*
unmanned
bezpomichnyi безпомічний *a.*
helpless
bezpomylkovyi безпомилковий
a. infallible
bezposerednii безпосередній *a*
direct
bezpryntsypnyi безпринципний
a. unprincipled
bezrezultatnyi безрезультатний
a. ineffective
bezrozsudnyi безрозсудний *a.*
reckless
bezshliubnist безшлюбність *n.*
celibacy
bezsmertia безсмертя *n.*
immortality
bezsmertnyi безсмертний *a.*
everlasting
bezsmertnyi безсмертний *a.*
immortal
bezsoromna diia безсоромна дія
n. indecency
bezsoromnyi безсоромний *a.*
lewd
bezsoromnyi безсоромний *a.*
shameless
bezstrashnyi безстрашний *a*
dauntless

bezstrashnyi безстрашний *a.*
venturous
bezsumnivnyi fakt безсумнівний
факт *n.* certainty
bezsyllia безсилля *n.* impotence
bezturbotnist безтурботність *n.*
nonchalance
bezturbotnyi безтурботний *a.*
gay
bezturbotnyi безтурботний *a.*
serene
bezumets безумець *n.* lunatic
bezvidpovidalnyi
безвідповідальний *a.* wanton
bezvykhidne polozhennia
безвихідне положення *n.*
stalemate
bezvykhidne stanovyshche
безвихідне становище *n.*
impasse
bezvynnyi безвинний *a.* innocent
bezzakonnyi беззаконний *a.*
lawless
bezzhalisnyi безжалісний *a.*
pitiless
bezzhurnyi безжурний *a.* cheerful
bi бі *pref* bi
bibliia біблія *n* bible
bibliohraf бібліограф *n*
bibliographer
bibliohrafiia бібліографія *+n*
bibliography
biblioteka бібліотека *n.* library
bibliotekar бібліотекар *n.* librarian
bida біда *n.* calamity
bidnist бідність *n.* necessity
bidnist бідність *n.* poverty
bidnyi бідний *a.* poor
bidolashnyi бідолашний *a.*
miserable
bidon бідон *n.* can
bihaty бігати *v.i.* run
bihty бігти *v.i* flee

bihty makhovym krokom бігти
маховим кроком *v.i.* stride
bihun бігун *n.* runner
bii бій *n* battle
biika бійка *n.* scuffle
biinytsia бійниця *n.* loop-hole
bil біль *n.* ache
bil u miazakh біль у м'язах *n.*
myalgia
bilia біля *prep* by
bilia біля *adv* by
bilka білка *n.* squirrel
bilok білок *n.* protein
bilsh nizh dostatnii більш ніж
достатній *a* abundant
bilshe більше *adv* more
bilshe toho більше того *adv.*
moreover
bilshist більшість *n* most
biluvatyi білуватий *a.* whitish
bilyi білий *a.* white
bilyty білити *v.t.* whitewash
bilyty vapnom білити вапном *v.t*
lime
bilyzna білизна *n* white
binokuliarnyi бінокулярний *n.*
binocular
biohraf біограф *n* biographer
biohrafiia біографія *n* biography
bioloh біолог *n* biologist
biolohiia біологія *n* biology
bioskop біоскоп *n* bioscope
birzhovyi біржовий *a.* stock
birzhovyi broker біржовий
брокер *n.* stag
bisyty бісити *v. t* enrage
bitseps біцепс *n* biceps
bity poperedu біти попереду *v.*
precede
biudzhet бюджет *n* budget
biuleten бюлетень *n* ballot
biuro бюро *n.* bureau
biurokrat бюрократ *n* bureaucrat

biurokratiia бюрократія *n.* Bureacracy

bizhenets біженець *n.* refugee

biznes бізнес *n* business

biznesmen бізнесмен *n* businessman

bizon бізон *n* bison

blahannia благання *n* adjuration

blahannia благання *n* cry

blahannia благання *n.* oration

blahannia благання *n.* plea

blahaty благати *v.t.* adiure

blahaty благати *v. t.* beg

blaho благо *n.* weal

blahochestia благочестя *n.* piety

blahochestyvyi благочестивий *a.* pious

blahodatnyi благодатний *a.* grateful

blahodiiannia благодіяння *n.* benefaction

blahodiinist благодійність *n.* philanthropy

blahodiinyi благодійний *a.* charitable

blahohoviinyi благоговійний *a.* reverent

blahohovinnia благоговіння *n.* awe

blahoprystoinist благопристойність *n* decorum

blahorodnyi благородний *adj* alin

blahoslovennia благословення *n* benison

blahoslovliaty благословляти *v. t* bless

blahotvornyi благотворний *a* beneficial

blahovolinnia благовоління *n.* goodwill

blakytnyi блакитний *a* blue

blazen блазень *n* buffoon

blazen блазень *n* fool

blazenskyi kovpak блазенський ковпак *n* foolscap

blazhenstvo блаженство *n* bliss

blef блеф *n* bluff

blefuvaty блефувати *v. t* bluff

blidnuty бліднути *v.i.* pale

blido-rozhevyi блідо-рожевий *a.* pinkish

blidyi блідий *a* pale

blindazh бліндаж *n* blindage

bliudo блюдо *n* dish

bliudtse блюдце *n.* saucer

bliuvota блювота *n* vomit

bliuznirskyi блюзнірський *a.* sacrilegious

blok блок *n* bloc

blokha блоха *n.* flea

blokuvannia блокування *v.t.* interlock

bloshytsia блошиця *n.* bug

bludyty блудити *v.i.* stray

blukaty блукати *v.i.* rove

blukaty bez mety блукати без мети *v.t.* ramble

blukaty navmannia блукати навмання *v.i.* meander

bluza блуза *n* blouse

blymaty блимати *v. t. & i* blink

blyshchaty блищати *v.i.* shine

blysk блиск *n* glitter

blyskotinnia блискотіння *n* flare

blyskucha mishura блискуча мішура *n.* glare

blyskuchyi блискучий *a* brilliant

blyskuchyi блискучий *a.* splendid

blyzhnii ближній *a.* near

blyzkist близькість *n.* proximity

blyzko близько *adv.* anigh

blyzniuk близнюк *n.* twin

boa боа *n.* necklet

bober бобер *n* beaver

bochka бочка *n.* bar

bochka бочка *n.* barrel

boh бог *n.* god
bohoslov богослов *n.* theologian
bohoslovia богослов'я *n* divinity
bohoslovia богослов'я *n.* theology
bohoslovskyi богословський *a.* theological
bohynia богиня *n.* goddess
boiahuz боягуз *n.* coward
boiahuzlyvyi боягузливий *a.* nerveless
boiahuztvo боягузтво *n.* cowardice
boiatysia боятися *v.t* dread
boiazkist боязкість *n.* timidity
boiazkyi боязкий *a.* timorous
boieprypasy боєприпаси *n.* ammunition
boiets боєць *n* militant
boikot бойкот *n* boycott
boikotuvaty бойкотувати *v. t.* boycott
boiovyi бойовий *a.* militant
boiovyi dukh бойовий дух *n.* morale
boiovyi poriadok бойовий порядок *n.* array
boks бокс *n* boxing
bolezaspokiilyvyi болезаспокійливий *a.* sedative
boliachka болячка *n* sore
boloto болото *n.* marsh
boloto болото *n.* swamp
bolotystyi болотистий *a.* marshy
bolvan болван *n.* loggerhead
bomba бомба *n* bomb
bombarduvalnyk бомбардувальник *n* bomber
bombarduvannia бомбардування *n* bombardment
bombarduvaty бомбардувати *v. t* bombard

bombyty бомбити *v. t* bomb
bordel бордель *n* brothel
bordiur бордюр *n.* welt
borets борець *n.* wrestler
borh борг *n* debt
borh борг *n.* score
borhovyi борговий *a.* obligatory
borhy борги *n.pl.* arrears
boroda борода *n* beard
boroda борода *n.* whisker
borodavka бородавка *n.* wart
boroshno борошно *n* flour
boroshnystyi борошнистий *a.* mealy
borotba боротьба *n* fight
borotba боротьба *n.* tussle
borotysia боротися *v. i.* battle
borotysia боротися *v. t.* combat
borotysia боротися *v.i.* tussle
borozna борозна *n.* furrow
borsuk борсук *n.* badger
borzhnyk боржник *n* debtor
borzhnyk za zastavnoiu боржник за заставною *n.* mortgagor
bos бос *n* boss
botanika ботаніка *n* botany
bovknuty бовкнути *v. t* blurt
bozhestvennist божественність *n.* godhead
bozhestvenyi божествений *a* divine
bozhestvo божество *n.* deity
bozhevillia божевілля *n.* frenzy
bozhevillia божевілля *n.* insanity
bozhevilnyi божевільний *a* crazy
bozhevilnyi божевільний *adj.* daft
brak брак *n.* paucity
brak брак *n.* scarcity
branets бранець *n.* captive
brashpyl брашпиль *v.t.* windlass
braslet браслет *n.* bangle
braslet браслет *n* bracelet
brat брат *n* brother

braterskyi братерський *a.* fraternal

bratovbyvstvo братовбивство *n.* fratricide

bratovbyvtsia братовбивця *n* cain

bratstvo братство *n* brotherhood

braty брати *v.t* take

braty na poruky брати на поруки *v. t.* bail

braty na sebe брати на себе *v.t.* incur

braty na vidhodivliu брати на відгодівлю *v.t.* agist

braty nazad брати назад *v.t.* resume

braty nazad брати назад *v.t.* revoke

braty pid sumniv брати під сумнів *v.t.* impeach

braty uchast брати участь *v.i.* partake

braty uchast u pikniku брати участь у пікніку *v.i.* picnic

braty uchast u skachkakh брати участь у скачках *v.i* race

braty v orendu брати в оренду *v.t.* rent

brekhaty брехати *v. t.* defame

brekhaty брехати *v.i* lie

brekhlyvyi брехливий *a.* mendacious

brekhnia брехня *n* lie

brekhun брехун *n.* liar

brendi бренді *n* brandy

briazkaltse брязкальце *n* rattle

briuky брюки *n. pl* trousers

brodiachyi бродячий *a* vagabond

brodiaha бродяга *n.* vagabond

brodinnia бродіння *n* fermentation

brodyty бродити *v.t* ferment

broker брокер *n* broker

brokkoli брокколі *n.* broccoli

bronia броня *n.* armour

bronza бронза *n. & adj* bronze

broshura брошура *n* brochure

broshura брошура *n* brochure

brova брова *n* brow

brud бруд *n* dirt

brudnyi брудний *a.* foul

brudnyty бруднити *v. t* blot

brudnytysia бруднитися *v.t.* soil

brukivka бруківка *n* causeway

brunka брунька *n* bud

brushchatka брущатка *n.* pitcher

brutalno povodytysia брутально поводитися *d* mistreat

brutalnyi брутальний *a* brutal

brutalnyi брутальний *a.* rude

brutto брутто *n.* gross

brydkyi бридкий *a.* horrible

brydkyi бридкий *a.* vile

brydzhi бриджі *n.* breeches

bryhada бригада *n.* brigade

bryhada бригада *n.* team

bryhadyr бригадир *n* brigadier

brytanskyi британський *adj* british

brytva бритва *n.* razor

bryz бриз *n* breeze

bryzhi брижі *n.* ripple

bryzkaty бризкати *v. t.* sprinkle

budennyi буденний *a.* workaday

bud-iakyi будь-який *adv.* either

bud-iakyi будь-який *a* every

budivelni lisy будівельні ліси *n.* scaffold

budivlia будівля *n* edifice

budivnytstvo будівництво *n* building

budka будка *n.* kennel

bud-khto будь-хто *n.* somebody

budova tila будова тіла *n* build

budova tila будова тіла *n.* habit

buduvaty будувати *v. t* build

budynochok будиночок *n.* lodge
budynok будинок *n.* home
budyty будити *v.t.* arouse
bufet буфет *n* cupboard
bufetna буфетна *n.* pantry
bufetnyk буфетник *n* drawer
bui буй *n* buoy
buinyi буйний *a.* rowdy
buinyi rist буйний ріст *n.* luxuriance
buivol буйвол *n.* buffalo
buivoliacha shkira буйволяча шкіра *n* buff
buk бук *n.* beech
buket букет *n* bouquet
buketyk kvitiv букетик квітів *n.* nosegay
bukhanets буханець *n.* loaf
bukhhalter бухгалтер *n* bookkeeper
bukhhalterska sprava бухгалтерська справа *n.* accountancy
bukhta бухта *n* bay
buklet буклет *n* booklet
buksuvaty буксувати *v.i.* skid
buksyr буксир *v.t.* tug
bukvalnyi буквальний *a.* literal
buldoh бульдог *n* bulldog
bunhalo бунгало *n* bungalow
bunt бунт *n.* rebellion
bunt бунт *n.* riot
buntivnyk бунтівник *n.* rebel
buntuvaty бунтувати *v. i* mutiny
burav бурав *n.* wimple
burchannia бурчання *n* growl
burchaty бурчати *v.i.* growl
bure vuhillia буре вугілля *n.* lignite
buria буря *n.* tempest
buriak буряк *n* beet
burian бур'ян *n.* weed

burkhlyvo aploduvaty бурхливо аплодувати *v.t* acclaim
burkhlyvo vyrazhaty protest бурхливо виражати протест *v. i.* clamour
burkhlyvyi бурхливий *a.* tempestuous
burkhlyvyi бурхливий *a.* uproarious
burmotannia бурмотання *n.* murmur
burmotaty бурмотати *v.i.* gabble
burulka бурулька *n.* icicle
bushuvaty бушувати *v.i.* rage
busynka бусинка *n* bead
buterbrod бутерброд *n.* sandwich
buttia буття *n* being
buty бути *v.t.* be
buty бути *v.i* exist
buty hidnym бути гідним *v. t.* deserve
buty korysnym бути корисним *v.t.* avail
buty nerishuchym бути нерішучим *v.i.* shilly-shally
buty nespravedlyvym бути несправедливим *v.t.* wrong
buty poserednykom бути посередником *v.i.* mediate
buty skhozhym бути схожим *v.t.* resemble
buty suddeiu бути суддею *v.t.*, umpire
buty u velykii kilkosti бути у великій кількості *v.i.* abound
buty v konflikti бути в конфлікті *v. i* conflict
buty v zmozi бути в змозі *v.* can
buty zadovolenym бути задоволеним *v.t.* consent3
buvai бувай *interj.* bye-bye
buzok бузок *n.* lilac
bych бич *n.* scourge

238

bychuvaty бичувати *v.t.* scourge
byk бик *n* bull
byk бик *n.* ox
bynt бинт *~n.* bandage
byntuvaty бинтувати *v.t* bandage
byttia биття *n.* throb
byty бити *v. t.* beat
byty kopytom бити копитом *n.* hoof
byty kozyrem бити козирем *v.t.* trump
byty lozynoiu бити лозиною *v.t.* switch
byty ostenem бити остенем *v.t.* spear
byty palytseiu бити палицею *v. i* bat
byty rukoiu бити рукою *v. t* cuff
byty strumenem бити струменем *v.i.* spout
byty strumynoiu бити струминою *v.i* flush
byty v baraban бити в барабан *v.i.* drum
bytysia битися *v.t* fight
bytysia битися *v.i.* pulse
bytysia битися *v.i.* scuffle
bytysia na dueli битися на дуелі *v. i* duel
byven бивень *n.* ivory

chaban чабан *n.* shepherd
chaharnyk чагарник *n.* shrub
chai чай *n* tea
chaika чайка *n* gull
chaika чайка *n.* gull
chainyk чайник *n.* kettle
chaklun чаклун *n.* sorcerer
chaklunka чаклунка *n.* hag
chaklunstvo чаклунство *n.* sorcery

chaklunstvo чаклунство *n.* witchcraft
chaklunstvo чаклунство *n.* witchery
chakluvaty чаклувати *v.t.* conjure
charivnist чарівність *n.* charm1
charivnist чарівність *n.* fascination
charivnist чарівність *n.* glamour
charivnyi чарівний *a.* winsome
charivnyk чарівник *n.* wizard
charuvaty чарувати *v. t* enchant
chary чари *n.* spell
chas час *n.* time
chas час *n.* while
chas do poludnia час до полудня *n* forenoon
chas liahaty spaty час лягати спати *n.* bed-time
chas vid chasu час від часу *adv.* occasionally
chasha чаша *n* bowl
chasha чаша *n* chaice
chashka чашка *n.* cup
chasnyk часник *n.* garlic
chasovyi часовий *n.* sentinel
chastka частка *n.* fraction
chastkovyi частковий *a.* partial
chasto часто *adv.* oft
chasto buvaty часто бувати *v.t.* haunt
chastota частота *n.* frequency
chastyi частий *a.* frequent
chastyna частина *n.* part
chastyna частина *n.* partition
chastyna частина *n* portion
chastyna частина *n.* residue
chastyna частина *n* stake
chavun чавун *n* cast-iron
chek чек *n.* cheque
chekannia чекання *n.* wait
chekaty чекати *v.t.* await
chekaty чекати *v. t* expect

chekaty чекати *v.i.* wait
chemnist чемність *n.* courtesy
chemnist чемність *n.* politeness
chemnist чемність *n.* urbanity
chemnyi чемний *a.* courteous
chempion чемпіон *n.* champion
chepliaty чепляти *v.i.* grapple
cherep череп *n.* skull
cherepakha черепаха *n.* tortoise
cherepakha черепаха *n.* turtle
chereshok черешок *n* stalk
cherevnyi черевний *a.* abdominal
cherevnyi tyf черевний тиф *n.* typhoid
cherevo черево *n* abdomen
cherez через *prep.* across
cherez через *prep.* along
cherez через *adv* over
cherez через *prep.* over
cherez через *prep.* through
cherez через *prep.* via
cherha черга *n.* queue
cherha черга *n* turn
cherhuvaty чергувати *v.t.* alternate
cherhuvatysia чергуватися *v.i.* rotate
chernets чернець *n.* monk
chernets чернець *n.* votary
chernetstvo чернецтво *n* monasticism
cherpaty черпати *v.t.* ladle
cherpaty lozhkoiu черпати ложкою *v.t.* spoon
cherstvist черствість *n.* obduracy
cherstvyi черствий *a.* callous
cherstvyi черствий *a.* stale
cherviak черв'як *n.* worm
chervone derevo червоне дерево *n.* mahogany
chervonity червоніти *v.i* blush
chervonity червоніти *v.t.* redden

chervonuvatyi червонуватий *a.* reddish
chervonyi червоний *a.* red
chervonyi kolir червоний колір *n.* red
chesnist чесність *n.* honesty
chesno чесно *adv.* fairly
chesnyi чесний *a.* honest
chest честь *n.* honour
chestoliubets честолюбець *n.* aspirant
chestoliubnyi честолюбний *a.* ambitious
chestoliubstvo честолюбство *n.* ambition
chetver четвер *n.* Thursday
chetvernyi четверний *a.* quadruple
chipkist чіпкість *n.* tenacity
chipkyi чіпкий *a.* tenacious
chipliannia чіпляння *n.* solicitation
chipliatysia чіплятися *v. t* cavil
chipliatysia чіплятися *v.t.* nag
chitkyi чіткий *a* distinct
chkhannia чхання *n* sneeze
chkhaty чхати *v.i.* sneeze
chlen член *n.* member
chlen profspilky член профспілки *n.* unionist
chlen tovarystva член товариства *n* co-partner
chlen zhuri член журі *n.* juror
chlenstvo членство *n.* membership
chmokane чмоканье *n* smack
chobit чобіт *n* boot
chokhol чохол *n.* sheet
cholo чоло *n.* front
cholovichyi чоловічий *a.* male
cholovichyi чоловічий *a.* manlike
cholovichyi чоловічий *a.* masculine

cholovichyi чоловічий *a.* virile
cholovik чоловік *n.* consort
cholovik чоловік *n* husband
cholovik чоловік *n* male
cholovik чоловік *n.* spouse
chomu чому *adv.* why
chorne derevo чорне дерево *n* ebony
chornobryvtsi чорнобривці *n.* marigold
chornorob чорнороб *n* coolie
chornorob чорнороб *n.* labourer
chornoshkiryi чорношкірий *n.* nigger
chornyi чорний *a* black
chornylo чорнило *n.* ink
chornysh чорниш *n.* slur
chornyty чорнити *v. t.* blacken
chortopolokh чортополох *n.* thistle
chotyrnadtsiat чотирнадцять *n.* fourteen
chotyry чотири *n.* four
chotyrykutnyi чотирикутний *a.* quadrangular
chotyrykutnyi чотирикутний *a.* quadrilateral
chotyrykutnyk чотирикутник *n.* quadrangle
chotyrynoha tvaryna чотиринога тварина *n.* quadruped
choven човен *n* boat
chovhannia човгання *n.* shuffle
chovhaty човгати *v.i.* shuffle
chovnyk човник *n.* shuttle
chrevo чрево *n.* womb
chub чуб *n* forelock
chudnyi чудний *a* rum
chudo чудо *n.* marvel
chudo чудо *n.* miracle
chudo чудо *n* wonder
chudotvornyi чудотворний *a.* miraculous

chudovyi чудовий *a.* remarkable
chudovyi чудовий *a.* wondrous
chudovysko чудовисько *n* beast
chuma чума *n.* plague
chutky чутки *n* bruit
chutlyvist чутливість *n.* sensibility
chutlyvyi чутливий *a.* sensitive
chutnyi чутний *a* audible
chuttia чуття *n.* antennae
chuttia чуття *v.t* nose
chuttievist чуттєвість *n.* sensuality
chuttievyi чуттєвий *a.* sensual
chuty чути *v.t.* hear
chuzhyi чужий *a.* vicarious
chvert чверть *n.* quarter
chy чи *conj.* whether
chyi чий *pron.* whose
chynovnyk чиновник *n* official
chynyty obstruktsiiu чинити обструкцію *v.t.* obstruct
chynyty opir чинити опір *v.t.* resist
chyselnyi чисельний *a.* numerical
chyselnyk чисельник *n.* numerator
chyslennishyi численніший *a.* more
chyslennyi численний *a.* numerous
chyslennyi численний *a.* vast
chyslo dvadtsiat число двадцять *n* twenty
chyslo dvanadtsiat число дванадцять *n* twelve
chyslo trydtsiat число тридцять *n.* thirty
chyslo trynadtsiat число тринадцять *n.* thirteen
chyslovyi числовий *a.* arithmetical
chystota чистота *n* clarity
chystota чистота *n* cleanliness

chystota чистота *n.* purity
chystyi чистий clean
chystyi чистий *a* clear
chystyi чистий *a* net
chystyi чистий *a* pure
chystyi чистий *a.* sheer
chystylnyk чистильник *n.* sweeper
chystylyshche чистилище *n.* purgatory
chystyty чистити *v. t* clean
chystyty чистити *v. t* cleanse
chystyty do biloho чистити до білого *v.t.* whiten
chystyty hubkoiu чистити губкою *v.t.* sponge
chystyty konia чистити коня *v.t* groom
chystyty shvabroiu чистити шваброю *v.t.* mop
chytach читач *n.* reader
chytaty читати *v.t.* read
chytaty lektsiiu читати лекцію *v* lecture

D

dacha дача *n* bower
dakh дах *n.* roof
daleka vidstan далека відстань *n* far
daleko далеко *adv.* far
dalekyi далекий *a* distant
dalekyi zviazok далекий зв'язок *n.* telecommunications
dali далі *adv.* onwards
dalnii дальній *a* far
dama дама *n.* dame
damba дамба *n* dam
dantyst дантист *n* dentist
dar дар *n.* donation
dar дар *n.* gift
daremnyi даремний *a.* worthless

daruvaty дарувати *v. t* bestow
daruvaty дарувати *v.t.* remember
data дата *n* date
datuvaty bilsh rannim chyslom датувати більш раннім числом *n* antedate
datuvaty piznishym chyslom датувати пізнішим числом *v.t.* post-date
daty liky дати ліки *v.t.* physic
daty poradu дати пораду *v. t.* counsel
daty prytulok дати притулок *v.t.* shelter
davaty давати *v.t.* afford
davaty давати *v.t.* impart
davaty khabar давати хабар *v. t.* bribe
davaty mozhlyvist давати можливість *v. t* enable
davaty na chai давати на чай *v.t.* tip
davaty obitnytsiu давати обітницю *v.t.* vow
davaty osichku давати осічку *v.i.* misfire
davaty osvitu давати освіту *v. t* educate
davaty perevahu давати перевагу *v.t.* advantage
davaty pokazannia давати показання *v.i.* testify
davaty pryvid давати привід *v.t* occasion
davaty sobi voliu давати собі волю *v.t.* indulge
davaty v borh давати в борг *v.t.* loan
davaty vidomosti давати відомості *v.t.* notify
davaty vidpochynok давати відпочинок *v.i.* repose

davaty vidsich давати відсіч *v.t.*
rebuff
davka давка *n.* jostle
davnii давній *a.* antique
dbailyvist дбайливість *n.*
solicitude
de де *conj.* where
de b ne bulo де б не було *adv.*
wherever
debatuvaty дебатувати *v. t.*
debate
debaty дебати *n.* debate
debet дебет *n* debit
debetuvaty дебетувати *v. t* debit
debosh дебош *n* debauch
defekt дефект *n* defect
defekt дефект *n.* shortcoming
defile дефіле *n.* defile
definitsiia дефініція *n* definition
defitsyt дефіцит *n* deficit
defitsytnyi дефіцитний *a.* scarce
defliatsiia дефляція *n.* deflation
dehraduvaty деградувати *v. t*
degrade
deist деїст *n.* deist
dekan декан *n.* dean
dekhto дехто *pron.* some
deklamatsiia декламація *n.*
recitation
deklamuvaty декламувати *v.t.*
recite
dekoratsii декорації *n.* scenery
dekoratsiia декорація *n*
decoration
dekoratyvnyi декоративний *a.*
ornamental
delehatsiia делегація *n*
delegation
delehuvaty делегувати *v. t*
delegate
delikatne делікатне *a.* ticklish
delta дельта *n* delta

demarkatsiia демаркація *n.*
demarcation
demokratiia демократія *n*
democracy
demokratychnyi демократичний
a democratic
demon демон *n.* demon
demonstratsiia демонстрація *n.*
demonstration
demonstruvaty демонструвати *v.*
t demonstrate
demonstruvaty smilyvist
демонструвати сміливість *v.t.*
stunt
demoralizuvaty деморалізувати
v. t. demoralize
den день *n* day
den vidpochynku день
відпочинку *n.* holiday
dendi денді *n* dandy
dennyi spektakl денний
спектакль *n.* matinee
depo депо *n* depot
deportuvaty депортувати *v.t.*
deport
depozyt депозит *n.* deposit
depresiia депресія *n* depression
deputat депутат *n* deputy
deputatsiia депутація *n.*
deputation
deren дерен *n.* sod
derevianyi дерев'яний *a.* wooden
derevo дерево *n.* tree
dertysia дертися *v. i* clamber
derzhava держава *n.*
commonwealth
derzhavnyi diiach державний
діяч *n.* statesman
derzhavnyi strii державний стрій
n. regime
derzhavnyi ustrii державний
устрій *n.* polity
des десь *adv.* somewhere

des poruch десь поруч *adv.*
hereabouts
desantnyi десантний *adj*
amphibious
deshcho дещо *adv.* something
deshevshaty дешевшати *v. t.*
cheapen
deshevyi дешевий *a* cheap
desiat десять *n.* ten
desiatkovyi десятковий *a*
decimal
desiatylittia десятиліття *n.*
decennary
desiatyna десятина *n.* tithe
desna десна *n.* gum
despot деспот *n* despot
detal деталь *n* detail
detali деталі *n.* belongings
detalizuvaty деталізувати *v. t*
detail
detalno rozrobliaty детально
розробляти *v. t* elaborate
detektyv детектив *a* detective
detektyvnyi детективний *n.*
detective
detonator детонатор *n.* trigger
detsillion деціліон *n.* decillion
devianosto дев'яносто *n.* ninety
devianostyi дев'яностий *a.*
ninetieth
deviat дев'ять *n.* nine
deviatnadtsiat дев'ятнадцять *n.*
nineteen
deviatnadtsiatoho
дев'ятнадцятого *a.* nineteenth
deviatsiia девіація *n* deviation
deviatyi дев'ятий *a.* ninth
deviz девіз *n.* motto
diadia дядя *n.* uncle
diafrahma діафрагма *n.* midriff
diahnostuvaty діагностувати *v. t*
diagnose
diahnoz діагноз *n* diagnosis

dialekt діалект *n* dialect
dialoh діалог *n* dialogue
diamant діамант *n* diamond
diapazon діапазон *n.* range
diia vazhelia дія важеля *n.*
leverage
diialnist діяльність *n.* activity
diialnyi діяльний *a.* live
diiaty діяти *v.i.* act
diiaty діяти *v.t.* operate
diiaty zanadto pospishno діяти
занадто поспішно *v.t.* rush
diieslovo дієслово *n.* verb
diieta дієта *n* diet
diievist дієвість *n* efficacy
diievyi дієвий *a* forceful
diisnist дійсність *n.* validity
diisnyi дійсний *a.* valid
dilianka ділянка *n.* plot
dilianka zemli ділянка землі *n*
dale
dilyty ділити *v.t.* portion
dilyty na sehmenty ділити на
сегменти *v.t.* segment
dilyty navpil ділити навпіл *v. t*
bisect
dilytysia ділитися *v.t.* share
dira діра *n* hole
diriavyty дірявити *v.t* hole
ditovbyvstvo дітовбивство *n.*
infanticide
diuim дюйм *n.* inch
diuzhyna дюжина *n* dozen
diva діва *n.* maiden
divchyna дівчина *n.* girl
divchynka дівчинка *n.* lass
diviziia дивізія *n* division
divka дівка *n.* wench
divochyi дівочий *a.* girlish
dizhka діжка *n.* tub
diznannia дізнання *n* interrogative
diznavannia дізнавання *n.*
recognition

diznavatysia дізнаватися *v.t.* recognize

dlia для *prep* for

dlia choho для чого *adv.* whither

dlubatysia длубатися *v.t.* sap

dno дно *n* bottom

do до *prep.* before

do до *prep.* pending

do до *prep.* till

do до *prep.* towards

do до *prep.* until

do до *prep.* up

do bereha до берега *adv.* ashore

do pobachennia до побачення *interj.* good-bye

do rechi до речі *adv* appositely

do splaty до сплати *a.* payable

do tsykh pir до цих пір *adv.* still

do tykh pir до тих пір *conj* until

doba доба *n* epoch

dobir добір *n* adoption

dobirnyi добірний *a* select

doblesnyi доблесний *a.* valiant

doblest доблесть *n.* prowess

doblest доблесть *n.* valour

dobre добре *adv.* well

dobre znaiomyi добре знайомий *adj.* conversant

dobrobut добробут *n.* wealth

dobrobut добробут *n.* welfare

dobrochesnist доброчесність *n.* virtue

dobrochesnyi доброчесний *a.* virtuous

dobrodiiannia добродіяння *n* boon

dobrodushno zhartuvaty добродушно жартувати *v.t.* banter

dobroiakisnyi доброякісний *a.* laudable

dobrosusidskyi добросусідський *a.* neighbourly

dobrota доброта *n.* goodness

dobrovilno добровільно *adv.* voluntarily

dobrovilnyi добровільний *a.* voluntary

dobrozychlyvist доброзичливість *n* benevolence

dobrozychlyvo доброзичливо *adv.* kindly

dobrozychlyvyi доброзичливий *adj.* amicable

dobrozychlyvyi доброзичливий *a* benevolent

dobryi добрий *a.* good

dobryvo добриво *n* fertilizer

dochirnia kompaniia дочірня компанія *a.* subsidiary

dochka дочка *n* daughter

dodatkovi vybory додаткові вибори *n* by-election

dodatkovo додатково *adv* extra

dodatkovyi додатковий *a.* additional

dodatkovyi додатковий *a.* other

dodatkovyi podatok додатковий податок *n.* surtax

dodatok додаток *n.* addition

dodatok додаток *n.* appendix

dodaty додати *v.t.* add

dodavaty додавати *v.t.* suffix

dohana догана *n.* rebuke

dohana догана *n.* reprimand

dohliad догляд *n.* care

dohliadach доглядач *n.* warden

dohliadaty доглядати *v.t.* woo

dohma догма *n* dogma

dohmatychnyi догматичний *a* dogmatic

dohmatychnyi догматичний *a.* oracular

dohot дьоготь *n.* tar

dohovir договір *n.* compact

doistorychnyi доісторичний *a.*
prehistoric
doity доїти *v.t.* milk
dok док *n.* dock
dokaz доказ *n* evidence
dokaz доказ *n.* proof
dokhid дохід *n.* income
dokhody доходи *n.* revenue
dokir докір *n.* reproach
dokir докір *n.* reproof
dokladaty zusyllia докладати
зусилля *v.i.* strive
dokladno докладно *adv.* minutely
dokoriaty докоряти *v.t.* reproach
dokoriaty докоряти *v.t* upbraid
dokory sovisti докори совісті *n.*
remorse
doktor доктор *n.* medico
doktorska stupin докторська
ступінь *n* doctorate
doktryna доктрина *n* doctrine
dokuchaty докучати *v.t.* vex
dokuchlyva liudyna докучлива
людина *n* barnacles
dokument документ *n* document
**dokument pro peredachu prava
vlasnosti** документ про
передачу права власності *n*
deed
dokument pro prava документ
про права *n.* muniment
dolar долар *n* dollar
dolaty долати *v.t.* surmount
dolaty долати *v.t.* transcend
dolia доля *n* destiny
dolon долонь *n.* palm
dolyna долина *n.* valley
domahatysia домагатися *v.t.*
attain
domahatysia uspikhu
домагатися успіху *v.i.* succeed
domashnia ptytsia домашня
птиця *n.* poultry

domashnia robota домашня
робота *n* domestic
domashnia tvaryna домашня
тварина *n.* pet
domashnii домашній *a* domestic
dominion домініон *n* dominion
dominuiuchyi домінуючий *a*
dominant
dominuvaty домінувати *v. t*
dominate
domovlenist домовленість *n.*
covenant
donkikhotskyi донкіхотський *a.*
quixotic
donor донор *n* donor
donos донос *n.* denunciation
donosyty доносити *v. t* denounce
donyzu донизу *adv* downward
doplata доплата *n.* surcharge
dopomahaty допомагати *v.t.*
assist
dopomahaty допомагати *v.t.* help
dopomahaty допомагати *v.t.*
support
dopomizhnyi допоміжний *a.*
auxiliary
dopomizhnyi mekhanizm
допоміжний механізм *n.*
auxiliary
dopomizhnyi zasob допоміжний
засоб *n.* supplement
dopomoha допомога *n* aid
dopomoha допомога *n.* succour
dopomohty допомогти *v.t* aid
dopovnennia доповнення *n.*
adjunct
dopovnenyi доповнений *a*
accomplished
dopovniuvaty доповнювати *v.t.*
supplement
dopushchennia допущення *n.*
admission
dopuskaty допускати *v.t.* admit

dopuskaty допускати *v.t.* own
dopuskaty vidkhylennia
допускати відхилення *v.t.*
waive
dopustymyi допустимий *a.*
admissible
dopytlyvyi допитливий *a.*
inquisitive
dopytuvaty допитувати *v.t.*
interrogate
dorechnist доречність *n.*
propriety
dorechno доречно *adj* apposite
dorechno доречно *a.* timely
dorechnyi доречний *a.*
appropriate
dorechnyi доречний *a.* pertinent
dorechnyi доречний *a.* well-timed
dorikaty дорікати *v.t.* rebuke
dorivniuvaty дорівнювати *v.*
t equal
dorivniuvaty дорівнювати *v.t.*
total
doroha дорога *n.* road
dorohotsinnyi дорогоцінний *a.*
precious
dorohotsinnyi kamin
дорогоцінний камінь *n.* jewel
dorohyi дорогий *a.* costly
dorosla liudyna доросла людина
n. adult
doroslyi дорослий *a* adult
doruchaty доручати *v. t.* commit
doruchaty доручати *v. t.* consign
doruchaty доручати *v. t* depute
doruchennia доручення *n.*
commission
doruchyty доручити *v.t.* vest
dosada досада *n.* annoyance
dosada досада *n* vexation
dosazhdaty досаджати *v.t.* annoy
doshch дощ *n* rain
doshchovyi дощовий *a.* moist

doshchovyi дощовий *a.* rainy
doshka дошка *n.* plank
doshliubnyi дошлюбний *adj.*
antenuptial
dosi досі *adv.* hitherto
dosiahaty досягати *v.t.* achieve
dosiahaty досягати *v.t.* obtain
dosiahaty naivyshchoi tochky
досягати найвищої точки *v.i.*
culminate
dosiahnennia досягнення *n.*
attainment
dosie досьє *n* file
doskonalyi досконалий *a.* perfect
doslidzhennia дослідження *n.*
examination
doslidzhuvaty досліджувати *v.t*
explore
doslivno дослівно *adv.* verbatim
doslivnyi дослівний *a.* verbatim
dostatnii достатній *a*
considerable
dostatnist достатність *n.*
sufficiency
dostatno достатньо *adv* enough
dostatok достаток *n.* affluence
dostatok достаток *n.* opulence
dostavka доставка *n* delivery
dostavliaty доставляти *v. t*
deliver
dostovirnyi достовірний *a.*
authentic
dostup доступ *n* access
dostup доступ *n.* admittance
dostupnyi доступний *a.*
obtainable
dosvichenyi досвічений *a*
conversant
dosvichenyi досвічений *a.*
versed
dosvid досвід *n* experience
dosvidchenyi povodyr
досвідчений повідар *n.* pilot

dosyt досить *adv.* enough
dosyt досить *adv.* pretty
dotep дотеп *n.* jest
dotepna vidpovid дотепна
відповідь *n.* repartee
dotepnist дотепність *n.* wit
dotepnyi дотепний *a.* witty
dotrymannia дотримання *n.*
adherence
dotrymannia дотримання *n.*
observance
dotrymuvatysia дотримуватися
v.i. adhere
dotsilnist доцільність *n*
advisability
dotsilnist доцільність *n.* suitability
dotsilnyi доцільний *a.* advisable
dotychna дотична *n.* tangent
dotyk дотик *n* touch
dotykovyi дотиковий *a.* tactile
dovesty довести *v.t.* vindicate
dovesty do bidnosti довести до
бідності *v.t.* impoverish
dovhastyi довгастий *a.* oblong
dovhastyi predmet довгастий
предмет *n.* oblong
dovho довго *adv* long
dovhonosyk довгоносик *n.* weevil
dovhoochikuvanyi
довгоочікуваний *a.* welcome
dovhota довгота *n.* longitude
dovhovichnist довговічність *n.*
longevity
dovhovichnyi довговічний *a*
durable
dovhozhytel довгожитель *n*
centenarian
dovhyi довгий *a.* long
dovichnyi довічний *a.* lifelong
dovid довід *n.* argument
dovidatysia z dosvidu
довідатися з досвіду *v. t.*
experience

dovidka довідка *n.* reference
dovidnyk довідник *n* directory
dovidnyk turysta довідник
туриста *n.* handbook
doviduvatysia довідуватися *v. t*
consult
dovilnyi довільний *a.* arbitrary
dovira довіра *n* confidence
dovira довіра *n* faith
dovirena osoba довірена особа
n confidant
dovirenist довіреність *n.* proxy
doviriaty довіряти *v. i* confide
dovirlyvist довірливість *adj.*
credulity
dovirlyvyi довірливий *a.* trustful
dovodyty доводити *v.t.* prove
dovzhyna довжина *n.* length
doza доза *n* dose
doza likiv доза ліків *v. t* drench
dozrivaty дозрівати *v.i.* ripen
dozvil дозвіл *n.* assent
dozvil дозвіл *n.* leave
dozvil дозвіл *n.* permission
dozvillia дозвілля *n.* leisure
dozvolenyi дозволений *a.* legal
dozvolenyi дозволений *a.*
permissible
dozvoliaty дозволяти *v.t.* allow
dozvoliaty дозволяти *v. i* consent
dozvoliaty demonstruvannia
дозволяти демонстрування *v.t.*
release
dozvolyty дозволити *v.t.* permit
drakhma драхма *n* dram
drakon дракон *n* dragon
drama драма *n* drama
dramaturh драматург *n* dramatist
dramatychnyi драматичний *a*
dramatic
drapiruvalnyk драпірувальник *n*
draper

drativlyvist дратівливість *n.*
petulance
drativlyvyi дратівливий *a.*
impatient
drativlyvyi дратівливий *a.*
irritable
drativnyi дратівний *a.* irksome
dratuvaty дратувати *v.t.* incense
dratuvaty дратувати *v.t.* irritate
drazhe драже *n.* comfit
drazhnyty дражнити *v.t.* rag
drazhnyty дражнити *v.t.* taunt
drenazh дренаж *n* drainage
drenazhna truba дренажна
труба *n.* culvert
drevnii древній *a.* immemorial
dribiazkovyi дріб'язковий *a.*
minute
dribna chastka дрібна частка *n.*
minim
dribnopomisne dvorianstvo
дрібнопомісне дворянство *n.*
gentry
dribnyi дрібний *a.* insignificant
dribnyi дрібний *a.* petty
dribnytsia дрібниця *n.* trifle
drimaty дрімати *v. i* doze
drimota дрімота *n.* doze
driuchok дрючок *n* cudgel
drizhdzhi дріжджі *n.* yeast
druhoriadnyi другорядний *a.*
tributary
druhosortnyi другосортний *a.*
middling
druhyi другий *a.* second
druk друк *n* print
drukarka друкарка *n.* typist
drukarska pomylka друкарська
помилка *n.* misprint
drukuvaty друкувати *v.t.* print
drukuvaty na mashyntsi
друкувати на машинці *v.t.* type

druzhni stosunky дружні
стосунки *n.* amity
druzhyna дружина *n.* wife
druzi друзі *n.* kith
dub дуб *n.* oak
dublikat дублікат *n* duplicate
dubliuvaty дублювати *v. t*
duplicate
dubylnyk дубильник *n.* tanner
dubyna дубина *n* bat
duel дуель *n* duel
duel дуель *n.* meeting
duha дуга *n* curve
dukh дух *n.* psyche
dukh дух *n.* spirit
dukhovenstvo духовенство *n*
clergy
dukhovnist духовність *n.*
spirituality
dukhovnyi духовний *a.* spiritual
dukhy духи *n.* perfume
dumaty думати *v.t.* think
dumka думка *n.* opinion
dupa дупа *n.* ass
duplo дупло *n.* cavern
duren дурень *n* blockhead
durist дурість *n* folly
durnuvatyi дурнуватий *a.*
sheepish
durnyi дурний *a.* mindless
durnyi дурний *a* stupid
duryty дурити *v.t* gull
duryty дурити *v.t* hoax
dush душ *n.* shower
dusha душа *n.* soul
dushevnokhvoryi
душевнохворий *a.* insane
dushyty душити *v.t.* stifle
dushyty душити *v.t* suffocate
dushytysia душитися *v. t.* choke
duty poryvamy дути поривами
v.t. pull
duzhe дуже *adv.* highly

duzhe poshyrenyi дуже поширений *a.* widespread
duzhe smachnyi дуже смачний *a* delicious
duzhe sylnyi дуже сильний *a.* herculean
duzhe tverda bryla дуже тверда брила *v. t* burk
duzhe zadovolenyi дуже задоволений *a* overjoyed
dva два *n.* two
dva tyzhni два тижні *n.* fort-night
dvadtsiata chastyna двадцята частина *n* twentieth
dvadtsiatyi двадцятий *a.* twentieth
dvadtsiatyi двадцятий *a.* twenty
dvanadtsiat дванадцять *n.* twelve
dvanadtsiata chastyna дванадцята частина *n.* twelfth
dvanadtsiatyi дванадцятий *a.* twelfth
dveri двері *n* door
dvichi двічі *adv.* twice
dvichi na misiats двічі на місяць *adj.* bimonthly
dviika двійка *a.* two
dviikovyi двійковий *adj* binary
dviinyk двійник *n.* counterpart
dviinyk двійник *n* double
dvir двір *n.* courtyard
dvobukvenyi двобуквений *adj* biliteral
dvoiezhenstvo двоєженство *n* bigamy
dvoistyi двоїстий *a* dual
dvoiuridnyi brat двоюрідний брат *n.* cousin
dvokhosovyi двохосьовий *adj* biaxial
dvokhsotrichchia двохсотріччя *adj* bicentenary
dvokrapka двокрапка *n* colon

dvomovnyi двомовний *a* bilingual
dvonohe двоноге *n* biped
dvorianstvo дворянство *n.* nobility
dvorianyn дворянин *n.* nobleman
dvorichnyi дворічний *adj* biennial
dvostatevyi двостатевий *adj.* bisexual
dvoznachnist двозначність *n.* ambiguity
dvoznachnyi двозначний *a.* ambiguous
dvuuholnyi двуугольний *adj.* biangular
dvyhun двигун *n* engine
dydaktychnyi дидактичний *a* didactic
dyiakon диякон *n.* deacon
dyiavol диявол *n* devil
dykhannia дихання *n* breath
dykhaty дихати *v. i.* breathe
dykist дикість *n.* savagery
dyktator диктатор *n* dictator
dyktsiia дикція *n* diction
dyktuvannia диктування *n* dictation
dyktuvaty диктувати *v. t* dictate
dykun дикун *n* savage
dykyi дикий *a.* barbarous
dylema дилема *n* dilemma
dyler дилер *n* dealer
dym дим *n.* smoke
dymchastyi димчастий *a.* smoky
dymetr диметр *n* diameter
dymity диміти *v.i.* smoke
dynamichnyi динамічний *a* dynamic
dynamika динаміка *n.* dynamics
dynamit динаміт *n* dynamite
dynastiia династія *n* dynasty
dynia диня *n.* melon
dyplom диплом *n* diploma
dyplomat дипломат *n* diplomat

dyplomatiia дипломатія *n* diplomacy
dyplomatychnyi дипломатичний *a* diplomatic
dyrektor директор *n.* director
dyrektor директор *n.* principal
dysertatsiia дисертація *n.* thesis
dyshlo дишло *a.* neap
dysk диск *n.* disc
dyskryminatsiia дискримінація *n* discrimination
dyskryminuvaty дискримінувати *v. t.* discriminate
dyskvalifikatsiia дискваліфікація *n* disqualification
dyskvalifikuvaty дискваліфікувати *v. t.* disqualify
dyspanser диспансер *n* dispensary
dyspersiia дисперсія *n.* variance
dystsyplina дисципліна *n* discipline
dytia дитя *n.* kid
dytiacha koliaska дитяча коляска *n.* perambulator
dytiache lizhko дитяче ліжко *n.* cot
dytiachyi дитячий *a.* childish
dytiachyi budynok дитячий будинок *n.* orphanage
dytiachyi sad дитячий сад *n.* kindergarten ;
dytyna дитина *n.* baby
dytyncha дитинча *n* cub
dytynstvo дитинство *n.* childhood
dyvan диван *n.* couch
dyvanna podushka диванна подушка *n* cushion
dyvizion дивізіон *n* battalion
dyvnyi дивний *a.* queer
dyvnyi дивний *a.* strange
dyvnyi дивний *a.* wonderful
dyvoplit дивопліт *n.* hedge

dyvovyzhnyi дивовижний *a.* outlandish
dyvuvannia дивування *n.* amazement
dyvuvaty дивувати *v.t.* amaze
dyvuvatysia дивуватися *v.i.* astound
dyvuvatysia дивуватися *v.i* marvel
dyvyna дивина *n.* oddity
dyvytysia дивитися *v.t.* gaze
dyvytysia skosa дивитися скоса *v.i.* squint
dyvytysia vseredynu дивитися всередину *v.i.* introspect
dyvytysia zakokhanymy ochyma дивитися закоханими очима *v.t.* ogle
dyzenteriia дизентерія *n* dysentery
dzerkalo дзеркало *n* mirror
dzhem джем *n.* jam
dzhentlmen джентльмен *n.* gentleman
dzherelo джерело *n.* origin
dzherelo джерело *n.* source
dzherelo enerhii джерело енергії *n.* generator
dzherelo kharchuvannia джерело харчування *n* breast
dzhunhli джунглі *n.* jungle
dzhut джут *n.* jute
dzhynsova tkanyna джинсова тканина *n.* jean
dzob дзьоб *n* beak
dzvenity дзвеніти *v.i.* jingle
dzvin дзвін *n* bell
dzvin дзвін *n.* toll
dzvinkyi potsilunok дзвінкий поцілунок *n.* smack
dzvinok дзвінок *n.* call
dzvonyty дзвонити *v.t.* telephone
dzyzhchannia дзижчання *n.* buzz

dzyzhchaty дзижчати *v. i* buzz

efekt ефект *n* effect
efektyvnist ефективність *n*
  efficiency
efektyvnyi ефективний *a*
  effective
efektyvnyi ефективний *a* efficient
efir ефір *n* ether
ehoistychnyi егоїстичний *a.*
  selfish
ehoizm егоїзм *n* ego
ekipazh екіпаж *n.* crew
ekipiruvannia екіпірування *n.* kit
ekipiruvaty екіпірувати *v. t* equip
ekonomichnyi економічний *a*
  economic
ekonomiia економія *n* economy
ekonomika економіка *n.*
  economics
ekonomnyi економний *a.* thrifty
ekonomyty економити *v.t.* spare
ekran екран *n.* screen
ekskursiia екскурсія *n.* excursion
ekspansiia експансія *n.*
  expansion
ekspedytsiia експедиція *n*
  expedition
eksperiment експеримент *n*
  experiment
ekspert експерт *n* expert
ekspluatuvaty експлуатувати *v.*
  t exploit
eksponat експонат *n.* exhibit
ekstraordynarnyi
  екстраординарний *a.*
  extraordinary
ekstremalnyi екстремальний *a*
  extreme
ekstremist екстреміст *n* extremist
ekvator екватор *n* equator

ekvivalentnyi еквівалентний *a*
  equivalent
ekzamenator екзаменатор *n*
  examiner
ekzamenovanyi екзаменований
  n examinee
el ель *n* ale
elastychnyi еластичний *a* elastic
elehantnist елегантність *n*
  elegance
elehantnyi елегантний *adj*
  elegant
elehiia елегія *n* elegy
elektorat електорат *n*
  constituency
elektromotor електромотор *n.*
  motor
elektrychna napruha електрична
  напруга *n.* voltage
elektrychnyi електричний *a*
  electric
elektrychnyi strum електричний
  струм *n* current
elektryfikuvaty електрифікувати
  v. t electrify
elektryka електрика *n* electricity
element елемент *n* element
elementarnyi елементарний *a*
  elementary
elementarnyi елементарний *a.*
  simple
elf ельф *n* elf
emal емаль *n* enamel
emansypatsiia емансипація *n.*
  emancipation
emblema емблема *n* emblem
embrion ембріон *n* embryo
emotsiia емоція *n* emotion
emotsiinyi емоційний *a* emotional
enerhiia енергія *n.* energy
enerhiinyi енергійний *a* energetic
entomolohiia ентомологія *n.*
  entomology

entsyklopediia енциклопедія *n.*
encyclopaedia
entuziazm ентузіазм *n*
enthusiasm
epichna poema епічна поема *n*
epic
epidemiia епідемія *n* epidemic
epihrama епіграма *n* epigram
epilepsiia епілепсія *n* epilepsy
epiloh епілог *n* epilogue
epitafiia епітафія *n* epitaph
epizod епізод *n* episode
epokha епоха *n* era
erotychnyi еротичний *a* erotic
eroziia ерозія *n* erosion
ese есе *n.* essay
eseist есеїст *n* essayist
esentsiia есенція *n* essence
eskadron ескадрон *n.* squadron
eskiz ескіз *n.* sketch
estetychnyi естетичний *a.*
aesthetic
estetyka естетика *n.pl.* aesthetics
etap етап *n.* stage
etychnyi етичний *a* ethical
etyka етика *n.* ethics
etyket етикет *n* etiquette
etyketka етикетка *n.* tally
etymolohiia етимологія *n.*
etymology
evakuatsiia евакуація *n*
evacuation
evakuiuvaty евакуювати *v. t*
evacuate

F

fabryka фабрика *n* factory
faeton фаетон *n* chaise
fail файл *n* file
fakel факел *n.* torch
fakh фах *n* feat
faksymile факсиміле *n* facsimile

fakt факт *n* fact
faktor фактор *n* factor
faktychno фактично *adv.* actually
faktychnyi фактичний *a.* actual
fakultet факультет *n* faculty
falsyfikatsiia фальсифікація *n*
forgery
fanatychnyi фанатичний *a*
fanatic
fanatyk фанатик *n* bigot
fanatyk фанатик *n* fanatic
fanatyk фанатик *n.* zealot
fanatyzm фанатизм *n* bigotry
fantastychnyi фантастичний *a*
fantastic
fantastychnyi фантастичний *a.*
weird
fantazer фантазер *n.* visionary
fantaziinyi фантазійний *v.t* fancy
fantom фантом *n.* phantom
farba фарба *n.* paint
farbuvaty фарбувати *v. t* dye
farbuvaty фарбувати *v.t.* paint
farbuvaty za trafaretom
фарбувати за трафаретом *v.i.*
stencil
farfor фарфор *n.* china
farfor фарфор *n.* porcelain
farmatsevt фармацевт *n* druggist
fars фарс *n* farce
fartukh фартух *n.* apron
fasad фасад *n* facade
fatalnyi фатальний *a* fatal
fatum фатум *n* fate
fauna фауна *n* fauna
favoryt фаворит *n* favourite
favoryt фаворит *n.* minion
faza фаза *n.* phase
federalnyi федеральний *a*
federal
federatsiia федерація *n*
federation
feia фея *n* fairy

fenomenalnyi феноменальний *a*.
phenomenal
feodalnyi феодальний *a* feudal
ferma ферма *n* farm
ferment фермент *n* ferment
fermer фермер *n* farmer
feston фестон *n* festoon
fial фіал *n*. phial
fiasko фіаско *n* fiasco
fihliar фігляр *n*. mummer
fihura фігура *n* figure
fihura фігура *n*. stature
fihuralnyi фігуральний *a*
figurative
fiksuvaty фіксувати *v.t* fix
fiktsiia фікція *n* figment
fiktyvnyi фіктивний *a* sham
filantrop філантроп *n*.
philanthropist
filantropichnyi філантропічний
a. philanthropic
filiia філія *n* branch
filoloh філолог *n*. philologist
filolohichnyi філологічний *a*.
philological
filolohiia філологія *n*. philology
filosof філософ *n*. philosopher
filosofiia філософія *n*. philosophy
filosofskyi філософський *a*.
philosophical
filtr фільтр *n* filter
filtruvaty фільтрувати *v.t* filter
finansova sprava фінансова
справа *n* finance
finansovyi фінансовий *a* financial
finansuvaty фінансувати *v.t*
finance
finansyst фінансист *n* financier
fioletovyi фіолетовий *adj*. purple
fioletovyi kolir фіолетовий колір
n. violet
firma фірма *n*. firm

fisharmoniia фісгармонія *n*.
harmonium
fiskalnyi фіскальний *a* fiscal
fistula фістула *n* fistula
fizionomiia фізіономія *n*.
physiognomy
fizychna vada фізична вада *n*
handicap
fizychnyi фізичний *a*. physical
fizyk фізик *n*. physicist
fizyka фізика *n*. physics
flakon флакон *n*. vial
flanel фланель *n* flannel
fleita флейта *n* flute
fliaha фляга *n* flask
flihel флігель *n*. outhouse
flirt флірт *n* flirt
flirtuvaty фліртувати *v.i* flirt
fliuid флюїд *n* fluid
flora флора *n* flora
flot флот *n* fleet
foiie фойє *n*. lobby
fokalnyi фокальний *a* focal
fokus фокус *n* focus
fokusnyk фокусник *n*. juggler
fokusuvatysia фокусуватися *v.t*
focus
folha фольга *v.t* foil
fon фон *n*. background
fond фонд *n*. fund
fonetychnyi фонетичний *a*.
phonetic
fonetyka фонетика *n*. phonetics
fontan фонтан *n*. fountain
fora v tenisi фора в тенісі *n*
bisque
forma форма *n* form
forma форма *n* mould
forma форма *n*. shape
formalnist формальність *n*.
technicality
formalnyi формальний *a* formal
format формат *n* format

formula формула *n* formula
formuliuvaty формулювати *v.t*
  formulate
formuvannia формування *n*
  formation
formuvaty polk формувати/полк
  v.t. regiment
fortetsia фортеця *n.* fortress
fortetsia фортеця *n.* stronghold
fosfat фосфат *n.* phosphate
fosfor фосфор *n.* phosphorus
foto фото *n* photo
fotohraf фотограф *n.*
  photographer
fotohrafichnyi фотографічний *a.*
  photographic
fotohrafiia фотографія *n*
  photograph
fotohrafuvannia
  фотографування *n.*
  photography
fotohrafuvaty фотографувати *v.t.*
  photograph
fotokadr фотокадр *n.* still
frahment фрагмент *n.* fragment
frakht фрахт *n.* freight
fraktsiia фракція *n* faction
fraktsiinyi фракційний *a* factious
frantsuzka mova французька
  мова *n* French
frantsuzkyi французький *a.*
  French
fraza фраза *n.* phrase
frazeolohiia фразеологія *n.*
  phraseology
freska фреска *n.* mural
frukt фрукт *n.* fruit
fruktovyi sad фруктовий сад *n.*
  orchard
fu фу *interj* fie
fufaika фуфайка *n.* jersey

fundamentalnyi
  фундаментальний *a.*
  fundamental
funktsiia функція *n.* function
funktsioner функціонер *n.*
  functionary
funktsionuvaty функціонувати *v.i*
  function
funt фунт *n.* pound
furazh фураж *n* fodder
furhon фургон *n.* van
futbolnyi miach футбольний
  м'яч *n* oval
fyrkaty фиркати *v.i.* snort

graty ґрати *n.* grate
gudzyk ґудзик *n* button

habardyn габардин *n.* whipcord
hachok гачок *n.* crotchet
hadaty гадати *v. t* conjecture
hadaty гадати *v.t.* presume
hadaty гадати *v.t.* repute
hadyna гадина *n.* toad
hai гай *n.* wood
haikovyi kliuch гайковий ключ *n.*
  wrench
hak гак *n.* hook
halaktyka галактика *n.* galaxy
halantnist галантність *n.* gallantry
halantnyi галантний *a.* gallant
halas галас *n* babel
halaslyvyi гасливий *a.* hilarious
halaslyvyi гасливий *a.*
  tumultuous
halereia галерея *n.* gallery
haliavyna галявина *n.* lawn
halka галька *n.* pebble
halmo гальмо *n* brake

halmuvaty гальмувати *v. t* brake
halon галон *n.* gallon
halop галоп *n.* gallop
halvanizuvaty гальванізувати *v.t.*
    galvanize
hamanets гаманець *n.* wallet
hanba ганьба *n* affront
hanba ганьба *n.* infamy
hanba ганьба *n.* odium
hanbyty ганьбити *v.* asperse
hanchirka ганчірка *n* duster
hanebnyi ганебний *a.* shameful
hanhster гангстер *n.* gangster
hanok ганок *n.* porch
harantiia гарантія *n.* warranty
harantiia vid zbytkiv гарантія від
    збитків *n.* indemnity
harantuvaty гарантувати *v. t*
    ensure
harazh гараж *n.* garage
harbuz гарбуз *n.* pumpkin
harchannia гарчання *n.* snarl
harchaty гарчати *v.i.* snarl
hariachkovyi oznob гарячковий
    озноб *n* ague
hariachnist гарячність *n.*
    vehemence
hariachyi гарячий *a* fervent
harmata гармата *n.* cannon
harmoniia гармонія *n.* harmony
harmoniinyi гармонійний *a.*
    harmonious
harnenkyi гарненький *a* pretty
harnyi гарний *a.* handsome
hartuvaty гартувати *v.t.* quench
has гас *n.* kerosene
haslo гасло *n.* slogan
hasyty гасити *v.t* extinguish
hatka гатка *n.* hurdle1
havan гавань *n.* harbour
havkannia гавкання *n.* woof
havkaty гавкати *v.i.* yap
haz газ *n.* gas

hazeta газета *n.* gazette
hazopodibnyi газоподібний *adj.*
    aeriform
hemoroi геморой *n.* piles
henerator генератор *n* dynamo
henii геній *n.* genius
heohraf географ *n.* geographer
heohrafichnyi географічний *a.*
    geographical
heohrafiia географія *n.*
    geography
heoloh геолог *n.* geologist
heolohichnyi геологічний *a.*
    geological
heolohiia геологія *n.* geology
heometriia геометрія *n.* geometry
heometrychnyi геометричний *a.*
    geometrical
hermetyzuvaty герметизувати
    v.t. pressurize
heroi герой *n.* hero
heroichnyi героїчний *a.* heroic
heroinia героїня *n.* heroine
heroizm героїзм *n.* heroism
hertsoh герцог *n* duke
herundii герундій *n.* gerund
het геть *adv.* away
hibon гібон *n.* gibbon
hibryd гібрид *n* hybrid
hibrydnyi гібридний *a.* hybrid
hidnist гідність *n* dignity
hidnyi гідний *a.* worthy
hidnyi pokhvaly гідний похвали
    a. praiseworthy
hihant гігант *n.* giant
hihantskyi гігантський *a.* gigantic
hihantskyi гігантський *a.*
    tremendous
hihiiena гігієна *n.* hygiene
hihiienichnyi гігієнічний *a.*
    hygienic
hiiena гієна *n.* hyaena, hyena
hildiia гільдія *n.* guild

hilka гілка *n* spray
hilochka гілочка *n.* sprig
himn гімн *n* anthem
himnast гімнаст *n.* gymnast
himnastychnyi гімнастичний *a.* gymnastic
himnastychnyi zal гімнастичний зал *n.* gymnasium
himnastyka гімнастика *n.* gymnastics
hiperbola гіпербола *n.* hyperbole
hipnotyzm гіпнотизм *n.* hypnotism
hipnotyzuvaty гіпнотизувати *v.t.* hypnotize
hipnotyzuvaty гіпнотизувати *v.t.* mesmerize
hipnoz гіпноз *n.* mesmerism
hipoteza гіпотеза *n.* hypothesis
hirchytsia гірчиця *n.* mustard
hirkota гіркота *n.* affliction
hirkyi гіркий *a* bitter
hirlianda гірлянда *n* anadem
hirska vershyna гірська вершина *n.* alp
hist гість *n.* guest
hitara гітара *n.* guitar
hladkyi гладкий *a.* sleek
hlasnist гласність *n.* publicity
hlasnyi гласний *n.* vowel
hlaukoma глаукома *n.* glaucoma
hlava глава *n.* chapter
hlazur глазур *n* glaze
hlechyk глечик *n.* jug
hliadach глядач *n.* on-looker
hliansuvatyi глянсуватий *a.* lustrous
hlianuty глянути *v.i* look
hlid глід *n.* hawthorn
hliser глісер *n.* glider
hlitseryn гліцерин *n.* glycerine
hliukoza глюкоза *n.* glucose
hlobalnyi глобальний *a.* global

hlobus глобус *n.* globe
hlosarii глосарій *n.* glossary
hlukhyi глухий *a* deaf
hlukhyi глухий *a.* hollow
hlukhyi stuk глухий стук *n.* thud
hlumytysia глумитися *v.i.* jeer
hlushnyk глушник *n.* silencer
hlushyty глушити *v.t.* muffle
hluzlyvo posmikhnutysia глузливо посміхнутися *v.i* sneer
hluzuvannia глузування *n.* wipe
hlyboka tuha глибока туга *n.* yearning
hlybokyi глибокий *a.* deep
hlybyna глибина *n* depth
hlyna глина *n* argil
hlynozem глинозем *n* clay
hnaty гнати *v. t* distil
hnii гній *n.* pus
hnit гніт *n.* wick
hnitiuchyi гнітючий *a.* oppressive
hnityty гнітити *v.t.* obsess
hnityty гнітити *v.t.* oppress
hniv гнів *n.* anger
hnivnyi гнівний *a.* irate
hnizdo гніздо *n.* nest
hnizdytysia гніздитися *v.t.* nest
hnobytel гнобитель *n.* oppressor
hnuchkist гнучкість *n.* versatility
hnuchkyi гнучкий *a* facile
hnuchkyi гнучкий *a* flexible
hnutysia гнутися *v. t* bow
hnyl гниль *n.* rot
hnyty гнити *v.i.* rot
hobelen гобелен *n.* tapestry
hoduvannia годування *n* feed
hoduvaty годувати *v.t* feed
hoduvaty hrudmy годувати грудьми *v.t.* suckle
hodyna година *n.* hour
hodynnyk годинник *n.* clock
hodytysia годитися *v.t* fit

hoidalky гойдалки *n* swing
hoidaty гойдати *v.i.* sway
hoidaty гойдати *v.t.* dandle
hoidatysia гойдатися *v. t* dangle
hoidatysia гойдатися *v.i.* oscillate
holf гольф *n.* golf
holinnia гоління *n* shave
holka голка *n.* needle
holod голод *n* dearth
holodna smert голодна смерть *n.* starvation
holodnyi голодний *a.* hungry
holodovka голодовка *n* famine
holoduvannia голодування *n* fast
holoduvaty голодувати *v.i* fast
holos голос *n.* voice
holosno hovoryty голосно говорити *v.i.* shout
holosuvannia голосування *n.* poll
holosuvaty голосувати *v.i.* ballot
holova голова *n.* head
holova komety голова комети *n.* coma
holoveshka головешка *n* brand
holovna pidtrymka головна підтримка *n.* mainstay
holovnyi головний *a.* basic
holovnyi головний *a.* cardinal
holovnyi головний *a.* chief
holovnyi bil головний біль *n.* headache
holovnym chynom головним чином *adv.* mainly
holovolomka головоломка *n.* puzzle
holovoriz головоріз *n.* thug
holovuiuchyi головуючий *n* chairman
holovuvaty головувати *v.i.* preside
holub голуб *n* dove
holub голуб *n.* pigeon
holubyty голубити *v.t* fondle

holyi голий *a.* bare
holyi голий *a.* nude
holytysia голитися *v.t.* shave
homeopat гомеопат *n.* homoeopath
homeopatiia гомеопатія *n.* homeopathy
homilka гомілка *n.* ankle
homin гомін *n* din
honchar гончар *n.* potter
honcharni vyroby гончарні вироби *n.* pottery
honh гонг *n.* gong
honky гонки *n.* race
honorar гонорар *n* fee
honytva гонитва *n.* pursuit
hora гора *n.* mount
horb горб *n.* hunch
horbok горбок *n.* hillock
hordist гордість *n.* pride
hordovytist гордовитість *n.* arrogance
hordovytyi гордовитий *a.* haughty
hordyi гордий *a.* proud
hore горе *n.* grief
horezvisnyi горезвісний *a.* notorious
horikh горіх *n* nut
hority горіти *v. t* burn
horiucha rechovyna горюча речовина *a.* inflammable
horiuvaty горювати *v.t.* grieve
horlianka горлянка *n.* gourd
horlo горло *n.* throat
horlovyi горловий *a.* guttural
horn горн *n.* furnace
horobets горобець *n.* sparrow
horokh горох *n.* pea
horoskop гороскоп *n.* nativity
horshchyk горщик *n.* pot
hortannyi гортанний *a.* throaty
horyla горила *n.* gorilla

horyshche горище *n*. loft
horystyi гористий *a*. mountainous
horyzont горизонт *n*. horizon
Hospoda Господа *n*. Messrs
hospodar господар *n*. host
hospodar господар *n*. proprietor
hostrokintsevyi гострокінцевий
,*a*. pungent
hostrota гострота *n*. keenness
hostryi гострий *adj* argute
hostryi bil гострий біль *n*. pang
hostynnist гостинність *n*.
hospitality
hostynnist гостинність *n*
welcome
hostynnyi гостинний *a*.
- hospitable
hotel готель *n*. hotel
hotivka готівка *n*. cash
hotovnist готовність *n*.
willingness
hotovyi готовий *a*. ready
hotuvaty готувати *v. t* cook
hovirkyi говіркий *a*. talkative
hovoryty говорити *v.i*. talk
hovoryty natiakamy говорити
натяками *v.t*. intimate
hovoryty zahadkamy говорити
загадками *v.i*. riddle
hra гра *n*. game
hrabizh грабіж *n* plunder
hrabizhnyk грабіжник *n*. robber
hrabuvaty грабувати *v.t*. rob
hradatsiia градація *n*. gradation
hrafichnyi графічний *a*. graphic
hrafik графік *n*. chart
hrafik графік *n* diagram
hrafstvo графство *n*. shire
hrafynia графиня *n*. countess
hrak грак *n*. rook
hralna karta гральна карта *n*.
card

hralna karta гральна карта *n*.
play card
hralna kist гральна кість *n* die
hralni kosti гральні кості *n*. dice
hram грам *n*. gramme
hramatyka граматика *n*. grammar
hramatysty граматисти *n*.
grammarian
hramofon грамофон *n*.
gramophone
hramota грамота *n* charter
hramotnist грамотність *n*. literacy
hran грань *n* edge
hranata граната *n*. grenade
hrandioznyi грандіозний *a*. grand
hranychnyi граничний *a*.
marginal
hranychnyi граничний *a* overall
hranytsia границя *n*. limit
hratsiia грація *n*. grace
hraty грати *v.i* game
hraty na fleiti грати на флейті *v.i*
flute
hraty v azartni ihry грати в
азартні ігри *v.i*. gamble
hraty v kosti грати в кості *v. i*.
dice
hratysia гратися *v.i*. sport
hravets гравець *n*. gambler
hravets bytkoiu гравець биткою
n. batsman
hraviruvaty гравірувати *v. t*
engrave
hravitatsiia гравітація *n*.
gravitation
hrebin гребінь *n* comb
hrebinets гребінець *n* crest
hreblia гребля *n*. barrage
hrebty гребти *v.t*. row
hrebty veslom гребти веслом *v.i*.
paddle
hretska mova грецька мова *n*.
Greek

hretskyi грецький *a* Greek
hriaz грязь *n.* mire
hriaznulia грязнуля *n.* slattern
hrikh гріх *n.* sin
hrilka грілка *n.* damsel
hrim грім *n.* thunder
hrish гріш *n.* mite
hrishnyi грішний *a.* sinful
hrishnyk грішник *n.* sinner
hrishyty грішити *v.i.* sin
hrity гріти *v.t.* warm
hrity na sontsi гріти на сонці *v.t.* sun
hritysia грітися *v.i.* bask
hriukaty грюкати *v.i.* rumble
hriznyi грізний *a* formidable
hrobnytsia гробниця *n* cist
hromada громада *n.* fraternity
hromadianstvo громадянство *n* citizenship
hromadianyn громадянин *n* citizen
hromadskist громадськість *n.* public
hromadskyi громадський *a.* public
hromizdkyi громіздкий *a* bulky
hromovyi громовий *a.* thunderous
hromyty громити *v.t.* smash
hroshi гроші *n.* money
hroshi гроші *n.* pelf
hroshovyi грошовий *a.* pecuniary
hroshovyi perekaz грошовий переказ *n.* remittance
hroshovyi podarunok грошовий подарунок *n.* gratuity
hrotesk гротеск *a.* grotesque
hroza гроза *n.* storm
hrozovyi грозовий *a.* stormy
hrubyi грубий *a* coarse
hrubyi грубий *a* unmannerly
hruden грудень *n* december

hrudka грудка *n.* clot
hrudna zaloza грудна залоза *n.* mamma
hrudnyi грудний *a.* mammary
hrudy груди *n* bosom
hrum грум *n.* groom
hrunt грунт *n.* soil
hruntovka грунтовка *n.* primer
hrupa група *n.* group
hrupa ministriv група міністрів *n.* cabinet
hrupa z desiaty група з десяти *n* decade
hrupuvaty групувати *v.t.* group
hrusha груша *n.* pear
hruzylo грузило *n.* lead
hryb гриб *n.* mushroom
hrybok грибок *n.* fungus
hrymasy гримаси *n* antic
hrymity гриміти *v.i.* thunder
hryp грип *n.* influenza
hryva грива *n.* mane
hryzha грижа *n.* hernia
hryzty гризти *v.t.* nibble
hryzun гризун *n.* rodent
huava гуава *n.* guava
huba губа *n.* lip
hubernator губернатор *n.* governor
hubka губка *n.* sponge
hubnyi губний *a.* labial
huchne vitannia гучне вітання *n* acclaim
huchni veseloshchi гучні веселощі *n.* hilarity
huchnyi гучний *a.* loud
hudinnia гудіння *n* hum
hudity гудіти *v. i* hum
huliaka гуляка *n.* reveller
hulianka гулянка *n.* jollity
huliannia гуляння *n.* revel
huma гума *n.* rubber

humanitarii гуманітарій *a*
humanitarian
humanitarnyi гуманітарний *a*
classical
humannyi гуманний *a.* humane
humor гумор *n.* humour
humoryst гуморист *n.* humorist
humorystychnyi гумористичний
a. humorous
hurkit гуркіт *n.* rumble
hurkotity гуркотіти *v.i.* grumble
hurtka гуртка *n.* mug
hurtozhytok гуртожиток *n.* hostel
husak гусак *n.* goose
husenytsia гусениця *n* caterpillar
hushcha гуща *n* middle
hushchavyna гущавина *n.* thicket
husto густо *adv.* thick
hustonaselenyi густонаселений
a. populous
hustyi густий *a* dense
huvernantka гувернантка *n.*
governess
hvaltuvaty гвалтувати *v.t.* rape
hvozdyka гвоздика *n* clove
hvynt гвинт *n.* screw
hvyntivka гвинтівка *n* rifle
hykannia гикання *n.* hoot
hykavka гикавка *n.* hiccup
hynuty гинути *v.i.* perish
hyrlo shakhty гирло шахти *n.*
outset

i і *conj.* and
i odyn i druhyi і один і другий
pron both
i tak dali і так далі *a* etcetera
ideal ідеал *n* ideal
ideal ідеал *n.* nonpareil
idealist ідеаліст *n.* idealist

idealistychnyi ідеалістичний *a.*
idealistic
idealizm ідеалізм *n.* idealism
idealizuvaty ідеалізувати *v.t.*
idealize
idealnyi ідеальний *a.* ideal
ideia ідея *n.* idea
identychnist ідентичність *n.*
identity
identychnyi ідентичний *a.*
identical
identyfikatsiia ідентифікація *n.*
indentification
identyfikuvaty ідентифікувати
v.t. identify
idioma ідіома *n.* idiom
idioma ідіома *n.* locution
idiomatychnyi ідіоматичний *a.*
idiomatic
idiot ідіот *n.* idiot
idiotskyi ідіотський *a.* idiotic
idiotyzm ідіотизм *n.* ideocy
idol ідол *n.* idol
idolopoklonnyk ідолопоклонник
n. idolater
ihnoruvaty ігнорувати *v.t.* ignore
ihra sliv ігра слів *n.* quibble
ihrashka іграшка *n.* toy
iiena Ієна *n.* Yen
iierarkhiia ієрархія *n.* hierarchy
iklo ікло *n.* tusk
iliuminatsiia ілюмінація *n.*
illumination
iliustratsiia ілюстрація *n.*
illustration
iliustrovanyi ілюстрований *a.*
pictorical
iliustruvaty ілюструвати *v.t.*
illustrate
iliuziia ілюзія *n.* illusion
imbyr імбир *n.* ginger
imennyk іменник *n.* noun

imenuvaty іменувати *v.t.*
nominate
imenytyi іменитий *a* eminent
imia ім'я *n.* name
imitator імітатор *n* mimic
imituvaty імітувати *v.t* mimic
immihrant іммігрант *n.* immigrant
immihratsiia імміграція *n.*
immigration
immihruvaty іммігрувати *v.i.*
immigrate
imovirnyi імовірний *a.* possible
imperator імператор *n* emperor
imperatrytsia імператриця *n*
empress
imperializm імперіалізм *n.*
imperialism
imperiia імперія *n* empire
imperskyi імперський *a.* imperial
import імпорт *n.* import
importuvaty імпортувати *v.t.*
import
impozantnyi імпозантний *a.*
imposing
impuls імпульс *n.* impact
impulsyvnist імпульсивність *n.*
impetuosity
impulsyvnyi імпульсивний *a.*
impulsive
imunizuvaty імунізувати *v.t.*
immunize
imunnyi імунний *a.* immune
inakshe інакше *adv.* alias
inakshyi інакший *pron.* other
indiiskyi індійський *a.* Indian
indychka індичка *n.* turkey
indyho індиго *n.* indigo
indykator індикатор *n.* indicator
indyvidualizm індивідуалізм *n.*
individualism
indyvidualnist індивідуальність
n. individuality
inertnyi інертний *a.* inert

infantilnyi інфантільний *a.*
infantile
infektsiinyi інфекційний *a.*
infectious
informator інформатор *n.*
informer
informatsiia інформація *n.*
information
informatsiinyi інформаційний *a.*
informative
inhrediient інгредієнт *n.*
ingredient
initsial ініціал *n.* initial
initsiatyva ініціатива *n.* initiative
initsiatyvnist ініціативність *n*
enterprise
inkryminuvaty інкримінувати *v.t.*
incriminate
inodi іноді *adv.* sometimes
inozemets іноземець *n* foreigner
inozemna mova іноземна мова
n. lingo
inozemnyi іноземний *a* foreign
insektytsyd інсектицид *n.*
insecticide
inshyi інший *a* another
inshyi інший *a* else
inspektor інспектор *n.* inspector
inspektsiia інспекція *n.* inspection
inspektuvannia інспектування *n.*
survey
instantsiia інстанція *n.* instance
instinktyvnyi інстінктивний *a.*
intrinsic
instruktazh інструктаж *n.*
instruction
instruktor інструктор *n.* instructor
instrument інструмент *n.*
instrument
instrumentalist інструменталіст
n. instrumentalist

instrumentalnyi інструментальний *a.* instrumental

instsenuvaty інсценувати *v.t.* stage

instynkt інстинкт *n.* instinct

instynktyvnyi інстинктивний *a.* instinctive

instytut інститут *n.* institute

insynuatsiia інсинуація *n.* insinuation

intelekt інтелект *n.* intellect

intelektualnyi інтелектуальний *a.* inner

intelihent інтелігент *n.* intellectual

intelihentsiia інтелігенція *n.* intelligentsia

intensyvnist інтенсивність *n.* intensity

intensyvnyi інтенсивний *a.* intensive

interes інтерес *n.* interest

interpretator інтерпретатор *n* exponent

interval інтервал *n.* interim

interventsiia інтервенція *n.* intervention

introspektsiia інтроспекція *n.* introspection

intryha інтрига *n* intrigue

intryhuvaty інтригувати *v.t.* intrigue

intsoliatsiia інтсоляція *n.* installation

intsydent інцидент *n.* incident

intuitsiia інтуїція *n.* insight

intuitsiia інтуїція *n.* intuition

intuityvnyi інтуїтивний *a.* intuitive

intymnyi інтимний *a.* intimate

invalid інвалід *n* invalid

investuvaty інвестувати *v.t.* invest

investytsii інвестиції *n.* investment

inzhener інженер *n* engineer

inzhyr інжир *n* fig

irlandska mova ірландська мова *n.* Irish

irlandskyi ірландський *a.* Irish

ironichnyi іронічний *a.* ironical

ironiia іронія *n.* irony

iryska іриска *n.* toffee

irzha іржа *n.* rust

irzhannia іржання *n.* neigh

irzhaty іржати *v.i.* neigh

irzhavity іржавіти *v.i* rust

irzhavyi іржавий *a.* rusty

iskra іскра *n.* spark

iskra іскра *n.* spark

iskrinnia іскріння *n.* sparkle

iskrytysia іскритися *v.i.* scintillate

iskrytysia іскритися *v.i.* spark

iskrytysia іскритися *v.i.* sparkle

isnuvannia існування *n* existence

isnuvannia існування *n.* subsistence

isnuvaty існувати *v.i.* prevail

isnuvaty існувати *v.i.* subsist

ispanets іспанець *n.* Spaniard

ispanska mova іспанська мова *n.* Spanish

ispanskyi іспанський *a.* Spanish

isteriia істерія *n.* hysteria

isterychnyi істеричний *a.* hysterical

istoriia історія *n.* history

istoriia історія *n.* tale

istorychnyi історичний *a* . historic

istoryk історик *n.* historian

istotnyi істотний *a* essential

istynnyi істинний *a.* true

italiiska movu італійська мову *n.* Italian

italiiska solomka італійська соломка *n.* leghorn

italiiskyi італійський *a.* Italian
ity lehko i shvydko іти легко і
швидко *v.t.* trip
izhoi ізгой *n.* outlaw
izium ізюм *n.* raisin
izoliator ізолятор *n.* insulator
izoliatsiia ізоляція *n.* isolation
izoliatsiia ізоляція *n.* segregation
izoliuvaty ізолювати *v.t.* isolate
izoliuvaty ізолювати *a.* secluded
izoliuvatysia ізолюватися *v.t.*
segregate

kabala кабала *n* bondage
kaban кабан *n* boar
kabare кабаре *n.* cabaret
kabel кабель *n.* cable
kabinet кабінет *n.* closet
kabinet кабінет *n.* parlour
kachaty качати *v.t.* pitch
kachka качка *n* canard
kachka качка *n.* duck
kadmii кадмій *n* cadmium
kadylo кадило *n* censer
kadyty кадити *v. t* cense
kafe кафе *n.* cafe
kafedra кафедра *a.* pulpit
kafedralnyi sobor кафедральний
собор *n.* minster
kaiannyk каянник *a.* repentant
kaiattia каяття *n.* compunction
kaidany кайдани *n* bond
kaidany кайдани *n* fetter
kakhel кахель *n.* tile
kaktus кактус *n.* cactus
kal кал *n* dung
kalambur каламбур *n.* pun
kalamburyty каламбурити *v.i.*
pun
kalamutyty каламутити *v.t.*
puddle

kalendar календар *n.* calendar
kalibr калібр *n* bore
kalichyty калічити *v.t.* lame
kalihrafiia каліграфія *n*
calligraphy
kalii калій *n.* potassium
kalika каліка *n* cripple
kalitstvo каліцтво *n.* mutilation
kaliuzha калюжа *n.* puddle
kalkuliator калькулятор *n*
calculator
kaloriia калорія *n.* calorie
kaltsii кальцій *n* calcium
kamera камера *n.* camera
kamerher камергер *n*
chamberlain
kamfora камфора *n.* camphor
kamiana ukladka кам'яна
укладка *n.* masonry
kamianystyi кам'янистий *a.* stony
kamin камінь *n.* stone
kaminna doshka камінна дошка
n. mantel
kamlot камлот *n* camlet
kampaniia кампанія *n.* campaign
kamvolnyi камвольний *n.*
worsted
kanal канал *n.* canal
kanalizatsiia каналізація *n.*
sewerage
kanava канава *n* ditch
kanchuk канчук *n* lash
kandydat кандидат *n.* candidate
kanistra каністра *n.* canister
kanton кантон *n* canton
kantseliariia канцелярія *n*
chancery
kantseliarski tovary канцелярські товари *n.*
stationery
kantsler канцлер *n.* chancellor
kapannia капання *n* drip
kapaty капати *v. i* drip

kapeliukh капелюх *n.* hat
kapeliushnyk капелюшник *n.* milliner
kapitalist капіталіст *n.* capitalist
kapitalnyi remont капітальний ремонт *n.* overhaul
kapitan капітан *n.* captain
kapituliatsiia капітуляція *n* surrender
kapituliuvaty капітулювати *v. t* capitulate
kapiushon капюшон *n.* hood
kapkan капкан *n.* trap
kaplytsia каплиця *n.* chapel
kapot капот *n* bonnet
kapryz каприз *n.* caprice
kapsulnyi капсульний *adj* capsular
kapusta капуста *n.* cabbage
karakuli каракулі *n* scrawl
karalnyi каральний *a.* punitive
karat карат *n.* carat
karaty карати *v. t.* castigate
karaty карати *v.t.* punish
karaul караул *n.* sentry
karavan караван *n.* caravan
karbid карбід *n.* carbide
karbuvannia monety карбування монети *n* coinage
karbuvaty карбувати *v.t.* mint
kardamon кардамон *n.* cardamom
kardynal кардинал *n.* cardinal
karier кар'єр *n.* quarry
kariera кар'єра *n.* career
karioznyi каріозний *adj* carious
karkannia каркання *n.* caw
karkaty каркати *v. i.* caw
karliuchky карлючки *n.* scribble
karlyk карлик *n.* midget
karlykovyi карликовий *n.* pygmy
karnaval карнавал *n* carnival
karnyi карний *a.* penal

karta карта *n* map
karton картон *n.* cardboard
kartonka картонка *n* carton
kartoplia картопля *n.* potato
kartyna картина *n.* picture
karykatura карикатура *n.* caricature
kaseta касета *n.* cassette
kasha каша *n.* cereal
kashalot кашалот *n.* sperm
kashel кашель *n.* cough
kashliaty кашляти *v. i.* cough
kashne кашне *n.* muffler
kashtan каштан *n.* chestnut
kaskad каскад *n.* cataract
kaskad каскад *n.* waterfall
kasta каста *n* caste
kastorove maslo касторове масло *n.* castor oil
kasuvalnyi касувальний *a.* irritant
kasyr касир *n.* cashier
kat кат *n.* executioner
kataloh каталог *n.* catalogue
kataloh каталог *n.* schedule
katastrofa катастрофа *n* disaster
katastrofichnyi катастрофічний *a* disastrous
katatysia na chovni кататися на човні *v.i* boat
katatysia na kovzanakh кататися на ковзанах *v.t.* skate
katehorichnyi категорічний *a.* categorical
katehoriia категорія *n.* category
katok каток *v.i.* slide
katolitska zhinocha shkola католіцька жіноча школа *n* convent
katolytskyi католицький *a.* catholic
katuvannia катування *n.* torture
katuvaty катувати *v.t.* torture
kava кава *n* coffee

kavaler кавалер *n* chevalier
kavaler кавалер *n* gallant
kavaleriia кавалерія *n.* cavalry
kavaleryst кавалерист *n.* trooper
kavun кавун *n.* water-melon
kazhan кажан *n* bat
kaznacheistvo казначейство *n.* treasury
kedr кедр *n.* cedar
kelykh келих *n.* goblet
kepka кепка *n.* cap
kepkuvaty кепкувати *v.i.* jest
kepskyi кепський *a.* wretched
keramika кераміка *n* ceramics
kerivna posada керівна посада *n.* leadership
kerivnyk керівник *n.* leader
kerivnyk керівник *n.* superintendent
kerivnyk konferentsii керівник конференції *n* convener
kerivnytstvo керівництво *n.* governance
kerivnytstvo керівництво *n.* guidance
kermo кермо *n.* helm
kerovanyi керований *a.* manageable
keruvaty керувати *n* conduct
ketchup кетчуп *n.* ketchup
khabar хабар *n* bribe
khabarnyk хабарник *ns.* barrator
khalat халат *n.* robe
khalat халат *n.* smock
khalatnist халатність *n.* negligence
khalatnyi халатний *a.* negligent
khalupka халупка *n.* shanty
kham хам *n* cad
khandryty хандрити *v.i.* mope
khanzha ханжа *n* canter
khanzha ханжа *n.* noble
khanzha ханжа *n.* prude

khaos хаос *n.* chaos
khaotychnyi хаотичний *adv.* chaotic
khapaty хапати *v.t.* grab
kharakter характер *n.* character
kharakter характер *n.* kidney
kharakter характер *n.* mettle
kharakteryzuvaty характеризувати *v. t* define
kharchuvannia харчування *n.* nourishment
kharchuvannia харчування *n.* nutrition
khata хата *n* house
khatyna хатина *n.* cabin
khatyna хатина *n.* hut
khaziain хазяїн *n.* master
khid хід *n* stroke
khimichnyi хімічний *a.* chemical
khimichyty хімічити *v.i* fiddle
khimiia хімія *n.* chemistry
khimik хімік *n.* chemist
khimikat хімікат *n.* chemical
khinin хінін *n.* quinine
khiromant хіромант *n.* palmist
khiromantiia хіромантія *n.* palmistry
khirurh хірург *n.* surgeon
khirurhiia хірургія *n.* surgery
khlib хліб *n* bread
khliv хлів *n.* cote
khlopchyk хлопчик *n* boy
khlopchyk хлопчик *n.* youngster
khlopets хлопець *n* fellow
khlopets хлопець *n.* lad
khlor хлор *n* chlorine
khloroform хлороформ *n* chloroform
khlostaty хльостати *v.t.* lash
khlynuty хлинути *v.i.* surge
khlynuty хлинути *v.i.* well
khmara хмара *n.* cloud
khmarnist хмарність *a.* overcast

khmarnyi хмарний *a* cloudy
khmurytysia хмуритися *v.i* frown
khmurytysia хмуритися *v.i.* scowl
khnykaty хникати *v.i.* whimper
khobi хобі *n.* hobby
khocha хоча *conj.* albeit
khocha хоча *conj.* although
khocha хоча *adv* even
khocha хоча *conj.* nevertheless
khocha хоча *conj.* though
khocha хоча *conj.* when
khoda хода *n.* gait
khoda хода *n.* step
khoda хода *n* tread
khodovyi ходовий *a.* salable
khodyty ходити *v.i.* pace
khodyty ходити *v.i.* walk
khodyty navshpynky ходити навшпиньки *v.t.* tip
khokei хокей *n.* hockey
khol хол *n.* lounge
kholera холера *n.* cholera
kholod холод *n.* chill
kholod холод *n* cold
kholodnokrovnist холоднокровність *n.* composure
kholodnyi холодний *a* cold
kholodnyi холодний *a.* frigid
kholodylnyk холодильник *n* cooler
kholodylnyk холодильник *n.* fridge
kholodylnyk холодильник *n.* refrigerator
kholostiak холостяк *n.* bachelor
kholostiak холостяк *n.* single
khomut хомут *n* clamp
khor хор *n* choir
khor хор *n.* chorus
khoral хорал *n* chant
khorobrist хоробрість *n* bravery
khorobrist хоробрість *n.* courage

khorobryi хоробрий *a* brave
khorobryi хоробрий *a* daring
khoroshyi хороший *a.* well
khortytsia хортиця *n.* greyhound
khotity хотіти *v.t.* want
khotity хотіти *v.t.* wish
khotity pyty хотіти пити *v.i.* thirst
khovaty ховати *v. t.* bury
khovaty ховати *v. t.* conceal
khovaty ховати *v.t* hide
khovaty ховати *v.t.* secrete
khram храм *n.* temple
khrebet хребет *n.* backbone
khrebet хребет *n.* ridge
khrebet хребет *n.* spine
khreshchennia хрещення *n.* baptism
khrest хрест *n* cross
khrestyty хрестити +*v.t.* baptize
khronichnyi хронічний *a.* chronic
khronika хроніка *n.* chronicle
khronohraf хронограф *n* chronograph
khronolohiia хронологія *n.* chronology
khropinnia хропіння *n* snore
khropity хропіти *v.i.* snore
khrypkyi хрипкий *a.* hoarse
Khrystos Христос *n.* Christ
khrystyianskyi християнський *a.* Christian
khrystyianskyi svit християнський світ *n.* Christendom
khrystyianstvo християнство *n.* Christianity
khrystyianyn християнин *n* Christian
khto хто *pron.* who
khto b ne хто б не *pron.* whoever
khtos хтось *pron.* somebody
khtos хтось *pron.* someone
khtyvyi хтивий *a.* lascivious

khtyvyi хтивий *a.* lustful
khtyvyi хтивий *a.* voluptuous
khudnuty худнути *v.i.* slim
khudoba худоба *n.* cattle
khudozhnii художній *a.* artistic
khudozhnyk художник *n.* artist
khudozhnyk художник *n.* painter
khudyi худий *a.* lank
khudyi худий *n.* lean
khudyi худий *a.* scanty
khulihan хуліган *n* bully
khulihan хуліган *n.* hooligan
khulihan хуліган *n.* ruffian
khulihanskyi хуліганський *a.* obscene
khustka хустка *n.* kerchief
khutro хутро *n* bonten
khutro хутро *n.* fur
khvala хвала *n* laud
khvala хвала *n.* praise
khvalko хвалько *n* bouncer
khvalko хвалько *n* brag
khvalkuvatyi хвалькуватий *a.* tall
khvalyty хвалити *v. t* compliment
khvalyty хвалити *v.t.* praise
khvastaty хвастати *v.i* boast
khvastaty хвастати *v. i* brag
khvastaty хвастати *v.i.* swagger
khvastoshchi хвастощі *n* boast
khvastoshchi хвастощі *n.* vainglory
khvirtka хвіртка *n.* wicket
khvist хвіст *n.* stern
khvist хвіст *n.* tail
khvority хворіти *v.i.* ache
khvority хворіти *v.t.* pain
khvoroba хвороба *n.* ailment
khvoroba хвороба *n.* illness
khvoroba хвороба *n.* malady
khvoroba хвороба *n.* sickness
khvoroblyvyi хворобливий *a.* morbid

khvoroblyvyi хворобливий *a.* painful
khvoroblyvyi хворобливий *a.* sickly
khvoryi хворий *a.* ill
khvoryi хворий *a.* sick
khvyli хвилі *n.* surge
khvylia хвиля *n.* tide
khvylia хвиля *n.* wave
khvyliastist хвилястість *n.* undulation
khvyliuvannia хвилювання *n* commotion
khvyliuvannia хвилювання *n* disquiet
khvyliuvannia хвилювання *n.* fret
khvyliuvaty хвилювати *v. t* excite
khvyliuvaty хвилювати *v.t.* perturb
khvylyna хвилина *n.* minute
khyba хиба *n* fault
khykhykaty хихикати *v.i.* giggle
khylytysia хилитися *v.i.* slope
khymernyi химерний *adj* bizarre
khymernyi химерний *a.* quaint
khymernyi химерний *a.* whimsical
khytatysia хитатися *v.i.* stagger
khytatysia хитатися *v.i.* vacillate
khytatysia хитатися *v.i* wobble
khytkyi хиткий *a.* rickety
khytkyi хиткий *a.* shaky
khytrist хитрість *n* cunning
khytrist хитрість *n* deceit
khytrist хитрість *n.* ruse
khytrist хитрість *n.* stratagem
khytrist хитрість *n.* trickery
khytrist хитрість *n.* wile
khytryi хитрий *a* crafty
khytryi хитрий *a* cunning
khytryi хитрий *a.* sly
khytryi хитрий *a.* tricky
khytryi хитрий *a.* wily

268

khyzhyi хижий *adj* accipitral
khyzuvatysia хизуватися *v.t.*
 parade
kil кіл *n.* pale
kilka кілька *a* several
kilkisnyi кількісний *a.* quantitative
kilkist кількість *n.* quantity
kilochok кілочок *n.* peg
kiltse кільце *n.* ring
kiltsiuvaty кільцювати *v.t* girdle
kilvater кільватер *n* wake
kimnata кімната *n.* chamber
kin кінь *n.* steed
kinchatysia кінчатися *v. t* end
kinchatysia кінчатися *v.i.* expire
kinchyk pera кінчик пера *n.* nib
kinets кінець *n* last
kino кіно *n.* movies
kinoteatr кінотеатр *n.* cinema
kinovar кіновар *n* cinnabar
kintsevyi кінцевий *a.* ultimate
kintsivka кінцівка *n.* limb
kir кір *n* measles
kishka кішка *n.* cat
kistka кістка *n.* bone
kit кіт *n.* tomcat
kiuveta кювета *n.* cuvette
kivsh ківш *n.* ladle
kladovyshche кладовище *n.*
 churchyard
klapan клапан *n.* valve
klapot клапоть *n* patch
klapot клапоть *n.* rag
klaptyk клаптик *n.* scrap
klas клас *n* class
klasty класти *v.t.* lay
klasty krai класти край *v.t.*
 repress
klasty na polytsiu класти на
 полицю *v.t.* rack
klasty na stil класти на стіл *v.t.*
 table

klasty ne na mistse класти не на
 місце *v.t.* misplace
klasty u mishok класти у мішок
 v. i. bag
klasty v bank класти в банк *v. t*
 deposit
klasychnyi класичний *a* classic
klasyfikatsiia класифікація *n*
 classification
klasyfikuvaty класифікувати *v. t*
 classify
klasyk класик *n* classic
klatsannia клацання *n.* click
klatsaty клацати *v.t.* snap
klei клей *n.* adhesive
klei клей *n.* glue
kleikyi клейкий *a.* adhesive
kleity клеїти *v.t.* paste
klepaty клепати *v.t.* rivet
klerk клерк *n* clerk
klerykalnyi клерикальний *a*
 clerical
kliamka клямка *n.* latch
kliap кляп *n.* gag
kliient клієнт *n..* client
klimaks клімакс *n.* climax
klimat клімат *n.* climate
klinika клініка *n.* clinic
klishch кліщ *n* mite
klit кліть *n.* crate
klityna клітина *n.* cage
klitynnyi клітинний *adj* cellular
kliuch ключ *n* clue
kliuch ключ *n.* key
kliuvannia клювання *n* nibble
kliuvaty клювати *v.i.* peck
kliuvok клювок *n.* peck
klopitkyi клопіткий *a.*
 troublesome
klopotannia клопотання *n.*
 petition
klopotatysia клопотатися *v.t.*
 solicit

kloun клоун *n* clown
klub клуб *n* club
klubok клубок *n.* clew
klykaty кликати *v. t.* call
klyn клин *n.* wedge
kmitlyvist кмітливість *n.* acumen
kmitlyvyi кмітливий *a.* apprehensive
kmitlyvyi кмітливий *a.* intelligent
kniaziuvannia князювання *n* reign
kniazivskyi князівський *a.* princely
knyha книга *n* book
knyhoprodavets книгопродавець *n* book-seller
knyzhkovyi книжковий *n.* bookish
knyzhkovyi khrobak книжковий хробак *n* book-worm
koalitsiia коаліція *n* coalition
kobalt кобальт *n* cobalt
kobra кобра *n* cobra
kobyla кобила *n.* mare
kochehar кочегар *n.* stoker
kochivnyk кочівник *n.* nomad
kochovyi кочовий *a.* nomadic
kod код *n* code
kodlo кодло *n.* bantling
koefitsiient коефіцієнт *n.* coefficient
koika койка *n* berth
kokain кокаїн *n* cocaine
koketka кокетка *n.* minx
kokhanets коханець *n.* lover
kokhanka коханка *n.* paramour
kokhanyi коханий *n* beloved
kokos кокос *n* coconut
kokosovi volokna кокосові волокна *n* coir
kokpit кокпіт *n.* cock-pit
koks кокс *v. t* coke
kolechko колечко *n.* ringlet
koledzh коледж *n* college

koleha колега *n* colleague
kolektor колектор *a.* manifold
kolektsiia колекція *n* collection
kolektsionuvaty колекціонувати *v. t* collect
kolektyvnyi колективний *a.* collective
koleso колесо *a.* wheel
koliaska коляска *n.* carriage
koliia колія *n.* rut
kolino коліно *n.* knee
kolir колір *n* colour
kolir oblychchia колір обличчя *n* complexion
koliuchist колючість *n* gibe
koliuchka колючка *n.* barb
koliuchyi колючий *a.* barbed
kolo коло *n.* circle
kolo коло *n.* circumference
koloda колода *n* block
koloda колода *n.* log
Kolon Колон *n* colon
kolona колона *n* column
kolonialnyi колоніальний *a* colonial
koloniia колонія *n* colony
kolonizatsiia колонізація *n.* settlement
kolonizuvaty колонізувати *v.t.* subjugate
kolorova kapusta кольорова капуста *n.* cauliflower
kolosalnyi колосальний *a.* stupendous
koloty колоти *n.* prick
kolovorot коловорот *n.* wimble
koly коли *conj.* now
koly коли *adv.* when
koly b ne коли б не *adv. conj* whenever
kolykhaty колихати *v.t.* lull
koly-nebud коли-небудь *adv* ever
kolys колись *adv.* sometime

kolyshnia vykhovanka колишня
виховання *n* alumna
kolyshnii колишній *a* former
kolyska колиска *n* cradle
kolyskova колискова *n.* lullaby
kolyvannia коливання *n.*
hesitation
kolyvannia коливання *n.* variation
kolyvaty коливати *v.t.* rock
kolyvatysia коливатися *v.i.*
hesitate
kolyvatysia коливатися *v.i.* waver
kolyvnyi коливний *a.* hesitant
kom ком *n.* clod
koma кома *n* comma
komakha комаха *n.* insect
komanda команда *n* command
komanduvaty командувати *v. t*
command
komandyr командир *n*
commander
komar комар *n.* mosquito
kombinatsiia комбінація *n*
combination
kombinuvaty комбінувати *v. t*
combine
komediant комедіант *n.*
comedian
komediia комедія *n.* comedy
komendant комендант *n*
commandant
komendantska hodyna
комендантська година *n*
curfew
komentar коментар *n* comment
komentar коментар *n*
commentary
komentator коментатор *n*
commentator
komentuvaty коментувати *v. i*
comment
kometa комета *n* comet
komfort комфорт *n.* comfort1

komichnyi комічний *a* comic
komik комік *n* comic
komir комір *n* collar
komisioner комісіонер *n.*
middleman
komitet комітет *n* committee
komiunike комюніке *n.*
communiqué
komivoiazher комівояжер *n.*
traveller
komora комора *n.* ambry
kompaniia компанія *n* bunch
kompaniia компанія *n.* company
kompas компас *n* compass
kompensatsiia компенсація *n*
compensation
kompensuvaty компенсувати *v.t*
compensate
kompetentnist компетентність *n*
competence
kompetentnyi компетентний *a.*
competent
kompetentsiia компетенція *n.*
purview
kompiliuvaty компілювати *v. t*
compile
kompleks комплекс *n* complex
kompleksnyi комплексний *a*
complex
kompliment комплімент *n.*
compliment
kompozytor композитор *n*
compositor
komprometuvaty
компрометувати *v. t*
compromise
kompromis компроміс *n*
compromise
komu кому *pron.* whom
komunalnyi комунальний *a*
communal
komunikatsiia комунікація *n.*
communication

komunizm комунізм *n* communism

konduktor кондуктор *n* conductor

kondyter кондитер *n* confectioner

kondyterski vyroby кондитерські вироби *n* confectionery

konferentsiia конференція *n* conference

konfidentsiinyi конфіденційний *a*. confidential

konfiskatsiia конфіскація *n* confiscation

konfiskuvaty конфіскувати *v. t* confiscate

konflikt конфлікт *n*. conflict

konflikt конфлікт *n*. tangle

konfrontatsiia конфронтація *n*. confrontation

konhres конгрес *n* congress

koniaka коняка *n*. horse

koniuktura кон'юктура *n*. conjuncture

koniunktyva кон'юнктива *n*. conjunctiva

konkretnyi конкретний *a*. specific

konkurentospromozhnyi конкурентоспроможний *a* competitive

konkursna propozytsiia конкурсна пропозиція *n* bid

konkuruvaty конкурувати *v. i* compete

konservant консервант *n*. preservative

konservator консерватор *n* conservative

konservator консерватор *n*. square

konservatyvnyi консервативний *a* conservative

konservuvaty консервувати *v. t* conserve

konservy консерви *n*. preserve

konsolidatsiia консолідація *n* consolidation

konsoliduvaty консолідувати *v. t.* consolidate

konspekt конспект *n*. conspectus

konspekt конспект *n*. precis

konspekt конспект *n*. summary

konspekt конспект *n*. syllabus

konstatatsiia констатація *n*. statement

konstebl констебль *n* constable

konstruiuvaty конструювати *v. t.* construct

konstytutsiia конституція *n* constitution

konsultatsiia консультація *n* consultation

konsultuvaty консультувати *v.t.* advise

kontakt контакт *n*. contact

kontaktuvaty контактувати *v. t* contact

kontekst контекст *n* context

kontrabandyst контрабандист *n*. smuggler

kontrakt контракт *n* contract

kontrast контраст *n* contrast

kontratseptsiia контрацепція *n*. contraception

kontrol контроль *n* control

kontroler контролер *n*. controller

kontroler контролер *n*. supervisor

kontroliuvaty контролювати *v. t* control

kontroliuvaty контролювати *v.t.* supervise

kontsentratsiia концентрація *n*. concentration

kontsentruvatysia концентруватися *v. t* concentrate

kontseptsiia концепція *n* concept

kontsert концерт *n*. concert

kontur контур *n* contour
kontuziia контузія *v.t.* contuse
kontynent континент *n* continent
kontynentalnyi континентальний *a* continental
kontynhent vybortsiv контингент виборців *n* electorate
konus конус *n* taper
konvert конверт *n* envelope
konvoi конвой *n* escort
konyk коник *n* fad
konyk коник *n.* hobby-horse
kooperatyvnyi кооперативний *a* co-operative
koordynatsiia координація *n* co-ordination
koordynovanyi координований *a* co-ordinate
koordynuvaty координувати *v.t* co-ordinate
kopaty копати *v.t.* dig
kopaty lopatoiu копати лопатою *v.t.* spade
kopiia копія *n* copy
kopiia копія *n.* repetition
kopiiuvaty копіювати *v. t* copy
kopiiuvaty копіювати *v.t.* imitate
koprolohiia копрологія *n.* coprology
kora кора *n.* bark
korabelnyi khronometr корабельний хронометр *n.* watch
koral корал *n* coral
korchyty корчити *v.i.* writhe
kordon кордон *n* border
korespondent кореспондент *n.* correspondent
korespondentsiia кореспонденція *n* mail
koriandr коріандр *n.* coriander
korin корінь *n.* root

korinnyi zub корінний зуб *n.* molar
korivnyk корівник *n* byre
kornet корнет *n.* cornet
korobka коробка *n* box
korol король *n.* king
koroleva королева *n.* queen
korolivskyi королівський *a.* regal
korolivstvo королівство *n.* kingdom
korolivstvo королівство *n.* realm
korona корона *n* crown
koronatsiia коронація *n* coronation
korosta короста *n.* scabies
korotenka pisenka коротенька пісенька *n* lay
korotko коротко *adv.* short
korotkochasnyi короткочасний *a.* momentary
korotkozorist короткозорість *n.* myopia
korotkozoryi короткозорий *a.* myopic
korotkyi короткий *a.* brief
korova корова *n.* cow
koroziinyi корозійний *adj.* corrosive
korporatsiia корпорація *n* corporation
korporatsiia корпорація *n.* incorporation
korporatyvnyi корпоративний *adj.* corporate
korpus корпус *n* corps
korsazh корсаж *n* bodice
korychnevyi коричневий *a* brown
korychnevyi kolir коричневий колір *n* brown
korydor коридор *n.* corridor
Korynf Коринф *n.* Corinth
koryslyvist корисливість *n.* lucre

koryslyvyi корисливий *a.* mercenary

korysnist корисність *n.* utility

korysnyi корисний *a.* healthy

korysnyi корисний *a.* helpful

korysnyi корисний *a.* profitable

korystuvannia користування *n.* usage

korytsia кориця *n* cinnamon

korytysia коритися *v.t.* obey

kosa коса *n.* scythe

koshenia кошеня *n.* kitten

koshmar кошмар *n.* nightmare

koshtorys кошторис *n.* estimate

koshtovnist коштовність *n* gem

koshtovnosti коштовності *n.* jewellery

koshtuvaty коштувати *v.t.* cost

koshty кошти *n* means

koshyk кошик *n.* basket

kosmetychnyi косметичний *a.* cosmetic

kosmetyka косметика *n.* cosmetic

kosmichnyi космічний *adj.* cosmic

kosookist косоокість *n* squint

kostenity костеніти *v.t.* ossify

kostium костюм *n.* suit

kosulia косуля *n.* roe

kosyi косий *a.* oblique

kosyty косити *v.t.* scythe

kotedzh котедж *n* cottage

kotroho котрого *a.* implicit

kotushka котушка *n.* reel

kotyty котити *v.i.* roll

kovadlo ковадло *n.* anvil

koval коваль *n* blacksmith

koval коваль *n.* smith

kovbania ковбаня *n.* slough

kovdra ковдра *n* blanket

kovkyi ковкий *a.* malleable

kovtaty ковтати *v.t.* swallow

kovtok ковток *n.* gulp

kovtok ковток *n.* swallow

kovzannia ковзання *v.i.* slip

kovzaty ковзати *n* slide

koza коза *n.* goat

kozel vidpushchennia козел відпущення *n.* scapegoat

Kozerih Козеріг *n* Capricorn

kozhen кожен *a* each

kozhukh кожух *n.* casing

kozyr козир *n.* trump

krab краб *n* crab

kradena rich крадена річ *v.i.* steal

kradizhka крадіжка *n.* theft

kradizhka zi zlomom крадіжка зі зломом *n* burglary

kradkoma крадькома *adv.* stealthily

krai край *n* brim

kraievyd краєвид *n.* view

kraina країна *n.* country

krainii крайній *a.* last1

krainii крайній *a.* outside

krainist крайність *n* emergency

krainy Pivdnia країни Півдня *n.* south

krainy Zakhodu країни Заходу *n.* occident

krakh крах *n.* wreck

kramar крамар *n.* tradesman

kran кран *n.* tap

krapaty крапати *v. i* drop

kraplia крапля *n* drop

krasa краса *n* beauty

krashchaty кращати *v. t* brighten

krashchyi кращий *a* better

krasnomovnyi красномовний *a* eloquent

krasnomovstvo красномовство *n* eloquence

krasty красти *v.t.* pilfer

krastysia крастися *v.i.* sneak

krasunia красуня *n* belle

krasyvyi красивий *a* beautiful
kravatka краватка *n* tie
kravets кравець *n.* tailor
kredo кредо *n.* creed
kredyt кредит *n* credit
kredytor кредитор *n* creditor
kredytor po zastavnii кредитор по заставній *n.* mortgagee
kreiser крейсер *n* cruiser
krematsiia кремація *n* cremation
kremuvaty кремувати *v. t* cremate
kren крен *n.* lurch
krenytysia кренитися *v.i.* lurch
kreslennia креслення *n* draft
kreslennia креслення *n* drawing
Krez Крез *n.* croesus
kriakaty крякати *v.i.* quack
krim крім *prep* besides
krim toho крім того *adv* besides
kripak кріпак *n.* serf
kriposnyi riv кріпосний рів *n.* moat
kripyty кріпити *v.t.* furl
kriz крізь *adv* around
krok крок *n.* pitch
krokhmal крохмаль *n.* starch
krokhmalyty крохмалити *v.t.* starch
krokodyl крокодил *n* crocodile
krokuvaty крокувати *v.t.* advance
kroliachyi sadok кролячий садок *n.* warren
krolyk кролик *n.* rabbit
kronshtein кронштейн *n.* corbel
kropitkyi кропіткий *a.* painstaking
kropyva кропива *n.* nettle
kropyvianyk кропив'яник *n.* wren
krov кров *n* blood
krovoprolyttia кровопролиття *n* bloodshed
krovotochyty кровоточити *v. i* bleed

kruhla duzhka кругла дужка *n.* parenthesis
kruhliak кругляк *n.* rubble
kruhlyi круглий *a.* round
kruhom кругом *adv* about
kruhoobih кругообіг *n.* circuit
kruhovoi круговой *a* circular
kruhovorot круговорот *n* circulation
kruiz круїз *v.i.* cruise
krupnyi крупний *a.* large
krupy крупи *n.* grain
krushyty крушити *v. t* distress
krutyi крутий *a.* steep
krutyty v rukakh крутити в руках *v.i.* toy
kruzhliannia кружляння *n.* spin
kruzhliaty кружляти *v.i.* whirl
krychaty кричати *v. i* cry
kryk крик *n.* bawl
krykhitka крихітка *n* crumb
krykhitnyi крихітний *a.* tiny
krykhkyi крихкий *a.* frail
krykhkyi крихкий *a.* slight
krykhta крихта *n.* chit
krylatyi крилатий *adj.* aliferous
krylo крило *v.t.* annex
krylo крило *n.* wing
kryminalne peresliduvannia кримінальне переслідування *n.* prosecution
kryminalnyi кримінальний *a* criminal
krynytsia криниця *n.* well
kryptohrafiia криптографія *n.* cryptography
kryshka кришка *n.* lid
kryshtal кришталь *n* crystal
kryshyty кришити *v. t* chop
kryshyty кришити *v. t* crumble
kryterii критерій *n* canon
kryty крити *v.t.* roof

kryty kakhlem крити кахлем *v.t.* tile
kryty solomoiu крити соломою *v.t.* thatch
krytychnyi критичний *a* critical
krytyk критик *n* critic
krytyka критика *n* criticism
krytykuvaty критикувати *v. t* criticize
kryva крива *n.* graph
kryvava biinia кривава бійня *n* carnage
kryvavyi кривавий *a* bloody
kryvda кривда *n.* offence
kryvdnyk кривдник *n.* offender
kryvdyty кривдити *v.t.* aggrieve
kryvliaka кривляка *n.* monkey
kryvyi кривий *adj* anfractuous
kryvyi кривий *a.* wry
kryza криза *n* crisis
kryzhanyi крижаний *a.* icy
kserokopiiuvaty ксерокопіювати *v.t.* xerox
kseroks ксерокс *n.* xerox
ksylofon ксилофон *n.* xylophone
kub куб *n* cube
kubichnyi кубічний *a* cubical
kublo кубло *n* dive
kubok кубок *n* beaker
kubovydnyi кубовидний *adj.* cubiform
kucher кучер *n* coachman
kudkudakaty кудкудакати *v. i* cackle
kudy куди *adv.* where
kukhar кухар *n* cook
kukhnia кухня *n.* kitchen
kukhonna plyta кухонна плита *n* cooker
kukhovarstvo куховарство *n.* concoction
kukhovaryty куховарити *v. t* concoct

kukurikaty кукурікати *v. i* crow
kukurudza кукурудза *n.* maize
kulak кулак *n* fist
kulbaba кульбаба *n.* dandelion
kulhavyi кульгавий *a.* lame
kulia куля *n* bullet
kulinarne mystetstvo кулінарне мистецтво *n.* cuisine
kulminatsiia кульмінація *n.* superlative
kult культ *n* cult
kultura культура *n* culture
kulturnyi культурний *a* cultural
kumivstvo кумівство *n.* nepotism
kumkannia кумкання *n.* croak
kunytsia куниця *n.* marten
kupa купа *n.* heap
kupaty купати *v. t* bathe
kupe купе *n.* compartment
kupets купець *n.* merchant
Kupidon Купідон *n* Cupid
kupivlia купівля *v.t.* purchase
kuplet куплет *n.* couplet
kupol купол *n* dome
kupuvaty купувати *v. t.* buy
kurcha курча *n.* chicken
kurhan курган *n.* mound
kurier кур'єр *n.* courier
kurierskyi кур'єрський *a* express
kurka курка *n.* hen
kurkuma куркума *n.* curcuma
kurkuma куркума *n.* turmeric
kurort курорт *n* resort
kurs курс *n.* course
kursant курсант *n.* cadet
kursyv курсив *n.* italics
kursyvnyi курсивний *a.* italic
kurtka куртка *n.* jacket
kurtyzanka куртизанка *n.* courtesan
kushak кушак *n.* girdle
kushch кущ *n* bush
kushtuvaty куштувати *v.t.* sip

kut кут *n.* angle
kutovyi кутовий *a.* angular
kuvalda кувалда *n.* maul
kuvaty кувати *v.t* forge
kuznia кузня *n* forge
kvadratnyi квадратний *a* square
kvalifikatsiia кваліфікація *n.* qualification
kvalifikuvaty кваліфікувати *v.i.* qualify
kvantovyi квантовий *n.* quantum
kvaplyvist квапливість *n* hurry
kvapyty квапити *v.t.* hurry
kvapyty квапити *v.i.* speed
kvartyra квартира *n.* apartment
kvasolia квасоля *n.* bean
kvintesentsiia квінтесенція *n.* quintessence
kvitka квітка *n* flower
kvitnykar квітникар *n* florist
kvituchyi квітучий *a.* prime
kvorum кворум *n.* quorum
kvota квота *n.* quota
kvytok квиток *n.* ticket
kydannia кидання *n* casting
kydaty кидати *v.t.* throw
kydaty zi stukom кидати зі стуком *v.t.* slam
kydok кидок *n.* bound
kyi кий *n.* staff
kylym килим *n.* carpet
kylymok килимок *n.* rug
kyndzhal кинджал *n.* baslard
kyndzhal кинджал *n.* dagger
kyparys кипарис *n* cypher cypress
kypinnia кипіння *n* boil
kypity кипіти *v.i.* boil
kypity na povilnomu vohni кипіти на повільному вогні *v.i.* simmer
kyrka кирка *n.* pick

kyrkomotyka киркомотика *n.* mattock
kysen кисень *n.* oxygen
kyshechnyk кишечник *n.* bowel
kyshenia кишеня *n.* pocket
kyshka кишка *n.* intestine
kyshkovyi кишковий *adj.* alvine
kyshkovyi кишковий *a.* intestinal
kyslota кислота *n* acid
kyslotnist кислотність *n.* acidity
kyslyi кислий *a* acid
kystovyi кистьовий *adj* carpal
kyt кит *n.* whale
kytovyi vus китовий вус *n.* baleen
kytytsia китиця *n* cluster
kyvaty holovoiu кивати головою *v.i.* nod
kyvok кивок *n.* beck

labirynt лабіринт *n.* labyrinth
laboratoriia лабораторія *n.* laboratory
ladan ладан *n.* incense
lahidnyi лагідний *a.* meek
lahodyty лагодити *v.t.* mend
lahuna лагуна *n.* lagoon
laiaty лаяти *v.t.* scold
laiatysia лаятися *v. t.* damn
laiatysia лаятися *v.t.* swear
laika лайка *n.* invective
laika лайка *n.* malediction
laika лайка *n.* obscenity
laim лайм *n.* lime
lak лак *n.* varnish
lakei лакей *n.* lackey
lakeiskyi лакейський *a.* menial
lakhmitnyk лахмітник *n.* tatter
lakonichnyi лаконічний *a.* laconic
laktometr лактометр *n.* lactometer

laktoza лактоза *n.* lactose
lakuvaty лакувати *v.t.* varnish
lama лама *n.* lama
lamaty ламати *v. t* break
lampa лампа *n.* bulb
lan лань *n* doe
lando ландо *n.* barouche
landshaft ландшафт *n.* landscape
lantset ланцет *a.* lancet
lantsiuh ланцюг *n* chain
lapa лапа *n.* paw
laska ласка *n.* endearment
lasoshchi ласощі *n.* dainty
lastivka ластівка *n.* swallow
lataty латати *v.t.* patch
latentnyi латентний *a.* latent
latun латунь *n.* brass
laureat лауреат *n* laureate
lava лава *n* bench
lava лава *n.* lava
lavanda лаванда *n.* lavender
lavr лавр *n.* laurel
lavyna лавина *n* billow
lebid лебідь *n.* swan
lebidka лебідка *n.* winch
led ледь *adv.* barely
ledachyi ледачий *a.* sluggish
ledar ледар *n.* loafer
ledar ледар *n.* sluggard
ledariuvaty ледарювати *v.i.* laze
ledariuvaty ледарювати *v.i.* loaf
ledarstvo ледарство *n.* idleness
ledi леді *n.* lady
ledve ne ледве не *adv.* nearly
lehalnist легальність *n.* legality
lehenda легенда *n.* legend
lehendarnyi легендарний *a.* legendary
lehion легіон *n.* legion
lehioner легіонер *n.* legionary
lehka koliaska легка коляска *n* chariot

lehke легке *n* lung
lehkist легкість *n* ease
lehkovazhnist легковажність *n* flippancy
lehkovazhnyi легковажний *a.* frivolous
lehkyi легкий *a* easy
lehkyi son легкий сон *n.* nap
lehkyi tuman легкий туман *n.* haze
lehshe легше *n.* lighter
leitenant лейтенант *n.* lieutenant
leksykohrafiia лексикографія *n.* lexicography
leksykon лексикон *n.* lexicon
lektor лектор *n.* lecturer
lektsiia лекція *n.* lecture
leleka лелека *n.* stork
lementuvaty лементувати *v.i.* yell
leopard леопард *n.* leopard
lepet лепет *n.* babble
lepetaty лепетати *v.i.* babble
lestoshchi лестощі *n* adulation
lestyty лестити *v.t* flatter
letalnyi летальний *a.* lethal
letarhichnyi летаргічний *a.* lethargic
letity летіти *v.i* fly
Lev Лев *n.* Leo
lev лев *n* lion
levynyi левиний *a* leonine
levytsia левиця *n.* lioness
lezhaty лежати *v.i.* lie
lezhyt hlyboko useredyni лежить глибоко усередині *a.* inmost
lezo лезо *n.* blade
liakaty лякати *v.t.* intimidate
lialka лялька *n* doll
lialka лялька *n.* puppet
liapas ляпас *n.* slap
liapaty ляпати *v. i.* clap
liapka ляпка *n.* blot

liaskannia ляскання *n.* pope
liberalizm лібералізм *n.* liberalism
liberalnyi ліберальний *a.* liberal
lichylnyi ochkiv лічильний очків
  n. scorer
lid лід *n.* ice
lift ліфт *n.* lift
liha ліга *n.* league
likar лікар *n* doctor
likarnia лікарня *n.* hospital
likarskyi лікарський *a.* medicinal
likarskyi retsept лікарський
  рецепт *n.* prescription
likhovisnyi ліховісний *a.* baleful
likhtar ліхтар *n.* lantern
likot лікоть *n* ancon
likuvalnyi лікувальний *a.*
  remedial
likuvannia лікування *n.* physic
likuvaty лікувати *v.t.* treat
likvidatsiia ліквідація *n.*
  liquidation
likviduvaty ліквідувати *v.t.*
  liquidate
liky ліки *n* cure
liky ліки *n.* medicament
liliia лілія *n.* lily
lin лінь *n.* laziness
linchuvaty лінчувати *v.t.* lynch
linhva franka лінгва франка *n.*
  lingua franca
linhvist лінгвіст *n.* linguist
linhvistychnyi лінгвістичний *a.*
  linguistic
liniia лінія *n.* line
liniiuvaty лініювати *v.t.* line
linoshchi лінощі *n.* sloth
linyvyi лінивий *n.* lazy
linza лінза *n.* lens
lipyty ліпити *v.t.* model
lira ліра *n.* lyre
lirychnyi ліричний *a.* lyric

lirychnyi virsh ліричний вірш *n.*
  lyric
liryk лірик *n.* lyricist
lis ліс *n* forest
lisnychyi лісничий *n.* ranger
lisnyk лісник *n* forester
lisnytstvo лісництво *n* forestry
lisomaterialy лісоматеріали *n.*
  timber
lisovyi лісовий *a.* sylvan
lisy ліси *n.* woods
lisysta mistsevist лісиста
  місцевість *n.* woodland
litak літак *n.* plane
litalnyi aparat літальний апарат
  n. aircraft
litaty літати *v.i.* navigate
literator літератор *n.* litterateur
literatura література *n.* literature
literaturnyi літературний *a.*
  literary
litnii літній *a.* aged
lito літо *n.* summer
litopysets літописець *n.* annalist
litopysi літописі *n.pl.* annals
litr літр *n.* litre
litsenziat ліцензіат *n.* licensee
litsenziia ліцензія *n.* licence
litsenzuvaty ліцензувати *v.t.*
  license
liturhiinyi літургійний *a.* liturgical
liubiaznist люб'язність *n.*
  amiability
liubiaznyi люб'язний *a.* amiable
liubiaznyi люб'язний *a.* urbane
liubliachyi люблячий *a.*
  affectionate
liubliachyi люблячий *a.* loving
liubov любов *n* love
liubovnyi zviazok любовний
  зв'язок *n* amour
liubytel любитель *n.* amateur
liubyty любити *v.t.* like

liubyty любити *v.t.* love
liudskyi людський *a.* human
liudskyi rid людський рід *n.* mankind
liudstvo людство *n.* humanity
liudy люди *n.* people
liudyna людина *n.* man
liudyna людина *n.* person
liudyna neznatnoho pokhodzhennia людина незнатного походження *n.* commoner
liudyna, pohlynena zemnymy interesamy людина, поглинена земними інтересами *n.* worldling
liudynopodibnyi людиноподібний *adj.* anthropoid
liuk люк *n.* manhole
liut лють *n.* fury
liut лють *n.* wrath
liutnia лютня *n.* lute
liutserna люцерна *n.* lucerne
liutyi лютий *n* February
liutyi лютий *a* ferocious
livak лівак *n* leftist
livo ліво *adv.* left
livreia ліврея *n.* livery
livyi лівий *a.* left
lizhko ліжко *n* bed
lliane nasinnia лляне насіння *n.* linseed
lob лоб *n* forehead
lodianyk na palychtsi льодяник на паличці *n.* lollipop
lodovyk льодовик *n.* glacier
loharyfm логарифм *n.* logarithim
lohichne poiasnennia логічне пояснення *n.* rationale
lohichnist логічність *n.* consistence,-cy
lohichnyi логічний *a* consequent

lohichnyi логічний *a.* logical
lohik логік *n.* logician
lohika логіка *n.* logic
loialnist лояльність *n* fidelity
loialnist лояльність *n.* loyalty
loialnyi лояльний *a.* loyal
lokalizuvaty локалізувати *v.t.* localize
lokh льох *n.* vault
lokomotyv локомотив *n.* locomotive
lokon локон *n.* curl
lopata лопата *n.* shovel
losion лосьйон *n.* lotion
loskotaty лоскотати *v.t.* tickle
lotereia лотерея *n.* lottery •
lotos лотос *n.* lotus
lovyty ловити *v. t.* catch
lovyty na bleshniu ловити на блешню *v.i.* spin
lovyty sitkoiu ловити сіткою *v.t.* net
loza лоза *n.* rod
loza лоза *n.* twig
lozhka ложка *n.* spoon
luchka лучка *n.* meadow
luchnyk лучник *n* archer
luh луг *n* alkali
luh луг *n.* mead
luk dlia strilby лук для стрільби *n* bow
lukavist лукавість *n* duplicity
lukavyty лукавити *v. t* dodge
luna луна *n* echo
lunaty лунати *v. t* echo
lunatyk лунатик *n.* somnambulist
lupa лупа *n* dandruff
luptsiuvaty лупцювати *v. t* belabour
lushpaika лушпайка *n.* husk
lychyna личина *n.* guise
lykho лихо *n* evil
lykhodii лиходій *n* fiend

lykhomanka лихоманка *n* fever
lykhoslivia лихослів'я *n*. slander
lykhvar лихвар *n*. usurer
lykhvarstvo лихварство *n*. usury
lykhyi лихий *a* evil
lymon лимон *n*. lemon
lymonad лимонад *n*. lemonade
lymonnyi лимонний *adj*. citric
lynka линька *v.i.* moult
lypka hriaz липка грязь *n*. ooze
lypkyi липкий *n*. sticky
lyshe лише *conj*. only
lysk лиск *n*. gloss
lyskuchyi лискучий *a*. glossy
lyskuchyi лискучий *a*. shiny
lyst лист *n* letter
lyst лист *n*. message
lystia листя *n* foliage
lystochok листочок *n*. leaflet
lystok листок *n*. leaf
lystonosha листоноша *n*.
  postman
lystopad листопад *n*. november
lysukha лисуха *n*. coot
lysyi лисий *a*. bald
lysytsia лисиця *n*. fox
lytsar лицар *n*. knight
lytsarskyi лицарський *a*.
  chivalrous
lytsarstvo лицарство *n*. chivalry
lytse лице *n* face
lytsemir лицемір *n*. hypocrite
lytsemirnyi лицемірний *a*.
  hypocritical
lytsemirstvo лицемірство *n*.
  hypocrisy
lytsova storona лицьова
  сторона *n* outside
lytsovyi лицьовий *a* facial
lyty лити *v.i.* pour
lytysia литися *v.i.* rain
lytysia zlyvoiu литися зливою *v.t.*
  shower

lyzaty лизати *v.t.* lick
lzhesvidchennia лжесвідчення
  n. perjury
lzhesvidchyty лжесвідчити *v.i.*
  perjure

**m`iakush** м`якуш *n*. mush
mah маг *n*. magician
mahazyn магазин *n*. shop
mahichnyi магічний *a*. magical
mahistral магістраль *n*. artery
mahistratura магістратура *n*.
  magistracy
mahnat магнат *n*. magnate
mahnetyt магнетит *n*. loadstone
mahnetyzm магнетизм *n*.
  magnetism
mahnit магніт *n*. magnet
mahnitnyi магнітний *a*. magnetic
maiachyty маячити *v.i.* loom
maiak маяк *n* beacon
maiatnyk маятник *n*. pendulum
maibutnie майбутнє *n* future
maibutnii майбутній *a* after
maibutnii майбутній *a*. future
maidanchyk майданчик *n*.
  ground
maie pohanu reputatsiiu має
  погану репутацію *a*. infamous
maietok маєток *n*. manor
maino майно *n*. baggage
maino майно *n* estate
maino майно *n*. property
maior майор *n* major
maister майстер *n* foreman
maister vesluvannia майстер
  веслування *n*. oarsman
maisternia майстерня *n*.
  workshop
maisternist майстерність *n*.
  mastery

maisternyi майстерний *a.* skilful
maizhe майже *adv.* almost
maizhe майже *adv* much
maizhe майже *prep.* nigh
maket макет *n.* model
makh мах *n* bout
makhaty махати *v.i.* wag
makhaty krylamy махати крилами *v.t* flutter
makler маклер *n.* jobber
maksymalnyi максимальний *a.* maximum
maksymizuvaty максимізувати *v.t.* maximize
maksymum максимум *n* maximum
mala velychyna мала величина *n* small
malenkyi маленький *a.* less
malenkyi kovtok маленький ковток *n.* sip
malia маля *n.* babe
malia маля *n* child
maliariia малярія *n.* malaria
malist малість *n.* smallness
maliuvaty малювати *v.t* draw
maliuvaty малювати *v.t.* picture
maliuvaty olivtsem малювати олівцем *v.t.* pencil
maliuvaty portret малювати портрет *v.t.* portray
malo мало *adv.* little
malo ne мало не *prep.* near
malo toho мало того *adv.* nay
malovnychyi мальовничий *a.* picturesque
malvaziia мальвазія *n.* malmsey
malyi малий *a.* least
malynovyi kolir малиновий колір *n* crimson
mama мама *n* mum
mamasha мамаша *n* mummy
mamont мамонт *n.* mammoth

mandat мандат *n.* mandate
mandrivka мандрівка *n.* trip
mandrivnyk мандрівник *n.* rover
mandruvaty мандрувати *v.i.* stroll
mandruvaty мандрувати *v.i.* travel
mandruvaty мандрувати *v.i.* wander
mandry мандри *n* stroll
maneken манекен *n.* mannequin
manera манера *n.* manner
manera hovoryty манера говорити *n.* parlance
manevr маневр *n.* manoeuvre
manevruvaty маневрувати *v.i.* manoeuvre
manho манго *n* mango
manhusta мангуста *n.* mongoose
maniakalnyi syndrom маніакальний синдром *n* mania
manifest маніфест *n.* manifesto
maniia манія *n* craze
maniiak маніяк *n.* maniac
manikiur манікюр *n.* manicure
manipuliatsiia маніпуляція *n.* manipulation
manipuliuvaty маніпулювати *v.t.* manipulate
manirnist манірність *n.* mannerism
manna манна *n.* manna
manorialnyi маноріальний *a.* manorial
mantiia мантія *n* mantle
manzheta манжета *n* cuff
mara мара *n.* wraith
marafon марафон *n.* marathon
marhanets марганець *n.* manganese
marharyn маргарин *n.* margarine
marharytka маргаритка *n* daisy

marionetka маріонетка *n.* marionette

marker маркер *n.* marker

marmelad мармелад *n.* marmalade

marmur мармур *n.* marble

marnist марність *n.* futility

marno марно *adv.* vainly

marnoslavnyi марнославний *a.* vainglorious

marnoslavstvo марнославство *n* conceit

marnotratnist марнотратність *n* extravagance

marnotratnyi марнотратний *a* extravagant

marnotratnyi марнотратний *a.* wasteful

marnovirstvo марновірство *n.* superstition

marnuvaty марнувати *v.t.* waste

marnyi марний *a* empty

marnyi марний *a* fond

marnyi марний *a.* futile

marnyi марний *a.* vain

marochnyi марочний *n.* vintage

maroder мародер *n.* marauder

maroderstvuvaty мародерствувати *v.i.* maraud

Mars Марс *n* Mars

marsh марш *n* march

marshal маршал *n* marshal

marshrut маршрут *n.* route

marshyruvaty марширувати *v.i* march

marynuvaty маринувати *v.t* pickle

maryty марити *v.i.* rave

marzha маржа *n.* margin

masa маса *n.* mass

masa маса *n.* mountain

masazh масаж *n.* massage

masazhuvaty масажувати *v.t.* massage

masazhyst масажист *n.* masseur

mashyna shvydkoi dopomohy машина швидкої допомоги *n.* ambulance

maska маска *n.* mask

maskarad маскарад *n.* masquerade

maskuvannia маскування *n* disguise

maskuvaty маскувати *v. t* disguise

maskuvaty маскувати *v.t.* mask

maslianystyi маслянистий *a.* oily

maslo масло *n* butter

maslorobnia маслоробня *n* dairy

masnyi масний *a* fat

masove vbyvstvo масове вбивство *n.* massacre

masove vynyshchennia масове винищення *n.* holocaust

masshtab масштаб *n.* scale

masturbuvaty мастурбувати *v.i.* masturbate

mastylo мастило *n* grease

mastyty мастити *v.t.* lubricate

masyvnyi масивний *a.* massive

mat мат *n* mate

matador матадор *n .* matador

match матч *n.* match

matematychnyi математичний *a.* mathematical

matematyk математик *n.* mathematician

matematyka математика *n* mathematics

materevbyvchyi матеревбивчий *a.* matricidal

materevbyvstvo матеревбивство *n.* matricide

material матеріал *n* material

materializm матеріалізм *n.* materialism

materializuvaty матеріалізувати *v.t.* materialize
materiia матерія *n* fabric
materynskyi материнський *a.* motherly
materynstvo материнство *n.* maternity
materynstvo материнство *n.* motherhood
matinka матінка *n* mother
matka матка *n.* uterus
matovyi матовий *a* dim
matrats матрац *n.* mattress
matrimonialnyi матрімоніальний *a.* matrimonial
matros матрос *n.* sailor
matryarkh матриарх *n.* matriarch
matrytsia матриця *n* matrix
maty мати *v.t.* have
maty koryst мати користь *v. t.* benefit
maty mozhlyvist мати можливість *v* may
maty na uvazi мати на увазі *v.t* mean
maty namir мати намір *v.t.* intend
maty nepravylne uiavlennia мати неправильне уявлення *v.t.* misconceive
**maty pevni obov`iazky** мати певні обов`язки *v.t.* suppose
maty prysmak мати присмак *v.t.* smack
maty skhylnist мати схильність *v.i.* tend
maty spravu мати справу *v.i.* traffic
mavpa мавпа *n* ape
mavpiachyi мавпячий *a.* apish
mavpuvaty мавпувати *v.t.* ape
mavzolei мавзолей *n.* mausoleum
maz мазь *n.* ointment
mazaty мазати *v.t.* anoint

mazaty мазати *v. t* butter
mazaty dohtem мазати дьогтем *v.t.* tar
mazok мазок *n.* daub
mech меч *n.* sword
mechet мечеть *n.* mosque
med мед *n.* honey
medal медаль *n.* medal
medalion медальйон *n.* locket
medalist медаліст *n.* medallist
mediana медіана *a.* median
medovi soty медові соти *n.* honeycomb
medovyi misiats медовий місяць *n.* honeymoon
medsestra медсестра *n.* nurse
medychnyi медичний *a.* medical
medykament медикамент *n* drug
medytatyvnyi медитативний *a.* meditative
medytsyna медицина *n.* medicine
mehafon мегафон *n.* megaphone
mehalit мегаліт *n.* megalith
mehalitychnyi мегалітичний *a.* megalithic
mehera мегера *n.* vixen
mekhanichnyi механічний *a.* mechanical
mekhanik механік *n.* mechanic
mekhanika механіка *n.* mechanics
mekhanizm механізм *n.* mechanism
melankholiia меланхолія *n.* melancholia
melankholiinyi меланхолійний *a.* melancholic
melioruvaly меліорували *v.t.* meliorate
melnyk мельник *n.* miller
melodiia мелодія *n.* melody
melodiinyi мелодійний *a.* melodious

melodrama мелодрама *n.*
melodrama
melodramatychnyi
мелодраматичний *а.*
melodramatic
membrana мембрана *n.*
membrane
memorandum меморандум *n*
memorandum
memorial меморіал *n.* memorial
memorialnyi меморіальний *а*
memorial
memuary мемуари *n.* memoir
menedzher менеджер *n.*
manager
meni мені *pron.* me
meninhit менінгіт *n.* meningitis
meniu меню *n.* menu
menopauza менопауза *n.*
menopause
mensh za vse менш за все *adv.*
least
menshe менше *adv.* less
menshist меншість *n.* minority
menshyi менший *а.* lesser
menstrualnyi менструальний *а.*
menstrual
menstruatsii менструації *n.*
menses
menstruatsiia менструація *n.*
menstruation
mentalitet менталітет *n.* mentality
mer мер *n.* mayor
merekhtinnia мерехтіння *n* flicker
merekhtity мерехтіти *v.t* flicker
merezha мережа *n.* network
merezhyvnyi мереживний *а.* lacy
merezhyvo мереживо *n.* lace
merhel мергель *n.* marl
merkantylnyi меркантильний *а.*
mercantile
mersyryzuvaty мерсиризувати
v.t. mercerise

mertvo-blidyi мертво-блідий *а.*
ghastly
mertvyi мертвий *а* dead
merydian меридіан *а.* meridian
merzennyi мерзенний *а*
despicable
merzliakuvatyi мерзлякуватий *а*
chilly
merzota мерзота *n* filth
merzotnyi мерзотний *а* filthy
meshkanets мешканець *n.*
inmate
meshkaty мешкати *v. i* dwell
mesiia месія *n.* messiah
meta мета *n.* aim
metafizychnyi метафізичний *а.*
metaphysical
metafizyka метафізика *n.*
metaphysics
metafora метафора *n.* metaphor
metal метал *n.* metal
metalevyi металевий *а.* metallic
metalnyi метальний *а* projectile
metalnyi spys метальний спис *n.*
javelin
metalurhiia металургія *n.*
metallurgy
metamorfoza метаморфоза *n.*
metamorphosis
metannia метання *n* toss
metaty метати *v. t.* cast
metaty метати *v.t.* toss
metaty ikru метати ікру *v.i.* spawn
metelyk метелик *n* butterfly
metempsykhoz метемпсихоз *n.*
rebirth
meteor метеор *n.* meteor
meteornyi метеорний *а.* meteoric
meteoroloh метеоролог *n.*
meteorologist
meteorolohiia метеорологія *n.*
meteorology
metod метод *n* device

metod метод *n.* method
metodychnyi методичний *a.* methodical
metr метр *n.* meter
metr метр *n.* metre
metropoliia метрополія *n.* metropolis
metrychnyi метричний *a.* metric
metushlyvist метушливість *n.* vanity
metushnia метушня *n.* fuss
metushnia метушня *n.* turmoil
metushytysia метушитися *v.i* fuss
mezalians мезальянс *n.* misalliance
mezha межа *n* boundary
mezha межа *n.* verge
mezhuvaty межувати *v.t* border
mezonin мезонін *n.* mezzanine
miach м'яч *n.* ball
miakist м'якість *n.* lenience, leniency
miakot plodu м'якоть плоду *n.* pulp
miakyi м'який *a.* gentle
miasnyk м'ясник *n* butcher
miaso м'ясо *n.* meat
miasystyi м'ясистий *a.* pulpy
miata м'ята *n.* mint
miatnyi м'ятний *n* mint
miaz м'яз *n.* muscle
miazystyi м'язистий *a.* muscular
mid мідь *n* copper
midnyk мідник *n.* tinker
mif міф *n.* myth
mifichnyi міфічний *a.* mythical
mifolohichnyi міфологічний *a.* mythological
mifolohiia міфологія *n.* mythology
mihrant мігрант *n.* migrant
mihratsiia міграція *n.* migration
mihren мігрень *n.* migraine

mihruvaty мігрувати *v.i.* migrate
mii мій *pron.* mine
mii мій *a.* my
mikhur міхур *n* bubble
mikhy міхи *n.* bellows
mikrob мікроб *n.* germ
mikrofilm мікрофільм *n.* microfilm
mikrofon мікрофон *n.* microphone
mikrokhvylova pich мікрохвильова піч *n.* microwave
mikrometr мікрометр *n.* micrometer
mikroskop мікроскоп *n.* microscope
mikroskopichnyi мікроскопічний *a.* microscopic
mikroskopiia мікроскопія *n.* micrology
miliard мільярд *n* billion
milion мільйон *n.* million
milioner мільйонер *n.* millionaire
militsiia міліція *n.* militia
mility міліти *v.t.* shoal
milkyi мілкий *a.* shallow
mim мім *n.* mime
mimichnyi мімічний *a.* mimic
mimika міміка *n* mimicry
mimikriia мімікрія *n.* mimesis
minaret мінарет *n.* minaret
mineral мінерал *n.* mineral
mineralnyi мінеральний *a* mineral
mineraloh мінералог *n.* mineralogist
mineralohiia мінералогія *n.* mineralogy
miniatiura мініатюра *n.* miniature
miniatiurnyi мініатюрний *a.* miniature
miniaty міняти *v.t.* barter1
miniaty міняти *v.t.* supersede

minimalnyi мінімальний *a.*
minimal
minimalnyi мінімальний *a*
minimum
minimizuvaty мінімізувати *v.t.*
minimize
minimum мінімум *n.* minimum
ministerstvo міністерство *n.*
ministry
ministr міністр *n.* minister
minlyvist мінливість *n.* vicissitude
minlyvyi мінливий *a* fickle
minlyvyi мінливий *a.* wayward
minus мінус *n* minus
miozis міозіс *n.* myosis
mira міра *n.* measure
mirazh міраж *n.* mirage
miriady міріади *n.* myriad
mirkuvannia міркування *n.*
speculation
mirkuvaty міркувати *v.t.* meditate
mirylo мірило *n* criterion
mishanyna мішанина *n.*
miscellany
mishok мішок *n.* sack
mishura мішура *n.* tinsel
misiachnyi місячний *a.* lunar
misiats місяць *n.* month
misiats місяць *n.* moon
misiia місія *n.* mission
misioner місіонер *n.* missionary
misis місіс *n..* missis, missus
miska mytnytsia міська митниця
n. octroi
miskyi міський *a.* urban
mist міст *n* bridge
mistechko містечко *n.* town
mister містер *n.* mister
mistkist місткість *n.* capacity
mistkyi місткий *a.* ample
mistkyi місткий *a.* roomy
misto місто *n* city
mistse місце *n.* lieu

mistse місце *n.* place
mistse dii місце дії *n.* locale
mistse podii місце подій *n* arena
mistse prozhyvannia місце
проживання *n.* residence
mistse roztashuvannia місце
розташування *n.* location
mistse zustrichi місце зустрічі *n.*
venue
mistsepolozhennia
місцеположення *n.* locus
mistsevist місцевість *n.* locality
mistsevyi місцевий *a.* indigenous
mistsevyi місцевий *a.* local
mistsevyi zhytel місцевий
житель *n* native
mistseznakhodzhennia
місцезнаходження *adv.*
whereabout
mistychnyi містичний *a.* mystic
mistyfikatsiia містифікація *n.*
hoax
mistyfikuvaty містифікувати *v.t.*
mystify
mistyk містик *n* mystic
mistyt містить *a.* inclusive
mistytsyzm містицизм *n.*
mysticism
mistyty містити *v.t.* contain
mistyty v sobi містити в собі *v.t.*
imply
mistyty v sobi містити в собі *v.t.*
presuppose
mitla мітла *n* broom
mits міць *n.* power
mitsnist міцність *n.* strength
mitsnyi міцний *a* firm
mitsnyi міцний *a.* sound
mizantrop мізантроп *n.*
misanthrope
mizernyi мізерний *a.* minuscule
mizh між *prep.* amongst
mizh між *prep* between

mizhnarodnyi міжнародний *a.*
international
mliavist млявість *n.* lethargy
mliavyi млявий *a* flat
mlyn млин *n.* mill
mnozhene множене *n.*
multiplicand
mnozhennia множення *n.*
multiplication
mnozhynnist множинність *n.*
multiplicity
mnozhynnyi множинний *a.*
multiple
mnozhyty na chotyry множити
на чотири *v.t.* quadruple
mobilizuvaty мобілізувати *v.t.*
mobilize
mobilnist мобільність *n.* mobility
mobilnyi мобільний *a.* mobile
mochka vukha мочка вуха *n.*
lobe
mochytysia мочитися *v.i.* urinate
moda мода *n* fashion
modalnist модальність *n.*
modality
model модель *n* make
modernizuvaty модернізувати
v.t. modernize
modni tovary модні товари *n.*
millinery
modnyi модний *a* fashionable
moduliuvaty модулювати *v.t.*
modulate
modyfikatsiia модифікація *n.*
modification
modystka модистка *n.* milliner
mohty могти *v. t.* can
mohutnii могутній *adj.* mighty
mohutnist могутність *n.* might
mohyla могила *n.* grave
mohyla могила *n.* tomb
mohylnyk могильник *n.* mortuary
mokh мох *n.* moss

mokhove boloto мохове болото
n. moor
mokrota мокрота *n.* sputum
mokryi мокрий *a.* wet
mol моль *n.* mole
molekula молекула *n.* molecule
molekuliarnyi молекулярний *a.*
molecular
moliarnyi молярний *a* molar
molochnyi молочний *a.* milch
molochnyi молочний *a.* milky
molod молодь *n* young
molodist молодість *n.*
adolescence
molodshyi za zvanniam
молодший за званням *n.* junior
molodyi молодий *a.* junior
moloko молоко *n.* milk
molotarka молотарка *n.* thresher
molotok молоток *n.* hammer
moloty молоти *v.t.* mill
molotyty молотити *v.t.* thrash
molytva молитва *n.* prayer
molyty молити *v. t.* entreat
molytysia молитися *v.i.* pray
moment момент *n.* moment
monakhynia монахиня *n.* nun
monarkh монарх *n.* monarch
monarkhiia монархія *n.*
monarchy
monastyr монастир *n.* cloister
monastyr монастир *n.* monastery
moneta монета *n* coin
monetnyi монетний *a.* monetary
monohamiia моногамія *n.*
monogamy
monohinnyi моногінний *a.*
monogynous
monohrafiia монографія *n.*
monograph
monohrama монограма *n.*
monogram

monokhromatychnyi монохроматичний *a.* monochromatic

monokl монокль *n.* monocle

monokuliar монокуляр *a.* monocular

monolit моноліт *n.* monolith

monoloh монолог *n.* monologue

monopoliia монополія *n.* monopoly

monopolist монополіст *n.* monopolist

monopolizuvaty монополізувати *v.t.* monopolize

monoteist монотеїст *n.* monotheist

monoteizm монотеїзм *n.* monotheism

monotonnist монотонність *n* monotony

monstr монстр *n.* monster

monumentalnyi монументальний *a.* monumental

moral мораль *n.* moral

moralist мораліст *n.* moralist

moralizuvaty моралізувати *v.t.* moralize

moralnist моральність *n.* morality

moralnyi моральний *a.* moral

morda морда *n.* muzzle

more море *a.* profound

more море *n.* sea

morekhidnyi морехідний *a.* nautic(al)

moreplavets мореплавець *n.* voyager

morfii морфій *n.* morphia

morh морг *n.* morgue

morhanatychnyi морганатичний *a.* morganatic

morhannia моргання *n* wink

moriak моряк *n.* mariner

morkva морква *n.* carrot

moroz мороз *n.* frost

morshchyty морщити *v.t.* wrinkle

morshchytysia морщитися *v. i* cockle

morshchytysia морщитися *v.i.* wince

morska sazhen морська сажень *n* fathom

morskyi морський *a.* marine

morzh морж *n.* walrus

moskvych москвич *n.* muscovite

mostyty мостити *v.t.* pave

mostyty kamenem мостити каменем *v.t.* stone

mot мот *n.* spendthrift

motalna mashyna мотальна машина *n.* winder

motaty мотати *v.i.* reel

motel мотель *n.* motel

motok priazhi моток пряжі *n.* skein

motornyi моторний *adj.* deft

motoroshnyi моторошний *a.* uncanny

motuzka мотузка *n.* rope

motuzka мотузка *v.t.* string

motyka мотика *v.t.* hack

motyv мотив *n.* motif

motyv мотив *n.* motive

motyv мотив *n.* tune

motyvatsiia мотивація *n.* motivation

motyvuvaty мотивувати *v* motivate

mova мова *n* discourse

movchannia мовчання *n.* quiet

movchaznyi мовчазний *a.* mum

movchaznyi мовчазний *a.* mute

movnyi мовний *a.* lingual

movoznavstvo мовознавство *n.* linguistics

mozaika мозаїка *n.* mosaic

mozhlyvist можливість *n.* occasion
mozhlyvist можливість *n.* probability
mozhlyvo можливо *adv.* perhaps
mozhlyvyi можливий *a.* hypothetical
mozok мозок *n* brain
mriachyty мрячити *v. i* drizzle
mriiaty мріяти *v. i.* dream
mriilyvist мрійливість *n.* reverie
msprytnyi мспритний *a* slick
mstyty мстити *v.t.* avenge
mstyvyi мстивий *a.* revengeful
muchenyk мученик *n.* martyr
muchenytstvo мучеництво *n.* martyrdom
muchyty мучити *v. t* bedevil
muchytysia мучитися *v.t.* agonize
mudrets мудрець *n.* sage
mudrist мудрість *n.* wisdom
mudrosti zub мудрості зуб *n.* wisdom-tooth
mudryi мудрий *a.* sage
mudryi мудрий *a.* wise
muka мука *n.* torment
muka мука *n.* worry
mukannia мукання *n.* low
mukaty мукати *v.i* moo
mukha муха *n* fly
mul мул *n.* mule
mulat мулат *n.* mulatto
muliar муляр *n.* mason
muliar муляр *n.* paddy
mulla мулла *n.* mullah
multfilm мультфільм *n.* cartoon
mumiia мумія *n.* mummy
munitsypalitet муніципалітет *n.* municipality
munitsypalnyi муніципальний *a.* municipal
murakha мураха *n* ant
murkotannia муркотання *n.* purr

murkotity муркотіти *v.i.* purr
mushka мушка *n* foresight
mushket мушкет *n.* musket
mushketer мушкетер *n.* musketeer
mushtabel муштабель *n.* maulstick
muskus мускус *n.* musk
muslin муслін *n.* muslin
muson мусон *n.* monsoon
mustanh мустанг *n.* mustang
mutatsiia мутація *n.* mutation
mutatsiinyi мутаційний *a.* mutative
muza муза *n* muse
muzei музей *n.* museum
muzhnii мужній *a.* manly
muzhnist мужність *n* manliness
muzhyk мужик *n* boor
muzychnyi музичний *a.* musical
muzyka музика *n.* music.
muzykant музикант *n.* musician
myhannia мигання *n.* twinkle
myhdal мигдаль *n.* almond
myhdalyna мигдалина *n.* tonsil
myinyk мийник *n.* washer
mylia миля *n.* mile
mylna pina мильна піна *n.* lather
mylnyi мильний *a.* soapy
mylo мило *n.* soap
myloserdia милосердя *n.* charity
myloserdia милосердя *n.* mercy
myloserdnyi милосердний *a.* merciful
mylostynia милостиня *n.* alms
mylostyvo милостиво *adv* benignly
mylostyvyi милостивий *adj* benign
mylostyvyi милостивий *a.* gracious
mylovydnist миловидність *n.* prettiness

mylyi милий *a* dear
mymovoli мимоволі *adv.* unwittingly
mymryty мимрити *v.i.* mutter
mynule минуле *n.* antecedent
mynulyi минулий *a.* past
mynushchyi минущий *a.* transitory
mynuty минути *n* escape
myr мир *n.* peace
myrianyn мирянин *n.* layman
myrnyi мирний *a.* peaceful
myroliubnyi миролюбний *a.* pacific
myrovyi poserednyk мировий посередник *n.* compounder
myrra мирра *n.* myrrh
myrskyi мирський *a.* mundane
myrt мирт *n.* myrtle
mysha миша *n.* mouse
myslennia мислення *n* thought
myslytel мислитель *n.* thinker
myslyty мислити *v.i.* reason
myslyvets мисливець *n.* hunter
myslyvskyi sobaka мисливський собака *n.* hound
mystetstvo мистецтво *n.* art
mystetstvo мистецтво *n.* workmanship
myt мить *n.* instant
myto мито *n* toll
mytra митра *n.* mitre
mytropolyt митрополит *n.* metropolitan
myttievyi миттєвий *a.* instant
myty мити *v.t.* wash
myty shampunem мити шампунем *v.t.* shampoo
mzhychka мжичка *n* drizzle

na на *adv.* on
na на *prep.* on
na bortu на борту *adv* aboard
na hirshe на гірше *adv.* backward
na pershyi pohliad на перший погляд *adv.* prima facie
na pivnich на північ *adv.* north
na pivnich на північ *adv.* northerly
na shchastia на щастя *adv.* luckily
na shcho на що *conj.* whereat
na skhid на схід *adv* east
na sotniu на сотню *adv.* per cent
na viddali на віддалі *adv.* apart
na vidminu vid на відміну від *prep* unlike
na vodi на воді *adv.* afloat
na zakhid на захід *adv.* west
na zakhid на захід *adv.* westerly
na zakinchennia на закінчення *adv.* lastly
na zhal на жаль *interj.* alas
na zvoroti на звороті *adv.* overleaf
nabahato набагато *adv.* better
nabih набіг *n.* irruption
nabir набір *n* set
nablyzhatysia наближатися *v.i.* near
nabob набоб *n.* nabob
nabrydaty набридати *v. t* bore
nabrydaty набридати *v. t* bother
nabukhaty набухати *v.i.* swell
nabuttia набуття *n* commencement
nabuttia chynnosti набуття чинності *n* acquest
nabuvaty набувати *v.t.* acquire
nabyvaty набивати *v.t.* pad
nabyvka набивка *n.* gasket

nachalnyk начальник *n.* senior
nachebto начебто *adv.* like
nachis начіс *n* nap
nachynnia начиння *n.* utensil
nachytanyi начитаний *a.* well-read
nad над *prep.* above
nadannia надання *n.* provision
nadaty formu надати форму *v.t* shape
nadavaty надавати *v.t.* grant
nadavaty надавати *v. t* entrust
nadavaty dvorianskyi tytul надавати дворянський титул *v. t.* ennoble
nadavaty kvadratnu formu надавати квадратну форму *v.t.* square
nadavaty pravo надавати право *v. t.* entitle
nadavaty vidtinok надавати відтінок *v.t.* tinge
nadavaty zhorstkosti надавати жорсткості *v.t.* stiffen
nadavaty zhytlo надавати житло *v.t* house
nadhrobna plyta надгробна плита *n.* ledger
nadiahaty namordnyk надягати намордник *v.t* muzzle
nadiia надія *n* hope
nadiia надія *n.* reliance
nadiina liudyna надійна людина *n.* trusty
nadiinyi надійний *a.* reliable
nadiinyi надійний *a.* sterling
nadil наділ *n.* allotment
nadiliaty наділяти *v.t.* allot
nadity naruchnyky надіти наручники *v.t* handcuff
nadivaty pokryshku надівати покришку *v.t.* tire

nadkhodyty надходити *v. i.* behave
nadkhodyty надходити *v.t.* reach
nadliudskyi надлюдський *a.* superhuman
nadlyshkovyi надлишковий *a.* redundant
nadlyshok надлишок *n* abundance
nadlyshok надлишок *n* excess
nadmir надмір *n.* plenty
nadmirna kilkist надмірна кількість *n.* superabundance
nadmirnist надмірність *n* extreme
nadmirnist надмірність *n.* redundance
nadmirno napruzhuvaty надмірно напружувати *v.t.* tax
nadmirno optymistychnyi надмірно оптимістичний *a.* roseate
nadmirnyi надмірний *a.* prodigal
nadmirnyi надмірний *a.* undue
nadpryrodnyi надприродний *a.* supernatural
nadpysuvaty надписувати *v. t.* endorse
naduty надути *v.i.* blow
naduvannia надування *n.* inflation
nadzvukovyi надзвуковий *a.* supersonic
nadzvychaino shchedryi надзвичайно щедрий *a.* munificent
nafarshyruvaty нафарширувати 2 *v.t.* stuff
nafta нафта *n.* petroleum
nahaduiuchyi нагадуючий *a.* reminiscent
nahaduvannia нагадування *n.* reminder

nahaduvaty нагадувати *v.t.*
remind
nahar na svichtsi нагар на свічці
n. snuff
nahliad нагляд *n.* oversight
nahliadach наглядач *n.* overseer
nahliadaty наглядати *v.t.*
invigilate
nahori нагорі *adv* above
nahoroda нагорода *n.* award
nahorodyty ordenom нагородити
орденом *v.t.* star
nahorodzhuvaty нагороджувати
v.t. award
nahorodzhuvaty ordenamy
нагороджувати орденами *v. t*
decorate
nahota нагота *n.* nudity
nahrabovane награбоване *n.*
prey
nahromadzhuvaty
нагромаджувати *v.t* heap
naiavnist наявність *n.* presence
naiavnyi наявний *a* available
naibilsh найбільш *adv.* most
naiblyzhchyi найближчий *a.*
proximate
naichastishe найчастіше *adv.*
often
naihirshe найгірше *n.* worst
naihirshyi найгірший *a* worst
naihlybshyi найглибший *a.*
innermost
naimach наймач *n.* lessee
naimanets найманець *n.* hireling
naimannia наймання *n.* hire
naimaty наймати *v. t* employ
nainyzhchyi riven найнижчий
рівень *n.* nadir
naitonshyi найтонший *a.*
superfine
naivazhlyvishyi найважливіший
a. momentous

naividdalenishyi
найвіддаленіший *a.* utmost
naivnist наївність *n.* naivete
naivnyi наївний *a.* naive
naivyshcha tochka найвища
точка *n* sublime
naivyshchyi найвищий *a.*
superlative
nakaz наказ *n.* conge
nakazovyi наказовий *a.*
imperative
nakazuvaty наказувати *v.t* order
nakazuvaty наказувати *v.t.*
prescribe
nakazuvaty наказувати *v.t.*
require
nakhaba нахаба *n.* swine
nakhabnyi нахабний *a.*
impertinent
nakhabstvo нахабство *n.*
insolence
nakhlibnyk нахлібник *n*
dependant
nakhyl нахил *n* bias
nakhylennia нахилення *n.*
inclination
nakhyliaty нахиляти *v.t.* slant
nakladaty aresht накладати
арешт *v.t.* sequester
nakladaty veto накладати вето
v.t. veto
nakladennia накладення *n.*
imposition
naklasty накласти *v.t.* impose
nakleika наклейка *n.* sticker
nakleity наклеїти *v.t.* stick
nakleiuvaty наклеювати *v.t.* affix
naklep наклеп *n* defamation
naklepnytskyi наклепницький *a.*
slanderous
nakoloty наколоти *v.t.* prick
nakonechnyk наконечник *n.* tip
nakydaty накидати *v.t.* sketch

nakydatysia накидатися *v.i.*
pounce
nakydka накидка *n.* cape
nakyp накип *n.* ream
nalashtovuvaty налаштовувати
v.t. tune
nalezhaty належати *v. i* belong
nalezhne належне *n* due
nalezhnyi належний *adv* due
nalezhnyi належний *a* due
nalezhnyi належний *a.* proper
nalezhnyi належний *a.* requisite
nalezhnyi належний *a.* sufficient
nalezhnym chynom належним
чином *adv* duly
nalezhnym chynom належним
чином *adv* right
naliakaty налякати *v.t.* frighten
naliakaty налякати *v.t.* scare
naliakaty налякати *v.t.* startle
namahatysia намагатися *v.t.*
attempt
namatsuvaty намацувати *v.t.*
grope
namet намет *n.* tent
namichatysia намічатися *v.i.*
teethe
namir намір *n* animus
namir намір *n.* design
namir намір *n.* purpose
namir намір *n.* scope
namylyty намилити *v.t.* soap
namysto намисто *n.* necklace
nanosnyi наносний *a.* superficial
nanosyty наносити *v.t.* inflict
nanosyty na kartu наносити на
карту *v.t.* map
nanosyty smuhy наносити смуги
v.t. stripe
nanyzuvaty нанизувати *v.t* thread
napad напад *n.* assault
napadaty нападати *v.t.* attack

napakhuvaty parfumamy
напахувати парфумами *v.t.*
perfume
naparnyk напарник *n.* mate
napererik наперерік *prep.* athwart
naperstok наперсток *n.* thimble
napii напій *n* beverage
napolehlyvist наполегливість *n.*
perseverance
napolehlyvyi наполегливий *a.*
insistent
napoliahaty наполягати *v.t.* insist
napoval наповал *adv.* outright
napravliaty направляти *v. t* direct
napravliaty na mistse roboty
направляти на місце роботи
v.t. station
napriam напрям *n* direction
napruha напруга *n* strain
napruzhenist напруженість *n.*
tension
napruzhenyi напружений *a.*
strenuous
napruzhuvaty напружувати *v. t*
bend
napys напис *n.* inscription
narada нарада *n* deliberation
narazhaty na nebezpeku
наражати на небезпеку *v.t.*
imperil
narechena наречена *n* bride
nariad наряд *n.* attire
nariadnist нарядність *n.* gaiety
nariadzhaty наряджати *v.t.* attire
narikannia нарікання *n.*
lamentation
narikaty нарікати *v.t.* murmur
narizaty skybkamy нарізати
скибками *v.t.* slice
narizaty u dovzhynu нарізати у
довжину *v.t.* slit
narizno нарізно *adv.* asunder
narkoman наркоман *n.* addict

narkotychnyi наркотичний *n.* narcotic
narkoz наркоз *n.* narcosis
narochnyi нарочний *n* express
narodnyi народний *a.* vernacular
narodzhennia народження *n* bearing
narodzhennia народження *n.* inception
narodzhenyi pislia smerti batka народжений після смерті батька *a.* posthumous
narodzhuvaty народжувати *v. t* beget
naroshchuvaty koru нарощувати кору *v.t.* bark
nartsys нарцис *n* narcissus
nartsys zhovtyi нарцис жовтий *n.* daffodil
naruchnyk наручник *n.* handcuff
naruha наруга *n.* outrage
narukavnyk нарукавник *a* armlet
naryv нарив *n* blain
naselennia населення *n.* population
naseliaty населяти *v.t.* inhabit
naseliaty населяти *v.t.* populate
nash наш *pron.* our
nashchadky нащадки *n.* posterity
nashchadok нащадок *n* descendant
nasinnia насіння *n.* seed
nasinnievyi насіннєвий *a.* seminal
naskochyty наскочити *v.t.* surprise
naskok наскок *n* pounce
naslidky наслідки *n.* repercussion
naslidok наслідок *n* consequence
naslidok наслідок *n.* outcome
naslidok наслідок *n.* progeny
naslidok наслідок *n.* sequel

nasliduvach наслідувач *n.* imitator
nasliduvannia наслідування *n.* imitation
nasliduvanyi наслідуваний *a.* heritable
nasliduvaty наслідувати *v.i* mime
nasmikhatysia насміхатися *v.i.* gibe
nasmishka насмішка *n.* ridicule
nasmishnyk насмішник *n.* joker
nasoloda насолода *n.* luxury
nasoloda насолода *n* relish
nasolodzhuvatysia насолоджуватися *v.t.* relish
nasos насос *n.* pump
naspravdi насправді *adv.* really
nastavnyk наставник *n.* mentor
nastii настій *n* extract
nastoianka настоянка *n.* tincture
nastoiatel настоятель *n* prior
nastoiatelka настоятелька *n.* prioress
nastorozhenist настороженість *n.* alertness
nastorozhenyi насторожений *a.* alert
nastorozhenyi насторожений *a.* wary
nastrii настрій *n.* mood
nastrii настрій *n.* sentiment
nastroiuvaty настроювати *v. t* bias
nastup наступ *n.* attack
nastup наступ *n* offensive
nastupnist наступність *n.* succession
nastupnyi наступний *a.* forthcoming
nastupnyi наступний *a.* next
nastupnyi наступний *a.* successive
nastupnyi наступний *a.* ulterior

nastupnyi den наступний день *n.* morrow

nastupnyk наступник *n.* successor

nastylaty doshky настилати дошки *v.t.* plank

nastylaty palubu настилати палубу *v. t* deck

nastylaty pidlohu настилати підлогу *v.t* floor

nastyrlyvist настирливість *n.* molestation

nasuvaietsia насувається *a.* imminent

nasychennia насичення *n.* saturation

nasychuvaty насичувати *v.t.* satiate

nasylaty neshchastia насилати нещастя *v.t.* plague

nasylnytskyi насильницький *a* forcible

nasylnytskyi насильницький *a.* violent

nasylstvo насильство *n.* violence

nasylu насилу *adv.* hardly

nasyp насип *n* embankment

natalnyi натальний *a.* natal

natiahuvaty натягувати *v.t.* strain

natiak натяк *n* allusion

natiak натяк *n.* hint

natiakaty натякати *v.i* hint

natilna bilyzna натільна білизна *n.* underwear

natkhnennia натхнення *n.* inspiration

natkhnennyi натхненний *a.* animate

natovp натовп *n* crowd

natrapyty натрапити *v.t.* jostle

natsiia нація *n.* nation

natsionalistychnyi націоналістичний *n.* nationalist

natsionalizatsiia націоналізація *n.* nationalization

natsionalizm націоналізм *n.* nationalism

natsionalizuvaty націоналізувати *v.t.* nationalize

natsionalnist національність *n.* nationality

natsionalnyi національний *a.* internal

natsionalnyi національний *a.* national

naturalist натураліст *n.* naturalist

naturalizuvaty натуралізувати *v.t.* naturalize

natyraty натирати *v.t.* smear

natysk натиск *n.* onrush

natysk натиск *n.* onset

natyskaty pedal натискати педаль *v.t.* pedal

nauka наука *n.* science

naukovets науковець *n.* scientist

naukovyi науковий *a* academic

navala навала *n.* invasion

navaliuvaty навалювати *v.t.* pile

navantazhennia навантаження *n.* load

navantazhuvaty навантажувати *v.t.* load

navazhuvatysia наважуватися *v.t.* risk

navchalnyi навчальний *n.* tutorial

navchalnyi plan навчальний план *n* curriculum

navchalnyi sudovyi protses навчальний судовий процес *n.* moot

navchannia навчання *n.* learning

navchannia навчання *n.* training

navchaty навчати *v.t.* teach

navedennia наведення *n* offer

navedenyi u poriadok наведений у порядок *a.* trim

naverkh наверх *adv.* upward
naviazlyva ideia нав'язлива ідея
n. obsession
naviazuvaty нав'язувати *v. t.*
enforce
navidnyi навідний *a.* suggestive
navihator навігатор *n.* navigator
navihatsiia навігація *n.* navigation
naviiaty навіяти *v.t.* waft
naviiuvaty навіювати *v.t.* inspire
navis навіс *n* shed
navkolo навколо *adj.* ambient
navkolo навколо *adv.* round
navkolyshnie seredovyshche
навколишнє середовище *n.*
environment
navmysne vbyvstvo навмисне
вбивство *n.* murder
navmysnist навмисність *n.*
premeditation
navmysno навмисно *adv.*
purposely
navmysno vvodyty v omanu
навмисно вводити в оману *v. t*
deceive
navmysnyi навмисний *a.*
intentional
navodyty dokazy наводити
докази *v.t.* adduce
navpaky навпаки *adv.* vice-versa
navriad chy навряд чи *adv.* ill
navriad chy навряд чи *adv.*
scarcely
navyk навик *n.* skill
nazad назад *adv.* back
nazavzhdy назавжди *adv* forever
nazdohnaty наздогнати *v.t.*
overtake
nazhyty нажити *v.t.* profit
nazhyvka наживка *n* bait
nazovni назовні *prep* outside
nazovni назовні *adv* outward
nazva назва *n.* title

nazvanyi batko названий батько
n. parent
nazvaty назвати *v.t.* name
ne не *conj* nor
ne не *adv.* not
ne buty не бути *v.t* absent
ne diiaty не діяти *v.i.* slumber
ne doviriaty не довіряти *v.t.*
mistrust
ne dozvoliaty не дозволяти *v. t.*
debar
ne dozvoliaty не дозволяти *v.t*
forbid
ne liubyty не любити *v. t* dislike
ne pidkoriatysia не підкорятися
v. t disobey
ne podobatysia не подобатися *v.*
t displease
ne potrapyty не потрапити *v.t.*
miss
ne skhodytysia v pohliadakh
не сходитися в поглядах *v. i*
disagree
ne skhvaliuvaty не схвалювати
v. t disapprove
ne vidpovidaty не відповідати
v.t. mismatch
neabyiakyi неабиякий *a.* hefty
neaktyvnyi неактивний *a.* silent
neakuratno pysaty неакуратно
писати *v.t.* scribble
nebahatoslivnyi небагатослівний
a. terse
nebazhannia небажання *n.*
reluctance
nebesa небеса *n.* heaven
nebesnyi небесний *adj* celestial
nebezpechnist небезпечність *n.*
insecurity
nebezpechnyi небезпечний *a*
dangerous
nebezpechnyi небезпечний *a.*
insecure

nebezpeka небезпека *n.* danger
nebezpeka небезпека *n.* jeopardy
nebezpeka небезпека *n* menace
nebo небо *n.* sky
nechemnist нечемність *n.* indiscretion
nechesno нечесно *adv* malafide
nechesnyi нечесний *a* dirty
nechesnyi нечесний *a* dishonest
nechistokrovnyi нечістокровний *a* mongrel
nechutlyvist нечутливість *n.* insensibility
nechutlyvyi нечутливий *a.* insensible
nechutnyi нечутний *a.* inaudible
nechuvanyi нечуваний *a* fabulous
nechyslennyi нечисленний *a* few
nechystota нечистота *n.* impurity
nechystyi нечистий *a.* impure
nedarma недарма *adv.* justly
nedavnii недавній *a.* latter
nedavnii недавній *a.* new
nedavno недавно *adv.* recently
nedbailyvyi недбайливий *n.* slothful
nedbalyi недбалий *a.* careless
nedbalyi недбалий *a.* nonchalant
nedbalyi недбалий *a.* slipshod
nediisnyi недійсний *a.* invalid
nediisnyi недійсний *a.* void
nediiuchyi недіючий *a.* inoperative
nedilia неділя *n.* Sunday
nedohliad недогляд *n.* omission
nedoidannia недоїдання *n.* malnutrition
nedolik недолік *n* blemish
nedootsiniuvaty недооцінювати *v.t.* misjudge
nedopalok недопалок *n.* stub
nedorechna veselist недоречна веселість *n.* levity

nedorechnist недоречність *n.* impropriety
nedorechnyi недоречний *a.* inopportune
nedorechnyi недоречний *a.* irrelevant
nedorohyi недорогий *a.* inexpensive
nedoskonalist недосконалість *n.* imperfection
nedoskonalyi недосконалий *a* faulty
nedostacha недостача *n.* shortage
nedostatnii недостатній *adj.* deficient
nedostupnyi недоступний *a.* impenetrable
nedosvidchenist недосвідченість *n.* inexperience
nedotorkannyi недоторканний *a.* sacrosanct
nedoumkuvatyi недоумкуватий *a.* silly
nedovira недовіра *n.* mistrust
nedozvolenyi недозволений *a.* illicit
nedruh недруг *n* foe
nedystsyplinovanist недисциплінованість *n.* indiscipline
nef неф *n.* nave
nehaino негайно *adv.* straightway
nehainyi негайний *a.* instantaneous
neharazdy негаразди *n.* adversity
nehatyv негатив *n.* negative
nehatyvnyi негативний *a* minus
nehidnyk негідник *n.* wretch
nehnuchkyi негнучкий *a.* inflexible
nehnuchkyi негнучкий *n.* stiff

nehostynnyi негостинний *a.*
inhospitable
nehovirkyi неговіркий *a.* taciturn
nehr негр *n.* negro
nehramotnist неграмотність *n.*
illiteracy
nehrytianka негритянка *n.*
negress
neiaskravyi неяскравий *a.* sullen
neiasnyi неясний *a* equivocal
neiasnyi неясний *a.* indescribable
neiasnyi неясний *a.* indistinct
neilon нейлон *n.* nylon
neimovirnyi неймовірний *a.*
incredible
neimovirnyi неймовірний *a.*
unlikely
neitralizm нейтралізм *n.* non-
alignment
neitralizuvaty нейтралізувати *v.t.*
neutralize
neitralnyi нейтральний *a.* neutral
neitron нейтрон *n.* neutron
nekhtuvaty нехтувати *v. t.* disdain
nekhtuvaty нехтувати *v.t.* slight
nekompetentnyi некомпетентний
a. incompetent
nekonkuruiuchyi неконкуруючий
a complementary
nekroloh некролог *a.* obituary
nekromant некромант *n.*
necromancer
nekropol некрополь *n.* necropolis
nektar нектар *n.* nectar
nekultyvovanyi некультивований
a. wild
nekvaplyvo неквапливо *adv.*
leisurely
nekvaplyvyi неквапливий *a.*
leisurely
neliudianist нелюдяність *n*
barbarity

neliudskyi нелюдський *a.*
inhuman
nelohichnyi нелогічний *a.* illogical
neloialnyi нелояльний *a* disloyal
nematerialnyi нематеріальний *a.*
immaterial
nemich неміч *n.* infirmity
nemichnyi немічний *a.* infirm
nemitsnyi неміцний *a* flimsy
nemovlia немовля *n.* infant
nemozhlyvist неможливість *n.*
impossibility
nemozhlyvist prochytaty
неможливість прочитати *n.*
illegibility
nemozhlyvyi неможливий *a.*
impossible
nemyloserdnyi немилосердний
adj. merciless
nemynuchyi неминучий *a.*
inevitable
nenadiinyi ненадійний *a.*
unreliable
nenadovho ненадовго *adv.*
awhile
nenalezhna povedinka
неналежна поведінка *n.*
misbehaviour
nenasytno ненаситно *a.*
insatiable
nenasytnyi ненаситний *a.*
voracious
nenavydity ненавидіти *v.t.* abhor
nenavydity ненавидіти *v.t.* hate
nenavydity ненавидіти *v.t.* loathe
nenavyst ненависть *n.* hate
nenazhera ненажера *n.*
cormorant
nenormalnyi ненормальний *a*
abnormal
neobachnyi необачний *a.* rash
neobdumanyi необдуманий *a.*
haphazard

neobdumanyi необдуманий *a.*
inconsiderate
neoberezhnyi необережний *a.*
imprudent
neobgruntovanyi
необґрунтований *a.* unjust
neobhruntovanyi
необгрунтований *a.* invalid
neobkhidna umova необхідна
умова *n.* requirement
neobkhidne необхідне *a.* needful
neobkhidnist необхідність *n.*
must
neobkhidnist необхідність *n.*
need
neobkhidno необхідно *n.*
necessary
neobkhidnyi необхідний *a.*
indispensable
neoboviazkovyi необов'язковий
a. optional
neobroblenyi необроблений *a*
crude
neobroblenyi необроблений *a.*
rough
neobtesanyi необтесаний *a.*
uncouth
neodnakovyi неоднаковий *a.*
matchless
neofitsiinyi неофіційний *a.*
informal
neokhainyi неохайний *a.*
slatternly
neokhainyi неохайний *a.* slovenly
neokhoche zhodzhuvatysia
неохоче згоджуватися *v.i.*
acquiesce
neokhochyi неохочий *a.* loath
neolitychnyi неолітичний *a.*
neolithic
neonovyi неоновий *n.* neon
neosiazhnyi неосяжний *a.*
immense

neosvichenyi неосвічений *a.*
ignorant
neotsinennyi неоцінений *a.*
invaluable
neparnyi непарний *a.* odd
neperebornyi непереборний *a.*
insurmountable
neperekhidnyi неперехідний *a.*
(verb) intransitive
neperekhidnyi неперехідний *a.*
neuter
neperemozhnyi непереможний
a. invincible
neperenosnyi непереносний *a.*
intolerable
neperevershuvanyi
неперевершуваний *a.* peerless
neplatospromozhnyi
неплатоспроможний *a.*
insolvent
nepodalik неподалік *adv.*
thereabouts
nepodilnyi неподільний *a.*
indivisible
nepokhytnyi непохитний *a.*
adamant
nepokhytnyi непохитний *a.*
resolute
nepokirlyvyi непокірливий *a.*
insubordinate
nepokirnyi непокірний *a.* unruly
nepokirnyi непокірний *a.*
untoward
nepokora непокора *n.*
insubordination
nepomirnist непомірність *n.*
surfeit
nepomitno vseliaty непомітно
вселяти *v.t.* insinuate
nepomitnyi непомітний *a.*
obscure
nepopravnyi непоправний *a.*
irrecoverable

neporiadnyi непорядний *a.*
indecent
neporivniannyi непорівнянний *a.*
incomparable
neporozuminnia непорозуміння
n misapprehension
neporozuminnia непорозуміння
n. mistake
neporozuminnia непорозуміння
n. misunderstanding
neporushnyi непорушний *a.* still
neposhtyvyi непоштивий *a*
discourteous
nepotribnyi непотрібний *a.*
needless
nepovaha неповага *n* disrespect
nepovnolitnii неповнолітній *a.*
minor
nepovnolitnii pidlitok
неповнолітній підліток *n* minor
nepovnotsinnist неповноцінність
n. inferiority
nepovnyi неповний *a* .
incomplete
nepovtornyi неповторний *a.*
inimitable
nepratsezdatnyi непрацездатний
a disabled
nepravomirnyi неправомірний *a.*
wrongful
nepravosuddia неправосуддя *n.*
injustice
nepravylna nazva неправильна
назва *n.* misnomer
nepravylne неправильне *n.*
misdirection
nepravylne kerivnytstvo
неправильне керівництво *n.*
mismanagement
nepravylne uiavlennia
неправильне уявлення *n.*
misconception

nepravylni administratyvni dii
неправильні адміністративні
дії *n.* maladministration
nepravylnist неправильність *n.*
irregularity
nepravylno неправильно *adv.*
wrong
nepravylno adresuvaty
неправильно адресувати *v.t.*
misdirect
nepravylno tlumachyty
неправильно тлумачити *v.t.*
misconstrue
nepravylno zrozumity
неправильно зрозуміти *v.t.*
misunderstand
nepravylnyi неправильний *a*
anomalous
nepravylnyi неправильний *a*
erroneous
nepravylnyi неправильний *a.*
illegitimate
nepriamyi непрямий *a.* indirect
neprofesiinyi непрофесійний *a.*
lay
neprokhidnist непрохідність *n.*
obstruction
neprokhidnyi непрохідний *a.*
impassable
nepromokalnyi непромокальний
a. watertight
nepronyknyi непроникний *a*
proof
neprozorist непрозорість *n.*
opacity
neprozoryi непрозорий *a.*
opaque
nepryborkanyi неприборканий *a.*
indomitable
neprydatnyi непридатний *a.*
inapplicable
nepryiazn неприязнь *n* dislike

nepryiaznyi неприязний *a.*
inimical
nepryiemnist неприємність *n.*
nuisance
nepryiemno volohyi неприємно
вологий *adj.* dank
nepryiemnyi неприємний *a.*
disagreeable
nepryiemnyi неприємний *a.*
obnoxious
nepryiemnyi неприємний *a.*
wicked
nepryiemnyi zvuk неприємний
звук *n.* jar
nepryiniattia неприйняття *n.*
rejection
neprykhovanyi неприхований *a.*
obvious
neprykhylnist неприхильність *a.*
indisposed
neprykhylnyi неприхильний *a.*
averse
neprykhylnyi неприхильний *a.*
reluctant
neprymyrennyi непримиренний
a. irreconcilable
neprypustymyi неприпустимий
a. inadmissible
neprytomnist непритомність *n.*
swoon
neprytomnity непритомніти *v.i*
swoon
Neptun Нептун *n.* Neptune
nepysmennyi неписьменний *a.*
illiterate
nepytushcha liudyna непитуща
людина *n.* teetotaller
nepytushchyi непитущий *a.*
teetotal
neratsionalnyi нераціональний
a. irrational
nerazni obrysy неразні обриси
n blur

nerehuliarnyi нерегулярний *a.*
irregular
nerehuliarnyi нерегулярний *a.*
occasional
nerishuchist нерішучість *n.*
indecision
nerishuchyi нерішучий *n.* shilly-
shally
nerivnist нерівність *n* disparity
neroba нероба *n.* idler
nerozbirlyvo pysaty
нерозбірливо писати *v.t.* scrawl
nerozbirlyvyi нерозбірливий *a.*
indiscriminate
nerozchynnyi нерозчинний *n.*
insoluble
nerozdilnyi нероздільний *a.*
inseparable
nerozsudlyvist нерозсудливість
n. imprudence
nerozsudlyvyi нерозсудливий *a*
foolish
nerozumnyi нерозумний *a.*
witless
nerukhomist нерухомість *n.*
stillness
nerukhomyi нерухомий *a.*
motionless
nerushymyi нерушимий *a.*
imperishable
Nerv Нерв *n.* Nerve
nervovyi нервовий *a.* nervous
nerzhaviiuchyi нержавіючий *a.*
stainless
neshchadnyi нещадний *a.*
ruthless
neshchaslyvyi нещасливий *a.*
unhappy
neshchasnyi нещасний *a* forlorn
neshchasnyi нещасний *a.*
unfortunate
neshchasnyi vypadok нещасний
випадок *n.* misadventure

neshchasnyi vypadok нещасний випадок *n.* mishap
neshchastia нещастя *n.* tribulation
neshchyrist нещирість *n.* insincerity
neshchyryi нещирий *a.* insincere
neskhozhyi несхожий *a* dissimilar
neskhozhyi na несхожий на *a* unlike
neskhvalennia несхвалення *n* disapproval
neskhvalennia несхвалення *n.* objection
neskinchennist нескінченність *n.* infinity
neskinchennyi нескінченний *a.* interminable
neskinchennyi нескінченний *a.* perpetual
neskladnist нескладність *n* facility
neskorochenyi нескорочений *a.* full
neskromne нескромне *a.* immodest
neskromnist нескромність *n.* immodesty
neskromnyi нескромний *a.* indiscreet
neslukhnianyi неслухняний *a.* naughty
nesmachnyi несмачний *a.* insipid
nespliachyi несплячий *a.* wakeful
nespodivanka несподіванка *n.* sudden
nespokii неспокій *n* botheration
nespokiinyi неспокійний *a.* uneasy
nespravedlyvyi несправедливий *a* crook
nespravnyi несправний *a.* wrong

nespromozhnist неспроможність *n.* bankruptcy
nespryiatlyvyi несприятливий *a* adverse
nespryiniatlyvist несприйнятливість *n.* immunity
nestabilnyi нестабільний *adj.* astatic
nestacha нестача *n.* lack
nestalist несталість *n.* instability
nestandartnyi нестандартний *a.* outsize
nestatky нестатки *n.* hardship
nesterpnyi нестерпний *a.* insupportable
nesterpnyi нестерпний *a.* repugnant
nesterpnyi bil нестерпний біль *n.* throe
nestiamnyi нестямний *a.* rampant
nestiikist нестійкість *n.* insistence
nestravnyi нестравний *a.* indigestible
nesty нести *v. t* bring
nestyhlyi нестиглий *a.* immature
nestyhlyi нестиглий *a.* verdant
nesumlinnist несумлінність *n.* dishonesty
nesumlinnyi несумлінний *a.* malafide
nesuvoryi несуворий *a.* mild
nesvidomyi несвідомий *a.* automatic
nesvoiechasnyi несвоєчасний *a.* injudicious
netaktovnyi нетактовний *a* clumsy
neterpymist нетерпимість *n.* impatience
neterpymyi нетерпимий *a.* intolerant
netochnyi неточний *a.* inexact

netolerantnist нетолерантність *n.* intolerance
netri нетрі *n.* slum
neuperedzhenist неупередженість *n.* impartiality
neuperedzhenyi неупереджений *a.* impartial
neuspikh неуспіх *n* failure
neutstvo неуцтво *n.* ignorance
neuvazhnyi неуважний *a.* inattentive
nevarenyi неварений *a.* raw
nevblahannyi невблаганний *a.* inexorable
nevdacha невдача *n.* mischance
nevdacha невдача *n.* misfortune
nevdachlyvyi невдачливий *a.* luckless
nevdakha невдаха *n* underdog
nevdalyi невдалий *a.* maladroit
nevdiachnist невдячність *n.* ingratitude
nevdiachnyi невдячний *a.* thankless
nevdovolenist невдоволеність *n* displeasure
nevdovolennia невдоволення *n* dissatisfaction
nevelyka kilkist невелика кількість *n.* little
nevelykyi невеликий *a.* small
nevhaslyi невгаслий *a.* living
nevianuchyi нев'янучий *a.* perennial
nevidchutnyi невідчутний *a.* intangible
nevidomist невідомість *n.* obscurity
nevidpovidalnyi невідповідальний *a.* irresponsible
nevidpovidnist невідповідність *n.* maladjustment

nevidpovidnyi невідповідний *a.* improper
nevidstupnyi невідступний *a.* relentless
nevirno невірно *adv.* amiss
nevirno nazyvaty невірно називати *v.t.* miscall
nevirnyi невірний *a.* incorrect
nevlovymyi невловимий *a* elusive
nevmilo pratsiuvaty невміло працювати *v. t* bungle
nevmilyi невмілий *a.* incapable
nevpynnyi невпинний ~*a.* ceaseless
nevroloh невролог *n.* neurologist
nevrolohiia неврологія *n.* neurology
nevroz невроз *n.* neurosis
nevtrymnyi невтримний *adv.* headlong
nevvichlyvyi неввічливий *a.* impolite
nevybahlyvyi невибагливий *a.* lowly
nevydymyi невидимий *a.* invisible
nevyhadlyvyi невигадливий *a.* plain
nevyhnutyi невигнутий *a.* straight
nevylikovnyi невиліковний *a.* incurable
nevymovnyi невимовний *a.* nefandous
nevynnist невинність *n.* innocence
nevypravnyi невиправний *a.* incorrigible
nevyznachenist невизначеність *n.* vagueness
nevyznachenyi невизначений *a.* indefinite

nevyznachenyi artykl невизначений артикль *art* an
nevzhe невже *adv.* indeed
nezabarom незабаром *adv.* shortly
nezadovilnyi незадовільний *a.* insufficient
nezadovolenist незадоволеність *n* discontent
nezadovolenyi незадоволений *a.* malcontent
nezaimana незаймана *n.* virgin
nezaimanist незайманість *n.* virginity
nezaimanyi незайманий *a.* intact
nezainiatyi незайнятий *a.* idle
nezakhyshchenyi незахищений *a.* indefensible
nezakonne pryvlasnennia незаконне привласнення *n.* misappropriation
nezakonnyi незаконний *a.* illegal
nezalezhnist незалежність *n.* independence
nezalezhno незалежно *adv.* solo
nezalezhnyi незалежний *a.* irrespective
nezamizhnia незаміжня *a* maiden
nezaperechnyi незаперечний *a.* irrefutable
nezapliamovanyi незаплямований *a.* spotless
nezavershenyi незавершений *a.* imperfect
nezbahnenyi незбагнений *a.* marvellous
nezchyslennyi незчисленний *a.* countless
nezdatnist нездатність *n* disability
nezdatnist нездатність *n.* incapacity
nezdatnyi нездатний *a.* unable
nezdibnist нездібність *n.* inability

nezdiisnennist нездійсненність *n.* impracticability
nezdiisnennyi нездійсненний *a.* impracticable
nezdorovyi нездоровий *a.* unwell
nezduzhannia нездужання *n.* malaise
nezhrabnyi незграбний *a.* awkward
nezhyvyi неживий *a.* inanimate
nezlichenni незліченні *a.* incalculable
nezlichennyi незліченний *a* myriad
nezlichnyi незлічний *a.* innumerable
nezmirnyi незмірний *a.* immeasurable
neznachnist незначність *n.* insignificance
neznachnyi незначний *a.* puny
neznaiomets незнайомець *n.* stranger
neznannia незнання *n.* nescience
nezrilist незрілість *n.* immaturity
nezrilyi незрілий *adj* callow
nezrilyi незрілий *a.* puerile
nezrivniannyi незрівнянний *a.* nonpareil
nezrozumilyi незрозумілий *a.* inexplicable
nezruchnist незручність *n* discomfort
nezruchnyi незручний *a.* inconvenient
nezvazhaiuchy na незважаючи на *conj.* notwithstanding
nezviazno hovoryty незв'язно говорити *v.t.* maunder
nezviaznykh незв'язних *a.* incoherent
nezvychainist незвичайність *n.* singularity

nezzakonno pryvlasniuvaty незаконно привласнювати *v.t.* misappropriate

ni ні *a.* no

ni odyn ні один *adv.* none

niavkannia нявкання *n.* mew

niavkaty нявкати *v.i.* mew

nich ніч *n.* night

nichnyi нічний *a.* nocturnal

nichnyi metelyk нічний метелик *n.* moth

nichoho нічого *adv.* nothing

nide ніде *adv.* nowhere

nihilizm нігілізм *n.* nihilism

nihot ніготь *n.* nail

niiakyi ніякий *adv.* no

nikchema нікчема *n.* nonentity

nikchema нікчема *n.* nought

nikel нікель *n.* nickel

nikhto ніхто *pron.* nobody

nikoly ніколи *adv.* never

nikotyn нікотин *n.* nicotine

nimb німб *n.* nimbus

nimfa німфа *n.* nymph

nimyi німий *a* dumb

nis ніс *n.* nose

nisenitnyi нісенітний *a.* nonsensical

nisenitnyi нісенітний *a.* quarrelsome

nisenitnytsia нісенітниця *n.* nonsense

nisha ніша *n.* niche

nishcho ніщо *n.* zero

niuans нюанс *n.* nuance

niukh нюх *n.* smell

niukhaty нюхати *v.t.* smell

nivechyty нівечити *v.t.* mutilate

nizdria ніздря *n.* nostril

nizh ніж *n.* knife

nizhno vorkuvaty ніжно воркувати *v. i* coo

nizhnyi ніжний *n.* soft

nizhnyi ніжний *a* tender

nizhytysia ніжитися *v.i.* loll

nochnushka ночнушка *n.* nightie

noha нога *n* foot

noha нога *n.* leg

nomenklatura номенклатура *n.* nomenclature

nomer номер *n.* number

nominal номінал *n.* par

nominalnyi номінальний *a.* nominal

nora нора *n* burrow

norka норка *n.* mink

norma норма *n.* norm

norma норма *n.* regulation

normalizuvaty нормалізувати *v.t.* normalize

normalnist нормальність *n.* normalcy

normalnyi нормальний *a.* normal

normalnyi нормальний *a.* sane

normuvannia нормування *n.* measurement

norovlyvyi норовливий *a.* restive

nosha ноша *n* burden

noshi ноші *n.* litter

nosok носок *n.* toe

nosorih носоріг *n.* rhinoceros

nosova kistka носова кістка *n* nasal

nosovychok носовичок *n.* handkerchief

nosovyi носовий *a.* nasal

nostalhiia ностальгія *n.* nostalgia

nosyk носик *n.* spout

nosylky носилки *n.* sedan

nosylky носилки *n.* stretcher

nosylnyk носильник *n.* carrier

nosytysia носитися *v.i* scamper

notarius нотаріус *n.* notary

novator новатор *n.* innovator

novitnii новітній *a.* up-to-date

novonavernenyi новонавернений *n* convert
novovvedennia нововведення *n.* innovation
novyi новий *a.* novel
novyi protektor новий протектор *n.* retread
novynka новинка *n.* novelty
novyny новини *n.* news
novyny новини *n. pl.* tidings
nozhnyi braslet ножний браслет *n* anklet
nozhytsi ножиці *n.* scissors
nozhytsi ножиці *n. pl.* shears
nudha нудьга *n.* tedium
nudnyi нудний *a.* lifeless
nudota нудота *n.* nausea
nudotnyi нудотний *a.* mawkish
nudyty нудити *v.t.* vomit
nudytysia нудитися *v.i.* pine
nul нуль *n.* nil
nulovyi нульовий *a.* null
numeruvaty storinky нумерувати сторінки *v.t.* page
nutroshchi нутрощі *n.* entrails
nuzhda нужда *n* distress
nyshchivnyi udar нищівний удар *n* smash
nyshporyty нишпорити *v.i.* fumble
nytka нитка *n.* thread
nytsyi ниций *a.* low
nyzhche нижче *adv* below
nyzhche нижче *prep* below
nyzhche нижче *v.t.* lower
nyzhchyi нижчий *a* under
nyzhnia spidnytsia нижня спідниця *n.* petticoat
nyzhnii нижній *a.* nether
nyzkopoklonstvo низькопоклонство *n.* sycophancy
nyzkyi низький *a.* ignoble

nyzkyi низький *a.* short
nyzyna низина *n.* low

oazys оазис *n.* oasis
**ob`iekt** об`єкт *n.* object
**ob`iekt zazdroshchiv** об`єкт заздрощів *n* envy
**ob`iekt znevahy** об`єкт зневаги *n.* scorn
**ob`iem** об`єм *n.* volume
obbyty оббити *v.t.* stud
obbyvka оббивка *n.* padding
obchyslennia обчислення *n.* calculation
obchysliuvaty обчислювати *v.t.* rate
obdarovanyi обдарований *a.* gifted
obdumanyi обдуманий *a* deliberate
obdyraty обдирати *v.t.* peel
obdyraty обдирати *v.t.* rook
obdyvliatysia обдивлятися *v.t.* survey
oberezhnist обережність *n.* safeguard
oberezhnyi обережний *adj.* circumspect
oberezhnyi обережний *a.* watchful
oberihaty оберігати *v.t.* reserve
oberihaty оберігати *v.t.* retain
obernuty обернути *v.t.* wrap
obertalnyi обертальний *a.* rotary
obertannia обертання *n.* rotation
obertaty обертати *v.t.* reverse
obertatysia обертатися *v.i.* revolve
obez- обез- *pref.* be
obezholovyty обезголовити *v. t.* behead

obezzbroiuvaty обеззброювати *v. t* disarm

obgruntovanyi обґрунтований *a.* reasonable

obgruntovuvaty обґрунтовувати *v.t.* substantiate

obhorodzhuvaty tynom обгороджувати тином *v.t* hurdle2

obhortka обгортка *n* wrap

obhovorennia обговорення *n.* counsel

obhovoriuvaty обговорювати *v. i* deliberate

obhovoriuvaty обговорювати *v. t.* discuss

obid обід *n.* lunch

obid обід *n.* rim

obidaty обідати *v.i.* lunch

obiednannia об'єднання *n.* unification

obiednanyi об'єднаний *a.* incorporate

obiednuvaty об'єднувати *v.t.* unite

obiekt об'єкт *n.* target

obiektyvnyi об'єктивний *a.* objective

obiemystyi об'ємистий *a.* voluminous

obiiednannia обйєднання *n* rally

obiimatysia обійматися *v.t.* pet

obiimy обійми *n* embrace

obiiniaty обійняти *v. t.* embrace

obitnytsia обітниця *n.* vow

obitsianka обіцянка *n* promise

obitsiaty обіцяти *v.t* promise

obiznanyi обізнаний *a.* adept

obiznanyi обізнаний *a.* proficient

obkhid обхід *n* bypass

obkhodyty обходити *v.t.* skirt

obkladannia обкладання *n.* assessment

obkladaty обкладати *v.t.* levy

obkladaty podatkom обкладати податком *v.t.* geld

obkraiaty обкраяти *v.t.* lop

oblachaty облачати *v.t.* robe

obladnannia обладнання *n* equipment

oblahorodzhuvaty облагороджувати *v.t* dignify

oblast область *n* domain

obliahaty облягати *v. t* besiege

obliamovuvaty облямовувати *v.t* fringe

oblihatsiia облігація *n.* obligation

obliteratsiia облітерація *n.* obliteration

obloha облога *n.* siege

obluda облуда *n* deception

oblychchia обличчя *n.* countenance

oblyzuvannia облизування *n* lick

obman обман *n.* imposture

obmaniuvaty обманювати *v.t.* juggle

obmanshchyk обманщик *n.* impostor

obmazuvaty обмазувати *v. t.* daub

obmezhennia обмеження *n.* infringement

obmezhennia обмеження *n.* restriction

obmezhenyi обмежений *adj.* borne

obmezhuvalnyi обмежувальний *a.* restrictive

obmezhuvaty обмежувати *v. t* confine

obmezhuvaty обмежувати *v.t.* straiten

obmin обмін *n* exchange

obmin rechovyn обмін речовин *n.* metabolism

obminiuvaty обмінювати *v. t* exchange

obminiuvatysia обмінюватися *v.* interchange

obmirkovuvaty обмірковувати *v. t* consider

obmirkovuvaty обмірковувати *v.t.* premeditate

obmotaty обмотати *v.t.* wind

obmovliaty обмовляти *v.t.* backbite

obmundyruvannia обмундирування *n* clothing

obmundyruvannia обмундирування *n.* outfit

obmundyruvaty обмундирувати *v.t* outfit

obmyvannia обмивання *n* ablution

obnosyty rovom обносити ровом *v.t.* moat

obnosyty stinoiu обносити стіною *v.t.* wall

obolonka оболонка *n.* shell

oborka оборка *n.* frill

oborona оборона *adv.* defensive

oboroniaty обороняти *v. t* defend

oboronozdatnyi обороноздатний *a.* tenable

oborotna storona оборотна сторона *n* reverse

oborotnyi оборотний *a.* negotiable

oboviazkovyi обов'язковий *a* compulsory

obozhniuvannia обожнювання *n.* adoration

obozhniuvanyi обожнюваний *a.* adorable

obozhniuvaty обожнювати *v.t.* adore

obpaliuvaty обпалювати *v.t.* singe

obramovuvaty обрамовувати *v.t.* frame

obraty обрати *v. t* elect

obraz образ *n.* image

obraza образа *n* hurt

obraza образа *n.* snub

obrazhaty ображати *v.t.* abuse

obrazhaty ображати *v.t.* offend

obrazlyve hluzuvannia образливе глузування *n* taunt

obrazlyvyi образливий *a.* touchy

obrazyty образити *v.t.* affront

obriad обряд *n.* rite

obrobka обробка *n* manufacture

obrobliaty обробляти *v. t* cultivate

obrubok обрубок *n.* stump

obrubuvaty обрубувати *v.t* stump

obruchyty обручити *v. t* betroth

obrys обрис *n.* outline

observatoriia обсерваторія *n.* observatory

obshyvaty paneliamy обшивати панелями *v.t.* panel

obsiah обсяг *n* bulk

obsluhovuvannia обслуговування *n.* service

obsluhovuvaty обслуговувати *v.t* service

obstanovka обстановка *n.* furniture

obstavliaty обставляти *v.t.* furnish

obstavyna обставина *n* circumstance

obstavyny, shcho vypravdovuiut обставини, що виправдовують *n.* justification

obstriliuvaty artyleriiskym vohnem обстрілювати артилерійським вогнем *v. t.* cannonade

obstupaty обступати *v.t.* surround

obtiazhenyi обтяжений *a.* fraught

obtiazhlyvyi обтяжливий *a*
burdensome
obtiazhlyvyi обтяжливий *a.*
weighty
obtiazhuvaty обтяжувати *v. t*
burden
obtikannia обтікання *n.*
circumfluence
obtsukrovuvaty обцукровувати
v.t. sugar
obumovlenyi обумовлений *a*
conditional
obumovliuvaty обумовлювати *v.*
t. calumniate
oburennia обурення *n.*
indignation
oburenyi обурений *a.* indignant
oburiuvatysia обурюватися *v.t.*
resent
obval обвал *v. i* collapse
obvodyty обводити *v. t.* encircle
obvynuvach обвинувач *n.*
prosecutor
obvynuvachenyi обвинувачений
n. accused
obvynuvachyty обвинувачити
v.t. accuse
obvynuvalnyi akt обвинувальний
акт *n.* indictment
obvyvaty обвивати *v.t.* wreathe
obydva обидва *adj.* both
obzherlyvist обжерливість *n.*
gluttony
ocheret очерет *n.* rush
ochevydets очевидець *n.*
spectator
ochevydnyi очевидний *a.* evident
ochikuvannia очікування *n.*
expectation
ochikuvaty очікувати *v.i* abide
ochne yabluko очне яблуко *n*
eyeball
ochnyi очний *a.* ocular

ocholiuvaty очолювати *v.t.*
spearhead
ochyshchaty очищати *v. t* clear
ochyshchaty vid shkarlupy
очищати від шкарлупи *v.t.* shell
ochyshchatysia очищатися *v.t.*
purify
ochyshchennia очищення *n*
clearance
ochyshchennia kyshechnyka
очищення кишечника *n.*
purgation
ochysnyi очисний *a* purgative
ochysnyi zavod очисний завод
n. refinery
oda ода *n.* ode
oderzhuvach одержувач *n.*
receiver
oderzhuvach platezhu
одержувач платежу *n.* payee
oderzhuvaty одержувати *v.t.*
score
odiah одяг *n.* costume
odiahaty одягати *v.t.* bedight
odiahatysia одягатися *v.t* garb
odiiannia одіяння *n.* garb
odioznyi одіозний *a.* odious
odkrovennia одкровення *n.*
revelation
odnak однак *adv.* notwithstanding
odnakovyi однаковий *a* equal
odnakovyi однаковий *a.* same
odnochasnyi одночасний *a.*
simultaneous
odnomanitnyi одноманітний *a.*
monotonous
odnoridnyi однорідний *a.*
homogeneous
odnoskladove slovo
односкладове слово *n.*
monosyllable
odnoskladovyi односкладовий
a. monosyllabic

odnostainist одностайність *n.*
unanimity
odnostainyi одностайний *a.*
unanimous
odnostoronnii односторонній *a*
ex-parte
odr одр *n* bier
odruzhennia одруження *n.*
wedding
odruzhuvatysia одружуватися
v.t. marry
odruzhyty одружити *v.t.* wed
oduriuvaty одурювати *v.t.* trick
odurmaniuvaty одурманювати
v.t. intoxicate
odyn один *pron.* one
odyn odnoho один одного *pron.*
each
odynadtsiat одинадцять *n* eleven
odynychnyi одиничний *a.*
singular
odynytsia одиниця *n.* unit
ofis офіс *n.* office
ofitser офіцер *n.* officer
ofitsiant офіціант *n.* waiter
ofitsiantka офіціантка *n.* waitress
ofitsiine rozporiadzhennia
офіційне розпорядження *n.*
requisition
ofitsiino офіційно *adv.* officially
ofitsiino praznachuvaty
na posadu офіційно
празначувати на посаду *v.t.*
install
ofitsiino vvodyty na posadu
офіційно вводити на посаду *n.*
induction
ofitsiinyi офіційний *a.* official
ofitsioznyi офіціозний *a.* officious
ohirok огірок *n* cucumber
ohliad огляд *n* browse
ohliadaty оглядати *v.t.* review
ohlianuty оглянути *v.t.* view

ohlushaty оглушати *v.t.* stun
oholene tilo оголене тіло *n* nude
oholenyi оголений *a.* naked
oholiuvaty оголювати *v.t.* bare
oholoshennia оголошення *n.*
announcement
oholoshuvaty оголошувати *v.t.*
announce
oholoshuvaty оголошувати *v.t.*
publicize
oholoshuvaty poza zakonom
оголошувати поза законом *v.t.*
attaint
oholoshuvaty poza zakonom
оголошувати поза законом *v.t*
outlaw
ohornuty огорнути *v.t* mantle
ohorodzhuvaty огороджувати *v.t*
fence
ohorozha огорожа *n.* enclosure
ohortaty огортати *v. t* envelop
ohriadnyi огрядний *a* gross
ohuzok огузок *n.* rear
ohyda огида *n.* horror
ohydnyi огидний *a.* heinous
ohynaty огинати *v.t.* round
okean океан *n.* ocean
okeanichnyi океанічний *a.*
oceanic
okhainist охайність *n.* tidiness
okhainyi охайний *a.* tidy
okholodyty охолодити *v.t.*
refrigerate
okholodzhennia охолодження *n.*
refrigeration
okholodzhuvaty охолоджувати
v. i. cool
okhorona охорона *n.* guard
okhoronets охоронець *n.*
bodyguard
okhoroniaty охороняти *v.i.* guard
oklad оклад *n.* salary
oko око *n* ogle

oko око *n* eye
okolytsi околиці *n.* surroundings
okolytsia околиця *n.* outskirts
okozamyliuvannia
  окозамилювання *n* eyewash
okremo окремо *adv.* aside
okremyi окремий *a.* separate
okreslyty окреслити *v.t.* outline
okruh округ *n* district
oksamyt оксамит *n.* velvet
oktava октава *n.* octave
okulist окуліст *n.* oculist
okultnyi окультний *a.* occult
okun окунь *n.* perch
okupant окупант *n.* occupier
okynuty pohliadom окинути
  поглядом *v.i.* glance
olen олень *n* deer
oleniachyi rih оленячий ріг *n.*
  antler
oliharkhiia олігархія *n.* oligarchy
oliia олія *n.* oil
oliinytsia олійниця *n.* churn
olimpiada олімпіада *n.* olympiad
oliudniuvaty олюднювати *v.t.*
  humanize
olivets олівець *n.* pencil
olovo олово *n.* tin
olyvkovyi оливковий *n.* olive
omana омана *n* fallacy
omanlyvyi оманливий *adj*
  bimenasl
omar омар *n.* lobster
omeha омега *n.* omega
omela омела *n.* mistletoe
omlet омлет *n.* omelette
omolodzhennia омолодження *n.*
  rejuvenation
omolodzhuvatysia
  омолоджуватися *v.t.* rejuvenate
on tam он там *adv.* yonder
on toi он той *a.* yonder
onimilyi онімілий *a.* numb

onovlennia оновлення *n.* renewal
onovyty оновити *v.t.* refresh
opadaty опадати *v. t* diminish
opal опал *n.* opal
opera опера *n.* opera
operator оператор *n.* operator
operatsii операції *n.* interchange
operatsiia операція *n.* operation
operatyvnyi оперативний *a.*
  operative
operizuvaty оперізувати *v.t.*
  begird
opik опік *n* burn
opik опік *n* singe
opika опіка *v* custody
opikun опікун *n.* trustee
opir опір *n.* resistance
opir опір *n.* revolt
opium опіум *n.* opium
oplachuvaty оплачувати *v.t.*
  remunerate
oplakuvaty оплакувати *v. t* bewail
oplata оплата *n* pay
oplata pratsi оплата праці *n.*
  remuneration
oplesky оплески *n.* applause
oplot оплот *n.* support
opodatkovuvanyi
  оподатковуваний *a.* taxable
opodatkuvannia оподаткування
  n. taxation
opokhyle polozhennia опохиле
  положення *n.* tilt
oponent опонент *n.* opponent
opora опора *n* crutch
oportunizm опортунізм *n.*
  opportunism
opovidach оповідач *n.* teller
opovidannia оповідання *n.*
  narrative
opovidannia оповідання *n.* story
opovidaty оповідати *v.t.* narrate
opozytsiia опозиція *n.* opposition

opozytsioner опозиціонер *n*
malcontent
oprominiuvaty опромінювати *v.t.*
illuminate
oprotestuvannia опротестування
n. protestation
opryliudnyty оприлюднити *v. t*
divulge
optom оптом *adv.* wholesale
optova torhivlia оптова торгівля
n. wholesale
optovyi оптовий *a* wholesale
optovyk оптовик *n.* wholesaler
optsiia опція *n.* option
optsion опціон *n.* refusal
optychnyi оптичний *a.* optic
optyk оптик *n.* optician
optymalnyi оптимальний *a*
optimum
optymist оптиміст *n.* optimist
optymistychnyi оптимістичний *a.*
optimistic
optymizm оптимізм *n.* optimism
optymum оптимум *n.* optimum
opublikuvannia опублікування *n.*
publication
opuklist опуклість *n.* prominence
opuklyi опуклий *a* arch
opuskaty опускати *v.t.* avale
opustyty опустити *v.t.* omit
opys опис *n* description
opys опис *n.* portrait
opysovyi описовий *a* descriptive
opysuvaty описувати *v. t*
describe
opysuvaty описувати *v.t.* report
orach орач *n.* ploughman
orakul оракул *n.* oracle
oranzhereia оранжерея *n.*
greenery
orator оратор *n.* orator

oratorske mystetstvo
ораторське мистецтво *n.*
oratory
oratorskyi ораторський *a.*
oratorical
oraty орати *v.t.* plough
oraty орати *v.t.* till
orbita орбіта *n.* orbit
orda орда *n.* horde
order ордер *n.* warrant
orel орел *n* eagle
orenda оренда *n.* lease
orendar орендар *n.* tenant
orhan орган *n.* organ
orhanichne dobryvo органічне
добриво *n.* manure
orhanichnyi органічний *a.*
organic
orhanizatsiia організація *n.*
organization
orhanizm організм *n.* organism
orhanizuvaty організувати *v.t.*
organize
orhiia оргія *n* debauchery
oriientovnyi орієнтовний *a.*
tentative
oriientuvaty орієнтувати *v.t.*
orient
oriientuvatysia орієнтуватися *v.t.*
orientate
orkestr оркестр *n.* orchestra
orkestrovyi оркестровий *a.*
orchestral
ornament орнамент *n.* ornament
ornyi орний *adj* arable
ortodoksalnist ортодоксальність
n. orthodoxy
ortodoksalnyi ортодоксальний *a.*
orthodox
oryhinal оригінал *n* original
oryhinalnist оригінальність *n.*
originality
osa оса *n.* wasp

osel осел *n* donkey
oseledets оселедець *n.* herring
oselennia v seli оселення в селі *n.* rustication
oselia оселя *n* dwelling
oseredok осередок *n.* cell
oshchadlyvist ощадливість *n.* thrift
oshchadlyvyi ощадливий *a* economical
oshchadlyvyi ощадливий *a.* prudent
oshukanets ошуканець *n.* swindler
oshukuvannia ошукування *n.* swindle
oshukuvaty ошукувати *v.t.* swindle
osiazhnyi осяжний *a.* tangible
osichka осічка *n.* miss
osin осінь *n.* autumn
oskarzhuvaty оскаржувати *v. t* contest
oskolok осколок *n.* splinter
oskverniaty оскверняти *v.t.* profane
oslabliaty ослабляти *v.t.* abate
oslabliaty opir protyvnyka ослабляти опір противника *v.t.* soften
osliachyi ослячий *adj.* asinine
osnova основа *n.* base
osnovnyi основний *a* main
osnovnyi основний *a* staple
osnovnyi ton основний тон *n.* tonic
osnovy hromadianskosti основи громадянськості *n* civics
osoba особа *n.* wight
osoba, shcho daie harantiiu особа, що дає гарантію *n.* warrantor

osoba, shcho zaimaie posadu особа, що займає посаду *n.* incumbent
osoba, yaka zazhyla durnoi slavy особа, яка зажила дурної слави *n.* notoriety
osoba, yakii daietsia harantiia особа, якій дається гарантія *n.* warrantee
osoblyvist особливість *n.* peculiarity
osoblyvist особливість *n.* trait
osoblyvo особливо *adv.* singularly
osoblyvyi особливий *a* especial
osobniak особняк *n.* mansion
osobovyi особовий *a* finite
osobystist особистість *n.* personality
osobysto особисто *adv.* bodily
osobystyi особистий *a.* individual
ostannii останній *a.* recent
ostannim chasom останнім часом *adv.* lately
ostatochnyi остаточний *a* final
ostoron осторонь *adv.* aloof
ostriv острів *n.* island
ostrivets острівець *n.* isle
ostrivnyi острівний *a.* insular
osud осуд *n* blame
osudnist осудність *n.* sanity
osudzhuvaty осуджувати *v. t.* censure
osushennia осушення *n* arefaction
osushuvaty осушувати *v. t* drain
osviachennia освячення *n.* sanctification
osviachuvaty освячувати *v.t.* sanctify
osvichenist освіченість *n.* accomplishment
osvichenyi освічений *a.* literate

osvidchennia освідчення *n.* proposal
osvita освіта *n* education
osvitlennia освітлення *n.* lightening
otochennia оточення *n.* milieu
otochuvaty оточувати *v. t* enclose
otochyty kiltsem оточити кільцем *v.t.* ring
otrotstvo отроцтво *n* boyhood
otruinist отруйність *n.* virulence
otruinyi отруйний *a.* poisonous
otruity отруїти *v.t.* poison
otruta отрута *n.* poison
otrymannia отримання *n.* receipt
otrymuvaty отримувати *v.t.* receive
otrymuvaty zadovolennia отримувати задоволення *v. t* enjoy
otset оцет *n.* vinegar
otsiniuvaty оцінювати *v.t.* price
otsinka оцінка *n.* appreciation
otvir отвір *n.* aperture
ovalnyi овальний *a.* oval
ovatsiia овація *n.* ovation
Oven Овен *n* aries
overdraft овердрафт *n.* overdraft
oves овес *n.* oat
ovoch овоч *n.* vegetable
ovochevyi овочевий *a.* vegetable
ovolodity soboiu оволодіти собою *v.t.* rally
ovolodivaty оволодівати *v.t.* possess
ozbroiennia озброєння *n.* armament
ozbroiuvaty озброювати *v.t.* arm
ozdoblennia оздоблення *n.* ornamentation
ozdoblennia оздоблення *n* trim
ozdobliuvaty оздоблювати *v.t.* ornament

ozero озеро *n.* lake
ozhyrinnia ожиріння *n.* obesity
ozhyvliaty оживляти *v. t.* enliven
ozhyvyty оживити *v.t.* animate
ozlobliaty озлобляти *v. t* embitter
oznachaty означати *v.i.* matter
oznaiomyty ознайомити *v.t.* initiate
oznaka ознака *n* feature
oznaka ознака *n.* omen

pachka пачка *n* batch
padaty падати *v.i.* fall
padaty nyts падати ниць *v.t.* prostrate
padinnia падіння *n* fall
padliuka падлюка *n.* scoundrel
pafos пафос *n.* pathos
pahin пагін *n* sprout
pahoda пагода *n.* pagoda
pahorb пагорб *n.* hill
pai пай *n.* share
paket пакет *n.* packet
pakhnuty пахнути *v.i.* smack
pakhta пахта *n* buttermilk
pakt пакт *n.* pact
pakuvalnyk пакувальник *n.* wrapper
palaiuchyi палаючий *adv.* ablaze
palaiuchyi палаючий *adv.* aglow
palankin паланкін *n.* palanquin
palatka палатка *n* booth
palats палац *n.* palace
palatsovyi палацовий *a.* palatial
palaty палати *v.i* blaze
palets палець *n* finger
palia паля *n.* pile
palia паля *n.* stilt
palitra палітра *n.* palette
palkist палкість *n* fervour

palko bazhaty палко бажати *v.t.* crave

palkyi палкий *a.* ardent

palma пальма *n.* palm

palomnyk паломник *n.* pilgrim

palomnytstvo паломництво *n.* pilgrimage

palto пальто *n* coat

paluba палуба *n* deck

palychka паличка *n.* wand

palytsia палиця *n.* stick

palyty палити *v.t.* scorch

palyvo паливо *n.* fuel

pamflet памфлет *n.* pamphlet

pamfletyst памфлетист *n.* pamphleteer

pamiat пам'ять *n.* memory

pamiataty пам'ятати *v.t.* mind

pamiatnyi пам'ятний *a.* memorable

pamiatnyk пам'ятник *n.* monument

pan пан *n.* lord

panatseia панацея *n.* panacea

panchishni vyroby панчішні вироби *n.* hosiery

panehiryk панегірик *n.* panegyric

panel панель *n.* panel

pani пані *n.* mistress

panichna vtecha панічна втеча *n.* stampede

panichno tikaty панічно тікати *v.i* stampede

panika паніка *n.* panic

paniruvaty панірувати *v. t. & i* breaden

panorama панорама *n.* panorama

panorama панорама *n.* prospect

panskyi панський *a.* lordly

panteist пантеїст *n.* pantheist

panteizm пантеїзм *n.* pantheism

pantera пантера *n.* panther

pantomima пантоміма *n.* pantomime

panuvannia панування *n* domination

panuvannia панування *n.* prevalence

panuvaty панувати *v.t.* rule

paperovyi zmii паперовий змій *n.* kite

papir папір *n.* paper

papliuzhyty паплюжити *v.t.* slander

papliuzhyty паплюжити *v.t.* violate

papskyi папський *a.* papal

papstvo папство *n.* papacy

papuha папуга *n.* parrot

par пар *n* steam

para пара *n* couple

para пара *n.* pair

parad парад *n.* parade

paradoks парадокс *n.* paradox

paradoksalnyi парадоксальний *a.* paradoxical

parafin парафін *n.* paraffin

parafraz парафраз *n.* paraphrase

parahon парагон *n.* paragon

parahraf параграф *n.* item

paralelizm паралелізм *n.* parallelism

paralelnyi паралельний *a.* parallel

paralelohram паралелограм *n.* parallelogram

paralich параліч *n.* paralysis

paralitychnyi паралітичний *a.* paralytic

paralizuvaty паралізувати *v.t.* paralyse

parashut парашут *n.* parachute

parashutyst парашутист *n.* parachutist

parasolka парасолька *n.* umbrella

parazyt паразит *n.* parasite

parazytnyi паразитний *a.* spurious

parcha парча *n* brocade

pari парі *n.* wager

pariia парія *n.* leper

park парк *n.* park

parkan паркан *n* fence

parkuvaty паркувати *v.t.* park

parlament парламент *n.* parliament

parlamentarii парламентарій *n.* parliamentarian

parlamentskyi парламентський *a.* parliamentary

parodiia пародія *n.* parody

parodiia пародія *n.* skit

parodiiuvaty пародіювати *v.t.* parody

parol пароль *n.* watchword

paroplav пароплав *n.* steamer

paropodibnyi пароподібний *a.* vaporous

parostok паросток *n.* sapling

parta парта *n* desk

partiia партія *n.* consignment

partner партнер *n.* partner

partnerstvo партнерство *n.* partnership

partyzan партизан *n.* guerilla

partyzaniv партизанів *a.* partisan

partyzanskyi партизанський *n.* partisan

parusyna парусина *n.* canvas

paryruvannia парирування *n.* parry

paryruvaty парирувати *v.t.* parry

parytet паритет *n.* parity

paryty парити *v.i.* soar

pasazhyr пасажир *n.* passenger

pasha паша *v.t.* pasture

pasika пасіка *n.* apiary

paskvil пасквіль *n.* libel

pasmo пасмо *n* strand

pasovyshchi пасовищі *n.* lea

pasovyshchi пасовищі *n.* pasture

pasport паспорт *n.* passport

pasta паста *n.* paste

pastelnyi пастельний *n.* pastel

pastka пастка *n.* snare

pastoralnyi пасторальний *a.* pastoral

pastukh пастух *n.* herdsman

pastva паства *n.* sheep

pasty пасти *v.i.* graze

pasyvnyi пасивний *a.* passive

patent патент *n* patent

patentovanyi патентований *a.* patent

patentovanyi zasob патентований засіб *n.* nostrum

patentuvaty патентувати *v.t.* patent

patetychnyi патетичний *a.* pathetic

patly патли *n.* manes

patoka патока *n* molasses

patriot патріот *n.* patriot

patriotychnyi патріотичний *a.* patriotic

patriotyzm патріотизм *n.* patriotism

patron патрон *n.* cartridge

patronazh патронаж *n.* patronage

patrul патруль *n* patrol

patruliuvaty патрулювати *v.i.* patrol

patsiient пацієнт *n* patient

pauza пауза *n.* pause

pava пава *n.* peahen

pavilion павільйон *n.* pavilion

pavuk павук *n.* spider

pavutyna павутина *n* cobweb

pavutynnyi павутинний *a.* webby

pavych павич *n.* peacock
paz паз *n.* notch
pazur пазур *n* claw
pechal печаль *n.* sorrow
pechatka печатка *n.* seal
pechenia печеня *n* roast
pechera печера *n.* cave
pechinka печінка *n.* liver
pechyvo печиво *n* biscuit
pedahoh педагог *n.* pedagogue
pedahohika педагогіка *n.* pedagogy
pedal педаль *n.* pedal
pedant педант *n.* pedant
pedantychnist педантичність *n.* pedantry
pedantychnyi педантичний *n.* pedantic
pederast педераст *n.* sodomite
pekar пекар *n.* baker
pekarnia пекарня *n* bakery
pekelnyi пекельний *a.* infernal
peklo пекло *a.* hell
pekty пекти *v.t.* bake
pekuchyi пекучий *a.* hot
pekuchyi bil пекучий біль *n* smart
peliustka пелюстка *n.* petal
pelka пелька *n* yap
penka пенька *n.* hemp
penni пенні *n.* penny
pensiia пенсія *n.* pension
pensioner пенсіонер *n.* pensioner
penzlyk пензлик *n* brush
perchyty перчити *v.t.* pepper
perebilshennia перебільшення *n.* exaggeration
perebilshuvaty перебільшувати *v.t.* amplify
perebilshuvaty перебільшувати *v. t.* exaggerate
perebuvannia перебування *n* stay

perebyty tsinu перебити ціну *v.t.* outbid
peredacha передача *n.* transmission
peredaty передати *v.t* hand
peredavach передавач *n.* transmitter
peredavaty передавати *v.t* forward
peredavaty po radio передавати по радіо *v.t.* radio
peredavaty po telebachenniu передавати по телебаченню *v.t.* telecast
peredavaty v suborendu передавати в суборенду *v.t.* sublet
peredbachaty передбачати *v.t* forestall
peredbachennia передбачення *n.* foreknowledge
peredbachennia передбачення *n.* prescience
peredbachlyvist передбачливість *n* forethought
peredbachlyvyi передбачливий *a.* cautious
peredbachuvanyi передбачуваний *a.* would-be
peredbachyty передбачити *v.t.* anticipate
peredbachyty передбачити *v.t* foresee
peredchasnyi передчасний *a.* premature
peredchasnyi передчасний *a.* previous
peredchuttia передчуття *n.* premonition
peredchuvaty передчувати *v.t.* apprehend
peredmistia передмістя *n.* suburb

peredmova передмова *n* foreword

perednia lapa передня лапа *n* foreleg

perednii передній *a* front

peredovyi передовий *a* foremost

peredovyi передовий *a.* forward

peredovytsia передовиця *n* editorial

peredozuvannia передозування *n.* overdose

peredplichchia передпліччя *n* forearm

peredrukovuvaty передруковувати *v.t.* reprint

peredshliubnyi передшлюбний *a.* premarital

peredumova передумова *n.* presupposition

pereduvaty передувати *v.t.* antecede

peredvishchaty передвіщати *v.t.* portend

peredzvin передзвін *n.* jingle

perehaniaty переганяти *v.t.* still

perehaniaty litaky переганяти літаки *v.t* ferry

perehliad перегляд *n.* revision

perehliadaty переглядати *v.t.* revise

perehlianuty переглянути *v.t.* peruse

perehovory переговори *n.* negotiation

perehovory переговори *n.* parley

perehravaty перегравати *v.t.* overact

pereimaty переймати *v.t.* adopt

perekazuvaty переказувати *v.t.* paraphrase

perekhid перехід *n.* trek

perekhidnyi перехідний *n.* transitive

perekhidnyi period перехідний період *n.* transition

perekhopliuvannia перехоплювання *n.* interception

perekhopyty перехопити *v.t.* intercept

perekhrestia перехрестя *n.* intersection

perekhytryty перехитрити *v.t.* outwit

pereklad переклад *n.* translation

perekladach перекладач *n.* interpreter

perekladnyi перекладний *a.* transferable

perekladyna перекладина *n.* girder

perekladyny перекладини *n.* rung

pereklychka перекличка *n.* roll-call

pereklyk переклик *n* muster

perekonanist переконаність *n* conviction

perekonannia переконання *n.* persuasion

perekonanyi переконаний *a* earnest

perekonanyi kholostiak переконаний холостяк *n* agamist

perekonaty переконати *v. t* convince

perekonlyvyi переконливий *adj.* cogent

perekonuvaty переконувати *v.i.* dehort

perekonuvaty переконувати *v.t.* reassure

perekruchuvaty перекручувати *v.t.* sophisticate

perekryttia перекриття *n* overlap

perekryvaty перекривати *v.t.*
overlap
perekydannia перекидання *n.*
somersault
perekydaty перекидати *v.t.*
overthrow
perekydatysia перекидатися *v. i.*
capsize
pereliakanyi переляканий *a.*
afraid
perelit переліт *n* flight
pereliub перелюб *n.* adulteration
pereliubstvuvaty
перелюбствувати *v.t.*
adulterate
perelyvannia переливання *n.*
supervision
perelyvatysia cherez krai
переливатися через край *v.t*
overrun
peremahaty перемагати *v.t.*
vanquish
peremezhovuvaty
перемежовувати *v.t.* punctuate
peremishchaty переміщати *v.t.*
shift
peremishchennia переміщення
n. permutation
peremizhnyi переміжний *a.*
alternate
peremoha перемога *n.* victory
peremohty перемогти *v. t.* defeat
peremohty перемогти *v.t.* worst
peremozhets переможець *n.*
victor
peremozhnyi переможний *a.*
victorious
peremychky перемички *n.* lintel
peremykach перемикач *n.* switch
peremykaty перемикати *v. t*
commute
peremyria перемир'я *n.* truce

perenesennia перенесення *n.*
transfer
perenesty перенести *v.* born
perenosnyi переносний *a.*
portable
perenosyty переносити *v.t* bear
pereobtiazhuvaty
переобтяжувати *v.t.*
overburden
pereotsiniuvaty переоцінювати
v.t. overrate
perepel перепел *n.* quail
pereplutaty переплутати *v.t.* mull
perepochynok перепочинок *v.t.*
bait
perepolokh переполох *v.i.* stir
perepona перепона *n.* obstacle
perepovnenyi переповнений *a.*
replete
pereprava переправа *n* ferry
perepravliaty переправляти *v. t.*
convey
perepustka перепустка *n.* permit
perepys перепис *n.* census
perepysuvaty переписувати *v. t.*
enumerate
pererobliaty переробляти *v.t.*
alter
pererobliaty переробляти *v. t.*
change
pererva перерва *n.* interruption
perervaty перервати *v.i* abort
pereryvaty переривати *v.t.*
interrupt
pereryvchastyi переривчастий
a fitful
peresadzhuvaty пересаджувати
v.t graft
pereselennia переселення *n.*
transmigration
pereseliaty переселяти *v.t.*
transplant

pereseliatysia переселятися *v.i.*
trek
pereshkoda перешкода *n*
drawback
pereshkodzhaiuchyi
перешкоджаючий *a.*
obstructive
pereshkodzhaty перешкоджати
v.i. interfere
pereshkodzhaty перешкоджати
v.t. thwart
peresidaty пересідати *v.t.*
transfer
peresliduvannia переслідування
n. pursuance
peresliduvaty переслідувати *v.t.*
victimize
peresliduvaty v sudovomu
poriadku переслідувати
в судовому порядку *v.t.*
prosecute
perestaratysia перестаратися *v.t.*
overdo
perestavaty переставати *v. i.*
cease
perestrilka перестрілка *n.*
skirmish
perestromliuvaty
перестромлювати *v.t.* spike
perestupaty переступати *v.t.*
transgress
peresuvannia пересування *n.*
movement
peresuvaty пересувати *v.t.* shunt
peresuvatysia пересуватися *v.t*
ambulate
peresuvatysia kolonoiu
пересуватися колоною *v.i.* file
peresyliuvaty пересилювати *v.t.*
overpower
peresyliuvaty пересилювати *v.t.*
overrule
perets перець *n.* pepper

perets chervonyi перець
червоний *n* capsicum
perets hostryi перець гострий *n.*
chilli
peretvorennia перетворення *n.*
reduction
peretvoriuvaty перетворювати *v.*
t convert
peretvoriuvaty na ridynu
перетворювати на рідину *v.t.*
liquefy
peretvoriuvaty v hotivku
перетворювати в готівку *v. t.*
cash
peretvoriuvatysia
перетворюватися *v.t.* pivot
peretvoriuvatysia na otset
перетворюватися на оцет *v.*
acetify
peretvoryty na miaku masu
перетворити на м'яку масу *v.t.*
pulp
peretyn перетин *n.* crossing
peretynaty перетинати *v. t* cross
peretynatysia перетинатися *v.t.*
intersect
perevaha перевага *n.* advantage
perevaha перевага *n* start
perevaliuvannia перевалювання
n. preponderance
perevaliuvaty перевалювати *v.i.*
preponderate
perevantazhennia
перевантаження *n* overload
perevantazhuvaty
перевантажувати *v.t.* overload
perevariuvaty переварювати *v.*
t. digest
perevazhannia переважання *n.*
predominance
perevazhaty переважати *v.i.*
predominate

perevazhuvaty переважувати *v.t.*
outweigh
perevernutyi перевернутий *a.*
topsy turvy
perevershuvaty перевершувати
v.t. out-balance
perevershuvaty chyselno
перевершувати чисельно *v.t.*
outnumber
perevershyty перевершити *v.t.*
outdo
perevertaty перевертати *v.t.*
invert
perevertaty перевертати *v.t.*
subvert
perevezennia перевезення *n.*
cartage
pereviriaty перевіряти *v.t.*
validate
pereviriaty zvitnist перевіряти
звітність *v.t.* audit
perevirka перевірка *n.* verification
pereviryty перевірити *v.t.* verify
perevizny zasoby перевізни
засоби *n* conveyance
perevodyty переводити *v.t.*
translate
perevorot переворот *n.* upheaval
perevozyty перевозити *v.t.*
transport
perevtoma перевтома *n.*
overwork
perevtomliuvatysia
перевтомлюватися *v.i.*
overwork
perevydannia перевидання *n.*
reprint
perevyshchennia перевищення
n. surplus
perevyshchuvaty перевищувати
v.t exceed
perevyshchuvaty перевищувати
v.i excel

perevyshchuvaty перевищувати
v.t. top
perevytrachaty перевитрачати
v.t. overdraw
perezariad перезаряд *n*
overcharge
perezariadzhaty перезаряджати
v.t. overcharge
perezhovuvaty пережовувати *v.t.*
masticate
perezhyty пережити *v.t.* outlive
perforuvaty перфорувати *v.t.*
perforate
period період *n.* period
periodychne vydannia
періодичне видання *n.*
periodical
periodychnyi періодичний *a.*
periodical
perlyna перлина *n.* pearl
pero перо *n* feather
perpendykuliar перпендикуляр
n. perpendicular
perpendykuliarnyi
перпендикулярний *a.*
perpendicular
persh перш *adv.* before
pershoriadnyi першорядний *n.*
paramount
pershyi перший *a* first
pershyi перший *a.* premier
pershyi prymirnyk перший
примірник *n* first
personal персонал *n.* personnel
personalnyi персональний *a.*
personal
personazh персонаж *n.*
personage
personifikatsiia персоніфікація
n. personification
perspektyva перспектива *n.*
opportunity

perspektyvnyi перспективний *a.* prospective
perspektyvy перспективи *n.* possibility
persyk персик *n.* peach
peruka перука *n.* wig
perukar перукар *n.* barber
pervisnyi первісний *a.* primeval
pervynnyi первинний *a.* primary
peryferiia периферія *n.* periphery
peryla перила *n.* rail
pestytsyd пестицид *n.* pesticide
pestyty пестити *v. t.* caress
pestytysia пеститися *v.t* endear
pesymist песиміст *n.* pessimist
pesymistychnyi песимістичний *a.* pessimistic
pesymizm песимізм *n.* pessimism
petelka петелька *n* eyelet
petlia петля *n.* loop
pevna kilkist певна кількість *n.* aliquot
pevnyi певний *a* decisive
pevnyi певний *a* definite
pianino піаніно *n.* piano
pianist піаніст *n.* pianist
pianytsia п'яниця *n* bibber
piat п'ять *n* five
piata п'ята *n.* heel
piatdesiat п'ятьдесят *n.* fifty
piatnadtsiat п'ятнадцять *n* fifteen
piatnytsia п'ятниця *n.* Friday
piatykutnyk п'ятикутник *n.* pentagon
piavka п'явка *n.* leech
pich піч *n.* oven
pich піч *n.* stove
pid під *prep* beneath
pid під *prep.* under
pid під *prep.* underneath
pid chas під час *prep* during
pid uklon під уклон *adv* downwards

pidbadoriuvaty підбадьорювати *v. t* encourage
pidbir підбір *n* match
pidboriddia підборіддя *n.* chin
pidburiuvalnyi підбурювальний *a.* seditious
pidburiuvannia підбурювання *n.* instigation
pidburiuvannia do zakolotu підбурювання до заколоту *n.* sedition
pidburiuvaty підбурювати *v.t.* abet
pidburiuvaty підбурювати *v.t* foment
piddatlyvist піддатливість *v.t.* give
piddatlyvyi піддатливий *a.* supple
piddavaty піддавати *v.t.* subject
piddavaty nebezpetsi піддавати небезпеці *v. t.* endanger
piddavaty nebezpetsi піддавати небезпеці *v.t.* peril
piddavaty ostrakizmu піддавати остракізму *v.t.* ostracize
piddavaty sumnivu піддавати сумніву *v.t* query
piddavatysia піддаватися *v.i.* succumb
pidfarbovuvaty підфарбовувати *v.t.* tincture
pidhaniaty підганяти *v. t* bustle
pidhliadaty підглядати *v.i.* peep
pidhonka підгонка *n* fit
pidhotovchyi підготовчий *a.* preparatory
pidhotovchyi zakhid підготовчий захід *n* preliminary
pidhotovka підготовка *n.* preparation
pidhotovliaty підготовляти *v.t.* prepare

pidiom підйом *n.* climb1
pidiom підйом *n.* rise
pidiomnyi kran підйомний кран
n crane
pidkabluchnyk підкаблучник *n.*
henpecked
pidkazka підказка *n.* tip
pidkazuvaty підказувати *v.t.*
suggest
pidkhid підхід *n.* approach
pidkhodyty підходити *v.t.*
approach
pidkhozhyi підхожий *a* eligible
pidkladaty podushku підкладати
подушку *v. t* cushion
pidkladka підкладка *n* lining
pidkladka підкладка *n* pillow
pidkorennia підкорення *n.*
subjugation
pidkoriatysia підкорятися *v. i*
comply
pidkotyty підкотити *v.t.* wheel
pidkresliuvaty підкреслювати *v.t.*
underline
pidkydaty підкидати *v.t.* palm
pidlabuznyk підлабузник *n.*
sycophant
pidlehlyi підлеглий *a.* inferior
pidlehlyi підлеглий *n* subordinate
pidleshchuvatysia
підлещуватися *v.t.* wheedle
pidlisok підлісок *n.* coppice
pidlist підлість *n.* meanness
pidlitkovyi vik підлітковий вік *n.*
teens
pidlitok підліток *n.* teenager
pidloha підлога *n* floor
pidlokitnyk підлокітник *n* elbow
pidlyi підлий *a.* abject
pidlyi підлий *a.* nefarious
pidmaister підмайстер *n.*
apprentice
pidmitannia підмітання *n.* sweep

pidmitaty підмітати *v.i.* sweep
pidmorhuvaty підморгувати *v.i.*
wink
pidnebinnia піднебіння *n.* palate
pidnebinnyi піднебінний *a.*
palatal
pidnesenist піднесеність *n.* fort
pidnesenist піднесеність *n.*
sublimity
pidnesennia піднесення *n*
elevation
pidnesenyi піднесений *a.* sublime
pidneslyvist піднесливість *n.*
servility
pidniaty підняти *v.t.* hoist
pidniatyi піднятий *a* erect
pidnimaty піднімати *v.i.* heave
pidnimaty піднімати *v.t.* uplift
pidnimaty na smikh піднімати на
сміх *v.t.* ridicule
pidnimaty za dopomohoiu
vazhilia піднімати за
допомогою важіля *v.t.* lever
pidnimaty zakolot піднімати
заколот *v.i.* rebel
pidnimatysia підніматися *v.i.*
scramble
pidnos піднос *n.* tray
pidnoshennia підношення *n.*
offering
pidnosyty підносити *v.t.* present
pidnosytysia підноситися *v.i.*
tower
pidopichna osoba підопічна
особа *n.* ward
pidopichnyi підопічний *n.*
responsibility
pidoshva підошва *n.* sole
pidozra підозра *n.* surmise
pidozra підозра *n.* suspicion
pidozrilyi підозрілий *a.* suspect
pidozriuvanyi підозрюваний *n*
suspect

pidozriuvaty підозрювати *v.t.*
suspect
pidpal підпал *n* arson
pidperizuvaty підперізувати *v.t.*
gird
pidpirka підпірка *n.* prop
pidporiadkovanist
підпорядкованість *n*
dependence
pidporiadkovuvaty
підпорядковувати *v.t.*
subordinate
pidporiadkuvannia
підпорядкування *n.* conformity
pidpryiemstvo підприємство *n.*
venture
pidpylyi підпилий *a.* tipsy
pidpyraty підпирати *v.t.* prop
pidpys підпис *n.* signature
pidpysaty підписати *v.t.* sign
pidpyska підписка *n.* subscription
pidpysuvatysia підписуватися
v.t. subscribe
pidrakhovuvaty підраховувати *v.
t.* count
pidrakhovuvaty підраховувати
v.t. reckon
pidrakhovuvaty holosy
підраховувати голоси *v.t.* poll
pidrakhuvaty підрахувати *v.t.*
tally
pidriadnyi підрядний *a.*
subordinate
pidriadnyk підрядник *n* contractor
pidrizaty підрізати *v.t.* prune
pidroblenyi підроблений *a* bogus
pidrobliaty підробляти *a.*
counterfeit
pidrobliuvach підроблювач *n.*
counterfeiter
pidruchnyk підручник *a.* tutorial
pidrumianiuvaty підрум'янювати
v.t. toast

pidryvaty підривати *v.t.*
undermine
pidryvna diialnist підривна
діяльність *n.* subversion
pidryvnyi підривний *a.*
subversive
pidshtovkhnuty підштовхнути
v.t. nudge
pidshyty підшити *v.t* file
pidslipuvatyi підсліпуватий *n.*
purblind
pidslukhovuvaty підслуховувати
v.t. overhear
pidsolodzhuvaty підсолоджувати
v.t. sweeten
pidstava підстава *n.* basement
pidstava підстава *n.* cause
pidsterihaty підстерігати *v.t.*
waylay
pidstupnist підступність *n.* guile
pidsudnyi підсудний *n* defendant
pidsumok підсумок *n.* total
pidsumovuvaty підсумовувати
v.t. summarize
pidsushuvaty підсушувати *v.t.*
parch
pidsyliuvach підсилювач *n*
amplifier
pidtekst підтекст *n.* undertone
pidtochuvaty підточувати *v.t.* fret
pidtrymka підтримка *n* behalf
pidtrymuvaty підтримувати *v.t.*
maintain
pidtrymuvaty підтримувати *v.t.*
second
pidtrymuvaty vohon
підтримувати вогонь *v.t.* stoke
pidtverdzhennia підтвердження
n confirmation
pidtverdzhuvaty підтверджувати
v.t. corroborate
pidviazka підв'язка *n.* garter

pidvodna techiia підводна течія *n*. undercurrent
pidvodnyi підводний *a* submarine
pidvodnyi choven підводний човен *n*. submarine
pidvyshchennia підвищення *v.t.* raise
pidvyshchuietsia підвищується *adv*. up
pidvyshchuvaty підвищувати *v.t.* heighten
pidvyshchuvaty po sluzhbi підвищувати по службі *v. t* elevate
pidzemnyi підземний *a*. subterranean
pidzemnyi svit підземний світ *n*. underworld
pidzhaty піджати *v.t.* purse
piedestal п'єдестал *n*. pedestal
pihmei пігмей *n*. pigmy
piimannia піймання *n*. catch
piimaty v pastku піймати в пастку *v.t.* snare
piimaty v siti піймати в сіті *v.t* mesh
pik пік *n*. peak
pikantnist пікантність *n*. poignancy
pikantnyi пікантний *a*. piquant
pikantnyi пікантний *a*. poignant
piket пікет *n*. picket
piketuvaty пікетувати *v.t.* picket
pikhota піхота *n*. infantry
pikhotynets піхотинець *n*. peon
pikhva піхва *n*. vagina
pikhvy піхви *n*. scabbard
pikiruvannia пікірування *n* swoop
pikluvannia піклування *n*. wardship
pikluvatysia піклуватися *v. i.* care
piknik пікнік *n*. picnic
pilhovyi пільговий *a*. preferential

piliulia пілюля *n*. pill
pilot пілот *n*. aviator
pilotuvaty пілотувати *v.t.* pilot
pina піна *n* foam
pioner піонер *n*. pioneer
pioreia піорея *n*. pyorrhoea
piramida піраміда *n*. pyramid
pirat пірат *n*. pirate
piratstvo піратство *n*. piracy
pirnannia пірнання *n* plunge
pirnaty пірнати *v. i* dive
pishchanyi піщаний *a*. sandy
pishokhid пішохід *n*. pedestrian
pislia після *prep*. since
pislia після *prep* upon
pislia choho після чого *conj*. whereupon
pislia vsikh після всіх *adv*. last
pisnia пісня *n*. song
pisnyi пісний *a* fast
pisok пісок *n*. sand
pistolet пістолет *n*. pistol
pisuar пісуар *n*. urinal
pit піт *n*. perspiration
pit піт *n*. sweat
piton пітон *n*. python
piure пюре *n*. mash
pivden південь *n*. south
pivdennyi південний *a*. south
piven півень *n* cock
pivkulia півкуля *n*. hemisphere
pivnich північ *n*. north
pivnichnyi північний *a*. northerly
pivnoch північ *n*. midnight
piznannia пізнання *n*. knowledge
piznii пізній *a*. late
pizno пізно *adv*. late
pkhaty пхати *v.t.* jab
pkhykannia пхикання *n* whine
plachushchyi плачущий *a*. tearful
plakalnyky плакальники *n*. mourner
plakat плакат *n*. poster

plakaty плакати *v.i.* weep
plaksyvyi плаксивий *a.*
lachrymose
plan план *n.* plan
planeruvaty планерувати *v.t.*
plane
planeta планета *n.* planet
planetarnyi планетарний *a.*
planetary
plantatsiia плантація *n.* plantation
planuvaty планувати *v.t.* plan
plany na maibutnie плани на
майбутнє *n.* outlook
plashch плащ *n.* cloak
plata плата *n.* premium
plata za prostii плата за простій
n. demurrage
platan платан *n.* sycamore
platforma платформа *n.* platform
plato плато *n.* plateau
platonichnyi платонічний *a.*
platonic
platospromozhnist
платоспроможність *n.* solvency
plattia плаття *n* dress
plattia плаття *n.* frock
plattiana shafa платтяна шафа
n. wardrobe
platyty платити *v.t.* pay
platyty vdruhe платити вдруге
v.t. repay
plavaty плавати *v.i* float
plavaty na yakhti плавати на яхті
v.i yacht
plavaty v chomus плавати в
чомусь *v.i.* swim
plavets плавець *n.* swimmer
plavka плавка *n* fuse
plavlennia плавлення *n.* fusion
plavno rukhatysia плавно
рухатися *v.t.* glide
plavnyi плавний *a.* smooth
plavnyk плавник *n* fin

plavuchist плавучість *n*
buoyancy
plavuchyi плавучий *a.* natant
plavylna chasha плавильна
чаша *n.* crevet
plavylnia плавильня *n.* foundry
plavyty плавити *v.t.* fuse
plazuvaty плазувати *v. i* creep
plebistsyt плебісцит *n.* plebiscite
pleche плече *n.* shoulder
plekaty плекати *v. t.* cherish
plekaty плекати *v.t.* mother
plemia плем'я *n.* tribe
pleminnyi племінний *a.* tribal
pleminnyk племінник *n.* nephew
pleminnytsia племінниця *n.*
niece
plentatysia плентатися *v. t* crawl
pleskaty плескати *v.i.* pop
pleskaty yazykom плескати
язиком *v.t.* jabber
pleskatysia плескатися *v.i.*
splash
plesty intryhy плести інтриги *v.t.*
plot
plesty z ocheretu плести з
очерету *v. t.* cane
pletinnia плетіння *n.* wicker
pliama пляма *n.* smear
pliamkaty плямкати *v.t.* munch
pliamochka плямочка *n.* speck
pliamuvaty плямувати *v.t.* spot
pliashka пляшка *n* bottle
pliazh пляж *n* beach
plidnyi плідний *a.* fruitful
plidnyi плідний *a.* prolific
plitka плітка *n.* gossip
pliumazh плюмаж *n* aigrette
plius плюс *n* plus
pliushch плющ *n* ivy
pliuvalnytsia плювальниця *n.*
spittoon
pliuvaty плювати *v.i.* spit

pliuvok плювок *n* spittle
plivka плівка *n* film
plodyty плодити *v.t.* propagate
ploshcha площа *n* area
ploshcha zemli v akrakh площа землі в акрах *n.* acreage
ploshchyna площина *n* flat
ploskyi плоский *a* level
ploskyi плоский *a.* plane
plot плоть *n* flesh
plotskyi плотський *a.* sensuous
pluh плуг *n.* plough
plutanyna плутанина *n.* maze
plutaty плутати *v.t.* muddle
plyn плин *n* lapse
plyta плита *n.* plate
plyvun пливун *n.* quicksand
pnevmoniia пневмонія *n.* pneumonia
po по *prep.* around
po по *prep* down
po batkovi по батькові *a.* paternal
po vsomu по всьому *adv.* throughout
pobachennia побачення *n.* appointment
pobachennia побачення *n.* tryst
pobachyty побачити *v.t.* sight
pobichnyi побічний *a.* incidental
pobilka побілка *n.* whitewash
pobizhnyi побіжний *a.* fugitive
poblazhlyvist поблажливість *n.* indulgence
poblazhlyvyi поблажливий *a.* indulgent
poblyzu поблизу *adv.* near
poboiuvannia побоювання *n.* anticipation
poboiuvannia побоювання *n.* misgiving
poboiuvatysia побоюватися *v.i* fear
pobornyk поборник *n.* protagonist

pobyty побити *v.t.* wallop
pochatkivets початківець *n.* novice
pochatkovyi початковий *a.* initial
pochatkovyi початковий *a.* original
pochatok початок *n.* beginning
pochatok початок *n.* prime
pochesnyi почесний *a.* honorary
pochet почет *n.* suite
pochuttia почуття *n* feeling
pochuttia obrazy почуття образи *n.* resentment
pochuttia spushenosti почуття спушеності *n.* void
pochynaty починати *v.t.* auspicate
pochynatysia починатися *v. t* commence
pochytaty почитати *v.t.* revere
podacha подача *n.* innings
**podacha m`iacha** подача м`яча *n.* serve
podahra подагра *n.* gout
podali подалі *adv.* further
podalshyi подальший *a* further
podarunok подарунок *n.* present
podarunok na pamiat подарунок на пам'ять *n.* keepsake
podatok податок *n* duty
podatok na nadprybutok податок на надприбуток *n.* supertax
podavaty подавати *v.i.* provide
podavaty miach подавати м'яч *v.i* bowl
podavaty prokhannia подавати прохання *v.t.* petition
podiaka подяка *n.* gratitude
podiaka подяка *n.* thanks
podiakuvaty подякувати *v.t.* thank
podibnist подібність *n.* likeness

podibno подібно *adv* alike
podibnyi подібний *a.* analogous
podibnyi do zhinky подібний до
  жінки *a* effeminate
podiia подія *n.* happening
podil поділ *n.* separation
podilyty navpil поділити навпіл
  v.t. halve
podobatysia подобатися *v.i.*
  please
podolaty подолати *v.t.* overcome
podorozh подорож *n* travel
podorozhnii подорожній *n.*
  wayfarer
podorozhnyk подорожник *n.*
  plantain
podorozhuvaty подорожувати
  v.i. journey
podovzhuvaty подовжувати *v.t.*
  lengthen
podraznyk подразник *n.* irritant
podriapaty подряпати *v.t.* scratch
podriapyna подряпина *n.* scratch
podribniuvaty подрібнювати *v.t.*
  pound
podrimaty подрімати *v.i.* nap
podrizaty zhyvoplit подрізати
  живопліт *v.t* hedge
podruzhnii подружній *n.* spousal
podruzhzhia подружжя *n.*
  matrimony
podushka подушка *n.* pad
poduv подув *n.* whiff
podviinyi подвійний *a* double
podviria подвір'я *n.* yard
podvoity подвоїти *v.t.* redouble
podvyh подвиг *n.* coup
podvyh подвиг *n* exploit
podyv подив *n* daze
poet поет *n.* poet
poetesa поетеса *n.* poetess
poetychnist поетичність *n.* poetry
poetychnyi поетичний *a.* poetic

poetyka поетика *n.* poetics
poeziia поезія *n.* poesy
pohan погань *n.* muck
pohana robota погана робота *n*
  bungle
pohana slava погана слава *n*
  disrepute
pohane stavlennia погане
  ставлення *n.* misuse
pohane upravlinnia погане
  управління *n.* misrule
pohano погано *adv.* badly
pohano povodytysia погано
  поводитися *v.i.* misbehave
pohanyi поганий *a.* sinister
pohanyty поганити *v.t.* pollute
pohashaty погашати *v.t.* satisfy
pohashennia погашення *n.*
  redemption
pohirshuvaty погіршувати *v.t.*
  worsen
pohladzhuvaty погладжувати *v.t.*
  stroke
pohliad погляд *n* gaze
pohliad nazad погляд назад *n.*
  retrospect
pohlynaty поглинати *v.t* absorb
pohlynennia поглинення *n.*
  merger
pohoda погода *n* weather
pohodzhenist погодженість *n.*
  conformity
pohodzhuvatysia погоджуватися
  v.i. agree
pohodzhuvatysia погоджуватися
  v.t. concede
pohonia погоня *v. t.* chase1
pohonych sloniv погонич слонів
  n. mahout
pohrabuvannia пограбування *n.*
  robbery
pohrabuvaty пограбувати *v.t.*
  plunder

pohrib погріб *n* cellar
pohrozhuvaty погрожувати *v.t.* threaten
poias пояс *n.* waistband
poiasnennia пояснення *n* explanation
poiasniuvaty пояснювати *v. t.* explain
poiasok kolony поясок колони *n* annulet
poiava поява *n* appearance
poiednuvaty поєднувати *v.t.* mate
poity поїти *v.t.* water
poizd поїзд *n.* train
poizdka поїздка *n.* journey
poizdka поїздка *n* ride
pokaiannia покаяння *n.* repentance
pokarannia покарання *n.* punishment
pokaz показ *n.* signification
pokazannia показання *n.* testimony
pokazhchyk покажчик *n.* index
pokaznyi показний *a.* conspicuous
pokaznyk показник *n.* quotient
pokazuvaty показувати *v.t.* show
pokazuvaty zhestom показувати жестом *v.i.* motion
pokazuvatysia показуватися *v.i.* appear
pokhid похід *n* crusade
pokhmuryi похмурий *a.* moody
pokhmuryi похмурий *a.* woebegone
pokhmuryi pohliad похмурий погляд *n.* frown
pokhmuryi vyhliad похмурий вигляд *n.* scowl
pokhodzhennia походження *n.* ancestry

pokhoron похорон *n.* funeral
pokhoronna pisnia похоронна пісня *n.* monody
pokhoronne bahattia похоронне багаття *n.* pyre
pokhovannia поховання *n.* sepulture
pokhvala похвала *n* commendation
pokhvalnyi похвальний *a.* commendable
pokhvalnyi похвальний *a* creditable
pokhyloho viku похилого віку *a* elderly
pokhylyi похилий *adj.* declivous
pokhytuvannia похитування *n.* stagger
pokirnist покірність *n.* acquiescence
pokirnist покірність *n.* humility
pokirnyi покірний *a* dutiful
pokirnyi покірний *a.* submissive
pokladatysia покладатися *v.i.* rely
pokladenyi покладений *a* incumbent
poklasty покласти *v.t.* put
poklasty kinets покласти кінець *v.t* abolish
pokloniatysia поклонятися *v.t.* worship
pokloninnia поклоніння *n.* worship
pokloninnia odnomu Bohu поклоніння одному Богу *n.* monolatry
poklykannia покликання *n.* calling
poklykaty покликати *v.t.* summon
pokoivka покоївка *n.* maid
pokolinnia покоління *n.* generation

pokora покора *n.* submission
pokrovytel покровитель *n.* patron
pokryshka покришка *n.* cover
pokryty покрити *v.t.* sheet
pokryty sazheiu покрити сажею *v.t.* soot
pokrytyi lystiam покритий листям *a.* leafy
pokrytyi shvamy покритий швами *a.* seamy
pokryvalo покривало *n.* coverlet
pokryvaty bryzhamy покривати брижами *v.t.* ripple
pokryvaty merezheiu покривати мережею *v.t.* net
pokryvaty metalom покривати металом *v.t.* plate
pokryvaty olovom покривати оловом *v.t.* tin
pokryvaty shkiroiu покривати шкірою *v.t* skin
pokryvaty tonkoiu plivkoiu покривати тонкою плівкою *v.t* film
pokupets покупець *n.* buyer
pokupka покупка *n.* purchase
poky поки *n. conj.* till
poky поки *conj.* while
pokydaty покидати *v.t.* abandon
pokydky покидьки *n.* refuse
pola пола *n.* lap
pole поле *n* field
polehshennia полегшення *n.* alleviation
polehshennia полегшення *n.* relief
polehshuvaty полегшувати *v.t.* appease
polehshuvaty полегшувати *v. t* ease
polehshuvaty полегшувати *v.t* facilitate

polehshuvaty полегшувати *v.i.* lighten
poliahaty полягати *v. i* consist
Poliarna zirka Полярна зірка *n.* loadstar
poliarnyi полярний *n.* polar
polihamiia полігамія *n.* polygamy
polihamnyi полігамний *a.* polygamous
polihlot поліглот *n.* polyglot1
polipshennia поліпшення *n.* improvement
polipshuvaty поліпшувати *v. t* better
polipshuvatysia поліпшуватися *v.t.* ameliorate
polirovka поліровка *n* polish
poliruvaty полірувати *v.t.* polish
polit політ *n.* voyage
politeist політеїст *n.* polytheist
politeistychnyi політеїстичний *a.* polytheistic
politekhnichnyi політехнічний *a.* polytechnic
politekhnikum політехнікум *n.* polytechnic
politseiskyi поліцейський *n.* policeman
politsiia поліція *n.* police
politychnyi політичний *a.* politic
polityk політик *n.* politician
polityka політика *n.* policy
polityka політика *n.* politics
polius полюс *n.* pole
poliuvannia полювання *n.* chase2
poliuvannia полювання *n* hunt
poliuvaty полювати *v.t.* hunt
polk полк *n.* regiment
polkovnyk полковник *n.* colonel
polo поло *n.* polo
poloh полог *n.* canopy
polokhatysia полохатися *v.i.* shy

polokhlyvyi полохливий *a.* timid
polomka поломка *n* breakage
polonennia полонення *n.* captivity
polonenyi полонений *a.* captive
polonyty полонити *v. t.* captivate
polosa полоса *n.* strip
poloskaty полоскати *v.i.* gargle
polotno полотно *n.* linen
poloty полоти *v.t.* weed
polovyi hravets na livii storoni vid boulera v kryketi польовий гравець на лівій стороні від боулера в крикеті *n.* mid-off
polovyi hravets na pravii storoni vid boulera v kryketi польовий гравець на правій стороні від боулера в крикеті *n.* mid-on
polovyna половина *n.* half
polovynnyi половинний *a* half
polozhennia положення *n.* case
poluden полудень *n.* midday
poluden полудень *n.* noon
polumia полум'я *n* blaze
polumia полум'я *n* flame
polumianity полум'яніти *v.i* flame
polunytsia полуниця *n.* strawberry
polyn полин *n.* wormwood
pomaranchevyi помаранчевий *a* orange
pomerty померти *v. i* decease
pomerty померти *v. i* die
pomiakshennia пом'якшення *n.* mitigation
pomiakshuvaty пом'якшувати *v.t.* alleviate
pomiakshuvatysia пом'якшуватися *v.i.* relent
pomichaty помічати *v.t.* remark
pomichnyk помічник *n* help
pomidor помідор *n.* tomato

pomirnist помірність *n.* temperance
pomirnyi помірний *a* medium
pomirnyi помірний *a.* moderate
pomishchaty поміщати *v.t.* place
pomishchaty poseredyni поміщати посередині *v.t.* sandwich
pomist поміст *n.* dais
pomitno помітно *adj* perceptible
pomitnyi помітний *a.* appreciable
pomnozhyty помножити *v.t.* multiply
pompeznist помпезність *n.* pomposity
pompeznyi помпезний *a.* pompous
pomsta помста *n.* revenge
pomsta помста *n.* vengeance
pomstytysia помститися *v.i.* retaliate
pomyliatysia помилятися *v. i* err
pomyliatysia помилятися *v.t.* mistake
pomylka помилка *n* error
pomylka помилка *n.* miscarriage
pomylkova dumka помилкова думка *n.* misbelief
pomylkovyi помилковий *a.* inaccurate
pomyluvannia помилування *n.* pardon
pomyluvaty помилувати *v.t.* pardon
ponad понад *adv.* beyond
ponadnormovyi понаднормовий *adv.* overtime
ponadnormovyi chas понаднормовий час *n* overtime
ponedilok понеділок *n.* Monday
ponevoliuvaty поневолювати *v.t.* enslave
poni поні *n.* pony

poniattia поняття *n.* notion
ponosyty поносити *v.t.* vilify
po-novomu по-новому *adv.* anew
ponuryi понурий *a.* morose
ponyzhuvaty понижувати *v.t.* abase
poperechnyi поперечний *a* cross
poperechyna поперечина *n.* spoke
poperednii попередній *a.* preliminary
poperednyk попередник *n* forerunner
poperednyk попередник *n.* predecessor
poperedu попереду *adv.* ahead
poperedzhaty попереджати *v.t.* warn
poperedzhaty zazdalehid попереджати заздалегідь *v.t* forewarn
poperedzhennia попередження *n.* notification
poperedzhuvalnyi попереджувальний *a.* precautionary
poperek поперек *n.* loin
po-pershe по-перше *adv* first
popil попіл *n.* ash
popleskuvannia поплескування *n* pat
poplin поплін *n.* poplin
popovniuvaty поповнювати *v.t.* replenish
popravky поправки *n.pl.* amends
poprosyty попросити *v.t.* request
populiarnist популярність *n.* popularity
populiarnist популярність *n.* vogue
populiarnyi популярний *n* pop
populiarnyi популярний *a.* popular

populiaryzuvaty популяризувати *v.t.* popularize
popusk попуск *n.* connivance
popyt попит *n* request
porada порада *n* advice
poranennia поранення *n.* wound
poranyty поранити *v.t.* wound
poratysia поратися *v.t* handle
porazka поразка *n.* affection
poriadok порядок *n.* order
poriatunok порятунок *n* rescue
poriatunok порятунок *n.* salvation
porih поріг *n.* threshold
porivnialnyi порівняльний *a* comparative
porivniannia порівняння *n* comparison
porivniannia порівняння *n.* simile
porivniuiuchy z порівнюючи з *prep.* versus
porivniuvaty порівнювати *v. t* compare
porivniuvaty порівнювати *v.t.* parallel
poriz поріз *n* cut
porochnyi порочний *a.* vicious
poroda порода *n* breed
porodzhuvaty породжувати *v.t.* generate
poroshok порошок *n.* powder
poroshyty порошити *v.t.* dust
porozhnia poroda порожня порода *n* spoil
porozhnie mistse порожнє місце *n.* nothing
porozhnii порожній *a* blank
porozhnyna порожнина *n.* cavity
porshen поршень *n.* piston
port порт *n.* port
portal портал *n.* portal
portatyvnyi портативний *a.* handy
portfel портфель *n.* portfolio

portovi mytni zbory портові митні збори *n.* wharfage
portret портрет *n* portrayal
portretnyi zhyvopys портретний живопис *n.* portraiture
portsiia порція *n.* allowance
portyk портик *n.* portico
poruch поруч *adv.* nigh
poruch z поруч з *prep.* beside
poruchchia поруччя *n.* railing
poruchytel поручитель *n.* guarantee
poruchytelstvo поручительство *n.* surety
porushennia порушення *n* breach
porushennia travlennia порушення травлення *n.* indigestion
porushuvaty порушувати *v.t.* incite
porushuvaty spravu порушувати справу *v.t.* sue
porushuvaty zakon порушувати закон *v.t.* outrage
pory пори *n.* pore
porynaty поринати *v.t.* plunge
poselenets поселенець *n.* settler
poserednii посередній *a.* ordinary
poserednist посередність *n.* mediocrity
poserednyk посередник *n.* intermediary
poserednyk посередник *n.* mediator
poserednytstvo посередництво *n.* mediation
poserednytstvo посередництво *n.* mediation
posharpanyi пошарпаний *a.* threadbare
poshest пошесть *n.* pestilence

poshkodzhennia пошкодження *n.* damage
poshkodzhuvaty пошкоджувати *v. t.* damage
poshta пошта *n.* mail
poshtmeister поштмейстер *n.* postmaster
poshtove viddilennia поштове відділення *n.* post-office
poshtovi vytraty поштові витрати *n.* postage
poshtovkh поштовх *n.* push
poshtovyi поштовий *a.* postal
poshuk пошук *n.* quest
poshuky пошуки *n* rummage
poshyrennia поширення *n.* spread
poshyrenyi поширений *a.* prevalent
poshyriuvaty поширювати *v.t.* shed
poshyriuvaty chutky поширювати чутки *v.t.* rumour
poshyriuvatysia поширюватися *v.i.* spread
posiahannia посягання *n.* trespass
posiahaty посягати *v.t.* infringe
posibnyk посібник *n* manual
poslablennia послаблення *n.* abatement
poslabliaty послабляти *v.t.* mitigate
poslabliuvaty послаблювати *v. t.* enfeeble
poslabliuvaty послаблювати *v.t.* weaken
poslannia послання *n.* missive
poslaty послати *v.t.* send
poslatysia послатися *v.t.* refer
poslidovnist послідовність *n.* sequence

poslidovno послідовно *adv*
consecutively
poslidovnyi послідовний *adj.*
consecutive
poslidovnyk послідовник *n*
follower
posliduvaty послідувати *v.t* follow
posluzhlyvyi послужливий *adj.*
complacent
posluzhlyvyi послужливий *adj.*
complaisant
posmertnyi посмертний *a.* post-
mortem
posmiiuvatysia посміюватися *v.*
i chuckle
posmikhatysia посміхатися *v.i.*
smile
posmikhovysko посміховисько
n. scoff
posol посол *n.* ambassador
posolstvo посольство *n* embassy
pospikh поспіх *n.* haste
pospishaty поспішати *v.i.* hasten
pospishnyi поспішний *a* snap
post пост *n.* post
postachalnyk постачальник *n.*
supplier
postachannia постачання *n.*
procurement
postachaty постачати *v.t.* supply
postanova постанова *n* bylaw,
bye-law
postava постава *n.* posture
postavliaty proviziiu поставляти
провізію *v. i* cater
postiine mistse prozhyvannia
постійне місце проживання *n*
domicile
postiinyi постійний *a* abiding
postilni prynalezhnosti постільні
приналежності *n.* bedding
postril постріл *n.* shot

postskryptum постскриптум *n.*
postscript
postupalnyi поступальний *a.*
onward
postupatysia поступатися *v.t.*
surrender
postupka поступка *n* concession
postupovyi поступовий *a.*
gradual
posud посуд *n.* crockery
posukha посуха *n* dry
posviachuvaty v lytsari
посвячувати в лицарі *v.t.*
knight
posylannia посилання *n.* link
posylaty povidomlennia
посилати повідомлення *v.t.*
notice
posylatysia посилатися *v.t* link
posylatysia na посилатися на *v.t.*
allege
posyliuvaty посилювати *v.t.*
reinforce
posyliuvatysia посилюватися *v.t.*
intensify
posylka посилка *n.* parcel
posylnyi посильний *n.*
messenger
posypaty посипати *v.t.* strew
potai prosuvatysia потай
просуватися *v.i.* stalk
potainyi потайний *a.* secretive
potash поташ *n.* potash
potentsial потенціал *n.* potential
potentsiia потенція *n.* potency
potentsiinist потенційність *n.*
potentiality
potentsiinyi потенційний *a.*
potential
potertyi потертий *a.* shabby
potiah потяг *n.* appetence
potik потік *n* flow
potim потім *adv.* next

potity потіти *v.i.* perspire
potity потіти *v.i.* sweat
potmianity потьмяніти *v. t* dim
potochnyi поточний *a* current
potochnyi поточний *a* routine
potomstvo потомство *n.* offspring
potreba потреба *n* want
potrebuvaty потребувати *v.t.* need
potreby потреби *adv.* needs
po-tretie по-третє *adv.* thirdly
potribne потрібне *n* requisite
potribnyi потрібний *a* necessary
potriinyi потрійний *a.* triplicate
potriskuvaty потріскувати *v.t.* crackle
potroiennia потроєння *n.* triplication
potroiuvaty потроювати *v.t.,* triple
potsilunok поцілунок *n.* kiss
poturannia потурання *n.* condonation
potuzhnyi потужний *a.* potent
potuzhnyi потужний *a.* powerful
potvornist потворність *n.* ugliness
potvornyi потворний *a.* hideous
potvornyi потворний *a.* ugly
potylytsia потилиця *n.* nape
povaha повага *n* deference
povaha повага *n.* respect
povalennia повалення *n* overthrow
povalyty повалити *v.i.* topple
povazhaty поважати *v. t* esteem
povazhaty поважати *v. t* honour
povazhnyi поважний *a.* venerable
povchalna baza повчальна база *n* apologue
povchaty повчати *v.i.* sermonize
povedinka поведінка *n* behaviour
poverennnia повереннння *n.* resumption

poverkh поверх *n.* storey
poverkhnevyi поверхневий *a.* outward
poverkhnia поверхня *n.* surface
poverkhovist поверховість *n.* superficiality
poverkhovyi поверховий *a* cursory
povernennia повернення *n.* return
povernennia do zhyttia повернення до життя *n.* revival
povernuty повернути *v.i.* return
povertaty повертати *v.t.* restore
povertaty hroshi повертати гроші *n.* refund
povertatysia повертатися *v.i.* revert
poviazanyi z ictoriieiu пов'язаний з історією *a.* historical
poviazanyi z politykoiu пов'язаний з політикою *a.* political
poviazanyi z prylyvom пов'язаний з приливом *a.* tidal
poviazka пов'язка *n* deligate1
poviazuvaty пов'язувати *v.t* bind
povidomlennia повідомлення *n.* intimation
povidomliaty повідомляти *v.t.* inform
povidomliaty po telebachenniu повідомляти по телебаченню *v.t.* televise
poviia повія *n.* strumpet
povilnist повільність *n.* slowness
povilno повільно *adv.* slowly
povilnyi повільний *a* slow
povin повінь *n* flood
povirenyi повірений *n.* solicitor
povist повість *n.* novelette
povistka повістка *n.* agenda

povitria повітря *n* air

povitriana kulia повітряна куля *n.* balloon

povitrianyi повітряний *a.* aerial

povitrianyi повітряний *a.* airy

povna lozhka повна ложка *n.* spoonful

povnistiu повністю *adv* entirely

povnistiu повністю *adv.* wholly

povnistiu ruinuvaty повністю руйнувати *n.* wrack

povnolitnii повнолітній *a.* major

povnolittia повноліття *n.* majority

povnota повнота *n.* fullness

povnyi повний *a* complete

povnyi повний *adj.* crass

povnyi повний *a* downright

povnyi повний *a* utter

povnyi bazhannia повний бажання *a.* solicitous

povnyi komplekt повний комплект *n* complement

povody поводи *n.* rein

povodzhennia поводження *n.* treatment

povstalyi повсталий *a.* insurgent

povstanets повстанець *n.* insurgent

povstannia повстання *n.* uprising

povstavaty повставати *v.i.* revolt

povtorennia повторення *n.* reiteration

povtorennia повторення *n.* relapse

povtoriuvanyi повторюваний *a.* recurrent

povtoriuvaty повторювати *v.t.* repeat

povtoryty повторити *v.t.* reiterate

povynen повинен *v.* must

povz повз *prep.* past

povzannia повзання *n* crawl

povzty повзти *v.i.* snake

povzucha roslyna повзуча рослина *n* creeper

poza поза *n.* pose

poza поза *prep.* without

poza mezhamy поза межами *a.* outdoor

pozadu позаду *adv* after

pozadu позаду *prep* behind

pozashliubne spivzhyttia позашлюбне співжиття *n.* concubinage

pozashliubnyi позашлюбний *a* bastard

pozbavlennia позбавлення *n* forfeiture

pozbavlennia voli позбавлення волі *n.* confinement

pozbavlennia zhyttia позбавлення життя *n.* homicide

pozbavlenyi позбавлений *a* devoid

pozbavlenyi holovy позбавлений голови *adj.* acephalous

pozbavlenyi prostoty позбавлений простоти *a.* sophisticated

pozbavliaty позбавляти *v.t.* denude

pozbavliaty позбавляти *v.t.* relieve

pozbavliaty zakonnoi syly позбавляти законної сили *v.t.* invalidate

pozbavyty позбавити *v. t* deprive

pozbavyty vlady позбавити влади *v. t* depose

pozbutysia позбутися *v.t* forfeit

pozdorovlennia поздоровлення *n* congratulation

pozdorovliaty поздоровляти *v. t* congratulate

pozdorovliaty поздоровляти *v.t* hail

pozhadlyvist пожадливість *n.*
avidity
pozhadlyvyi пожадливий *a.*
greedy
pozhertvuvannia пожертвування
n. sacrifice
pozhovtity пожовтіти *v.t.* yellow
pozhvavlennia пожвавлення *n*
animation
pozhvavyty пожвавити *v.t.* wake
pozhylets пожилець *n.* occupant
pozhynaty пожинати *v.t.* reap
pozhyvnist поживність *n.*
richness
pozhyvnyi поживний *a.* nutritive
pozikhannia позіхання *n.* yawn
pozikhaty позіхати *v.i.* gape
pozikhaty позіхати *v.i.* yawn
poznachaty позначати *v. i* denote
poznachaty позначати *v.t.* label
poznachaty позначати *v.t* mark
poznachennia позначення *n.*
notation
poznachka позначка *n.* mark
poznaiomyty познайомити *v.t.*
acquaint
pozolota позолота *a.* gilt
pozov позов *n* claim
pozovna позовна *n.* count
pozuvaty позувати *v.i.* pose
pozychaty позичати *v.t.* lend
pozyka позика *n.* loan
pozytsiia позиція *n.* position
pozytyvnyi позитивний *a.* plus
pozytyvnyi позитивний *a.*
positive
pozyvach позивач *n* claimant
pozyvach позивач *n.* plaintiff
ppohane povodzhennia ппогане
поводження *n.* mal-treatment
prabatko прабатько *n* forefather
prachka прачка *n.* laundress

prahmatychnyi прагматичний *a.*
pragmatic
prahmatyzm прагматизм *n.*
pragmatism
prahnennia прагнення *n.*
aspiration
prahnennia прагнення *n.*
intention
prahnuchyi прагнучий *adj.* athirst
prahnuty прагнути *v.t.* aspire
prahnuty прагнути *v.i.* hanker
praktychni znannia практичні
знання *n.* lore
praktychnyi практичний *a.*
practical
praktyka практика *n.* practice
praktykuiuchyi likar
практикуючий лікар *n.*
practitioner
pralnia пральня *n.* laundry
prannia прання *n* wash
prapor прапор *n.* banner
praska праска *n.* iron
pratsia праця *n.* labour
pratsiuvaty працювати *v.i.* labour
pratsiuvaty nasosom працювати
насосом *v.t.* pump
pratsiuvaty stameskoiu
працювати стамескою *v. t.*
chisel
pratsiuvaty, yak rab працювати,
як раб *v.i.* slave
pratsivnyk працівник *n* employee
pratsovytyi працьовитий *a.*
industrious
praty прати *v. t* erase
praty i prasuvaty прати і
прасувати *v.t.* launder
pravda правда *n.* truth
pravdopodibnist
правдоподібність *n.*
verisimilitude

338

pravdopodibnyi правдоподібний *a.* probable
pravdyvist правдивість *n.* veracity
pravdyvyi правдивий *a.* truthful
pravednyi праведний *a.* godly
pravliachyi правлячий *n.* ruling
pravo право *n* right
pravoporushennia правопорушення *n.* violation
pravyi правий *a.* right
pravylno правильно *adv* aright
pravylnyi правильний *a* correct
pravylo правило *n.* rule
pravytel правитель *n.* ruler
pravyty правити *v.t.* rein
preambula преамбула *n.* preamble
predmet предмет *n.* matter
predmet bazhannia предмет бажання *n* desire
predmet odiahu предмет одягу *n.* garment
predmet zakhoplennia предмет захоплення *n.* admiration
predmety odiahu предмети одягу *n.* apparel
predok предок *n.* ancestor
predstavliaty представляти *v.t.* submit
predstavnyk представник *n.* representative
predstavnytskyi представницький *a.* representative
predykat предикат *n.* predicate
prefekt префект *n.* prefect
preferentsiia преференція *n.* preference
prefiks префікс *a.* particle
prefiks префікс *n.* prefix
prekrasnyi прекрасний *a.* admirable

prekrasnyi прекрасний *a.* lovely
prelat прелат *n.* prelate
preliudiia прелюдія *n.* prelude
premiera прем'єра *n.* premiere
premier-ministr прем'єр-міністр *n* premier
premiia премія *n* bonus
prepodobnyi преподобний *a.* reverend
prerohatyva прерогатива *n.* prerogative
presa преса *n* press
prestyzh престиж *n.* prestige
prestyzhnyi престижний *a.* prestigious
pretendent претендент *n* nominee
pretenziinist претензійність *n.* pretension
pretenziinyi претензійний *a.* pretentious
pretsedent прецедент *n.* precedent
preventyvnyi превентивний *a.* preventive
prezentatsiia презентація *n.* presentation
prezumptsiia презумпція *n.* presumption
prezydent президент *n.* president
prezydentskyi президентський *a.* presidential
prezyrlyva usmishka презирлива усмішка *n* sneer
prezyrlyvyi презирливий *a* contemptuous
prezyrstvo презирство *n* contempt
priakha пряха *n.* spinner
priama kyshka пряма кишка *n.* rectum
priamo прямо *adv.* straight

priamokutnyi прямокутний *a.* rectangular

priamokutnyk прямокутник *n.* rectangle

priamota прямота *n.* integrity

priamyi прямий *a* through

prianyi пряний *a.* spicy

priazha пряжа *n.* yarn

priazhka пряжка *n* buckle

priorytet пріоритет *n.* precedence

prizvyshche прізвище *n.* surname

prizvysko прізвисько *n.* alias

pro про *prep* about

proba проба *n.* hallmark

probachnyi пробачний *a.* venial

probachyty пробачити *v.t.* remit

probih пробіг *n.* mileage

probii пробій *n.* rupture

probil пробіл *n* blank

probizhka пробіжка *n* scamper

problema проблема *n.* trouble

problematychnyi проблематичний *a.* problematic

problysk проблиск *n.* ray

probudzhuvatysia пробуджуватися *v.t.* awake

probyratysia пробиратися *v.i.* wade

probyty пробити *v.t.* punch

probyvaty otvir пробивати отвір *v.t.* puncture

prochyshchaty прочищати *v.t.* purge

prochytannia прочитання *n.* perusal

prodavaty продавати *v.t.* sell

prodavaty v rozdrib продавати в роздріб *v.t.* retail

prodavaty z auktsionu продавати з аукціону *v.t.* auction

prodavets продавець *n.* salesman

prodazh продаж *n.* sale

prodazhnist продажність *n.* venality

prodazhnyi продажний *a.* venal

prodovzhennia продовження *n.* continuation

prodovzhuvaty продовжувати *v. i.* continue

prodovzhuvatysia продовжуватися *v.i.* last

prodovzhyty продовжити *v.i.* proceed

prodovzhyty продовжити *v.t.* prolong

produkt продукт *n.* product

produktsiia продукція *n.* produce

produktsiia продукція *n.* production

produktyvnist продуктивність *n.* performance

produktyvnist продуктивність *n.* productivity

produktyvnyi продуктивний *a.* productive

proekt проект *n.* project

proektor проектор *n.* projector

proektsiia проекція *n* plane

proektsiia проекція *n.* projection

proektuvaty проектувати *v. t.* design

profanuvaty профанувати *v.t.* profile

profesiia професія *n.* profession

profesiia професія *n.* vocation

profesiinyi професійний *a.* professional

profesor професор *n.* professor

profil профіль *n.* profile

prohalyna прогалина *n.* lacuna

prohnoz прогноз *n* forecast

prohnoz прогноз *n.* prediction

prohnozuvaty прогнозувати *v.t.* predict

proholoshennia проголошення *n.* proclamation

proholoshuvaty проголошувати *v.t.* proclaim

prohrama програма *n.* programme

prohrama програма *v.t.* project

prohres прогрес *n.* advancement

prohres прогрес *n.* progress

prohresuvaty прогресувати *v.i.* progress

prohresyvnyi прогресивний *a.* progressive

prohulianka прогулянка *n* ramble

prohulianka za muzhi mista прогулянка за мужі міста *n.* outing

prohulnyk прогульник *n.* shirker

proiasnennia прояснення *n* clarification

proiasnyty прояснити *v. t* clarify

proiav прояв *n* display

proiavliaty проявляти *v. t* display

proizd проїзд *n.* thoroughfare

prokaza проказа *n.* lark

prokaza проказа *n.* leprosy

prokazhenyi прокажений *a.* leprous

prokhach прохач *n.* petitioner

prokhannia прохання *n.* entreaty

prokhidnyi прохідний *a.* practicable

prokhodyty проходити *v. t* elapse

prokhodyty проходити *v.i.* pass

prokhodyty stroiem проходити строєм *v.i* troop

prokhodzhennia проходження *n.* passage

prokhodzhuvatysia проходжуватися *v.t.* saunter

prokholodnyi прохолодний *a* cool

prokladaty shliakh прокладати шлях *v.t.* pioneer

prokladaty shliakh прокладати шлях *v.t.* work

prokladaty tunel прокладати тунель *v.i.* tunnel

prokliattia прокляття *n* curse

prokliatyi проклятий *a.* accursed

proklin проклін *n.* damnation

proklynaty проклинати *v. t* curse

prokol прокол *n.* puncture

prokoliuvaty проколювати *v.t.* pierce

proktor проктор *n.* proctor

prokuror прокурор *n.* attorney

prokysaty прокисати *v.t.* sour

prokyslyi прокислий *a.* sour

proloh пролог *n.* preface

proloh пролог *n.* prologue

prolom пролом *n.* fracture

prolom пролом *n* gap

prolyvaty проливати *v.i.* spill

prolyvnyi проливний *a.* torrential

promainuty промайнути *v.t.* zip

promakh промах *n* blunder

promakhuvatysia промахуватися *v.i* blunder

promenystyi променистий *a.* radiant

promin промінь *n* beam

promizhnyi проміжний *adj.* annectant

promizhnyi проміжний *a.* intermediate

promizhok проміжок *n.* interval

promochyty промочити *v.t.* wet

promova промова *n.* speech

promovets промовець *n.* spokesman

promyslova pich dlia sushinnia промислова піч для сушіння *n.* kiln

pronos пронос *n* diarrhoea

pronosne проносне *n.* purgative

pronosnyi проносний *a* laxative

pronosnyi zasib проносний засіб *n.* laxative

pronosytysia zi svystom проноситися зі свистом *v.i.* whiz

pronykaiuchyi проникаючий *a.* ingrained

pronykaty проникати *v.t.* penetrate

pronyklyvist проникливість *n.* sagacity

pronyklyvyi проникливий *a.* shrewd

pronyknennia проникнення *n.* vision

pronyrlyvyi пронирливий *a.* nosy

pronyzlyvo krychaty пронизливо кричати *v. i* bray

pronyzlyvyi пронизливий *a.* shrill

pronyzlyvyi kryk пронизливий крик *n* yell

pronyzuvaty пронизувати *v.t.* saturate

pronyzuvaty spysom пронизувати списом *v.t.* lance

propahanda пропаганда *n.* propaganda

propahandyst пропагандист *n.* propagandist

propoloskaty прополоскати *v.t.* rinse

proponuvaty пропонувати *v. t* enact

proponuvaty tsinu пропонувати ціну *v.t* bid

proponuvaty vykonannia uhody пропонувати виконання угоди *v.t.* tender

proportsiia пропорція *n.* proportion

proportsiinyi пропорційний *a.* proportional

propovid проповідь *n.* gospel

propovidnyk проповідник *n.* preacher

propoviduvaty проповідувати *v.i.* preach

propozytsiia пропозиція *n* tender

propusk пропуск *n* pass

propuskaty пропускати *v.i.* skip

propyshchaty пропищати *v. i* cheep

prorakhunok прорахунок *n.* miscalculation

prorakhuvatysia прорахуватися *v.t.* miscalculate

prorochyi пророчий *a.* prophetic

prorok пророк *n.* prophet

prorokuvaty пророкувати *v.t.* prophesy

proroshchuvannia пророщування *n.* germination

prorostaty проростати *v.i.* sprout

prorosty прорости *v.i.* germinate

prorotstvo пророцтво *n.* prophecy

prorubuvaty прорубувати *v.t.* hew

proryv прорив *n* break

proryv прорив *n.* penetration

proryvaty проривати *v.t.* rupture

proshchalnyi pryiom hostei прощальний прийом гостей *n* farewell

proshchannia прощання *n.* adieu

proshchaty прощати *v.t* excuse

proshchavai! прощавай! *interj.* farewell

proshchavai(te)! прощавай(те)!
interj. adieu
proshchupuvaty прощупувати
v.t. probe
proshtovkhuvatysia
проштовхуватися *v.t.* shoulder
prosivaty просівати *v.t.* sift
proslavliannia прославляння *n.*
apotheosis
proslavliaty прославляти *v.t.* laud
proso просо *n.* millet
prosochuvannia просочування
n. leakage
prosochuvaty просочувати *v.t.*
pervade
prosochuvatysia просочуватися
v.i. seep
prosodiia просодія *n.* prosody
prospekt проспект *n.* avenue
prostak простак *n.* simpleton
prostatstvo простацтво *n.*
naivety
prostiahatysia простягатися *v.t.*
span
prostir простір *n.* space
prostir za mezhamy chohos
простір за межами чогось *n*
without
prostodushnist простодушність
n. simplicity
prostoliudyn простолюдин *n.*
jack
prostorovyi просторовий *a.*
spatial
prostoryi просторий *a.* spacious
prostota простота *n.* rusticity
prostratsiia прострація *n.*
prostration
prostrochenyi прострочений *a.*
overdue
prostrochuvaty прострочувати
v.i. procrastinate

prostupok проступок *n.*
misconduct
prostyi простий *a.* artless
prostyi простий *a.* straightforward
prostyi narod простий народ *n.*
populace
prostymyi простимий *a.*
pardonable
prostytutka проститутка *n.*
prostitute
prostytutsiia проституція *n.*
prostitution
prosuvannia просування *n.*
promotion
prosuvatysia vpered
просуватися вперед *v.i.* wriggle
prosvichuvaty renthenivskymy
promeniamy просвічувати
рентгенівськими променями
v.t. x-ray
prosvishchaty просвіщати *v. t.*
enlighten
prosvit просвіт *n.* glimpse
prosvit просвіт *n.* rent
prosyty просити *v.t.* ask
prosyty просити *v.t.* implore
prote проте *adv.* nonetheless
protehuvannia протегування *n.*
protection
protehuvaty протегувати *v.t.*
patronize
protest протест *n.* protest
protestuvaty протестувати *v.i.*
protest
protiahom протягом *conj.* for
protoka протока *n.* strait
protoptuvaty протоптувати *v.t.*
tread
prototyp прототип *n.* prototype
protsedura процедура *n.*
procedure
protses процес *n.* process
protsesiia процесія *n.* procession

protsvitaiuchyi процвітаючий *a.* prosperous
protsvitannia процвітання *n.* prosperity
protsvitaty процвітати *v.i.* prosper
proty проти *prep.* against
proty- проти- *pref.* contra
protydiiaty протидіяти *v.t.* counteract
protylezhnyi протилежний *a.* opposite
protyotruta протиотрута *n.* mithridate
protyrichchia протиріччя *n* contradiction
protyrichchia v zakoni протиріччя в законі *n.* antinomy
protyroienyi протироєний *a.* triple
protystavliaty протиставляти *v.t.* contrapose
protystoiaty протистояти *v. t* counter
protyvnyi противний *a.* nasty
protyvnyk противник *n.* adversary
proverbialnyi провербіальний *a.* proverbial
provesty провести *v.t.* guide
provesty opytuvannia провести опитування *v.t.* quiz
provesty rozvidku провести розвідку *v.i* scout
provezennia провезення *n.* portage
proviant провіант *n.* victuals
provid провід *n.* wire
providentsialne провіденціальне *a.* providential
providna pozytsiia провідна позиція *n.* lead
providnyi провідний *a* principal

providnyk провідник *n.* porter
provintsializm провінціалізм *n.* provincialism
provintsiia провінція *n.* province
provintsiinyi провінційний *a.* provincial
provisnyk провісник *n.* vaccinator
provodka проводка *n.* wiring
provodyty проводити *v.t.* pursue
provodyty проводити *v.t.* usher
provodyty проводити *v.t.* while
provodyty liniiu проводити лінію *v.t.* line
provodyty spivbesidu проводити співбесіду *v.t.* interview
provodyty vidbir проводити відбір *v.t.* select
provodyty zymu проводити зиму *v.i* winter
provokatsiia провокація *n.* provocation
provokatsiinyi провокаційний *a.* provocative
provokuvaty провокувати *v.t.* provoke
provozyty kontrabandoiu провозити контрабандою *v.t.* smuggle
provulok провулок *n.* row
provydets провидець *n.* seer
provydinnia провидіння *n.* providence
provyna провина *n.* guilt
provyna провина *n.* transgression
provynytysia провинитися *v.i.* trespass
proza проза *n.* prose
prozaichnyi прозаїчний *a.* prosaic
prozhyvannia проживання *n.* habitation
prozhyvaty проживати *v. t* bide
prozhyvaty проживати *v.i.* reside

prozorlyvyi прозорливий *a.*
sagacious
prozoryi прозорий *a.* transparent
prozvaty прозвати *v.t.* nickname
pry при *prep.* at
pry smerti при смерті *adj.* alamort
pry tsomu при цьому *conj*
however
pryberezhnyi прибережний *a.*
littoral
prybii прибій *n.* surf
pryblyzno приблизно *a.*
approximate
pryborkaty приборкати *v. t* daunt
pryborkuvaty приборкувати *v. t*
curb
prybulets прибулець *a.* alien
prybutkovyi прибутковий *a.*
lucrative
prybuttia прибуття *n.* arrival
prybuty прибути *v.i.* arrive
prybyralnyk vulyts
прибиральник вулиць *n.*
orderly
prybyraty прибирати *v.t.* remove
prybyvaty прибивати *v.t* hammer
prychal причал *n.* moorings
prychastia причастя *n.* supper
prychisuvaty причісувати *v. t*
dress
prychyna причина *n.* reason
prychynnist причинність *n*
causality
prychynnyi причинний *adj.*
causal
prydane придане *n* dowry
prydatnist придатність *n.*
aptitude
prydatnyi придатний *a*
convenient
prydatnyi придатний *n* fitter
prydatnyi придатний *a.* suitable

prydatnyi dlia roboty придатний
для роботи *a.* workable
prydatnyi dlia yizhy придатний
для їжи *a* edible
prydatnyi dlia zhytla придатний
для житла *a.* habitable
prydatok придаток *n.* appendage
prydbannia придбання *n.*
acquirement
prydushennia придушення *n.*
suppression
prydushuvaty придушувати *v.t.*
nail
prydvornyi придворний *n.*
courtier
pryhaduvannia пригадування *n*
anamnesis
pryhaniaty приганяти *v.i* surface
pryhladzhuvaty пригладжувати
v.t. smooth
pryhnichennia пригнічення *n.*
oppression
pryhnichuvaty пригнічувати *v. t*
deject
pryhnobliuvaty пригноблювати
v. t depress
pryhoda пригода *n.* occurrence
pryholomshlyvyi
приголомшливий *a.* terrific
pryholomshuvaty
приголомшувати *v.t.* stupefy
pryholomshyty приголомшити *v.*
t bemuse
pryholosnyi приголосний *n.*
consonant
pryhoshchannia пригощання *n*
treat
pryhvynchuvaty пригвинчувати
v.t. screw
pryiatel приятель *n* chum
pryiatel приятель *n.* friend
pryiatel приятель *n.* pal

pryiednannia приєднання *n.*
affiliation
pryiednatysia приєднатися *v.t.*
rejoin
pryiednuvaty приєднувати *v.t.*
append
pryiednuvatysia приєднуватися
v.t. accede
pryiednuvatysia приєднуватися
v.t. join
pryiemne provedennia chasu
приємне проведення часу *n.*
pastime
pryiemnyi приємний *a.* cosy
pryiemnyi приємний *a.* glad
pryiemnyi приємний *a.* pleasant
pryimaty приймати & accept
pryiniatnyi прийнятний *a*
acceptable
pryiniattia прийняття *n*
acceptance
pryiniattia yizhy прийняття їжи
n. meal
pryiniaty duzhe velyku dozu
прийняти дуже велику дозу *v.t.*
overdose
pryiom прийом *n.* reception
pryiom hostei прийом гостей *n.*
party
prykazka приказка *n* byword
prykhid прихід *n.* advent
prykhid прихід *n.* parish
prykhodyty приходити *v. i.* come
prykhodyty na dopomohu
приходити на допомогу *v.t.*
succour
prykhodyty v hosti приходити в
гості *v.t.* visit
prykhovanyi прихований *a* inside
prykhovuvaty приховувати *v.t.*
veil
prykhylnist прихильність *n*
favour1

prykhylnyk прихильник *n*
devotee
prykhylnyk прихильник *n.* stickler
prykhylnyk suvoroi dystsypliny
прихильник суворої
дисципліни *n.* martinet
pryklad приклад *n* example
prykladaty прикладати *v.t.* adhibit
prykmeta прикмета *n.* token
prykmetnyk прикметник *n.*
adjective
prykoliuvaty приколювати *v.t.* pin
prykrasa прикраса *n* dressing
prykrashaty прикрашати *v.t.*
adorn
prykrashaty прикрашати *v. t*
beautify
prykrashaty прикрашати *v.t.* gild
prykrashaty hirliandoiu
прикрашати гірляндою *v.t.*
garland
prykripliuvaty kilochkom
прикріплювати кілочком *v.t.*
peg
prykryi прикрий *a* deplorable
prykryty прикрити *v.t.* screen
prykydatysia прикидатися *v.t*
feign
prylad прилад *n.* appliance
prylavok прилавок *n.* counter
prylehlyi прилеглий *a.* adjacent
pryliahaty прилягати *v* abutted
prylypannia прилипання *n.*
adhesion
prylypaty прилипати *v. i.* cling
prymaniuvaty приманювати *v.t.*
lure
prymanka приманка *n.* lure
prymara примара *n.* spectre
prymarnyi примарний *a.*
visionary
prymishchennia приміщення *n.*
accommodation

prymishchennia приміщення *n.* room

prymitka примітка *n.* note

prymitnyi примітний *a.* notable

prymityvnyi примітивний *a.* primitive

prymkha примха *n.* vagary

prymkha примха *n.* whim

prymorskyi приморський *a.* maritime

prymus примус *n* compulsion

prymushuvaty примушувати *v.t* force

prymushuvaty примушувати *v.t* urge

prymusovyi примусовий *a.* mandatory

prymusyty примусити *v.t* block

prymykaty примикати *v.t.* adjoin

prymyrennia примирення *n.* reconciliation

prymyriaty примиряти *v.t.* conciliate

prymyriaty примиряти *v.t.* reconcile

prymyrytel примиритель *n.* lubricant

prynada принада *n.* attraction

prynalezhnist приналежність *n* appurtenance

prynalezhnist do cholovichoi stati приналежність до чоловічої статі *n.* virility

prynesty принести *v.t* fetch

prynosyty приносити *v.t.* get

prynosyty v zhertvu приносити в жертву *v.t.* sacrifice

prynter принтер *n.* printer

prynts принц *n.* prince

pryntsesa принцеса *n.* princess

pryntsyp принцип *n.* principle

pryntsyp принцип *n.* tenet

prynyzhenist приниженість *n.* humiliation

prynyzhennia приниження *n* abasement

prynyzhuvaty принижувати *v.t.* humiliate

prynyzyty принизити *v.t.* snub

prypadok припадок *n* fit

prypii припій *n.* solder

pryplyv приплив *n.* influx

pryplyv приплив *n.* tributary

prypravliaty приправляти *v.t.* spice

prypushchennia припущення *n.* supposition

prypuskaty припускати *v.t.* surmise

prypynennia припинення *n* defeat

prypynennia припинення *n.* termination

prypynennia viiskovykh dii припинення військових дій *n.* armistice

prypyniaty припиняти *v. t* discontinue

prypyniaty припиняти *v.t.* leave

prypyniaty припиняти *v.t.* terminate

prypys припис *n.* injunction

prypysanyi приписаний *adj.* adscript

prypysuvaty приписувати *v.t.* ascribe

prypysuvaty приписувати *v.t.* attribute

pryrechennia приречення *n.* predestination

pryrikaty прирікати *v. t.* doom

pryrist приріст *n.* increment

pryroda природа *n.* nature

pryrodno природно *adv.* naturally

pryrodnyi природний *a.* natural

pryruchaty приручати *v.t.* tame
pryshch прищ *n* acne
pryshchyk прищик *n.* spot
pryshporyty пришпорити *v.t.* spur
prysiaha присяга *n.* oath
prysiazhnyi присяжний *n.*
  juryman
prysidaty присідати *v.i.* duck
pryskiplyvyi прискіпливий *adj*
  censorious
pryskorennia прискорення *n*
  acceleration
pryskoriuvaty прискорювати *v.t*
  accelerate
pryskoriuvaty прискорювати *v. t*
  boost
pryslivia прислів'я *n.* adage
pryslivia прислів'я *n.* proverb
pryslivnyk прислівник *n.* adverb
pryslivnykovyi прислівниковий
  a. adverbial
prysmak присмак *n.* smack
pryspiv приспів *n* refrain
prystavaty приставати *v.t.* molest
prystavliaty speredu
  приставляти спереду *v.t.* prefix
prystoinist пристойність *n*
  decency
prystoinyi пристойний *a.* seemly
prystosovuvaty пристосовувати
  v.t accommodate
prystrasnyi пристрасний *a.*
  passionate
prystrast пристрасть *n.* appetite
prystrii пристрій *n* establishment
prystup приступ *n* flush
prysviachuvaty присвячувати *v.t.*
  consecrate
prysypliaty присипляти *v.t.*
  sedate
prytcha притча *n.* parable
prytiahaty do sudu притягати до
  суду *v.* arraign

pryton притон *n* den
prytuliaty притуляти *v.i.* lean
prytulok притулок *n.* haven
prytupliatysia притуплятися *v.
  t.* dull
prytysnutysia притиснутися *v.i.*
  nestle
prytysnutysia притиснутися *v.*
  nuzzle
pryvablyvyi привабливий *a.*
  attractive
pryvablyvyi привабливий *a.*
  lovable
pryval привал *n* halt
pryvatnist приватність *n.*
  particular
pryvatnyi приватний *a.* private
pryvchaty привчати *v.t.* accustom
pryvchaty привчати *v. t.* habituate
pryvertaty привертати *v. t*
  engage
pryvertaty uvahu привертати
  увагу *v.t.* preoccupy
pryvesty v poriadok привести в
  порядок *v.t.* trim
pryviaz прив'язь *n.* tether
pryviazaty прив'язати *v.t.* tether
pryvid привід *n.* preposition
pryvilei привілей *n* benefit
pryvilei привілей *n.* franchise
pryvilei привілей *n.* privilege
pryvitannia привітання *n.*
  salutation
pryvitaty привітати *v.t.* salute
pryvitno pryimaty привітно
  приймати *v.t* welcome
pryvitnyi привітний *a.* affable
pryvlasnennia привласнення *n.*
  acquisition
pryvlasniuvaty привласнювати
  v.t. appropriate
pryvlasnyty привласнити *v.t.*
  pocket

pryvnesenyi привнесений *adj*
adscititious
pryvodyty u vidchai приводити у
відчай *v. t* dishearten
pryvodyty v liut приводити в
лють *v.t.* infuriate
pryvodyty v poriadok приводити
в порядок *v.t.* tidy
pryvodyty v skladne
stanovyshche приводити в
складне становище *v.t.* puzzle
pryvodyty v zamishannia
приводити в замішання *v.t.*
nonplus
pryz приз *n.* prize
pryznachaty призначати *v.t.*
allocate
pryznachaty pensiiu призначати
пенсію *v.t.* pension
pryznachatysia призначатися *v.t.*
mean
pryznachennia призначення *n*
destination
pryznachennia призначення *n.*
intent
pryzovnyi призовний *a.* military
pryzovnyk призовник *n.* recruit
pryzupynennia призупинення *n.*
suspension
pryzupyniaty призупиняти *v.t.*
suspend
psalom псалом *n.* psalm
psevdonim псевдонім *n.*
pseudonym
pshenytsia пшениця *n.* wheat
psuietsia псується *a.* incorruptible
psuvannia псування *n.* corruption
psuvaty псувати *v.t.* vitiate
psykhiatr психіатр *n.* psychiatrist
psykhiatriia психіатрія *n.*
psychiatry
psykhiatrychna likarnia
психіатрична лікарня *n* asylum

psykhichnyi психічний *a.* psychic
psykholoh психолог *n.*
psychologist
psykholohichnyi психологічний
a. psychological
psykholohiia психологія *n.*
psychology
psykhopat психопат *n.*
psychopath
psykhoterapiia психотерапія *n.*
psychotherapy
psykhoz психоз *n.* psychosis
ptakh птах *n* bird
ptakholov птахолов *n.* fowler
ptashenia пташеня *n.* nestling
ptashnyk пташник *n.* aviary
ptashynyi klei пташиний клей *n*
birdlime
ptytsia птиця *n.* fowl
publika публіка *n.* audience
publikatsiia публікація *n.*
prospectus
publikuvaty публікувати *v.t:*
publish
puchok пучок *n.* wisp
pudryty пудрити *v.t.* powder
pudynh пудинг *n.* pudding
pukh пух *n* over
pukhkyi пухкий *adv.* full
pukhlyna пухлина *n.* tumour
pukhyr пухир *n* bleb
pulover пуловер *n.* pullover
puls пульс *n.* pulse
pulsatsiia пульсація *n.* pulsation
pulsuvaty пульсувати *v.i.* pulsate
punkt пункт *n.* paragraph
punktualnist пунктуальність *n.*
nicety
punktualnyi пунктуальний *a.*
punctual
punktuatsiia пунктуація *n.*
punctuation
punsh пунш *n.* punch

purkhannia пурхання *n* flutter
puryst пурист *n.* purist
purytanskyi пуританський *a.*
  puritanical
purytanyn пуританин *n.* puritan
pushynka пушинка *n* flock
puskaty korinnia пускати коріння
  v.i. root
puskaty pid ukis пускати під укіс
  v. t. derail
pustelia пустеля *n* desert
pustodzvin пустодзвін *n.*
  windbag
pustoporozhnie пустопорожнє *a.*
  indolent
pustoshchi пустощі *n.* frolic
pustota пустота *n.* hollow
pustotlyvyi пустотливий *a.*
  mischievous
pustun пустун *n.* villain
pustuvaty пустувати *v.i.* frolic
pustyn пустинь *n.* hermitage
pustyr пустир *n* barren
puta пута *n.* shackle
puzyr пузир *n* blister
pyiachyty пиячити *v.i.* revel
pyiatyka пиятика *n.* revelry
pykhatyi пихатий *a.* insolent
pykhtinnia пихтіння *n.* pant
pyl пил *n* dust
pyliaty пиляти *v.t* file
pyliaty пиляти *v.t.* saw
pylnist пильність *n.* vigilance
pylno dyvytysia пильно
  дивитися *v.i* glare
pylnyi пильний *a.* vigilant
pylnyi pohliad пильний погляд
  n. stare
pylok пилок *n.* pollen
pyrih пиріг *n.* cake
pyrkhannia пирхання *n.* snort
pysaty писати *v.t.* write

pysaty pamflety писати
  памфлети *v.t.* lampoon
pysaty paskvili писати пасквілі
  v.t. libel
pyshatysia пишатися *v.t.* pride
pyshchaty пищати *v.i* pipe
pyshnist пишність *n.* pageantry
pyshnota пишнота *n.* pomp
pyshnyi пишний *a.* luxuriant
pyshnyi пишний *a.* magnificent
pysmennyk письменник *n.* writer
pysmove svidchennia письмове
  свідчення *n* affidavit
pytalnyi питальний *a.*
  interrogative
pytannia питання *n.* interrogation
pytannia питання *n.* question
pytaty питати *v.t.* question
pytvo питво *n* drink
pyvo пиво *n* beer
pyvovarnia пивоварня *n* brewery

R

rab раб *n.* slave
rab chohos раб чогось *n.* thrall
rabolipnyi раболіпний *a.*
  subservient
rabolipstvo раболіпство *n.*
  subservience
rabolipstvuvaty раболіпствувати
  v. i. cringe
rabolipstvuvaty раболіпствувати
  v. i. crouch
rabovlasnytstvo рабовласництво
  n. slavery
rabskyi рабський *a.* servile
rabskyi рабський *a.* slavish
rabstvo рабство *n.* thralldom
rada рада *n.* council
radiatsiia радіація *n.* radiation
radii радій *n.* radium
radio радіо *n.* radio

radioperedacha радіопередача *n* broadcast
radiopryimach радіоприймач *n* wireless
radisnyi радісний *a.* mirthful
radist радість *n.* glee
radity радіти *v.i.* rejoice
radius радіус *n.* radius
radnyk радник *n.* councillor
radnyk радник *n.* counsellor
raduvaty радувати *v.t.* gladden
radykalnyi радикальний *a.* radical
radyty радити *v.t.* recommend
radytysia радитися *v. i* confer
rahu z miasa z ovochamy рагу з м'яса з овочами *n.* hotchpotch
rai рай *n.* paradise
raion район *n* corner
rak рак *n.* cancer
raketa ракета *n.* missile
rakhit рахіт *n.* rickets
rakhunok рахунок *n.* account
rakhunok-faktura рахунок-фактура *n.* invoice
rakhuvaty рахувати *v.t.* compute
rakovyna раковина *n* sink
rama рама *n* frame
rana рана *n.* injury
randevu рандеву *n.* rendezvous
ranets ранець *n.* satchel
ranh ранг *n.* rank
ranishe раніше *adv* formerly
rankova zoria ранкова зоря *n* aurora
rannie dytynstvo раннє дитинство *n.* infancy
rannii ранній *a* early
rano рано *adv* early
ranok ранок *n.* morning
rapira рапіра *n.* rapier
raptova zlyva раптова злива *n.* spate

raptovo раптово *adv.* suddenly
raptovyi раптовий *a* abrupt
rasovyi расовий *a.* racial
rasyzm расизм *n.* racialism
ratsion раціон *n.* ration
ratsionalizuvaty раціоналізувати *v.t.* rationalize
ratsionalnist раціональність *n.* rationality
ratsionalnyi раціональний *a* expedient
ratyfikuvaty ратифікувати *v.t.* ratify
ratyshche ратище *n.* shaft
ravlyk равлик *n.* snail
raz раз *adv.* once
raz na dva tyzhni раз на два тижні *adj* bi-weekly
raz na tyzhden раз на тиждень *adv.* weekly
razmeliuvaty размелювати *v.i.* grind
razom разом *adv.* together
reabilitatsiia реабілітація *n.* rehabilitation
reabilituvaty реабілітувати *v.t.* rehabilitate
reahuvannia реагування *n.* response
reahuvaty реагувати *v.i.* react
reaktsiia реакція *n.* reaction
reaktsiinyi реакційний *a.* reactionary
reaktyvnyi dvyhun реактивний двигун *n.* jet
reaktyvnyi snariad реактивний снаряд *n.* rocket
realist реаліст *n.* realist
realistychnyi реалістичний *a.* realistic
realizatsiia реалізація *n.* realization
realizm реалізм *n.* realism

realnist реальність *n.* reality
realnyi реальний *a.* real
rebernyi реберний *adj.* costal
rebro ребро *n.* rib
rechovyi речовий *a.* material
rechovyna речовина *n.* stuff
redahuvaty редагувати *v. t* edit
redaktorckii редакторскій *a* editorial
redys редис *n.* radish
referendum референдум *n.* referendum
refleks рефлекс *n.* reflex
reflektornyi рефлекторний *a* reflex
reflektyvnyi рефлективний *a.* reflective
reforma реформа *n.* reform
reformator реформатор *n.* reformer
reformuvannia реформування *n.* reformation
reformuvaty реформувати *v.t.* reform
reheneratsiia регенерація *n.* regeneration
reheneruvaty регенерувати *v.t.* regenerate
rehion регіон *n.* region
rehionalnyi регіональний *a.* regional
rehit регіт *n.* laughter
rehuliarnist регулярність *n.* regularity
rehuliarnyi регулярний *a.* regular
rehuliator регулятор *n.* regulator
rehuliuvannia регулювання *n.* alignment
rehuliuvaty регулювати *v.t.* temper
reid рейд *n.* raid
reiestr реєстр *n.* register

reiestrator реєстратор *n.* recorder
reiestratsiia реєстрація *n.* registration
reiestratura реєстратура *n.* registry
reiestruvaty реєструвати *v.t.* incorporate
reiestruvaty реєструвати *v.t.* register
reika рейка *n.* lath
reituzy рейтузи *n.* pantaloon
reket рекет *n.* racket
reklama реклама *n* advertisement
reklamnyi lystok рекламний листок *n.* handbill
reklamuvannia рекламування *n* boost
reklamuvaty рекламувати *v.t.* advertise
rekomendatsiia рекомендація *n.* recommendation
rekomenduvaty рекомендувати *v. t* commend
rektifikuvaty ректіфікувати *v.i.* rectify
rektyfikatsiia ректифікація *n.* purification
rekviiem реквієм *n.* requiem
rekvizuvaty реквізувати *v.t.* requisition
relaksatsiia релаксація *n.* relaxation
rele реле *n.* relay
relevantnist релевантність *n.* relevance
relevantnyi релевантний *a.* relevant
relihiia релігія *n.* religion
relihiinyi релігійний *a.* religious
relikviia реліквія *n.* relic
remeslo ремесло *n* craft
remin ремінь *n* belt

reminets ремінець *n.* strap
remisiia ремісія *n.* remission
remisnyk ремісник *n.* artisan
remont ремонт *n.* renovation
remontuvaty ремонтувати *v.t.*
  overhaul
renesans ренесанс *n.*
  renaissance
renthen рентген *n.* x-ray
renthenivskyi рентгенівський *a.*
  x-ray
repatriant репатріант *n* repatriate
repatriatsiia репатріація *n.*
  repatriation
repatriiuvaty репатріювати *v.t.*
  repatriate
repelent репелент *n* repellent
repetyruvaty репетирувати *v.t.*
  rehearse
repetytor репетитор *n.* tutor
repetytsiia репетиція *n.* rehearsal
replika репліка *n* cue
reporter репортер *n.* reporter
represiia репресія *n.* repression
reproduktsiia репродукція *n.*
  replica
reptyliia рептилія *n.* reptile
reputatsiia репутація *n.*
  reputation
resheto решето *n.* riddle
reshitka решітка *n.* lattice
respublika республіка *n.* republic
respublikanets республіканець *n*
  republican
respublikanskyi
  республіканський *a.* republican
restavruvaty реставрувати *v.t.*
  renovate
restoran ресторан *n.* restaurant
restoratsiia ресторація *n.*
  restoration
resurs ресурс *n.* resource

retelni poshuky ретельні пошуки
  n research
retelnyi ретельний *a* careful
retelnyi ретельний *a* thorough
retrospektsiia ретроспекція *n.*
  retrospection
retrospektyvnyi
  ретроспективний *a.*
  retrospective
retsept рецепт *n.* recipe
retsesiia рецесія *n.* recession
retsydyv рецидив *n.* recurrence
retsydyvuvaty рецидивувати *v.i.*
  recur
retsypiient реципієнт *n.* recipient
retushuvaty ретушувати *v.t.*
  retouch
rev рев *n.* roar
reverans реверанс *n.* obeisance
reversyvnyi реверсивний *a.*
  reversible
revinnia ревіння *n* bray
revity ревіти *v. i* bellow
revmatychnyi ревматичний *a.*
  rheumatic
revmatyzm ревматизм *n.*
  rheumatism
revnoshchi ревнощі *n.* jealousy
revnyi ревний *a.* zealous
revnyvyi ревнивий *a.* jealous
revokatsiia ревокація *n.*
  revocation
revoliutsiia революція *n.*
  revolution
revoliutsiinyi революційний *a.*
  revolutionary
revoliutsioner революціонер *n*
  revolutionary
revolver револьвер *n.* revolver
rezerv резерв *n.* store
rezervuar резервуар *n.* basin
rezervuvannia резервування *n.*
  reservation

rezhym режим *n.* mode
reziume резюме *n.* resume
rezonans резонанс *n.* resonance
rezonansnyi резонансний *a.* resonant
rezultat результат *n.* result
rezydent резидент *n* resident
riabyty рябити *v.t.* ruffle
riad ряд *n.* row
riasnity рясніти *v.i.* teem
riasnyi рясний *a* fertile
riasnyi рясний *a.* profuse
riativnyk рятівник *n.* saviour
riatuvaty рятувати *v.t.* rid
riatuvaty sudno рятувати судно *v.t.* salvage
rich річ *n.* thing
richechka річечка *n.* rivulet
richka річка *n.* river
richnyi річний *adj* aestival
richnytsia річниця *n.* anniversary
richyshche річище *n* channel
rid рід *n.* gender
ridka yizha рідка їжа *n* liquid
ridkisnyi рідкісний *a.* rare
ridkisnyi рідкісний *a.* sparse
ridko рідко *adv.* seldom
ridkyi рідкий *a.* liquid
ridna mova рідна мова *n.* vernacular
ridnia рідня *n.* kin
ridnyi рідний *a.* native
rifmopletstvo ріфмоплетство *n.* crambo
rih ріг *n.* horn
rik рік *n.* year
rikoshetuvaty рікошетувати *v.i.* rebound
ripa ріпа *n.* turnip
rishaty рішати *v.t.* resolve
rishennia рішення *n* decision
rishennia рішення *n* decree

rishuche bratysia рішуче братися *v.t* fling
rishuchist рішучість *n* dash
rishuchist рішучість *n.* resolution
rishuchyi рішучий *a.* manful
rishymist рішимість *n.* determination
riv рів *n.* trench
riven рівень *n.* level
riven zapasiv рівень запасів *n.* stocking
rivnia рівня *n* equal
rivniannia рівняння *n* equation
rivnist рівність *n* equality
rivnomirnyi рівномірний *a* even
rivnostoronnii рівносторонній *a* equilateral
rivnosylnyi рівносильний *a.* tantamount
rivnyi рівний *n.* peer
rivnyna рівнина *n.* plain
rizak різак *n* colter
rizanyna різанина *n.* slaughter
rizaty різати *v. t* cut
rizba різьба *n.* imagery
Rizdvo Різдво *n* Christmas
Rizdvo Різдво *n.* Xmas
rizhok ріжок *n* bugle
rizko padaty різко падати *v.i.* slump
rizko zaperechuvaty різко заперечувати *v.t.* retort
rizkyi різкий *adj* absonant
rizkyi різкий *a.* acute
rizkyi різкий *a.* smart
rizkyi rukh різкий рух *n.* jerk
rizkyi vypad різкий випад *n.* shy
riznomanitnist різноманітність *n.* variety
riznomanitnyi різноманітний *a* diverse
riznomanitnyi різноманітний *a.* miscellaneous

riznomanitnyi різноманітний *a.*
multiform
riznostoronnii різносторонній *a.*
versatile
riznovyd різновид *n.* kind
riznyi різний *a.* sundry
riznytsia різниця *n* difference
roaznoshchyk роазнощик *n.*
vendor
robitnyk робітник *n.* worker
robochyi робочий *n.* workman
robot робот *n.* robot
robota робота *n.* job
robota робота *n.* work
robotodavets роботодавець *n*
employer
robyty робити *v. t* do
robyty робити *v.t.* make
robyty dohanu робити догану *v.t.*
reprimand
robyty eskiz робити ескіз *v. t*
draft
robyty hnuchkym робити
гнучким *v.t.* limber
robyty karnym робити карним
v.t. penalize
robyty krashchym робити
кращим *v.t.* reclaim
robyty nedbalo робити недбало
v. t botch
robyty neobkhidnym робити
необхідним *v.t.* necessitate
robyty neprydatnym робити
непридатним *v. t* disable
robyty ochevydnym робити
очевидним *v.t.* manifest
robyty pauzu робити паузу *v.i.*
pause
robyty pereklyk робити переклик
v.t. muster
robyty pobytym робити побитим
v.t. stereotype

robyty podorozh робити
подорож *v.i.* voyage
robyty pokupky робити покупки
v.i. shop
robyty poperedzhennia робити
попередження *v. t.* caution
robyty rivnym робити рівним *v.t.*
level
robyty shcheplennia робити
щеплення *v.t.* inoculate
robyty shcho-nebud u vidpovid
робити що-небудь у відповідь
v.i. respond
robyty skladky робити складки
v.t. crimple
robyty syrotoiu робити сиротою
v.t orphan
robyty tonkym робити тонким
v.t. thin
robyty tverdym робити твердим
v.t. harden
robyty vodonepronyknym
робити водонепроникним *v.t.*
waterproof
robyty vstup робити вступ *v.t.*
preface
robyty vybir робити вибір *v.i.* opt
robyty vylazku робити вилазку
v.i. sally
robyty vypad робити випад *v.i*
lunge
robyty zhyttievym робити
життєвим *v.t.* vitalize
robyty zyhzahy робити зигзаги
v.i. zigzag
robytysia робитися *v.t.* grow
rodiuchist родючість *n* fertility
rodiuchyi родючий *a* rank
rodiuchyi родючий *a.* rich
rodovid родовід *n.* lineage
rodovid родовід *n.* pedigree
rodych родич *n.* relative
rodychka родичка *n.* relation

rodzynka родзинка *n.* zest
rohivka рогівка *n* cornea
rohonosets рогоносець *n.*
  cuckold
roialist рояліст *n.* royalist
roialti роялті *n.* royalty
roitysia роїтися *v.i.* swarm
rokhkannia рохкання *n.* grunt
rokhkaty рохкати *v.i.* grunt
rol роль *n.* role
rom ром *n.* rum
roman роман *n* novel
romanist романіст *n.* novelist
romantychnyi романтичний *a.*
  romantic
romantyka романтика *n.*
  romance
ropa ропа *v.t.* leach
rosa роса *n.* dew
roslyi рослий *a.* stalwart
roslyna рослина *n.* plant
roslynnist рослинність *n.*
  vegetation
roslynnyi slyz рослинний слиз *n.*
  mucilage
rosomakha росомаха *n.* glutton
rot рот *n.* mouth
rovisnyk ровісник *n.* precursor
rozarii розарій *n.* rosary
rozbavlenyi розбавлений *a* dilute
rozbavliaty розбавляти *v. t* dilute
rozbazariuvaty розбазарювати
  v.t. squander
rozbihatysia розбігатися *v. t*
  disperse
rozbii розбій *n.* dacoity
rozbiinychaty розбійничати *v.t*
  pirate
rozbiinyk розбійник *n.* bandit
rozbirlyvo розбірливо *adv.* legibly
rozbirlyvyi розбірливий *a.* legible
rozbizhnist розбіжність *n.*
  disagreement

rozbrat розбрат *n.* strife
rozbyty vshchent розбити вщент
  v.t. rout
rozbyty z hriukotom розбити з
  грюкотом *v. i* crash
rozbyvaty tabir розбивати табір
  v. i. camp
rozcharovuvaty розчаровувати *v.*
  t. disappoint
rozchyn розчин *n.* solution
rozchyniaty розчиняти *v.t*
  dissolve
rozchynnist розчинність *n.*
  solubility
rozchynnyi розчинний *a.* soluble
rozchynnyk розчинник *n* solvent
rozdacha роздача *n.* dealing
rozdaty роздати *v. i* deal
rozdavaty роздавати *v. t*
  distribute
rozdavliuvaty роздавлювати *v.t*
  mash
rozdavliuvaty роздавлювати *v.t.*
  squash
rozdavyty роздавити *v. t* crush
rozdil розділ *n.* section
rozdiliaty розділяти *v. t* divide
rozdiliaty розділяти *v.t.* partition
rozdilyty na chotyry розділити
  на чотири *v.t.* quarter
rozdobuty роздобути *v.t.* procure
rozdratuvannia роздратування
  n. ire
rozdratuvannia роздратування *n.*
  irritation
rozdribna torhivlia роздрібна
  торгівля *n.* retail
rozdribnyi роздрібний *a* retail
rozdribnyi torhovets роздрібний
  торговець *n.* retailer
rozdum роздум *n.* rumination
rozdvoiuvatysia роздвоюватися
  v. t. double

rozdyraty роздирати *v.t.* tear
rozetka розетка *n.* socket
rozfarbovuvaty розфарбовувати
v. t colour
rozhevyi рожевий *a* pink
rozhevyi рожевий *n.* pink
rozhliad розгляд *n.* approval
rozhliad розгляд *n* consideration
rozhliad розгляд *n* review
rozhliad розгляд *n.* scrutiny
rozhliadaty розглядати *v. t* examine
rozhortaty розгортати *v.t.* deploy
rozhrabuvaty розграбувати *v.t.* ransack
rozhrom розгром *n* rout
roziasnyty роз'яснити *v.i.* irradiate
rozibratysia розібратися *v.t.* grasp
roziednaty роз'єднати *v.t.* insulate
roziednuvaty роз'єднувати *v. t* disconnect
rozihrash розіграш *n.* bam
rozihrash розіграш *n* draw
rozivdka розівдка *n* exploration
rozkaiuvatysia розкаюватися *v.i.* repent
rozkazaty розказати *v.t.* tell
rozkhvaliuvaty розхвалювати *v. t.* extol
rozkish розкіш *n.* superfluity
rozkishnyi розкішний *a.* sumptuous
rozkladannia розкладання *n.* decomposition
rozkladaty розкладати *v. t.* decompose
rozkleiuvaty розклеювати *v.t.* post
rozkol розкол *n.* secession
rozkoliuvaty розколювати *v.i.* split

rozkoliuvaty розколювати *v.t.* sunder
rozkoliuvatysia розколюватися *v.t* fracture
rozkopka розкопка *n.* excavation
rozkopuvaty розкопувати *v.t.* unearth
rozkryty розкрити *v. t* disclose
rozkrytyi розкритий *a.* open
rozkryvatysia розкриватися *v.t.* unfold
rozkvartyruvannia розквартирування *n.* cantonment
rozkvit розквіт *n* bloom
rozkvit розквіт *n.* heyday
rozkvitaty розквітати *v.i.* bloom
rozkydaty розкидати *v.t.* scatter
rozlad розлад *n* discord
rozlad розлад *n.* frustration
rozladnuvaty розладнувати *v.t.* frustrate
rozluchaty розлучати *v. t* divorce
rozluchennia розлучення *n* divorce
rozlyvochna mashyna розливочна машина *n* bottler
rozmir розмір *n.* gauge
rozmir розмір *n.* size
rozmiriaty розміряти *v.t.* proportion
rozmistyty розмістити *v.t.* locate
rozmnozhuvalnyi aparat розмножувальний апарат *n* cyclostyle
rozmnozhuvaty розмножувати *v. t* cyclostyle
rozmova розмова *n* talk
rozmovliaty розмовляти *v. i.* chat2
rozorennia розорення *n.* ruin
rozpad розпад *n* decay
rozpiattia розп'яття *n.* rood

rozplata розплата *n.* wage
rozplavlenyi розплавлений *a.*
molten
rozplidnyk розплідник *n.* nursery
rozplyvchastyi розпливчастий *a.*
vague
rozpochynaty розпочинати *v.t.*
begin
rozpodil розподіл *n* distribution
rozpodiliaty розподіляти *v.t.*
apportion
rozpodiliaty розподіляти *v.i.*
participate
rozporiadzhennia
розпорядження *n* disposal
rozporoshuvaty розпорошувати
v.t. spray
rozpovid розповідь *n.* narration
rozpovidach розповідач *n.*
narrator
rozpovidaty розповідати *v.t.*
recount
rozpovidnyi розповідний *a.*
narrative
rozprostertyi розпростертий *a.*
prostrate
rozpushchenyi розпущений *a.*
licentious
rozpusnyi розпусний *a.* profligate
rozpusnyk розпусник *n*
debauchee
rozpusta розпуста *n.* profligacy
rozputnyi розпутний *a.* immoral
rozpytuvaty розпитувати *v.t.*
inquire
rozrada розрада *n.* balsam
rozrakhovuvaty розраховувати *v.*
t. calculate
rozrakhunok розрахунок *n.*
computation
rozrakhunok розрахунок *n*
estimation

rozrakhuvaty za chasom
розрахувати за часом *v.t.* time
rozriadzhaty розряджати *v. t*
discharge
rozrizaty розрізати *v.t.* rip
rozrizniaty розрізняти *v. i*
distinguish
rozrobliaty karier розробляти
кар'єр *v.i.* quarry
rozrostannia tkanyny
розростання тканини *n*
accrementition
rozrostatysia розростатися *v.i*
flourish
rozryv розрив *n* abruption
rozryvaty розривати *v.t.* sever
rozshchepliuvannia
розщеплювання *n* split
rozshchepliuvaty розщеплювати
v.t. splinter
rozshchepliuvaty na tonki shary
розщеплювати на тонкі шари
v.t. laminate
rozshuk розшук *n.* search
rozshyriuvaty розширювати *v. t*
enlarge
rozshyriuvatysia розширюватися
v.t. widen
rozsichennia розсічення *n*
dissection
rozsikaty розсікати *v. t* dissect
rozsil розсіл *n* brine
rozsistysia розсістися *v.i.* lounge
rozslabliatysia розслаблятися
v.t. relax
rozsliduvannia розслідування *n.*
investigation
rozsliduvaty розслідувати *v.t.*
investigate
rozstavliaty za velychynoiu
розставляти за величиною *v.t.*
size

rozstavyty z promizhkamy розставити з проміжками *v.t.* space

rozstroiuvatysia розстроюватися *v.t.* shatter

rozsud розсуд *n* discretion

rozsudlyvist розсудливість *n.* prudence

rozsudlyvyi розсудливий *a.* judicious

rozsudlyvyi розсудливий *a.* rational

rozsypchastyi розсипчастий *a* crisp

roztashovanyi useredeni krainy розташований усередені країни *a.* inland

roztashovuvaty розташовувати *v. t* dispose

roztashovuvatysia розташовуватися *v.t.* pair

roztiah розтяг *n* wrick

roztiahnennia suhloba розтягнення суглоба *n.* sprain

roztiahnuty zviazky розтягнути зв'язки *v.t.* sprain

roztiahuvannia розтягування *n* stretch

roztiahuvaty розтягувати *v.t.* stretch

roztrachuvaty розтрачувати *v.t.* spend

roztriskuvannia розтріскування *v. i* crack

roztsiniuvaty розцінювати *v.t.* appraise

roztsiniuvaty розцінювати *v.t.* regard

roztyrannia розтирання *n* rub

rozum розум *n.* judgement

rozum розум *n.* mind

rozuminnia розуміння *n.* apprehension

rozuminnia розуміння *n* comprehension

rozumnyi розумний *a.* clever

rozumovyi розумовий *a.* intellectual

rozumovyi розумовий *a.* mental

rozv`iazuvaty розв'язувати *v.t.* loosen

rozvaha розвага *n.* fun

rozval розвал *n* downfall

rozvantazhuvannia розвантажування *n.* discharge

rozvantazhyty розвантажити *v.t.* unburden

rozvazhaty розважати *v. t* entertain

rozvazhlyvyi розважливий *a.* prudential

rozvedennia розведення *n.* propagation

rozviazka розв'язка *n.* upshot

rozviaznist розв'язність *n* swagger

rozviazuvaty розв'язувати *v.t.* loose

rozvidka розвідка *n.* intelligence

rozvidnyk розвідник *n.* guide

rozvidnyk розвідник *n* scout

rozvodyty розводити *v.t* breed

rozvytok розвиток *n.* development

rozvytok розвиток *n* evolution

rozvyvaty розвивати *v. t.* develop

rozvyvaty розвивати *v.t.* expand

rozzbroiennia роззброєння *n.* disarmament

rozzhariuvatysia розжарюватися *v.i.* glow

rozziavyvshy rot роззявивши рот *adv.*, agape

rtut ртуть *n.* mercury

rtut ртуть *n.* quicksilver

rtutnyi ртутний *a.* mercurial

rubaty рубати *v.t.* slash
rubaty miaso рубати м'ясо *v.t.* mince
rubaty shableiu рубати шаблею *v.t.* sabre
rubets рубець *n* wake
rubin рубін *n.* ruby
rubizh рубіж *n.* frontier
rubl рубль *n.* rouble
ruchatysia ручатися *v.t* guarantee
ruchatysia za ручатися за *v.i.* vouch
ruchatysia za ручатися за *v.t.* warrant
ruchka ручка *n.* pen
ruchna robota ручна робота *n.* handicraft
ruchna robota ручна робота *n.* handiwork
ruchnyi ручний *a.* manual
ruchnyi ручний *a.* tame
ruda руда *n.* ore
rudyment рудимент *n.* rudiment
rudymentarnyi рудиментарний *a.* rudimentary
ruinuvannia руйнування *n* destruction
ruinuvaty руйнувати *v.t.* wreck
ruinuvatysia руйнуватися *v. i* decay
ruka рука *n.* arm
ruka рука *n* hand
rukav рукав *n* sleeve
rukavychka рукавичка *n.* glove
rukavytsia рукавиця *n.* gauntlet
rukavytsia рукавиця *n.* mitten
rukh рух *n.* motion
rukhatysia рухатися *v.t.* move
rukhatysia khvylepodibno рухатися хвилеподібно *v.i.* undulate

rukhatysia nazad i vpered рухатися назад і вперед *v.t.* shuttle
rukhatysia z hudinniam рухатися з гудінням *v.i.* zoom
rukhlyvyi рухливий *a.* agile
rukhome maino рухоме майно *n.* movables
rukhomyi рухомий *a.* movable
rukoiatka рукоятка *n.* handle
rukopashna рукопашна *n.* melee
rukopys рукопис *n.* manuscript
rulka рулька *n.* shin
rulon рулон *n.* roll
rumianets рум'янець *n* blush
rumianyi рум'яний *a.* rosy
runo руно *n* fleece
rupiia рупія *n.* rupee
rusalka русалка *n.* mermaid
rushiina syla рушійна сила *n.* momentum
rushiina syla рушійна сила *n.* mover
rushnyk рушник *n.* towel
ruta рута *v.t.* rue
rutyna рутина *n.* routine
rvaty рвати *v.t.* gather
rvaty рвати *v.t.* lacerate
rvaty na shmatky рвати на шматки *v.t* tatter
ryba риба *n* fish
rybalka рибалка *n* fisherman
rychaty ричати *v.i.* roar
rydannia ридання *n* sob
rydaty ридати *v.i.* sob
rydykiul ридикюль *n.* purse
ryksha рикша *n.* rickshaw
rylo рило *n.* snout
ryma рима *n.* rhyme
rymuvaty римувати *v.i.* rhyme
rynok ринок *n* market
rynok ринок *v.t* market
rys рис *n.* rice

rys рись *n* trot
rytm ритм *b.* rhythm
rytmichnyi ритмічний *a.* rhythmic
rytorychnyi риторичний *a.* rhetorical
rytoryka риторика *n.* rhetoric
rytual ритуал *n.* ritual
rytualnyi ритуальний *a.* ritual
ryty рити *v. t.* excavate
rytysia ритися *v.i.* rummage
ryvok ривок *n.* hitch
ryvok ривок *n* spurt
ryzyk ризик *n.* peril
ryzyk ризик *n.* risk
ryzyknuty ризикнути *v.t.* venture
ryzykovanyi ризикований *a.* risky
ryzykuvaty ризикувати *v.t.* jeopardize

sabotazh саботаж *n.* sabotage
sabotuvaty саботувати *v.t.* sabotage
sad сад *n.* garden
sadivnyk садівник *n.* gardener
sadivnyk садівник *n.* grower
sadivnytstvo садівництво *n.* horticulture
sadno садно *n* graze
sadyba садиба *n.* barton
sadyst садист *n.* sadist
sadyzm садизм *n.* sadism
sadzhaty саджати *v.t.* plant
sadzhaty u vulyk саджати у вулик *n.* hive
sait сайт *n.* site
sake саке *n.* sake
sakharinovyi сахаріновий *a.* saccharine
sakharyn сахарин *n.* saccharin
salat салат *n.* salad
saliut салют *n* salute

salo сало *n.* bacon
salo сало *n.* tallow
sam сам *pron.* myself
samist самість *n.* self
samit саміт *n.* summit
samitnyk самітник *n.* hermit
samitnyk самітник *n.* recluse
samka самка *n* bitch
samoderzhavnyi самодержавний *a* autocratic
samoderzhavstvo самодержавство *n* autocracy
samoderzhets самодержець *n* autocrat
samohubnyi самогубний *a.* suicidal
samohubstvo самогубство *n.* suicide
samoobman самообман *n* flattery
samorodok самородок *n.* nugget
samostiinyi самостійний *a.* independent
samota самота *n.* solitude
samotnii самотній *a.* alone
samotnii самотній *a.* single
samotnist самотність *n.* loneliness
samovdovolenyi самовдоволений *a.* smug
samoviddanyi самовідданий *a.* selfless
samovpevnenist самовпевненість *n.* assumption
samozakokhanist самозакоханість *n.* narcissism
samozrechennia самозречення *n.* renunciation
samyi самий *a.* most
samytsia самиця *n* female
sanatorii санаторій *n.* sanatorium
sanchata санчата *n.* skate
sandal сандал *n.* sandal

sandalove derevo сандалове дерево *n.* sandalwood
sanhvinichnyi сангвінічний *a.* sanguine
sanitarnyi санітарний *a.* sanitary
sanktsiia санкція *n.* sanction
sanktsionuvaty санкціонувати *v.t* approbate
sanktsionuvaty санкціонувати *v. t* confirm
sanktsionuvaty санкціонувати *v.t.* sanction
sapfir сапфір *n.* sapphire
sarai сарай *n.* barn
sarana сарана *n.* locust
sardonichnyi сардонічний *a.* sardonic
sarkastychnyi саркастичний *a.* sarcastic
sarkazm сарказм *n.* sarcasm
sarzha саржа *n.* serge
satana сатана *n.* satan
satyra сатира *n.* satire
satyrychnyi сатиричний *a.* satirical
satyryk сатирик *n.* satirist
savan саван *n.* shroud
sazha сажа *n.* soot
secha сеча *n.* urine
sechovyi сечовий *a.* urinary
sechovyi mikhur сечовий міхур *n* bladder
sechovypuskannia сечовипускання *n.* urination
sehment сегмент *n.* segment
seif сейф *n.* safe
seismichnyi сейсмічний *a.* seismic
sekret секрет *n.* secret
sekretar секретар *n.* secretary
sekretariat секретаріат *n.* secretariat (e)
sekretnist секретність *n.* secrecy

sekretnyi секретний *a.* secret
sekretsiia секреція *n.* secretion
seksapilnyi сексапільний *a.* sexy
seksualnist сексуальність *n.* sexuality
seksualnyi сексуальний *a.* sexual
sekta секта *n.* schism
sekta секта *n.* sect
sektantskyi сектантський *a.* sectarian
sektor сектор *n.* sector
sekunda секунда *n* second
selektyvnyi селективний *a.* selective
selezinka селезінка *n.* spleen
selianstvo селянство *n.* peasantry
selianyn селянин *n.* peasant
selianyn селянин *n* rustic
seliuk селюк *n* carl
seliuk селюк *n* churl
selo село *n.* village
selyshche селище *n.* hamlet
selyshche селище *a.* township
semestr семестр *n.* semester
semestrovyi семестровий *a.* terminal
seminar семінар *n.* seminar
semyrichnyi семирічний *a* seven
senat сенат *n.* senate
senator сенатор *n.* senator
senatorskyi сенаторський *a.* senatorial
sens сенс *n.* meaning
sens сенс *n.* purport
sens сенс *n.* sense
sensatsiinyi сенсаційний *a.* sensational
sententsiia сентенція *n.* maxim
sentymentalni сентиментальнй *a* maudlin

sentymentalnyi сентиментальний *a.* sentimental
separatyst сепаратист *n.* secessionist
sepsys сепсис *n.* sepsis
septychnyi септичний *a.* septic
ser сер *n.* sir
serdyty сердити *v.i.* rouse
sered серед *prep.* among
sered серед midst
sereda середа *n.* Wednesday
serednia velychyna середня величина *n.* average
serednii середній *a.* mediocre
serednii середній *a.* mid
serednii середній *a.* middle
serednii rid середній рід *n* neuter
serednovichnyi середньовічний *a.* medieval
serednovichnyi середньовічний *a.* medieval
serednyk середник *n.* mullion
seredyna lita середина літа *n.* midsummer
serial серіал *n.* serial
seriia серія *n.* series
seriinyi серійний *a.* serial
serioznist серйозність *n.* gravity
serioznyi серйозний *a* serious
serp серп *n.* sickle
serpen серпень *n.* August
sertse серце *n.* heart
sertsebyttia серцебиття *n.* palpitation
sertsepodibnyi серцеподібний *adj.* cordate
sertsevo серцево *adv.* heartily
sertsevyi серцевий *adjs* cardiacal
sertsevyi серцевий *a* cordial
sertyfikat сертифікат *n.* certificate
servetka серветка *n.* napkin
serzhant сержант *n.* sergeant

sesiia сесія *n.* session
sestra сестра *n.* sister
sestrynskyi сестринський *a.* sisterly
sestrynstvo сестринство *n.* sisterhood
sezon сезон *n.* season
sezonnyi сезонний *a.* seasonal
sfera сфера *n.* sphere
sferychnyi сферичний *a.* spherical
shabash шабаш *n.* sabbath
shablia шабля *n.* sabre
shablon шаблон *n.* pattern
shafa шафа *n.* locker
shafran шафран *n.* saffron
shafrannyi шафранний *a* saffron
shakal шакал *n.* jackal
shakh i mat шах і мат *n* checkmate
shakhrai шахрай *n.* knave
shakhrai шахрай *n.* rascal
shakhrai шахрай *n.* sharper
shakhraiskyi шахрайський *a.* fraudulent
shakhraiskyi шахрайський *a.* roguish
shakhraistvo шахрайство *n.* cheat
shakhraistvo шахрайство *n.* fraud
shakhraistvo шахрайство *n.* knavery
shakhraistvo шахрайство *n.* roguery
shakhraiuvaty шахраювати *v. t.* cheat
shakhta шахта *n* mine
shakhtar шахтар *n.* miner
shal шаль *n.* shawl
shalenity шаленіти *v.i.* rampage
shalenstvo шаленство *n.* rampage

shalenyi шалений *adv.* amuck
shalenyi шалений *a* fierce
shalenyi шалений *a.* frantic
shalenyi шалений *a.* vehement
shamkaty шамкати *v.i.* mumble
shampun шампунь *n.* shampoo
shana шана *n* esteem
shanoblyvyi шанобливий *a.* respectful
shanoblyvyi шанобливий *a.* reverential
shanovnyi шановний *a.* honourable
shans шанс *n.* chance
shansy шанси *n.* odds
shantazh шантаж *n* blackmail
shantazhuvaty шантажувати *v.t* blackmail
shanuvalnyk шанувальник *n.* suitor
shanuvalnyk шанувальник *n.* worshipper
shanuvannia шанування *n.* homage
shanuvannia шанування *n.* reverence
shanuvannia шанування *n.* veneration
shanuvaty шанувати *v.t.* hallow
shanuvaty шанувати *v.t.* respect
shanuvaty шанувати *v.t.* venerate
shar шар *n* coating
shar шар *n.* layer
shar шар *n.* orb
shar шар *n* ply
shar шар *n.* stratum
sharf шарф *n.* scarf
sharf шарф *n.* throw
sharlatan шарлатан *n* quack
sharlatanstvo шарлатанство *n.* quackery
sharm шарм *n* spell
shatun шатун *n.* pitman

shchabel щабель *n.* round
shchaslyvyi щасливий *a.* fortunate
shchaslyvyi щасливий *a.* happy
shchaslyvyi щасливий *a.* joyful, joyous
shchaslyvyi щасливий *a.* lucky
shchastia щастя *n.* happiness
shchebet щебет *n.* twitter
shchebetaty щебетати *v.i.* twitter
shchedrist щедрість *n* bounty
shchedrist щедрість *n.* generosity
shchedrist щедрість *n.* liberality
shchedro razdavaty щедро раздавати *v.t.* lavish
shchedryi щедрий *a* bountiful
shchedryi щедрий *a.* generous
shchedryi щедрий *a.* lavish
shchedryi dar щедрий дар *n.* largesse
shchelepa щелепа *n.* jaw
shcheplennia щеплення *n.* graft
shcheplennia щеплення *n.* inoculation
shchetyna щетина *n* bristle
shchilnist щільність *n* density
shchilnyi щільний *a.* compact
shchilnyi щільний *a* consistent
shchilnyi щільний *a.* tough
shchilyna щілина *n.* opening
shchilyna щілина *n.* slit
shchipka щіпка *n.* pinch
shcho що *conj.* that
shcho що *interj.* what
shcho що *pron.* which
shcho b ne що б не *pron.* whatever
shcho lezhyt v osnovi що лежить в основі *adj.* basal
shcho maie formu vukha що має форму вуха *adj.* auriform
shcho maie tsinnist що має цінність *n.* worth

shcho maie zvychai що має звичай *a.* wont

shcho ne maie nomera що не має номера *a.* numberless

shcho ne maie plodiv що не має плодів *adj.* acarpous

shcho perebuvaie v rusi що перебуває в русі *adv.* astir

shcho perekhodyt z odnoho mistsia na inshe що переходить з одного місця на інше *adj* ambulant

shcho perevazhaie що переважає *a.* predominant

shcho perevershuie що перевершує *a.* transcendent

shcho rozchyniaie що розчиняє *a.* solvent

shcho styraietsia що стирається *a.* washable

shcho tryvaie rik що триває рік *a.* yearly

shcho tryvaie vsiu nich що триває всю ніч *a* overnight

shcho tuzhyt що тужить *a.* wistful

shcho vyklykaie strakh що викликає страх *a.* awful

shcho vyklykaie vidrazu що викликає відразу *a.* loathsome

shcho za що за *pron.* what

shchob щоб *adv.* that

shchob... ne щоб... не *conj.* lest

shchodenna hazeta щоденна газета *n.* daily

shchodenno щоденно *adv* adays

shchodenno щоденно *adv.* daily

shchodennyi щоденний *a* daily

shchodennyk щоденник *n* diary

shchohla щогла *n.* mast

shchoka щока *n* cheek

shchokvartalnyi щоквартальний *a.* quarterly

shchomisiachno щомісячно *adv* monthly

shchomisiachnyi щомісячний *a.* monthly

shchomisiachnyk щомісячник *n* monthly

shchorichna renta щорічна рента *n.* annuity

shchorichno щорічно *adv.* yearly

shchorichnyi щорічний *a.* annual

shchos щось *n.* aught

shchos щось *pron.* something

shchos podibne щось подібне *n.* like

shchotyzhnia щотижня *adv.* weekly

shchur щур *n.* rat

shchypaty щипати *v.t* nip

shchypaty щипати *v.t.* pinch

shchyptsi щипці *n. pl.* tongs

shchyrist щирість *n.* sincerity

shchyroserdnyi щиросердний *a.* sincere

shchyryi щирий *a.* candid

shchyryi щирий *a.* frank

shchyryi щирий *a.* whole-hearted

shchyt щит *n.* shield

shchzabezpechuvaty instrumentamy щзабезпечувати інструментами *v.t.* implement

shchzhoda щзгода *n.* compliance

shedevr шедевр *n.* masterpiece

shelf шельф *n.* shelf

shelma шельма *n.* rogue

shepeliavist шепелявість *n* lisp

shepeliavyty шепелявити *v.t.* lisp

shepit шепіт *n* whisper

shepotity шепотіти *v.t.* whisper

shershen шершень *n.* hornet

shevron шеврон *n.* stripe

shist шість *n., a* six

shistdesiat шістьдесят *n., a.* sixty

shistdesiatyi шістдесятий *a.* sixtieth

shistnadtsiat шістнадцять *n., a.* sixteen

shistnadtsiatyi шістнадцятий *a.* sixteenth

shkandybaty шкандибати *v.i.* waddle

shkapa шкапа *n.* jade

shkapa шкапа *n.* nag

shkarpetka шкарпетка *n.* sock

shkatulka шкатулка *n* casket

shkidlyvyi шкідливий *a.* injurious

shkidlyvyi шкідливий *a.* noxious

shkidlyvyi шкідливий *a.* pernicious

shkidnyk шкідник *n.* pest

shkidnyk шкідник *n.* wrecker

shkiper шкіпер *n.* skipper

shkira шкіра *n.* cutis

shkira шкіра *n.* leather

shkira шкіра *n.* skin

shkirianyi zavod шкіряний завод *n.* tannery

shkirka шкірка *n.* peel

shkiv шків *n.* pulley

shkoda шкода *n.* harm

shkoda шкода *n* ill

shkoduvaty шкодувати *v.t.* grudge

shkodyty шкодити *v.i* blast

shkodyty шкодити *v.t* harm

shkola школа *n.* school

shkval шквал *n.* gust

shlam шлам *n.* silt

shlanh шланг *n.* hose

shliakh шлях *n* medium

shliakh шлях *n.* path

shliakh шлях *n.* way

shliakhetnist шляхетність *n.* splendour

shliakhetnyi шляхетний *a.* noble

shlifuvalnyk шліфувальник *n.* grinder

shliub шлюб *n.* marriage

shliub шлюб *n.* wedlock

shliubnyi шлюбний *a* conjugal

shliubnyi шлюбний *a.* marriageable

shliubnyi шлюбний *a.* nubile

shliubnyi шлюбний *a.* nuptial

shliuz шлюз *n.* sluice

shlondra шльондра *n.* slut

shlondra шльондра *n.* whore

shlopaty шльопати *v.t.* pat

shlopaty шльопати *v.t.* slap

shlunkovyi шлунковий *a.* gastric

shlunok шлунок *n.* stomach

shmahaty шмагати *v.t.* lambaste

shmatochok шматочок *n.* morsel

shmatok шматок *n* bit

shmatok шматок *n.* lump

shmatok шматок *n.* mouthful

shmatok шматок *n.* piece

shmatok шматок *n.* slab

shmatuvaty шматувати *v.t.* mangle

shnek шнек *n.* auger

shnur шнур *n* cord

shnuruvaty шнурувати *v.t.* lace

shofer шофер *n.* chauffeur

shok шок *n.* shock

shokolad шоколад *n* chocolate

shokuvaty шокувати *v.t.* horrify

shokuvaty шокувати *v.t.* scandalize

shokuvaty шокувати *v.t.* shock

sholom шолом *n.* helmet

shorstkuvatyi шорсткуватий *a.* rugged

shorty шорти *n. pl.* shorts

shose шосе *n.* highway

shostyi шостий *a.* sixth

shotlandets шотландець *n.* Scot

shotlandskyi шотландський *a.*
scotch
shou шоу *n.* show
shov шов *n.* joint
shov шов *n.* seam
shovk шовк *n.* silk
shovkovyi шовковий *a.* silken
shovkovystyi шовковистий *a.*
silky
shovkovytsia шовковиця *n.*
mulberry
shpora шпора *n.* spur
shpryts шприц *n.* syringe
shpurliaty шпурляти *v.t.* shove
shpyhun шпигун *n* emissary
shpyhun шпигун *n.* spy
shpyhuvaty шпигувати *v.i.* spy
shpyl шпиль *n.* steeple
shpylka шпилька *n.* pin
shpylka шпилька *n.* spike
shpylka шпилька *n.* stud
shpynat шпинат *n.* spinach
shpyndel шпиндель *n.* spindle
shram шрам *n* scar
shryft Brailia шрифт Брайля *n*
braille
shtamp штамп *n.* imprint
shtamp штамп *n.* stamp
shtampuvaty штампувати *v.t.*
manufacture
shtatyv штатив *n.* tripod
shtofkhaty штофхати *v.t.* spurn
shtorm шторм *n.* gale
shtovkhannia штовхання *n.*
shove
shtovkhaty штовхати *v.t.* jog
shtovkhaty штовхати *v.t.* poke
shtovkhaty штовхати *v.t.* push
shtraf штраф *n* fine
shtraf штраф *n* forfeit
shtraf штраф *n.* penalty
shtrafuvaty штрафувати *v.t* fine

shtrafuvaty штрафувати *v.t.*
surcharge
shtrykhuvaty штрихувати *v.t.*
shade
shtuchnyi штучний *a.* artificial
shtuchnyi штучний *a* false
shtukaturka штукатурка *n.*
plaster
shtukaturyty штукатурити *v.t.*
plaster
shturmuvaty штурмувати *v.*
assail
shturmuvaty штурмувати *v.i.*
storm
shukaty шукати *v.t.* search
shukaty шукати *v.t.* seek
shum шум *n.* ado
shum шум *n* clamour
shum шум *n.* hubbub
shum шум *n.* noise
shum шум *n.* tumult
shum шум *n.* uproar
shum шум *n.* whir
shumno svarytysia шумно
сваритися *v. t* brangle
shumnyi шумний *a.* noisy
shuntuvalnyi шунтувальний *a.*
shut
shvabra швабра *n.* mop
shvartuvatysia швартуватися *v.t*
moor
shveitsar швейцар *n.* usher
shveitsarets швейцарець *n.*
swiss
shveitsarskyi швейцарський *a*
swiss
shvets швець *n* cobbler
shvets швець *n* sewer
shvydke zbilshennia швидке
збільшення *n.* proliferation
shvydkist швидкість *n.* gear
shvydkist швидкість *n.* rapidity
shvydkist швидкість *n.* speed

shvydkist швидкість *n.* velocity
shvydko швидко *adv.* apace
shvydko швидко *adv.* speedily
shvydko poshyriuvatysia
швидко поширюватися *v.i.*
proliferate
shvydko vykonuvaty швидко
виконувати *v. t.* expedite
shvydkoplynnyi швидкоплинний
a. temporal
shvydkopsuvnyi швидкопсувний
a. perishable
shvydkyi швидкий *a* fast
shvydkyi швидкий *a.* lively
shvydkyi швидкий *a.* prompt
shvydkyi швидкий *a.* quick
shvydkyi швидкий *a.* rapid
shvydkyi швидкий *a.* speedy
shvydkyi швидкий *a.* swift
shvydkyi pohliad швидкий
погляд *n.* glance
shvydkyi pohliad швидкий
погляд *n* peep
shvydshe швидше *adv.* rather
shvydshe, nizh швидше, ніж *conj*
before
shybenyk шибеник *n.* romp
shybenyk шибеник *n.* tomboy
shybenytsia шибениця *n.* .
gallows
shyfer шифер *n.* slate
shyfr шифр *n.* cipher, cipher
shyia шия *n.* neck
shykuvaty v sherenhu шикувати
в шеренгу *v.t.* rank
shylinh шилінг *n.* shilling
shympanze шимпанзе *n.*
chimpanzee
shyna шина *n.* tyre
shynel шинель *n.* overcoat
shynok шинок *n.* saloon
shyp шип *n.* thorn
shypinnia шипіння *n* hiss

shypinnia шипіння *n.* sizzle
shypity шипіти *v.i* hiss
shypity шипіти *v.i.* sizzle
shyroko широко *adv.* wide
shyrokyi широкий *a* broad
shyrokyi широкий *a.* general
shyrokyi широкий *a.* wide
shyrota широта *n.* latitude
shyryna ширина *n* breadth
shyryna ширина *n.* width
shyshka шишка *n.* cone
shyty шити *v.t.* sew
shyty шити *v.t.* tailor
siaiania сяяня *n* shine
siaiaty сяяти *v. i* beam
siaiuchyi сяючий *a.* refulgent
siaiuchyi сяючий *a.* resplendent
siaivo сяйво *n.* radiance
siaivo сяйво *n.* refulgence
sich січ *v.t.* whip
sidalo сідало *n.* roost
sidlaty сідлати *v.t.* saddle
sidlo сідло *n.* saddle
siiaty сіяти *v.t.* seed
siiaty сіяти *v.t.* sow
siiesta сієста *n.* siesta
sik сік *n* juice
sil сіль *n.* salt
silske hospodarstvo сільське
господарство *n* agriculture
silskohospodarskyi
сільськогосподарський *a*
agricultural
silskyi сільський *a.* rural
silskyi сільський *a.* rustic
silskyi zhytel сільський житель
n. villager
sim сім *n.* seven
simdesiat сімдесят *n., a* seventy
simdesiatyi сімдесятий *a.*
seventieth
simeinyi сімейний *a.* marital
simia сім'я *n* family

simnadtsiat сімнадцять *n.* seventeen

simnadtsiatyi сімнадцятий *a.* seventeenth

sino сіно *n.* hay

sirchanyi сірчаний *a.* sulphuric

sirka сірка *n.* sulphur

siryi сірий *a.* grey

sisty na korabel сісти на корабель *v. t.* board

sisty na milynu сісти на мілину *v.i.* strand

sit сіть *n.* net

siti сіті *n.* mesh

sitkivka сітківка *n.* retina

siudy сюди *adv.* hither

siurpryz сюрприз *n.* surprise

skakaty скакати *v.t.* gallop

skakaty скакати *v.i.* spring

skalp скальп *n* scalp

skamianilist скам'янілість *n.* fossil

skandal скандал *n* scandal

skanuvaty сканувати *v.t.* scan

skarb скарб *n.* treasure

skarbnyk скарбник *n.* treasurer

skarby скарби *n.* riches

skarha скарга *n* complaint

skarha скарга *n.* grievance

skarhy скарги *n* lament

skarzhytysia скаржитися *v. i* complain

skasovuvaty скасовувати *v.t.* lift

skasovuvaty скасовувати *v.t.* repeal

skasovuvaty скасовувати *v.t.* vacate

skasuvannia скасування *n* cancellation

skasuvannia скасування *n* repeal

skasuvaty скасувати *v.t.* nullify

skaz сказ *n.* rabies

skazaty сказати *v.t.* say

skazhenist скаженість *n.* rage

skazhenyi скажений *a.* furious

skelet скелет *n.* skeleton

skelia скеля *n.* rock

skeptychnyi скептичний *a.* sceptical

skeptyk скептик *n.* sceptic

skeptytsyzm скептицизм *n.* scepticism

skhema схема *n.* scheme

skhid схід *n* east

skhid схід *n.* orient

skhidnyi східний *a* east

skhidnyi східний *a* eastern

skhidnyi східний *a.* oriental

skhody сходи *n.* ladder

skhodynka сходинка *n.* stair

skhodyty сходити *v.t.* ascend

skhodzhennia сходження *n.* ascent

skholastychnyi схоластичний *a.* scholastic

skhopliuvaty схоплювати *v.t.* grip

skhovyshche сховище *n.* refuge

skhovyshche сховище *n.* repository

skhovyshche сховище *n.* vault

skhozhist схожість *n.* resemblance

skhozhist схожість *n.* similitude

skhozhyi схожий *a.* alike

skhozhyi схожий *a.* like

skhozhyi схожий *a.* similar

skhozhyi na mamonta схожий на мамонта *a* mammoth

skhreshchuvaty схрещувати *v.t* fold

skhvalennia схвалення *n.* approbation

skhvalennia схвалення *n* rush

skhvalnyi vyhuk схвальний вигук *n.* cheer

skhyblenyi схиблений *a.* lunatic

skhyl схил *n* slant
skhyl схил *n.* slope
skhyliaty схиляти *v.i.* incline
skhylnist схильність *n* bent
skhylnist схильність *n.* proclivity
skhylnyi схильний *a.* intent
skhylnyi схильний *a.* prone
skhylnyi схильний *a.* willing
skipetr скіпетр *n.* sceptre
sklad склад *n.* storage
sklad склад *n.* syllable
sklad склад *v.t* warehouse
sklad tovariv склад товарів *n.* godown
sklad zbroi склад зброї *n.* armoury
skladalnyk складальник *n* collector
skladannia складання *n* composition
skladannia tablyts складання таблиць *n.* tabulation
skladaty складати *v. t* compose
skladaty складати *v. t* constitute
skladaty складати *v.t.* sum
skladaty koshtorys складати кошторис *v. t* estimate
skladaty v yamu складати в яму *v.t.* pit
skladaty virshy складати вірши *v.t.* versify
skladaty zakonoproekt складати законопроект *n* draught
skladenyi складений *a* compound
skladka складка *n* crease
skladka складка *n* fold
skladnist складність *n.* complication
skladnyi складний *a* difficult
skladnyi складний *a.* multiplex
skladovyi складовий *adj.* component
skladovyi складовий *a.* syllabic

sklasty rozklad скласти розклад *v.t.* schedule
skleiuvaty склеювати *v.t.* conglutinat
sklep склеп *n.* sepulchre
skliar скляр *n.* glazier
sklo скло *n.* glass
sklobii склобій *n.* cullet
sklykannia скликання *n.* convocation
sklykaty скликати *v. t* convene
sklykaty скликати *v.t.* convoke
sklyty склити *v.t.* glaze
sknara скнара *n.* miser
sknara скнара *n.* niggard
sknarist скнарість *n* cupidity
skoba скоба *n* brace
skoba скоба *n.* staple
skopuvaty скопувати *v.t.* trench
skorbota скорбота *n.* woe
skorbotnyi скорботний *n.* mournful
skoriaty скоряти *v.t.* subdue
skoro скоро *adv.* anon
skoro скоро *adv.* soon
skorochennia скорочення *n* abridgement
skorochennia скорочення *n.* breviary
skorochennia скорочення *n.* retrenchment
skorochuvaty скорочувати *v.t* abridge
skorochuvaty скорочувати *v.t.* abbreviate
skorochuvaty скорочувати *v. t* contract
skorochuvaty скорочувати *v. t* curtail
skorochuvaty скорочувати *v.t.* shorten
skorochuvatysia скорочуватися *v. t* dwindle

skorochuvatysia скорочуватися *v.i* shrink

skorpion скорпіон *n.* scorpion

skorynka скоринка *n.* crust

skotch скотч *n.* scotch

skotokrad скотокрад *n* abactor

skotokradstvo скотокрадство *n* abaction

skovuvaty сковувати *v.t* fetter

skovznuty сковзнути *n.* slip

skripliuvaty pidpysom скріплювати підписом *v. t.* countersign

skripyty скріпити *v.t.* tag

skromnist скромність *n* modesty

skromnyi скромний *a.* frugal

skromnyi скромний *a.* humble

skromnyi скромний *a.* modest

skronia скроня *n* temple

skrutne stanovyshche скрутне становище *n.* predicament

skrutne stanovyshche скрутне становище *n.* quandary

skrutnyi скрутний *a.* needy

skrutnyi скрутний *a.* onerous

skryp скрип *n* creak

skryp скрип *n* squeak

skrypal скрипаль *n.* violinist

skrypity скрипіти *v. i* creak

skrypity скрипіти *v.i.* squeak

skrypka скрипка *n* fiddle

skrypka скрипка *n.* violin

skrypuchyi скрипучий *a.* strident

skrytnist скритність *n.* reticence

skubty скубти *v.t.* pluck

skulptor скульптор *n.* sculptor

skulptura скульптура *n.* sculpture

skulpturnyi скульптурний *a.* sculptural

skupchennia narodu скупчення народу *n* confluence

skupchuvaty скупчувати *v.t.* amass

skupchuvatysia скупчуватися *v.i* flock

skupist скупість *n.* avarice

skupyi скупий *a.* mean

skupyi скупий *a.* miserly

skupyi скупий *a.* niggardly

skupyi скупий *a.* stingy

skupyty скупити *v.t* engross

skuter скутер *n.* scooter

skuvaty скувати *v.t.* shackle

skybochka скибочка *n.* slice

skyd скид *n* uplift

skydaty скидати *v.t.* oust

skydaty z tronu скидати з трону *v. t* dethrone

skyhlyty скиглити *v.i.* whine

skynuty shkiru скинути шкіру *v.t.* slough

skypydar скипидар *n.* turpentine

skyrtuvaty скиртувати *v.t.* mow

slabka istota слабка істота *n.* weakling

slabka pidozra слабка підозра *n.* inkling

slabkist слабкість *n* debility

slabkist слабкість *n.* laxity

slabkist слабкість *n.* weakness

slabkyi слабкий *a* delicate

slabkyi слабкий *a* faint

slabkyi слабкий *a* feeble

slabkyi слабкий *a.* impotent

slabkyi слабкий *a.* lax

slabkyi слабкий *a.* little

slabkyi слабкий *a.* slack

slabkyi слабкий *a.* weak

slabnuty слабнути *v.i* faint

slaboumnyi слабоумний *n.* moron

slabshaty слабшати *v.i.* languish

slabshaty слабшати *v.t.* slacken

slabyna слабина *n.* slacks

slastoliubets сластолюбець *n.* sensualist

slastoliubets сластолюбець *n.* voluptuary
slava слава *n* fame
slava слава *n.* glory
slava слава *n.* hail
slava слава *n.* lustre
slava слава *n.* renown
slavetna liudyna славетна людина *n* celebrity
slavetnyi славетний *a* famous
slavnyi славний *a* decent
slavnyi славний *a.* glorious
slavyty славити *v.t.* glorify
slenh сленг *n.* slang
slid слід *v.t.* trace
slid слід *n.* track
slid слід *n.* vestige
slidstvo слідство *n.* inquest
sliduvaty слідувати *v.i* ensue
slipe zakhoplennia сліпе захоплення *n.* infatuation
slipen сліпень *n.* gadfly
slipota сліпота *n* ablepsy
slipota сліпота *n* amauriosis
slipota сліпота *n* blindness
slipuchyi blysk сліпучий блиск *n* dazzle
slipyi сліпий *a* blind
sliuda слюда *n.* mica
sloika слойка *n.* puff
slon слон *n* elephant
slota сльота *n.* slush
slotavyi сльотавий *a.* slushy
slovesnyi словесний *a.* verbal
slovesnyi словесний *a.* wordy
slovnyk словник *n* dictionary
slovnyk словник *n.* vocabulary
slovo слово *n.* say
slovo слово *n.* word
slovo chesti слово честі *n.* parole
sloza сльоза *n.* tear
sloza сльоза *n.* tear
sluha слуга *n* menial

sluha слуга *n.* servant
slukh слух *n.* hearsay
slukh слух *n.* rumour
slukhach слухач *n.* listener
slukhaty слухати *v.i.* listen
slukhnianist слухняність *n.* obedience
slukhnianyi слухняний *a.* obedient
slukhovyi слуховий *adj.* auditive
sluzhyty служити *v.t.* serve
sluzhyty podushkoiu служити подушкою *v.t.* pillow
sluzhyty vstupom служити вступом *v.t.* prelude
slyna слина *n.* saliva
slyna слина *n* spit
slynyty слинити *v. t* beslaver
slyva слива *n.* plum
slyz слиз *n.* mucus
slyz слиз *n.* slime
slyzkyi слизький *a.* slippery
slyzovyi слизовий *a.* mucous
slyzovyi слизовий *a.* slimy
smachnyi смачний *a.* palatable
smachnyi смачний *a.* tasty
smachnyi смачний *a.* toothsome
smahliavyi смаглявий *a.* swarthy
smak смак *n* flavour
smak смак *n.* liking
smak смак *n.* savour
smak смак *n.* taste
smakuvaty смакувати *v.t.* savour
smarahd смарагд *n* emerald
smazhene смажене *n* fry
smazhenyi смажений *a* roast
smazhyty смажити *v.t.* fry
smazhyty смажити *v.t.* roast
smerch смерч *n.* whirlwind
smerdity смердіти *v.i.* stink
smert смерть *n* death
smert смерть *n* decease
smert смерть *n.* end

smert смерть *n.* exit
smertelnyi смертельний *a* deadly
smertnist смертність *n.* mortality
smertnyi смертний *n* mortal
smertnyi смертний *a.* mortal
smiiatysia сміятися *v.i* laugh
smikh сміх *n.* laugh
smilyvist сміливість *n* boldness
smilyvist сміливість *n.* daring
smilyvist сміливість *n.* intrepidity
smilyvyi сміливий *a.* courageous
smilyvyi сміливий *a.* spirited
smishnyi смішний *a* comical
smishnyi смішний *a.* laughable
smishnyi смішний *a.* ridiculous
smishnyi смішний *a.* zany
smittia сміття *n.* garbage
smittia сміття *n.* rubbish
smittia сміття *n.* trash
smittiar сміттяр *n.* scavenger
smity сміти *v. i.* dare
smoh смог *n.* smog
smoktaty смоктати *v.t.* suck
smorid сморід *n.* stench
smorid сморід *n* stink
smorodyna смородина *n.* currant
smykannia смикання *n* pluck
smykannia смикання *n.* pull
smyrennist смиренність *n.* lowliness
smyslovyi смисловий *a.* notional
snariad снаряд *n.* projectile
snasti снасті *n.* tackle
snidanok сніданок *n* breakfast
snih сніг *n.* snow
snip сніп *n.* sheaf
snizhnyi сніжний *a.* snowy
snob сноб *n.* snob
snobistskyi снобістський *v* snobbish
snobizm снобізм *n.* snobbery
snuvaty снувати *v.t.* whisk
sobaka собака *n* dog

sobor собор *n.* cathedral
sochevytsia сочевиця *n.* lentil
sochytysia сочитися *v.i.* trickle
sodomiia содомія *n.* sodomy
sofa софа *n.* sofa
sofist софіст *n.* sophist
sofizm софізм *n.* sophism
sohodni сьогодні *adv.* today
sohodni vvecheri сьогодні ввечері *adv.* tonight
sohodnishnii vechir сьогоднішній вечір *n.* to-night
sohordniashnii den сьогордняшній день *n.* today
soiuz союз *n.* union
soiuznyk союзник *n.* ally
sokhnuty сохнути *v. i.* dry
sokhnuty сохнути *v.i.* wither
sokil сокіл *n* falcon
sokilnyk сокільник *n* hawker
sokovytyi соковитий *a.* juicy
sokovytyi соковитий *a.* lush
sokyra сокира *n.* axe
sokyrka сокирка *n.* hatchet
soldat солдат *v.i.* soldier
solidnyi солідний *a.* massy
solinnia соління *n.* pickle
solist соліст *n.* soloist
solnyi сольний *a.* solo
solnyi kontsert сольний концерт *n.* recital
solo соло *n* solo
solod солод *n.* malt
solodkist солодкість *n.* sweetness
solodkyi солодкий *a.* luscious
solodkyi солодкий *a.* sweet
solodovyi otset солодовий оцет *n* alegar
soloma солома *n.* straw
soloma солома *n.* thatch
solonist солоність *n.* salinity
solonyi солоний *a.* salty

solovei соловей *n.* nightingale
solovyi сольовий *a.* saline
solyty солити *v.t.* condite
solyty солити *v.t* salt
somnabulizm сомнабулізм *n.*
lunacy
somnambulizm сомнамбулізм *n.*
somnambulism
somyi сьомий *a.* seventh
son сон *n* dream
son сон *n* rest
son сон *n.* sleep
son сон *n.* slumber
sonet сонет *n.* sonnet
sonia соня *n.* sleeper
soniachnyi сонячний *a.* solar
soniachnyi сонячний *a.* sunny
sonlyvist сонливість *n.*
somnolence
sonlyvyi сонливий *a.* somnolent
sonnyi сонний *a.* sleepy
sontse сонце *n.* sun
sopinnia сопіння *n* sniff
sopity сопіти *v.i.* sniff
soplo сопло *n.* nozzle
sorochka сорочка *n.* shirt
sorochyty сорочити *v. t* beguile
sorok сорок *n.* forty
soroka сорока *n.* magpie
sorokonizhka сороконіжка *n.*
centipede
sorom сором *n.* shame
soromiazlyvyi сором'язливий *a.*
bashful
soromyty соромити *v.t.* abash
soromyty соромити *v.t.* shame
sort сорт *a* kind
sort сорт *n.* sort
sortuvaty сортувати *v.t.* assort
sortuvaty сортувати *v.t* grade
sortuvaty сортувати *v.t* sort
sosna сосна *n.* pine
sosok сосок *n.* nipple

sosok сосок *n.* teat
sotnia сотня *n.* hundred
sotsialist, sotsialistychnyi
соціаліст, соціалістичний *n,a*
socialist
sotsializm соціалізм *n* socialism
sotsialnyi соціальний *n.* social
sotsiolohiia соціологія *n.*
sociology
sous соус *n.* sauce
sova сова *n.* owl
sovisno совісно *a.* ashamed
sovist совість *n* conscience
sovok совок *n.* trowel
spad спад *n.* slump
spadaty спадати *v.i.* subside
spadkoiemets спадкоємець *n.*
heir
spadkoiemne maino спадкоємне
майно *n.* patrimony
spadkovist спадковість *n.*
heredity /
spadkovyi спадковий *a.* ancestral
spadkovyi спадковий *a.*
hereditary
spadshchyna спадщина *n.*
heritage
spadshchyna спадщина *n.*
legacy
spaika спайка *n.* commissure
spalakh спалах *n* burst
spalakh спалах *n* flash
spalakh спалах *n.* outbreak
spalakh спалах *n.* outburst
spalne mistse спальне місце *n*
bunk
spaniiel спанієль *n.* spaniel
spantelychuvaty спантеличувати
v. t. baffle
spantelychuvaty спантеличувати
v.t. perplex
spariuvatysia спарюватися *v. t*
couple

sparovuvatysia спаровуватися
v.i. copulate
spaty спати *v.i.* sleep
spazm спазм *n.* spasm
spazmatychnyi спазматичний *a.*
spasmodic
speka спека *n* glow
speka спека *n.* heat
spekotnyi спекотний *a.* sultry
spekotnyi спекотний *a.* torrid
spektakl спектакль *n.* play
spekuliant спекулянт *n.* profiteer
spekuliatsiia спекуляція *n.*
jobbery
spekuliuvaty спекулювати *v.i.*
profiteer
spekuliuvaty спекулювати *v.i.*
speculate
sperechannia сперечання *n.*
altercation
sperechatysia сперечатися *v.t.*
argue
sperechatysia сперечатися *v.i*
bet
sperechatysia сперечатися *v. t*
bicker
sperechatysia сперечатися *v. i*
dispute
sperechatysia сперечатися *v.i.*
wrangle
sperma сперма *n.* semen
spetsialist спеціаліст *n.* specialist
spetsializatsiia спеціалізація *n.*
specialization
spetsializuvatysia
спеціалізуватися *v.i.* specialize
spetsialnist спеціальність *n.*
speciality
spetsialnyi спеціальний *a* extra
spetsialnyi спеціальний *a.*
special
spetsii спеції *n.* spice
spetsodiah спецодяг *n.* overall

spetsyfikatsiia специфікація *n.*
specification
spianinnia сп'яніння *n.*
intoxication
spidnytsia спідниця *n.* skirt
spiker спікер *n.* speaker
spilkuvannia спілкування *n.*
intercourse
spilkuvatysia спілкуватися *v. t*
commune
spilkuvatysia спілкуватися *v. t*
communicate
spilkuvatysia спілкуватися *v.t.*
converse
spilkuvatysia спілкуватися *v.t.*
intermingle
spilne navchannia спільне
навчання *n.* co-education
spilno спільно *adv.* jointly
spilnyk спільник *n* accomplice
spilnyk спільник *n.* associate
spilyi спілий *a.* mellow
spir спір *n* controversy
spir спір *n* dispute
spiral спіраль *n.* spiral
spiralnyi спіральний *a.* spiral
spirnyi спірний *a.* objectionable
spirytualist спіритуаліст *n.*
spiritualist
spirytyzm спіритизм *n.*
spiritualism
spishno спішно *adj.* post
spishnyi спішний *a* immediate
spivak співак *n.* singer
spivak співак *n.* songster
spivaty співати *v.i.* sing
spivbesida співбесіда *n.*
interview
spivchuttia співчуття *n*
compassion
spivchuttia співчуття *n*
condolence
spivchuttia співчуття *n.* sympathy

spivchuvaty співчувати *v. t*
commiserate
spivchuvaty співчувати *v. i.*
condole
spivchuvaty співчувати *v.i.*
sympathize
spivisnuvannia співіснування *n*
co-existence
spivisnuvaty співіснувати *v. i*
co-exist
spivmeshanka співмешанка *n*
concubine
spivmeshkaty співмешкати *v. t*
cohabit
spivochyi ptakh співочий птах *n.*
warbler
spivpadaty співпадати *v.i.* match
spivpratsiuvaty співпрацювати *v.*
i collaborate
spivpratsiuvaty співпрацювати *v.*
i co-operate
spivrobitnytstvo співробітництво
n collaboration
spivrobitnytstvo співробітництво
n co-operation
spivrozmirnyi співрозмірний *a.*
proportionate
spivuchasnyk співучасник *n*
accessory
spivvidnoshennia
співвідношення *n.* ratio
spivzvuchchia співзвуччя *n.*
consonance
splachuvaty сплачувати *v.t.*
reimburse
splata сплата *n.* payment
splata сплата *n.* repayment
splata borhu сплата боргу *n.*
satisfaction
splavliaty сплавляти *n.* alloy
splesk сплеск *n* splash
spliachyi сплячий *adv.* asleep

spodivatysia сподіватися *v.t.*
hope
spohad спогад *n.* recollection
spohad спогад *n.* reminiscence
spohliadannia споглядання *n*
contemplation
spohliadaty споглядати *v. t*
contemplate
spohliadaty споглядати *v.i.* muse
spoiuvaty споювати *n.* soldier
spokii спокій *n.* calm
spokii спокій *n.* repose
spokii спокій *n.* tranquility
spokii спокій *n.* serenity
spokiinyi спокійний *a.* peaceable
spokiinyi спокійний *a.* placid
spokiinyi спокійний *a.* secure
spokiinyi спокійний *a.* tranquil
spokusa спокуса *n* allurement
spokusa спокуса *n.* temptation
spokushaty спокушати *v. t.* court
spokushaty спокушати *v. t.*
debauch
spokushaty спокушати *v. t.* entice
spokushaty спокушати *n.* seduce
spokushaty спокушати *v.t.* tempt
spokuslyvyi спокусливий *a*
seductive
spokusnyk спокусник *n.* tempter
spokuta спокута *n.* atonement
spokutuvaty спокутувати *v.i.*
atone
spoluchennia сполучення *n*
compound
spoluchnyi сполучний *a* binding
spoluka сполука *n* compound
sponsor спонсор *n.* sponsor
sponsoruvaty спонсорувати *v.t.*
sponsor
spontannist спонтанність *n.*
spontaneity
spontannyi спонтанний *a.*
spontaneous

sponukannia спонукання *n.*
incentive
sponukannia спонукання *n.*
inducement
sponukannia спонукання *n* urge
sponukaty спонукати *v.t* goad
sponukaty спонукати *v.t.* induce
sponukaty спонукати *v.t.* instigate
sponukaty спонукати *v.t.* prompt
sporadychnyi спорадичний *a.*
sporadic
sporiadzhaty споряджати *v.t.*
apparel
sporiadzhennia спорядження *n.*
munitions
sporidnenist спорідненість *n*
affinity
sporidnenist спорідненість *n.*
kinship
sporidnenyi споріднений *a.* akin
sporidnenyi споріднений *adj*
cognate
sporozhnyty спорожнити *v* empty
sport спорт *n.* sport
sportsmen спортсмен *n.*
sportsman
sportyvnyi спортивний *a.*
sportive
sporudyty спорудити *v. t* erect
sporudzhennia спорудження *n*
construction
sporudzhennia спорудження *n*
erection
sporudzhuvaty споруджувати *v.t.*
rear
sposib zhyttia спосіб життя *n*
living
sposterezhennia спостереження
n. observation
sposterezhennia спостереження
n. surveillance

**sposterezhennia za tymy,
khto prokhodyt ispyt**
спостереження за тими, хто
проходить іспит *n.* invigilation
sposterezhlyvyi спостережливий
a. observant
sposterihaty спостерігати *v.t.*
observe
sposterihaty спостерігати *v.t*
shadow
sposterihaty спостерігати *v.t.*
watch
spotvoriuvaty спотворювати *v. t.*
corrupt
spotvoriuvaty спотворювати *v. t*
distort
spotvoriuvaty спотворювати *v.t.*
mar
spotvoriuvaty спотворювати *v.t.*
misrepresent
spotvoriuvaty спотворювати *v.t.*
uglify
spotykatysia спотикатися *v.i.*
stumble
spovid сповідь *n* confession
spoviduvaty сповідувати *v. t.*
confess
spoviduvaty сповідувати *v.t.*
profess
spovilnennia сповільнення *n.*
moderation
spovilniuvaty сповільнювати *v.t.*
retard
spovishchaty сповіщати *v.t.*
apprise
spovishchaty сповіщати *v.t*
herald
spovnenyi hidnosti сповнений
гідності *a.* stately
spovniuvaty сповнювати *v.t.*
overwhelm
spozhyvannia споживання *n*
consumption

spozhyvannia споживання *n* expenditure
spozhyvaty споживати *v. t* consume
spraha спрага *n.* thirst
sprahlyi спраглий *adj.* appetent
sprahlyi спраглий *a.* thirsty
sprava справа *n.* affair
sprava справа *n* concern
sprava справа *n* deal
sprava справа *n* file
sprava справа *n.* proposition
spravedlyvist справедливість *n.* justice
spravedlyvyi справедливий *a* equitable
spravedlyvyi справедливий *a* fair
spravedlyvyi справедливий *a.* just
spravedlyvyi справедливий *a.* righteous
spravnyi справний *a.* serviceable
spravytysia справитися *v. i* cope
spravzhnii справжній *a.* genuine
spravzhnii справжній *a.* present
spravzhnii справжній *a.* veritable
spravzhnii справжній *a.* very
spriamovuvaty спрямовувати *v.i.* turn
spriamuvatysia vnyz спрямуватися вниз *v.i.* swoop
sprintovat спрінтовать *v.i.* sprint
sproba спроба *n.* attempt
sproba спроба *n* effort
sproba спроба *v.i* endeavour
sproba спроба *n* try
sprobuvaty спробувати *v.i.* try
spromozhnii спроможній *a* able
sproshchennia спрощення *n.* simplification
sprostiahaty спростягати *v. t* extend

sprostovuvaty спростовувати *v.t.* confute
sprostovuvaty спростовувати *v. t* disprove
sprostovuvaty спростовувати *v.t.* stale
sprostuvannia спростування *n.* refutation
sprostuvaty спростувати *v.t.* refute
sprostyty спростити *v.t.* simplify
sprychyniaty bezlad спричиняти безлад *v. t* clutter
spryiannia сприяння *n.* abetment
spryiannia сприяння *n.* assistance
spryiatlyvyi сприятливий *a.* auspicious
spryiatlyvyi сприятливий *a* congenial
spryiatlyvyi сприятливий *a* favourable
spryiatlyvyi сприятливий *a.* opportune
spryiatlyvyi сприятливий *a.* wholesome
spryiaty сприяти *v. t* contribute
spryiaty сприяти *v.t* favour
spryiaty сприяти *v.t* further
spryiaty сприяти *v.i.* minister
spryiaty сприяти *v.t.* promote
spryiaty zaienniu сприяти заєнню *v.i.* heal
spryimaty сприймати *v.t.* perceive
spryiniatlyvyi сприйнятливий *a.* perceptive
spryiniatlyvyi сприйнятливий *a.* receptive
spryiniattia сприйняття *n.* perception
sprynt спринт *n* sprint

spryntsiuvaty спринцювати *v.t.*
syringe
sprytnist спритність *n.* agility
sprytnist спритність *n.* readiness
sprytnist спритність *n.* sleight
sprytnyi спритний *a.* nimble
sprytnyi спритний *a.* resourceful
sprytnyk спритник *n.* trickster
spusk спуск *n.* descent
spusk спуск *n.* launch
spuskaty спускати *v.t.* launch
spustoshennia спустошення *n.*
havoc
spustoshennia спустошення *n.*
ravage
spustoshuvaty спустошувати *v.t.*
depredate
spustoshuvaty спустошувати *v.t.*
ravage
spyna спина *n.* back
spynnyi спинний *a.* spinal
spyrtohorilchanyi zavod
спиртогорілчаний завод *n*
distillery
spys спис *n.* lance
spys спис *n.* spear
spysok список *n* bill
spysok список *n.* list
sriblo срібло *n.* silver
sriblyty сріблити *v.t.* silver
sribnyi срібний *a* silver
ssavets ссавець *n.* mammal
stabilizatsiia стабілізація *n.*
stabilization
stabilizuvatysia стабілізуватися
v.t. stabilize
stabilnist стабільність *n.* stability
stabilnyi стабільний *a.* stable
stadion стадіон *n.* stadium
stado стадо *n.* herd
stainia стайня *n* stable
stal сталь *n.* steel
stalist сталість *n.* permanence

stalyi сталий *a* constant
stameska стамеска *n* chisel
stan стан *n.* fortune
stan стан *n.* state
stan nepevnosti стан непевності
n. abeyance
stan povnoi bezporadnosti стан
повної безпорадності *n.* palsy
stan sprav стан справ *n.* juncture
stan viiny стан війни *n*
belligerency
standart стандарт *n.* norm
standart стандарт *n.* standard
standartnyi стандартний *a*
standard
standartyzatsiia стандартизація
n. standardization
standartyzuvaty
стандартизувати *v.t.*
standardize
stanovyty становити *v.i* amount
stantsiia станція *n.* station
stara diva стара діва *n.* spinster
starannia старання *n* endeavour
starannist старанність *n*
diligence
starannyi старанний *a* diligent
starannyi старанний *a* eager
starannyi старанний *a.* studious
starechyi старечий *a.* senile
stareznyi старезний *a.* antiquated
starist старість *n.* senility
starodavnii стародавній *a.*
ancient
staromodnyi старомодний *a.*
outmoded
starosta староста *n* elder
starosta староста *n.* monitor
starovyna старовина *n.* antiquity
starshyi старший *a* elder
starshyi старший *a.* senior
starshynstvo старшинство *n.*
priority

starshynstvo старшинство *n.* superiority
staryi старий *a.* old
stat стать *n.* sex
statechnyi статечний *a.* sedate
statechnyi статечний *a.* staid
stateva zrilist статева зрілість *n.* puberty
statevyi chlen статевий член *n.* penis
statsionarnyi стаціонарний *a.* stationary
stattia стаття *n* article
stattia стаття *n* clause
statuia статуя *n.* statue
statura статура *n.* physique
status статус *n.* status
statut статут *n.* statute
staty na yakir стати на якір *v.t* harbour
statychnyi статичний *n.* static
statyka статика *n.* statics
statysia статися *v.t.* happen
statyst статист *n.* mute
statystychnyi статистичний *a.* statistical
statystyk статистик *n.* statistician
statystyka статистика *n.* statistics
stavaty ставати *v. i* become
stavaty mitsnym ставати міцним *v.t.* toughen
stavka ставка *n* bet
stavka ставка *n.* rate
stavlennia ставлення *n.* attitude
stavnyi ставний *a.* lofty
stavok ставок *n.* pond
stavyty ставити *v.t.* impute
stavyty ставити *v.t* set
stavyty ставити *v.t.* stake
stavyty chyslo ставити число *v. t* date
stavyty initsialy ставити ініціали *v.t* initial

stavyty kapkany ставити капкани *v.t.* trap
stavyty kran ставити кран *v.t.* tap
stavyty krapky nad ставити крапки над *v. t* dot
stavyty liudei (do harmaty) ставити людей (до гармати) *v.t.* man
stavyty na kartu ставити на карту *v.t* hazard
stavyty naholos ставити наголос *v.t* stress
stavyty pechatku ставити печатку *v.t.* seal
stavyty pechatku ставити печатку *v.i.* stamp
stavyty pidmetku ставити підметку *v.t* sole
stavyty po poriadku ставити по порядку *v.t.* range
stavyty umovoiu ставити умовою *v.t.* stipulate
stavyty v stainiu ставити в стайню *v.t.* stable
stavytysia ставитися *v.i.* pertain
stavytysia ставитися *v.t.* relate
stavytysia druzhno ставитися дружньо *v. t.* befriend
stavytysia neseriozno ставитися несерйозно *v.i* trifle
stazhyst стажист *v.t.* intern
stazhyst стажист *n.* probationer
stazhyst стажист *n.* trainee
steblo стебло *n.* stalk
steblo стебло *n.* stem
stehno стегно *n* hip
stehno стегно *n.* thigh
stelazh стелаж *n.* rack
stelia стеля *n.* ceiling
stenohrafiia стенографія *n.* stenography
stenohrafistka стенографістка *n.* stenographer

step степ *n.* steppe
stereotyp стереотип *n.* stereotype
stereotypnyi стереотипний *a.* stereotyped
sterlinh стерлінг *n.* sterling
sternia стерня *n.* stubble
sterpity стерпіти *v.t.* stomach
sterpnyi стерпний *a* endurable
sterty стерти *v. t* efface
sterviatnyk стерв'ятник *n.* vulture
sterylizatsiia стерилізація *n.* sterilization
sterylizuvaty стерилізувати *v.t.* sterilize
sterylnist стерильність *n.* sterility
sterylnyi стерильний *a.* sterile
stetoskop стетоскоп *n.* stethoscope
stezhka стежка *n.* lane
stezhka стежка *n.* trail
stiah стяг *n* flag
stiahnuty remenem стягнути ременем *v.t.* strap
stibaty стібати *v.t.* thresh
stibok стібок *n.* stitch
stichni vody стічні води *n.* sewage
stichnyi стічний *a.* waste
stih стіг *n.* rick
stiikist стійкість *n.* steadiness
stiikyi стійкий *a.* persistent
stiikyi стійкий *a.* resistant
stiikyi стійкий *a.* staunch
stiikyi стійкий *a.* steadfast
stiikyi стійкий *a.* steady
stiikyi стійкий *a.* sturdy
stiikyi prykhylnyk стійкий прихильник *n* stalwart
stiilo стійло *n.* stall
stil стіл *n.* table
stilets стілець *n.* chair
stilets стілець *n.* stool

stina стіна *n.* wall
stinnyi стінний *a.* mural
stiuard стюард *n.* steward
sto tysiach сто тисяч *n* lac, lakh
stobana kovdra стьобана ковдра *n.* quilt
stobaty стьобати *v.t* flog
stobaty стьобати *v.t.* stitch
stohin стогін *n* groan
stohin стогін *n.* moan
stohnaty стогнати *v.i.* groan
stohnaty стогнати *v.i.* lament
stohnaty стогнати *v.i.* moan
stohradusnyi стоградусний *a.* centigrade
stoiachyi стоячий *n.* standing
stoiak стояк *n.* stand
stoiak стояк *n* strut
stoiaty стояти *v.i.* stand
stoiaty na kolinakh стояти на колінах *v.i.* kneel
stoiaty oblychchiam do стояти обличчям до *v.t* face
stoichnyi стоїчний *n.* stoic
stokratnyi стократний *n. & adj* centuple
stoliar столяр *n.* joiner
stolitnii столітній *adj.* centennial
stolittia століття *n.* century
stolychnyi столичний *a.* capital
stolychnyi столичний *a.* metropolitan
stolytsia столиця *n.* capital
stomlenyi стомлений *a.* weary
stomliuiuchyi стомлюючий *a.* laborious
stomliuvaty стомлювати *v.t* fatigue
stomliuvaty стомлювати *v.t.* weary
stomliuvatysia стомлюватися *v.i.* weary
stop стоп *n* stop

stopor стопор *n.* throttle
storichchia сторіччя *n.* centenary
storinka сторінка *n.* page
storona сторона *n.* side
storona u spravi сторона у справі *n.* litigant
storona, shcho vyhrala сторона, що виграла *n.* winner
storona, yaka pidpysalasia сторона, яка підписалася *n.* signatory
storonnia liudyna стороння людина *n.* outsider
storozh сторож *n.* keeper
stos стос *n.* pack
stosovnyi do viiny стосовний до війни *a.* warlike
stosuvatysia стосуватися *v. t* concern
stosuvatysia стосуватися *v. t* encompass
stovbur стовбур *n.* trunk
stovp стовп *n.* pillar
stovp стовп *n* post
stovpotvorinnia стовпотворіння *n.* pandemonium
straik страйк *n* strike
straikari страйкарі *n.* striker
straikuvaty страйкувати *v.t.* strike
strakh страх *n* fear
strakh страх *n.* scare
strakhatysia страхатися *a* dread
strakhovka страховка *n.* insurance
strakhovyshche страховище *n* bogle
strakhuvannia страхування *n.* assurance
strakhuvaty страхувати *v.t.* insure
strashennyi страшенний *a.* terrible
strashnyi страшний *a.* fearful

strata страта *n* execution
strateh стратег *n.* strategist
stratehichnyi стратегічний *a.* strategic
stratehiia стратегія *n.* strategy
stratyty стратити *v.t.* decimate
stratyty стратити *v. t* execute
straus страус *n.* ostrich
strazh страж *n.* guardian
strazhdannia страждання *n.* anguish
strazhdannia страждання *n.* pain
strazhdaty страждати *v.t.* suffer
stremeno стремено *n.* stirrup
stres стрес *n.* stress
strichka стрічка *n.* band
strichka стрічка *n.* ribbon
strichka стрічка *n.* tape
strila стріла *n* arrow
strila стріла *n.* dart
strilianyna стрілянина *n* shoot
striliaty стріляти *v.t.* shoot
striliaty z hvyntivky стріляти з гвинтівки *v.t.* rifle
striliaty zalpamy стріляти залпами *v.t* volley
strimchak стрімчак *n.* cliff
strimka ataka стрімка атака *n.* onslaught
strimkyi стрімкий *a.* impetuous
strofa строфа *n.* stanza
strohist строгість *n.* rigour
strohist строгість *n.* severity
strohist строгість *n.* stringency
stroiovyi стройовий *a.* combatant
strok davnosti строк давності *n.* limitation
strokatyi строкатий *a.* motley
strokatyi строкатий *a.* plural
strokovyi строковий *a.* terminable
strop строп *n.* sling
struchok стручок *n.* pod

struhachka стругачка *n.* sharpener
struhaty стругати *v.t.* whittle
struktura структура *n.* structure
strukturnyi структурний *a.* structural
strumin струмінь *n.* spray
strumochok струмочок *n.* streamlet
strumok струмок *n.* brook
strumok струмок *n.* creek
struna струна *n.* chord
strunkyi стрункий *a.* shapely
strunkyi стрункий *n.* slender
strybaty стрибати *v.* i hop
strybaty стрибати *v.i* jump
strybaty стрибати *v.i.* leap
strybaty perevertom стрибати перевертом *v.i.* somersault
strybok стрибок *n* hop
strybok стрибок *n.* jump
strybok стрибок *n* leap
strybok стрибок *n* skip
stryhty ovets стригти овець *v.t* fleece
stryhuchyi lyshai стригучий лишай *n.* ringworm
stryktura стриктура *n.* stricture
strymanyi стриманий *a.* reticent
strymanyi стриманий *a.* temperate
strymuvannia стримування *n.* inhibition
strymuvaty стримувати *v.t.* moderate
strymuvaty стримувати *v.t.* restrain
strymuvaty стримувати *v.i.* stay
stryzhen стрижень *n.* pivot
stryzhka стрижка *n* coif
stsena сцена *n.* scene
stsena сцена *n.* spectacle
stsenarii сценарій *n.* script

stsenichnyi сценічний *a.* scenic
stsyntylliatsyia сцинтилляция *n.* scintillation
student студент *n.* student
student студент *n.* undergraduate
studiia студія *n.* studio
stukaty стукати *v.t.* knock
stukaty стукати *v.t.* thump
stuknuty стукнути *v.t.* bang
stupin ступінь *n* degree
stupin ступінь *n.* extent
stupin ступінь *n.* grade
stupnuty ступнути *v.i.* step
stverdnyi ствердний *a* affirmative
stverdzhuvaty стверджувати *v.t.* affirm
stverdzhuvaty стверджувати *v.t* state
stvorennia створення *n* creation
stvorennia створення *n.* invention
stvorinnia створіння *n* creature
stvoriuvaty створювати *v. t* create
styhlyi стиглий *a* ripe
styhmat стигмат *n.* stigma
stykhnuty стихнути *v.t.* quiet
styl стиль *n.* language
styl стиль *n.* style
stymul стимул *n.* goad
stymul стимул *n.* stimulus
stymuliator стимулятор *n.* stimulant
stymuliuvaty стимулювати *v.t.* propel
stymuliuvaty стимулювати *v.t.* stimulate
stypendiia стипендія *n.* stipend
styskannia стискання *n* grasp
styskaty стискати *v. t.* compress
styskaty стискати *v.t.* constrict
styskaty стискати *v.t.* throttle
stysle chyslo стисле число *n* multiple

styslist стислість *n* brevity
styslo zapysaty стисло записати *v.t.* jot
styslyi стислий *a* concise
stysnuty стиснути *v.t.* squeeze
**sub`iekt** суб`єкт *n* entity
subiektyvnyi суб'єктивний *a.* subjective
sublimuvaty сублімувати *v.t.* sublimate
subordynatsiia субординація *n.* subordination
subota субота *n.* Saturday
subprodukty субпродукти *n* by-product
substantsiia субстанція *n.* substance
subsydiia субсидія *n.* subsidy
subsydiiuvaty субсидіювати *v.t.* subsidize
suchasnist сучасність *n.* modernity
suchasnyi сучасний *a* contemporary
suchasnyi сучасний *a.* modern
suchkorub сучкоруб *n* limber
sud суд *n.* court
suddia суддя *n.* judge
suddia суддя *n.* magistrate
suddivskyi суддівський *a.* magisterial
sudno судно *n.* ship
sudno судно *n.* vessel
sudnoplavnyi судноплавний *a.* navigable
sudochynstvo судочинство *n.* judicature
sudoustrii судоустрій *n.* judiciary
sudova povistka судова повістка *n.* summons
sudovchynstvo судовчинство *n.* proceeding
sudovo karanyi prostupok судово караний проступок *n.* misdemeanour
sudovyi судовий *a.* judicial
sudovyi nakaz судовий наказ *n.* writ
sudovyi nakaz pro peredachu areshtovanoho do sudu dlia nalezhnoho sudovoho rozhliadu судовий наказ про передачу арештованого до суду для належного судового розгляду *n.* habeas corpus
sudovyi protses судовий процес *n.* litigation
sudovyi prystav судовий пристав *n.* bailiff
sudovyi rozhliad судовий розгляд *n.* trial
sudovyi rozporiadnyk судовий розпорядник *n.* referee
sudynna obolonka судинна оболонка *n* choroid
sudyty судити *v.i.* judge
sudytysia судитися *v.t.* litigate
sufiks суфікс *n.* suffix
sufler суфлер *n.* prompter
suietnyi суєтний *a.* worldly
suk сук *n* bough
sukhar сухар *n* cracker
sukhyi сухий *adj.* arid
sukhyi сухий *a* dry
sukhyi сухий *a.* husky
suknia сукня *n.* gown
sukupnist сукупність *n.* constellation
sukupnist сукупність *n.* totality
suky суки *n.* lop
suma сума *n* amount
suma сума *n.* sum
sumarno сумарно *adv.* summarily
sumarnyi сумарний *a* summary
sumbur сумбур *n.* welter

sumchastyi сумчастий *n.*
marsupial
sumiattia сум'яття *n.* tumble
sumish суміш *n* blend
sumish суміш *n.* mixture
sumisnyi сумісний *adj.* compliant
sumisnytstvo сумісництво *n.*
plurality
sumka сумка *n.* bag
sumka сумка *n.* pouch
sumlinno сумлінно *adv* bonafide
sumlinnyi сумлінний *a* bonafide
sumniv сумнів *n* distrust
sumniv сумнів *n* doubt
sumniv сумнів *n.* query
sumnivatysia сумніватися *v. t.*
distrust
sumnivatysia сумніватися *v. i*
doubt
sumnivnyi сумнівний *а.*
questionable
sumnivnyi сумнівний *a.* uncertain
sumnyi сумний *a.* grievous
sumnyi сумний *a.* lamentable
sumnyi сумний *a.* pitiful
sumnyi сумний *a.* rueful
sumnyi сумний *a.* sad
sumnyi сумний *n.* woeful
sumovaty сумовати *v.t.* sadden
sumovytyi сумовитий *a* cheerless
sumuvaty сумувати *v.i* long
sumuvaty сумувати *v.i.* mourn
sup суп *n.* soup
superechka суперечка *n.* contest
superechka суперечка *n.* wrangle
superechyty суперечити *v. t*
contradict
superechyty суперечити *v. t*
contrast
superechyty суперечити *v.t.*
gainsay
supermen супермен *n.* superman

supernychaty суперничати *v.t.*
rival
supernychaty суперничати *v.i.*
vie
supernyk суперник *n* agonist
supernyk суперник *n.* rival
supernytstvo суперництво *n.*
rivalry
suprotyvnyi супротивний *a*
contrary
suprovid супровід *n*
accompaniment
suprovidne maino супровідне
майно *n.* paraphernalia
suprovodzhuvaty
супроводжувати *v.t.*
accompany
suprovodzhuvaty
супроводжувати *v. t* escort
suputnyk супутник *n.* companion
suputnyk супутник *n.* satellite
suputnyk супутник *n.* sputnik
surmyty сурмити *v. t* blare
susha суша *n.* land
susid сусід *n.* neighbour
susidstvo сусідство *n.*
neighbourhood
susidstvo сусідство *n.* vicinity
suspilstvo суспільство *n.*
community
suspilstvo суспільство *n.* society
sut суть *n* content
sut суть *n.* gist
sutinkovyi сутінковий *n* dusk
sutinky сутінки *n* twilight
sutulist сутулість *n* stoop
sutulytysia сутулитися *v.i.* stoop
sutychka сутичка *n* collision
sutychka сутичка *n* combat1
sutychka сутичка *n.* encounter
sutychka сутичка *n.* grapple
suvenir сувенір *n.* memento
suvenir сувенір *n.* remembrance

suvenir сувенір *n.* souvenir
suveren суверен *n.* sovereign
suverenitet суверенітет *n.* sovereignty
suverennyi суверенний *a* sovereign
suvii сувій *n.* scroll
suvoryi суворий *a.* austere
suvoryi суворий *a.* rigorous
suvoryi суворий *a.* stern
suvoryi суворий *a.* strict
suvoryi суворий *a.* stringent
svarka сварка *n* fray
svarka сварка *n.* quarrel
svaryty сварити *v. t.* chide
svarytysia сваритися *v. i. & n* brawl
svarytysia сваритися *v.i.* quarrel
svavilnyi свавільний *a.* headstrong
sverbity свербіти *v.i.* itch
sverbizh свербіж *n.* itch
sverdlo свердло *n* drill
sverdlyty свердлити *v. t.* drill
svetr светр *n.* sweater
Sviashchenne pysannia Священне писання *n.* scripture
sviashchennyi священний *a.* heavenly
sviashchennyi священний *a.* sacred
sviashchenstvo священство *n.* priesthood
sviashchenyk священик *a.* ministrant
sviashchenyk священик *n.* parson
sviashchenyk священик *n.* priest
sviatist святість *n.* sanctity
sviatkovyi святковий *a* festive
sviatkuvannia святкування *n.* celebration
sviatkuvannia святкування *n.* commemoration
sviatkuvaty святкувати *v. t. & i.* celebrate
sviatkuvaty святкувати *v.t.* solemnize
sviato свято *n* festival
sviato свято *n.* jubilee
sviatotatstvo святотатство *n.* sacrilege
sviatyi святий *a.* holy
sviatyi святий *n.* saint
sviatyi святий *a.* saintly
sviatylyshche святилище *n.* sanctuary
svichka свічка *n.* candle
svidchyty свідчити *v.i.* witness
svidchyty proty свідчити проти *v.i.* militate
svidok свідок *n.* witness
svidok, yakyi daie pokazannia pid prysiahoiu свідок, який дає показання під присягою *n.* deponent
svidomyi свідомий *a.* aware
svidotstvo свідоцтво *n.* testimonial
svit світ *n.* world
svitanok світанок *n* dawn
svitaty світати *v. i.* dawn
svitlist світлість *n.* lordship
svitlo світло *n.* light
svitlyi світлий *a* light
svitski liudy світські люди *n.* ton
svitskyi світський *a.* profane
svitylo світило *n.* lamp
svitytsia світиться *a.* luminous
svizhyi свіжий *a.* fresh
svoboda свобода *n.* freedom
svoboda свобода *n.* liberty
svoiaky свояки *n.* in-laws
svoiechasno своєчасно *adv* pat

svoiechasnyi своєчасний *a.* seasonable

svoieridnyi своєрідний *a.* peculiar

svynarnyk свинарник *n.* sty

svynia свиня *n.* pig

svynia свиня *n.* sow

svyniache salo свиняче сало *n.* lard

svynka свинка *n.* mumps

svyntsevyi свинцевий *a.* leaden

svynyna свинина *n.* pork

svyst kuli свист кулі *n.* zip

svystity свистіти *v.i.* whistle

svystok свисток *n* whistle

svyta свита *n.* retinue

svydchyty свідчити *v.t.* attest

sydiachyi сидячий *a.* sedentary

sydinnia сидіння *n.* seat

sydity сидіти *v.t.* seat

sydity сидіти *v.i.* sit

sydity navpochipkakh сидіти навпочіпках *v.i.* squat

syhara сигара *n* cheroot

syhara сигара *n.* cigar

syhareta сигарета *n.* cigarette

syhnal сигнал *n.* signal

syhnalizuvaty сигналізувати *v.t.* signal

syhnalnyi сигнальний *v.t* alarm

syhnalnyi сигнальний *a.* signal

syla сила *n* force

syla сила *n.* verve

syla dukhu сила духу *n.* fortitude

syla inertsii сила інерції *n.* inertia

syla voli сила волі *n.* will

sylf сильф *n.* sylph

sylna storona сильна сторона *n.* forte

sylne bazhannia сильне бажання *n.* longing

sylno сильно *adv.* sharp

sylnodiinyi сильнодійний *a* drastic

sylnyi сильний *a.* strong

sylnyi сильний *a.* vigorous

sylnyi udar сильний удар *v.t.* whack

syluet силует *n.* silhouette

symetriia симетрія *n.* symmetry

symetrychnyi симетричний *a.* symmetrical

symfoniia симфонія *n.* symphony

sympatychnyi симпатичний *a.* sympathetic

sympozium симпозіум *n.* symposium

symptom симптом *n.* symptom

symptomatychnyi симптоматичний *a.* symptomatic

symuliuvaty симулювати *v.i.* sham

symvol символ *n.* symbol

symvolichnyi символічний *a.* symbolic

symvolizm символізм *n.* symbolism

symvolizuvaty символізувати *v.t.* symbolize

syn син *n.* son

syniak синяк *n* bruise

synii kolir синій колір *n* blue

synonim синонім *n.* synonym

synonimichnyi синонімічний *a.* synonymous

synopsys синопсис *n.* synopsis

syntaksys синтаксис *n.* syntax

syntetychnyi синтетичний *a.* synthetic

syntetychnyi produkt синтетичний продукт *n* synthetic

syntez синтез *n.* synthesis

sypatysia сипатися *v.i* hail

syr сир *n.* cheese
syr сир *n* curd
syrena сирена *n.* siren
syrity сиріти *v. t.* damp
syrop сироп *n.* syrup
syrota сирота *n.* orphan
syryi сирий *a.* humid
systema система *n.* system
systematychnyi систематичний *a.* systematic
systematyzuvaty систематизувати *v.t.* systematize
sytist ситість *n.* satiety
syto сито *n.* sieve
sytuatsiia ситуація *n.* situation

T

ta, shcho narodzhuvala та, що народжувала *a.* multiparous
tabir табір *n.* camp
tabirnyi табірний *adj* castral
tabletka таблетка *n.* tablet
tablychnyi табличний *a.* tabular
tabu табу *n.* taboo
tabuliator табулятор *n.* tabulator
taiemna uhoda таємна угода *n* collusion
taiemnychyi таємничий *a.* mysterious
taiemnyi таємний *adj.* clandestine
taiemnytsia таємниця *n* dark
taiemnytsia таємниця *n* enigma
taiemnytsia таємниця *n.* mystery
taifun тайфун *n.* typhoon
tainstvo таїнство *n.* sacrament
tainyk тайник *n* cache
taitysia таїтися *v.i.* lurk
tak так *adv.* so
tak так *adv.* yes
tak chy inakshe так чи інакше *adv.* anyhow

tak samo, yak так само, як *conj* both
tak yak так як *conj.* as
takhta тахта *n.* ottoman
takozh також *adv.* also
takozh також *adv.* likewise
taksi таксі *n.* cab
taksi таксі *n.* taxi
takt такт *n.* tick
taktovnist тактовність *n.* tact
taktovnyi тактовний *a.* tactful
taktyk тактик *n.* tactician
taktyka тактика *n.* tactics
takyi такий *a.* such
takym chynom таким чином *conj.* so
takym chynom таким чином *adv.* thus
talant талант *n.* talent
taliia талія *n.* waist
talisman талісман *n.* mascot
talisman талісман *n.* talisman
tam там *adv.* there
tamarynd тамаринд *n.* tamarind
tanets танець *n* dance
tanker танкер *n.* tanker
tantsiuvaty танцювати *v. t.* dance
tanuty танути *v.i.* melt
tanuty танути *v.i* thaw
tapochky тапочки *n. pl* slipper
taranyty таранити *v.t.* ram
tarhan тарган *n* cockroach
taryf тариф *n.* tariff
tasma тасьма *n.* string
tasma тасьма *n.* web
tato, tatus тато, татусь *n* dad, daddy
tatuiuvannia татуювання *n.* tattoo
tatuiuvaty татуювати *v.i.* tattoo
taverna таверна *n.* tavern
teatr театр *n.* theatre
teatralnyi театральний *a.* theatrical

teist теїст *n.* theist
teizm теїзм *n.* theism
tekhnichne obsluhovuvannia технічне обслуговування *n.* maintenance
tekhnichnyi технічний *a.* scientific
tekhnichnyi технічний *n.* technical
tekhnik технік *n.* technician
tekhnika техніка *n.* technique
tekhnoloh технолог *n.* technologist
tekhnolohichnyi технологічний *a.* technological
tekhnolohiia технологія *n.* technology
tekst текст *n.* text
tekstovyi текстовий *n.* textual
tekstura текстура *n.* texture
tekstylnyi текстильний *a.* textile
tekty текти *v.i* flow
tekty текти *v.i.* leak
tekty текти *v.i.* stream
tekuchyi текучий *a* fluid
telebachennia телебачення *n.* television
telefon телефон *n.* phone
telefon телефон *n.* telephone
telehrafiia телеграфія *n.* telegraphy
telehrafist телеграфіст *n.* telegraphist
telehrafnyi телеграфний *n.* telegraph
telehrafnyi телеграфний *a.* telegraphic
telehrafuvaty телеграфувати *v.t.* telegraph
telehrafuvaty телеграфувати *v.t.* wire
telehrama телеграма *n.* telegram
telepat телепат *n.* telepathist
telepatiia телепатія *n.* telepathy

telepatychnyi телепатичний *a.* telepathic
telepen телепень *n.* laggard
teleperedacha телепередача *n.* telecast
teleskop телескоп *n.* telescope
teleskopichnyi телескопічний *a.* telescopic
telia теля *n.* calf
tema тема *n.* subject
tema тема *n.* theme
tema тема *n.* topic
tematychnyi тематичний *a.* thematic
temnity темніти *v.i.* darkle
temno-bordovyi темно-бордовий *a* maroon
temno-bordovyi kolir темно-бордовий колір *n.* maroon
temnyi темний *a.* backward
temnyi темний *a* dark
temnyi темний *a.* gloomy
temnyi темний *a.* shadowy
temnyi темний *a.* sombre
temp темп *n* pace
temperament темперамент *n.* temperament
temperamentnyi темпераментний *a.* temperamental
temperatura температура *n.* temperature
tendentsiia тенденція *n.* tendency
tendentsiia тенденція *n.* trend
tender тендер *n* tender
tenditnyi тендітний *a.* brittle
tenditnyi тендітний *a.* fragile
tenditnyi тендітний *a.* slight
teneta тенета *n. pl.* toils
tenis теніс *n.* tennis
teokratiia теократія *n.* theocracy
teorema теорема *n.* theorem

teoretychnyi теоретичний *a.* theoretical
teoretyk теоретик *n.* theorist
teoretyzuvaty теоретизувати *v.i.* theorize
teoriia теорія *n.* theory
teplo тепло *n.* warmth
teplovyi тепловий *a.* thermal
teplyi теплий *a.* lukewarm
teplyi теплий *a.* warm1
terapevt терапевт *n.* physician
terapiia терапія *n.* therapy
terasa тераса *n.* terrace
terier тер'єр *n.* terrier
termin термін *n.* term
termin orendy термін оренди *n.* tenancy
terminal термінал *n* terminal
terminolohichnyi термінологічний *a.* terminological
terminolohiia термінологія *n.* terminology
terminovist терміновість *n.* urgency
terminovyi терміновий *a.* urgent
termometr термометр *n.* thermometer
termos (kolba) термос (колба) *n.* thermos (flask)
ternystyi тернистий *a.* thorny
teror терор *n.* terror
teroryst терорист *n.* terrorist
teroryzm тероризм *n.* terrorism
teroryzuvaty тероризувати *v.t.* terrorize
terpinnia терпіння *n.* patience
terpity терпіти *v.t.* tolerate
terpliachist терплячість *n.* endurance
terpliachyi терплячий *a.* patient
terpymist терпимість *n.* tolerance
terpymist терпимість *n.* toleration

terpymyi терпимий *a.* lenient
terpymyi терпимий *a.* tolerable
tertia тертя *n.* friction
terty терти *v.t* grate
terty терти *v.t.* rub
terytorialnyi територіальний *a.* territorial
terytoriia територія *n.* territory
terzaty терзати *v.t* maul
terzaty терзати *v.i.* prey
tesliar тесляр *n.* carpenter
tesliarski roboty теслярські роботи *n.* carpentry
test тест *n* test
testuvaty тестувати *v.t.* test
tezka тезка *n.* namesake
ti, khto ті, хто *dem. pron.* that
tiaha тяга *n.* traction
tiahar тягар *n.* onus
tiahar тягар *n.* tax
tiahty тягти *v. t* drag
tiahty тягти *v.t.* manhandle
tiahtysia тягтися *v.i.* plod
tiahtysia тягтися *v.i.* toil
tiamushchyi тямущий *a* docile
tiara тіара *n.* tiara
tiazhity тяжіти *v.i.* gravitate
tikaty тікати *v. i* decamp
tikaty тікати *v.i* escape
tilesnyi тілесний *a* corporal
tilky тільки *adv.* just
tilky тільки *adv.* only
tilky тільки *conj.* yet
tilo тіло *n* body
tilo тіло *n.* solidarity
tin тінь *n.* ghost
tin тінь *n.* shade
tin тінь *n.* shadow
tipatysia тіпатися *v.i.* pant
tisnyi zviazok тісний зв'язок *n.* intimacy
tisto тісто *n* dough
titka тітка *n.* aunt

tiulen тюлень *n.* seal
tiurban тюрбан *n.* turban
tiuremnyk тюремник *n.* jailer
tiuremnyk тюремник *n.* warder
tiurma тюрма *n.* prison
tiutiun тютюн *n.* tobacco
tkach ткач *n.* weaver
tkanyna тканина *n* cloth
tkanyna тканина *n* textile
tkanyna тканина *n.* tissue
tkatskyi verstat ткацький
верстат *n* loom
tkaty ткати *v.t.* weave
tlity тліти *v.i.* smoulder
tlumachyty тлумачити *v.t.*
interpret
tmianist тьмяність *v.t.* tarnish
tmianyi тьмяний *a.* lacklustre
tmianyi тьмяний *a.* wan
tochka точка *n* dot
tochka точка *n.* point
tochka zoru точка зору *n* angle
tochka zoru точка зору *n.*
standpoint
tochna kopiia точна копія *n.* ditto
tochnist точність *n.* accuracy
tochnist точність *n.* precision
tochnist точність *n.* punctuality
tochnyi точний *a.* accurate
tochnyi точний *a* exact
tochnyi точний *a.* precise
tochnyi postril точний постріл *n*
bull's eye
tochyty точити *v.t.* sharpen
tochyty точити *v.t.* whet
todi тоді *adv.* then
todishnii тодішній *a* then
toha тога *n.* toga
toi той *pron.* such
toi той *rel. pron.* that
toi, khto boretsia той, хто
бореться *n* combatant1

toi, khto ne pidkhodyt той, хто
не підходить *n.* misfit
toi, khto pidtrymuie
kandydaturu той, хто
підтримує кандидатуру *n.*
seconder
toi, kto slidkuie za tym, shchob
studenty ne spysuvaly pid
chas ispytiv той, кто слідкує
за тим, щоб студенти не
списували під час іспитів *n.*
invigilator
toi, shcho ne maie tsentru той,
що не має центру *adj* acentric
toi, shcho ne znaie той, що не
знає *a.* unaware
toi, shcho vidnosytsia
do Arystofana той, що
відноситься до Аристофана
adj aristophanic
toi, shcho vtomliuie той, що
втомлює *a.* tiresome
toi, shcho vysoko lytaie той, що
високо літає *adj* altivalent
toi, shcho zablukav той, що
заблукав *adv.,* astray
toi, shcho zasluhovuie dovyry
той, що заслуговує довіри *a.*
trustworthy
toi, shcho zhyvytsia derevynoiu
той, що живиться деревиною
a. xylophagous
toi, shcho znakhodytsia v stani
viiny той, що знаходиться в
стані війни *a* belligerent
toi, shcho zrostaie той, що
зростає *adj.* adnascent
tokar токар *n.* turner
tokarnyi verstat токарний
верстат *n.* lathe
toksychna rechovyna токсична
речовина *n.* intoxicant

tolerantnyi толерантний *a.* tolerant
tom том *n.* tome
tomu тому *adv.* ago
tomu тому *adv.* since
tomu тому *adv.* therefore
tomu shcho тому що *conj.* because
ton тон *n.* tone
tonizuiuchyi тонізуючий *a.* tonic
tonkist тонкість *n.* subtlety
tonko spryimaiuchyi тонко сприймаючий *a.* keen
tonkyi тонкий *a* fine
tonkyi тонкий *a.* slim
tonkyi тонкий *a.* subtle
tonkyi тонкий *a.* thin
tonkyi muslin тонкий муслін *n.* mull
tonna тонна *n.* tonne
tonuty тонути *v.i* drown
tonzura тонзура *n.* tonsure
topaty топати *v.t.* conculcate
topaz топаз *n.* topaz
topohraf топограф *n.* topographer
topohrafichnyi топографічний *a.* topographical
topohrafiia топографія *n.* topography
topolia тополя *n.* poplar
toptaty топтати *v.t.* trample
topyty топити *v.i.* sink
torf торф *n.* turf
torh торг *n* auction
torhivlia торгівля *n* commerce
torhivlia торгівля *n.* trade
torhovets торговець *n.* monger
torhovets торговець *n.* seller
torhovets торговець *n.* trader
torhovets kantseliarskym pryladdiam торговець канцелярським приладдям *n.* stationer

torhovyi торговий *a* commercial
torhuvaty торгувати *v.i* trade
torhuvatysia торгуватися *v.i.* haggle
torkaty lapoiu торкати лапою *v.t.* paw
torkatysia торкатися *v.t.* touch
torkatysia noskom торкатися носком *v.t.* toe
tornado торнадо *n.* tornado
torpeda торпеда *n.* torpedo
torpeduvaty торпедувати *v.t.* torpedo
torzhestvo торжество *n.* jubilation
tost тост *n.* pledge
tost тост *n.* toast
totalnyi тотальний *a.* total
totozhnist тотожність *n.* oneness
totozhnist тотожність *n.* similarity
tovar товар *n.* commodity
tovar товар *n* good
tovar товар *n.* merchandise
tovarnyi товарний *a.* marketable
tovaroobmin товарообмін *n.* barter2
tovarysh товариш *n.* comrade
tovarysh товариш *n.* helpmate
tovaryskist товариськість *n.* joviality
tovaryskist товариськість *n.* sociability
tovaryskyi товариський *a.* jovial
tovaryskyi товариський *a.* sociable
tovarystvo товариство *n.* confraternity
tovkotnecha товкотнеча *n.* throng
tovkty v stupi товкти в ступі *v.t.* mortar
tovpytysia товпитися *v.t.* mob
tovpytysia товпитися *v.t.* throng
tovstyi товстий *a.* stout

tovstyi товстий *a.* thick
tradytsiia традиція *n.* tradition
tradytsiinyi традиційний *a.* traditional
trafaret трафарет *n.* stencil
trahediia трагедія *n.* tragedy
trahichnyi трагічний *a.* tragic
trahik трагік *n.* tragedian
traiektoriia траєкторія *n.* trace
trakt тракт *n* tract
traktat трактат *n.* tract
traktat трактат *n.* treatise
traktor трактор *n.* tractor
traktyr трактир *n.* inn
tramvai трамвай *n.* tram
trans транс *n.* trance
transformatsiia трансформація *n.* transformation
transformuvaty трансформувати *v.t.* transfigure
transformuvaty трансформувати *v.t.* transform
transkrybuvaty транскрибувати *v.t.* transcribe
transkryptsiia транскрипція *n.* transcription
transliuvaty транслювати *v. t* broadcast
transport транспорт *n.* traffic
transport транспорт *n.* transport
transportuvannia транспортування *n.* transportation
tranzyt транзит *n.* transit
trapliatysia траплятися *v. t* befall
trapliatysia траплятися *v.t.* offer
traur траур *n.* mourning
trava трава *n* grass
trava трава *n.* herb
traven травень *n.* May
travlennia травлення *n* digestion
treiler трейлер *n.* trailer
trel трель *n* warble

tremtinnia тремтіння *n* quake
tremtinnia тремтіння *n* shake
tremtinnia тремтіння *n* shudder
tremtinnia тремтіння *n.* tremor
tremtity тремтіти *v.i.* quake
tremtity тремтіти *v.i.* shiver
tremtity тремтіти *v.i.* tremble
trener тренер *n* coach
trenuvannia тренування *n.* tuition
trenuvaty тренувати *v.t.* train
trepet трепет *n.* quiver
trepet трепет *n.* thrill
treteiskyi sud третейський суд *n.* arbitration
treteiskyi suddia третейський суддя *n.* arbitrator
treteiskyi suddia третейський суддя *n.* umpire
tretii третій *a.* third
tretii третій *a* three
tretyna третина *n.* third
triasinnia трясіння *n.* jolt
triaska тряска *n.* jumble
triasovyna трясовина *n* bog
triasty трясти *v.t.* jolt
triasty трясти *v.i.* shake
triastysia трястися *v.t.* jumble
triitsia трійця *n.* trinity
trio тріо *n.* trio
triplikat тріплікат *n* triplicate
tripotity тріпотіти *v.i.* palpitate
tripotity тріпотіти *v.i.* quiver
tripotity тріпотіти *v.t.* thrill
tripotity тріпотіти *v.i.* throb
trishchaty тріщати *v. i* blether
trishchaty тріщати *v. i* brustle
trishchaty тріщати *n. & v. i* clack
trishchaty тріщати *v.i.* rattle
trishchyna тріщина *n* cleft
trishchyna тріщина *n* fissure
trishchyna тріщина *n* flaw
trishchyna тріщина *n.* rift
trishky трішки *n.* modicum

trisk тріск *n* crack
triuk трюк *n* trick
triumf тріумф *n.* triumph
triumfalnyi тріумфальний *a.* triumphal
triumfuiuchyi тріумфуючий *a.* triumphant
triumfuvaty тріумфувати *v. i* exult
triumfuvaty тріумфувати *v.i.* triumph
trofei трофей *n.* loot
trofei трофей *n.* trophy
troianda троянда *n.* rose
trokhy трохи *adv.* somewhat
tron трон *n.* throne
tropichna lykhomanka тропічна лихоманка *n.* dengue
tropichnyi тропічний *a.* tropical
tropik тропік *n.* tropic
trotuar тротуар *n.* pavement
truba труба *n.* chimney
truba труба *n.* pipe
truba труба *n.* trumpet
trubchastyi трубчастий *a.* tubular
trubka трубка *n.* tube
trudnoshchi труднощі *n* difficulty
trudovyi stazh трудовий стаж *n.* seniority
truna труна *n* coffin
trup труп *n* corpse
trupa трупа *n.* troupe
truskyi труський *a.* jerky
try три *n.* three
trybuna трибуна *n.* rostrum
trybunal трибунал *n.* tribunal
trychi тричі *adv.* thrice
trydtsiat тридцять *n.* thirty
trydtsiatyi тридцятий *a.* thirtieth
trykolirnyi триколірний *a.* tricolour
trykolisnyi velosyped триколісний велосипед *n.* tricycle

trykolor триколор *n* tricolour
trykutnyi трикутний *a.* triangular
trykutnyk трикутник *n.* triangle
trymaty тримати *v.t* hold
trymaty тримати *v.t.* keep
trymaty pid vartoiu тримати під вартою *v. t* detain
trymaty v pevnykh mezhakh тримати в певних межах *v.t.* restrict
trymatysia триматися *v. t.* carry
trynadtsiat тринадцять *n.* thirteen
trynadtsiata chastyna тринадцята частина *n* thirtieth
trynadtsiatyi тринадцятий *a.* thirteenth
trystoronnii тристоронній *a.* tripartite
tryvala vorozhnecha тривала ворожнеча *n.* feud
tryvale nedoidannia тривале недоїдання *n* hunger
tryvalist тривалість *n* duration
tryvalist тривалість *a.* lasting
tryvalyi тривалий *a.* lengthy
tryvialnyi тривіальний *a.* trivial
tryvkyi тривкий *a.* substantial
tryvoha тривога *n* alarm
tryvoha тривога *n* anxiety
tryvozhytysia тривожитися *v.t.* trouble
trysk тріск *n* crash
tsarevbyvstvo царевбивство *n.* regicide
tsariuvaty царювати *v.i.* reign
tsarskyi царський *a.* royal
tseberka цеберка *n.* pail
tsehla цегла *n* brick
tsehla povitrianoho sushinnia цегла повітряного сушіння *n.* adobe
tselibat целібат *n.* celibacy
tsement цемент *n.* cement

tsementuvaty цементувати *v. t.* cement

tsent цент *n* cent

tsentr центр *n* center

tsentr центр *n* centre

tsentr центр *n.* thick

tsentr uvahy центр уваги *n.* limelight

tsentralnyi центральний *a.* central

tsentralnyi центральний *n.* midland

tsenzor цензор *n.* censor

tsenzura цензура *n.* censorship

tsenzura цензура *n.* censure

tsenzuruvaty цензурувати *v. t.* censor

tserebralnyi церебральний *adj* cerebral

tseremonialnyi церемоніальний *a.* ceremonial

tseremoniia церемонія *n.* ceremony

tseremonnyi церемонний *a.* ceremonious

tserkovnyi himn церковний гімн *n.* hymn

tserkovnyi storozh церковний сторож *n.* beadle

tserkva церква *n.* church

tsiatka цятка *n.* mottle

tsiatochka цяточка *n.* mote

tsikavist цікавість *n* curiosity

tsikavyi цікавий *a* curious

tsikavyi цікавий *a.* interesting

tsikavyi цікавий *a.* nosey

tsikavytysia цікавитися *v.i.* wonder

tsil ціль *n.* objective

tsile ціле *n* whole

tsilespriamovanyi цілеспрямований *a* outright

tsiliushchyi цілющий *a* curative

tsiliushchyi цілющий *a.* salutary

tsilkom цілком *adv* all

tsilkom цілком *a* bodily

tsilkom цілком *adv.* fully

tsilkom цілком *adv.* quite

tsilkom цілком *adv.* stark

tsilkovytyi цілковитий *a.* mere

tsiluvaty цілувати *v.t.* kiss

tsilyi цілий *a* entire

tsilyi цілий *a.* whole

tsilyna цілина *n* virgin

tsilyna цілина *n.* wilderness

tsilyty цілити *v.i.* aim

tsina ціна *n.* expense

tsina ціна *n.* price

tsinnist цінність *n.* value

tsinnyi цінний *a.* useful

tsinnyi цінний *a.* valuable

tsinuvaty цінувати *v.t.* value

tsipok ціпок *n.* cane

tskuvannia цькування *n.* persecution

tskuvaty sobakamy цькувати собаками *v. t* dog

tsnotlyvist цнотливість *n.* chastity

tsnotlyvyi цнотливий *a.* chaste

tsokaty цокати *v.i.* tick

tsokotity цокотіти *v. t.* chatter

tsukaty цукати *n.* sweetmeat

tsukerka цукерка *n.* candy

tsukerka цукерка *n* sweet

tsukor цукор *n.* sugar

tsukrovyi diabet цукровий діабет *n* diabetes

tsutsenia цуценя *n.* puppy

tsutsenia цуценя *n.* whelp

tsvil цвіль *n.* mildew

tsvirinkannia цвірінькання *n* chirp

tsvirinkaty цвірінькати *v.i.* chirp

tsvirkun цвіркун *n* cricket

tsvisty цвісти *v.i* blossom

tsvisty цвісти *v.i.* thrive
tsvitinnia цвітіння *n* blossom
tsvyntar цвинтар *n.* cemetery
tsybulia цибуля *n.* onion
tsybulia-porei цибуля-порей *n.* leek
tsyferblat циферблат *n.* dial
tsyfra цифра *n* digit
tsyfra цифра *a.* numeral
tsykl цикл *n* cycle
tsyklichnyi циклічний *a* cyclic
tsyklon циклон *n.* cyclone
tsylindr циліндр *n* cylinder
tsynik цинік *n* cynic
tsynk цинк *n.* zinc
tsynovka циновка *n.* mat
tsyrk цирк *n.* circus
tsyrkuliar циркуляр *n.* circular
tsyrkuliuvaty циркулювати *v. i.* circulate
tsysterna цистерна *n.* tank
tsytadel цитадель *n.* citadel
tsytata цитата *n.* quotation
tsytuvaty цитувати *v.t.* quote
tsyvilizatsiia цивілізація *n.* civilization
tsyvilizuvaty цивілізувати *v. t* civilize
tsyvilna osoba цивільна особа *n* civilian
tsyvilnyi цивільний *a* civic
tsyvilnyi цивільний *a* civil
tualet туалет *n.* lavatory
tualet туалет *n.* toilet
tuberkuloz туберкульоз *n.* tuberculosis
tudy туди *adv.* thither
tuflia туфля *n.* shoe
tuhyi тугий *a.* tight
tuman туман *n* fog
tuman туман *n.* mist
tuman туман *n.* vapour
tumannist туманність *n.* nebula

tumannyi туманний *a.* hazy
tumannyi туманний *a.* misty
tumbler тумблер *n.* tumbler
tunel тунель *n.* tunnel
tupyi тупий *a* blunt
tupyi тупий *a* dull
tupyi тупий *a.* obtuse
tupyk тупик *n* deadlock
tur тур *n.* tour
turbina турбіна *n.* turbine
turbotlyvyi турботливий *a.* respective
turbulentnist турбулентність *n.* turbulence
turbulentnyi турбулентний *a.* turbulent
turbuvaty турбувати *v.t.* ail
turbuvaty турбувати *v. t* commove
turbuvaty турбувати *v. t* disturb
turbuvaty турбувати *v.t.* harass
turbuvatysia турбуватися *v.i.* worry
turnir турнір *n.* tournament
turyst турист *n.* tourist
turyzm туризм *n.* tourism
tushkovane miaso тушковане м'ясо *n.* stew
tushkuvaty тушкувати *v.t.* stew
tut тут *adv.* here
tut i dali тут і далі *adv.* hereafter
tuz туз *n* ace
tuzhlyvyi тужливий *adj* melancholy
tuzhyty тужити *v.i.* yearn
tvan твань *n.* mud
tvaryna тварина *n.* animal
tvaryna тварина *n* brute
tvaryna, shcho maie bahato nih тварина, що має багато ніг *n.* multiped
tvarynnyi тваринний *a* beastly
tverdity твердіти *v. t* concrete

tverdo твердо *adv.* surely
tverdyi твердий *a.* harsh
tverdyi твердий *a.* severe
tverdyi твердий *n* solid
tverdyty твердити *v. i* contend
tverdzhennia твердження *n.* allegation
tverdzhennia твердження *n* contention
tverezist тверезість *n.* sobriety
tverezyi тверезий *a.* sober
tvorchyi творчий *adj.* creative
tvorchyi творчий *a.* imaginative
tvorets творець *n* creator
tvorets творець *n.* originator
tvoryty творити *v.t.* pen
tychok тичок *n* dig
tychok тичок *n.* poke
tyhr тигр *n.* tiger
tyhrytsia тигриця *n.* tigress
tyk тик *n.* teak
tykaty тикати *v.t.* thrust
tykhyi тихий *a.* quiet
tylna storona ruky тильна сторона руки *n.* backhand
tym chasom тим часом *adv.* meanwhile
tym ne mensh тим не менш *adv.* however
tym samym тим самим *adv.* thereby
tymchasove perebuvannia тимчасове перебування *n* sojourn
tymchasove zhytlo тимчасове житло *n.* lodging
tymchasovo prozhyvaty тимчасово проживати *v.i.* sojourn
tymchasovo zhyty тимчасово жити *v.t.* lodge
tymchasovyi тимчасовий *a.* casual

tymchasovyi тимчасовий *a.* provisional
tymchasovyi тимчасовий *a.* temporary
tyniatysia тинятися *v.i.* roam
tyniatysia bez dila тинятися без діла *v.i.* loiter
typ тип *n.* cast
typ тип *n.* type
typovyi типовий *a.* typical
tyrada тирада *n.* tirade
tyran тиран *n.* tyrant
tyraniia тиранія *n.* tyranny
tysha тиша *n* hush
tysha тиша *n.* silence
tysiacha тисяча *n.* chiliad
tysiacha тисяча *n.* thousand
tysiachnyi тисячний *a* thousand
tysiacholittia тисячоліття *n.* millennium
tysk тиск *n.* pressure
tysniava тиснява *n* squash
tytanichnyi титанічний *a.* titanic
tytr титр *n.* caption
tyzhden тиждень *n.* week
tyzhnevyi тижневий *a.* weekly

u у *prep.* in
u у *prep.* into
u lizhku у ліжку *adv.* abed
u podyvi у подиві *adv* agaze
u poli у полі *adv.* afield
u seredyni у середині *adv.* inside
u vohni у вогні *adv.* aflame
uberihaty уберігати *v.t.* save
ubliudok ублюдок *n.* bastard
ubohyi убогий *a.* meagre
ubohyi убогий *a.* scant
ubohyi убогий *a* spare
ubohyi убогий *a.* squalid
uboztvo убозтво *n.* misery

uboztvo убозтво *n.* squalor
ubrannia убрання *n.* clothes
ubuvaty убувати *v.i.* wane
ubyty убити *v.t.* slay
ubyvtsia убивця *n.* murderer
uchasnyk учасник *n.* participant
uchasnyk учасник *n.* voter
uchasnyk biiky учасник бійки *n.* belligerent
uchasnyk hry учасник гри *n.* player
uchasnyk perehovoriv учасник переговорів *n.* negotiator
uchasnyk torhiv учасник торгів *n.* bidder
uchast участь *n.* participation
uchen учень *n.* learner
uchora учора *adv.* yesterday
uchuvaty учувати *v.t.* scent
uchytel учитель *n.* preceptor
udacha удача *n.* godsend
udacha удача *n.* luck
udalyni удалині *adv.* afar
udar удар *n.* bang
udar удар *n* beat
udar удар *n* blow
udar удар *n* hit
udar удар *n* slam
udar удар *n.* stab
udar удар *n* thrust
udar nohoiu удар ногою *n.* kick
udariaty ударяти *v.t.* hit
udariaty pro zemliu ударяти про землю *v.i.* dap
udariatysia iz hlukhym stukom ударятися із глухим стуком *v.i.* thud
udavannia удавання *n.* pretence
udavannia удавання *n* sham
udavanyi удаваний *adj* mock
udavaty удавати *v.t.* assume
udobriuvaty удобрювати *v.t* fertilize

udobriuvaty удобрювати *v.t.* manure
udobriuvaty kompostom удобрювати компостом *n* compost
udoskonalennia удосконалення *n.* perfection
udoskonaliuvaty удосконалювати *v.t.* perfect
udoskonaliuvaty удосконалювати *v.t.* refine
udostal удосталь *adv.* galore
udostoiuvaty удостоювати *v.t.* grace
udostoiuvaty удостоювати *v.t.* vouchsafe
udrukovane удруковане *v.t.* imprint
udushennia удушення *n.* strangulation
udushennia удушення *n.* suffocation
uhlyb krainy углиб країни *adv.* inland
uhoda угода *n.* agreement
uhoda угода *n.* bargain
uhoda угода *n.* consent
uhoda угода *n.* convention
uhoda угода *n* fix
uhoda угода *n.* transaction
uhoda угода *n.* treaty
uiava уява *n* fancy
uiava уява *n.* imagination
uiavliaty уявляти *v.t.* imagine
uiavnyi уявний *a.* imaginary
uidlyvyi уїдливий *a.* caustic
uidlyvyi уїдливий *a.* waspish
ukaz указ *n.* ordinance
ukazuvaty указувати *v.t.* point
ukhyliannia ухиляння *n* evasion
ukhyliatysia ухилятися *v.t.* shirk
ukhylnyi ухильний *a.* tortuous
ukladach укладач *n* draftsman

ukladach укладач *n.* former
ukladaty укладати *v. t* conclude
ukladaty укладати *v. t* encase
ukladaty укладати *v.t.* infer
ukladaty укладати *v.t.* stow
ukladaty pari укладати парі *v.i.* wager
ukladaty uhodu укладати угоду *v.t.* bargain
uklin уклін *n* bow
ukomplektuvaty shtat укомплектувати штат *v.t.* staff
ukripliuvaty укріплювати *v.t.* steady
ukryttia укриття *n.* hide
ukryttia укриття *n.* lee
ukryttia укриття *n.* shelter
ukus укус *n* bite
ukus укус *n.* sting
ulamky уламки *n* debris
ulamky уламки *n.* wreckage
ulamok zuba уламок зуба *n.* snag
ulan улан *n.* lancer
uliublene mistse улюблене місце *n* haunt
uliublenets улюбленець *n* darling
uliublenyi улюблений *a* beloved
uliublenyi улюблений *a* darling
uliublenyi улюблений *a* favourite
uliuliukaty улюлюкати *v.i* hoot
ultymatum ультиматум *n.* ultimatum
uminnia уміння *n.* proficiency
umova умова *n* condition
umova умова *n* prerequisite
umova умова *n.* proviso
umova умова *n.* stipulation
umovliaty умовляти *v. t* coax
umovne zvilnennia uviaznenoho z viaznytsi умовне звільнення ув'язненого з в'язниці *v.t.* parole

umyrotvoriaty умиротворяти *v.t.* pacify
unikalnyi унікальний *a.* unique
unison унісон *n.* unison
universalnist універсальність *n.* universality
universalnyi універсальний *a.* universal
universytet університет *n.* university
untsiia унція *n.* ounce
unykaty уникати *v.i* abscond
unykaty уникати *v.t.* avoid
unykaty уникати *v. t* elude
unykaty уникати *v. t* evade
unykaty уникати *v.t.* shun
unyknuty уникнути *n.* avoidance
uosoblennia уособлення *n.* impersonation
uosoblennia уособлення *n.* incarnation
uosobliuvaty уособлювати *v.t.* impersonate
uosobliuvaty уособлювати *v.t.* personify
uosobliuvaty уособлювати *v.t.* typify
upakovka упаковка *n.* packing
upakovuvaty упаковувати *v.t.* pack
upakuvannia упакування *n.* package
upered уперед *adv* forward
uperedzhenist упередженість *n.* partiality
uperedzhennia упередження *n.* prejudice
uperedzhenyi упереджений *a.* interested
uperedzhenyi упереджений *a* unfair
uperemish упереміш *adv.* pell-mell

399

upertist упертість *n.* obstinacy
upertyi упертий *a.* stubborn
upodibniuvaty уподібнювати *v.t.* liken
uporiadkovanyi упорядкований *a.* orderly
uporiadkovuvaty упорядковувати *v.t.* adjust
uporskuvannia упорскування *n.* injection
upovilnennia уповільнення *n.* retardation
upovnovazhenyi уповноважений *n.* assignee
upovnovazhenyi уповноважений *n.* commissioner
upovnovazhuvaty уповноважувати *v.t.* accredit
upovnovazhuvaty уповноважувати *v.t.* assign
upovnovazhuvaty уповноважувати *v.t.* authorize
upovnovazhyty уповноважити *v.t* empower
upravliaty управляти *v.t.* administer
upravliaty управляти *v.t.* govern
upravliaty управляти *v.t.* lead
upravliaty управляти *v.t.* manage
upravliaty управляти *v.t.* steer
upravliaty управляти *v.t.* superintend
upravlinnia управління *n.* administration
upravlinnia управління *n* board
upravlinnia управління *n.* government
upravlinnia управління *n.* management
upravlinskyi управлінський *a.* managerial
upriazh упряж *n.* harness

upuskaty z uvahy упускати з уваги *v.t.* overlook
upyratysia упиратися *v.i.* persevere
ura ура *interj.* hurrah
urahan ураган *n.* hurricane
urazlyvyi уразливий *a.* vulnerable
urehulovuvaty урегульовувати *v.t.* regulate
urizuvaty урізувати *v.t.* retrench
urna урна *n* urn
urochysta promova урочиста промова *a.* inaugural
urochyste vidkryttia урочисте відкриття *n.* inauguration
urochystist урочистість *n.* solemnity
urochystyi урочистий *a.* solemn
urodzhenyi уроджений *a.* inborn
urok урок *n.* lesson
urozhai урожай *n* crop
urozhai урожай *n.* harvest
urvaty урвати *v.t.* snatch
uryvchastyi уривчастий *a* curt
uryvchastyi уривчастий *a.* sketchy
usadka усадка *n.* shrinkage
usamitnennia усамітнення *n.* privacy
usamitnennia усамітнення *n.* seclusion
usamitniuvatysia усамітнюватися *v.t.* seclude
useredniuvaty усереднювати *v.t.* average
useredyni усередині *prep.* inside
useredynu усередину *adv.* inwards
ushchelyna ущелина *n.* ravine
usiliakyi усілякий *a.* various
usiudy усюди *prep.* throughout
uskladnennia ускладнення *n.* impediment

uskladnennia ускладнення *n.* perplexity

uskladniuvaty ускладнювати *v.t.* aggravate

uskladniuvaty ускладнювати *v. t* complicate

uskladniuvaty ускладнювати *v. t* embarrass

uskladniuvaty ускладнювати *v.t.* handicap

uskladniuvaty ускладнювати *v.t.* involve

usmishka усмішка *n.* smile

usno усно *adv.* orally

usno усно *adv.* verbally

usno усно *adv.* viva-voce

usnyi усний *a.* oral

usnyi усний *a* viva-voce

usnyi ispyt усний іспит *n* viva-voce

uspadkovuvaty успадковувати *v.t.* inherit

uspadkuvannia успадкування *n.* inheritance

uspikh успіх *n.* joy

uspikh успіх *n.* success

uspishnyi успішний *a* successful

ustanova установа *n.* foundation

ustanova установа *n.* institution

ustanovka установка *n* mount

ustrytsia устриця *n.* oyster

usunennia усунення *n* elimination

usushka усушка *n.* wastage

usuvaty усувати *v. t* eliminate

usuvaty усувати *v.t* remedy

usvidomliuvaty усвідомлювати *v.* acknowledge

usvidomliuvaty усвідомлювати *v.t.* appreciate

usvidomliuvaty усвідомлювати *v.t.* sense

usypalnytsia усипальниця *n.* shrine

utikach утікач *n.* fugitive

utikha утіха *n* consolation

utishaty утішати *v.t.* solace

utopichnyi утопічний *a.* utopian

utopiia утопія *n* . utopia

utrudnene dykhannia утруднене дихання *n.* gasp

utrymannia утримання *n.* retention

utrymannia утримання *n* upkeep

utrymuvach reiestru утримувач реєстру *n.* registrar

utrymuvaty утримувати *v.t.* deduct

utrymuvaty утримувати *v.t.* withhold

utrymuvatysia утримуватися *v.i.* abstain

utrymuvatysia утримуватися *v.i.* refrain

utrymuvatysia vid утримуватися від *v.t* forgo

utvoriuvaty утворювати *v.t.* form

utyl утиль *n.* junk

utylitarnyi утилітарний *a.* utilitarian

utylizatsiia утилізація *n.* utilization

utylizuvaty утилізувати *v.t.* utilize

uvaha увага *n.* attention

uvaha увага *n* heed

uvaha увага *n.* regard

uvazhno ohliadaty уважно оглядати *v.t.* inspect

uvazhnyi уважний *a.* attentive

uvazhnyi уважний *a.* considerate

uvazhnyi уважний *a.* mindful

uvertiura увертюра *n.* overture

uviaznenyi ув'язнений *n.* prisoner

uviazniuvaty ув'язнювати *v.t.* imprison

uvichniuvaty увічнювати *v.t.* perpetuate

uvichnyty увічнити *v.t.* immortalize

uvihnutyi увігнутий *adj.* concave

uzahalnennia узагальнення *n.* abstraction

uzakonyty узаконити *v.t.* legalize

uzberezhzhia узбережжя *n* coast

uzbichchia узбіччя *n* curb

uzda узда *n* bridle

uzdovzh уздовж *adv.* along

uzhalyty kropyvoiu ужалити кропивою *v.t.* nettle

uzhodzhennia узгодження *n.* concord

uzhodzhuvaty узгоджувати *v.t.* accord

uzmoria узмор'я *n.* offing

uzurpatsiia узурпація *n.* usurpation

uzurpuvaty узурпувати *v.t.* usurp

v в *prep.* within

v chomu в чому *adv.* wherein

v hori в горі *adv.* aloft

v inshomu vypadku в іншому випадку *adv.* otherwise

v kintsevomu rakhunku в кінцевому рахунку *adv.* ultimately

v kupi в купі *adv* aheap

v mezhakh в межах *adv.* within

v pershu cherhu в першу чергу *adv.* primarily

v riad в ряд *adv* abreast

v rozdrib в роздріб *adv.* retail

v rusi в русі *adv.* afoot

v seredeni в середені *prep.* amid

v toi chas yak в той час як *conj.* whereas

v znachnii miri в значній мірі *adv.* substantially

vabyty вабити *v.t.* beckon

vada вада *n* demerit

vaha вага *n.* weight

vahannia вагання *n* demur

vahatysia вагатися *v. t* demur

vahitna вагітна *a.* pregnant

vahitnist вагітність *n.* pregnancy

vahomishyi вагоміший *a.* prior

vahomist вагомість *n.* weightage

vahomyi вагомий *a.* grave

vahon вагон *n.* wagon

vahon tramvaia вагон трамвая *n.* car

vailuvatyi вайлуватий *a.* ungainly

vakansiia вакансія *n.* vacancy

vakantnyi вакантний *a.* vacant

vaktsyna вакцина *n.* vaccine

vaktsynatsiia вакцинація *n.* vaccination

vaktsynuvaty вакцинувати *v.t.* vaccinate

vakuum вакуум *n.* vacuum

val вал *n.* rampart

valiatysia валятися *v.i.* wallow

valiuta валюта *n* currency

valiutuvannia валютування *n.* valuation

valka валка *n.* stream

valun валун *n* boulder

valyk валик *n.* roller

valyty валити *v.t* fell

vanna ванна *n* bath

vantazh вантаж *n.* cargo

vantazhivka вантажівка *n.* lorry

vantazhnyi avtomobil вантажний автомобіль *n.* truck

vantazhyty вантажити *v.t.* lade

vantazhyty na korabel вантажити на корабель *v. t* embark

vapno вапно *n.* lime

vartist вартість *n.* cost

vartist proizdu вартість проїзду *n* fare
vartyi вартий *a* worth
varvar варвар *n.* barbarian
varvarskyi варварський *a.* barbarian
varvarskyi варварський *a.* savage
varvarstvo варварство *n.* barbarism
varyty pyvo варити пиво *v. t.* brew
vat ват *n.* watt
vaucher ваучер *n.* voucher
vazektomiia вазектомія *n.* vasectomy
vazelin вазелін *n.* vaseline
vazhil важіль *n.* lever
vazhka pratsia важка праця *n.* toil
vazhka robota важка робота *v.i.* moil
vazhko dykhaty важко дихати *v.i* gasp
vazhko stupaty важко ступати *v.t.* lump
vazhkyi важкий *a.* arduous
vazhkyi важкий *a.* muggy
vazhkyi udar важкий удар *n.* thump
vazhlyvist важливість *n.* importance
vazhlyvyi важливий *a.* important
vazhlyvyi важливий *a.* responsible
vazhyty важити *v.t.* weigh
vbrannia вбрання *n.* vestment
vbyraty вбирати *v.t.* soak
vbyty вбити *v.t.* assassinate
vbyvaty вбивати *v.t.* kill
vbyvaty вбивати *v.t.* murder
vbyvchyi вбивчий *a.* murderous

vbyvstvo вбивство *n* assassination
vbyvstvo batka вбивство батька *n.* patricide
vbyvtsia вбивця *n.* assassin
vchenist вченість *n.* scholarship
vchenyi вчений *a.* learned
vchenyi вчений *n.* scholar
vchora вчора *n.* yesterday
vchyniaty zmovu вчиняти змову *v. i.* conspire
vchynok вчинок *n.* action
vchytel вчитель *n.* teacher
vchyty вчити *v.t.* instruct
vchytysia вчитися *v.i.* learn
vdacha вдача *n.* temper
vdalist вдалість *n* felicity
vdaryty nohoiu вдарити ногою *v.t.* kick
vdavaty вдавати *v.t.* pretend
vdavatysia вдаватися *v.i.* resort
vdiachnyi вдячний *a.* thankful
vdivets вдівець *n.* widower
vdobavok вдобавок *adv.* withal
vdoskonalenyi вдосконалений *a* elaborate
vdoskonaliuvaty вдосконалювати *v.t.* improve
vdova вдова *n.* widow
vdumlyvyi вдумливий *a.* thoughtful
vduvaty вдувати *v.i.* puff
vdvichi вдвічі *a.* twofold
vdykh вдих *n.* respiration
vdykhaty вдихати *v.i.* inhale
vdykhaty вдихати *v.i.* respire
vecheria вечеря *n* dinner
vecheriaty вечеряти *v. t.* dine
vechir вечір *n* evening
vedmid ведмідь *n* bear
vehetarianets вегетаріанець *n.* vegetarian

vehetarianskyi вегетаріанський *a* vegetarian

velity веліти *v.t.* will

Vellinhton Веллінгтон *n.* wellington

velosyped велосипед *n.* bicycle

velosypedyst велосипедист *n* cyclist

velych велич *n.* grandeur

velychavist величавість *n.* stateliness

velycheznyi величезний *a* enormous

velycheznyi величезний *a.* huge

velycheznyi величезний *a.* monstrous

velychnist величність *n.* majesty

velychnyi величний *a.* august

velychnyi величний *a.* majestic

velychyna величина *n.* magnitude

velyka kilkist велика кількість *n.* prodigality

velyka kilkist велика кількість *n.* profusion

velykden великдень *n* easter

velykodushnist великодушність *n.* magnanimity

velykodushnyi великодушний *a.* magnanimous

velykyi великий *a* big

velykyi krok великий крок *n* stride

velykyi palets великий палець *n.* thumb

velykyi vidkladnyi komir великий відкладний комір *n.* rabato

vena вена *n.* vein

ventyliator вентилятор *n.* ventilator

ventyliatsiia вентиляція *n.* ventilation

ventyliatsiinyi вентиляційний *n.* vent

ventyliuvaty вентилювати *v.t.* ventilate

veranda веранда *n.* veranda

verba верба *n.* willow

verbliud верблюд *n.* camel

verbovyi prut вербовий прут *n.* withe

verbuvaty вербувати *v.t.* recruit

verdykt вердикт *n.* verdict

veredlyvyi вередливий *a.* capricious

veresen вересень *n.* September

vereshchaty верещати *v.i.* shriek

veresk вереск *n.* shriek

verkhivka верхівка *n.* apex

verkhivka верхівка *n.* tip

verkhnia chastyna верхня частина *n.* top

verkhnia shchelepa верхня щелепа *n.* maxilla

verkhnii верхній *a.* upper

verkhnii shar верхній шар *n.* top

verkhovenstvo верховенство *n.* supremacy

verkhovnyi верховний *a.* supreme

vershky вершки *n* cream

vershnyk вершник *n.* rider

vershyna вершина *n.* pinnacle

versiia версія *n.* version

verstat верстат *n.* lathe

verstat верстат *n.* tool

vertity вертіти *v.t.* wind

vertykalno вертикально *a.* upright

vertykalnyi вертикальний *a.* vertical

ves весь *a.* all

vesela pisnia весела пісня *n* carol

veselist веселість *n* festivity

veselist веселість *n.* mirth
veseloshchi веселощі *n.* merriment
veselyi веселий *a* merry
vesillia весілля *n.* nuptials
vesliar весляр *n.* oar
veslo весло *n* paddle
vesluvannia веслування *n* row
vesna весна *n* spring
vesnianyi весняний *a.* vernal
vest вест *n.* west
vestovyi вестовий *a.* western
vesty вести *v. t* conduct
vesty вести *v.t* head
vesty вести *v.t.* transact
vesty napolehlyvu borotbu вести наполегливу боротьбу *v.i.* wrestle
vesty perehovory вести переговори *v.t.* negotiate
vesty perehovory вести переговори *v.i* parley
vesty viinu вести війну *v.t.* wage
vesty viinu вести війну *v.i.* war
veteran ветеран *n.* veteran
veterynarnyi ветеринарний *a.* veterinary
veto вето *n.* veto
vezty na avtomobili везти на автомобілі *v.i.* motor
vhamovuvaty вгамовувати *v.t.* allay
vhamovuvaty вгамовувати *v.t.* mortify
vholos вголос *adv.* aloud
vhoru вгору *adv.* upwards
vianuty в'янути *v.i* fade
viazanka в'язанка *n* faggot
viazaty в'язати *v.t.* knit
viazaty u vuzly в'язати у вузли *v.t.* bale
viaznytsia в'язниця *n.* jail
vibratsiia вібрація *n.* oscillation

vibratsiia вібрація *n.* vibration
vibruvaty вібрувати *v.i.* vibrate
vich-na-vich віч-на-віч *n.* tete-a-tete
vichnist вічність *n* eternity
vichnozelena roslyna вічнозелена рослина *n* evergreen
vichnozelenyi вічнозелений *a* evergreen
vichnyi вічний *a* eternal
vid від *prep.* from
vidbiliuvaty відбілювати *v. t. & i* blanch
vidbiliuvaty відбілювати *v. t* bleach
vidbutysia відбутися *v.i.* stem
vidbuvaty відбувати *v. i.* depart
vidbuvatysia відбуватися *v.i.* occur
vidbyraty відбирати *v.t.* pick
vidbyraty probu відбирати пробу *v.t.* sample
vidbytok відбиток *n* cachet
vidbyvach відбивач *n.* reflector
vidbyvaty відбивати *v.t.* repulse
vidbyvaty hodynnyi відбивати годинний *v.t.* toll
vidbyvatysia відбиватися *v.i.* struggle
vidchai відчай *n* despair
vidchaidushna holova відчайдушна голова *n.* bayard
vidchaidushnyi відчайдушний *a* desperate
vidchutnyi відчутний *a.* palpable
vidchutnyi відчутний *a.* sensible
vidchuttia відчуття *n.* sensation
vidchuvaty відчувати *v.t* feel
vidchuvaty brak відчувати брак *v.t.* lack
vidchuvaty hostryi bil відчувати гострий біль *v.t.* sting

vidchuvaty sylnyi bil відчувати сильний біль *v.i* smart
vidchuzhuvaty відчужувати *v.t.* alienate
viddacha віддача *n.* recoil
viddalenyi віддалений *a.* remote
viddalenyi vid moria віддалений від моря *a.* interior
viddanist відданість *n* dedication
viddanist відданість *n* devotion
viddannia віддання *n.* subjection
viddaty віддати *v.t.* render
viddavaty na muky віддавати на муки *v.t.* tantalize
viddavaty perevahu віддавати перевагу *v.t.* prefer
viddavatysia віддаватися *v. t* devote
viddilennia відділення *n* department
viddilennia відділення *n.* severance
viddilnyi віддільний *a.* separable
viddrukovuvaty віддруковувати *v.t.* impress
vidhaluzhennia відгалуження *n.* offshoot
vidibrannia dytyny vid hrudei відібрання дитини від грудей *n* ablactation
vidibraty відібрати *v.t.* single
vidiity відійти *v.i.* retreat
vidkhody відходи *n.* waste
vidkhozhe mistse відхоже місце *n.* latrine
vidkhylennia відхилення *n.* aberrance
vidkhyliaty відхиляти *v. t.* decline
vidkhyliatysia відхилятися *v. i* deviate
vidkladaty відкладати *v.t.* adjourn
vidkladennia відкладення *n.* adjournment

vidklasty відкласти *v.t.* shelve
vidklykannia відкликання *n.* recall
vidklykaty відкликати *v.t.* countermand
vidklykaty відкликати *v.t.* recall
vidkryte more відкрите море *n* main
vidkryto відкрито *adv.* openly
vidkryttia відкриття *n.* discovery
vidkryty відкрити *v.t.* open
vidkrytyi відкритий *adv.* ajar
vidkrytyi відкритий *a.* free
vidkryvaty відкривати *v. t.* dedicate
vidkydaty відкидати *v.t.* negative
vidkydaty відкидати *v.t.* reject
vidluchaty відлучати *v.t.* wean
vidluchyty vid tserkvy відлучити від церкви *v. t.* excommunicate
vidlyha відлига *n* thaw
vidlyty відлити *v. i* ebb
vidlyv відлив *n* ebb
vidlyvaty u formu відливати у форму *v.t.* mould
vidma відьма *n.* witch
vidminiuvatysia відмінюватися *v.t. & i.* conjugate
vidminnist відмінність *n* distinction
vidminnyi відмінний *a* different
vidminnyi відмінний *a.* excellent
vidminyty відмінити *v.t.* undo
vidmiriaty відміряти *v.t* mete
vidmitka відмітка *n* check
vidmova відмова *n* abnegation
vidmova відмова *n.* repulse
vidmova відмова *n* no
vidmovka відмовка *n* pretext
vidmovliaty відмовляти *v. t* dissuade
vidmovliaty відмовляти *v.t.* refuse

vidmovliaty sobi v chomu-nebud відмовляти собі в чому-небудь *v. t* abnegate
vidmovliatysia відмовлятися *v.t.* forsake
vidmovliatysia відмовлятися *v.t.* relinquish
vidmovliatysia vid perekonan відмовлятися від переконань *v.i.* backslide
vidmovyty відмовити *v.t.* persuade
vidniaty відняти *v.t.* subtract
vidnimannia віднімання *n.* subtraction
vidnimaty віднімати *v. t.* bereave
vidnimaty vid hrudei віднімати від грудей *v. t* ablactate
vidnosnyi відносний *a.* relative
vidnovlennia відновлення *n.* reinstatement
vidnovliuvaty відновлювати *v.t.* redress
vidnovliuvaty відновлювати *v.t.* reinstate
**vidnovliuvaty u pam`iati** відновлювати у пам`яті *v.t.* retrace
vidnovyty відновити *v.t.* renew
vidnovyty protektor відновити протектор *v.t.* retread
vidobrazhaty відображати *v.t* fend
vidobrazhaty відображати *v.t.* mirror
vidobrazhaty відображати *v.t.* reflect
vidobrazhennia відображення *n.* reflection
vidokremlene mistse відокремлене місце *n.* recess
vidokremlennia відокремлення *n.* insulation

vidokremlenyi відокремлений *a.* lone
vidokremliuvaty відокремлювати *v.t.* part
vidokremliuvaty відокремлювати *v.t.* separate
vidokremliuvatysia відокремлюватися *v.i.* secede
vidoma liudyna відома людина *n.* notability
vidomyi відомий *a.* well-known
vidosoblenist відособленість *n.* insularity
vidplachuvaty відплачувати *v.t.* requite
vidplata відплата *n.* nemesis
vidplata відплата *n.* retaliation
vidpochynok відпочинок *n.* recreation
vidpochyvaty відпочивати *v.i.* rest
vidpovid відповідь *n.* rejoinder
vidpovidach відповідач *n.* accountant
vidpovidach відповідач *n.* respondent
vidpovidalne polozhennia відповідальне положення *n.* trust
vidpovidalnist відповідальність *n.* liability
vidpovidalnyi відповідальний *a* accountable
vidpovidaty відповідати *v. i* correspond
vidpovidaty vzaiemnistiu відповідати взаємністю *v.t.* reciprocate
vidpovidnist відповідність *n.* correspondence
vidpovidno відповідно *adv.* accordingly

vidpovidnyi відповідний *a.*
apposite
vidpovisty відповісти *v.t* answer
vidpravliaty відправляти *v.t.* post
vidpravliaty відправляти *v.t.*
transmit
vidpravliaty poshtoiu
відправляти поштою *v.t.* mail
vidpravliatysia відправлятися *v.t.*
repair
vidpuskaty відпускати *v. t.*
dismiss
vidpuskaty na voliu відпускати
на волю *v.t.* enfranchise
vidpuskna hramota відпускна
грамота *n.* manumission
vidpustka відпустка *n.* vacation
vidradzhuvaty відраджувати *v. t.*
discourage
vidrakhuvannia відрахування *n*
remand
vidrakhuvaty відрахувати *v.t.*
remand
vidraza відраза *n.* abhorrence
vidraza відраза *n.* aversion
vidrazlyvyi відразливий *a.*
repulsive
vidrazu відразу *adv.* instantly
vidriadzhannia відряджання *n*
detachment
vidriadzhaty відряджати *v. t*
detach
vidrikatysia відрікатися *v.t,*
abdicate
vidrizniatysia відрізнятися *v. i*
differ
vidro відро *n* bucket
vidrodzhennia відродження *n.*
resurgence
vidrodzhuvaty відроджувати *v.i.*
revive
vidryv відрив *n.* avulsion

vidryvnyi talon відривний талон
n. coupon
vidryzhka відрижка *n* belch
vidshkodovuvaty
відшкодовувати *v.t.* refund
vidshkoduvannia відшкодування
n. recompense
vidshkoduvannia відшкодування
n. recovery
vidshkoduvannia відшкодування
n redress
vidshkoduvannia відшкодування
n. remedy
vidshkoduvaty відшкодувати *v.t.*
recoup
vidshtovkhuvannia
відштовхування *n.* repulsion
vidshtovkhuvaty відштовхувати
v.t. repel
vidsich відсіч *n.* rebuff
vidsivaty відсівати *v.t.* sieve
vidskochyty відскочити *v.i.* recoil
vidskok відскок *n.* rebound
vidsorbuvaty відсьорбувати *v.i.*
sup
vidsotok відсоток *n.* percentage
vidstalyi відсталий *n.* straggler
vidstan відстань *n* distance
vidstan відстань *n* walk
vidstavaty відставати *v.i.* straggle
vidstavka відставка *n.* resignation
vidstii відстій *n.* sediment
vidstoiuvaty відстоювати *v.t.*
assert
vidstrochka відстрочка *n.*
postponement
vidstrochka відстрочка *n.*
prolongation
vidstrochuvaty відстрочувати *v.t.*
prorogue
vidstupaty відступати *v.i.* recede
vidsutnii відсутній *a* absent
vidsutnist відсутність *n* absence

vidsutnist відсутність *n.* privation
vidsutnist smaku відсутність смаку *n.* insipidity
vidteper відтепер *adv.* henceforward
vidterminovuvaty відтерміновувати *v.t.* postpone
vidtik відтік *n* drain
vidtiniaty відтіняти *v.t.* tint
vidtinok відтінок *n.* tinge
vidtodi відтоді *adv.* thereafter
vidtsentrovyi відцентровий *adj.* centrifugal
vidtvorennia відтворення *n* reproduction
vidtvoriuvalnyi відтворювальний *a.* reproductive
vidtvoriuvaty відтворювати *v.t.* reproduce
vidvantazhennia відвантаження *n.* shipment
vidvazhnyi відважний *adj.* hardy
vidvazhnyi відважний *a.* intrepid
vidvedennia відведення *n.* withdrawal
vidvernennia відвернення *n.* prevention
vidvertaty відвертати *v.t.* ward
vidvertist відвертість *n.* candour
vidvertyi відвертий *a.* outspoken
vidvesty відвести *v.t.* avert
vidviduvach відвідувач *n.* attendant
vidviduvach відвідувач *n.* visitor
vidviduvanist відвідуваність *n.* attendance
vidviduvannia відвідування *n.* visit
vidviduvaty відвідувати *v.t.* attend
vidvolikaty відволікати *v. t* divert
vidvyslyi відвислий *a* flabby

vidznachaty відзначати *v. t.* commemorate
vidzyv відзив *n* reply
vihvam вігвам *n.* wigwam
viia вія *n* eyelash
viialo віяло *n* fan
viiannia віяння *n* waft
viiaty віяти *v.t.* winnow
viina війна *n.* war
viiska війська *n* military
viiskovi dii військові дії *n.* warfare
viiskovo-morskyi військово-морський *a.* naval
viiskovo-morskyi flot військово-морський флот *n.* navy
viiskovyi військовий *a.* martial
vik вік *n.* age
vikarii вікарій *n.* vicar
vikha віха *n.* milestone
vikno вікно *n.* window
vikonna rama віконна рама *n.* chess
vikonne sklo віконне скло *n.* pane
viktoryna вікторина *n.* quiz
vil віл *n* bullock
villa вілла *n.* villa
vilnodumets вільнодумець *n.* libertine
vilnyi вільний *a* fluent
vilnyi вільний *a.* loose
vilnyi chas вільний час *n.* leisure
vin він *pron.* he
vinchaty вінчати *v. t* crown
vinochok віночок *n.* coronet
vinok вінок *n.* garland
vinok вінок *n.* wreath
vinyk віник *n* whisk
vira віра *n* belief
virnist вірність *n.* allegiance
virno вірно *adv.* aright

virnopiddanyi вірнопідданий *n.* loyalist

virnyi вірний *a* faithful

virolomstvo віроломство *n.* perfidy

virolomstvo віроломство *n.* treachery

virospovidannia віросповідання *n* creed

virsh вірш *n.* poem

virshomaz віршомаз *n.* poetaster

virshomaz віршомаз *n.* rhymester

virshovanyi riadok віршований рядок *n.* verse

virshuvannia віршування *n.* versification

virshyk віршик *n.* clink

virtualnyi віртуальний *a* virtual

virtuoznyi віртуозний *a.* masterly

virus вірус *n.* virus

viryty вірити *v. t* believe

viryty вірити *v.t* trust

vis вісь *n.* axis

vis вісь *n.* axle

vishaty вішати *v.t.* hang

vishaty вішати *v.i.* swing

vishaty pid steliu вішати під стелю *v.t.* sky

visim вісім *n* eight

visimdesiat вісімдесят *n* eighty

visimdesiatyrichnyi вісімдесятирічний *a.* octogenarian

visimdesiatyrichnyi staryi вісімдесятирічний старий *n.* octogenarian

visimnadtsiat вісімнадцять *n* eighteen

visk віск *n.* wax

viski віскі *n.* whisky

visnyk вісник *n.* herald

vispa віспа *n.* smallpox

vistria вістря *n.* spearhead

vitalni vyhuky вітальні вигуки *n* acclamation

vitalnia вітальня *n* drawing-room

vitamin вітамін *n.* vitamin

vitaty вітати *v. t.* cheer

vitatysia вітатися *v.t.* greet

viter вітер *n.* wind

vitriak вітряк *n.* windmill

vitrianyi вітряний *a.* windy

vitrylo вітрило *n.* sail

vitse-korol віце-король *n.* viceroy

vivsianka вівсянка *n.* porridge

vivtar вівтар *n.* altar

vivtsia вівця *n* ewe

viyzvoliaty виизволяти *v.t.* liberate

viz віз *n.* wain

vizok візок *n.* cart

vizualizuvaty візуалізувати *v.t.* visualize

vizualnyi візуальний *a.* visual

vizyter візитер *n* caller

vkazivka вказівка *n.* indication

vkazivka вказівка *n.* suggestion

vkazivnyi palets вказівний палець *n* forefinger

vkazuvaty вказувати *v.t.* indicate

vkhid вхід *n* entrance

vkhodyty входити *v. t* enter

vkladannia вкладання *n.* insertion

vkladaty вкладати *v.t.* attach

vkladennia вкладення *n.* attachment

vkliuchaty включати *v. t* comprehend

vkliuchaty включати *v.t.* include

vkliuchennia включення *n.* inclusion

vkrai вкрай *adv.* utterly

vkryvaty вкривати *v. t* clothe

vlada влада *n.* authority

vlada влада *n* sway

vlashtovuvaty влаштовувати *v.t.* arrange

vlashtuvaty rizanynu влаштувати різанину *v.t.* massacre

vlashtuvatysia влаштуватися *v.i.* perch

vlasnist власність *n.* ownership

vlasnyi власний *a.* own

vlasnyi zhinkam власний жінкам *n.* womanish

vlasnyk власник *n.* owner

vlasnytskyi власницький *a.* proprietary

vlastyvyi властивий *a.* inherent

vlastyvyi materi властивий матері *a.* maternal

vlastyvyi vchenym властивий вченим *a.* scholarly

vlastyvyi zhinkam властивий жінкам *a* feminine

vliublyvyi влюбливий *a.* amorous

vlyvannia вливання *n.* infusion

vlyvaty вливати *v.t.* infuse

vlyvaty po kraplyni вливати по краплині *v.t.* instil

vmishchuvaty вміщувати *v.t.* store

vmity povodytysia вміти поводитися *v.t.* wield

vmyraiuchyi вмираючий *a.* moribund

vnesok внесок *n* contribution

vnochi вночі *adv.* nightly

vnosyty do spysku вносити до списку *v. t* enrol

vnosyty do spysku вносити до списку *v.t.* list

vnutrishnia storona внутрішня сторона *n.* inside

vnutrishnii внутрішній *a.* indoor

vnutrishnii внутрішній *a.* inward

vnutrishnii monoloh внутрішній монолог *n.* soliloquy

vnutrishnist внутрішність *n.* interior

vnyz вниз *adv* down

vnyzu внизу *adv* beneath

vnyzu внизу *adv* under

voda вода *n.* water

voden водень *n.* hydrogen

vodianyi водяний *n.* merman

vodianystyi водянистий *a.* watery

vodii водій *n* driver

vodoima водойма *n.* reservoir

Vodolii Водолій *n.* aquarius

vodonepronykna tkanyna водонепроникна тканина *n* waterproof

vodonepronyknyi водонепроникний *a.* waterproof

vodoprovidnyk водопровідник *n.* plumber

vodospad водоспад *n.* cascade

vodozlyv водозлив *n.* weir

vodyty avtomobil водити автомобіль *v. t* drive

vohkist вогкість *n* damp

vohnennyi вогненний *a* fiery

vohnyshche вогнище *n.* hearth

vohon вогонь *n* fire

voin воїн *n.* warrior

voiovnychyi войовничий *a* bellicose

vokalist вокаліст *n.* vocalist

vokalnyi вокальний *a.* vocal

vokzal вокзал *n.* terminus

volan волан *n.* shuttlecock

volaty волати *v.i.* low

volaty волати *v.i.* scream

volaty волати *v.i.* wail

voleiu-nevoleiu волею-неволею *adv.* perforce

volia воля *n.* volition

volochinnia волочіння *n* drag

volochyty волочити *v.t.* trail

volodinnia володіння *n.* hold

volodinnia володіння *n*. tenure
volodity володіти *v.t*. master
voloha волога *n*. moisture
volohist вологість *n*. humidity
volohist вологість *n*. wetness
volohyi вологий *a* damp
volokno волокно *n* fibre
volonter волонтер *n*. volunteer
voloskyi horikh волоський горіх *n*. walnut
volossia волосся *n* hair
volt вольт *n*. volt
volynka волинка *n*. bagpipe
vona вона *pron*. she
vono воно *pron*. it
vorkuvannia воркування *n* coo
vorochatysia ворочатися *v.i*. tumble
voroh ворог *n* enemy
vorohuvaty ворогувати *v.t*. antagonize
voron ворон *n*. raven
vorona ворона *n* crow
vorota ворота *n*. gate
vorozhe stavlennia вороже ставлення *n*. hostility
vorozhist ворожість *n* animosity
vorozhnecha ворожнеча *n* enmity
vorozhyi ворожий *a*. hostile
vorozhyi ворожий *a*. virulent
vorsuvaty ворсувати *v.t*. tease
vorushytysia ворушитися *v. i. & n* budge
vosha воша *n*. louse
voshchyty вощити *v.t*. wax
voskovanyi воскований *adj*. cerated
vosma chastyna myli восьма частина милі *n*. furlong
vosmykutnyi восьмикутний *a*. octangular
vosmykutnyk восьмикутник *n*. octagon

vostanskyi востанський *a*. rebellious
vovk вовк *n*. wolf
vovna вовна *n*. wool
vovniana materiia вовняна матерія *n* woollen
vovnianyi вовняний *a*. woollen
vozhd вождь *n*. chieftain
vozytysia возитися *v.i*. romp
vpadaty впадати *v.i*. lapse
vpered вперед *adv*. forth
vpertyi впертий *a*. mulish
vpertyi впертий *a*. obstinate
vpevnenyi впевнений *a*. confident
vpevnenyi впевнений *a*. sure
vpiddavaty honinniam впіддавати гонінням *v.t*. persecute
vplutuvaty вплутувати *v.t*. implicate
vplyv вплив *n*. influence
vplyvaty впливати *v.t*. affect
vplyvaty впливати *v. t* effect
vplyvova osoba впливова особа *v.t*. influence
vplyvovyi впливовий *a*. influential
vpoperek впоперек *adv*. across
vporiadkuvannia впорядкування *n*. arrangement
vprava вправа *n*. exercise
vpravliatysia вправлятися *v.t*. practise
vpravnyi вправний *a*. artful
vpravnyi maister вправний майстер *n* craftsman
vpravnyi strilets вправний стрілець *n*. marksman
vprovadzhuvaty впроваджувати *v.t*. inculcate
vpysuvaty вписувати *v.t*. inscribe
vrakhovuiuchy врахозуючи *prep*. considering

vrazhaiuchyi вражаючий *a.*
impressive
vrazhaty вражати *v.t.* astonish
vrazhaty вражати *v.t.* invade
vrazhennia враження *n.*
impression
vrazhenyi zhakhom вражений
жахом *a.* aghast
vrazlyvyi вразливий *a.* intense
vrehuliuvannia врегулювання *n.*
adjustment
vrehuliuvaty врегулювати *v.i.*
settle
vreshti-resht врешті-решт *adv.*
eventually
vrivnovazhenist врівноваженість
n poise
vrivnovazhuvaty врівноважувати
v.t. poise
vrodzhenyi вроджений *a.* innate
vse все *pron* all
vse mozhlyve все можливе *n*
utmost
vsebichnyi всебічний *a*
comprehensive
vseliaty poboiuvannia вселяти
побоювання *v.t.* misgive
vseliaty shanoblyvyi strakh
вселяти шанобливий страх *v.t.*
overawe
vsemohutnii всемогутній *a.*
almighty
vsemohutnist всемогутність *n.*
omnipotence
vseosiazhnyi всеосяжний *a.*
integral
vseredeni всередені *adv.* within
vseredyni всередині *adv.* indoors
vsesvit всесвіт *n.* universe
vsesylnyi всесильний *a.*
omnipotent
vsevidannia всевідання *n.*
omniscience

vseznaiuchyi всезнаючий *a.*
omniscient
vshanovuvaty вшановувати *v.i*
feast
vsi всі *n* all
vsi razom всі разом *adv.*
altogether
vsistysia na sidalo всістися на
сідало *v.i.* roost
vsiu nich всю ніч *adv.* overnight
vsiudysushchist всюдисущість
n. omnipresence
vsiudysushchyi всюдисущий *a.*
omnipresent
vsmoktuvannia всмоктування *n.*
suck
vspiniuvaty вспінювати *v.t* foam
vstanovlenyi встановлений *a* set
vstanovliuvaty встановлювати
v.t. mount
vstanovliuvaty встановлювати
v.t. specify
vstanovliuvaty mezhi
встановлювати межі *v.t.* limit
vstanovyty встановити *v.t* finger
vstavaty вставати *v.* rise
vstavaty na chyius storonu
вставати на чиюсь сторону *v.i.*
side
vstavliaty вставляти *v.t.* insert
vstavliaty kameni вставляти
камені *v.t.* jewel
vstup вступ *n* accession
vstup вступ *n* entry
vstupaty u soiuz вступати у
союз *v.t.* ally
vstupaty v taiemni vidnosyny
вступати в таємні відносини
v.i. tamper
vstupnyi вступний *a.* introductory
vsuperech всупереч *prep.*
notwithstanding
vsypaty всипати *v. t* bestrew

vtamuvaty втамувати *v.t.* slake
vtecha втеча *n.* run
vtekty втекти *v. i* elope
vtilennia втілення *n* embodiment
vtilenyi втілений *a.* incarnate
vtiliuvaty втілювати *v. t.* embody
vtiliuvaty втілювати *v.t.* incarnate
vtim втім *adv.* though
vtishaty втішати *v. t* comfort
vtishaty втішати *v.t.* soothe
vtoma втома *n* fatigue
vtomlenyi втомлений *a.* weary
vtomlyvyi втомливий *a.* trying
vtorhatysia вторгатися *v.t.* intrude
vtorhnennia вторгнення *n.* intrusion
vtorynna syrovyna вторинна сировина *n.* salvage
vtorynnyi вторинний *a.* secondary
vtrachaty втрачати *v.t.* lose
vtrata втрата *n* bereavement
vtrata втрата *n.* loss
vtraty втрати *n.* casualty
vtruchannia втручання *n.* interference
vtruchannia втручання *n.* interjection
vtruchatysia втручатися *v.i.* intervene
vtulka втулка *n.* hub
vtykaty втикати *v.t.* stab
vtyskuvaty втискувати *v. t* cram
vudyty вудити *v.i* fish
vuhillia вугілля *n* coal
vuhlets вуглець *n.* carbon
vuhor вугор *n.* pimple
vukho вухо *n* ear
vulharnist вульгарність *n.* vulgarity
vulharnyi вульгарний *a.* vulgar
vulkan вулкан *n.* volcano

vulkanichnyi вулканічний *a.* volcanic
vulychnyi khlopchyk вуличний хлопчик *n.* urchin
vulyk вулик *n.* beehive
vulytsia вулиця *n.* street
vus вус *n.* moustache
vusa вуса *n.* mustache
vushna sirka вушна сірка *n* cerumen
vusyk вусик *n.* cornicle
vuzkyi вузький *a.* narrow
vuzlovyi punkt вузловий пункт *n.* node
vuzol вузол *n* bundle
vvazhaty вважати *v.i.* deem
vvazhaty vynnym вважати винним *v. t* blame
vvazhaty za вважати за *v.t.* account
vvedennia введення *n.* input
vverhaty u morok ввергати у морок *v. t* benight
vverkh dnom вверх дном *adv* topsy turvy
vvesty v omanu ввести в оману *v.t.* hoodwink
vvichlyvist ввічливість *n.* complaisance
vvichlyvyi ввічливий *adj.* bland
vviriaty ввіряти *v.t.* consign
vvodyty вводити *v.t.* inject
vvodyty v omanu вводити в оману *v.t.* misguide
vvodyty v posadu вводити в посаду *v.t.* induct
vvodytysia вводитися *v.i* mix
vybachaty вибачати *v.t* forgive
vybachatysia вибачатися *v.i.* apologize
vybachennia вибачення *n.* apology
vybir вибір *n.* selection

vyblyskuvaty виблискувати *v.t*
flash
vyblyskuvaty виблискувати *v.i.*
glitter
vyblyskuvaty виблискувати *v.i.*
twinkle
vyboina вибоїна *n.* groove
vyboina вибоїна *n.* pitfall
vyboistyi вибоїстий *adj* bumpy
vyborche pravo виборче право
n. suffrage
vyborets виборець *n.* constituent
vybory вибори *n* election
vybudovuvaty вибудовувати *v.t*
marshal
vybudovuvaty v liniiu
вибудовувати в лінію *v.t.* align
vybukh вибух *n* blast
vybukh вибух *n.* explosion
vybukh pochuttiv вибух почуттів
n. passion
vybukhnuty вибухнути *v. t.*
explode
vybukhova rechovyna вибухова
речовина *n.* explosive
vybukhovyi вибуховий *a*
explosive
vybyraty вибирати *v. t.* choose
vybyvaty z kolii вибивати з колії
v.t. unsettle
vychavliuvaty вичавлювати *v.t*
wring
vycherpuvaty вичерпувати *v. t.*
exhaust
vyd вид *n.* perspective
vyd вид *n.* species
vyd dyialnosti вид дияльності *n.*
occupation
vydacha видача *n* grant
vydalennia видалення *n.* removal
vydalyty видалити *v. t* delete
vydannia видання *n* edition

vydatky na zbilshennia
vartosti vlasnosti видатки на
збільшення вартості власності
n betterment
vydatnyi видатний *a.* laureate
vydatnyi видатний *a.* pre-eminent
vydavaty видавати *v. t* emit
vydavaty dekret видавати
декрет *v. i* decree
vydavaty zakony видавати
закони *v.i.* legislate
vydavets видавець *n* editor
vydavets видавець *n.* publisher
vydiliaty виділяти *v.t* accent
vydiliaty виділяти *v.t* evolve
vydiliaty moloko виділяти
молоко *v.i.* lactate
vydiliatysia виділятися *v.i.* ooze
vydilyty виділити *v.t.* void
vydnyi видний *a.* prominent
vydnyi видний *a.* sightly
vydobutok видобуток *n* booty
vydovbuvaty видовбувати *v.t*
hollow
vydovyshche видовище *n.*
entertainment
vydovyshche видовище *n.*
pageant
vydozmina видозміна *n.*
transfiguration
vydra видра *n.* otter
vyduzhuvaty видужувати *v.t.*
recover
vydymist видимість *n.* visibility
vydymyi видимий *a.* apparent
vydyrannia видирання *n*
scramble
vydyratysia видиратися *v.i* climb
vyhadanyi вигаданий *a* fictitious
vyhadaty вигадати *v. t* devise
vyhadka вигадка *n* fiction
vyhaduvaty вигадувати *v.t*
fabricate

vyhaniaty виганяти *v.t.* banish
vyhidnyi вигідний *a.* remunerative
vyhnanets вигнанець *n.* outcast
vyhnannia вигнання *n.* expulsion
vyhnaty вигнати *v. t.* eject
vyhoda вигода *n.* profit
vyhodovuvaty dytynu вигодовувати дитину *v.t* nurse
vyhotovlennia виготовлення *n* fabrication
vyhotovliaty v trokh prymirnykakh виготовляти в трьох примірниках *v.t.* triplicate
vyhrash виграш *n* gain
vyhrash виграш *n* win
vyhrashnyi виграшний *a.* advantageous
vyhrashnyi виграшний *a.* meritorious
vyhraty виграти *v.t.* win
vyhribaty вигрібати *v.t.* shovel
vyhribna yama вигрібна яма *n.* cesspool
vyhuk вигук *n* exclamation
vyhuk вигук *n.* outcry
vyhuk вигук *n.* shout
vyhukuvaty вигукувати *v.i* exclaim
vyhyn вигин *v.t.* twist
vyhynannia вигинання *n* wriggle
vyhynaty вигинати *v. t* curve
vyhynaty spynu вигинати спину *v.i* bog
vyiav sumnivu вияв сумніву *n.* impeachment
vyiav zakhoplennia вияв захоплення *n.* rapture
vyiavlennia виявлення *n.* manifestation
vyiavliaty виявляти *v. t* detect
vyiavliaty виявляти *v. t* exhibit
vyiavliaty виявляти *v.t.* signify

vyimaty z pikhov виймати з піхов *v.t.* unsheathe
vyizd виїзд *n* drive
vykhid вихід *n* yield
vykhid na pensiiu вихід на пенсію *n.* retirement
vykhodyty виходити *n.* issue
vykhodyty na виходити на *v.t* front
vykhor вихор *n* whirl
vykhovannia виховання *n.* nurture
vykhovuvaty виховувати *v.t.* foster
vykhvaliannia вихваляння *n.* glorification
vykladaty викладати *v. t* expose
vykliuchaty виключати *v. t* except
vykliuchaty, ne rakhuiuchy виключати, не рахуючи *v.t* bar
vyklyk виклик *n.* challenge
vyklykaty викликати *v. t.* challenge
vyklykaty nevdovolennia викликати невдоволення *v. t.* dissatisfy
vyklykaty revnoshchi викликати ревнощі *v.t.* jaundice
vyklykaty zakhoplennia викликати захоплення *v. t* enrapture
vykonannia виконання *n.* achievement
vykonannia виконання *n.* acting
vykonavets виконавець *n.* performer
vykonuvaty виконувати *v.t.* fulfill
vykonuvaty виконувати *v.t.* perform
vykonuvaty oboviazky виконувати обов'язки *v.i.* officiate

vykoriniuvaty викорінювати *v. t* eradicate

vykorystannia використання *n.* use

vykorystovuvaty використовувати *v.t.* use

vykradaty викрадати *v.t.* abduct

vykradennia викрадення *n* abduction

vykrasty викрасти *v.t.* kidnap

vykresliuvaty викреслювати *v.t.* obliterate

vykrut викрут *n* elusion

vykrutas викрутас *v.i.* quibble

vykup викуп *n.* ransom

vykupovuvaty викуповувати *v.t.* ransom

vykydaty викидати *v.t.* spurt

vykyden викидень *adv* abortive

vykynuty викинути *v.i.* miscarry

vylazka вилазка *n.* sally

vylikovnyi виліковний *a* curable

vylikovuvaty виліковувати *v. t.* cure

vylit виліт *n* departure

vylochnyi kliuch вилочний ключ *n.* spanner

vyluchaty вилучати *v. t.* exempt

vyluchaty z obihu вилучати з обігу *v.t.* demonetize

vylyvok виливок *n* mould

vymahaty вимагати *v. t* claim

vymia вим'я *n.* udder

vymir вимір *n* dimension

vymiriuvalnyi вимірювальний *a.* metrical

vymiriuvaty вимірювати *v. t* determine

vymiriuvaty вимірювати *v.t* measure

vymiriuvaty hlybynu вимірювати глибину *v.t* fathom

vymiriuvaty hlybynu вимірювати глибину *v.i.* sound

vymirnyi вимірний *a.* measurable

vymochuvaty вимочувати *v.t.* steep

vymoha вимога *n* demand

vymova вимова *n.* pronunciation

vymovliaty вимовляти *v.t.* pronounce

vymovliaty вимовляти *v.t.* voice

vymovliaty z shypinniam вимовляти з шипінням *v.* assibilate

vympel вимпел *n.* streamer

vymuchenyi вимучений *a.* laboured

vymykaty вимикати *v. t* exclude

vynahoroda винагорода *n.* gratification

vynahoroda винагорода *n.* honorarium

vynahoroda винагорода *n.* reward

vynahorodzhuvaty винагороджувати *v.t.* recompense

vynahorodzhuvaty винагороджувати *v.t.* reward

vynakhid винахід *n.* artifice

vynakhidlyvyi винахідливий *a.* inventive

vynakhidnyk винахідник *n.* inventor

vynakhodyty винаходити *v.t.* invent

vyniatkovyi винятковий *a* exclusive

vyniatkovyi винятковий *a.* particular

vyniatkovyi винятковий *a* sole

vyniatok виняток *n* exception

vynnyi винний *a* culpable

vyno вино *n.* wine

vynohrad виноград *n.* grape
vynohradna loza виноградна
лоза *n.* vine
vynosyty na noshakh виносити
на ношах *v.t.* litter
vynosyty treteiske rishennia
виносити третейське рішення
v.t. arbitrate
vynosyty vypravdalnyi vyrok
виносити виправдальний
вирок *v.t.* acquit
vynosyty vyrok виносити вирок
v.t. adjudge
vynuvatets винуватець *n* culprit
vynuvatyi винуватий *a.* guilty
vynykaty виникати *v.i.* arise
vypad випад *n.* lunge
vypadkovist випадковість *n.*
contingency
vypadkovyi випадковий *a*
accidental
vypadok випадок *n* accident
vypadok випадок *n* event
vyparovuvaty випаровувати *v. i*
evaporate
vyparovuvatysia випаровуватися
v.t. vaporize
vyperedzhaty випереджати *v.t.*
outrun
vyperedzhaty випереджати *v.t.*
surpass
vyplachuvaty виплачувати *v.t.*
redeem
vyplavliaty виплавляти *v.t.* smelt
vyplodok виплодок *n.* spawn
vypravdannia виправдання *n.*
acquittal
vypravdovuvaty виправдовувати
v.t. justify
vypravdovuvaty po sudu
виправдовувати по суду *v.t.*
assoil

vypravlennia виправлення *n*
correction
vypravlennia виправлення *n*
reclamation
vypravliaty виправляти *v. t*
correct
vypravliaty виправляти *v. t*
exercise
vypravnyi виправний *a*
reformatory
vypravnyi zaklad виправний
заклад *n.* reformatory
vypravyty виправити *a.* reparable
vypriamlennia випрямлення *n.*
rectification
vypriamliaty випрямляти *v.t.*
straighten
vypriamytysia випрямитися *v.t.*
right
vyprobnyi termin випробний
термін *n.* probation
vyprobovuvaty випробовувати *v.*
t. essay
vyprobuvannia випробування *n.*
ordeal
vyprobuvaty випробувати *v.t.*
taste
vyprominiuvaty випромінювати
v.t. radiate
vypuklyi випуклий *a.* salient
vypusk випуск *n.* instalment
vypusk випуск *v.t.* number
vypuskaty випускати *v.i.* graduate
vypuskaty par випускати пар *v.i.*
steam
vypusknyi випускний *n* graduate
vypyvaty випивати *v. t* drink
vypyvka випивка *v. i* booze
vypzvoliaty випзволяти *v.t* free
vyr вир *n.* whirlpool
vyraz вираз *n.* expression
vyraz oblychchia вираз обличчя
n. visage

vyrazhaty виражати *v.t.* term
vyrazhaty slovamy виражати словами *v.t.* utter
vyrazka виразка *n.* ulcer
vyrazkovyi виразковий *a.* ulcerous
vyraznyi виразний *a* emphatic
vyraznyi виразний *a.* sharp
vyrikaty вирікати *v.t.* mouth
vyrishalnyi вирішальний *adj.* crucial
vyrishennia вирішення *n* answer
vyrishuvaty вирішувати *v. t* decide
vyrishyty вирішити *v.t.* solve
vyrivniuvaty вирівнювати *v. t* even
vyrizaty вирізати *v. t.* carve
vyrobliaty виробляти *v.t.* produce
vyrobnychyi виробничий *a.* industrial
vyrobnyk виробник *n.* maker
vyrobnyk виробник *n* manufacturer
vyrobnytstvo виробництво *n.* industry
vyroby вироби *n. pl.* ware
vyrok вирок *n* condemnation
vyrok вирок *n.* sentence
vyroshchuvaty вирощувати *v.t.* nurture
vyrostaty z виростати з *v.t.* outgrow
vyrubka вирубка *n* slash
vyruchka виручка *n.* proceeds
vyrushaty v dorohu вирушати в дорогу *v.t.* start
vyruvaty вирувати *v.i.* seethe
vyrvaty вирвати *v.t.* wrest
vyryvaty z korenem виривати з коренем *v.t.* uproot
vysadka висадка *n.* landing

vysadzhuvaty висаджувати *v.i.* land
vyselennia виселення *n* eviction
vyseliaty виселяти *v. t* evict
vyshche вище *prep.* afore
vyshchist вищість *n.* pre-eminence
vyshchoi yakosti вищої якості *a.* superb
vyshchyi вищий *a.* superior
vyshtovkhuvaty виштовхувати *v. t.* expel
vyshukanist вишуканість *n.* refinement
vyshykovuvaty v boiovyi poriadok вишиковувати в бойовий порядок *v.t.* array
vyshyvannia вишивання *n* embroidery
vyskochka вискочка *n.* upstart
vysliv вислів *n* dictum
vysliv вислів *n.* saw
vyslovliuvannia висловлювання *n.* utterance
vyslovliuvaty висловлювати *v. t.* express
vyslovliuvaty dumku висловлювати думку *v.t.* opine
vyslovliuvaty slovamy висловлювати словами *v.t* word
vyslovliuvatysia висловлюватися *v.i.* speak
vyslovyty висловити *v.t.* phrase
vyslyzaty вислизати *v. t.* bilk
vysmiiuvaty висміювати *v.t.* satirize
vysnazhenyi виснажений *a.* haggard
vysnazhlyvyi виснажливий *a.* tedious
vysnazhuvaty виснажувати *v.t.* depauperate

vysnovok висновок *n.* conclusion
vysoka yakist висока якість *n.* excellence
vysoke polozhennia високе положення *n* eminance
vysokist високість *n.* Highness
vysoko tsinuvaty високо цінувати *v.t.* prize
vysoko tsinuvaty високо цінувати *v.t.* treasure
vysokyi високий *a.* high
vysota висота *n.* altitude
vystachyty вистачити *v.i.* suffice
vystavka виставка *n.* exhibition
vystezhuvaty вистежувати *v.t.* track
vystupaty proty виступати проти *v.t.* oppose
vystupaty v sudi виступати в суді *v.i.* plead
vysuvannia висування *n.* nomination
vysuvaty висувати *v.t.* propose
vysuvaty висувати *v.t.* propound
vysuvaty obvynuvachennia висувати обвинувачення *v.t.* indict
vysuvaty vymohu висувати вимогу *v. t* demand
vysvitliuvaty висвітлювати *v.t.* alluminate
vysydzhuvaty висиджувати *v.i.* incubate
vysylka висилка *n.* banishment
vysypnyi tyf висипний тиф *n.* typhus
vyterpity витерпіти *v.t.* endure
vytiahaty витягати *v. t* extract
vytiahuvaty витягувати *v.t.* retrieve
vytik витік *n.* leak
vytikannia витікання *n* expiry
vytikaty витікати *v.i.* result

vytisniaty витісняти *v. t* displace
vytivka витівка *n* mischief
vytonchenist витонченість *n.* sophistication
vytonchenyi витончений *a.* dainty
vytonchenyi витончений *a.* nice
vytonchenyi витончений *a.* polite
vytrachaty витрачати *v. t* expend
vytrata витрата *n* consumption
vytrebuvannia витребування *n.* vindication
vytrebuvaty spravu z nyzhchoho sudu do vyshchoho витребувати справу з нижчого суду до вищого *v. t* evoke
vytrishchatysia витріщатися *v.i.* stare
vytrymuvaty витримувати *v.t.* withstand
vytryvalist витривалість *n.* stamina
vyttia виття *n* wail
vyty вити *v.t.* howl
vytyraty витирати *v.t.* wipe
vytyraty rushnykom витирати рушником *v.t.* towel
vyvaliuvaty вивалювати *v.t.* tip
vyvchaty вивчати *v.t.* scrutinize
vyvchaty вивчати *v.i.* study
vyvchennia вивчення *n.* inquisition
vyvchennia вивчення *n.* study
vyvedennia виведення *n.* inference
vyverhaty вивергати *v. t* belch
vyverhatysia вивергатися *v. i* erupt
vyvershennia вивершення *n.* completion
vyvert виверт *n* dodge
vyvertkyi верткий *a.* shifty

vyverzhennia виверження *n*
eruption
vyvezennia вивезення *n* export
vyvitriuvaty вивітрювати *v.t.*
weather
vyvodok виводок *n* brood
vyvodyty виводити *v. t.* derive
vyvodyty z rivnovahy виводити з
рівноваги *v.t.* upset
vyvozyty вивозити *v. t.* export
vyvykhnuty вивихнути *v.t.*
wrench
vyzhyvannia виживання *n.*
survival
vyzhyvaty виживати *v.i.* survive
vyznachaty визначати *v.t.* assess
vyznachaty
mistseznakhodzhennia
визначати місцезнаходження
v.t. position
vyznachennia визначення *n.*
attribute
vyznachnyi визначний *a.*
noteworthy
vyznannia визнання *n.*
acknowledgement
vyznanty vynnym визнанти
винним *v. t.* convict
vyznavaty визнавати *v.t.* avow
vyznavaty визнавати *v. t.* declare
vyzvolennia визволення *n.*
liberation
vyzvolytel визволитель *n.*
liberator
vzahali взагалі *adv.* any
vzaiemnyi взаємний *a.* mutual
vzaiemodiia взаємодія *n.*
interplay
vzaiemodiia взаємодія *n.* liaison
vzaiemorozuminnia
взаєморозуміння *n.* rapport

vzaiemozalezhnist
взаємозалежність *n.*
interdependence
vzaiemozalezhnyi
взаємозалежний *a.*
interdependent
vzaiemozviazok взаємозв'язок *n.*
correlation
vzhe вже *adv.* already
vzhe вже *adv.* yet
vzhyvaty вживати *v.t.* undertake
vzhyvaty vidpovidnykh zakhodiv
вживати відповідних заходів
v.i. reply
vzirets взірець *n.* sample
vzuvaty взувати *v.t.* shoe
vzvod взвод *n.* platoon

ya я *pron.* I
yabluko яблуко *n.* apple
yachmin ячмінь *n.* barley
yachmin na otsi ячмінь на оці *n.*
stye
yadernyi ядерний *a.* nuclear
yadro ядро *n.* core
yadro ядро *n.* nucleus
yahnia ягня *n.* lamb
yahniatko ягнятко *n.* lambkin
yaiechko яєчко *n.* testicle
yaiechnyi bilok яєчний білок *n*
albumen
yaiechnyk яєчник *n.* ovary
yaitse яйце *n* egg
yak як *adv.* as
yak як *adv.* how
yak як *n.* yak
yak maty як мати *adj.* motherlike
yak pravylo як правило *adv.*
generally
yakhta яхта *n.* yacht

yakii vidpovidaie zvychaiu якій
відповідає звичаю *a.* usual
yakir якір *n.* anchor
yakirna stoianka якірна стоянка
n anchorage
yakisnyi якісний *a.* qualitative
yakist якість *n.* quality
yakoho mozhno vidstezhyty
якого можно відстежити *a.*
traceable
yakos якось *adv.* somehow
yakshcho якщо *conj.* if
yakshcho ne якщо не *conj.*
unless
yakyi який *pron.* as
yakyi який *a.* that
yakyi який *a.* what
yakyi який *a* which
yakyi b ne який б не *pron*
whichever
yakyi dme z pivnochi який дме з
півночі *a.* northern
yakyi dopovniuie який доповнює
a. supplementary
yakyi doroho koshtuie який
дорого коштує *a* expensive
yakyi holosuie «za» який
голосує «за» *a.* content
**yakyi korystuietsia
nedotornkanistiu** який
користується недоторнканістю
a. inviolable
yakyi liubyt rozkish який любит
розкіш *a.* luxurious
yakyi maie pidozru який має
підозру *a.* suspicious
**yakyi maie pravo na zvilnennia
z uviaznennia pid zastavu**
який має право на звільнення
з ув'язнення під заставу *a.*
bailable
yakyi maietsia na uvazi який
мається на увазі *a.* tacit

yakyi mistyt zoboviazannia
який містить зобов'язання *a.*
promissory
yakyi narodzhuietsia який
народжується *a.* nascent
yakyi navivaie tuhu який навіває
тугу *a.* lonely
yakyi ne beretsia do uvahy
який не береться до уваги *a.*
negligible
yakyi ne pamiataie який не
пам'ятає *a.* oblivious
yakyi nese vidpovidalnist який
несе відповідальність *a.*
answerable
yakyi obyraie який обирає *adj.*
constituent
yakyi pasuie який пасує *a*
becoming
yakyi perebuvaie na rozhliadi
який перебуває на розгляді *a.*
subjudice
yakyi pidliahaie skasuvanniu
який підлягає скасуванню *a.*
revocable
yakyi postiino meshkaie який
постійно мешкає *a.* resident
yakyi rozhliadaietsia який
розглядається *a* pending
yakyi sluzhyt do vyrazhennia
який служить до вираження *a.*
expressive
yakyi spodivaietsia який
сподівається *a.* hopeful
yakyi spuskaietsia який
спускається *a* downward
**yakyi stosuietsia vyboriv u
senat** який стосується виборів
у сенат *a* senatorial
yakyi usvidomliuie який
усвідомлює *a* conscious
yakyi vazhko chytaietsia який
важко читається *a.* illegible

yakyi vidbuvsia do narodzhennia який відбувся до народження *adj.* antenatal

yakyi vidchuvaie який відчуває *a.* sentient

yakyi vidrodzhuietsia який відроджується *a.* resurgent

yakyi vidshtovkhuie який відштовхує *a.* repellent

yakyi vilno teche який вільно тече *a.* affluent

yakyi vkazuie який вказує *a.* indicative

yakyi vykhodyt na pivnich який виходить на північ *a* north

yakyi vymahaietsia zazdalehid який вимагається заздалегідь *a.* prerequisite

yakyi vyplyvaie який випливає *a.* subsequent

yakyi yde lyshe vid odniiei storony який йде лише від однієї сторони *a* ex-parte

yakyi ye blyzniukom який є близнюком *a* twin

yakyi zadovolniaietsia який задовольняється *a.* satiable

yakyi zberihaie який зберігає *a.* retentive

yakyi zlyvaietsia який зливається *adj.* confluent

yakyi-nebud який-небудь *a.* any

yakyis якийсь *a* certain

yakyis якийсь *a.* some

yalovychyna яловичина *n* beef

yalyna ялина *n* fir

yama яма *n.* pit

yamka ямка *n* bunker

yamka pid hrudmy ямка під грудьми *n* anticardium

yanhol янгол *n* angel

yarlyk ярлик *n.* label

yarlyk ярлик *n.* tag

yarmarok ярмарок *n.* fair

yarmo ярмо *n.* yoke

yarus ярус *n.* tier

yashchirka ящірка *n.* lizard

yashchyk ящик *n* ark

yashchyk ящик *n* chest

yaskravist яскравість *n* brilliance

yaskravo spalakhnuty яскраво спалахнути *v.i* flare

yaskravo-chervonyi яскраво-червоний *a.* vermillion

yaskravo-chervonyi kolir яскраво-червоний колір *n.* vermillion

yaskravyi яскравий *a* bright

yaskravyi яскравий *a.* gaudy

yaskravyi яскравий *a.* gorgeous

yaskravyi яскравий *a.* lucent

yaskravyi яскравий *a.* vivid

yasla ясла *n.* crib

yasla ясла *n.* manger

yasnist ясність *n.* lucidity

yasno ясно *adv* clearly

yasnovelmozhnist ясновельможність *n* excellency

yasnyi ясний *a.* lucid

yastrub яструб *n* hawk

yavno явно *adv* downright

yavnyi явний *a.* explicit

yavnyi явний *a.* manifest

yavnyi явний *a.* overt

yavyshche явище *n.* phenomenon

yazyk язик *n.* tongue

ye є *v. t* eat

yednist єдність *n.* unity

yedynyi єдиний *a.* one

yedynyi єдиний *a.* only

yeher єгер *n.* huntsman

yemnyi ємний *a.* capacious

yepyskop єпископ *n* bishop

yeretyk єретик *n.* miscreant

Yevanheliie Євангеліє *n.* gospel

yevnukh євнух *n* eunuch
yevrei єврей *n.* Jew
yidalnia їдальня *n.* canteen
yidkist їдкість *n.* pungency
yii їй *pron.* her
yii її *a* her
yikh їх *a.* their
yikhaty zaliznytseiu їхати
   залізницею *v.t.* rail
yikhnii їхній *pron.* theirs
yim їм *pron.* them
yistivne їстівне *n.* eatable
yistivnyi їстівний *a* eatable
yizdyty їздити *v.t.* ride
yizdyty na taksi їздити на таксі
   v.i. taxi
yizha їжа *n* food
ymovirnist ймовірність *n.*
   likelihood
ymovirno ймовірно *adv.* probably
ymovirnyi ймовірний *a* credible
yoho його *pron.* his
yolop йолоп *n* dunce
yolop йолоп *n.* gander
yomen йомен *n.* yeoman
yomu йому *pron.* him
yota йота *n.* jot
yty йти *v.i.* go
yty dobrovilno йти добровільно
   v.t. volunteer
yty na pensiiu йти на пенсію *v.i.*
   retire
yty pid vitrylamy йти під
   вітрилами *v.i.* sail
yty ryssiu йти риссю *v.i.* trot
yty u vidstavku йти у відставку
   v.t. resign
yudol юдоль *n.* vale
yula юла *n.* whirligig
yunak юнак *n.* youth
yunatskyi юнацький *a.* juvenile
yunyi юний *a.* adolescent
yunyi юний *a.* young

yunyi юний *a.* youthful
Yupiter Юпітер *n.* jupiter
yurba юрба *n.* mob
yurysdyktsiia юрисдикція *n.*
   jurisdiction
yurysprudentsiia юриспруденція
   n. jurisprudence
yuryst юрист *n.* jurist
yuryst юрист *n.* lawyer
yushka юшка *n* broth
yuvelir ювелір *n.* goldsmith
yuvelir ювелір *n.* jeweller
yzobar изобар *n.* isobar

Z

z з *prep.* with
z druhoho boku з другого боку
   adv. again
z harnymy maneramy з гарними
   манерами *a.* mannerly
z hotovnistiu з готовністю *adv.*
   readily
z obmezhenoiu vidpovidalnistiu
   з обмеженою відповідальністю
   a. limited
z pivdnia з півдня *a.* southerly
z tsoho chasu з цього часу *adv.*
   henceforth
z tykh pir з тих пір *conj.* since
za за *prep.* after
za за *prep.* beyond
za bort за борт *adv.* overboard
za khvylynu за хвилину *adv.*
   presently
za kordonom за кордоном *adv*
   abroad
za mezhamy за межами *adv*
   outside
za mezhi за межі *adv* outwards
za minusom за мінусом *prep.*
   minus

za vyniatkom за винятком *prep*
except
za vyniatkom за винятком *prep*
save
za vyrakhuvanniam за
вирахуванням *adv.* less
zaareshtovuvaty
заарештовувати *v.t.* arrest
zaareshtuvaty заарештувати *v.t.*
nab
zaarkanyty заарканити *v.t.* noose
zabalzamuvaty забальзамувати
v. t embalm
zabavliaty забавляти *v.t.* amuse
zabavnyi забавний *n.* funny
zabezpechenyi забезпечений *a.*
well-to-do
**zabezpechuvaty postiinym
dokhodom** забезпечувати
постійним доходом *v. t* endow
zabiiaka-korotun забіяка-
коротун *n.* bantam
zabludlyi заблудлий *a* stray
zabobonnyi забобонний *a.*
superstitious
zaborhuvaty заборгувати *v.t* owe
zaborona заборона *n.* ban
zaborona заборона *n.* prohibition
zaboronenyi заборонений *a*
taboo
zaboroniaiuchyi забороняючий
a. prohibitory
zaboroniaty забороняти *v.t.*
inhibit
zaboroniaty забороняти *v.t.*
suppress
zaboroniaty забороняти *v.t.*
taboo
zaboronnyi заборонний *a.*
prohibitive
zabrudnennia забруднення *n.*
pollution

zabrudniuvaty забруднювати *v.t.*
contaminate
zabrudnyty забруднити *v.t.* stain
zabryzkuvaty brudom
забризкувати брудом *v. t*
bemire
zabudkuvatyi забудькуватий *a*
forgetful
zabudovuvaty забудовувати *v. t.*
encumber
zabuttia забуття *n.* oblivion
zabuvaty забувати *v.t* forget
zabyraty nahrabovane dobro
забирати награбоване добро
v.i. loot
zabyty забити *v.t.* injure
zabyvaty забивати *v. t* butcher
zacharovuvaty зачаровувати *v.t.*
spell
zacharovuvaty pohliadom
зачаровувати поглядом *v.t*
fascinate
zacharuvaty зачарувати *v.t*
bewitch
zad зад *n* buttock
zadacha задача *n.* problem
zadaty robotu задати роботу *v.t.*
task
zadavaty ton задавати тон *v.t.*
tone
zadnii prokhid задній прохід *n.*
anus
zadovilnyi задовільний *a.*
satisfactory
zadovolenist задоволеність *n*
contentment
zadovolennia задоволення *n.*
content
zadovolennia задоволення *n*
enjoyment
zadovolennia задоволення *n.*
pleasure

zadovolenyi задоволений *a.*
jubilant
zadovolniaty задовольняти *v. t*
content
zadovolniaty задовольняти *v.t*
uphold
zadovolniaty vymoham
задовольняти вимогам *v.t.* suit
zadubilyi задубілий *n.* stark
zadukha задуха *n* apnoea
zadum задум *n* conception
zadumuvaty задумувати *v. t*
conceive
zadushlyvyi задушливий *a.* stuffy
zadushyty задушити *v.t.* strangle
zadykhnutysia задихнутися *v.t.*
smother
zadyraty задирати *v. t.* bully
zahadka загадка *n.* conundrum
zahalna dumka загальна думка
n. repute
zahalne mistse загальне місце *a.*
commonplace
zahalne mistse загальне місце *a.*
humdrum
zahalnyi загальний *a.* common
zahar загар *n., a.* tan
zahartovuvaty загартовувати *v.t.*
season
zahin загін *n.* squad
zahin dlia khudoby загін для
худоби *n.* bawn
zahlushka заглушка *n.* plug
zahlushyty заглушити *v.t.* silence
zahoiennia загоєння *n.* repair
zaholovnyi заголовний *a.* titular
zaholovok заголовок *n.* heading
zahoriaty загоряти *v.i.* tan
zahoritysia загорітися *v.t.* kindle
zahornuty v savan загорнути в
саван *v.t.* shroud
zahortaty v paket загортати в
пакет *v.t.* parcel

zahostrennia загострення *n.*
aggravation
zahostrenyi загострений *adj.*
cultrate
zahotovliuvaty pro zapas
заготовлювати про запас *v.t.*
pot
zahroza загроза *n.* hazard
zahroza загроза *n.* threat
zahrozhuvaty загрожувати *v.t*
menace
zahrozlyvyi загрозливий *a.*
ominous
zahybel загибель *n* doom
zahybel загибель *v.t.* ruin
zaiava заява *n* declaration
zaiavnyk заявник *n.* applicant
zaiets заєць *n.* hare
zaikannia заїкання *n* stammer
zaikatysia заїкатися *v.i.* stammer
zaimannia займання *n.*
inflammation
zaimaty stiilo займати стійло *v.t.*
stall
zaimaty vysoke stanovyshche
займати високе становище *v.t.*
throne
zaimatysia chyms poverkhovo
займатися чимсь поверхово *v.*
i. dabble
zaimatysia khliborobstvom
займатися хліборобством *v.i.*
tilt
zaimatysia prostytutsiieiu
займатися проституцією *v.t.*
prostitute
zaimennyk займенник *n.* pronoun
zainiatist зайнятість *n*
employment
zainiatyi зайнятий *a* busy
zaivyi зайвий *a* excess
zaivyi зайвий *a.* superabundant
zaivyi зайвий *a.* superfluous

zakhid захід *n* decline
zakhidnyi західний *a.* occidental
zakhidnyi західний *a.* west
zakhidnyi західний *a.* westerly
zakhody bezpeky заходи
безпеки *n.* precaution
zakhoplennia захоплення *n.*
seizure
zakhoplenyi захоплений *a*
enthusiastic
zakhoplenyi захоплений *a.* lyrical
zakhopliuiuchyi захоплюючий *a.*
spectacular
zakhopliuvaty захоплювати *v. t.*
delight
zakhopliuvaty захоплювати *v.t.*
occupy
zakhopliuvaty syloiu
захоплювати силою *v. t.*
capture
zakhopliuvatysia захоплюватися
v.t. admire
zakhoronennia захоронення *n*
burial
zakhvat захват *n* delight
zakhvataty захватати *v.t.* thumb
zakhvoriuvanist захворюваність
n morbidity
zakhvoriuvannia захворювання
n disease
zakhyshchaty захищати *v.t.*
advocate
zakhyshchaty захищати *v. t.*
champion
zakhyshchaty захищати *v.t.*
protect
zakhysnyi захисний *a.* protective
zakhysnyk захисник *n.* pleader
zakhysnyk захисник *n.* protector
zakinchennia закінчення *n* finish
zakinchuvaty закінчувати *v.t*
finish

zakinchuvatysia закінчуватися
v.i. issue
zakladaty закладати *v. t.*
establish
zakladka закладка *n.* book-mark
zaklepka заклепка *n.* rivet
zakliuchnyi заключний *a*
conclusive
zaklopotanist заклопотаність *n.*
preoccupation
zaklopotanyi заклопотаний *a.*
anxious
zaklyk заклик *n.* appeal
zaklykaty закликати *v.t.* invoke
zaklynannia заклинання *n.*
invocation
zaklynaty заклинати *v. t.* charm2
zaklynaty заклинати *v.i.* conjure
zakokhuvaty закохувати *v. t*
enamour
zakolot заколот *n.* insurrection
zakolot заколот *n.* mutiny
zakolotnyi заколотний *a.*
mutinous
zakon закон *n.* law
zakonnist законність *n.*
legitimacy
zakonnyi законний *a.* justifiable
zakonnyi законний *a.* lawful
zakonnyi законний *a.* statutory
zakonodavcha vlada
законодавча влада *n.*
legislature
zakonodavchyi законодавчий *a.*
legislative
zakonodavets законодавець *n.*
legislator
zakonodavstvo законодавство *n.*
legislation
zakononarodzhenyi
закононароджений *a.*
legitimate
zakrep закреп *n.* constipation

zakresliuvannia закреслювання *v. t.* cancel
zakripliuvaty закріплювати *v.i.* strut
zakripliuvaty kanatom закріплювати канатом *v. t.* cable
zakripliuvaty klynom закріплювати клином *v.t.* wedge
zakripyty snastiamy закріпити снастями *v.t.* tackle
zakrut закрут *n* bight
zakrutyty закрутити *n.* twist
zakrutyty holovu закрутити голову *v.t.* infatuate
zakryttia закриття *n.* closure
zakryty закрити *v. t* close
zakrytyi закритий *a.* close
zakryvaty закривати *v. t.* cover
zakryvaty kryshkoiu закривати кришкою *v. t.* cap
zakulisnyi закулісний *a.* underhand
zakuska закуска *n.* snack
zakusky ta napoi закуски та напої *n.* refreshment
zal зал *n.* hall
zal dlia hliadachiv зал для глядачів *n.* auditorium
zalezhaty залежати *v.t.* addict
zalezhaty залежати *v. i.* depend
zalezhna teritoriia залежна теріторія *n.* possession
zalezhnist залежність *n.* addiction
zalezhnyi залежний *a* dependent
zalezhnyi залежний *a* subject
zaliakuvannia залякування *n.* harassment
zaliakuvannia залякування *n.* intimidation
zaliakuvaty залякувати *v. t.* cow
zaliznyi залізний *v.t.* iron

zaliznytsia залізниця *n.* railway
zalomliuvaty заломлювати *v.t. & i.* deflect
zaloza залоза *n.* gland
zalp залп *n.* volley
zaluchaty залучати *v.t.* attract
zaluchennia залучення *n.* implication
zalyshaty залишати *v. t.* desert
zalyshaty shram залишати шрам *v.t.* scar
zalyshatysia залишатися *v.i.* remain
zalyshatysia v bezvykhidnomu stanovyshchi залишатися в безвихідному становищі *v.t* maroon
zalyshkovyi залишковий *a.* permanent
zalyshkovyi залишковий *a.* residual
zalyshky залишки *n.* remains
zalyshok залишок *n.* remainder
zalyshyty залишити *v.t.* jack
zalytsiannia залицяння *n.* courtship
zalyvaty заливати *v.t.* whelm
zalyvatysia заливатися *v.i.* warble
zamakh замах *n.* stroke
zamaniuvaty заманювати *v.t.* allure
zamanyty заманити *v. t.* entrap
zametil заметіль *n* blizzard
zamiaty зам'яти *v.i* falter
zamina заміна *n.* change
zamina заміна *n.* substitution
zaminiuvaty замінювати *v.t.* replace
zaminnyk замінник *n.* substitute
zaminyty замінити *v.t.* substitute
zamishchennia заміщення *n.* replacement

428

zamishuvannia замішування *n*
confusion
zamishuvaty замішувати *v. t*
entangle
zamiskyi заміський *a.* suburban
zamizhnia zhinka заміжня жінка
n. matron
zamochuvannia замочування *n.*
soak
zamok замок *n.* castle
zamok замок *n.* lock
zamorozhuvaty заморожувати
v.i. freeze
zamovchuvannia замовчування
n. default
zamovchuvaty замовчувати *v. t*
bemask
zamovnyk замовник *n* customer
zamozhnyi заможний *a.* wealthy
zamuliuvatysia замулюватися
v.t. silt
zamykaty замикати *v.t* key
zamykaty na zamok замикати на
замок *v.t* lock
zamykaty na zasuv замикати на
засув *v. t* bolt
zamyshliaty замишляти *v.t.*
purpose
zamyslenyi замислений *a.*
pensive
zamyslyty замислити *v.i.* scheme
zanadto занадто *adv.* too
zanedbanyi занедбаний *a.*
lonesome
zanedbanyi занедбаний *a.*
solitary
zanepad занепад *n* blight
zanepad занепад *n* decline
zanepadnytskyi занепадницький
a decadent
zanepokoiennia занепокоєння *n.*
suspense
zaniattia заняття *n.* occupancy

zanos занос *n* skid
zanosyty snihom заносити
снігом *v.i.* snow
zanurennia занурення *n.* dip
zanurennia занурення *n.*
immersion
zanuriuvaty занурювати *v.t.*
immerse
zanuriuvatysia занурюватися *v.*
t dip
zanuryty занурити *v.t.* ship
zaokhochuvaty заохочувати *v. t.*
embolden
zapakh запах *n.* odour
zapakh запах *n.* scent
zapal запал *n.* ardour
zapalenyi запалений *a.* sore
zapaliuvaty запалювати *v.t* fire
zapaliuvatysia запалюватися *v.i.*
inflame
zapalnyi запальний *a.* hasty
zapamorochennia
запаморочення *n* swim
zapamorochlyva shvydkist
запаморочлива швидкість *n*
breakneck
zapamorochlyvyi
запаморочливий *a.* giddy
zapas запас *n* supply
zapashnyi запашний *a.* odorous
zapasni chastyny запасні
частини *n.* spare
zapasnyi запасний *a* duplicate
zapeklyi запеклий *n.* arrant
zaperechennia заперечення *n*
denial
zaperechennia заперечення *n.*
negation
zaperechennia заперечення *n.*
retort
zaperechnyi заперечний *a.*
negative

zaperechuvaty заперечувати *v. t.* deny

zaperechuvaty заперечувати *v.t.* object

zapevniaty запевняти *v.t.* pledge

zapiastok зап'ясток *n.* wrist

zapii запій *n.* spree

zapikatysia запікатися *v. t* clot

zapiznilyi запізнілий *adj.* belated

zapizniuvatysia запізнюватися *v.i.* lag

zaplisnilyi запліснілий *a.* mouldy

zaplutanyi заплутаний *a.* intricate

zaplutuvaty заплутувати *v. t* bewilder

zaplutuvaty заплутувати *v.t.* tangle

zapobihaty запобігати *v.t.* prevent

zapobizhnyi запобіжний *a.* preservative

zapochatkovuvaty започатковувати *v.t.* originate

zapodiiuvaty заподіювати *v.t* cause

zapodiiuvaty bil заподіювати біль *v.t.* hurt

zapodiiuvaty bil заподіювати біль *v.t.* torment

zapopadlyvyi запопадливий *adj* alacrious

zapovid заповідь *n.* precept

zapovidaty заповідати *v. t.* bequeath

zapovit заповіт *n.* testament

zapovniuvaty заповнювати *v.t* fill

zapozychuvaty запозичувати *v. t* borrow

zapriahaty запрягати *v.t* harness

zapriahty запрягти *v.t.* yoke

zaprohramuvaty запрограмувати *v.t.* programme

zaproshennia запрошення *n.* invitation

zaproshuvaty запрошувати *v.t.* invite

zaprovadzhuvaty novovvedennia запроваджувати нововведення *v.t.* innovate

zapynky запинки *n.* stumble

zapys запис *n.* record

zapysuvaty записувати *v.t.* record

zapysuvatysia записуватися *v. t.* book

zapyt запит *n.* inquiry

zarakhuvaty do vyshchoho navchalnoho zakladu зарахувати до вищого навчального закладу *v.t.* matriculate

zaraz зараз *adv.* forthwith

zaraz зараз *adv.* now

zaraza зараза *n.* taint

zarazhaty заражати *v.t.* infect

zarazhennia зараження *n.* infection

zarazlyvyi заразливий *a* contagious

zarazyty заразити *v.t.* taint

zariad заряд *n.* charge

zariadzhaty заряджати *v. t.* charge

zarikatysia зарікатися *v.t.* forswear

zarizaty зарізати *v.t.* slaughter

zarobliaty заробляти *v. t* earn

zarobotok заwork заработок *n* emolument

zarodzhennia зародження *n.* birth

zarozumilist зарозумілість *n* egotism

zarozumilyi зарозумілий *a.* arrogant

zarplatnia зарплатня *n.* livelihood

zarubka зарубка *n.* nick

zaruchnyk заручник *n.* hostage
zaruchyny заручини *n.* betrothal
zaruchyny заручини *n.* plight
zasadyty lisom засадити лісом
v.t. afforest
zaseliaty заселяти *v.t.* people
zashmorh зашморг *n.* noose
zasib засіб *n.* mean
zasidka засідка *n.* ambush
zasknilyi заскнілий *a.* obdurate
zaslanets засланець *n.* exile
zaslaty заслати *v. t* exile
zaslipliuvaty blyskom
засліплювати блиском *v. t.*
dazzle
zaslona заслона *n* curtain
zasluha заслуга *n.* merit
zasluhovuvaty заслуґовувати *v.t*
merit
zasluzhenyi заслужений *a.*
veteran
zasmoktuvaty засмоктувати *v.t*
engulf
zasmuchenyi засмучений *a.*
sorry
zasmuchuvaty засмучувати *v.t.*
afflict
zasmuchuvatysia засмучуватися
v.i. sorrow
zasnovnyk засновник *n.* founder
zasnovuvaty засновувати *v.t.*
found
zasnuvaty заснувати *v.t.* base
zasob peresuvannia засоб
пересування *n.* vehicle
zasoby do isnuvannia засоби до
існування *n.* sustenance
zaspokiilyve заспокійливе *n*
sedative
zaspokiilyvyi заспокійливий *adj*
calmative
zaspokoiennia заспокоєння *n.*
calm

zaspokoiennia заспокоєння *n.*
solace
zaspokoity заспокоїти *v.t.*
assuage
zaspokoiuvaty заспокоювати *v. t.* calm
zaspokoiuvaty заспокоювати *v. t*
console
zaspokoiuvaty заспокоювати *v.t.*
quell
zaspokoiuvatysia
заспокоюватися *v.t.* tranquillize
zastarilyi застарілий *a.* outdated
zastava застава *n.* bail
zastavliaty заставляти *v.t.*
mortgage
zastavna заставна *n.* mortgage
zastavne pravo заставне право
n. lien
zasterezhennia застереження *n.*
admonition
zasterezhennia застереження *n.*
caution
zasterezhennia застереження *n.*
warning
zasterezhlyvyi застережливий *a.*
monitory
zasterihaty застерігати *v.t.*
admonish
zastibaty застібати *v. t.* button
zastibka застібка *n* clasp
zastii застій *n.* stagnation
zastiinyi застійний *a.* stagnant
zastoiuvatysia застоюватися *v.i.*
stagnate
zastosovnist застосовність *n.*
application
zastosovnyi застосовний *a.*
applicable
zastosovuvaty застосовувати *v.t.*
apply
zastrakhuvaty застрахувати *v.t.*
secure

zastup заступ *n.* spade
zastupnyk заступник *n.* vice
zastupnytstvo заступництво *n.*
auspice
zasudyty засудити *v. t.* condemn
zasudzhuvaty засуджувати *v.t.*
sentence
zasuv засув *n* bolt
zasuv засув *n* lock
zasuvka засувка *n* snap
zasvichuvaty засвічувати *v.t.*
light
zasvidchuvaty засвідчувати *v. t.*
certify
zasvoiennia засвоєння *n*
assimilation
zasvoiuvaty засвоювати *v.*
assimilate
zasypaty засипати *v.t.* ply
zatemnennia затемнення *n*
eclipse
zatemniuvaty затемнювати *v.t.*
obscure
zatiahnuty затягнути *v.t.* tighten
zatiahuvaty затягувати *v.t.* tie
zatiniuvaty затінювати *v.t.*
overshadow
zatkhlyi затхлий *a.* musty
zatmariuvaty затьмарювати *v.t.*
outshine
zatoka затока *n.* gulf
zatopliaty затопляти *v.t* flood
zatopliuvaty затоплювати *v.t.*
swamp
zatopliuvatysia затоплюватися
v.i. submerge
zator затор *n* blockade
zatovarennia затоварення *n* glut
zatrymka затримка *n* stoppage
zatrymuvaty затримувати *v.t. &*
i. delay
zatrymuvaty затримувати *v.t.*
impede

zatrymuvatysia затримуватися
v.i. linger
zatsukrovuvaty зацукровувати *v.*
t. candy
zatuliaty затуляти *v.t.* shield
zatumaniuvaty затуманювати *v.*
t blear
zatverdzhennia затвердження *n*
affirmation
zatverdzhuvaty затверджувати
v.t. appoint
zatverdzhuvaty затверджувати
v.t. approve
zatvor затвор *n.* shutter
zatychka затичка *n* spill
zatykaty затикати *n.* cork
zatykaty затикати *v.t.* plug
zatykaty rot затикати рот *v.t.* gag
zatyshne mistechko затишне
містечко *n.* snug
zatyshne mistse затишне місце
n. cosier
zatyshnyi затишний *adj.* cozy
zatyshnyi kutochok затишний
куточок *n.* nook
zatyshshia затишшя *n.* lull
zatyskaty затискати *v.t.* jam
zatysnennia затиснення *n* grip
zaukhvalyi заухвалий *a.* petulant
zauvazhennia зауваження *n.*
remark
zauvazhennia, zroblene «pro
sebe» зауваження, зроблене
«про себе» *n.* aside
zauvazhyty зауважити *v.t.* note
zavada завада *n.* hindrance
zavaliuvaty tovaramy
завалювати товарами *v.t.* glut
zavarnyi krem заварний крем *n*
custard
zavazhaty заважати *v.t.* hinder
zavazhaty заважати *v.t.* prohibit
zavbachaty завбачати *v.t* foretell

zavbachennia завбачення *v.t*
forecast
zavbachlyvyi завбачливий *a.*
provident
zavchasno завчасно *adv.*
beforehand
zavdannia завдання *n* errand
zavdannia завдання *n.* goal
zavdannia завдання *n.* task
zavdavaty obrazy завдавати
образи *v.t.* insult
zaverbuvatysia завербуватися *v.*
t enlist
zavershennia завершення *n.*
close
zavershuvaty завершувати *v. t*
complete
zaviazaty perestrilku зав'язати
перестрілку *v.t.* skirmish
zaviazaty vuzlom зав'язати
вузлом *v.t.* knot
zaviaznuty v bahniutsi
зав'язнути в багнюці *v.t.* mire
zaviazuvaty зав'язувати *v.t* fasten
zaviazuvaty ochi зав'язувати очі
v. t blindfold
zaviduvannia завідування *n.*
superintendence
zaviriaty завіряти *v.t.* assure
zavisa завіса *n.* veil
zavoiovuvaty завойовувати *v. t*
conquer
zavoiuvannia завоювання *n*
conquest
zavolikatysia заволікатися *n.*
gloom
zavolodity заволодіти *v.t.* seize
zavorushennia заворушення *n*
unrest
zavtra завтра *adv.* tomorrow
zavtrashnii den завтрашній день
n. tomorrow
zavydnyi завидний *a* enviable

zavyvannia завивання *n* howl
zavyvaty завивати *v.t.* wave
zavzhdy завжди *adv* always
zavziatist завзятість *n.*
persistence
zavziattia завзяття *n.* zeal
zavziatyi завзятий *a.* mettlesome
zazdalehid ozbroiuvatysia
заздалегідь озброюватися *v.t*
forearm
zazdrisnyi заздрісний *a* envious
zazdrist заздрість *n* grudge
zazdryty заздрити *v. t* envy
zazikhaty зазіхати *v. i* encroach
zaznachyty зазначити *v. t.* check
zaznavaty зазнавати *v.t.* undergo
zaznavaty nevdachi зазнавати
невдачі *v.i* fail
zazvychai зазвичай *adv.*
ordinarily
zbahachuvaty збагачувати *v. t*
enrich
zbentezhenyi збентежений *adv*
ablush
zberezhennia збереження *n.*
preservation
zberihach зберігач *n* custodian
zberihaty зберігати *v. t* enshrine
zberihaty na skladi зберігати на
складі *v.t.* stock
zberihatysia зберігатися *v.i.*
persist
zbihatysia збігатися *v. i* coincide
zbilshennia збільшення *n.*
augmentation
zbilshennia zobrazhennia
збільшення зображення *n.*
zoom
zbilshuvaty збільшувати *v.t.*
augment
zbilshuvaty збільшувати *v.t.*
magnify

zbilshuvatysia збільшуватися *v.i.*
accrue
zbilshuvatysia збільшуватися *n*
increase
zbir збір *n.* meet
zbirnyk збірник *n.* digest
zbochenets збоченець *v.t.*
pervert
zbochenist збоченість *n.*
perversity
zbochennia збочення *n.*
perversion
zbochenyi збочений *a.* perverse
zbory збори *n.* forum
zbroia зброя *n.* gun
zbroienosets зброєносець *n.*
henchman
zbroienosets зброєносець *n.*
squire
zbudlyvyi збудливий *a.*
inflammatory
zbudzhennia збудження *n.*
impulse
zbudzhennia збудження *n.* tense
zbudzhenyi збуджений *adj.* agog
zbudzhenyi збуджений *a.* tense
zbyrach starovynnykh rechei
збирач старовинних речей *n.*
antiquary
zbyrach vrozhaiu збирач
врожаю *n.* harverster
zbyrannia збирання *n.* levy
zbyraty збирати *v.t.* aggregate
zbyraty material збирати
матеріал *v.i.* research
zbyratysia збиратися *v.t.*
assemble
zbyratysia natovpom збиратися
натовпом *v.i* mass
zbytok збиток *n* disadvantage
zbytok збиток *n* wane
zbyty збити *v. t* down
zbyvaty збивати *v. t. & i.* churn

zbyvaty z shliakhu збивати з
шляху *v.t.* mislead
zcheplennia зчеплення *n* clutch
zcheplenyi зчеплений *a* coherent
zdatnist здатність *n* ability
zdatnist do volovoho rukhu
здатність до вольового руху *n.*
conation
zdatnist vidchuvaty здатність
відчувати *n.* sentience
zdatnyi здатний *a.* capable
zdatnyi do zcheplennia здатний
до зчеплення *adj* cohesive
zdaty здати *v.t.* yield
zdavaty v orendu здавати в
оренду *v.t.* lease
zdavaty vnaim здавати внайм
v.t. let
zdavatysia здаватися *v.i.* seem
zdavyty здавити *v.t.* press
zdibnist здібність *n.* capability
zdibnyi здібний *a.* apt
zdiimatysia здійматися *v.i* billow
zdiisnennia здійснення *n.*
fulfilment
zdiisnennist здійсненність *n.*
practicability
zdiisnennyi здійсненний *a*
feasible
zdiisniavaty nahliad здійснявати
нагляд *v.t.* oversee
zdiisniuvaty здійснювати *v.t.*
accomplish
zdiisniuvaty nabih здійснювати
набіг *v.t.* raid
zdiisniuvaty poizdku
здійснювати поїздку *v.i.* tour
zdiisniuvaty poshuk здійснювати
пошук *v.t* quest
zdiisnyty здійснити *v.t.* realize
zdobuvaty здобувати *v.t.* gain
zdobych здобич *n.* capture
zdobych здобич *n.* kill

zdohad здогад *n* conjecture
zdohadka здогадка *n.* guess
zdohaduvatysia здогадуватися
 v.i guess
zdorovia здоров'я *n.* health
zdorovyi здоровий *a.* hale
zdorovyi здоровий *a.* lusty
zdorovyi здоровий *a.* robust
zdravytsia здравиця *n.* wassail
zdryhatysia здригатися *v.i.*
 shudder
zduttia здуття *n* swell
zdyraty здирати *v.t.* strip
zdyvovanyi pohliad здивований
 погляд *n.* goggles
zdyvuvannia здивування *n.*
 astonishment
zdyvuvaty здивувати *v. t* daze
zebra зебра *n.* zebra
zefir зефір *n.* zephyr
zelenyi зелений *a.* green
zelenyi kolir зелений колір *n*
 green
zemlerobstvo землеробство *n.*
 husbandry
zemleryika землерийка *n.* shrew
zemletrus землетрус *n*
 earthquake
zemlia земля *n* earth
zemlia pid parom земля під
 паром *n* fallow
zemlianyi земляний *a* earthly
zemnyi земний *a* earthen
zenit зеніт *n.* zenith
zenitnyi зенітний *a.* anti-aircraft
zerniatko зернятко *n.* kernel
zerno зерно *n* corn
zhaba жаба *n.* frog
zhadanyi жаданий *a.* wishful
zhadaty жадати *v.t.* covet
zhadibnist жадібність *n.* greed
zhadibno жадібно *adv* avidly
zhadibnyi жадібний *adj.* avid

zhadka згадка *n.* mention
zhadoba pomsty жадоба помсти
 v.t. revenge
zhaduvaty згадувати *v. t* cite
zhaduvaty згадувати *v.t.* mention
zhaha жага *n.* lust
zhaket жакет *n.* jerkin
zhakh жах *n.* fright
zhakhaty жахати *v.t.* terrify
zhakhlyvo monotonnyi жахливо
 монотонний *a.* monostrous
zhakhlyvyi жахливий *a*
 abominable
zhakhlyvyi жахливий *a* dire
zhakhlyvyi жахливий *a* flagrant
zhal жаль *n* regret
zhalibnyi жалібний *a.* piteous
zhalist жалість *n.* pity
zhality жаліти *v.t.* pity
zhaliuhidni hroshi жалюгідні
 гроші *n.* pittance
zhaliuhidnyi жалюгідний *a.* paltry
zhaliuhidnyi жалюгідний *a.*
 pitiable
zhalkuvaty жалкувати *v.i.* regret
zhaloby жалоби *v.t* groove
zhalyty жалити *v. t.* bite
zharhon жаргон *n.* jargon
zhart жарт *n.* joke
zhart жарт *n.* prank
zhart жарт *n.* witticism
zhartivlyva besida жартівлива
 бесіда *n.* banter
zhartivlyvist жартівливість *n.*
 pleasantry
zhartivlyvyi жартівливий *a.*
 jocular
zhartivnyk жартівник *n* wag
zhartuvaty жартувати *v.i.* joke
zharty жарти *n.* raillery
zhaslyi згаслий *a* extinct
zhasmyn жасмин *n.* jasmine,
 jessamine

zhburliaty жбурляти *v.t.* hurl
zhburnuty жбурнути *v. i.* dash
zhebrak жебрак *n* beggar
zhebrakuvaty жебракувати *v. i* cadge
zhele желе *n.* jelly
zhenykh жених *n.* bridegroom
zhereb жереб *n.* lot
zherebets жеребець *n.* stallion
zhertovnyi жертовний *a.* sacrificial
zhertva жертва *n.* victim
zhertvoprynesennia жертвопринесення *n.* oblation
zhertvuvaty жертвувати *v. t* donate
zherty жерти *n.* gobble
zhest жест *n.* gesture
zhezl жезл *n* baton
zhidno згідно *prep.* per
zhidno z згідно з *conj.* after
zhinka жінка *n.* woman
zhinocha sorochka жіноча сорочка *n* chemise
zhinochnist жіночність *n.* womanhood
zhinochyi жіночий *a* female
zhinochyi monastyr жіночий монастир *n.* nunnery
zhmenia жменя *n.* handful
zhnets жнець *n.* reaper
zhoda згода *n.* accord
zhoda згода *n.* consensus
zhoden жоден *a.* neither
zhoden жоден *pron.* none
zhodnyi згодний *a.* agreeable
zhodom згодом *adv.* afterwards
zhodzhuvatysia згоджуватися *v.i.* assent
zholob жолоб *n.* gutter
zholodnity зголодніти *v.i.* starve
zholud жолудь *n.* acorn
zhorstkyi жорсткий *a.* hard

zhorstkyi жорсткий *a.* rigid
zhorstokist жорстокість *n* cruelty
zhorstokyi жорстокий *a* abusive
zhorstokyi жорстокий *a* cruel
zhortaty згортати *v.t.* convolve
zhovch жовч *n* bile
zhovchnist жовчність *n* acrimony
zhovirlyvyi зговірливий *a* amenable
zhovta farba жовта фарба *n* chrome
zhovten жовтень *n.* October
zhovtianytsia жовтяниця *n.* jaundice
zhovtok жовток *n.* yolk
zhovtuvatyi жовтуватий *a.* yellowish
zhovtyi жовтий *a.* yellow
zhovtyzna жовтизна *n* yellow
zhraia зграя *n.* shoal
zhraia зграя *n.* swarm
zhraia зграя *n.* troop
zhribaty v kupu згрібати в купу *v.t.* bank
zhrytsia жриця *n.* priestess
zhubnyi згубний *a.* maleficent
zhubnyi згубний *a.* perilous
zhuinu tvaryna жуйну тварина *n.* ruminant
zhuinyi жуйний *a.* ruminant
zhuk жук *n* beetle
zhuri журі *n.* jury
zhurnal журнал *n.* journal
zhurnalist журналіст *n.* journalist
zhurnalistyka журналістика *n.* journalism
zhurtovanyi згуртований *a.* solid
zhushchuvaty згущувати *v. t* condense
zhustyty згустити *v.i.* thicken
zhut жуть *n* dread
zhuvaty жувати *v. t* chew

zhuvaty zhuiku жувати жуйку *v.i.* ruminate

zhvaltuvannia згвалтування *n.* rape

zhvavist жвавість *n.* alacrity

zhvavist жвавість *n.* vivacity

zhvavyi жвавий *adj* brisk

zhvavyi жвавий *a.* jolly

zhylet жилет *n.* waistcoat

zhyletka жилетка *n.* vest

zhylyi жилий *a.* inhabitable

zhyn згин *n* bend

zhynaty згинати *v.t.* arch

zhyr жир *n* fat

zhyraf жираф *n.* giraffe

zhyrnyi жирний *a.* greasy

zhyrovyk жировик *n.* wen

zhytel житель *n.* inhabitant

zhytel Skhodu житель Сходу *n* oriental

zhyteli hrafstva жителі графства *n.* county

zhytlo житло *n* abode

zhytnytsia житниця *n.* granary

zhyto жито *n.* rye

zhyttia життя *n* life

zhyttia liudyny життя людини *n.* past

zhyttieradisnyi життєрадісний *a.* vivacious

zhyttievist життєвість *n.* vitality

zhyttievo vazhlyvyi життєво важливий *a.* vital

zhyttiezdatnyi життєздатний *a.* viable

zhyty жити *v.i.* live

zhyty rozpusno жити розпусно *v.t.* womanise

zhyty v seli жити в селі *v.t.* rusticate

zhyva ohorozha жива огорожа *n* quick

zhyvit живіт *n* belly

zhyvopys живопис *n.* painting

zhyvyi живий *a* alive

zhyvylnyi живильний *a.* nutritious

zhyvytsia живиця *n.* sap

zhyvyty живити *v.t.* nourish

zhyvyty syly живити сили *v.t.* sustain

zi smakom зі смаком *a.* tasteful

ziasovuvaty з'ясовувати *v.t.* ascertain

ziasuvaty з'ясувати *v. t* elucidate

ziavytysia з'явитися *v. i* emerge

ziednanyi з'єднаний *adj.* conjunct

ziednaty shvamy з'єднати швами *v.t.* seam

ziednuvaty з'єднувати *v. i* compound

ziednuvaty з'єднувати *v.t.* piece

ziednuvatysia з'єднуватися *v. t.* connect

zihrivaty зігрівати *v.t* heat

ziity зійти *v. i.* descend

zinytsia зіниця *n.* pupil

zipsovanyi зіпсований *adj* addle

zipsovanyi зіпсований *a.* bad

zipsovanyi зіпсований *a.* corrupt

zir зір *n.* sight

zirka зірка *n.* star

zirkopodibnyi зіркоподібний *adj.* asteroid

zirochka зірочка *n.* asterisk

zishchuliuvatysia зіщулюватися *v.i.* cower

zishtovkhuvaty зіштовхувати *v. i.* collide

zishtovkhuvatysia зіштовхуватися *v. t.* clash

zistavliaty зіставляти *v.t.* correlate

zitkhannia зітхання *n.* sigh

zitkhaty зітхати *v.i.* sigh

zitknennia зіткнення *n.* clash

ziuidovyi зюйдовий *a.* southern

zkhrustkyi зхрусткий *adj.* crump
zla satyra зла сатира *n.* lampoon
zlakovyi злаковий *a* cereal
zlamuvaty зламувати *v. i.* burst
zlamuvaty зламувати *v.i.* pry
zlehka злегка *adv.* lightly
zlipok зліпок *n.* mould
zlisnyi злісний *a.* malignant
zlisnyi злісний *a.* venomous
zlist злість *n.* spite
zlizty злізти *v.i.* alight
zloba злоба *n.* venom
zlochyn злочин *n* crime
zlochyn злочин *n.* misdeed
zlochynets злочинець *n* criminal
zlodii злодій *n.* thief
zlodiistvo злодійство *n.* snatch
zlodiuzhka злодюжка *n* sneak
zloiakisnist злоякісність *n.* malignancy
zloiakisnyi злоякісний *a* malign
zlomshchyk зломщик *n* burglar
zlopamiatnist злопам'ятність *n.* rancour
zloslovyty злословити *v.t.* malign
zlovisnyi зловісний *a.* inauspicious
zlovmysnyi зловмисний *a.* malicious
zlovmysnyk зловмисник *n.* malefactor
zlovzhyvannia зловживання *n* abuse
zlovzhyvannia зловживання *n.* misapplication
zlovzhyvannia doviroiu зловживання довірою *n.* malpractice
zlovzhyvaty зловживати *v.t.* misuse
zlydar злидар *n.* pauper
zlydennyi злиденний *a.* sordid
zlyi злий *a.* angry

zlyi umysel злий умисел *n.* malice
zlyttia злиття *n* amalgamation
zlyttia злиття *n.* junction
zlyva злива *n* downpour
zlyva злива *n.* torrent
zlyvatysia зливатися *v.t.* amalgamate
zlyvatysia зливатися *v.t.* merge
zmahannia змагання *n.* competition
zmahatysia змагатися *v. t* emulate
zmashchuvannia змащування *n.* lubrication
zmashchuvaty змащувати *v.t* oil
zmastyty змастити *v.t* grease
**zmenshene im`ia** зменшене ім`я *n.* nickname
zmenshennia зменшення *n.* decrement
zmenshuvaty зменшувати *v.t.* delibate
zmenshuvatysia зменшуватися *v.t* lessen
zmenshyty зменшити *v.t.* reduce
zmiia змія *n.* serpent
zmiiovyk змійовик *n.* serpentine
zmina зміна *n* alteration
zmina зміна *n.* amendment
zmina зміна *n* conversion
zmina зміна *n* shift
zmina polozhennia зміна положення *n.* move
zminiaty зміняти *v.t.* relay
zminiuvanyi змінюваний *a.* variable
zminiuvaty змінювати *v.t.* modify
zminiuvatysia змінюватися *v.t.* vary
zminnyi змінний *a.* alternative
zminnyi змінний *a.* removable
zminnyi змінний *a.* varied

zminyty змінити *v.t.* amend
zmishchennia зміщення *n* offset
zmishuvaty змішувати *v. t* blend
zmishuvaty змішувати *v. t*
confuse
zmishuvatysia змішуватися *v.t.*
mingle
zmist зміст *n.* aliment
zmitsniuvaty зміцнювати *v.t.*
strengthen
zmorshka зморшка *n.* wrinkle
zmova змова *n.* conspiracy
zmovliatysia змовлятися *v. t*
concert2
zmovnyk змовник *n.* conspirator
zmushuvaty змушувати *v. t*
compel
zmushuvaty zamovchaty
змушувати замовчати *v.i* hush
zmuzhnilist змужнілість *n.*
manhood
znachennia значення *n.*
significance
znachnyi значний *a* great
znachnyi значний *a.* sizable
znachok значок *n.* badge
znaiomstvo знайомство *n.*
acquaintance
znaiomstvo знайомство *n.*
introduction
znaiomyi знайомий *a* familiar
znaiomyty знайомити *v.t.*
introduce
znaiuchyi знаючий *a* expert
znak знак *n.* sign
znakhodytsia v borhu
знаходиться в боргу *a.*
indebted
znakhodyty знаходити *v. t*
discover
znakhodyty знаходити *v.t* find
znakhodyty знаходити *v.t.* see

znamenytist знаменитість *n.*
luminary
znamenytyi знаменитий *a.*
outstanding
znamenytyi знаменитий *a.*
renowned
znannia знання *n* cognizance
znariaddia знаряддя *n.*
implement
znariaddia знаряддя *n.* weapon
znaty знати *v.t.* know
znaty знати *v.t.* understand
znavets знавець *n.* adept
znedolenyi знедолений *a* outcast
znedolyty знедолити *v.t.* widow
znekhtuvaty знехтувати *v. t*
disregard
znenatska зненацька *adv.*
unawares
znetsiniuvaty знецінювати *v.t.i.*
depreciate
znetsiniuvatysia знецінюватися
v. t erode
znevaha зневага *n* disregard
znevaha зневага *n* neglect
znevazhannia зневажання *n*
disdain
znevazhaty зневажати *v. t*
despise
znevazhaty зневажати *v.t.* neglect
znevazhaty зневажати *v.t.* scorn
znevira зневіра *n* dejection
znevira зневіра *n.* melancholy
zneviriatysia зневірятися *v. i*
despair
zniattia зняття *n* dismissal
zniaty kontrol зняти контроль *v.t.*
decontrol
znimaty знімати *v.t* hire
znimaty знімати *v.t.* withdraw
znimaty z posady знімати з
посади *v.t.* sack
znoshenyi зношений *a.* worn

znosyty зносити *v. t.* demolish
znosyty зносити *v.t.* wear
znovu знову *adv.* afresh
znovu robyty знову робити *v.i.* relapse
znovu zibraty знову зібрати *v.t.* recollect
znushchannia знущання *n.* insult
znushchannia знущання *n.* mockery
znushchatysia знущатися *v.i.* mock
znushchatysia знущатися *v.i.* scoff
znykaty зникати *v.i.* vanish
znyknennia зникнення *n* disappearance
znyknennia зникнення *n.* output
znyknuty зникнути *v. i* disappear
znyshchennia знищення *n* annihilation
znyshchuvaty знищувати *v.t.* annihilate
znyshchuvaty знищувати *v. t* devour
znyshchyty знищити *v. t* destroy
znyzhennia зниження *n* decrease
znyzhka знижка *n* discount
znyzhuvaty знижувати *v. t* decrease
znyzhuvaty yakist знижувати якість *v. t.* debase
znyzu знизу *adv.* underneath
znyzuvannia знизування *n* shrug
znyzuvaty plechyma знизувати плечима *v.t.* shrug
zob зоб *n.* craw
zoboviazannia зобов'язання *n.* engagement
zoboviazanyi зобов'язаний *a.* liable
zoboviazuvaty зобов'язувати *v.t.* oblige

zobovzannia зобов'зання *n* must
zobrazhaty зображати *v. t.* depict
zobrazhaty зображати *v.t.* represent
zobrazhennia зображення *n* effigy
zobrazhennia зображення *n.* representation
zobrazyty зобразити *v.t* figure
zodiak зодіак *n* zodiac
zoik зойк *n* scream
zoloto золото *n.* gold
zolotyi золотий *a.* golden
zona зона *n.* zone
zonalnyi зональний *a.* zonal
zond зонд *n* probe
zooloh зоолог *n.* zoologist
zoolohichnyi зоологічний *a.* zoological
zoolohiia зоологія *n.* zoology
zoopark зоопарк *n.* zoo
zorianyi зоряний *a.* starry
zorianyi зоряний *a.* stellar
zoseredzhenyi зосереджений *a.* rapt
zovni зовні *adv.* out
zovni зовні *adv.* outwardly
zovnishnii зовнішній *a* external
zovnishnii зовнішній *a.* outer
zovnishnii slukhovyi prokhid зовнішній слуховий прохід *n* alveary
zovnishnist зовнішність *n.* look
zovnishnist зовнішність *n.* semblance
zovsim зовсім *adv.* through
zozulia зозуля *n* cuckoo
zposylatysia зposилатися *v.i.* allude
zrada зрада *n* betrayal
zradnyk зрадник *n.* snake
zradnyk зрадник *n.* traitor

zradnytskyi зрадницький *a.*
treacherous
zradnytstvo зрадництво *n.*
treason
zradzhuvaty зраджувати *v.t.*
betray
zrazok зразок *n.* specimen
zrechennia зречення *n* abdication
zrechennia зречення *n.*
repudiation
zrikatysia зрікатися *v.t.* renounce
zrikatysia зрікатися *v.t.* repudiate
zrilist зрілість *n.* maturity
zrilyi зрілий *a.* mature
zrist зріст *n.* height
zrity зріти *v.i* mature
zrivniaty iz zemleiu зрівняти із
землею *v.t.* raze
zrivniuvaty зрівнювати *v. t.*
equalize
zrivniuvaty зрівнювати *v. t* equate
zrobyty bezlad зробити безлад
v.i mess
zrobyty mat зробити мат *v.t.*
mate
zrobyty pomylku зробити
помилку *v.t.* misprint
zrobyty pryval зробити привал
v. t. halt
zrobyty znak зробити знак *v. t*
beckon
zroshchennia зрощення *n.*
concrescence
zroshennia зрошення *n.* irrigation
zroshuvaty зрошувати *v.t.* irrigate
zrostaiuchyi na derevyni
зростаючий на деревині *a.*
xylophilous
zrostannia зростання *n.* growth
zrostaty зростати *v.t.* increase
zrostaty hronamy зростати
гронами *v. i.* cluster

zrostatysia зростатися *v.t.*
accrete
zrozumilyi зрозумілий *a.*
intelligible
zrozumity nepravylno зрозуміти
неправильно *v.t.* misapprehend
zruchnist зручність *n.*
convenience
zruchnyi зручний *a* comfortable
zrushennia зрушення *v.t.* shear
zrymyi зримий *a.* visible
zryvaty зривати *v. t* disrupt
zub зуб *n.* tooth
zubets зубець *n* cog
zubnyi bil зубний біль *n.*
toothache
zubrinnia зубріння *n.* rote
zukhvala povedinka зухвала
поведінка *n* defiance
zukhvalist зухвалість *n.*
impertinence
zukhvalstvo зухвальство *n.*
hardihood
zukhvalyi зухвалий *a.* bold
zumovliuvaty зумовлювати *v.t.*
predetermine
zupyniaty rozvytok зупиняти
розвиток *n* dwarf
zupynka зупинка *n.* standstill
zupynka zrostannia зупинка
зростання *n* stunt
zupynyty зупинити *v.t.* stop
zustrichatysia зустрічатися *v.t.*
meet
zustrichne zvynuvachennia
зустрічне звинувачення *n.*
countercharge
zustrity зустріти *v. t* encounter
zusyllia зусилля *n* amplification
zusyllia зусилля *n* struggle
**zv`iazok** зв`язок *n* connection
zvaba зваба *n.* delusion
zvaba зваба *n.* seduction

zvabliuvaty заблювати *n.t.* delude

zvannia kapitana звання капітана *n.* captaincy

zvariuvannia зварювання *v.t.* solder

zvariuvannia зварювання *n* weld

zvaryty зварити *v.t.* weld

zvazhuvaty зважувати *v.t.* ponder

zvazhuvaty зважувати *v.t.* scale

zvedennia зведення *n* bulletin

zvelychuvaty звеличувати *v. t* exalt

zvernennia звернення *n.* recourse

zvernuty uvahu звернути увагу *v.t.* heed

zvernutysia звернутися *v.t.* address

zvertaty uvahu звертати увагу *v.t.* notice

zvertatysia звертатися *v.* advert

zveseliannia звеселяння *n* amusement

zviazaty motuzkoiu зв'язати мотузкою *v.t.* rope

zviazaty shnurom зв'язати шнуром *v.t* tape

zviazka зв'язка *n.* bale

zvid звід *n.* arch

zvidky звідки *adv.* whence

zvidnyk звідник *n.* bawd

zvidsy звідси *adv.* hence

zvidty звідти *adv.* thence

zvilnennia звільнення *n* release

zvilnennia vid oboviazku звільнення від обов'язку *n* excuse

zvilnenyi vid звільнений від *a* exempt

zvilniaty звільняти *v.t* absolve

zvilniaty звільняти *v. t* discard

zvilniaty звільняти *v.t.* manumit

zvilniaty звільняти *v.t.* quit

zvilniaty звільняти *v.t.* rescue

zviriachyi звірячий *a.* atrocious

zvirstvo звірство *n* atrocity

zvishchaty звіщати *v.i.* trumpet

zvit звіт *n.* report

zvodyty balans зводити баланс *v.t.* offset

zvodyty na prestol зводити на престол *v. t* enthrone

zvodyty sklepinnia зводити склепіння *v.i.* vault

zvodyty ukriplennia зводити укріплення *v.t.* fortify

zvodyty v tablytsiu зводити в таблицю *v.t.* tabulate

zvodyty z rozumu зводити з розуму *v.t* dement

zvodytysia зводитися *v.* amount

zvolikannia зволікання *n.* procrastination

zvolikaty зволікати *v.i.* slow

zvolozhuvaty зволожувати *v.t.* moisten

zvorotnyi зворотний *a* reflexive

zvorotnyi зворотний *a.* reverse

zvuchaty звучати *v.i.* resound

zvuchnist звучність *n.* sonority

zvuk звук *n* sound

zvuk rizhka звук ріжка *n.* clarion

zvukonasliduvannia звуконаслідування *n.* onomatopoeia

zvukovyi звуковий *a.* sonic

zvuzhuvaty звужувати *v.t.* narrow

zvuzhuvatysia do kintsia звужуватися до кінця *v.i.* taper

zvychai звичай *n.* custom

zvychaino звичайно *adv.* certainly

zvychaino звичайно *adv.* usually

zvychainyi звичайний *a.* average

zvychainyi звичайний *a* customary

zvychka звичка *n* wont
zvykhnutysia звихнутися *v.i.*
maddle
zvyklyi звиклий *a.* accustomed
zvyklyi do novykh umov звиклий
до нових умов *a.* wonted
zvynuvachennia звинувачення *n*
accusation
zvyvatysia звиватися *v.t.* crankle
zvyvystyi звивистий *a.* sinuous
zyhzah зигзаг *n.* zigzag
zyhzahopodibnyi
зигзагоподібний *a.* zigzag
zyma зима *n.* winter
zymivlia зимівля *n.* hibernation
zymovyi зимовий *a.* wintry
zzadu ззаду *adv* behind

Coleg y
Cymoedd
Learning Centre / Canolfan Dysgu
Aberdare Campus
Tel: 01685 887510

WITHDRAWN
* FROM *
STOCK